LAW, POLITICS
AND THE
JUDICIAL PROCESS
IN CANADA

FOURTH EDITION

F. L. MORTON, ed.
DAVE SNOW, ed.

University of Calgary Press
2500 University Drive NW
Calgary, Alberta
Canada T2N 1N4
press.ucalgary.ca

This book is available as an ebook. The publisher should be contacted for any use which falls outside the terms of that license.

Library and Archives Canada Cataloguing in Publication

   Law, politics, and the judicial process in Canada / F.L. Morton, ed., Dave Snow, ed. — Fourth edition.

Includes bibliographical references and index.
Issued in print and electronic formats.
ISBN 978-1-55238-990-4 (softcover).—ISBN 978-1-55238-991-1 (PDF).—
ISBN 978-1-55238-992-8 (EPUB).—ISBN 978-1-55238-993-5 (Kindle)

   1. Courts—Canada. 2. Judicial process—Canada. 3. Political questions and judicial power—Canada. I. Morton, F. L. (Frederick Lee), 1949-, editor II. Snow, Dave, 1985-, editor

KE8200.L39 2018   347.71'012   C2018-903592-7
KF8700.ZA2L39 2018   C2018-903593-5

The University of Calgary Press acknowledges the support of the Government of Alberta through the Alberta Media Fund for our publications. We acknowledge the financial support of the Government of Canada. We acknowledge the financial support of the Canada Council for the Arts for our publishing program.

Printed and bound in Canada by Friesens
♻ This book is printed on 57 lb 100% FSC paper

Copyediting by Ryan Perks
Cover design, page design, and typesetting by Melina Cusano

Table of Contents

3

The Canadian Judicial System   92

4

Judicial Recruitment and Selection   117

5

Judicial Independence, Ethics and Discipline

6

Interest Groups and Access to Judicial Power   243

7

Precedents, Statutes and Legal Reasoning   330

8

Judicial Decision-Making   370

9

Judicial Review and Federalism   405

10

Aboriginal Law and the Judicial Process   453

11

The Harper Conservatives and the   504
Canadian Judiciary

12

Reconciling Judicial Review and   573
Constitutional Democracy

Appendices

Index

Preface to the New Edition

2017 marked the thirty-fifth anniversary of the *Canadian Charter of Rights and Freedoms*. F.L. Morton completed the first edition of this book in May, 1984, the month the Supreme Court issued its first *Charter* decision. In the preface to that first edition, he speculated that the adoption of the *Charter* was going to "force the Canadian judiciary into a much more explicit political function than it had previously exercised." This was indeed speculation. No one knew at the time what the *Charter* would hold; its impact – if any – would be a function of judicial interpretation and choice. Given our judges' history of deference to elected governments and provincial opposition to the *Charter* (especially Quebec's), there were ample reasons to suspect no more than modest deviation from the *status quo ante*.

Today, in our fourth decade of "Charterland," Canadians live in a different legal and political world. There have been hundreds of *Charter* cases decided by the Supreme Court of Canada and thousands more by lower courts. The list of public policies shaped by the courts' interpretation of the *Charter* is long and still growing: Aboriginal rights and land claims, abortion, bilingualism, capital punishment, criminal procedure, electoral distribution, family law, LGBTQ rights, immigration and refugee determination, judicial ethics, judicial salaries, labour law, Quebec separatism, pornography, prisoner voting rights and Sunday closing laws. Since the third edition was published in 2002, we can add topics such as supervised injection sites, terrorism, third-party election advertising and health care. The Supreme Court has also reversed its early *Charter* precedent in recent years on issues such as assisted suicide, prostitution and collective bargaining.

While the Supreme Court's *Charter* decisions are the most visible and often dramatic indicators of the *Charter*'s impact, they represent only the tip of the iceberg of *Charter*-induced activities. The Court's *Charter* activism has been both a cause and an effect of numerous other changes in the legal and political systems: the docket and decision-making procedures of the Supreme Court, judicial appointments, law schools, legal scholarship, interest group activity and government expenditures. These changes are recounted in the revised introductions to each chapter and in over forty new readings that have been selected for the fourth edition. We are pleased to include the works of a new generation of scholars in this new edition, many of whom have grown up in a post-*Charter* Canada.

Two developments from the last fifteen years have so altered the judicial process that we have included in this edition two entirely new chapters. The first, Chapter 10, concerns the growing influence of Aboriginal law and the judicial process. Readings here, which only scratch the surface of this diverse field, include topics such as resource development, the duty to consult and Métis mobilization. The second, Chapter 11, concerns the strained relationship between Stephen Harper's Conservative government (2006–2015) and the courts. Readings in this chapter range from Harper's changes to lower court appointments, to the Supreme Court's incredible rejection of the appointment of Marc Nadon and the public recriminations between the Prime Minister and the Chief Justice that ensued.

The last fifteen years have also witnessed considerable changes to the way judges are appointed by federal and provincial governments. Chapter 4 has been updated substantially to detail the implications of these changes with an all-new introduction and six new readings. Canadian political scientists have also undertaken new approaches to studying judicial behaviour, which has led to an overhaul of the chapter on judicial decision-making (Chapter 8). Finally, judges themselves have not been immune from scandal, providing considerable grist for a revised Chapter 5 on judicial independence, ethics and discipline.

All of this new material means that we have had to remove several readings from this edition. We once again thank those authors whose work help shaped previous editions. For this edition, we are indebted to many people, first and foremost all of the contributing authors, without whom there would be no book. We have received permissions from all living contributors and their publishers, and every effort has been made to contact those whose readings continue to appear in this edition. We would also like to thank Mark Harding, Tom Bateman, Dennis Baker and Kate Puddister for their helpful suggestions on early drafts of the introductory chapters. We are also grateful for the support of Jerred Kiss, a research assistant at the University of Guelph. Finally, we want to thank the staff at the University of Calgary Press, especially Brian Scrivener. For any errors of omission or commission, we take full responsibility.

1

The Rule of Law in the Canadian Constitution

On December 4, 1946, Frank Roncarelli was informed by the Quebec Liquor Commission that the liquor licence for his Montreal restaurant had been revoked "forever." Mr. Roncarelli had not violated any Liquor Commission guidelines, nor had he been charged with or convicted of any criminal wrongdoing. The licence was revoked because, as Mr. Roncarelli and indeed everyone else knew, Maurice Duplessis, the Premier of Quebec, wanted to punish him for his membership in and financial support of the Jehovah's Witnesses. The Jehovah's Witnesses are an evangelizing, fundamentalist protestant sect that had outraged Duplessis and the French-Catholic majority in Quebec through their outspoken criticisms of the Catholic Church and its priests. The Duplessis government had begun a campaign of legal harassment against the Witnesses by arresting them for distributing their printed materials without a licence. Roncarelli frustrated this plan by regularly providing bail money for his arrested fellow-believers, who would then return to the streets. Roncarelli thus became a special target of the Quebec government's harassment.

After a thirteen-year legal battle, the Supreme Court of Canada finally ruled that the government of Quebec's treatment of Roncarelli had been arbitrary and illegal. Moreover, Duplessis could not hide behind the civil immunity normally enjoyed by state administrators under Quebec law. By grossly abusing his administrative discretion, Duplessis was deemed to have acted outside the law and was thus subject to being sued by Roncarelli for damages[1] (Reading 1.1). A majority of the Court held that in Canada there is a general right not to be punished by the arbitrary exercise of government power. A government, federal or provincial, can only move against an individual in accordance with known rules, and the Duplessis government had failed to meet this standard. In so ruling, the Supreme Court reasserted one of the fundamental principles of the "unwritten constitution" of Canada – "the rule of law."

The *Roncarelli* case was just the most recent chapter in a living tradition that can be traced back through the nineteenth-century writings of A.V. Dicey (Reading 1.4); the American Declaration of Independence of 1776 (Reading 1.3); the political theory of the seventeenth-century philosopher John Locke (Reading 1.2); and even to the fields of Runnymede in June, 1215, when the English nobles forced King John to sign *Magna Carta* and to agree to rule *per legem terrae* – that is, according to the laws of the land.[2]

Magna Carta marked the beginning of the "rule of law" tradition. The Glorious Revolution of 1688 deposed the Stuart kings and established Parliament's supremacy over the Crown. This landmark event initiated the practice of government that we now take for granted (too much so!) – representative government, or government by consent of the governed.

The second reading is from the writings of John Locke, often referred to as the "theorist of the Glorious Revolution." Locke's *Second Treatise on Government*, first published in 1690, has been the most influential defence and advocacy of "government by consent," or liberal democracy, ever written. In it, we find not only a defence of "government by consent of the governed," but also a restatement of the principle of *per legem terrae*. Locke explicitly declares that even the new sovereign, the legislature, must rule "by declared and received laws ... interpreted by known authorized judges."

A careful reading of the passage from Locke reveals that, in addition to these procedural restrictions, he imposes a second major restriction on the legislative, or "law-making," power of the state – "the law of Nature." This substantive restriction means that, not only must laws be duly enacted and fairly administered, but laws themselves must not violate the "natural rights" of individuals that exist by the "law of Nature." This law of nature is understood to transcend human society and to exist independently of the positive law of any given state.

This double limitation on just government was given its most striking and memorable articulation in the American Declaration of Independence of 1776, written primarily by Thomas Jefferson (Reading 1.3). The Americans justified their revolution, and subsequently founded their new republic, on the two fundamental principles of Locke's political theory: that "all men are by Nature equal," and that they possess certain inalienable (i.e., natural) rights. There is a critical tension between these two fundamental concepts of equality and liberty. The principle of natural equality essentially means that no person (or group of persons) is inherently so superior as to rule others without their consent. This banishes the traditional claims of priests, kings and nobles to rule on the basis of their alleged natural superiority, and replaces it with government by consent of the governed. In practice, this has meant some form of "majority rule" democracy. The principle of natural rights means that a just government cannot violate these rights, since the very purpose of government is to secure such rights. The tension arises from the fact that "majority rule" does not always produce laws that respect the rights of individuals or groups that are not part of the majority.

This tension is more of a theoretical problem than a practical one. Most of the time, the combined practice of "government by consent" and "the rule of law" is a strong guarantee that the twin requirements of equality and liberty will be met. It is unlikely that a governing majority will ever (knowingly) consent to policies that are destructive of their rights. The "rule of law" provides additional safeguards by deterring rulers from pursuing ends and using means that "they would not like to have known by the people, and own not willingly."[3] But what happens when the majority consents to laws that are destructive of the natural rights of a minority? What happens when government by the "consent of the governed" no longer "secures these rights"? Neither Locke nor Jefferson answered this question. The practical problem of reconciling "majority rule" with "minority rights" was left to the founders of new liberal democracies such as the United States and Canada.

Historically, modern liberal democracies have given institutional expression to the principles of equality and liberty in one of two ways: the British parliamentary or Westminster model and the American "separation of powers" model. Because of two major differences in the British and American systems, the courts in each have very different functions and characteristics. The American model is ultimately based on and organized by a single basic document – a written constitution. This single document sets down in writing "the rules governing the composition, powers and methods of operation of the main institutions of government, and the general principles applicable to their relations to the citizens."[4] By contrast, the Westminster model is based on an "unwritten constitution" – a combination of historically important statutes, the common law and numerous unwritten conventions and usages. (In 1998, Britain took a step in the direction of the American model by adopting the *Human Rights Act*. See below.) The second difference is that the American-style "written constitution" includes an enumeration of the fundamental rights and liberties of the individual against government, known collectively as the *Bill of Rights*. While individuals enjoy basically the same rights and freedoms under the traditional British parliamentary model of democracy, they are not "spelled out" in any single, basic document of government (i.e., they are not "constitutionally entrenched").

The result of these two differences is that under the American model of democracy, the courts, and especially the Supreme Court, play a more explicit and influential political role. Ever since the 1803 case of *Marbury v. Madison*, American courts have assumed the function of interpreting and enforcing "constitutional law" just as they do all other law. This "judicial review" of legislative and executive actions is intended to ensure that the latter conform to the procedures and limitations laid down in the Constitution. If government laws and actions do not conform, the Court declares them to be "unconstitutional," invalid and therefore without legal effect.

It is easy to see how, in theory at least, combining the American practice of judicial review with an entrenched bill of rights resolves the tension between liberty and equality, majority rule and minority rights. If the majority enacts a law that infringes a person's constitutional right, the individual can go to court and ask the judges to strike down the law as unconstitutional. This approach to protecting civil liberties was particularly effective in promoting racial justice in the United States during the 1950s and 1960s. While the more "democratic" (majoritarian) institutions of government refused to take action, the United States Supreme Court used the *Bill of Rights*' guarantee of "equal protection of the laws" to strike down the legal barriers of racial discrimination in American society. However, as the Supreme Court expanded its "judicial activism" into more and more areas of public policy and local government, serious questions began to arise about the "undemocratic" character of its use of judicial review. In protecting the "individual rights" side of the liberal equation, the Court was perceived as neglecting and even violating the equality requirement of government by consent of the governed.[5]

The British model of parliamentary supremacy combined with the "rule of law" tradition avoids this problem. There are no written constitutional prohibitions for the British courts to enforce against Parliament, and the courts do not interpret or enforce constitutional conventions, the "unwritten constitution."[6] The critics of parliamentary democracy, however, contend that it is prone to the opposite problem – that there is no adequate mechanism to protect individuals or minorities from democratic majorities that violate their rights. While this may be true in theory, in practice it has not proven to be a serious problem in either Great Britain or Canada. While Canada's record when it comes to civil liberties is far from perfect,[7] it remains much better than the vast majority of modern nation-states.

The key to the British parliamentary system's practical success is conveyed in the reading from Dicey on "the rule of law," and especially his quotation from Tocqueville (Reading 1.4). Comparing the governments of England and Switzerland, Tocqueville observed that, "In England there seems to be more liberty in the customs than in the laws of the people," while the opposite holds for Switzerland. For both Tocqueville and Dicey, the British condition is far preferable. For, in the long run, a society's customs, habits, beliefs – the moral quality of public opinion – is a more dependable guarantee of just laws than the "paper barriers" of constitutional "guarantees." Put very simply, a written constitution cannot "guarantee" that the laws of a democratic society will be any more just or fair than the people who make up that society.

The government of Canada was basically modelled after the British parliamentary system. The one important exception is the federal form of the union of the Canadian provinces, and the defining of the forms and limits of this union in a single, written document – the *British North America Act, 1867,* now known as the *Constitution Act, 1867.* This aspect of Canadian government is especially important for the courts because it has thrust upon them the function of judicial review, or "umpire" of the federal system.[8] Federalism aside, both levels of government in Canada were formed after the Westminster model, which entailed parliamentary supremacy within their respective spheres of jurisdiction.

Accordingly, until 1982 Canada followed the British approach to the protection of civil liberty – parliamentary supremacy combined with "the rule of law," and a healthy self-confidence in Canadians' basic sense of fairness and tolerance for diversity. Inevitably, the proximity of the United States has prompted constant comparisons. One of the most eloquent and forceful defences of the Anglo-Canadian approach to protecting civil liberties was given by the dean of Canadian political science, R. MacGregor Dawson. In discussing the various components of Canada's unwritten constitution, Dawson argued that

> The mere fact that a constitutional doctrine is not explicitly enunciated and formally committed to writing may affect the external appearance but not disturb the genuineness or force of that doctrine. Thus the broad tolerance which will permit differences of opinion and will disapprove of punitive or repressive measures against the dissenters is of as great constitutional significance and may conceivably under some circumstances afford an even more assured protection than an explicit guarantee of freedom of speech, written into a constitution, yet with no solid conviction behind it.[9]

The force of Dawson's argument notwithstanding, Canadian political leaders have been increasingly attracted to the American approach to protecting civil liberties. In 1960, the Diefenbaker government enacted the Canadian *Bill of Rights.* It took the form of a statute, not a constitutional amendment, and applied only to the federal government and not to the provinces.[10] Partly because of dissatisfaction with this document and partly in response to political developments within Canada during the 1970s, the Trudeau government undertook a major program of constitutional reform in 1980. Prime Minister Pierre Trudeau's constitutional agenda included "patriating" the *British North America Act*, along with an amending formula and a new *Charter of Rights* that applied to both levels of Canadian government. After a year and a half of political maneuvering, confrontation and finally compromise, modified versions of all three objectives were achieved.

The adoption of a constitutionally entrenched *Charter of Rights* (reproduced in Appendix C) fundamentally altered the Canadian system of government by placing explicit limitations on the law-making power of both levels of government. Parliament was no longer supreme; the Constitution was. Or almost. The *Charter* was not adopted in its original, "pure" form. Attachment to the tradition of parliamentary supremacy, combined with provincial suspicion and opposition, forced an important compromise. Added in the eleventh hour of constitutional negotiations between the federal government and the provinces, section 33 of the *Charter* allows both provincial legislatures and the federal Parliament to declare that a law will operate "notwithstanding" certain *Charter* provisions if they deem it necessary (see Chapter 12). Parliamentary supremacy was thus preserved, albeit in a qualified form.

In 1998, the United Kingdom took a step in the direction of its two former North American colonies by incorporating the European Convention for the Protection of Human Rights and Fundamental Freedoms into English domestic law by passing the *Human Rights Act*. This legislation allows the rights enumerated in the European Convention to be asserted and adjudicated in British courts. However, British political leaders were reluctant to abandon their three-hundred-year tradition of parliamentary sovereignty. In the end, they chose not to give British courts the power to declare laws invalid. Instead, the courts are instructed to interpret legislation in accordance with the Convention "as far as it is possible." However, if a judge finds an irreconcilable conflict between a statute and a provision of the Convention, the most the judge can do is issue a "declaration of incompatibility." This finding does not invalidate the law in question or prevent it from being enforced. However, it triggers a "fast track" procedure for Parliament to remedy the legal problem identified by the courts. In the final analysis, however, it rests with the government of the day whether or how to respond to a declaration of incompatibility.

Today, Canada finds itself somewhere between the traditional British and American models of liberal democracy. While each country has given its courts a role in interpreting and enforcing constitutional rights, they have structured the division of labour between courts and legislatures differently. In each instance, elected governments can have the final word, but with different degrees of difficulty. For the Americans to reverse a Supreme Court ruling on their *Bill of Rights* requires either a constitutional amendment or "packing the Court" with new appointments committed to overturning the disputed precedent. While there are several examples of both, neither occurs frequently, although the paramount importance of incoming judges' "judicial philosophy" was on display during the vicious political battle surrounding Antonin Scalia's replacement on the U.S. Supreme Court in 2016–2017. In theory, Canadian governments are armed with a more usable "check" on perceived judicial error – the section 33 "notwithstanding" clause. In practice, Canadian legislatures have been increasingly reluctant to invoke their section 33 power (although the Saskatchewan government introduced legislation to do so in 2017; see Chapter 12). Canadian legislatures have also used the less drastic remedy of simply re-enacting the impugned legislation with amendments. In the United Kingdom, a judicial declaration of incompatibility does not alter the legal status quo, so it remains at the discretion of the government of the day whether or if to respond. In practice, however, the U.K. Parliament has been highly deferential to courts following declarations of invalidity.[11]

Reading 1.5 shows where Canada fits on the continuum of Commonwealth countries that have adopted explicit bills of rights in the last thirty-five years. Given the high political price for using the notwithstanding clause, Canada today functions much more like the American "strong form" system of judicial review, where judicial interpretations are rarely challenged by legislative majorities. For these reasons, Mark Harding has argued that the Canadian system reflects a "clash of constitutionalisms." Political constitutionalists, on the one hand, suggest that rights can be best protected through the traditional political channels (elected legislators and governments). On the other hand, legal constitutionalists elevate the judiciary as the primary "custodian" in rights disputes.[12] While legal constitutionalists won the battle over whether Canada should have a constitutional bill of rights, debates persist among Canadian scholars (and even judges) about if and when legislative majorities should be able to displace a judicial ruling. The truth of this debate lies somewhere between the two contending positions, for as Dawson pointed out, "Written law and the conventions will normally complement one another and each becomes necessary to the proper functioning of the other."[13] The implications of these different divisions of labour between courts and legislatures is the focus of "dialogue theory" discussed in Chapter 12.

While this debate is ongoing, there is one undisputed fact about the effect of enumerating individual rights in a written constitution: it thrusts the courts, and the judges who constitute them, into a more explicit and influential political role. The power of judges is also influenced by a more recent debate: whether constitutional rights (and thus judicial review) apply only to what the government does or whether they extend to the actions of private citizens and businesses. This debate portends a second "clash of constitutionalisms," between the adherents of liberalism and post-liberalism. This clash is the focus of Thomas Bateman's contribution (Reading 1.6).

As Bateman describes, traditional liberal constitutionalism drew a sharp distinction between the public and the private, between state and civil society. The purpose of constitutionalism (and especially constitutional rights) was to protect the latter from the former. Constitutional rights applied only to "state action" – laws passed by legislators, executive orders and the conduct of "state agents" such as the police. By placing written (and thus judicially enforceable limits) on what (and how) the state may do, liberal constitutionalism sought to enhance the sphere of individual freedom (civil society) by limiting the scope of state powers.

Liberal constitutionalists therefore conceived of rights as "negative" (i.e., rights against government). So conceived, constitutional rights, and thus judicial review, do not apply to "private" actions – that is, relationships in the home, the workplace or between neighbours. While this was the original understanding behind the 1982 *Canadian Charter of Rights and Freedoms*, Bateman analyzes how the Supreme Court has chipped away at this understanding and advanced – but not yet embraced – a post-liberal constitutionalism that applies to both state and civil society. For the new edition of this book, Bateman provides an update to Reading 1.6, showing how the growth of *Charter* values in the Supreme Court's administrative law jurisprudence has pushed it in a post-liberal direction. Future decisions will determine whether post-liberalism has prevailed.

NOTES

1   For an excellent account of both the *Roncarelli* case and the larger conflict between the Jehovah's Witnesses and the Quebec government, see William Kaplan, *State and Salvation: The Jehovah's Witnesses and Their Fight for Civil Rights* (Toronto: University of Toronto Press, 1989).

2   The full text of s.39 of *Magna Carta* reads as follows: "No freeman shall be taken or (and) imprisoned or disseised or outlawed or exiled or in any way destroyed, nor will we go upon him nor send upon him, except by the lawful judgement of his peers or (and) by the law of the land." This eight-hundred-year-old rule is the direct ancestor of the 1982 *Charter of Rights and Freedoms*, whose preamble declares: "Whereas Canada is founded upon principles that recognize the supremacy of God and the rule of law." Section 7 of the *Charter* essentially restates the modern formulation of *per legem terrae*, that no person can be deprived of life, liberty or security of the person, except in accordance with the "principles of fundamental justice." Sections 8 through 14 then elaborate a number of other legal rights.

3   See Locke, *The Second Treatise*, Ch. 1, Reading 1.2.

4   Sir Ivor Jennings, *The Law and the Constitution*. 5th ed. (London: University of London Press, 1959), p. 33.

5   This problem is the subject of Chapter 12.

6   The Supreme Court of Canada's decision in the 1981 *Patriation Reference* was contrary to this generally accepted practice. In subsequent references concerning Quebec secession and Senate reform, the Supreme Court once again based its decision on unwritten principles. See Readings 2.4, 2.5 and 2.6.

7   See Thomas Berger, *Fragile Freedoms: Human Rights and Dissent in Canada* (Vancouver: Clarke, Irwin and Co., 1981).

8   This is the subject of Chapter 9.

9   R. MacGregor Dawson, *The Government of Canada*. 4th ed. (Toronto: University of Toronto Press, 1963), p. 70.

10   This is discussed in greater detail in Reading 12.3.

11   Stephen Gardbaum, *The New Commonwealth Model of Constitutionalism: Theory and Practice* (Cambridge: Cambridge University Press, 2013), pp. 174–176.

12   Mark S. Harding, *Clashing Constitutionalisms in the Bill-of-Rights Era: Strength, Reach and Rights Values* (PhD dissertation, University of Calgary, December 2017).

13   Dawson, *Government of Canada*, p. 71.

1.1

Roncarelli v. Duplessis

Supreme Court of Canada, [1959] S.C.R. 121

The judgment of Rand and Judson JJ. was delivered by RAND J.: – The material facts from which my conclusion is drawn are these. The appellant was the proprietor of a restaurant in a busy section of Montreal which in 1946 through its transmission to him from his father had been continuously licenced for the sale of liquor for approximately 34 years; he is of good education and repute and the restaurant was of a superior class. On December 4 of that year, while his application for annual renewal was before the Liquor Commission, the existing licence was cancelled and his application for renewal rejected, to which was added a declaration by the respondent that no future licence would ever issue to him. These primary facts took place in the following circumstances.

For some years the appellant had been an adherent of a rather militant Christian religious sect known as the Witnesses of Jehovah. Their ideology condemns the established church institutions and stresses the absolute and exclusive personal relation of the individual to the Deity without human intermediation or intervention.

The first impact of their proselytizing zeal upon the Roman Catholic church and community in Quebec, as might be expected, produced a violent reaction. Meetings were forcibly broken up, property damaged, individuals ordered out of communities, in one case out of the province, and generally, within the cities and towns, bitter controversy aroused. The work of the Witnesses was carried on both by word of mouth and by the distribution of printed matter, the latter including two periodicals known as "The Watch Tower" and "Awake," sold at a small price.

In 1945 the provincial authorities began to take steps to bring an end to what was considered insulting and offensive to the religious beliefs and feelings of the Roman Catholic population. Large scale arrests were made of young men and women, by whom the publications mentioned were being held out for sale, under local by-laws requiring a licence for peddling any kind of wares. Altogether almost one thousand of such charges were laid. The penalty involved in Montreal, where most of the arrests took place, was a fine of $40, and as the Witnesses disputed liability, bail was in all cases resorted to.

The appellant, being a person of some means, was accepted by the Recorder's Court as bail without question, and up to November 12, 1946, he had gone security in about 380 cases, some of the accused being involved in repeated offences. Up to this time there had been no suggestion of impropriety; the security of the appellant was taken as so satisfactory that at times, to avoid delay when he was absent from the city, recognizances were signed by him in blank and kept ready for completion by the Court officials. The reason for the accumulation of charges was the doubt that they could be sustained in law. Apparently the legal officers of Montreal, acting in concert with those of the Province, had come to an agreement with the attorney for the Witnesses to have a test case proceeded with. Pending that, however, there was no stoppage of the sale of the tracts and this became the annoying circumstance that produced the volume of proceedings.

On or about November 12 it was decided to require bail in cash for Witnesses so arrested and the sum set ranged from $100 to $300. No such bail was furnished by the appellant; his connection with giving security ended with this change of practice; and in the result, all of the charges in relation to which he had become surety were dismissed.

At no time did he take any part in the distribution of the tracts: he was an adherent of the group but nothing more. It was shown that he had leased to another member premises in Sherbrooke which were used as a hall for carrying on religious meetings: but it is unnecessary to do more than mention that fact to reject it as having no bearing on the issues raised. Beyond the giving of bail and being an adherent, the appellant is free from any relation that could be tortured into a badge of character pertinent to his fitness or unfitness to hold a liquor licence.

The mounting resistance that stopped the surety bail sought other means of crushing the propagandist invasion and among the circumstances looked into was the situation of the appellant. Admittedly an adherent, he was enabling these protagonists to be at large to carry on their campaign of publishing what they believed to be the Christian truth as revealed by the Bible; he was also the holder of a liquor licence, a "privilege" granted by the Province, the profits from which, as it was seen by the authorities, he was using to promote the disturbance of settled beliefs and arouse community disaffection generally. Following discussions between the then Mr. Archambault, as the personality of the Liquor Commission, and the chief prosecuting officer in Montreal, the former, on or about November 21, telephoned to the respondent, advised him of those facts, and queried what should be done. Mr. Duplessis answered that the matter was serious and that the identity of the person furnishing bail and the liquor licensee should be put beyond doubt. A few days later, that identity being established through a private investigator, Mr. Archambault again communicated with the respondent and, as a result of what passed between them, the licence, as of December 4, 1946, was revoked.

In the meantime, about November 25, 1946, a blasting answer had come from the Witnesses. In an issue of one of the periodicals, under the heading "Quebec's Burning Hate," was a searing denunciation of what was alleged to be the savage persecution of Christian believers. Immediately instructions were sent out from the department of the Attorney-General ordering the confiscation of the issue and proceedings were taken against one Boucher charging him with publication of a seditious libel.

It is then wholly as a private citizen, an adherent of a religious group, holding a liquor licence and furnishing bail to arrested persons for no other purpose than to enable them to be released from detention pending the determination of the charges against them, and with no other relevant considerations to be taken into account, that he is involved in the issues of this controversy.

The complementary state of things is equally free from doubt. From the evidence of Mr. Duplessis and Mr. Archambault alone, it appears that the action taken by the latter as the general manager and sole member of the Commission was dictated by Mr. Duplessis as Attorney-General and Prime Minister of the province; that that step was taken as a means of bringing to a halt the activities of the Witnesses, to punish the appellant for the part he had played not only by revoking the existing licence but in declaring him barred from one "forever," and to warn others that they similarly would be stripped of provincial "privileges" if they persisted in any activity directly or indirectly related to the Witnesses and to the objectionable campaign. The respondent felt that action to be his duty, something which his conscience demanded of him; and as representing the provincial government his decision became automatically that of Mr. Archambault and the Commission....

... In these circumstances, when the *de facto* power of the Executive over its appointees at will to such a statutory public function is exercised deliberately and intentionally to destroy the vital business interests of a citizen, is there legal redress by him against the person so acting? This calls for an examination of the statutory provisions governing the issue, renewal and revocation of liquor licences and the scope of authority entrusted by law to the Attorney-General and the government in relation to the administration of the Act....

... The provisions of the statute, which may be supplemented by detailed regulations, furnish a code for the complete administration of the sale and distribution of alcoholic liquors directed by the Commission as a public service, for all legitimate purposes of the populace. It recognizes the association of wines and liquors as embellishments of food and its ritual and as an interest of the public. As put in Macbeth, the "sauce to meat is ceremony," and so we have restaurants, cafés, hotels and other places of serving food, specifically provided for in that association.

At the same time the issue of permits has a complementary interest in those so catering to the public. The continuance of the permit over the years, as in this case, not only recognizes its virtual necessity to a superior class restaurant but also its identification with the business carried on. The provisions for assignment of the permit are to this most pertinent and they were exemplified in the continuity of the business here. As its exercise continues, the economic life of the holder becomes progressively more deeply implicated with the privilege while at the same time his vocation becomes correspondingly dependent on it.

The field of licenced occupations and businesses of this nature is steadily becoming of greater concern to citizens generally. It is a matter of vital importance that a public administration that can refuse to allow a person to enter or continue a calling which, in the absence of regulation, would be free and legitimate, should be conducted with complete impartiality and integrity; and that the grounds for refusing or cancelling a permit should unquestionably be such and such only as are incompatible with the purposes envisaged by the statute: the duty of a Commission is to serve those purposes and those only. A decision to deny or cancel such a privilege lies within the "discretion" of the Commission; but that means that decision is to be based upon a weighing of considerations pertinent to the object of the administration.

In public regulation of this sort there is no such thing as absolute and untrammelled "discretion," that is that action can be taken on any ground or for any reason that can be suggested to the mind of the administrator; no legislative Act can, without express language, be taken to contemplate an unlimited arbitrary power exercisable for any purpose, however capricious or irrelevant, regardless of the nature or purpose of the statute. Fraud and corruption in the Commission may not be mentioned in such statutes but they are always implied as exceptions. "Discretion" necessarily implies good faith in discharging public duty; there is always a perspective within which a statute is intended to operate; and any clear departure from its lines or objects is just as objectionable as fraud or corruption. Could an applicant be refused a permit because he had been born in another province, or because of the colour of his hair? The ordinary language of the legislature cannot be so distorted.

To deny or revoke a permit because a citizen exercises an unchallengeable right totally irrelevant to the sale of liquor in a restaurant is equally beyond the scope of the discretion conferred. There was here not only revocation of the existing permit but a declaration of a future, definitive disqualification of the appellant to obtain one: it was to be "forever." This purports to divest his citizenship status of its incident of membership in the class of those of the public to whom such a privilege could be extended. Under the statutory language here, that is not competent to the Commission and *a fortiori* to the government or the respondent: *McGillivray* v. *Kimber*. There is here an administrative tribunal which, in certain respects, is to act in a judicial manner; and even on the view of the dissenting justices in *McGillivray*, there is liability: what could be more malicious than to punish this licencee for having done what he had an absolute right to do in a matter utterly irrelevant to the *Liquor Act*? Malice in the proper sense is simply acting for a reason and purpose knowingly foreign to the administration, to which was added here the element of intentional punishment by what was virtually vocation outlawry.

It may be difficult if not impossible in cases generally to demonstrate a breach of this public duty in the illegal purpose served; there may be no means, even if proceedings against the Commission were permitted by the Attorney-General, as here they were refused, of compelling the Commission to justify a refusal or revocation or to give reasons for its action; on these questions I make no observation; but in the case before us that difficulty is not present: the reasons are openly avowed.

The act of the respondent through the instrumentality of the Commission brought about a breach of an implied public statutory duty toward the appellant; it was a gross abuse of legal power expressly intended to punish him for an act wholly irrelevant to the statute, a punishment which inflicted on him, as it was intended to do, the destruction of his economic life as a restaurant keeper within the province. Whatever may be the immunity of the Commission or its member from an action for damages, there is none in the respondent. He was under no duty in relation to the appellant and his act was an intrusion upon the functions of a statutory body. The injury done by him was a fault engaging liability within the principles of the underlying public law of Quebec: *Mostyn* v. *Fabrigas*, and under art. 1053 of the *Civil Code*. That, in the presence of expanding administrative regulation of economic activities, such a step and its consequences are to be suffered by the victim without recourse or remedy, that an administration according to law is to be superseded by action dictated by and according to the arbitrary likes, dislikes and irrelevant purposes of public officers acting beyond their duty, would signalize the beginning of disintegration of the rule of law as a fundamental postulate of our constitutional structure. An administration of licences on the highest level of fair and impartial treatment to all may be forced to follow the practice of "first come, first served," which makes the strictest observance of equal responsibility to all of even greater importance; at this stage of developing government it would be a danger of high consequence to tolerate such a departure from good faith in executing the legislative purpose. It should be added, however, that that principle is not, by this language, intended to be extended to ordinary governmental employment: with that we are not here concerned.

It was urged by Mr. Beaulieu that the respondent, as the incumbent of an office of state, so long as he was proceeding in "good faith," was free to act in a matter of this kind virtually as he pleased. The office of Attorney-General traditionally and by statute carries duties that relate to advising the Executive, including here, administrative bodies, enforcing the public law and directing the administration of justice. In any decision of the statutory body in this case, he had no part to play beyond giving advice on legal questions arising. In that role his action should have been limited to advice on the validity of a revocation for such a reason or purpose and what that advice should have been does not seem to me to admit of any doubt. To pass from this limited scope of action to that of bringing about a step by the Commission beyond the bounds prescribed by the legislature for its exclusive action converted what was done into his personal act.

"Good faith" in this context, applicable both to the respondent and the general manager, means carrying out the statute according to its intent and for its purpose; it means good faith in acting with a rational appreciation of that intent and purpose and not with an improper intent and for an alien purpose; it does not mean for the purposes of punishing a person for exercising an unchallengeable right; it does not mean arbitrarily and illegally attempting to divest a citizen of an incident of his civil status....

1.2

Of the Extent of the Legislative Power
John Locke, *The Second Treatise* (1690)

Cambridge and New York: Cambridge University Press, 1960. Edited by Peter Laslett. Reprinted with permission.

The great end of Mens entring into Society, being the enjoyment of their Properties in Peace and Safety, and the great instrument and means of that being the Laws establish'd in that Society; the first and fundamental positive Law of all Commonwealths, is the establishing of the Legislative Power; as the first and fundamental natural Law, which is to govern even the Legislative itself, is the preservation of the Society, and (as far as will consist with the publik good) of every person in it. This Legislative is not only the supream power of the Commonwealth, but sacred and unalterable in the hands where the Community have once placed it....

... Though the Legislative, whether placed in one or more, whether it be always in being, or only by intervals, tho' it be the Supream Power in every Common-wealth; yet,

First, It is not, nor can possibly be absolutely Arbitrary over the Lives and Fortunes of the People. For it being but the joynt power of every Member of the Society given up to that Person, or Assembly, which is Legislator, it can be no more than those persons had in a State of Nature before they enter'd into Society, and gave up to the Community.... Their Power in the utmost Bounds of it, is limited to the publik good of the Society. It is a Power, that hath no other end but preservation, and therefore can never have a right to destroy, enslave, or designedly to impoverish the Subjects. The Obligations of the Law of Nature, cease not in Society but only in many Cases are drawn closer, and have by Humane Laws known Penalties annexed to them, to inforce their observation. Thus the Law of Nature stands as an Eternal Rule to all Men, Legislators as well as others....

... Secondly, The Legislative, or Supream Authority, cannot assume to its self a power to Rule by extemporary Arbitrary Decrees, but is bound to dispense Justice, and decide the Rights of the Subject by promulgated standing Laws, and known Authoris'd Judges. For the Law of Nature being unwritten, and so no where to be found but in the minds of Men, they who through Passion or Interest shall miscite, or misapply it, cannot so easily be convinced of their mistake where there is no establish'd Judge: And so it serves not, as it ought, to determine the Rights, and fence the Properties of those that live under it, especially where every one is Judge, Interpreter, and Executioner of it too, and that in his own Case: And he that has right on his side, having ordinarily but his own single strength, hath not force enough to defend himself from Injuries, or to punish Delinquents. To avoid these Inconveniencies which disorder Mens Properties in the state of Nature, Men unite into Societies, that they may have the united strength of the whole Society to secure and defend their Properties, and may have standing Rules to bound it, by which every one may know what is his. To this end it is that Men give up all their Natural Power to the Society which they enter into, and the Community put the Legislative Power into such hands as they think fit, with this trust, that they shall be govern'd by declared Laws, or else their Peace, Quiet, and Property will still be at the same uncertainty, as it was in the state of Nature.

Absolute Arbitrary Power, or Governing without settled standing Laws, can neither of them consist with the ends of Society and Government, which Men would not quit the freedom of the state of Nature for, and tie themselves up under, were it not to preserve their Lives, Liberties and Fortunes; and by stated Rules of Right and Property to secure their Peace and Quiet.... And therefore whatever Form the Common-wealth is under, the Ruling Power ought to govern by declared and received Laws, and not by extemporary Dictates and undetermined Resolutions. For then Mankind will be in a far worse condition, than in the State of Nature, if they shall have armed one or a few Men with the joynt power of a Multitude, to force them to obey at pleasure the exorbitant and unlimited Decrees of their sudden thoughts, or unrestrain'd, and till that moment unknown Wills without having any measures set down which may guide and justifie their actions. For all the power the Government has, being only for the good of the Society, as it ought not to be *Arbitrary* and at Pleasure, so it ought to be exercised by *established and promulgated Laws*: that both the People may know their Duty, and be safe and secure within the limits of the Law, and the Rulers too kept within their due bounds, and not to be tempted, by the Power they have in their hands, to imploy it to such purposes, and by such measures, as they would not have known, and own not willingly.

... Thirdly, The Supream Power cannot take from any Man any part of his Property without his own consent....

... Fourthly, The Legislative cannot transfer the Power of Making Laws to any other hands. For it being but a delegated Power from the People, they, who have it, cannot pass it over to others. The People alone can appoint the Form of the Commonwealth, which is by Constituting the Legislative, and appointing in whose hands that shall be.

... These are the Bounds which the trust that is put in them by the Society, and the Law of God and Nature, have set to the Legislative Power of every Commonwealth, in all Forms of Government.

First, They are to govern, by promulgated establish'd Laws, not to be varied in particular Cases, but to have one Rule for Rich and Poor, for the Favourite at Court, and the Country Man at Plough.

Secondly, These Laws also ought to be designed for no other end ultimately but the good of the People.

Thirdly, they must not raise Taxes on the Property of the People, without the Consent of the People, given by themselves, or their Deputies. And this properly concerns only such Governments where the Legislative is always in being, or at least where the People have not reserv'd any part of the Legislative to Deputies, to be from time to time chosen by themselves.

Fourthly, The Legislative neither must nor can transfer the Power of making Laws to any Body else, or place it anywhere but where the People have.

1.3

The Declaration of Independence
Thomas Jefferson (1776)

When in the course of human events, it becomes necessary for one people to dissolve the political bands which have connected them with another, and to assume among the Powers of the earth, the separate and equal station to which the Laws of Nature and of Nature's God entitle them, a decent respect to the opinions of mankind requires that they should declare the causes which impel them to the separation.

We hold these truths to be self-evident, that all men are created equal, that they are endowed by their Creator with certain unalienable Rights, that among these are Life, Liberty and the pursuit of Happiness. That to secure these rights, Governments are instituted among Men, deriving their just powers from the consent of the governed, that whenever any Form of Government becomes destructive of these ends, it is the Right of the People to alter or to abolish it, and to institute new Government, laying its foundation on such principles and organizing its powers in such form, as to them shall seem most likely to effect their Safety and Happiness. Prudence, indeed, will dictate that Governments long established should not be changed for light and transient causes; and accordingly all experience hath shown, that mankind are more disposed to suffer, while evils are sufferable, than to right themselves by abolishing the forms to which they are accustomed. But when a long train of abuses and usurpations, pursuing invariably the same Object evinces a design to reduce them under absolute Despotism, it is their right, it is their duty, to throw off such Government, and to provide new Guards for their future security....

1.4

The Rule of Law
A.V. Dicey

Introduction to the Study of the Law of the Constitution, 7th ed. (1885). London: MacMillan, 1908, ch. 4. Reprinted with permission.

Two features have at all times since the Norman Conquest characterised the political institutions of England.

The first of these features is the omnipotence or undisputed supremacy throughout the whole country of the central government. This authority of the state or the nation was during the earlier periods of our history represented by the power of the Crown. The King was the source of law and the maintainer of order. The maxim of the Courts, *tout fuit in luy et vient de lui al commencement*, was originally the expression of an actual and undoubted fact. This royal supremacy has now passed into that sovereignty of Parliament which has formed the main subject of the foregoing chapters.

The second of these features, which is closely connected with the first, is the rule or supremacy of law. This peculiarity of our polity is well expressed in the old saw of the Courts, "*La ley est le plus haute inheritance, que le roy ad; car par la ley il même et toutes ses sujets sont rulés, et si la ley ne fuit, nul roi, et nul inheritance sera.*"

This supremacy of the law, or the security given under the English constitution to the rights of individuals looked at from various points of view, forms the subject of this part of this treatise.

Foreign observers of English manners, such for example as Voltaire, De Lolme, Tocqueville, or Gneist, have been far more struck than have Englishmen themselves with the fact that England is a country governed, as is scarcely any other part of Europe, under the rule of law; and admiration or astonishment at the legality of English habits and feeling is nowhere better expressed than in a curious passage from Tocqueville's writings, which compares the Switzerland and the England of 1836 in respect of the spirit which pervades their laws and manners.

"I am not about," he writes, "to compare Switzerland with the United States, but with Great Britain. When you examine the two countries, or even if you only pass through them, you perceive, in my judgment, the most astonishing differences between them. Take it all in all, England seems to be much more republican than the Helvetic Republic. The principal differences are found in the institutions of the two countries, and especially in their customs (*moeurs*)....

> The Swiss do not show the love of justice which is such a strong characteristic of the English. Their Courts have no place in the political arrangements of the country, and exert no influence on public opinion. The love of justice, the peaceful and legal introduction of the judge into the domain of politics, are perhaps the most standing characteristics of a free people.

> Finally, and this really embraces all the rest, the Swiss do not show at bottom that respect for justice, that love of law, that dislike of

using force, without which no free nation can exist, which strikes strangers so forcibly in England.

I sum up these impressions in a few words.

Whoever travels in the United States is involuntarily and instinctively so impressed with the fact that the spirit of liberty and the taste for it have pervaded all the habits of the American people, that he cannot conceive of them under any but a Republican government. In the same way it is impossible to think of the English as living under any but a free government. But if violence were to destroy the Republican institutions in most of the Swiss Cantons, it would be by no means certain that after rather a short state of transition the people would not grow accustomed to the loss of liberty. In the United States and in England there seems to be more liberty in the customs than in the laws of the people. In Switzerland there seems to be more liberty in the laws than in the customs of the country.

Tocqueville's language has a twofold bearing on our present topic. His words point in the clearest manner to the rule, predominance, or supremacy of law as the distinguishing characteristic of English institutions. They further direct attention to the extreme vagueness of a trait of national character which is as noticeable as it is hard to portray. Tocqueville, we see, is clearly perplexed how to define a feature of English manners of which he at once recognises the existence; he mingles or confuses together the habit of self-government, the love of order, the respect for justice and a legal turn of mind. All these sentiments are intimately allied, but they cannot without confusion be identified with each other. If, however, a critic as acute as Tocqueville found a difficulty in describing one of the most marked peculiarities of English life, we may safely conclude that we ourselves, whenever we talk of Englishmen as loving the government of law, or of the supremacy of law as being a characteristic of the English constitution, are using words which, though they possess a real significance, are nevertheless to most persons who employ them full of vagueness and ambiguity. If therefore we are ever to appreciate the full import of the idea denoted by the term "rule, supremacy, or predominance of law," we must first determine precisely what we mean by such expressions when we apply them to the British constitution.

When we say that the supremacy or the rule of law is a characteristic of the English constitution, we generally include under one expression at least three distinct though kindred conceptions....

... It means, in the first place, the absolute supremacy or predominance of regular law as opposed to the influence of arbitrary power, and excludes the existence of arbitrariness, of prerogative, or even of wide discretionary authority on the part of the government. Englishmen are ruled by the law, and by the law alone; a man may with us be punished for a breach of law, but he can be punished for nothing else.

It means, again, equality before the law, or the equal subjection of all classes to the ordinary law of the land administered by the ordinary Law Courts; the "rule of law" in this sense excludes the idea of any exemption of officials or others from the duty of obedience to the law which governs other citizens or from the jurisdiction of the ordinary tribunals; there can be with us nothing really corresponding to the "administrative law" (*droit administratif*) or the "administrative tribunals" (*tribunaux administratifs*) of France. The notion which lies at the bottom of the "administrative law" known to foreign countries is, that affairs or disputes in which the government or its servants are concerned are beyond the sphere of the civil Courts and must be dealt with by special and more or less official bodies. This idea is utterly unknown to the law of England, and indeed is fundamentally inconsistent with our traditions and customs.

The "rule of law," lastly, may be used as a formula for expressing the fact that with us the law of the constitution, the rules which in foreign countries naturally form part of a constitutional code, are not the source but the consequence of the rights of individuals, as defined and enforced by the Courts; that, in short, the principles of private law have with us been by the action of the Courts and Parliament so extended as to determine the position of the Crown and of its servants; thus the constitution is the result of the ordinary law of the land.

General propositions, however, as to the nature of the rule of law carry us but a very little way. If we want to understand what that principle in all its different aspects and developments really means, we must try to trace its influence throughout some of the main provisions of the constitution. The best mode of doing this is to examine with care the manner in which the law of England deals with the following topics, namely, the right to personal freedom; the right to freedom of discussion; the right of public meeting; the use of martial law; the rights and duties of the army; the collection and expenditure of the public revenue; and the responsibility of Ministers. The true nature further of the rule of law as it exists in England will be illustrated by contrast with the idea of *droit administratif*, or administrative law, which prevails in many continental countries. These topics will each be treated of in their due order. The object, however, of this treatise, as the reader should remember, is not to provide minute and full information, *e.g.* as to the *Habeas Corpus* Acts, or other enactments protecting the liberty of the subject; but simply to show that these leading heads of constitutional law, which have been enumerated, these "articles," so to speak of the constitution, are both governed by, and afford illustrations of, the supremacy throughout English institutions of the law of the land. If at some future day the law of the constitution should be codified, each of the topics I have mentioned would be dealt with by the sections of the code.

1.5

Strong- and Weak-Form Judicial Review

Rainer Knopff, Rhonda Evans, Dennis Baker and Dave Snow

From "Dialogue: Clarified and Reconsidered," *Osgoode Hall Law Journal* 54, no. 2 (2017), 605–640. Reprinted with permission.

Figure 1: Strong- and Weak-Form Review

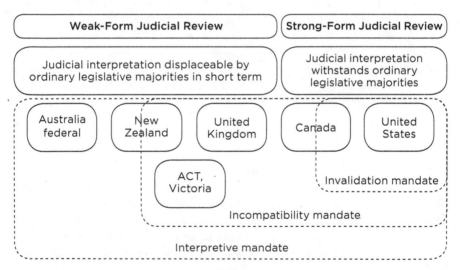

Interpretive Mandate:
Enjoyed by all courts in common-law liberal democracies and spans the continuum of weak- and strong-form systems. This includes the traditional judicial powers both to revise judge-made common law and to choose between plausibly available interpretations of statutes.

Incompatibility Mandate:
When courts, unable to find a rights-compatible interpretation of a law, can issue explicit statements of incompatibility.

Invalidation Mandate:
The authority to strike down and invalidate laws.

1.6

Liberal versus Post-Liberal Constitutionalism: Applying the *Charter* to Civil Society (Updated)

Thomas M.J. Bateman

Political Science, St. Thomas University. Updated for the 2018 edition.

Introduction

In their study of the new politics of the Canadian *Charter of Rights and Freedoms*, F.L. Morton and Rainer Knopff contend that a revolution is afoot, led, with active state assistance, by a coterie of interest groups and professional castes they call the "Court Party." They muster persuasive evidence to demonstrate that this political configuration has permeated not only the departments of the state but also the offices of the academy and the pages of the law journals.

Revolutions require more than the storming of the palace. They require a fundamental alteration of the principles of the regime. A revolution changes the moral fabric of the polity, reorienting citizens' habits and preferences. Is there evidence that the Court Party has proceeded beyond the occupation of the palace toward an alteration of the lives of citizens? In other words, have *Charter* norms penetrated civil society – those myriad institutions like family, workplace, church, school, and fraternal associations – where people live outside of the direct influence of the state?

This question begs others. What is the purpose of a *Charter* anyway? At bottom, is the *Charter* designed to limit action the state can take with respect to civil society and individual citizens? Or is it intended to announce a set of norms for all of society to embody? In one sense, these questions pose a false choice, since a constitution seeking to limit the scope of state action reflects principles informing the shape and purpose of a polity. But in another sense the questions imply a distinction between two different understandings of constitutionalism. The first, traditional liberal constitutionalism, distinguishes state from society and understands the constitution as a way to protect the latter from the former. The second is a more recent twentieth century variant urging the application of constitutional principles of liberty, equality, and due process on institutions regardless of their connections to the state.

The Supreme Court of Canada has been divided on the purpose of the *Charter*. More basically, it has been divided on the kind of constitutionalism the *Charter* should embody. Early *Charter* decisions reflect a traditional constitutionalism. But later decisions became longer, more complex, more riven with dissents based on divergent interpretive principles. One of the sources of divisions was a disquiet about traditional liberal constitutionalism. Decisions in the late 1980s and 1990s began to hint at a new understanding of the *Charter*. Judges are increasingly willing to apply the *Charter* to institutions beyond the state, and increasingly disposed to apply *Charter* norms "into" society, converting informal relationships into more formal, rule-bound ones based on judicially articulated principles of fairness, non-discrimination, and individual autonomy. However, the Court has not abandoned liberal constitutionalism for the new version. It goes back and forth, sensitive, apparently, to the circumstances of particular cases and to changes in Court personnel. If and when the Supreme Court of Canada finally drops liberal constitutionalism for a new post-liberal constitutionalism, the *Charter* revolution will have approached its consummation.

Post-Liberal Constitutionalism

Liberal constitutionalism is a set of political attitudes, an ideology, centred on the notion that legitimate government is limited, controlled government. Constitutionalism in the end is a counsel of political restraint on the part of all institutions of government. Constitutional government is constrained in what it can and should do. It is premised on a distinction between state and society. While a properly functioning society needs government to maintain order, enforce contracts, protect against external military threat, and address various forms of market failure, society functions best when citizens are free from the vicissitudes of arbitrary, ill-considered state meddling. Of course, ambitious and unscrupulous persons are found in government as well as civil society, and so the problem arises as to how the government not only can control excesses in civil society but also excesses of its own. And because the state has a monopoly on the legitimate use of coercion, it presents a unique threat to society. State power can threaten society as much as preserve it.

Constitutions are addressed to this problem. Constitutional mechanisms are all about "countervailance": power can only be checked by power, and the properly constructed constitution provides a set of checks and balances ensuring that the power of one state actor or state institution can be checked by the countervailing power of another. The doctrine of the "separation of powers" (more accurately, separate institutions sharing powers), for which the American Constitution is justly famous, is a cardinal constitutional idea. A judicially enforced bill of rights, of more recent vintage, is another.

In the beginning, bills of rights were intended to declare an absolute limit to what the state could do. They were a defence of individual persons and civil society against illegitimate state action. As the franchise was expanded and governments became sensitive to majority opinion, the bill of rights was upheld as an important bulwark against the reckless rule of the majority. So bills of rights were about the protection of property against expropriation, the protection of the due process rights (like the presumption of innocence until proven guilty) of accused offenders against overzealous police, and the protection of eccentric writers and religionists against majoritarian pressures to conform. In all these cases, the bill of rights marked out a region of non-interference around civil society beyond which the state was not to trespass. This liberal constitutionalism both reflected and supported a distinction between private and public realms. If you want to exclude women from your fraternal organization's membership, the liberal constitutionalist may resent your sexism but would defend your right to discriminate in this fashion in your private dealings.

Liberal constitutionalism has been attacked in a variety of ways. Critics argue that it relies on a right-wing ideology stressing the self-correcting, utility-maximizing wonders of the market which empirical evidence fails to confirm. When democratically elected governments sought to address market failure and unacceptable inequalities of wealth, judges in the early twentieth century vetoed such policies on increasingly anachronistic liberal constitutionalist principles, claiming employment matters were private relations beyond the reach of government. It is also claimed that the distinction between public and private realms is likewise an ideological construction that historically reinforced the subordination of women. Power is a problem not just of the state but of all manner of institutions: corporations, unions, and families. Confining principles of equality, liberty, and due process to the public, governmental realm does nothing to liberate women imprisoned in the domestic, "private" realm beyond the reach of such constitutional principles.

Criticisms like these led some to discard the liberal constitutionalist enterprise altogether. Others sought to revise liberal constitutionalism, to develop a new kind of constitutionalism which would provide the intellectual and moral foundation for the application of judicially enforced constitutional norms to institutions of civil society. The primary virtue of this new constitutionalism is that the application of constitutional norms "downward" into society need not await the action of the government. As the political history of liberal democracies of the twentieth century indicates, the line between state and society, public and private, has become fluid, subject to the willingness of state action to convert a formerly private matter into a public matter subject to legislative control. But what if the state refuses so to act?

Post-liberal constitutionalism is the solution. Judges need not await the formation of positive public policy. At the urging of a group or even an individual litigant, the private can be converted into the constitutional, subject to constitutional norms. For the new constitutionalists, the problem becomes: what regions of private choice should be exempt from judicial inquiry? If I must serve food at my restaurant to anyone who enters, can I nonetheless be allowed to decide on my marriage partner based on my racist preference for people of a certain skin colour or cultural background? Or are such manifestations of discriminatory preference incompatible with a democratic society, which requires the universal application of equality norms?

Constitutionalism and the Canadian *Charter*

An early draft of the Canadian *Charter* contained what is called an application provision, a section indicating what entities were bound by the terms of the *Charter*. *Charter* application is a threshold litigants initially have to clear before the courts can hear a *Charter* claim. The draft provision was crucially ambiguous and seemed to declare that not only government but "all matters within the authority of" government would be caught by *Charter* rights. According to three participants in the patriation debate,

> Since all the things that private citizens do are within the legislative jurisdiction of one level of government or another, the wording of the new application section turned the *Charter* not only into a constitutional document which restrained government, but a constitutional set of norms relating to the whole of social activity within the country. This was a radical transformation of the nature of the *Charter*.

Before the final draft was approved by the premiers, section 32 of the *Charter* was reworded to allay fears that the *Charter* was designed to apply to civil society institutions as well as the state proper. Representatives of the federal Department of Justice testifying before a special parliamentary committee on the constitution in 1981 were fairly clear that the *Charter* was to conform to the principles of a traditional constitutionalism: it would bind the government, not the whole of society. So settled did this issue seem to be that several constitutional scholars could insist immediately after the *Charter*'s entrenchment that it was a liberal constitutionalist instrument. As late as 1992, responding to suggestions that the *Charter* was transferring major social policy powers to the courts and undermining democracy in Canada, Peter Russell stressed the constraints on judicial decision making, a major one being the limits of *Charter* application:

> ... the *Charter* applies only to governments and legislatures. *Charter* rights and *Charter* freedoms can be claimed only against the actions of governments or legislatures. However the main barrier to full enjoyment or exercise of some rights, particularly equality rights, is not government action but government inaction in responding to problems emanating from the private sector and the very structure of society.

Russell's confidence is misplaced. While the Supreme Court of Canada has not rejected liberal constitutionalism, it is in the throes of a clash of constitutionalisms, uncomfortable with aspects of liberal constitutionalism but apparently wary of the consequences of traveling the new path of universal application of constitutional norms.

Toward a Post-Liberal Constitutionalism

The Supreme Court's *Charter* jurisprudence reveals several means by which liberal constitutionalism has been challenged: the expansion of the definition of "government" for the purposes of section 32 interpretation; the application of "*Charter* values" to the development of private law; and the development of a doctrine of "inaction" and "underinclusivity" in respect to section 15 equality rights claims. These mechanisms often arise together in the same cases but are analytically distinct and will be treated as such.

Defining "Government"

Section 32 of the *Charter* declares in part that the *Charter* applies "to the parliament and government of Canada ... and to the legislature and government of each province." How do we define government? In the era of the administrative state in which public expenditures consume over 40 percent of the GDP, it is hard to discern where the state stops and society begins. Equally, it is hard to determine when state influence over an entity becomes so overwhelming that the entity is then subsumed under the definition of government for the purposes of section 32. And is it possible for a part of an entity to be governmental for the purposes of section 32, while other parts of an entity escape *Charter* application?

Such issues were squarely presented to the Supreme Court for the first time in *McKinney v. University of Guelph* (1990). Eight university professors were subject to mandatory retirement according to university policies or collective agreements negotiated with faculty associations. They did not want to retire so they challenged (unsuccessfully) the mandatory retirement policy on the basis that it constituted age discrimination contrary to section 15 of the *Charter*. A crucial issue was whether the *Charter* applied to universities. For the majority, Gerard LaForest argued that universities are not sufficiently governmental to be caught by the *Charter*. Though they receive public moneys, are established by legislation, and are subject to myriad rules and regulations, they are, he wrote, independent civil society institutions. In order for an entity to be considered "government" for the purposes of section 32, there must be a clear nexus between government and the entity, and the entity must be subject to control and compulsion. It must be an instrument of public policy.

While universities did not qualify under this test, the Court has ruled that other entities like community colleges do fall within the *Charter*'s reach. Even community-based organizations like an Ontario sexual assault counseling centre was considered to be subject to the *Charter* by virtue only of its receipt of government grants.

Even if an entity is considered non-governmental, it may still be caught by the *Charter*. In *Stoffman* (1990), the Court held that the Vancouver General Hospital is not subject to the *Charter*. But in *Eldridge* (1997), the Court, in partial retreat, held that while an entity *in toto* may not be governmental, some of the acts which it performs may. Accordingly, the failure to provide interpretation services for deaf patients was considered contrary to section 15 of the *Charter*.

In addition, insofar as human rights legislation affects employment matters in private organizations, those matters are indirectly subject to *Charter* scrutiny. Human rights legislation, like all other legislation, is clearly subject to *Charter* scrutiny and courts have brought it into conformity with the *Charter* when they have found it constitutionally wanting. Even when a court has defined an institution to be non-governmental for purposes of *Charter* application, if the impugned activity (e.g., employment) of that institution is governed by human rights laws, then the *Charter* applies to the entity indirectly through the instrumentality of that law.

For example, in the *McKinney* case just discussed, whatever the status of universities for the purposes of *Charter* application, the fact that universities as employers are subject to the constraints of human rights legislation means that they are indirectly subject to *Charter* values. Universities are subject to human rights law; human rights law is subject to the *Charter*; ergo, universities are subject, albeit indirectly, to the *Charter*.

The *Charter* and Private Law

While legislation as positive acts of government are clearly subject to *Charter* scrutiny, courts do not simply interpret legislation. They are the custodians of the common law, a massive body of legal rules developed incrementally on a case-by-case basis independently of the legislative action of government. Legislation in an area of common law regulation has the effect of superceding common law rules; in the absence of state action, the common law prevails. Common law rules govern relationships between private persons – persons as contractors for goods or services or as tortfeasors, for example. Common law as a result is often called private law.

Should private law conform to *Charter* rights? The Supreme Court has been definitive on the point: yes and no. In the early, complicated case of *Dolphin Delivery* (1986), the Court was faced with a challenge to the constitutionality of a common law ban on secondary picketing. If a union is striking against company *A*, and *A* tries to stay in business by subcontracting its work out to company *B*, can the union conduct "secondary picketing" of *B*? While labour legislation has overturned much of the common law of employment, the legislation governing this particular case was silent on the matter. The union objected that the common law restriction on secondary picketing was contrary to the *Charter*'s protection of freedom of expression.

The Supreme Court, seeming to endorse liberal constitutionalist ideals, said that the *Charter* does not apply to the private law, even though private law is enforced by the courts which, on a common sense reading, are state institutions: "To regard a court order as an element of governmental intervention necessary to invoke the *Charter* would ... widen the scope of *Charter* application to virtually all private litigation." This was considered unacceptable. But the devil was in the details. First, the Court indicated, the *Charter* applies to private law when the government is party to a dispute. Second, as Justice McIntyre wrote for the Court:

Where ... private party "A" sues private party "B" relying on the common law and where no act of government is relied upon to support the action, the *Charter* will not apply. I should make it clear, however, that this is a distinct issue from the question whether the judiciary ought to apply and develop the principles of the common law in a manner consistent with the *fundamental values* enshrined in the Constitution. The answer to this question must be in the affirmative. In this sense, then, the *Charter* is far from irrelevant to private litigants whose disputes will be decided at common law.

So while *Charter rights* may not apply to private legal disputes, *Charter values* do. Subsequent case law suggests that there is precious little difference in practice between *Charter* rights and *Charter* values. When the Court wanted to alter common law rules to make them more egalitarian, *Charter* values enabled it to do so. In *Salituro* (1991), the common law rule that a person was incompetent to testify against his or her spouse was altered, with reliance upon *Charter* values, to allow that spouses irreconcilably separated were competent to do so.

In *Dobson* (1999), the Court was asked to develop tort law to allow a child to sue its mother for injuries sustained in a car accident *prior* to being born. Since the case raised the issue of the rights of a (yet) unborn child against his or her mother, *Dobson* had implications for the issue of abortion. (LEAF, for example, intervened against the claim of the child.) Here a majority of the Court held that, among other things, the *Charter* value of gender equality militated against such a development.

Charter values constitute a package of interpretive possibilities for judges more limitless than even the vaguely worded provisions of the *Charter* themselves. Litigants may be forgiven for their inability to guess whether *Charter* values will work for them or against them when they approach the bench. They can be assured, though, that regardless of positive state legislative action, the *Charter* will reach their private legal disputes.

State Inaction and Underinclusivity

Liberal constitutionalist theory suggests that the *Charter* is triggered only when the state acts. In the absence of the state action, the *Charter* does not apply. This comports with the previous discussion of the common law; whatever is not made a matter of public law remains the province of the common law. This view obviously constrains *Charter* application. And for critics of liberal constitutionalism, this is precisely the problem. For them, *Charter* norms, if they are to be given society-wide application, must be enforced by courts whether or not the state acts. At the distant but logical extreme, this implies a full-scale jurocracy, with popularly elected legislatures becoming irrelevant for public policy purposes.

The courts have not gone this far. But they have not shied away from declaring that when the state does enact programs that provide benefits to citizens, it cannot leave out persons who can claim the protection of section 15 of the *Charter*. In its 1999 ruling in *Law v. Canada*, the Court declared, "Underinclusive ameliorative legislation that excludes from its scope the members of a historically disadvantaged group will rarely escape the charge of discrimination."

It is worth pausing to consider the significance of this. Almost all of the thousands of laws and policies enforced by the state single out certain groups of people for special treatment. In this sense, almost every public policy discriminates against someone. Post-secondary students are entitled to tax deductions denied non-post-secondary students. Murderers are treated differently under the *Criminal Code* than are those convicted of manslaughter. Parents who send their children to daycares can claim favourable tax treatment while those who forego income to stay at home with their children cannot. Older people are entitled to state benefits to the exclusion of younger people. The ability to marry is confined to heterosexuals and monogamists. Adults are not allowed to have sex with children. Incestuous relationships are excluded from definitions of family. The list goes on. The point is that public policy is almost always selective. When is selectivity constitutionally benign and when is it constitutionally offensive?

In *Schachter* (1992), the father of a newborn sought parental leave benefits provided under the terms of the UI act. Benefits were available to natural mothers and adoptive parents but not natural fathers. Schachter claimed a section 15 violation. He won.

In *Miron v. Trudel* (1995), the issue was the restrictive definition of spouse in an insurance policy. Trudel was injured by an uninsured driver and as a result could no longer support his common law wife and family. His only recourse was to apply for benefits from his common law wife's insurance plan. The plan was held to extend to legally married spouses only. A 5–4 majority of the Supreme Court found this unconstitutionally underinclusive of common law spouses, granted the *Charter* claim, and read in common law spouse.

The *Eldridge* case, discussed earlier, concerned the failure of medical authorities acting under the terms of B.C. legislation to provide sign language interpretation services to deaf persons receiving medical care in that province. Eldridge was a deaf, pregnant woman to whom publicly funded signing services were denied because authorities did not consider them "medically required services" under the legislation. For a unanimous Court, LaForest found sign language interpretation so closely intertwined with the effective provision of medical services that it falls within the legislative definition of "medically required services." That provision, wrote LaForest, "impugns the state's failure to correct even those disadvantages it has not itself created." As an effects-oriented protection, section 15 prohibits "adverse effects of a facially neutral benefits scheme." Section 15 "makes no distinction between laws that impose unequal burdens and those that deny unequal benefits."

Perhaps the greatest strides have been made in relation to the equality rights of homosexuals. In *Knodel v. British Columbia* (1991), the issue before the B.C. Court of Appeal was the "restrictive" heterosexual definition of spouse in an employee benefits package for nurses. The homosexual partner of a nurse sought benefits on the nurse's death and was refused. The court found that definition of spouse to be unconstitutionally underinclusive of homosexual relationships. When the government "takes on an obligation and provides a benefit, section 15(1) makes denial of that benefit to other groups questionable." To remedy the defect, the court defined spouse inclusively.

The Supreme Court added sexual orientation to section 15's list of prohibited grounds of discrimination in *Egan* (1995) but narrowly upheld the heterosexual definition of spouse for the purposes of eligibility of spousal benefits under the *Old Age Security Act*. But in *Vriend* (1998), two years later, the Court rendered a stunning victory for homosexuals. Delwin Vriend was an instructor at a private Christian university college; when it was learned that he was gay, he was relieved of his duties. He protested to the Alberta Human Rights Commission but was told that the AHRC could not help him because the legislation did not prohibit discrimination on the basis of sexual orientation. Vriend then turned his sights on the Alberta government, alleging in court that the legislation was unconstitutionally underinclusive of this particular prohibited ground of discrimination. In other words, while the Alberta government acted to prohibit employment discrimination on some grounds (e.g., sex, age, colour, religion), it failed to include sexual orientation in that list. It therefore deprived Vriend and other homosexuals of the benefit of Alberta's human rights policy. The Supreme Court agreed with Vriend, and "read in" (i.e., judicially added) sexual orientation to the Alberta *Human Rights Act*.

Vriend provokes several questions. First, what if the state intended to leave sexual orientation out of the legislation? This was an easy question to answer. The Court heard evidence that the Alberta legislature considered and rejected proposed amendments to the law to add sexual orientation. For the Court, this was evidence enough that the legislature "acted" (though not in the form of legislation) to exclude homosexuals from a state benefit. Second, does *Vriend* mean that human rights legislation must mirror the protections of section 15 of the *Charter*? It seems so, Supreme Court comments in *Vriend* notwithstanding. An interesting problem with this is that section 15 prohibits discrimination on the basis of group characteristics that are unlisted in the provision. The courts since 1989 have added a few "analogous" grounds like citizenship and sexual orientation. It would seem that human rights legislation would be subject to judicial amendment each time the courts add a new prohibited ground to section 15 of the *Charter*. Critics claimed that this aspect of *Vriend* violated the principles of both federalism and democratic accountability.

Buoyed by their victory in *Vriend*, homosexual advocacy groups pressed the courts to declare unconstitutional underinclusive definitions of spouse in Ontario's *Family Law Act*. Ontario's NDP government in the early 1990s introduced legislation to give homosexual couples in conjugal relationships many of the same rights (and obligations) accorded heterosexual ones. That controversial legislation was defeated in a free vote by the legislature. But what cannot be done by the legislature may be done through the courts. *In M. v. H.* (1999), the Supreme Court essentially enacted the earlier legislation. The Court ruled that the omission of the right to sue for spousal support (in the event of a breakdown of a same-sex relationship) meant that the *Family Law Act* discriminated against homosexuals, contrary to section 15 of the *Charter*.

In the political economy of recognition and dignity, *M. v. H.* signals a major shift of political resources to homosexual advocacy groups. For all but one justice in the majority, evidence of legislative opposition to the extension of spousal rights to homosexuals did not figure in the section 15 analysis. It was simply the underinclusion of homosexual couples and the effects on their circumstances that governed the case....

[*Ed. note*: In 2005, the federal government passed legislation legalizing same-sex marriage.]

Section 15 jurisprudence in the 1990s has been concerned in part with the development of an underinclusivity doctrine. In its section 15 jurisprudence, the Supreme Court has rejected the older notion that it is state action that triggers *Charter* review. It has not yet accepted the full logic of such a move, which is to enforce a constitutional standard of public policy in the complete absence of evidence of state action.... When and if the Court does adopt such a post-liberal understanding of constitutionalism, the *Charter* revolution of which Morton and Knopff have written would be consummated....

2018 Addendum: *Charter* Values and the Administrative State

Since the above essay was written, the language of "*Charter* values" has dotted Supreme Court decisions with some regularity. Understandably, litigants find the flexibility of *Charter* values attractive, allowing them to craft creative arguments unbounded by more rigid rights. Perhaps to temper their enthusiasm, the Court limited the resort to *Charter* values in 2002, when it considered a case that turned on the proper interpretation of legislative provisions. In *Bell ExpressVu Limited Partnership v. Rex* (2002), the issue was whether the *Communications Act* allowed only licensed Canadian distributors of encrypted direct-to-home cable signals to offer the service. An American firm seeking to sell de-encryption devices to transmit American programming alleged that the law's ambiguity operated in its favour. The Supreme Court held that a series of well-established legal tools should be used to resolved ambiguities in the law. Only when these traditional tools fail should the courts resort to external aids like *Charter* values. "[T]o the extent this Court has recognized a '*Charter* values' interpretive principle, such principle can *only* receive application in circumstances of genuine ambiguity, i.e., where a statutory provision is subject to differing, but equally plausible, interpretations."

This decision might have dampened enthusiasm for using *Charter* values in the courts, but another development revived it. In advanced democracies with sprawling welfare bureaucracies like Canada, tens of thousands of decisions are made yearly about citizen entitlements to moneys and other entitlements. Persons have the right to appeal decisions they consider to be wrong. The sheer volume of such appeals would cripple the courts; and courts lack the particular policy expertise in various subject areas to dispose of appeals expeditiously. The solution adopted generations ago was the administrative agency, a body created by legislation and whose officers are appointed by the political executive. Such bodies are given discretion to make rules and to adjudicate conflicts arising from their application in particular cases. For instance, you may have been dismissed from your job and wish to claim Employment Insurance benefits. Your claim is refused. You can appeal that decision to a tribunal established under the *Act*. The original officer said you were fired and thus cannot claim benefits; on appeal, you show that you were in fact laid off, and so are entitled to them. The losing party in a tribunal proceeding can appeal to a court, and that court will review that decision applying a standard of review ranging from deference or reasonableness depending on the state of law and the nature of the issues. The appeal court does not retry the case, but it gives litigants the chance to argue that the tribunal's decision was faulty.

In *Doré v. Barreau du Québec* (2012), the Supreme Court addressed *Charter* values in this context. Gilles Doré was a Quebec lawyer who was subject to insulting and degrading comments by the judge in a case he was litigating. Doré wrote the judge a private letter that was equally insulting and immoderate. The judge was subject to a proceeding before the Canadian Judicial Council, at which the letter was made public. Doré was then brought before a disciplinary proceeding of the Quebec bar society, accused of conduct failing to uphold the standards of "moderation, objectivity, and dignity." He was found guilty and appealed the ruling, arguing that the decision infringed his *Charter* right to freedom of expression. The original tribunal sanctioned him; on appeal, another administrative tribunal upheld the decision, dismissing the *Charter* claim by arguing that when the *Charter* right is compared to the objectives of the law society rule, the limit on Doré's ability to speak freely was not unduly limited. Doré was unsatisfied with this somewhat casual assessment of his *Charter* rights. He wanted a more rigorous degree of constitutional scrutiny and appealed the tribunal's unwillingness to conduct a full *Oakes* test, a demanding test of the merits of the arguments in support of rules limiting his *Charter* rights.

Doré lost on appeals all the way up to the Supreme Court. He lost there, too, but the Court in an 8–0 decision clarified the standard for how administrative tribunals are to handle *Charter* claims. "It goes without saying," wrote Justice Abella, "that administrative decision-makers must act consistently with the values underlying the grant of discretion, including *Charter* values." In cases where an administrative tribunal declares a *law* contrary to a *Charter* right, its decision is reviewable by courts on the standard of correctness, the most demanding standard of judicial review. But if a particular *decision* of a tribunal is alleged to be contrary to the *Charter*, that decision is subject to judicial review on the standards of reasonableness. A court could reverse the decision only if it found the decision unreasonable on the facts. The Court set this latter standard, Abella wrote, because tribunals know particular facts and are policy experts in their fields and should be accorded deference by the courts. The upshot is that administrative tribunals have more freedom now to apply *Charter* values to the policies they enforce. "This allows the *Charter* to 'nurture' administrative law, by emphasizing that *Charter* values infuse the inquiry."

The new standard of review for *Charter* decisions made by administrative agencies will have important implications for post-liberal constitutionalism. In *Trinity Western University v. British Columbia College of Teachers* (2001) the Supreme Court heard an appeal which concerned whether the decision of the B.C. College of Teachers (BCCT) to deny accreditation of Trinity Western University's (TWU) School of Education was properly made. TWU is a Christian university whose students are required to sign a statement of faith which includes a provision to foreswear several sinful acts including sexual sins like fornication and homosexual relations. The BCCT argued that TWU B.Ed. graduates would be intolerant and would act contrary to values associated with equality rights protected by s. 15 of the *Charter*.

An 8–1 majority of the Court sided with TWU. Its reasoning is important. The majority held that the proper standard to apply to the BCCT decision is correctness. What the BCCT said in respect of the *Charter* warrants no deference. The BCCT's "expertise does not qualify it to interpret the scope of human rights nor to reconcile competing rights. It cannot be seriously argued that the determination of good character, which is an individual matter, is sufficient to expand the jurisdiction of the BCCT to the evaluation of religious belief, freedom of association and the right to equality generally." It went on to hold that the BCCT failed to balance religious freedom rights with equality rights and that there was precious little evidence in any case that TWU graduates have behaved badly in the world upon graduation. The majority wrote that although the community standards "are expressed in terms of a code of conduct rather than an article of faith, we conclude that a homosexual student would not be tempted to apply for admission, and could only sign the so-called student contract at a considerable personal cost. TWU is not for everybody; it is designed to address the needs of people who share a number of religious convictions."

TWU's 2001 victory was a win for traditional, liberal constitutionalism. The Court by its circuitous route advanced the principle that civil society in all its rough and messy variety is to be protected from the homogenizing tendencies of the administrative state. Put in different terms, it was a victory for "passive secularism" (see Ahmet T. Kuru, *Secularism and State Policies Toward Religion*, 2009), the view that secular societies are pluralistic societies and that it is not the state's prerogative to flatten that diversity.

In 2017, Trinity Western was before the Supreme Court again, this time defending its proposed law school against decisions by two provincial law societies to refuse to accredit the school due to TWU's allegedly "homophobic" statement of student conduct. (Three law societies refused to accredit TWU's law school. Nova Scotia's decision was not before the Court.) Much can be said for the view that the issues in 2017 were much the same as those in 2001 and that the decision should also be the same. But notice that since 2001 the Supreme Court has given administrative tribunals more latitude to apply *Charter* values according to their own lights; and the two law society decisions went against TWU. As important, political culture in Canada has shifted in ways that are averse to TWU's mission. Gay rights are much more entrenched in law and popular culture; "illiberal" Christian groups are increasingly objects of suspicion and ridicule. The politics of identity and "diversity" operate to cast dark clouds of suspicion on institutions like TWU. The secularism of the recent period is, in Kuru's term, much more "aggressive," unwilling to countenance even minoritarian departures from the gathering liberal ideological consensus. Courts sometimes lead in this gathering, sometimes follow. But they never depart.

1.7
Key Terms

Concepts

"All men are by nature equal"

Charter values

civil society

declaration of incompatibility

judicial review

liberal constitutionalism

natural law

natural right theory of government

parliamentary supremacy

per legem terrae

positive law

post-liberal constitutionalism

rule of law

state action

strong-form judicial review

unwritten constitution

weak-form judicial review

written constitution

Institutions, Events and Documents

A.V. Dicey, *The Law of the Constitution* (1885)

Bell ExpressVu Limited Partnership v. Rex, [2002] 2 S.C.R. 559

Canadian Bill of Rights (1960)

Canadian Charter of Rights and Freedoms (1982)

Constitution Act, 1867 (*British North American Act*, 1867)

Constitution of the United States of America (1788)

Doré v. Barreau du Québec, [2012] 1 S.C.R. 395

Declaration of Independence (1776)

Eldridge v. British Columbia, [1997] 3 S.C.R. 624

European Convention for the Protection of Human Rights and Fundamental Freedoms (1950)

Glorious Revolution of 1688

John Locke, *Second Treatise on Government* (1690)

Magna Carta (1215)

Roncarelli v. Duplessis, [1959] S.C.R. 121

Trinity Western University v. British Columbia College of Teachers, [2001] 1 S.C.R. 772

United Kingdom *Human Rights Act* (1998)

U.S. Bill of Rights (1791)

Vriend v. Alberta, [1998] 1 S.C.R. 493

2

Political Jurisprudence

This chapter addresses a deceptively simple set of questions. What do judges do? Do they just interpret and apply the law? Or, in the process of interpreting and applying the law, do judges also "make law"? If the answer to this final question is yes, then how do courts differ from legislatures? Ultimately, these questions take on a normative character: Should judges restrict themselves to declaring what the law is, as determined by statute and precedent? Or if a judge finds the relevant statutes and precedents inadequate or even "wrong," is the judge free to "make new law"?

These are old and much-debated questions, and they have been given very different answers by scholars and judges. There is some truth in each of these conflicting answers because the character of the judicial process varies from nation to nation, and indeed within a single nation. What is true of trial courts is not applicable to appeal courts, and what is true for torts and contracts does not apply to constitutional law. Different judges on the same court may conduct themselves according to different judicial philosophies.

Canadian legal and political thought traditionally held that judges do not, and should not, "make law" in any significant sense. "The law" was portrayed as something that already exists "out there"; the role of the judge is merely to find or "discover" its meaning and declare it to the interested parties. This view of judicial decision-making is known as the "declaratory model" and is closely associated with the British common law tradition from which it evolved. In both Britain and Canada, this view of judges as exercising "neither force nor will, but only judgement" was reinforced by the practice of parliamentary supremacy and the theory of legal positivism.

The parliamentary model of government stresses that only the representative legislature can "make law" because only the elected legislators have the consent of the people to govern. This understanding of just laws comes directly from the equality-consent dimension of liberal political theory, as articulated by John Locke in Reading 1.2 of the preceding chapter. According to this logic, it would be unjust and unjustifiable for judges to "make law," since judges are neither representative of nor responsible to the citizenry. This precise and limiting understanding of the judicial function has been reinforced by the theory of legal positivism. Legal positivism defines law as "the command of the sovereign," in this case the Queen in Parliament. This definition stresses the form and function of the law, not its content. The notion of judicial law-making is logically incompatible with this view.

The "declaratory model" of judging is drawn from British experience. This explains both its original dominance of Canadian jurisprudence and also its more recent decline. As we saw in Chapter 1, Canada differs from Great Britain by being a federal not a unitary state, and by having the boundaries of federalism defined in a "written constitution" – the *Constitution Act, 1867*.[1] Because of this difference, Canadian courts and judges have had to fulfill an important function virtually unknown in British legal experience until the new millennium – judicial review. Since its creation in 1875, the Supreme Court of Canada has acted as the "neutral umpire" of the federal division of powers between Ottawa and the provinces.

A constitutional law of federalism is political in a way other kinds of law are not. It defines and therefore limits the law-making powers of rival levels of government. Questions of constitutional law often arise in the context of heated political struggles between Ottawa and one or more provinces. Political passions run high, and all of Canada awaits the Court's decision with interest. Major government policy often hangs in the balance. In such circumstances, it becomes difficult to believe that judges are not aware of the policy consequences of their "legal" decisions and that these decisions are not influenced by the anticipation of their consequences. Indeed, in 1985 the Chief Justice of the Supreme Court of Canada, Brian Dickson, cautioned his fellow judges against adopting a "mechanical legalism," advising them instead to "be aware of the underlying principles and practical consequences of questions before [them], paying close attention to the policy aspects of each issue."[2] Under these circumstances, final appeal courts inevitably come to be regarded as hybrid institutions, part-judicial, part-political. This hybridity is now accepted wisdom, so much so that in his (ultimately successful) application to the Supreme Court of Canada in 2016, Justice Malcolm Rowe wrote that "Supreme Court judges ordinarily make law, rather than simply applying it" (see Reading 4.5).

In view of this dimension of Canadian law, it is not surprising that Canadian jurists began to be attracted by the "legal realism" theory of judging that had developed in the United States in the early decades of the twentieth century. The Americans had lived with the practice of judicial review since 1803. Moreover, the United States Supreme Court not only exercised judicial review over the boundaries of federalism but also enforced the more absolute limitations of the *Bill of Rights*. By the end of the nineteenth century, the Supreme Court had come to play an influential role in the major political issues of the day. The traditional "declaratory model" of judging, inherited with the common law from Great Britain, seemed increasingly to provide a less satisfactory explanation of what American courts and judges were actually doing in the area of constitutional law. A new generation of American jurists therefore began to rethink and reformulate the relationship between judges and law. Through the writings of men like Oliver Wendell Holmes, Benjamin Cardozo and Roscoe Pound, the "legal realism" theory of judging was developed.

The legal realists stressed the creative and personal connection between judges and law. Holmes declared that the law is "the prophecies of what the courts will do in fact, and nothing more pretentious."[3] Pound and Cardozo extended Holmes's critique by elaborating the subjective, personal dimension of judging. The key to this analysis was the "unfinished" quality of law, and the resulting discretion and freedom of the judge to give the law its practical meaning when applied to a novel set of circumstances.

The inescapably personal dimension of judging is explored in former Justice Bertha Wilson's discussion of the question, "Will women judges make a difference?" (Reading 2.3). Writing in 1990, Justice Wilson argued that, in certain areas of "judge-made law," gender does make a difference, and she claimed that women judges bring a "uniquely feminine perspective" to certain issues. American studies of gender differences in judging confirmed similar trends but also found that (for federally appointed judges) the partisan affiliation of the President making the appointments is also a relevant factor. This is not surprising, given the sharp conflict over federal judicial appointments between Republicans and Democrats since the Supreme Court's *Roe v. Wade* abortion decision in 1973. The Democrats have favoured judges who are willing to go beyond the original understanding of the Constitution, adopt the "living constitutionalist" approach (the American equivalent of the "living tree" approach; see Reading 12.3) and to·update constitutional meaning. Judges with this approach are open to using judicial review to create new rights, such as a woman's right to terminate a pregnancy. Republicans have supported judges with an "originalist" or textual philosophy. Originalists believe that since abortion is not mentioned in the Constitution, the issue should be left for elected legislatures to decide.

Justice Wilson's acceptance of the argument that a judge's gender may influence his or her decisions reveals the extent to which legal realism has triumphed, as do more recent data confirming the effect of gender differences at the Supreme Court of Canada. A number of quantitative studies from the last decade have confirmed that gender has emerged as "a significant new basis for cleavages" at the Supreme Court: gender differences were found to structure voting patterns in equality cases and non-unanimous free speech cases, while a subsequent study found male justices at the Supreme Court were more likely than female justices to support the criminally accused.[4] However, acceptance of the legal-realist view still leaves open the question of whether this is desirable or should be encouraged, especially as regards appeal court judges and especially in the area of constitutional law. The first generation of legal realists were almost all supporters of judicial self-restraint and deference to legislative judgments, while today many of their followers support a more activist exercise of judicial review.

The preceding example of Justice Wilson notwithstanding, Canadian jurists were initially unreceptive to the theory of judicial realism, which they considered an American idiosyncrasy. Predictably, it was the constitutional law decisions of Canada's first final court of appeal – the Judicial Committee of the Privy Council (JCPC), which was technically an advisory board to the Imperial Crown – that provoked the first appearance of judicial realism in Canadian legal and political thought. Beginning in the 1890s, the JCPC made a series of important constitutional decisions that progressively narrowed the scope of the federal government's legislative powers. This trend reached a climax in the mid-1930s, when the JCPC struck down a number of federal "New Deal" programs designed to cope with the economic and social devastation of the Great Depression. This provoked an angry reaction among some Canadian leaders, culminating in the *O'Connor Report* (1939) to the Senate, which advocated the abolition of appeals to the JCPC. The *O'Connor Report* argued that questions of Canadian constitutional law could be better answered by Canadian judges, judges with first-hand familiarity with the political and economic realities of Canadian life. Implicit in this argument was a tacit acceptance of the legal-realist view that a judge's personal background and political formation is an important factor in his or her legal decision-making. Because the goal of this movement was to make the Supreme Court the final court of appeal "of and for Canadians," it came to be known as "judicial nationalism."

In 1949, appeals to the JCPC were abolished, and the Supreme Court of Canada became the final and exclusive court of appeal for Canada. But this has not stopped the debate over the nature of the judicial process in Canada. The adoption in 1960 of the *Bill of Rights* stimulated new debate on this old issue. The *Bill of Rights*' broadly worded provisions – such as freedom of religion and equality before the law – seemed to invite and even require judicial choice and creativity in giving them practical application. By and large, the Canadian judiciary declined this invitation. Stressing the statutory (as opposed to constitutional) character of the 1960 *Bill of Rights* and the absence of any explicit qualification of the tradition of parliamentary supremacy, the Supreme Court gave a limited and traditional interpretation to its major provisions. Partly in response to the courts' cautious use of the *Bill of Rights*, the 1982 *Canadian Charter of Rights and Freedoms* was constitutionally entrenched and explicitly applies to both levels of government. The *Charter* raises the issue of proper judicial decision-making in an even more pointed and pressing manner.

The competing views of proper judicial conduct are the subject of Paul Weiler's 1967 article, "Two Models of Judicial Decision-Making" (Reading 2.1). One – the "adjudication of disputes" model – stresses the traditional understanding of the judicial function and the institutional characteristics that distinguish the judicial process from the legislative process. Weiler's second model – the "policy-making" model – asserts that there is no essential difference between judges and legislators, that "they make policy, or legislate, through essentially the same mode of reasoning."

Weiler's two models are not coterminous with the declaratory and judicial-realist theories of judging. While most informed observers now reject the declaratory model of judging, acceptance of judicial realism does not require acceptance of Weiler's "policy-making" model. Although some judicial law-making may be an inevitable by-product of judicial interpretation, many commentators argue that it is and should remain secondary to the main function of adjudication of disputes. Weiler's "two models" analysis provides a conceptual framework through which we can better evaluate recommendations that Canadian judges adopt a greater "policy-making" role, and it also demonstrates that different institutional consequences follow from the two different conceptions of judging. Traditional Canadian practices regarding judicial recruitment, judicial independence, jurisdiction, access to the courts, judicial fact-finding and modes of legal argument were all premised on the understanding that judges do not, and should not, "make law." As Canadian judges have moved away from the "adjudication of disputes" approach and toward a greater "policy-making" role, especially since the 1982 adoption of the *Charter*, the continued adequacy of traditional institutional practices has been challenged.[5] We can thus use Weiler's analytical framework to understand the traditional aspects of the judicial process and to evaluate the changes that have occurred in recent decades.

The next reading demonstrates the character of the debate over the proper role of the judiciary in Canadian law and politics. In the 1976 case of *Harrison v. Carswell*, we find a sharp disagreement over the judiciary's proper role between the then Chief Justice of Canada, Bora Laskin, and his successor as Chief Justice, Brian Dickson (Reading 2.2). The principal difference between Dickson's majority opinion and Laskin's dissent is not about the law but about the limits of the Supreme Court's responsibility. Both agree that the *Harrison* case raises a serious legal problem. But Laskin argues that the Supreme Court should solve it, while Dickson maintains that law reform is the business of the legislatures, not the courts. Astute observers may note the tension between the view Dickson articulated in 1976 and his statement from 1985, quoted above, in which he emphasized the importance of judges "paying close attention to the policy aspects of each issue." Did Dickson change his mind or was this shift a function of the changing judicial role following the *Charter*? The answer is likely a combination of both.

The last three readings in this chapter concern the political nature of the Supreme Court's jurisprudence and the Canadian Constitution. Michael Mandel's analysis of the Supreme Court's decision in the 1981 *Patriation Reference*[6] (Reading 2.4) provides strong evidence to support the judicial-realist school. The Supreme Court's decision in the *Patriation Reference* was arguably the most important it has ever made. It broke the political deadlock between the federal government and eight of the ten provinces and led to the adoption of the *Constitution Act, 1982*, of which the *Charter of Rights* was an integral part. At stake was whether Prime Minister Trudeau's plan to "patriate" the constitution unilaterally – that is, add an amending formula and the *Charter* to the Constitution without first obtaining the consent of all the provinces – was constitutionally permissible. While it was generally agreed that constitutional convention required the unanimous consent of the provinces for a formal amendment of this magnitude, it was also agreed that constitutional conventions were political matters and could not be recognized or enforced in courts of law. The federal lawyers argued that unilateral amendment was both constitutional (i.e., there was no convention of unanimity) and legal (i.e., even if there were such a convention, it could not be enforced by the courts). The opposing provinces argued that Trudeau's unilateralism was both unconstitutional and illegal (i.e., that it violated the convention and that the convention could be enforced by the courts). In the end, a sharply divided Supreme Court split the difference and ruled that the federal government's plan was legal but unconstitutional – that while it did not violate the letter of the law, it did violate constitutional convention.

Mandel shows that the division of the judges closely followed their political and regional affiliations. The three judges from Quebec all agreed that unilateralism was unconstitutional. The two judges who said that Trudeau's plan was both unconstitutional and illegal were Tory appointees from provinces that opposed the Liberal plan (Alberta and Nova Scotia). The three judges who took the other extreme – that unilateralism was both legal and constitutional – were all Trudeau appointees, two from Ontario, a province that supported the

Trudeau initiative. Of the seven-judge coalition that held unilateralism was legal, six were Trudeau appointees. "If we were paying attention," writes Mandel, this "gave us a good idea of what Canada could expect with the *Charter.*"

Seventeen years later, the Supreme Court was called on again to broker a constitutional dispute between Ottawa and Quebec. In the *Quebec Secession Reference*,[7] the Court was asked by the federal government whether Quebec had a right to secede unilaterally from Canada – that is, based on winning a Quebec-only referendum on secession and without any consent from or negotiations with the rest of Canada. Unlike the *Patriation Reference*, in this case the Court was unanimous. Thus, there were no (visible) disagreements among the justices that tracked along provincial or party-of-appointment lines. Does this mean that the *Quebec Secession Reference* was decided on strictly legal grounds and that the justices' political sympathies played no role? This seems unlikely, since the Court's ruling hardly mentions the relevant constitutional texts (the amending provisions in sections 38–41 of the *Constitution Act, 1982*). Rather, the Court discovered four new "foundational constitutional principles" – democracy, federalism, constitutionalism and the rule of law, and the protection of minorities – that it said underlie written constitutional rules and practice.

Skeptics have pointed out that if the Court had used the same four "foundational principles" to decide the 1981 *Patriation Reference* or the 1982 *Quebec Veto Reference*,[8] the results would have been different. Since only two of ten provinces were supporting Trudeau's unilateral initiative in 1981, this presumably would have failed the federalism principle. The following year, after Ottawa and all nine English-speaking provinces had consented to the *Constitution Act, 1982*, the Quebec government challenged its constitutional validity. At the time, the Supreme Court rejected Quebec's claim. However, if Quebec had been able to invoke the "protection of minorities" principle announced in 1998, presumably it would have prevailed in 1981.

Why in 1998 did the Supreme Court resort to unwritten "constitutional principles" that contradicted two of its most important constitutional precedents affecting Quebec? One interpretation is that the decision stems from political logic rather than legal logic. If the Court had simply followed precedent and the relevant written rules of constitutional amendment, its ruling would have been a crushing defeat for the separatist Parti Québécois (PQ) government, which would have then denounced the Court as a biased and illegitimate lackey of the federal Liberal Party. Instead, the Court used the newly discovered unwritten "constitutional principles" to craft a compromise decision. Significantly, when the Court released its decision, both Ottawa and the PQ government in Quebec claimed they had won. (In Reading 12.2, Beverley McLachlin, who was on the Court for the unsigned *Secession Reference*, defends the Court's use of unwritten principles.) The Court preserved its credibility and authority, especially in Quebec.

Robert Schertzer (Reading 2.5) argues that the Court's decision in the *Secession Reference* was an important example of the Court recognizing the legitimacy of multiple "models" of the federation: the pan-Canadian, provincial equality and multinational models. Rather than picking one model over the other, Schertzer argues that the Court in the *Secession Reference* accommodated all three. Moreover, the *Secession Reference* turned out to be a harbinger of things to come: In the subsequent decade, Schertzer found the Court was far more likely to recognize the legitimacy of multiple models than it was before. The case thus represents a "noticeable change in the court's general approach to federalism jurisprudence."

The third example of political jurisprudence explored in this chapter is the Supreme Court's 2014 *Reference re Senate Reform*,[9] in which the Court declared the Harper government's proposed Senate reforms unconstitutional. The Court ruled that Parliament could neither legislate non-binding, consultative elections for selecting senators, nor legislate term limits for senators without the consent of at least seven of the ten provinces. It also ruled that abolishing the Senate would require unanimous provincial consent. In Reading 2.6, F.L. Morton criticizes the Court for failing to constructively facilitate the reform of an institution whose political purpose has ceased to be useful. He contrasts the Court's decision with the *Patriation Reference* and the *Secession Reference*, both of which used "bold statecraft" and "questionable jurisprudence" to overcome political deadlock. Morton argues that the *Senate Reference* engaged in no such statecraft, and ignored the "foundational constitutional principles" of democracy and federalism the Court espoused in 1998.

While many believe the ruling has put an end to the Senate reform movement, Morton suggests that the Harper government should have simply turned the appointment of senators over to provincial premiers, the partisan dynamics of which could have led to provincial elections. However, after Harper was defeated in the 2015 election, Justin Trudeau's Liberal government soon introduced its own reform, whereby prospective senators are nominated by an independent committee. Although final discretion to appoint remains with the Prime Minister, this system is ostensibly designed to make senators non-partisan. However, a recent analysis found that the non-partisan senators voted with the Trudeau government 94.5 per cent of the time, raising questions about ideological diversity among appointees.[10] Whether even this limited reform will withstand constitutional scrutiny remains an open question, and depends on whether the courts will consider it a change to the "fundamental nature and role" of the Senate.

In each of these famous References – *Patriation, Secession* and *Senate* – the Supreme Court clearly engaged in political considerations. The legal-realist view of law-making undoubtedly shaped these decisions, yet each was restrained in its own way. Perhaps the best way to understand each of these foundational rulings is as an application of Professor James Gibson's legal-realist definition of judicial decisions as "a function of what they prefer to do, tempered by what they think they ought to do, but constrained by what they perceive is feasible to do."[11] In other words, judicial decisions – especially those involving constitutional law – are often a composite of law, politics and policy.

NOTES

1   Originally known and still commonly referred to as the *British North America Act*. Several other documents have been added to Canada's written constitution, most notably the *Constitution Act, 1982*.

2   "Dickson discourages mechanical legalism," *Globe and Mail*, Oct. 5, 1985, A4.

3   *Harvard Law Review* 10 (1897), p. 39.

4   Donald R. Songer, *The Transformation of the Supreme Court of Canada* (Toronto: University of Toronto Press, 2008), p. 209; Cynthia L. Ostberg and Matthew E. Wetstein, *Attitudinal Decision Making in the Supreme Court of Canada* (Vancouver: UBC Press, 2007), p. 22; Donald R. Songer, et al., *Law, Ideology, Collegiality: Judicial Behaviour in the Supreme Court of Canada* (Montreal/Kingston: McGill-Queen's University Press, 2012), pp. 144–145.

5   See Peter H. Russell, "Judicial Power in Canada's Political Culture," in *Courts and Trial: A Multidisciplinary Approach*, ed. M.L. Friedland (Toronto: University of Toronto Press, 1975), p. 75. This article was reprinted in the first edition of this book.

6   *Re: Resolution to amend the Constitution*, [1981] 1 S.C.R. 753.

7   *Reference re Secession of Quebec*, [1998] 2 S.C.R. 217.

8   *Re: Objection by Quebec to a Resolution to amend the Constitution*, [1982] 2 S.C.R. 793

9   *Reference re Senate Reform*, [2014] 1 S.C.R. 704.

10   Éric Grenier, "Why the Senate is unpredictable – and its independents not so independent," *CBC News*, June 19, 2017, http://www.cbc.ca/news/politics/grenier-senators-votes-1.4162949.

11   James L. Gibson, "From Simplicity to Complexity: The Development of Theory in the Study of Judicial Behavior," *Political Behavior* 5, no.1 (1983), p. 9.

2.1

Two Models of Judicial Decision-Making
Paul Weiler

Canadian Bar Review 46 (1968), 406–471. Reprinted with permission.

I. Introduction

The philosophy of the judicial process will soon be of great practical significance for the Canadian legal scene. The traditional, inarticulate, legal positivism of Canadian lawyers and judges is rapidly becoming outmoded by recent
developments. First, the determination of our new Prime Minister [*Ed. note*: In
1968 Pierre Trudeau had just become Prime Minister] to achieve an entrenched
Bill of Rights will, of necessity, confer on the courts the power and the duty
to make fundamental value judgments which cannot flow mechanically and
impersonally from the language of the document. Second, the British House
of Lords has decided to change its long-standing rule that its earlier precedents
could not be overruled. Presumably, and hopefully, the Canadian Supreme
Court will continue to imitate slavishly its English counterpart by following
this decision. Third, Canadian scholarship about the Supreme Court has begun to utilize some of the advanced techniques of the behavioural sciences
in order to study judicial decision-making. Two related developments should
follow. Our judges will grow increasingly conscious of the freedom and the
responsibility they have to develop and alter the law. Both academics and the
public will become aware of the fact of judicial power and then go on to question its legitimacy.

It is only too true that we will be decades behind the same course of developments in our neighbour to the south. There is a favourable cast to this situation. We have available to us a significant body of American experience, and
of jurisprudential reflection concerning it, which we can use in intelligently
understanding and evaluating the process of change that the Canadian judicial
process is likely to undergo. Moreover we can choose between at least two, substantially different conceptions of judicial decision-making which have been
elaborated in some detail in American legal thinking. One theory characterizes
the judicial function as, essentially, the "adjudication of disputes" within the
legal system. The other holds that at least some courts are primarily engaged in
"policy-making," in a manner largely indistinguishable from the other political
agencies in our society. It is my intention to draw together, in a systematic way,
these two very sophisticated theories, to show the conclusions which flow from
the insights that lie at the root of each "model," and to indicate the important

problems which, as yet, detract from the adequacy of each. In doing so, I shall also record the significance of many apparently unrelated phenomena within the Canadian judicial system.

What theoretical significance do I attach to the use of these models? Sociological theory tells us that the position of judge in any society carries with it a set of shared expectations about the type of conduct that is appropriate to that position. These expectations have reference not only to the proper *physical* behaviour of one who occupies that position but also to the mode of reasoning to be used in making his judicial decisions. There are several possible decision-making roles that can be proposed by society for its judges, each having different supporting reasons for their acceptance. Two of these roles are the subject of this article, "adjudicator" and "policy-maker." Both embody fundamental value choices for the society which, presumably, are made after some consideration of these competing justifications. Once the choice is made, the expectations that are connected with this one role must be shared by at least a substantial majority of the participants within the system in order that it have some institutional stability. Finally, the institutional position of the judge is reciprocally connected with society's wishes about how they should behave in their decision-making capacity. It is this connection between the role we give to our judges and the design of the structure within which they operate that the two models are intended to display.

Hence, the function of each model is to trace the institutional implications of each of these fundamental value judgments about the appropriate mission of the judge. One model is based on the value judgment that judges should make policy choices as a political actor; the other assumes it is desirable that judges confine their activity to the settlement of private disputes. As we shall see, there are real differences in the social arrangements which are most compatible with these two distinctive judgments about the appropriate judicial role. We should be able to verify the existence of these proposed differences in actual practice, or in recommendations about changes in the existing system. Moreover, not only do these theoretical models serve as a framework for explanations of how judges do behave, they also assist our appraisal of how judges ought to behave.

Finally, the use of these two schematic representations of the judicial process should serve to illuminate a significant moral problem that has surfaced recently in American legal discussion of the role of the judiciary. Once an institution has gained inertial force and power as a result of shared expectations about how it is and ought to operate, it is then available as an instrument for serving social purposes that are not compatible with the original model. Is it legitimate for those who believe in an alternative model of judicial behaviour to make covert use of the existing organization? To what extent will such "parasitic" utilization of one version of the judicial process induce actual changes in the existing system which make it more compatible with the form that naturally flows from a new conception of appropriate judicial decision-making? To these, and other problems, this article is addressed in a preliminary way.

II. The Adjudication of Disputes Model

The two models whose traits I am going to describe both agree in rejecting the viability and the desirability of the traditional Anglo-Canadian model of judicial decision-making. The latter suggests that a judge decides his cases by the somewhat mechanical application of legal rules which he finds *established* in the legal system. They are, in this sense, *binding* on him completely apart from his own judgment as to their fitness. This theory has a historical, if not a logical, relationship with the dictates of an Austinian, positivist conception of law and a rigid notion of the division of powers. The "adjudication of disputes" model shares, to some extent, the assumption that judges have a distinctive and limited function. However, it emphatically denies the conclusion that it is *possible* for a judge to be purely passive, and *desirable* that he makes decisions without a necessary exercise of his judgment about what the law ought to be.

As was stated earlier the purpose of the model is to show the necessary inter-relationship between the function which judicial decision-making is primarily intended to perform, the institutional characteristics which are implied by such a function, and the qualities in judicial decision-making which flow naturally from this institutional background. In short, the job we give judges to perform determines the design of the judicial process; the nature of the structure influences the manner in which judges carry out their tasks; the form of judicial action limits the issues judges may appropriately resolve. Hence the adjudication model rejects the tacit assumption, often made, of "institutional fungibility." The latter holds that the same substantive policies can and should be achieved in the same undifferentiated way, whatever be the organizational form in which various actors are allowed to strive for these ends. To the contrary, the specific institutional form of adjudication, by comparison with that of legislation, for instance, limits both the goals for which judges should strive and the means they should use for achieving these goals.

To summarize the model very briefly, it conceives of the judge as the adjudicator of specific, concrete disputes, who disposes of the problems within the latter by elaborating and applying a legal regime to facts, which he finds on the basis of evidence and argument presented to him in an adversary process. The body of rules and principles which are to govern the private conduct of the participants in the legal order are largely settled by forces outside adjudication, although the judge does play a collaborative role in articulating and elaborating these principles. However, the primary focus of adjudication is the settlement of disputes arising out of private lines of conduct, by evaluating such conduct in the light of established rules and principles. As we shall see, the whole institutional structure of adjudication – its incidence, access to it, the mode of participation in it, the bases for decision, and the nature of the relief available in it – are all defined by and flow naturally from this function. The key elements within the adjudicative model are (1) settlement of disputes, (2) the adversary process and (3) an established system of standards which are utilized in the process to dispose of the disputes.

Settlement of Concrete Disputes

The first characteristic of "adjudication" is that it has the function of settling disputes (between private individuals or groups, or the government and the individual). These disputes are not future-oriented debates over general policy questions, although, as we shall see, the latter can enter into the final resolution of the problem. Rather, the disputes which are necessary to set the process of adjudication in motion involve "controversies" arising out of a particular line of conduct which causes a collision of specific interests. There is no *logical* or *factual* necessity about this proposition. There can be exceptions and the question of defining the limits of the adjudicative function can be difficult and debatable in the marginal areas....

... To summarize, a court should confine itself to settling concrete, private disputes between individuals who apply to the adjudicator for the resolution of their problem.

An Adversary Process

An adversary process is one which satisfies, more or less, this factual description: as a prelude to the dispute being solved, the interested parties have the opportunity of adducing evidence (or proof) and making arguments to a disinterested and impartial arbiter who decides the case on the basis of this evidence and these arguments. This is by contrast with the public processes of decision by "legitimated power" and "mediation-agreement," where the guaranteed private modes of participation are voting and negotiation respectively. Adjudication is distinctive because it guarantees to each of the parties who are affected the right to prepare for themselves the representations on the basis of which their dispute is to be resolved.

The Need for Standards

… Why does the institution of adjudication require the existence of standards for decision? Of what type are these standards and what does it mean to say that they "exist"? Taking these questions in reverse order, in order that standards "exist," there must be a shared consensus between the adjudicator and the parties about what the standards are which the former is going to apply. Secondly, the parties must reasonably have expected, at the time they acted, that these standards would be used to evaluate their private conduct. Of course, some legal rules can be directed only to the arbiter himself dealing with purely remedial problems. We draw our standards from the legal order which regulates private conduct because a primary objective of the use of adjudication is to preserve the viability of this legal order by settling authoritatively the disputes arising within it. Successful adjudication requires that there be a shared consensus about these rules, especially insofar as they can be utilized to evaluate the conduct of the parties which gives rise to the dispute.

In order that adjudicative decisions be characterized by the quality of rationality which is a prerequisite for their moral force and acceptability, the arbiter must have some principles which he can utilize in explaining to himself and to the parties his reasons for deciding one way or the other. The arbiter is under a duty to articulate a reasoned basis for his decision (whether or not he writes an opinion), because he is not conceded the power of *enactment*. He is not considered to have a *legitimate* power to exercise a discretion to settle a matter just because it needs settling, and without giving reasons for deciding on the particular disposition he selects. Hence, he cannot merely confront an undifferentiated factual situation and decide by an intuitive "leap in the dark." He needs a set of ordering principles which enable him to make sense of the situation and abstract those relevant facets of it which can be organized into a reasoned argument.

Second, the adjudicative process can have the enhanced quality of rationality, which derives from its focusing on a specific, concrete dispute for decision, only if there are standards or principles which enable the adjudicator to single out the relevant, problematic facets of the situation on which he is going to concentrate his attention. If there is no framework of settled principles within which he can operate, and every aspect of every situation is always open to question, then the adjudicator will not be able to focus his attention on unresolved problems. Thus, he will not be able to attain a significantly higher quality of rationality in the solution which he produces for the problem.

Thirdly, to the extent that adjudication entails adversary participation, the presentation of proofs and arguments to the arbiter, the process is meaningless unless the parties can know before their preparation and presentation of the case the principles and standards which the arbiter is likely to find relevant to his disposition of the dispute. It is impossible to make an intelligent argument "in the air" and without any idea of which factors are considered relevant by the person whom one's argument is attempting to persuade. If a relatively passive attitude is necessarily conducive to impartiality (although this does not exclude some reciprocal clarification of views), and a high degree of rationality in result thus depends directly on the quality of the preparations and representation by each side, then a consensus of standards is needed in order that intelligent alternative positions are established and that an adequate "joinder of issue" results....

III. The Judicial Policy-Maker Model: The Judge as Political Actor

A second distinctive model of the judicial process has been developed in recent years, largely by American political scientists. Of course, it is not original in recognizing the inescapable fact that judicial decisions must involve the creative exercise of a court's judgment. It builds on the work of American Legal Realism, which showed that the mechanical application of rigid, automatic rules does not and cannot dispose of individual cases. Men, as judges, decide cases and this activity is one for which they are personally responsible.

However, as we have seen, the "adjudication" model also begins with this assumption. Judges must collaborate with other bodies in society in the development and elaboration of the law "as it ought to be." Yet this collaborative role is institutionally distinctive. The creative articulation of new legal rules is limited and incremental; it is based on a moving background of established legal principles; it is related to the dispute-settling focus of courts because the new rule must be appropriate for retrospective application to the facts giving rise to the instant case; finally, the adoption of the new rule must be justified in a reasoned opinion which establishes the probable "rightness" of the new rule. This whole set of limitations on judicial law-making is necessary in order to *legitimate* the final product. However, this legitimacy does not require a mechanical deduction of the rule from legal premises in which it somehow pre-exists, as in a "brooding omnipresence in the sky." The reasoning in the opinion is not of a logical-deductive type. Yet, it is supposed to be sufficiently communicable that it is open, in principle at least, to prior vicarious participation by the parties in the adversary process.

Many political scientists, by contrast, believe that judges should be perceived as political actors, continuously engaged in the formulation of policy for society. To say that judges are political actors is not simply to assert the truism that they are part of the governmental system, "authoritatively allocating values in society." Nor is it characteristic of only this model that judges exercise personal judgment in each decision they make and that no conclusions are automatic. What is distinctive is the thesis that judges make policy, or legislate, through essentially the same mode of reasoning as other actors in the governmental system. Moreover, at least for some courts, such political action is becoming, and is seen to be becoming, their primary concern, and adjudication of disputes is growing secondary.

Legislators have traditionally been contrasted with courts by the fact that society considers it acceptable for them to justify authoritative policy-making by reference to their own value preferences, or the interests of those who support or have access to them. Legislators do not feel institutionally committed to the formulation of new legal rules only if they can be justified by a reasoned opinion relating the development to accepted doctrinal premises. This model suggests that some courts also are not, and should not be, so institutionally committed.

The quality of political decision-making both influences and reflects the make-up of the institution within which it is carried on. If, as, and when judges become candid policy-makers, courts will take on a "political" character, and judges will be subjected to "political" pressures. The new orientation of the "policy-making" model should render appropriate for judges the same analysis that is applied to other political actors, as regards the recruitment of the men who make these decisions, the timing of their policy pronouncements, the influences brought to bear on the court, both internally and externally, and the success which attends its policy promulgation. The new model explains, in an illuminating way, many recent judicial phenomena that have followed the proposal and adoption of the new political role by some courts in some legal systems. Moreover, it shows the linkage of the various components in the judicial systems, as it becomes redesigned for its new institutional function. I shall compare the new model with the old, showing the changes we may expect in the existing system if and when judges turn from adjudication to concentrate on policy-making. I will not be interested in empirical proof, by scalogram analysis or otherwise, that courts do or do not make decisions based on "policy," rather than "law." Assuming that judges may internalize the role of "political actor" rather than "adjudicator," I hope to make clear the institutional significance of this fact....

IV. Conclusion
I do not believe it is possible yet to decide which of these models expresses a more appropriate role for judges in our society. Nor does either version furnish

a type of litmus test for discovering the nature of our present system. Probably, the various judiciaries in the common law are based on different mixtures of each role, however contradictory they may appear in the abstract. Our models are "ideal types," furnishing us with distinctive angles of vision on the same judicial reality, thus allowing us a more profound understanding and evaluation of tendencies within the existing system. Moreover, these two artificial constructs of the judicial process show us the practical significance of two as yet unresolved problems in legal philosophy. Is rational and communicable decision-making possible in choosing between social values? Is judicial choice about values that favour one interest over another a fair institution within a democracy?

In conclusion, I should emphasize my belief that the judicial process in Canada fits neither model as regards the appropriate mode of reasoning, although it is organized more or less along adjudicative lines. In fact, common law judging in Canada has truly been a wasteland of arid legalism, one that is only beginning to be relieved by a profounder vision of the scope of judicial action. For this reason alone, I am just as dubious about the desirability of judicial review of legislative action as about the present review of administrative action. Perhaps the proposal for a Canadian Bill of Rights should await the advent of judges who are products of a different legal education. It seems safe to predict that they will have been schooled in some version of the philosophies of judicial decision-making which I have sketched.

2.2

Harrison v. Carswell

Supreme Court of Canada, [1976] 2 S.C.R. 200

[*Ed. note*: In this case the Supreme Court was faced with a dispute between Harrison, the manager of a shopping centre in Winnipeg, and Carswell, a striking employee of one of the stores in the shopping centre. Carswell was participating in a lawful strike and was picketing on the sidewalk in front of her employer's store. Harrison informed her that picketing was not permitted in any area of the shopping centre, and asked her to leave. Carswell refused, and was arrested and convicted of petty trespass. The legal issue at stake in this case was the conflict between the traditional rights of private property (protected by the law of trespass) and the right to strike.]

The judgment of Laskin C.J. and Spence and Beetz J.J. was delivered by THE CHIEF JUSTICE (dissenting) – I would be content to adopt the reasons of Freedman C.J.M. and, accordingly, to dismiss this appeal without more if I did not feel compelled, in view of the course of argument, to add some observations bearing on the decision of this Court in *Peters v. The Queen* dismissing an appeal from the judgment of the Ontario Court of Appeal. The observations I am about to make about the *Peters* case carry into two areas of concern respecting the role of this Court as the final Court in this country in both civil and criminal causes. Those areas are, first, whether this Court must pay mechanical deference to *stare decisis* and, second, whether this Court has a balancing role to play, without yielding place to the Legislature, where an ancient doctrine, in this case trespass, is invoked in a new setting to suppress a lawful activity supported both by legislation and by a well-understood legislative policy....

... This Court, above all others in this country, cannot be simply mechanistic about previous decisions, whatever be the respect it would pay to such decisions. What we would be doing here, if we were to say that the *Peters* case, because it was so recently decided, has concluded the present case for us, would be to take merely one side of a debatable issue and say that it concludes the debate without the need to hear the other side.

I do not have to call upon pronouncements of members of this Court that we are free to depart from previous decisions in order to support the pressing need to examine the present case on its merits.

The judgment of Martland, Judson, Ritchie, Pigeon, Dickson, and de Grandpré, J.J. was delivered by Dickson J.

... The submission that this Court should weigh and determine the respective values to society of the right to property and the right to picket raises important and difficult political and socio-economic issues, the resolution of which must, by their very nature, be arbitrary and embody personal economic and social beliefs. It raises also fundamental questions as to the role of this Court under the Canadian constitution. The duty of the Court, as I envisage it, is to proceed in the discharge of its adjudicative function in a reasoned way from principled decision and established concepts. I do not for a moment doubt the power of the Court to act creatively – it has done so on countless occasions; but manifestly one must ask – what are the limits of the judicial function? There are many and varied answers to this question. Holmes J. said in *Southern Pacific Co. v. Jensen*, at p. 221: "I recognize without hesitation that judges do and must legislate, but they can do it only interstitially; they are confined from molar to molecular actions." Cardozo, *The Nature of the Judicial Process* (1921), p. 141, recognized that the freedom of the judge is not absolute in this expression of his review:

2: POLITICAL JURISPRUDENCE

This judge, even when he is free, is still not wholly free. He is not to innovate at pleasure. He is not a knight-errant, roaming at will in pursuit of his own ideal of beauty or of goodness. He is to draw his inspiration from consecrated principles.

The former Chief Justice of the Australian High Court, Sir Owen Dixon, in an address delivered at Yale University in September 1955, "Concerning Judicial Method," had this to say:

But in our Australian High Court we have had as yet no deliberate innovators bent on express change of acknowledged doctrine. It is one thing for a court to seek to extend the application of accepted principles to new cases or to reason from the more fundamental of settled legal principles to new conclusions or to decide that a category is not closed against unforeseen instances which in reason might be subsumed thereunder. It is an entirely different thing for a judge, who is discontented with a result held to flow from a long accepted legal principle, deliberately to abandon the principle in the name of justice or of social necessity or of social convenience. The former accords with the technique of the common law and amounts to no more than an enlightened application of modes of reasoning traditionally respected in the courts. It is a process by the repeated use of which the law is developed, is adapted to new conditions, and is improved in content. The latter means an abrupt and almost arbitrary change.

Society has long since acknowledged that a public interest is served by permitting union members to bring economic pressure to bear upon their respective employers through peaceful picketing, but the right has been exercisable in some locations and not in others and to the extent that picketing has been permitted on private property the right hitherto has been accorded by statute. For example, s. 87 of the *Labour Code of British Columbia Act*, 1973 (B.C.) (2nd Sess.), c. 122, provides that no action lies in respect of picketing permitted under the Act for trespass to real property to which a member of the public ordinarily has access.

Anglo-Canadian jurisprudence has traditionally recognized, as a fundamental freedom, the right of the individual to the enjoyment of property and the right not to be deprived thereof, or any interest therein, save by due process of law. The Legislature of Manitoba has declared in *The Petty Trespasses Act* that any person who trespasses upon land, the property of another, upon or through which he has been requested by the owner not to enter, is guilty of an offence. If there is to be any change in this statute law, if *A* is to be given the right to enter and remain on the land of *B* against the will of *B*, it would seem to me that such a change must be made by the enacting institution, the Legislature, which is representative of the people and designed to manifest the political will, and not by the Court.

2.3

Will Women Judges Really Make a Difference?
Justice Bertha Wilson

Osgoode Hall Law Journal 28, no. 3 (1990), 507–522. Reprinted with permission.

… Many have criticized as totally unreal the concept that judges are somehow superhuman, neutral, above politics and unbiased, and are able to completely separate themselves from their personal opinions and predispositions when exercising their judicial function.…

In his text, *The Politics of the Judiciary*, Professor Griffith caused a furor in legal and judicial circles in the United Kingdom when he questioned whether the English judiciary were capable of impartiality. He stated that for a judge to be completely impartial he or she would have to be like a political, economic and social eunuch and have no interests in the world outside the court. Because this is impossible, Griffith concludes that impartiality is an ideal incapable of realization. He says of the English judiciary:

> These judges have by their education and training and the pursuit of their profession as barristers acquired a strikingly homogeneous collection of attitudes, beliefs, and principles which to them represents the public interest.

The public interest, in other words, is perceived from the viewpoint of their own class. Chief Justice Nemetz has suggested that Professor Griffith's views may have some validity in Canada too, more particularly, Professor Griffith's view that judicial attitudes towards political and social issues reflect the lack of a proper understanding of the view of labour unions, minorities and the under-privileged.

Judge Rosalie Abella (Chair of the Ontario Law Reform Commission) also doubts that judicial impartiality is a realistic requirement. In her article, "The Dynamic Nature of Equality," she emphasizes that "[e]very decision-maker who walks into a courtroom to hear a case is armed not only with the relevant legal texts but with a set of values, common experiences and assumptions that are thoroughly embedded." [*Ed. note*: In March, 1992 Justice Minister Kim Campbell announced Judge Abella's appointment to the Ontario Court of Appeal.]

Judge Shientag refers to the fact that many judges believe that they have acted with the cold neutrality of an impartial judge when, in fact, they have completely failed to examine their prejudices and biases. He points out that the partiality and prejudice with which we are concerned is not overt, not something tangible on which the judge can put his or her finger. Yet by failing to appreciate this many judges are lulled into a false sense of security. Judge Sheintag emphasizes that progress will only be made when judges recognize this condition as part of the weakness of human nature. Then "[h]aving admitted the liability to prejudice, unconscious for the most part, subtle and nebulous at times, the next step is to determine what the judge, with his trained mind, can do to neutralize the incessant play of these obscure yet potent influences." Judge Sheintag concludes that "the judge who realizes, before listening to a case, that all men have a natural bias of mind and that thought is apt to be coloured by predilection, is more likely to make a conscientious effort at impartiality and dispassionateness than one who believes that his elevation to the bench makes him at once the dehumanized instrument of infallible logical truth."

But what has all this got to do with my subject: "Will women judges really make a difference?" It has a great deal to do with it and whether you agree or not will probably depend on your perception of the degree to which the existing law reflects the judicial neutrality or impartiality we have been discussing. If the existing law can be viewed as the product of judicial neutrality or impartiality, even though the judiciary has been very substantially male, then you may conclude that the advent of increased numbers of women judges should make no difference, assuming, that is, that these women judges will bring to bear the same neutrality and impartiality. However, if you conclude that the existing law, in some areas at least, cannot be viewed as the product of judicial neutrality, then your answer may be very different.

Two law professors at New York University, Professor John Johnston and Professor Charles Knapp, have concluded, as a result of their studies of judicial attitudes reflected in the decisions of judges in the United States, that United States judges have succeeded in their conscious efforts to free themselves from habits of stereotypical thought with regard to discrimination based on colour. However, they were unable to reach a similar conclusion with respect to discrimination based on sex and found that American judges had failed to bring to sex discrimination the judicial virtues of detachment, reflection and critical analysis which had served them so well with respect to other areas of discrimination.

They state:

> "Sexism" – the making of unjustified (or at least unsupported) assumptions about individual capabilities, interests, goals and social roles solely on the basis of sex differences – is as easily discernible in contemporary judicial opinions as racism ever was.

Professor Norma Wikler, a sociologist at the University of California, has reviewed a number of other studies of judicial attitudes by legal researchers and social scientists. These studies confirm that male judges tend to adhere to traditional values and beliefs about the "natures" of men and women and their proper roles in society. The studies show overwhelming evidence that gender-based myths, biases and stereotypes are deeply embedded in the attitudes of many male judges as well as in the law itself. Researchers have concluded that gender difference has been a significant factor in judicial decision-making, particularly in areas of tort law, criminal law and family law. Further many have concluded that sexism is the unarticulated underlying premise of many judgments in these areas, and that this is not really surprising having regard to the nature of the society in which the judges themselves have been socialized.

... So, where do we stand in Canada on this matter? As might be expected, feminist scholars in Canada have over the past two decades produced a vast quantity of literature on the subject, some of it very insightful, very balanced and very useful, and some of it very radical, quite provocative and probably less useful as a result. But all of it, it seems, is premised, at least as far as judicial decision-making is concerned, on two basic propositions: one, that women view the world and what goes on in it from a different perspective from men, and two, that women judges, by bringing that perspective to bear on the cases they hear, can play a major role in introducing judicial neutrality and impartiality into the justice system.

Taking my own personal experience as a judge of fourteen years' standing, working closely with my male colleagues on the bench, there are probably whole areas of the law on which there is no uniquely feminine perspective. This is not to say that the development of the law in these areas has not been influenced by the fact that the lawyers and the judges have all been men. Rather, the principles and the underlying premises are so firmly entrenched and so fundamentally sound that no good would be achieved by attempting to re-invent the wheel, even if the revised version did have a few more spokes in it. I have in mind areas such as the law of contract, the law of real property and the law applicable to corporations. In some other areas of the law, however, I think that a distinctly male perspective is clearly discernible. It has resulted in legal principles that are not fundamentally sound and that should be revisited when the opportunity presents itself. Canadian feminist scholarship has done an excellent job of identifying those areas and making suggestions for reform. Some aspects of the criminal law in particular cry out for change; they are based on presuppositions about the nature of women and women's sexuality that, in this day and age, are little short of ludicrous.

But how do we handle the problem that women judges, just as much as their male counterparts, are subject to the duty of impartiality? As was said at the outset, judges must not approach their task with preconceived notions about law and policy. They must approach it with detachment and, as Lord MacMillan said, purge their minds "not only of partiality to persons but of partiality to arguments." Does this then foreclose any kind of "judicial affirmative action" to counteract the influence of the dominant male perspective of the past and establish judicial neutrality through a countervailing female perspective? Is Karen Selick, writing recently in *The Lawyers Weekly*, correct when she argues that offsetting male bias with female bias would only be compounding the injustice? Does the nature of the judicial process itself present an insuperable hurdle so that the legislatures rather than the courts must be looked to for any significant legal change?

In part this may be so. Certainly, the legislature is the more effective instrument for rapid or radical change. But there is no reason why the judiciary cannot exercise some modest degree of creativity in areas where modern insights and life's experience have indicated that the law has gone awry. However, and this is extremely important, it will be a Pyrrhic victory for women and for the justice system as a whole if changes in the law come only through the efforts of women lawyers and women judges. The Americans were smart to realize that courses and workshops on gender bias for judges, male and female, are an essential follow-up to scholarly research and learned writing. In Canada, we are just beginning to touch the fringes.

... The Canadian Judicial Council and the Canadian Judicial Centre have both recognized the need for judicial education in this area and will include gender issues in their summer seminars for judges this year. I understand that the Centre hopes to subsequently present the program in a number of locations across the country, and the course materials will be available to all Canadian judges. I heartily endorse this initiative. It is a significant first step towards the achievement of true judicial neutrality. But it is only a first step and there is a long way to go.

I return, then, to the question of whether the appointment of more women judges will make a difference. Because the entry of women into the judiciary is so recent, few studies have been done on the subject. Current statistics, however, show that just over nine percent of federally appointed judges are women; it is reasonable to assume that more and more women will be appointed to the Bench as more and more women become licensed to practice law. Will this growing number of women judges by itself make a difference?

The expectation is that it will, the mere presence of women on the bench will make a difference. In an article "The Gender of Judges," Suzanna Sherry (an Associate Law Professor at the University of Minnesota) suggests that the mere fact that women are judges serves an educative function; it helps to shatter stereotypes about the role of women in society that are held by male judges and lawyers, as well as by litigants, jurors and witnesses.

... Some feminist writers are persuaded that the appointment of more women judges will have an impact on the process of judicial decision-making itself and on the development of the substantive law. As was mentioned earlier, this flows from the belief that women view the world and what goes on in it from a different perspective from men. Some define the difference in perspective solely in terms that women do not accept male perceptions and interpretations of events as the norm or as objective reality. Carol Gilligan (a Professor of Education at Harvard University) sees the difference as going much deeper than that. In her view, women think differently from men, particularly in responding to moral dilemmas. They have, she says, different ways of thinking about themselves and their relationships to others.

In her book, *In a Different Voice*, Gilligan analyses data she collected, in the form of responses from male and female participants in a number of different studies. These responses, she submits, support her central thesis that women see themselves as essentially connected to others and as members of a community; men see themselves as essentially autonomous and independent of others. Gilligan makes no claim about the origins of the differences she describes. She does, however, use the psychoanalytical work of Dr. Nancy Chodorow as a starting point. Chodorow postulates that gender differences arise from the fact that women do the mothering of children. Because the gender identity of male children is not the same as their mothers, they tend to distance and separate themselves from their mothers' female characteristics in order to develop their masculinity. Female children, on the other hand, define themselves through attachment to their mothers. Masculinity is therefore, according to Gilligan, defined through separation and individualism; femininity is defined through attachment and the formation of relationships. The gender identity of the male, she submits, is threatened by relationships while the gender identity of the female is threatened by separation.

Gilligan's work on conceptions of morality among adults suggests that women's ethical sense is significantly different from men's. Men see moral problems as arising from competing rights; the adversarial process comes easily to them. Women see moral problems as arising from competing obligations, the one to the other; the important thing is to preserve relationships, to develop an ethic of caring. The goal, according to women's ethical sense is not seen in terms of winning or losing but, rather, in terms of achieving an optimum outcome for all individuals involved in the moral dilemma. It is not difficult to see how this contrast in thinking might form the basis of different perceptions of justice.

There is merit in Gilligan's analysis. In part, it may explain the traditional reluctance of courts to get too deeply into the circumstances of a case, their anxiety to reduce the context of the dispute to its bare bones through a complex system of exclusionary evidentiary rules. This is one of the characteristic features of the adversarial process. We are all familiar with the witness on cross-examination who wants to explain his or her answer, who feels that a simple yes or no is not an adequate response, and who is frustrated and angry at being cut off with a half-truth. It is so much easier to come up with a black and white answer if you are unencumbered by a broader context which might prompt you, in Lord MacMillan's words, to temper the cold light of reason with the warmer tints of imagination and sympathy.

Gilligan's analysis may explain also the hostility of some male judges to permitting interveners in human rights cases. The main purpose of having interveners is to broaden the context of the dispute, to show the issue in a larger perspective or as impacting on other groups not directly involved in the litigation at all. But it certainly does complicate the issues to have them presented in polycentric terms.

... One of the important conclusions emerging from the Council of Europe's Seminar on Equality between Men and Women held in Strasbourg last November is that the universalist doctrine of human rights must include a realistic concept of masculine and feminine humanity regarded as a whole, that human kind *is* dual and must be represented in its dual form if the trap of an asexual abstraction in which human being is always declined in the masculine is to be avoided. If women lawyers and women judges through their differing perspectives on life can bring a new humanity to bear on the decision-making process, perhaps they *will* make a difference. Perhaps they will succeed in infusing the law with an understanding of what it means to be fully human.

2.4

Re Constitution of Canada, 1981: The Patriation Reference

Michael Mandel

The Charter of Rights and the Legalization of Politics in Canada (Toronto: Wall and Thompson, 1988), 24–34. Reprinted with permission.

[The constitutional reference cases of 1981 were] the third and by far most important aspect of the provincial counterattack. Three of the opposing provincial governments, Manitoba, Quebec, and Newfoundland, referred the question of the constitutionality of the federal proposal to their provincial supreme courts. But this was "constitutionality" with a difference. For in addition to the ordinary questions governments ask courts concerning matters of constitutional *legality*, each government asked a separate question about whether it was consistent with constitutional *convention* (understood as meaning, roughly, a historically recognized norm of political behaviour) for the federal government to approach the UK Parliament over such substantial provincial opposition.

Of course, everyone knew that the government's plan was *not* consistent with constitutional convention. What was extraordinary was to ask the courts to say so. Courts had sometimes ruled on conventions where doing so was necessary to resolve a question of law, but they had *never* done so where, as in this case, the supposed convention was completely detached from any legal question. Why?

The technical distinction between conventions and laws is that conventions are *unenforceable* in the courts. This means that the courts will not authorize the use of force to obtain obedience to conventions. But they will with laws. Why is this important? Because this regulation or authorization of the use of official force, this law *enforcement*, is not merely one of the functions of courts among many. It is their defining characteristic. Courts do not distinguish between the legal and the illegal in a vacuum or as an end in itself. Their determinations are a crucial part of the legitimate use of force in the modern state. The practical activity of the use of force by the state requires an institution capable of finally, efficiently, and authoritatively determining its legitimacy in any given case. The very idea of legality requires such an institution. That institution is the courts. Their word is law. But we do not need only one institution authorized to determine right and wrong or historical practice. Quite the contrary. We can do without "official" moralities and "official" histories. For a court to recognize a convention that by definition it will nevertheless not enforce is to do something that *anyone* has the authority to do. A court's opinion on the matter has no more formal, judicial, legal, or whatever-you-choose-to-call-it, authority than yours, mine, Pierre Trudeau's or René Lévesque's. If it is more persuasive, this is a political fact, not a legal one.

So when the courts were asked a separate question on constitutional convention, they were asked something outside of the realm of law and judging. Nevertheless, there was little reluctance on their part to answer it. Only one judge out of 22 refused out of a sense of judicial propriety. [*Ed. note*: The figure of 22 judges includes those who initially heard the reference in the Courts of Appeal.] As for the answers to the various questions, the three appellate courts were hopelessly divided, with Manitoba and Quebec (over dissents) in favour, and Newfoundland (unanimously) opposed. Of the 13 appellate judges who heard the cases, seven found in favour of the federal government and six against it. There was no avoiding referring the whole matter to the Supreme Court of Canada....

The arguments before the Supreme Court of Canada by a battery of constitutional lawyers in *Re Constitution of Canada* took only five days of late April 1981, amid what court historians claim was the most concentrated public attention in its history. However, the Court took the entire summer to prepare its decision, which was ready for release on September 28. Far from being reticent about its new role, the Court seemed eager for it, even too eager. It broke yet another tradition by allowing TV cameras into the courtroom for the first time, but the effect was ruined when one of the judges tripped a sound cable rendering the Chief Justice's reading of the judgment inaudible. What he had to say was hardly the stuff of high television ratings anyway. It was a dry recitation of the various questions put to the Court and their technical answers, confusing even for lawyers. The Supreme Court had many lessons to learn in public relations. What the decision would mean in political terms was also unclear at first. It was interpreted differently according to which side of the issue and which side of the Quebec border one was on. Quebec's *Le Devoir* headline was one way of looking at it: "Legal but unconstitutional," while Ontario's *Globe and Mail* headline was another: "PM's bid 'offends' but is legal." Both were technically correct: the legality of the plan was affirmed by a vote of seven judges to two, and its inconsistency with constitutional convention by a vote of six to three. A lot of the confusion came from the shifting alignments on the Court with some judges dissenting on one question yet joining the majority on the other. But closer examination shows the political logic of the decision. The Court voted almost perfectly along political and regional lines:

Table 1:

Judge	Province	Appointed	Legal	Conventional
Laskin	Ontario	Trudeau	Yes	Yes
Estey	Ontario	Trudeau	Yes	Yes
McIntyre	B.C.	Trudeau	Yes	Yes
Dickson	Manitoba	Trudeau	Yes	No
Beetz	Quebec	Trudeau	Yes	No
Lamer	Quebec	Trudeau	Yes	No
Chouinard	Quebec	Trudeau	Yes	No
Martland	Alberta	Diefenbaker	No	No
Ritchie	Alberta*	Diefenbaker	No	No

*[*Ed. note:* Justice Roland Ritchie was actually from Nova Scotia, not Alberta.]

This was a transparently political decision and gave us a good idea, if we were paying attention, of what Canada could expect with the *Charter.*

The reasoning of the judges was as revealing as their voting pattern. Of the two questions, the legality question was probably the easiest. As we have seen, for a court to hold an act of government illegal is, at least implicitly, to prohibit it. The majority argued that, however unconventional the federal government's action might be, there was nothing in the decided cases or the statutes authorizing a court actually to interfere with what was, after all, a mere request made by the Canadian Parliament to the UK Parliament. Whatever impact such a request might in fact have, it had no legal effect without a law being passed by the sovereign UK Parliament. Where could a court get the authority to *prohibit* a *request*? Furthermore, given the fact that the entire legal structure of Canada depended on a British enactment, what legal authority could a Canadian court have to refuse to recognize an amendment to the *BNA Act* by the Parliament that enacted it in the first place, however that amendment came to be proposed? The minority's answer was that the Court should, in effect, make up the authority so as to protect the fundamental federal structure of Canada. Courts had made things up before.

There was logic on both sides and certainly a lack of precedent had become increasingly unimportant to this court – that very day it would do a most unprecedented act. But to hold this action illegal, even if technically possible, would have been reckless on the part of the Court. What if Parliament were unable to achieve an agreement through patently unreasonable provincial intransigence? The Court would then have set up an insuperable legal obstacle to a constitutional amendment and would have found itself confronting an already popular plan (the *Charter*) as well as what could turn into a popular strategy (unilateralism). If, in such an event, Parliament went ahead despite the illegality, the Court would have had its *order* ignored with a consequent loss of prestige. And what then? Could it actually refuse to enforce the law once it returned? Shades of Roosevelt and 1937! Besides, it was unnecessary to go this far in light of the Court's answer on the convention question.

That there was a convention requiring more provincial consent than the federal government had obtained could not really be challenged. In fact, the historical record was that no amendments had been passed without the consent of *all* of the provinces affected, and this record strongly implied that this was indeed recognized as binding on the federal government. Indeed, the only legitimate questions concerned the requirement of unanimity and the Quebec veto. There was in fact no dissent from anyone on the Court that constitutional convention required more provincial support than had been obtained. What is intriguing about the convention question has nothing to do with the answers given to it nor the arguments offered by majority and minority for their respective conclusions. What is intriguing is the way the convention question was interpreted by each side, the way the answers of each side were presented, and, most intriguing of all, *that it was even answered.*

First, the way the question was interpreted. When it asked whether "the consent of the provinces" was necessary, did it mean *all* of the provinces or merely *some* of them? Each side interpreted this differently, but in the way that best suited its point of view on the outcome. It was as obvious to the majority that the question did *not* mean to refer to *all* of the provinces as it was to the minority that it *did*.

Majority:

It would have been easy to insert the words "all" into the question had it been intended to narrow its meaning. But we do not think it was so intended.

Minority:

From the wording of the questions and from the course of argument it is clear that the questions meant the consent of all the Provinces.... There is no ambiguity in the questions before the Court.

The only thing that was really clear, of course, was that if the majority wanted to cast doubt on the plan and the minority to approve it, interpreting the question in their respective ways made it easier for each side to achieve its respective goal. If they were only interested in the truth, each side would have given answers to each possible interpretation of the question. If this is not coincidence enough, there are the very obvious attempts by each side to give maximum impact to its respective position. The minority, which found the plan not contrary to constitutional convention, but nevertheless knew itself to have lost this issue, *minimized* the general importance of conventions:

> We cannot ... agree with any suggestion that the non-observance of a convention can properly be termed unconstitutional in any strict or legal sense.... In a federal State ... constitutionality and legality must be synonymous, and conventional rules will be accorded less significance than they may have in a unitary State such as the United Kingdom.

> With conventions or understandings he [the lawyer and law teacher] has no direct concern. They vary from generation to generation, almost from year to year.... The subject ... is not one of law but of politics, and need trouble no lawyer or the class of any professor of law.

The majority, on the other hand, went to great lengths to *maximize* the significance of its holding that the federal resolution, though legal, was contrary to convention: "[W]hile they are not laws, some conventions may be more important than some laws." Indeed, the majority went about as far as it could in this direction when it declared that conventions "form an integral part of the constitution and the constitutional system":

> That is why it is perfectly appropriate to say that to violate a convention is to do something which is unconstitutional although it entails no direct legal consequences. But the words "constitutional" and "unconstitutional" may also be used in strict legal sense, for instance with respect to a statute which is found *ultra vires* or unconstitutional. The foregoing may perhaps be summarized in an equation: constitutional conventions plus constitutional law equal the total Constitution of the country.

But one does not have to look any further for proof of the political nature of the case than to the fact that the Court agreed to answer the convention question at all. And this is the only point upon which it was unanimous! Remember that there was no precedent for the Court ruling on a convention question divorced from any legal question. Indeed, according to the Court's own definition, conventions "are not enforced by the courts." So, answering the convention question at all was out of line with the role of courts as ordinarily conceived. In answering the convention question, the Supreme Court of Canada acted "outside its legal function and [attempted] to facilitate a political outcome." It "intervened as another political actor, not as a court of law." What was the Court's defence of this action? The majority devoted a separate section of its reasons to the issue, but nothing it said really answered the question. We were told that the question was important (though "not confined to an issue of pure legality.... It has to do with a fundamental issue of constitutionality and legitimacy") and that courts should not "shrink" from answering a question "on account of the political aspects." But these are reasons for answering a *legal* question with political implications, not for answering a political question that has nothing to do with law. The minority argued that they had to answer because the majority answered, but also because the case was "unusual" and there had been extensive argument on the convention question. Perhaps the judge who came the closest to the truth was the Chief Justice of Manitoba, quoted by the majority in the Supreme Court, who said that the question "calls for an answer, and I propose to answer it." Put another way, the reasons given by the various judges to justify their willingness to answer the convention question, and characterized by one commentator as "inadequate" as, no doubt, technically they were, amounted to no more and no less than that they were answering it because they were *expected* to answer it.

Can anyone doubt that they were right about this? Outside of scholarly criticism of the legal credentials of the decision and the dangers such political behaviour might cause the Supreme Court, not a peep of political criticism was heard of the decision to answer the question. And, while it is impossible to say what would have happened had the convention question not been answered or had it been answered differently, it is clear that with the Court decision as it was, the federal government had no political hope of going ahead without at least another round of negotiations. For one thing, the NDP informed the government that it would now vote against the resolution without a new conference. In Britain, too, the decision was regarded as decisive.... The *Guardian* reported that even with strenuous Thatcher sponsorship, the Bill would now have a tough time. Though the outcome would obviously have been impossible to predict with certainty, it is clear that there would have been a serious battle in the British Commons and House of Lords had the federal government tried to go ahead with its original plan after the judgment.

But most important of all was that the whole *Charter* enterprise depended for its success on reverence for the Court. The reason Trudeau wanted the *Charter* in the first place was to use it against the unilingual tendencies of provincial governments in areas beyond federal control. He needed it now to use against the popular language legislation of the PQ government of Quebec. The idea was to entrench English language rights which directly contradicted the PQ's *Bill 101* so that the courts, ultimately the Supreme Court, would strike down the law as violating the *Charter of Rights*. Trudeau was going to trump democracy by claiming a greater legitimacy for the Supreme Court of Canada than for any mere government. How could he criticize the Court for going too far today when he needed it to go all the way tomorrow?

So the Supreme Court's decision all but forced the First Ministers' conference that began on November 2, 1981. In fact, it practically determined its outcome. This was due partly to the holding on legality, because the knowledge that a unilateral federal gambit would be legal and enforceable gave the provinces an extra incentive to be conciliatory and even to break ranks to achieve individual objectives. But most important of all to the final outcome was the clear indication given by both majority and minority on the convention question that constitutional convention did not require the unanimous, or even near unanimous, assent of the provinces. Both sides let everyone know that they would approve of much less. For the minority judges, the denial of a unanimity requirement was part and parcel with their dissent, but this would have been a fragile predictor without some expression on the question by the majority judges, and express themselves they did, once again completely without judicial excuse:

> It was submitted by counsel for Manitoba, Newfoundland, Quebec, Nova Scotia, British Columbia, Prince Edward Island and Alberta that the convention does exist [and] that it requires the agreement of all the Provinces....

> Counsel for Saskatchewan ... submitted that the convention does exist and requires a measure of provincial agreement....

> We wish to indicate at the outset that we find ourselves in agreement with the submissions made on this issue by counsel for Saskatchewan....

It seems clear that while the precedents taken alone point at unanimity, the unanimity principle cannot be said to have been accepted by all the actors in the precedents....

It would not be appropriate for the Court to devise in the abstract
a specific formula which would indicate in positive terms what
measure of provincial agreement is required....

It is sufficient for the Court to decide that at least a substantial measure of provincial consent is required.... Nothing more
should be said about this.

The Court had said more than enough already. It had introduced a completely "new element" into the equation, an element that was emphasized by the
Premiers of both British Columbia and Saskatchewan (two *opposing* provinces) in their televised opening speeches to the First Ministers' conference on
November 2. It was this element that made possible the ultimate exclusion of
Quebec, the only province with truly irreconcilable differences with Ottawa,
differences over entrenched minority language rights, not only Trudeau's bottom line but actually his *raison d'être*. It is clear that these specific rights, which
in their precision and prolixity read more like a tax statute than a constitution,
were the only non-negotiables for Trudeau. The grand rights and freedoms of
"conscience," "association," "fundamental justice," "equality," and so on, which
granted a purely general supervisory jurisdiction over legislation to the courts,
were expendable. Trudeau said as much after the referendum. And he proved
it in the resulting constitution where none of these grand individualistic rights
would be so precious as to be immune from legislative veto by use of s.33, the
"notwithstanding" clause. By contrast, language rights would be immune, and
at the same time, they would automatically render null and void the language
of education provisions of the PQ's *Bill 101*, the centrepiece of its program to
make the French language *the* language of Quebec.

In other words, unanimity among provinces and the federal government
was simply not achievable so long as Trudeau and Lévesque had to sign the
same document. The freedom from unanimity which the Supreme Court presumed to grant made possible the only conceivable agreement, one that would
exclude Quebec. Furthermore, the "deliberate vagueness" of the Court's formula gave the other provinces more than enough incentive to jump on the
federal bandwagon lest they be isolated with English Canada's anathema. This
seems in fact to have been what determined Manitoba's capitulation. It was the
only other province with a real interest in opposing entrenched language rights

(because of its relatively large and linguistically mistreated French minority) and, because of this, the only other province firmly opposed to a *Charter* at the time of the conference (Alberta had made its deal with the federal government on energy prices in September). An accord excluding Quebec did not necessarily entail the sneakiness of the night of November 4–5, 1981, during which, with all parties but Quebec involved, the compromise that was to be Canada's constitution was worked out and then presented as a *fait accompli* to a shocked René Lévesque the next morning at breakfast. That there would be an accord, however, and that it would exclude Quebec was about as inevitable as these things ever get.

The Court's role in the ultimate making of the deal and in its general contours was, therefore, a rather large one. Furthermore, the script required it consciously to stride outside of its judicial confines and directly into the political arena. But this, as we have tried to show, was not a random occurrence. For most of the century, everything, and more and more nearly everyone, had been grooming the Court for this part. In fact, the most obvious thing about the decision to answer the convention question was that this thoroughly non-traditional decision of the Court concerned the adoption of a law – a constitutionally entrenched *Charter of Rights and Freedoms* – that would invest the judiciary with essentially the same thoroughly non-traditional function, namely judging the *legitimacy* of jurisdictionally valid legislation. The *Charter of Rights and Freedoms* in fact transformed the Court into an institution charged with making the very sort of judgments which it made on the convention issue – though such judgments would henceforth be made under the formally satisfying umbrella of constitutional authority. So if we want to know why the Court would accept such a non-traditional role in determining the outcome of a major political crisis and why its acceptance of this role would in turn be accepted by all the other actors, the answer is that it would have been strange indeed for the Court, standing on the threshold of its new era, to have been too prudish to engage in the very kind of activity that would characterize that era, or to have been criticized for doing so. The decision on the convention should be regarded as the inauguration of a new era in which the judiciary is to play a central role in the political life of this country. The triumph of the legalization of politics can be dated, then, not from the formal entrenchment of the *Charter of Rights and Freedoms* on April 17, 1982, but from the decision on the convention question in *Re Constitution of Canada* some seven months earlier.

2.5

The Exemplar of the *Secession Reference*

Robert Schertzer

The Judicial Role in a Diverse Federation: Lessons from the Supreme Court of Canada (University of Toronto Press, 2016), 139–168. Reprinted with permission.

The *Secession Reference* represents the culmination of a tumultuous decade marked by considerable nationalist mobilization in Québec, heated intergovernmental conflict, and continuous constitutional negotiation. Following the patriation of the Constitution Act, 1982 without the signature of Québec was the *Quebec Veto Reference*, where the SCC told Québec the document was in force regardless of a perceived veto and special status for the province. A number of attempts followed that tried to bring the province into the constitutional fold, notably the Meech Lake Accord (which included a controversial clause recognizing Québec's distinct status) and the Charlottetown Accord (which included the "Canada Clause" recognizing Québec's distinct status along with Aboriginal rights to self-government and the equality of the provinces). Both of these attempts to amend the Constitution ultimately failed, the latter rejected by a pan-state referendum. Ironically, this process, which started as an attempt to accommodate Québec, actually exacerbated Québec–Canada relations and fuelled separatist sentiment. The result was a 1995 provincial referendum initiated by the Québec government seeking a mandate to secede.

With the federalist option winning the referendum by the slimmest of margins (securing only 50.6 per cent of the vote), the central government mobilized to combat separatist forces. A two-pronged strategy was implemented (so-called Plan A and Plan B). Plan A was to actively promote a united Canada and stress the benefit to Quebeckers of staying in the federation. Among other things, this took the form of appeasing "soft-nationalists" by recognizing Québec's distinct status through a motion in the House of Commons, committing to recognize a Québec veto over constitutional amendment proposals, and sponsoring pro-Canada activities in the province.

Plan B was to take a harder line that accentuated the costs associated with separation and made it difficult to achieve. The *Secession Reference* was a central component of Plan B. The reference, initiated by the central government, asked the court three related questions: (1) Can Québec legally, under Canadian constitutional law, unilaterally secede from Canada? (2) Under international law and the concept of self-determination does Québec have the right to unilaterally secede from Canada? (3) In the event of a conflict between domestic and international law, which would take precedence?

The validity of the entire court process was explicitly challenged by Québec. The province argued the move was an attempt to interfere in its domestic politics and constrain its democratic rights, while maintaining the SCC was biased against its position. Québec even refused to participate in the reference, and so the SCC had to appoint an *amicus curiae* (friend of the court) to defend the position in favour of unilateral secession. In addition, thirteen parties intervened in the decision, including the provinces of Manitoba and Saskatchewan, the governments of the Yukon and Northwest Territories, various Aboriginal groups (e.g., the Grand Council of the Crees and the Chiefs of Ontario) as well as other advocacy associations. The general thrust of the interventions was against the right of Québec to unilaterally secede. Nevertheless, the dynamic of conflict in the case was between the central government and the Québec government, represented through the *amicus curiae....*

The court's opinion rejected the *legal* right of Québec to unilaterally secede, under either Canadian or international law. However, Québec was given solace in the ruling. If a clear majority of Quebeckers voted for secession in a referendum with a clear question, a duty to negotiate in good faith would be placed upon both orders of government. Following the decision, both the central government and Québec claimed victory, the former stressing the legal aspect of the ruling and the need for clarity in any future referendums, the latter stressing the duty to negotiate following a referendum.

Because of this Solomonic approach (seen by many as a deft political move) and the issues raised by the reference, it is often heralded as the most important decision the court has ever made. What was at stake in the case was nothing less than the dissolution of the federation initiated by Québec. The case thus resonates with broader international issues: the unity of a state being challenged by a national minority group claiming a right to unilaterally secede, while the central government fights this endeavour. The reference thus forced the court to grapple with issues that directly challenge the legitimacy of the constitutional and federal system (including the role of the courts within the system). This extraordinary element no doubt led the court to shift its conception of the federation and the constitution....

Depiction of the Federation

In the *Secession Reference*, we see the court depict the federation in a way that recognizes the legitimacy of multiple models and the system as the process and outcome of negotiation in two related ways. First, it provides a *balanced depiction* of the federation ... to the extent it highlights how aspects of each of the three main federal models – pan-Canadian, provincial equality, and multinational – find support in the institutional and political structures of the federation.

For example, the pan-Canadian model finds support in the court's presentation of the nature of the federation and the role of the central government: "Canada as a whole is ... a democratic community in which citizens construct and achieve goals on a national scale through a federal government." This point is accentuated by the court's depiction of the constitution as an overlapping consensus that "was an act of nation-building." In line with this view, Canada operates on the premise of "constitutional supremacy" and "the *basic structure of our Constitution* ... contemplates the existence of certain political institutions, including freely elected legislative bodies at the federal and provincial level." The combination of statements here places the federation and the constitution above politics – as a consensus that takes place among one nation, which gives rise to the different orders of government, an understanding of the constitutional and federal system that closely aligns with the trimming approach and pan-Canadian model.

At the same time, the court's depiction of the federal and constitutional system recognizes the legitimacy of the provincial-equality model. While reflecting on the principle of federalism, the SCC consistently discusses the provinces as a block and as one of two orders of government, implying equality among them and with the central government. Also, the idea of the federation as a compact among equal provinces is a strong undercurrent of the decision. The court argues that without a federal system "neither the agreement of the delegates from Canada East nor that of the delegates from the maritime colonies could have been obtained." The point of the federation, in this view, is thus not to "weld the Provinces into one, nor to subordinate Provincial Governments to a central authority, but to establish a central government in which these Provinces should be represented, entrusted with exclusive authority only in affairs in which they had a common interest. Subject to this each Province was to retain its independence and autonomy and to be directly under the Crown as its head." It is clear here that the court elaborates upon an understanding of the federal and constitutional system that recognizes that the provinces have considerable autonomy as equal jurisdictions to pursue their own and collective self-interests (and thus draws from and reinforces that view that the federation is about facilitating the trading of interests).

There is also considerable support for an understanding of the federation and constitution in line with the multinational model. The court clearly states that the federation "facilitates the pursuit of collective goals by *cultural and linguistic minorities* which form the majority within a particular province. This is the case in Québec, where the majority of the population is French-speaking, and which possesses a *distinct culture*." Despite the above comments on the nature of the federation as a compact among equal provinces, the SCC also says that "the social and demographic reality of Québec explains the existence of the province of Québec as a political unit and indeed, was one of the essential reasons for establishing a federal structure for the Canadian union in 1867." The federal system, in this view, is "a legal response to the underlying political and cultural realities that existed at Confederation and continue to exist today." The adoption of "constitutional supremacy" cited above, when combined with comments saying the constitution is a tool to protect national minorities, thus also sustains a view of the federal and constitutional system as a framework segregating various nations in line with the multinational model.

These seemingly irreconcilable positions are not the product of faulty logic or incoherent reasoning; rather, when the decision is read carefully it is clear that support for one model is qualified in turn by important aspects from a competing model. For example, when weight is given to the idea of Canada as a mere quasi-federation (in line with a centralist pan-Canadian view) it is qualified by noting the importance of provincial autonomy and the federation as a compact among provinces; this view is then further qualified by highlighting that provincial autonomy is used to protect distinct cultural groups, their existence being the driving force behind confederation. The balancing of perspectives is indicative of the respect the SCC affords to the complexity of the issues at hand and its task of interpreting the constitution in the face of competing perspectives on it and the federation. The apparent support for each model is thus easier to grasp: it is about rejecting a singular perspective and seeking to embrace the complexity of the way the constitution and the federation are understood by key actors.

... [Second,] The court's view of the federation as the process and outcome of negotiation rests largely on the link it provides between democracy and federation, with the federation facilitating democracy and vice versa. In presenting democracy as a continual process of discussion, compromise, and negotiation among actors holding competing perspectives, it also presents the federation in the same light. The federal system in this view is not static – it is not a straitjacket – but, rather, is a process and outcome of contestation, and it is legitimate to the extent that it remains a democratic system of continual deliberation. It is in the relationship between democracy and the federation, then, that the court can coherently see the federal system as incorporating the competing federal models (viewed as contingent perspectives, with the federation representing the process and outcome of contestation between the subscribers of these contingent perspectives)....

This view of the federation, and the reconciliation of competing perspectives, is also closely linked to the court's understanding of the national character of Canada. In the reference, it is clear that the court recognizes the plurinational character of the state. Just as the competing perspectives are all legitimate, so too is their basis in differing self-selected identities. In other words, each conception put forth by the competing federal models (i.e., Canada as uninational or multinational) is legitimate, and in this way Canada is plurinational. As the SCC states: "[I]n Canada there may be different and equally legitimate majorities in different provinces and territories and at the federal level ... [T] he function of federalism is to enable citizens to participate concurrently in different collectivities and to pursue goals at both a provincial and a federal level." So, a picture of the state as comprising various sets of key political actors is painted, with each holding their own contingent perspectives on nationality and the federation....

Despite the support for the multinational model, acceptance of plurinationality helps to explain the court's avoidance of the controversial term "dualism" and reluctance to declare the Québécois "a people" under international law. In other words, the court does recognize a multinational Canada, but it identifies this *as one of the many views on nationality* that exist in Canada. The result is that the *Secession Reference* forces both the Québécois and the rest of Canada to question the validity of their particular national narratives as natural, universal, and true....

Outcome

The *Secession Reference* is a complex case that deals with many issues. Accordingly, there are a number of outcomes that stem from the decision.... First is the opinion that it is technically illegal for Québec to unilaterally secede. Second is the constitutional duty placed on both orders of government to negotiate, in good faith, with a government that wants to amend the constitution (i.e., secede). Third is the declaration that any referenda initiating negotiations related to secession needs to have a clear question, with a clear result. Fourth is the opinion that international law does not sanction Québec's unilateral secession....

Looking at these four points in tandem allows us to see that the court handed each jurisdiction a positive outcome, while mitigating negative outcomes. For example, deciding it is illegal for a province to unilaterally secede (under either Canadian or international law) is clearly a positive outcome for the central government, as is the ruling that only a clear reference question with a clear majority can trigger secession negotiations. These outcomes meet the objectives of the central government going into the case: to erect roadblocks for the secessionist movement. At the same time, the ruling that there is a constitutional duty to negotiate *in good faith* with a province seeking to secede also hands Québec a significantly positive outcome. This aspect of the opinion lends the secessionist movement legitimacy, pushing the other parties in the federation to recognize the validity of Québec's position in the face of a positive vote to secede (rather than simply being intransigent). The legitimacy the court affords Québec's position in this regard also helps to mitigate the negative outcome for it in the form of the illegality of unilateral secession and the clarity mandate (i.e., while Québec cannot unilaterally secede, if its people declare they want to leave the federation, the other members of the system have to work to make that a reality in good faith). Moreover, the court mitigates the negative aspects of the ruling for Québec by saying that, while *not granting legality* to the process, ultimately, the determinative element of any secession is if it is effective on a practical and political level. In addition, Aboriginal groups are handed a positive in the ruling for a duty to negotiate, with the court clearly saying that their interests need to be represented and accounted for in any negotiations that effect their lands and rights. Similarly, all other provinces also receive a positive element in the decision with the ruling that one of them alone could not legally alter or destroy the federal system and with the implication that any negotiations over secession would have all provinces represented at the table.

These outcomes also clearly have broader effects that reinforce the legitimacy of each of the main federal models. The ruling that under international law a sub-state unit cannot secede (and that Québec is not technically "a people" under international law) reinforces the superiority of the central government and a view of the provinces as subordinate territorial units in line with the pan-Canadian model. At the same time, giving all provinces a seat at the table in any negotiations over secession reinforces their status as equals in line with the provincial-equality model. Finally, ruling that there is a duty to negotiate with Québec, and the inclusion of Aboriginal interests in the process, reinforces a view of the federation as comprising and protecting national minorities....

Conclusion

The above discussion provides a comprehensive picture of the *Secession Reference* as an exemplar of a decision that recognizes and accounts for the contestation over nationality and the federation in Canada. It depicts the federation in an inclusive manner, with the court employing accepted forms of legal analysis that demonstrate how the federation reflects aspects of each federal model and as the process and outcome of negotiation. Building on this understanding of the federation, the decision reaches an outcome that rejects a zero-sum approach, while reinforcing the legitimacy of the inclusive depiction. And, running through the overall approach in the decision is the court's self-selected role as the facilitator of negotiation between conflicting parties, rather than the imposer of a particular solution. In this way, the reference both draws from, and reinforces, the federation as the process and outcome of negotiation between the subscribers of legitimate models. As a whole, then, the decision provides a benchmark for how the court can potentially generate legitimacy for the conflict-management process and the system more generally in the way it manages conflict over the federation....

The approach adopted in the *Secession Reference* represents a significant shift in its approach to federal arbitration. It stands in contrast to the proportion of the SCC's federal decisions that impose a federal model (i.e., those decisions that draw from and reinforce a single model in the depiction of the federation and the outcome). The shift in the character of this reference is most evident in the fact that some 64 per cent of the court's decisions prior to the reference impose a particular federal model, while only 25 per cent of those following it do so. The *Secession Reference* thus marks a noticeable change in the court's general approach to federalism jurisprudence....

Why did the court adopt such a significantly different approach in this particular case? ... the likeliest answer is that the court was forced to find a way to save the federation in the face of a direct challenge to the legitimacy of the constitutional and federal system. While all federalism jurisprudence involves conflict over the nature of the federation (i.e., over the way identities are recognized and power and resources are distributed), the uniqueness of the *Secession Reference* is the direct and serious nature of the conflict. The case was about a party to the federation challenging the survival of the system. Moreover, the court battle took place shortly after a near referendum victory for the separatist option. The *Secession Reference*, then, was one of the rare occasions where the entire legal and political system was in flux and in danger of dissolution. In the face of this crisis, the court was required – as the apex body of the legal system and the ultimate federal arbiter – to find an innovative way to rescue the legitimacy of the entire political and legal system....

In this way, the reference is best understood as an explicit attempt to generate and maintain legitimacy for the constitutional and federal system, as well as for its federal arbiter and the way in which it fulfils its role.... Rather than imposing a particular perspective ... the court turned to recognize, account for and manage the conflict that takes place over the federation. Seeing itself as part of the system of government as its federal arbiter, the court used what it had at hand to save the system: the law.

2.6

No Statecraft, Questionable Jurisprudence: How the Supreme Court Tried to Kill Senate Reform

F.L. Morton

University of Calgary School of Public Policy Research Papers 8, no. 21 (2015). Excerpt reprinted with permission.

Reform of the Senate has been a centre-piece of the Conservative Party's policy platform since its inception. A "Triple E" Senate – elected, equal and effective – was a founding policy of one of its two predecessor, the Reform Party. At the time of the reference, the Harper Government had won three successive federal elections in a row, with Senate reform as a policy priority. During this period – 2006 to the present – the Harper Government has introduced eight Senate reform bills. To explain and to expedite the first of these bills, Harper volunteered to testify before a Senate Committee, the first sitting Prime Minister ever to do so. Alberta has already held four Senate elections (1989, 1998, 2004, 2012) and Prime Minister Harper has appointed four of the winners of those elections to the Senate. In recent years, polls consistently show that an overwhelming majority of Canadians – as many as 90 percent – are ready to either reform the Senate (the Conservative Party's position) or abolish it (the NDP's position). But the Federal Liberal Party, Quebec and all four Atlantic provinces oppose the unilateral legislative reforms proposed by the Harper Government. The Quebec government had already referred the issue of unilateral federal reforms to the Senate to their own Supreme Court, which in turn had ruled against Ottawa.

Faced with a political and constitutional stalemate, the Government referred a set of six constitutional questions to the Supreme Court of Canada. [See sidebar] Harper's objective was to clarify what constitutional reforms the House and Senate acting alone could make WITHOUT involving the provincial governments and the risk of opening the Pandora's Box of the Meech Lake (1987) and Charlottetown (1992) Accords. The Government was looking to the Court for some practical guidance on the constitutional issues and a path forward to reforming or abolishing a scandal-plagued institution that is widely viewed as no longer performing any constructive role in Canadian politics.

Table 1:

Harper's Six Reference Questions and the Supreme Court's Answers

1. Can Parliament unilaterally amend the Constitution to set fixed terms for senators? *No.*

2. Can Parliament unilaterally amend the Constitution to allow Parliament to enact legislation to provide for consultative elections to identify potential nominees for appointment to the Senate? *No.*

3. Can Parliament unilaterally amend the Constitution to enact a framework for provincial governments to provide for consultative elections to identify potential nominees for appointment to the Senate? *No.*

4. Can Parliament unilaterally amend the Constitution to abolish the property qualifications for Senators? *Yes, except for Quebec.*

5. Can the Senate be abolished through the Section 38 amending formula—i.e., with the support of the federal government plus at least seven provinces with at least 50 per cent of Canada's population? *No.*

6. If the answer to Question 5 is negative, does the abolition of the Senate require using the Section 41 amending formula—unanimous consent of all the provinces plus the federal government? *Yes.*

Harper's use of the reference procedure to break this political and constitutional log-jam has parallels in the earlier *Patriation Reference* (1981) and *Quebec Secession Reference* (1998). In the former, then Prime Minister Pierre Trudeau was confronted with conflicting constitutional claims over his attempt at unilateral patriation of Canada's constitution. In the latter, then Prime Minister Jean Chretien was attempting to block Quebec's attempt at unilateral secession from Canada. Both these references were solid precedents for Harper to send his Senate reform questions to the Supreme Court. In both precedents, the Supreme Court had engaged in what Peter Russell has incisively described as "bold statecraft (if) questionable jurisprudence" to give partial victories to both sides of the conflicts and return the issues to the political arena for resolution. Harper clearly hoped that the Court would give him a green light to proceed unilaterally, but these precedents gave him reason to believe that the worst the Court would give him would be this kind of "half-loaf" result.

Instead, the Court slammed the door shut on Senate reform, save through a formal constitutional amendment involving most (section 38) or all (section 41) of the provinces. The Court's sweeping dismissal of the Government's proposed reforms would be completely acceptable if the law on the method of selecting senators were clear and compelling. In fact, the opposite is the case. There was a clear and simple interpretive path to allowing some form of consultative elections and returning the Senate reform issue back to the political forum – as the Court has done before, but chose not to here.

***

There are no hard "black letter" constitutional rules that dictated the Court's decision. A literal reading of section 42 of the *Constitution Act, 1982* – which requires the general amending formula (i.e. at least seven of the ten provinces with a total of 50 percent of Canada's population) for any changes to "the method of selecting Senators" – would allow for consultative elections. Subject to three specific qualifications – minimum age, property ownership and residency – all the constitution says about the "method of selecting Senators" is:

> The Governor General shall from Time to Time, in the Queen's Name … summon qualified Persons to the Senate; and … every Person so summoned shall become and be a Member of the Senate and a Senator.

Consultative elections do not change this process one iota.

Of course, this "method of appointing senators" is governed by the constitutional convention that the Governor General only "summons" individuals whom the Prime Minister has recommended.

The Court says very little about this convention – mentioning it briefly and only once – but its silence may not be surprising. This constitutional convention is founded on and reflects the Court's own "fundamental constitutional principle" of democracy. The consultative elections proposed by the Government would further strengthen this existing convention by making it more democratic. Is it the Court's role to say how much democracy is too much? No. The Court has said repeatedly that the development of constitutional conventions – both their waxing and their waning – is the sole responsibility of the elected branches of government, not the courts. So it's hardly surprising the Court chose to ignore the meaning and consequences of this convention. To have done so would have risked leading their reasoning to a result that the justices evidently did not want.

Consultative elections would not change this convention, but they would change the procedure used by the Prime Minister to recommend names. But even the use of consultative elections would be optional. And even if a Prime Minister chose to consult voters before recommending a name, he is not required to recommend the winner of such an election. This precedent is already well established. Both prime ministers Mulroney and Chretien ignored the winners of Alberta Senate elections, as was their constitutional right. None of the Senate reform bills proposed by the Harper Government would change this.

The Court's response to this argument is that it "privileges form over substance":

> It reduces the notion of constitutional amendment to a matter of whether or not the letter of the constitutional text is modified. This narrow approach is inconsistent with the broad and purposive manner in which the constitution is understood and interpreted.... While the provisions regarding the appointment of Senators would remain textually untouched, the Senate's fundamental nature and role as a complementary legislative body of sober second thought would be significantly altered.

The problem with this argument is that "privileging form over substance" – that is, favouring process over results – is at the core of what a written constitution and the rule of law is all about. A written constitution sends a message to all who exercise government powers – including judges: these are the rules that you must follow, even if they are inconvenient or obstruct what you deem a more just result. I am not saying the it is wrong for judges to engage in "purposive interpretation" of constitutional powers and rights; that is, go beyond the literal meaning of the text. But judicial fidelity to text is also a legitimate option, and so it would have been well within the scope of accepted constitutional norms to have interpreted this issue in a manner that supported the Government's Senate reform initiatives.

It also merits noting that when it comes to "privileging form over substance," the Court is no slouch. The justices turn a blind eye to the real world of Senate appointments. What exactly is the policy status quo that the Court is so righteously defending in the current Senate selection process? When a vacancy occurs, the Prime Minister summons the party's major fundraisers in that province and selects a worthy and generous supporter. So by entrenching the policy status quo, the Court in effect is preferring a selection process based on consulting with the governing party's fundraisers and major donors rather than with the people from that province. This hardly advances the "fundamental constitutional principle" of democracy. Ironically, the unintended effect of the Court's ruling may be to perpetuate a *de facto* privilege for those with property just as it was discarding the *de jure* property requirement.

Suffice it to say here that the Court could have easily accepted the so-called "narrow approach" of judicial loyalty to constitutional text – of privileging form over substance – and been within the norms of accepted judicial function. Indeed, it did precisely this in its ruling in the *Nadon Reference* only months earlier – a verbatim, literal interpretation of section 6 of the *Supreme Court Act*, blocking the Prime Minister's appointment of Marc Nadon to the Supreme Court because he was not a "current member" of the Quebec Bar Association. Why there and not here?

To conclude, the Court could have easily upheld the legality of consultative elections, but chose not to. In a case such as this, where a constitutional convention – appointment by the Prime Minister – has always supplemented the original textual rule, the Court should facilitate, not block, further development of that convention by the political branches of government. To justify doing the opposite in the *Senate Reference*, we should expect some strong evidence and persuasive arguments as to why. The Supreme Court's written opinion provides neither.

***

Rejecting what it disparages as a "narrow, textual" approach, the Court turns instead to judicial fidelity to the "framers' intent" to justify its blanket dismissal of the proposed reforms. Looking back to the Confederation debates, the Court finds that the non-elected Senate was central to the Senate's "fundamental nature and role" in Canada's "constitutional architecture." More specifically, the element of appointment, as opposed to election, is deemed central to ensuring that the Senate serves as "an independent, non-partisan body of sober second thought," and strengthens Canadian federalism by effectively representing provincial interests in the central government. On what the Court wrongly (see below) treats as a minor issue, the justices ruled that the Framers' requirement of property-ownership for Senate eligibility was not essential to either the independence of senators or their role as regional representatives, and so could be eliminated by simple statutory reform.

Both of these interpretations of the "Framers' intent" are problematic if not simply false. But first it must be remarked that the Court's sudden rediscovery of "Framers' intent" as a guide to constitutional interpretation is sharply inconsistent with its own recent practice.

Anyone familiar with the Court's *Charter of Rights* jurisprudence knows that the justices have routinely ignored "framers' intent" in cases involving abortion, sexual orientation, prisoner voting rights, labour law and Aboriginal rights. The judicial attempt to discern "Framers' intent" has been alternatively rejected as a "mission impossible" undertaking (i.e. Which framers? What evidence?); or worse, a "frozen concepts" approach that would render the constitution a legal straight-jacket, incapable of adapting to the economic and social changes that shape and reshape Canadian society

For several decades now, the Court has denigrated this "frozen concepts" approach to constitutional interpretation and embraced instead a broader, more flexible – and yes, more discretionary – approach. Whether under the rubric of "living tree" or "broad and purposive interpretation," the Supreme Court justices have routinely justified ignoring the Framers' intended meaning of various *Charter* rights and given themselves a free hand to "discover" new substantive meanings.

So the question must be asked: why, suddenly, in the *Senate Reform Reference*, is judicial fidelity to "framers' intent" the Rosetta Stone of constitutional meaning? This question becomes even more pressing when, in the very same decision, the Court rediscovers – however briefly – the interpretive magic of the "living tree" when it comes to removing the current property qualifications for Senators.

Advancing under the banner of "framers intent," the Court finds that the Canadian Founders intended the Senate's "fundamental role and nature" to be the "independence of the Senators" and how the Senate "engages the interests of the provinces." Since the unilateral removal of the property qualifications would affect neither, the Court reasons, it would simply "update the constitutional framework relating to the Senate without affecting the institution's fundamental role and nature." The Court ignores the paramount role that the Framers attached to the defense of property rights through an appointed Senate. In so doing, they unwittingly remove what for the Framers was the most important reason for having an appointed rather than an elected Senate. Was this because they got their history wrong, or just another example of their lack of interest in protecting property rights? Or more likely both.

Suffice it to say that if unilateral federal removal of the property requirements for Senators is simply a matter of "constitutional updating," then the

Court could just as easily applied the same low bar to consultative elections. But again it chose not to.

It is difficult not to conclude that the Court is guilty here of the same interpretative inconsistencies that Justice Moldaver criticized in his *Nadon* dissent: "cherry-picking" interpretive rules that support a pre-determined outcome. The common thread in both cases is that the Court chose interpretive rules that allowed it to reach conclusions that effectively blocked two different initiatives of the Harper Government.

✻✻✻

In addition to being contradictory and self-serving, the Court's elaboration of "Framers' intent" is also wrong when it comes to both bicameralism and federalism.

The Court repeatedly invokes the principle of "constitutional architecture" and the "Senate's fundamental nature and role" to defend the appointed Senate from the alleged dangers of consultative elections. Given the centrality of this concept to its decision, one would expect the Court to elaborate its meaning. But all we get is repeated invocations of that tired refrain used in high school civics courses that the Senate serves Canada as a chamber of "sober second thought." The only time the Court actually tries to give specific meaning to this is concept is their assertion that the Framers'

> intention was to make the Senate a thoroughly independent body … [from the House of Commons] in order to remove Senators from a partisan political arena that required unremitting consideration of short-term political objectives.

Suffice it to say that whatever the Framers' intentions may have been, the Senate has been neither independent nor non-partisan for the past 100 years. (And often not very sober either!) Today's Senate is a political rubber-stamp organized along strict party lines, and its members routinely follow the directions of the Prime Minister or party to whom they owe their seat.

Surely the justices who sit on the Court must know this, which may explain why they were content to keep their argument at the very general level of "constitutional architecture" and "sober second thought." But they are defending an institution that doesn't exist today, and may never have existed.

✻✻✻

Similarly, the Senate's "fundamental nature and role" is deemed to "engage the interests of the provinces." Again, the Court is suspiciously vague about exactly how the Senate "engages the interests of the provinces." According to their reading of the "Framers' intent," the Senate was "an integral part of the federal system" because it provided "a distinct form of representation for the regions ... and "assure[d] their voices would continue to be heard."

But again, there is a yawning gap between reality and whatever the Framers intended. Today there is virtually no communication between provincial Cabinet ministers (and senior civil servants) and their province's Senators. When the former journey to Ottawa, they go to meet with their federal counterparts – ministers and deputy ministers, not with Senators. I doubt that most provincial ministers could even name the senators from their respective provinces. The truth is that if the Senate were abolished tomorrow, nobody outside of Ottawa would notice and it would have no material effect on the functioning of Canadian federal politics.

We all understand that our Senators received their appointments thanks to the patronage of a current or former Prime Minister, and that when it comes to vote on any bills affecting the interest of the province, the whip ensures that party discipline will trump whatever provincial loyalties a Senator might have. Ironically, the consultative elections proposed by the Harper Government would break, or at least weaken, the yoke of party discipline and make Senators *more* effective voices for regional interests. For these reasons, the Court's defense of the Senate status quo on federalism grounds is even less persuasive than its bicameralism argument.

***

The Court can and should also be faulted for failing to live up to its own precedents of "bold statecraft, questionable jurisprudence" to break constitutional gridlock, as it had in the earlier *Patriation Reference* (1981) and *Quebec Secession Reference* (1998). The parallels between the *Senate Reform Reference* and these earlier landmark rulings are striking: high political stakes, high policy stakes, and high levels of partisan and regional conflict.

The political stakes were high in all three. In 1980, Trudeau had staked his entire political come-back on his promise of "renewed federalism" as he campaigned in the first Quebec secession referendum. The "patriation package" was his attempt to deliver – unilaterally if necessary – on that promise. In 1995, the Parti Quebecois had come within 1 percent of winning a majority on the second Quebec secession referendum, in part because of the convoluted and confusing wording of the referendum question. Smarting from charges he had almost allowed the separatists to destroy Canada, Prime Minister Chretien responded with the reference challenging the constitutional validity of any unilateral secession of a province from Canada. Reform of the Senate has been on the agenda of every round of mega-constitutional reform since the 1970s, but without resolution. As noted earlier, "Triple E" Senate reform – elected, equal and effective – has been a priority for Harper and the Reform/Conservatives since the 1980s.

The policy stakes were equally high. On the table in 1981 were a new *Charter of Rights* with enhanced judicial review; a new amending formula; and a new declaration of judicially enforceable rights for Anglophones in Quebec, Francophones outside of Quebec, and Aboriginals. In 1998, the possibility of a Canada without Quebec and an end to Canada as a bilingual nation was at stake. In 2014, the question was whether Canada could join the other major (and not so major) federal states of the world with a democratic and functional second chamber, or whether it was time to simply abolish the Senate altogether.

And all three cases featured high levels of partisan and/or regional conflict. Trudeau's attempt at unilateral patriation and reform of the constitution was strongly opposed by the "Gang of Eight" provinces and both opposition parties. The *Quebec Secession Reference* pitted a re-energized Quebec Prime Minister, Jean Chretien, (and the "Rest of Canada") against the charismatic Premier of Quebec, Lucien Bouchard. And while Harper had the support of Alberta and Saskatchewan for consultative elections, his attempts at unilateral Senate reform were opposed by Quebec, Ontario and all four Atlantic Provinces.

But this is where the parallels end. In the *Patriation Reference* and the *Quebec Secession Reference*, the Court found a way to give partial victories to both sides, and send the issue back to the political arena for resolution.

The unilateral constitutional changes proposed by Trudeau in 1980 went way beyond the modest "advisory" Senate elections proposed by the Harper Government. And they were much more strongly opposed by the "Gang of Eight" provinces than the current opponents of consultative elections. Yet the Court found a way to facilitate a political compromise. The Court's novel and counter-intuitive ruling – "unconstitutional but legal" – was hailed as a victory by both sides, and created an incentive for further political negotiations and compromise – which is exactly what happened. When the dust settled, both sides had made concessions, and all the provinces except Quebec agreed to an amended package of constitutional reforms, the *Constitution Act, 1982*.

In 1998, the Court was caught between a separatist government in Quebec that had just come within less than 1 percent of winning a secession referendum; and a federal government desperate to prevent this occurring again. The Court escaped this dilemma by discovering/inventing four new "foundational constitutional principles" – federalism, democracy, constitutionalism and the rule of law, and respect for minority rights. The Court then used these principles to weave a complicated compromise that gave a partial victory to both sides: The Feds got a ruling that unilateral secession would be unconstitutional. Quebec got a ruling that if the secession option were to receive a "clear majority on a clear question," then Feds/ROC would have a "constitutional obligation" to "negotiate in good faith." Both parties claimed victory. The Court left the details to be worked out by the respective parties. The result was the federal *Clarity Act*. It merits quoting the Court's parting wisdom in this ruling:

> We have interpreted the questions as relating to the constitutional framework within which political decisions may ultimately be made. Within that framework, the workings of the political process are complex, and can only be resolved by means of political judgments and evaluations. The Court has no supervisory role over the political aspects of constitutional negotiations.

But in the *Senate Reform Reference*, there was no such innovation, no giving a half-loaf to each side, no sending the issue back to the political arena for further negotiation and compromise. In short, no judicial statesmanship of the kind that Canadians have learned to expect from the nation's highest constitutional court.

Before leaving these unflattering comparisons, we should also ask why the Court is willing to attach so much constitutional significance to a majority vote in Quebec that would destroy Canada as we know it, but not to a majority vote that might elect a senator. If a "clear majority vote in Quebec on a clear question in favour of secession would confer democratic legitimacy on a secession initiative, which all the other participants in Confederation would have to recognize," then why would democratically elected senators not entail the same legitimacy and same obligation to respect?

Or to put it slightly differently, if it had been Quebec, not Alberta, that had held Senate elections, would the Supreme Court have ruled against popularly elected Senators from Quebec? How could it, given the Court's "clear majority on a clear question" precedent? Does the Court have a double standard – one for Quebec, another for the other nine provinces?

Indeed, the Court's ruling in the *Senate Reform Reference* has interesting implications for Quebec. If Harper's attempt to legislate relatively modest reforms to the Senate is unconstitutional, then what about the (euphemistically named) *Regional Veto Act*?

Passed in 1996 in the wake of the Quebec separatists' near victory in the 1995 secession referendum, the *Regional Veto Act* "restores" to Quebec what it claims to have "lost" in the 1982 *Constitution Act* – its "historical" power of unilateral veto over any constitutional amendment.

The "loss" of Quebec's historic constitutional veto has been fuel for separatist fires in Quebec since 1982. Twice since then subsequent federal governments tried to use constitutional amendments to "restore" this veto – in the Meech Lake (1987) and Charlottetown (1992) Accords. And twice this was defeated by the rest of Canada. The *Regional Veto Act* is a transparent attempt to do through the legislative back door what the new amending rules in the *Constitution Act, 1982* requires to be done through the constitutional front door.

If legislative tinkering with Senate reform is unconstitutional, then legislative amendments to the amending formula must certainly be unconstitutional. To actually test this hypothesis may be unwise, as it would risk provoking yet another national unity crisis. But it points to yet another deep flaw in the Supreme Court's judgment in the *Senate Reform Reference*.

***

To conclude, the Court had virtually unfettered discretion to decide this case however the justices wanted. The Court could have employed either a "narrow, textual approach" or the "living tree"/"broad and purposive" approach to open the door to some form of political compromise and legislative reform of the Senate. Instead, the Court "cherry-picked" its way to a contradictory and unpersuasive judgment and slammed the constitutional door on any incremental reforms. The Court failed to live up to its own precedents of "bold statecraft, questionable jurisprudence" to break a constitutional gridlock. Instead Canadians are stuck with a dysfunctional and discredited second chamber for at least another generation.

2.7
Key Terms

Concepts

adjudication of disputes model of judging
adversarial process
"bold statecraft, questionable jurisprudence"
"clear majority on a clear question"
constitutional convention
constitutional law
declaratory model of judging
"duty to negotiate"
foundational constitutional principles
"fundamental nature and role"
judicial nationalism
legal positivism
legal realism
multinational
plurinational
policy-making model of judging
"unconstitutional but legal"
uninational

Institutions, Events and Documents

Abolition of Appeals to the JCPC (1949)
Harrison v. Carswell [1976] 2 S.C.R. 200
Judicial Committee of the Privy Council (JCPC)
O'Connor Report (1939)
Reference re Secession of Quebec, [1998] 2 S.C.R. 217
Reference re Senate Reform, [2014] 1 S.C.R. 704
Re: Resolution to amend the Constitution, [1981] 1 S.C.R. 753
    (Patriation Reference)

3

The Canadian Judicial System

A distinctive feature of the Canadian judicial system is its unitary character. This distinguishes it from other federal nations such as the United States, which has a "dual court system." A dual court system parallels the division of legislative powers along federal lines by creating federal courts for federal law and state courts for state law. While the Canadian founders adopted the logic of federalism for the distribution of legislative authority, they did not apply it to the judiciary. Rather, they created a single judicial system to interpret and to apply both federal and provincial laws.

The Canadian judicial system's unitary character is illustrated by the judicial flow chart (Figure 1) in Reading 3.3. Both civil law, which is mainly provincial in origin, and criminal law, which is exclusively federal in origin, move from trial to appeal through the same system of courts. This unitary character is politically significant because it can mitigate the centrifugal forces of intergovernmental politics. Rather than accentuating regional differences, it promotes a continuity and uniformity of legal policy across the nation. However, the federal monopoly over appointing superior court judges, combined with long periods of Liberal Party dominance in Ottawa, have led some provinces – notably Quebec and Alberta – to demand that the power to appoint section 96 court judges be transferred to the provinces. In the United States, all state court judges are selected by the state, either by executive appointment, election or some combination of both. However, Ottawa has shown little interest in this proposal.

The unitary character of the Canadian judicial system is reinforced by the fact that it is the shared responsibility of both levels of government. The legal framework for this joint responsibility is laid out in sections 92(14) and 96–101 of the *Constitution Act, 1867* (see Reading 3.2). Section 92 allocates to the provinces the powers to make laws that provide for the "constitution, maintenance, and organization of provincial courts." Section 96 provides that the federal government "shall appoint the judges of the superior, district, and county courts in each province." These provisions create a joint federal-provincial responsibility for the section 96 courts, which are administered by the provinces but whose judges are appointed by the federal government. Section 96 courts also include provincial courts of appeal, the highest court in each province.

In the judicial hierarchy, there are two additional tiers of courts beside the section 96 or superior courts. Below are the section 92 courts, so-called because they are created, maintained and appointed wholly by the provincial governments, pursuant to section 92(14) of the *Constitution Act*. Although they are lower in the judicial hierarchy, these courts have extensive and diverse jurisdiction and they hear cases on a range of issues, including provincial offences, most family law and most criminal law offences. Separate from section 96 courts are section 101 courts, which are created, maintained and appointed wholly by the federal government. These courts, which include the Federal Court and the Federal Court of Appeal, operate separately from the section 96 court system. However, the top section 101 court – the Supreme Court of Canada – sits at the top of the judicial hierarchy for section 92, 96 and 101 courts.

The Judicial Committee of the Privy Council

Prior to Confederation, the Judicial Committee of the Privy Council (JCPC) served as the final court of appeal for the courts of all the British colonies, including Canada. It continued in this capacity under section 129 of the *Constitution Act, 1867*. The Privy Council served as final court of appeal for the entire British Empire. It was not a part of the regular English court system and did not hear appeals from English courts. It consisted of five judges drawn mainly from the law lords in the House of Lords.

Even after the Supreme Court was created in 1875, appeals to the Privy Council remained. In addition to appeals from Supreme Court decisions, there were also appeals from the Court of Appeal of each province. This latter possibility, known as a *per saltum* appeal, allowed parties to effectively bypass the Supreme Court of Canada, and therefore reduced the Supreme Court's prestige and influence. The Privy Council's decisions played a major role in shaping the constitutional development of Canada. Its interpretations of the federal division of powers significantly diminished the authority of the federal government while expanding that of the provinces. As discussed in Chapter 2, this trend, which reached a climax during the 1930s, provoked a reaction against the continued role of the Privy Council in Canadian public affairs. This "judicial nationalism" movement culminated in the abolition of appeals to the Privy Council in 1949. However, its pre-1949 decisions remain an important part of Canadian law, especially in the areas of federalism (see Reading 9.4).

Section 92 Courts

Section 92 courts can be described as both the least important and the most important courts in Canada. Their lack of status stems from their position as the lowest rung in the Canadian judicial hierarchy. They serve principally as trial courts for less serious offences and as courts of preliminary inquiry for more serious ones. Their decisions are always subject to review and reversal by "higher" courts. On the other hand, section 92 courts are critically important because of the high volume of litigation that they process each year. Described as the "workhorse" of the Canadian judicial system, these provincial courts handle over 95 per cent of all trials for federal offences.[1] For most Canadians, "a day in court" means a day in provincial court. The quality of justice in Canada is thus directly affected by the quality of the provincial court system. As a result of the somewhat belated recognition of their importance, there has been a conscious effort in the past several decades to improve the salaries and training of provincial court judges, the efficiency of court administration and even the physical setting of courtrooms and courthouses. The criminal law jurisdiction of the provincial courts is illustrated in the flow chart in Reading 3.4 (Figure 2). Section 92 courts hear all provincial offences and summary conviction offences, hybrid offences when the Crown chooses a summary charge, and they conduct all preliminary inquiries. In addition, they hear many indictable offences under the *Criminal Code*, and offences under the federal *Youth Criminal Justice Act*. Their civil law jurisdiction includes issues of minor civil claims and most family law.

Section 96 Courts

Each province (except Ontario) has a two-tier system of superior courts: a trial court of general criminal and civil jurisdiction and a corresponding appeal court. While the names of the lower tier of section 96 courts vary from province to province, their constitutional status is the same. In Alberta, Manitoba, New Brunswick and Saskatchewan, these courts are the Court of Queen's Bench; in British Columbia, Prince Edward Island, Newfoundland and Labrador and Nova Scotia, they are known as the Supreme Court; in Quebec, it is known as the Superior Court. Ontario is the only province that has retained an "intermediate-level" section 96 court (called the Divisional Court) between its lower-tier section 96 court (the Superior Court of Justice) and its Court of Appeal.[2] Several provinces also have family court divisions, unified family courts and/or probate courts at the section 96 trial level. In each province, the highest "tier" of section 96 court is called the Court of Appeal. The judges on all section 96 courts are appointed by the federal government.

The Court of Queen's Bench (or equivalent) is generally regarded as the cornerstone of the Canadian court system. Its prestige flows from its very broad criminal and civil jurisdiction and the fact that it is derived from the English superior courts of common law and equity. W.R. Lederman argues that the independence of these courts is part of the "unwritten constitution" inherited from Great Britain and that they could not be abolished or significantly altered without doing violence to the fundamental order of Canadian government (see Reading 5.1).

The criminal jurisdiction of the Court of Queen's Bench (or equivalent) includes the trial of the most serious indictable offences and appeals from all criminal trials initiated in section 92 courts. These courts also hear appeals from all summary conviction offences and lesser indictable offences (see Figure 2 in Reading 3.4). In terms of civil law, these section 96 courts hear appeals from section 92 courts on issues such as separation and guardianship disputes; they also hear all cases involving divorce (a federal jurisdiction) and all civil disputes whose monetary claims are too large for lower courts. They also hear appeals from juvenile and family courts and from some provincial administrative boards and tribunals. As a percentage of overall caseload, section 96 courts hear far more family law and civil law cases than criminal law cases, particularly compared with section 92 courts.

The Court of Appeal of each province is the highest provincial court. It sits principally to hear appeals from the Court of Queen's Bench or equivalent on questions of law, and its decisions are binding on all other courts within the province (unless overturned on appeal to the Supreme Court of Canada). The Court of Appeal also hears references from provincial governments (although the Supreme Court of British Columbia and the Court of Queen's Bench of Manitoba can also hear references in those provinces). The Chief Justice of the Court of Appeal serves as the Chief Justice of the province.

Section 101 Federal Courts

In addition to authorizing the creation of the Supreme Court, section 101 of the *Constitution Act, 1867*, also allows "for the establishment of any additional courts for the better administration of the laws of Canada." If it chose to, Parliament could use this authority to create an entirely new tier of federal courts, similar to those of the United States. In practice, it has not done so, but has created instead only a few federal courts of specialized jurisdiction. In 1875, Parliament created the Exchequer Court. In 1970, it was renamed the Federal Court and was given an expanded jurisdiction. The original jurisdiction of the Exchequer Court consisted of a collection of specialized areas of federal law

– admiralty law, copyright and trademark law, income and estate tax law, and citizenship and immigration law. It also heard civil claims against the Crown.

In 1970, the new Federal Court inherited this jurisdiction and, in addition, was given the function of supervising federal administrative law. The Federal Court has both a trial and an appellate division. The federal administrative law area has been largely hived off from the rest of the judicial system and made the special responsibility of the Federal Court. In 1983, Parliament created a new section 101 court, the Tax Court of Canada. It hears cases involving federal taxes and some federal fiscal policies, such as Old Age Security and the Canada Pension Plan. In 2003, the federal government divided the Federal Court's trial and appeal division in two and created the Federal Court of Appeal, which hears appeals from the Federal Court, the Tax Court of Canada and numerous federal administrative tribunals. There is the possibility of leave to appeal to the Supreme Court from all Federal Court of Appeal decisions.

In recent decades, there have been disputes concerning the extent of section 101 courts' jurisdiction, which is more limited in scope than section 96 courts. Ironically, the Supreme Court of Canada – itself a section 101 court – has restricted the scope of matters that can be heard in federal courts. This effort has culminated in *Windsor City v. Canadian Transit Co.* (2016),[3] in which a majority of the Supreme Court found that the Ontario Superior Court, rather than the Federal Court, was the appropriate venue to deal with a dispute between a federal agency and the city of Windsor, Ontario. Given the divided judgment in this case, such jurisdictional squabbles between section 96 and section 101 courts will likely continue.

The Supreme Court of Canada

At the summit of the judicial pyramid sits the Supreme Court of Canada. Since appeals to the JCPC were abolished in 1949, the Supreme Court has served as the final court of appeal for all matters of Canadian law. Its creation was authorized but not required by section 101 of the *Constitution Act, 1867*. Parliament, after considerable debate, exercised that power and enacted the *Supreme Court Act* in 1875.[4]

The Supreme Court has jurisdiction to hear appeals on all questions of criminal and civil law from the provincial courts of appeal and also accepts appeals from the Federal Court of Appeal. Since gaining control over most of its docket in 1975, the Court hears far fewer appeals "as of right," with far more being granted "leave to appeal." From 2010 to 2016, 23 per cent of the Supreme Court's cases were "as of right," while 77 per cent were granted leave to appeal, which means they were selected by the Court itself.[5] In Reading 3.1, the late Chief Justice Bora Laskin argues that the increasingly discretionary character of the Supreme Court's appellate jurisdiction changes the nature of the Court's function from that of traditional appellate review to one of "supervisory control." This represents a change of emphasis from concern for the individual case to overseeing the consistent development of Canadian law, especially in issues of public importance and national concern. As Ian Bushnell has observed,

> In the role of simply another review court, it is the litigant who is afforded access, and he brings the legal issue with him; when the court fulfills a law-making function, it is the legal problem that determines access, and the litigant is brought along with it.[6]

Gaining control of its docket has been one of the most important factors in the Supreme Court's rise in political prominence over the past four decades. This reform gave the Supreme Court considerable authority to influence the outcome of the leading political controversies of the day. The number of appeals by right dropped dramatically after 1975, while the number of cases accepted "by leave" of the Court soared. Applying the maxim that "you are what you do," Professor Peter McCormick concluded that by 2000, the Supreme Court had changed its function from that of an arbiter of economic disputes to a criminal and *Charter* adjudicator. Significantly, McCormick found that the origin of this shift occurred under the leadership of Chief Justice Laskin, the leading advocate of giving the Court control of its own docket.[7]

In the two decades prior to 1975, private law cases (mostly lawsuits between businesses) made up more than 50 per cent of the Court's caseload. That figure began dropping immediately following the reform; as of 2013, all private law cases constituted roughly 40 per cent of the Court's workload.[8] The Court has used its new discretion to hear many more criminal law cases, a category that represented only 15 per cent of its case load prior to 1975. Since the reform, criminal cases jumped to over 20 per cent on the Laskin Court (1973–1984); 37 per cent on the Dickson Court (1984–1990); and over 40 per cent on the Lamer Court (1990–1999). The other major new component of the Court's caseload is *Charter of Rights* cases. In the first two decades after the *Charter* became justiciable (1982), *Charter* cases accounted for approximately 20 per cent of the Court's decisions each year; in recent decades that number has dropped to roughly 10 per cent. In 2016, the percentage of criminal law cases heard by the Supreme Court (both *Charter* and non-*Charter*) was 41 per cent; the number of total *Charter* cases was 23 per cent (17 per cent criminal *Charter* cases and 6 per cent non-criminal).[9]

This does not mean that the Court accepts every *Charter* case that asks for leave to appeal. In fact, the number of applications for leave to appeal have been steadily dropping. In 2002, Roy Flemming found that the Court rejected four out of every five leave applications that it received, including *Charter* cases. From 2010 to 2015, the Court only granted leave in 11.5 per cent of applications, with a low of 9.2 per cent in 2010.[10] The Court uses a "public importance" test to determine which cases are granted leave. In practice, many of the factors in this test – a new legal issue, national interest, conflicting decisions at provincial courts and dissents in the cases being appealed – grant the Court a high degree of discretion. While the Supreme Court can now pick and choose which appeals to hear, there are several exceptions. One is the reference procedure, by which the federal government can ask the Court for an "advisory opinion" on any question of constitutional or statutory law. The number of references has decreased as a proportion of the total number of cases heard annually by the Court since the 1980s, although they frequently represent the most important cases (see Readings 2.4, 2.5, 2.6 and 6.1).

The original *Supreme Court Act* authorized the appointment of six judges and required that two of them be from Quebec; this was deemed necessary to accommodate civil law appeals from that province. Not to be outdone by her traditional rival, Ontario demanded equal treatment, and eventually a custom of having two Ontario judges on the Court came into being. The size of the Court was increased in 1927 to seven judges, and again in 1949, to nine. The number of Quebec and Ontario judges was increased to three, Quebec's by law and Ontario's by custom. Again by custom, the three remaining vacancies are normally filled by one judge from the Atlantic provinces and two from the Western provinces. While Justin Trudeau's government mused in 2016 about replacing Nova Scotia's Thomas Cromwell with someone who was not from Atlantic Canada, the reaction was strong, and Newfoundland and Labrador Justice Malcolm Rowe was eventually appointed (see Chapter 4). Justin Trudeau's second appointment also maintained the regional convention, as he replaced one Western Canadian judge (Beverley McLachlin) with another (Sheilah Martin). The endurance of the *de facto* practice of regional representation on the Supreme Court attests to its perception as an important "political" institution in the process of national government.

The Supreme Court is presided over by a Chief Justice, the highest judicial officer of Canada. Over time, customs developed to govern the appointment of the Chief Justice. A pattern of alternating the position between English-Canadian and French-Canadian judges developed and also of appointing the most senior judge in terms of service within each of these groups. Both of these customs were broken by Prime Minister Pierre Elliot Trudeau. In 1973, he appointed Bora Laskin, who had served considerably less time on the Court than several other anglophone members. In April, 1984, Trudeau again broke with tradition by appointing another anglophone, Brian Dickson, to succeed Laskin. These appointments cast some doubt on the continued validity of these traditions. However, in 1989, upon Dickson's retirement, Prime Minister Mulroney appointed Puisne Justice Antonio Lamer, the senior Quebec francophone on the Court, as Chief Justice. When Lamer retired in 2000, Prime Minister Chrétien appointed the anglophone judge with the most years of service, Beverley McLachlin, as the new Chief Justice. In December 2017, Justin Trudeau named the senior francophone judge, Quebec's Richard Wagner, as the successor to Chief Justice McLachlin. The Lamer, McLachlin and Wagner appointments suggest that there is still vitality in both conventions.

Because the Supreme Court was not constitutionally entrenched, for many years the perception was that Parliament could technically abolish it at any time. Many commentators have argued that this impugned the independence and thus the status of the Court. It was illogical, they argued, that the institution responsible for enforcing the constitutional protections against governments was not itself constitutionally protected. An attempt to change this situation was made in 1982. The *Constitution Act, 1982*, Section 41(d), declares that the composition of the Supreme Court (nine judges with three from Quebec) can only be changed by the unanimous consent of all the provincial legislatures and the federal Parliament. Section 42 requires that any changes to the Supreme Court other than its composition be done according to the new amending formula. These changes were intended to eliminate the Court's potential vulnerability to Parliament, yet they confused the situation by "constitutionalizing" an arrangement that existed only by statute, the *Supreme Court Act*. In doing so, these provisions thus put the cart before the horse. Some scholars argued that the effect of the 1982 amendments was to constitutionally entrench the entire *Supreme Court Act*, while others argued that the amendments could have no effect until or unless the Supreme Court itself was made part of the formal Constitution.

The 1987 Meech Lake Accord proposed to resolve this confusion by explicitly constitutionalizing the existence of the Supreme Court, including the requirement that three of the judges come from Quebec and that all new appointments be made from nomination lists submitted by the provinces. Because the Meech Lake Accord was not ratified, none of these amendments took effect, leaving the ambiguities created by the 1982 amendments unresolved for the time being. This all changed with the *Reference re Supreme Court Act* (2014),[11] when the Supreme Court itself had an opportunity to weigh in. As discussed in Reading 11.6, the Supreme Court declared that any changes to the *Supreme Court Act* affecting the Court's "composition" – including clarifications about the courts from which Quebec judges are appointed – require unanimous provincial consent. In so doing, it effectively constitutionalized much of the *Supreme Court Act*.

NOTES

1   Lori Hausegger, Matthew Hennigar and Troy Riddell, *Canadian Courts*. 2nd ed. (Don Mills, ON: Oxford University Press, 2015), pp. 34–35.

2   Hausegger, Hennigar and Riddell, *Canadian Courts*, p. 49.

3   *Windsor City v. Canadian Transit Co.,* [2016] 2 S.C.R. 617.

4   See Jennifer Smith, "The Origins of Judicial Review in Canada," Reading 9.1.

5   Supreme Court of Canada, "Statistics 2006–2016 – Category 3: Appeals Heard," 2017, http://www.scc-csc.ca/case-dossier/stat/cat3-eng.aspx.

6   S.I. Bushnell, "Leave to Appeal Applications to the Supreme Court of Canada: A Matter of Public Importance," *Supreme Court Law Review* 3 (1982), p. 488.

7   Peter McCormick, *Supreme at Last: The Evolution of the Supreme Court of Canada* (Toronto: James Lorimer, 2000).

8   Hausegger, Hennigar and Riddell, *Canadian Courts*, pp. 60–61.

9   Ibid.; Supreme Court of Canada, "Statistics 2006–2016," 2017.

10   Roy B. Flemming, "Agenda Setting: The Selection of Cases for Judicial Review in the Supreme Court of Canada," *Law, Politics and the Judicial Process in Canada.* 3rd ed. (Calgary: University of Calgary Press, 2002), pp. 546–554; Supreme Court of Canada, "Statistics 2006–2016," 2017.

11   *Reference re Supreme Court Act, ss. 5 and 6,* [2014] 1 S.C.R. 433.

3.1

The Role and Functions of Final Appellate Courts: The Supreme Court of Canada
Chief Justice Bora Laskin

Canadian Bar Review 53 (1975), 469–481. Reprinted with permission.

I

... I look upon the functions of the Supreme Court of Canada as those that arise out of its jurisdiction; the definition of its role depends on how that jurisdiction is exercised, how it uses its final appellate authority having regard to the kind and range of cases that come before it. The interaction between jurisdiction and role is obvious; and, inevitably, the judges' view of their role is bound to undergo definition and redefinition in the day-to-day grind of the court's business and in the periodic changes of its membership. One can envisage judges of the Supreme Court having some differences of opinion, probably slight ones, on the court's functions; any differences about its role are likely to be more serious.

II

The starting point for any consideration of the Supreme Court's functions and its role is that fact, a surprising one I am sure to foreign students of federalism, that the Supreme Court of Canada has no constitutional base. This marks it off immediately from such kindred courts as the Supreme Court of the United States and the High Court of Australia. The Supreme Court of Canada is a statutory creation of the Parliament of Canada under the power given that Parliament by section 101 of the British North America Act to constitute, maintain and organize "a general Court of Appeal for Canada." The size of the court, its jurisdiction, its procedure, indeed all questions touching its operation as a general court of appeal, an appellate court in short without any declared right to original jurisdiction, were left to the Government and Parliament of Canada to prescribe.

The size of the court, originally composed of six judges, with a seventh added in 1927 and two more added in 1949 upon the abolition of all appeals to the Privy Council from any appellate court in Canada, testifies both to population and regional growth in Canada, to the expansion of the business of the court and to its ultimate grave responsibility as a final appellate court. Of significance in its structure and operations was the provision of a quorum for sittings of the court, the number being fixed at five upon the creation of the court and remaining constant despite increase in its overall size. There could not, and even today there cannot be more than one Bench for the hearing of appeals; and I am thankful that this precludes having two Supreme Courts of Canada. Perhaps the only power a Chief Justice has is to assign the Bench for the hearing of appeals. Since my personal preference is to have the full court sit, and since the recent change in our jurisdiction enables the court to be selective in the cases that it will hear, I will not view with any regret the surrender of the power of assignment which, in any event, has been exercised with regard to the opinions of the other members of the court as to whether a panel of five or the full court should be assigned in any particular appeal.

The jurisdiction of the court, the scope of its appellate authority, was undoubtedly the most important matter that faced the Government and Parliament of Canada in creating the court in 1875. A number of models were available for consideration. There was the model of a national appellate court, functioning like an English appellate court, or like the House of Lords, with general jurisdiction (be it as of right or by leave) not limited to any class or classes of cases. There was, second, the model of a purely federal court, with an appellate jurisdiction limited to matters within or arising out of the exercise of federal legislative powers, including the validity of that exercise, but excluding constitutional issues arising under provincial legislation in view of the fact that appeals then lay directly to the Privy Council from provincial courts of appeal. There was, third, the model of a federal appellate court having also comprehensive appellate jurisdiction in all constitutional matters as ultimate Canadian expositor of the constitution, albeit there was a further appeal to the Privy Council. This was the model offered by the Supreme Court of the United States. There was, fourth, the model of a purely constitutional court and, fifth, the model of a federal and a constitutional court, with separate chambers for each of these functions, in adaptation of the chamber system found today in the *Cour de Cassation* of France.

Happily, in my view, the first model was chosen, thus adapting to federal Canada a system of appellate adjudication operative in unitary Great Britain but familiar to Canadians of Bench and Bar. To have adopted the federal model represented by the Supreme Court of the United States or some other such model, would have required at least consideration of, if not actual establishment of a system of federal courts of original jurisdiction. A dual court system such as obtains in the United States was resisted in Canada, save for the establishment of an Exchequer Court with a limited jurisdiction, and of Admiralty Courts. It was in the character of concurrent appointment as Exchequer Court judges that the judges of the Supreme Court of Canada were invested with original jurisdiction but this ceased when the Exchequer Court was set up on a separate base in 1887, ending a short first life and beginning a second one with a judge wholly its own, but with more added over the succeeding years.

Although the jurisdiction of the Exchequer Court was extended considerably when it was translated into the Federal Court of Canada in 1970, the latter is still a court of limited jurisdiction in federal matters. A serious and, in my view, unfortunate as well as an unnecessary upheaval in our Canadian system of judicature would result if the Government and Parliament of Canada moved now to federalize it at the level of original and intermediate appellate jurisdiction by withdrawing such jurisdiction in all federal matters from the provincial courts and reposing it in a federal court structure.

The Parliament of Canada has power to that end under section 101 of the British North America Act, the same section which authorized the creation of the Supreme Court of Canada. In authorizing as well (in its words) "the establishment of any additional Courts for the better administration of the laws of Canada," the section may be said to reflect some incongruity. On the one hand, it enabled Parliament to establish a "general," a truly national court of appeal whose authority was not limited to federal matters – the telling word is "general" – and, on the other hand to establish federal courts limited to jurisdiction in federal matters. To have exercised both grants of authority to the full, in the light of the fact that at Confederation in 1867 there were developed provincial courts habituated to adjudicate on matters that after Confederation were in terms of legislative power distributed between the central and provincial legislatures, would have created, and would now certainly create great tensions in federal-provincial relations. We can do without adding to those that already exist, although I am bound to add that tension to some degree is a by-product of federalism.

Parliament did exercise its authority to the full in establishing the Supreme Court of Canada in 1875 and in reconstituting the court in 1949 upon the abolition of all appeals in Canadian causes to the Privy Council. This makes good sense to me so long as the provincial courts are left, as they now are, to administer federal law as well as provincial law, indeed federal common law as well as provincial common law, save to the limited extent that judicial jurisdiction in federal matters has been reposed in the Federal Court of Canada, which has both a trial division and an appeal division in respect of those matters.

If there was any thought-out rationale for investing the Supreme Court of Canada with appellate authority from all provincial appellate courts, and in respect of provincial as well as federal matters cognizable in those courts, it was posited and, in my view, may be said to rest today on the following factors. First, there was and is the fact that particular litigation frequently involves issues that engage both federal and provincial matters which provincial courts have continued to handle without difficulty, and forum problems are, in general, avoided notwithstanding the hived-off jurisdiction of the Federal Court. Its jurisdiction is, on the whole, fairly distinct and has hitherto not created any intractable difficulties in forum selection, although some such questions have arisen. Second, there was and is the fact that the common law is largely the same in all the provinces outside of Quebec and that, subject to legislative changes, it ought to have a uniform operation in all those provinces, thus avoiding some possible conflict of laws problems; and, moreover, even in Quebec there are branches of the common law, as for example in the field of public law, that were and are common to it and to the other provinces of Canada. Third, there was and is the fact that many important branches of law, such as the criminal law, the law of negotiable instruments, the law of bankruptcy, the law of shipping, railway law, the law of patents and copyright have a national operation because they fall within exclusive federal competence; and even though they may interact in some respects with some aspects of the common law their interpretation and application must necessarily be uniform, and perhaps all the more so because of the interaction. Fourth, constitutional adjudication, involving the resolution of disputes as to the scope and reach of federal and provincial legislative powers must necessarily end in a court that can speak authoritatively for the whole of

Canada, and I may add here that there is equally a case to be made for final uniform resolution of questions touching the operation of public authorities.

Thus it was that upon the establishment of the Supreme Court of Canada we had in the main a one-stream two-tier system of appeals like that in Great Britain, although that country did not have to contend with federalism as we know it in Canada. To some extent, there is a three-tier system in respect of Ontario cases by reason of the recent establishment there of an intermediate appellate court, with a limited jurisdiction, operating between courts of first instance and the Ontario Court of Appeal. Should this innovation spread to other provinces it would not alter the force of the considerations which led to the establishment of the Supreme Court of Canada as a national court. Its character does not depend on the system of appeals within the judicial structure of any one or more provinces but, rather on how far beyond adjudication on federal matters and on constitutional matters its jurisdiction should extend.

The Government and the Parliament of Canada saw no need to water down the broad authority given to establish "a general Court of appeal for Canada"; and Parliament emphasized the breadth of its power by generous scope, especially in civil cases, for appeals as of right, appeals which the Supreme Court of Canada was obliged to hear, however local or private were the issues that they raised. This was appellate review in a traditional sense as distinguished from what I would term supervisory control.

Until the beginning of this year [1975] when appellate review was replaced by supervisory control (leave now being required in all non-criminal cases and in most criminal cases before an appeal will be entertained on the merits), appeals as of right in civil cases formed a large part of the Supreme Court's case load. I think this was one of the factors that led some scholarly students of the Supreme Court's work to urge federalization of its jurisdiction. Other factors were also raised in support of this position, such as the virtue of allocating judicial power along the same lines as legislative power, and the merit of leaving to final adjudication in the provincial courts legal issues reflecting local conditions and those based on provincial or municipal legislation.

I think that the amendments recently made to the Supreme Court's jurisdiction, making a previous requirement of leave (whether from the Supreme Court or the provincial appellate court) the general rule, have blunted the case that could formerly have been made and was made for limiting the Supreme Court of Canada to federal and constitutional issues. The four-pronged rationale which I mentioned earlier in this address as supporting a final appellate court with a general national jurisdiction is not, in my opinion, cogently answered by those who would reduce the court to a federal and constitutional institution. Still less is it answerable now that the Supreme Court is a supervisory tribunal rather than an appellate tribunal in the traditional sense. As a supervisory tribunal, it is fully able and would be expected to resist interference in purely local or private issues, and it is in fact enjoined to do so by the statutory formula which prescribes the requirements that must be met in order to obtain leave. The case for leave must be one with respect to which "the Supreme Court is of the opinion that any question involved therein is, by reason of its public importance or the importance of any issue of law or any issue of mixed law and fact involved in such question, one that ought to be decided by the Supreme Court or is, for any other reason, of such a nature or significance as to warrant decision by it."

The discretion given to the court under the foregoing formula is obvious, but it is a necessary control over the flow of cases that have already been before two courts. Now, even more in its supervisory role than in its heretofore more traditional appellate role, the Supreme Court's main function is to oversee the development of the law in the courts of Canada, to give guidance in articulate reasons and, indeed, direction to the provincial courts and to the Federal Court of Canada on issues of national concern or of common concern to several provinces, issues that may obtrude even though arising under different legislative regimes in different provinces. This is surely the paramount obligation of an ultimate appellate court with national authority. It is only under this umbrella that it can, in general, be expected to be sensitive to the correctness of the decisions in particular cases, whether they be between private litigants only or involve some government as a party.

I think I can risk saying that the mere fact that any level of government or any government agency is involved in a particular case is no more telling in favour of leave to appeal than the fact that litigation is private necessarily tells against the granting of leave. The issues in contention and, indeed, the issues which will be determinative of the appeal, however there may be others of importance in the case, and not the character of the parties, will guide the court in the exercise of its power to grant or refuse leave. Even where the court may be disposed to grant leave, it may do so, not at large, but by defining the specific question or questions on which it is prepared to have the case come forward.

III

I turn now to more debatable questions respecting the Supreme Court's exercise of its jurisdiction, questions going to its role as Canada's highest and final court on all justiciable matters. Two considerations affect any assessment of that role. One has to do with the kind of business that comes and will come before the court; the second has to do with the collegiality of the court, with the blend of individual independence of the judges *inter se* and their institutional responsibility. The bulk of the court's business is, and is likely to continue to be, the interpretation and application of statutes, some of which, as for example, parts of the Criminal Code and of the Quebec Civil Code, to take two illustrations, have long ago taken on what I may term a common law appearance. Two statutes, one, the British North America Act (and its amendments), only formally of that character (since it is Canada's chief written constitution), and the second, the Canadian Bill of Rights, a quasi-constitutional enactment are not, for interpretative purposes "statutes like other statutes" (to adopt well-known phraseology); and there is little doubt, certainly none in my mind, that the judicial approach to them, compelled by their character, has been different from that taken with respect to ordinary legislation. The generality of their language and their operative effect compel an approach from a wider perspective than is the case with ordinary legislation, especially legislation that is more precisely formulated.

The collegiality of the court touches a matter that may have a greater interest for the academic component of this assembly than for the practising Bar or members of the judiciary. It is theoretically open to each member of the Supreme Court of Canada, as it is theoretically open to each member of any appellate court, to write reasons in every case in which the member sits. Practical and institutional considerations militate against this; and so it is that when bare concurrences are filed with reasons proposed by a colleague, they may suggest some shift of position by the concurring judge who does not choose to write separate reasons, a shift on some matter subsidiary to or connected with the disposition of the main issue to which the concurrence was given.

Bare concurrences ought not to be taken as representing unqualified endorsement of every sentence of the reasons concurred in. Contextual approval, yes; and approval of the result, of course. After all the scrutiny and conferring on a set of proposed reasons are over, and after changes have been made in language and organization by the writer so far as he is willing to accommodate himself to the views of his colleagues, there may still remain in some colleague some questions about some parts of the reasons. However, he may decide on balance that there is no point in writing his own. In short, it is far safer and surer, if one would assess how a judge discharges his duties and how he regards his role and the role of the court, to assess him on what he himself writes and not on all of what is written by a colleague with whom he concurs in some particular case or cases.

There is no question that seems to have been as continuously and as strenuously considered, in relation to all courts and judges, and more particularly in relation to judges and courts of ultimate authority, as their law-making role. The Supreme Court of Canada began life at about the time Langdell and his case-law approach to the discovery of the "true legal rule" revolutionized legal studies in the United States. On the English side, before the nineteenth century was out the House of Lords had sanctified its own position as the expositor of the one true rule which, once declared, was alterable only by legislation. A quarter of a century later Cardozo was to tell us that at its highest reaches the role of the judge lay in creation and not in mere discovery. In this country, and perhaps in England too, we were inclined to think that creativity applied to what had not been previously considered and determined but, that accomplished in the highest court, creativity was spent and change was only for the legislature or for the constitutional amending process, as the case might be....

... Controversy has now ceased on the law-making role of judges, especially of judges of a final appellate court. Laymen may beg the question by consoling the dissenting judges of a divided court with the remark, "too bad the law was against you," but judges and lawyers know better. The late Lord Reid helped to bury the declaratory theory by remarking in a speech delivered in 1971 that law is not some known and defined entity secreted in Aladdin's cave and revealed if one uses the right password. We do not believe in fairy tales any more, said Lord Reid, and Lord Diplock did not doubt, when speaking for the Privy Council in an Australian appeal in 1974, that "when for the first time a court of final instance interprets [a statute] as bearing one of two or more possible meanings ... the effect of the exercise of its interpretative role is to make law." Such controversy as there is today in judicial law-making in a final court concerns the appropriateness of the occasion or of the case for enunciating a new rule of law and, even more important, the appropriateness of the occasion or of the case for upsetting an existing rule and substituting a different one in its place.

Neither here nor in any of the countries whence come our distinguished guests is *stare decisis* now an inexorable rule for our respective final courts. In this country, what appeared to be at times an obsessiveness about it came partly at least from our link with English law which also involved the ascendancy of English courts, so that *stare decisis* amounted to a form of ancestor worship. We are now able to view it as simply an important element of the judicial process, a necessary consideration which should give pause to any but the most sober conclusion that a previous decision or line of authority is wrong and ought to be changed. Such a conclusion is not likely to be arrived at by any judge or number of judges without serious reflection on its conformity or consistency with other principles that are part of the institutional history or the institutional patterns of the court. None of us operates without constraints that are both personal and institutional, born of both training and experience and of traditions of the legal system of which the court is a part.

When everything considered relevant has been weighed and an overruling decision commends itself to a judge, he ought not at that stage to stay his opinion and call upon the legislature to implement it. This is particularly true in respect of those areas of the law which are judge-made, and to a degree true in respect of those areas where legislation is involved which is susceptible of a number of meanings. A final court must accept a superintending responsibility for what it or its predecessors have wrought, especially when it knows how little time legislatures today have (and also, perhaps, little inclination) to intrude into fields of law fashioned by the courts alone, although legislatures may, of course, under the prodding of law reform agencies and of other public influences, from time to time do.

The role of the courts, the role of a final court, in the interpretation of legislation, bringing into play the relation between the legislative and the judicial arms of government, is of a different dimension, in my view, than the role played in the promulgation of judge-made law. The dimension comes from the dominant political and legal principle under which our courts operate, which is that, constitutional issues apart, Parliament and the provincial legislatures are the supreme, certainly the superior law-making bodies. On constitutional issues, issues concerning the division of distribution of legislative power, the courts, and ultimately the Supreme Court of Canada, have the final word (subject to constitutional amendment). This is a critical role, so critical for exercises of legislative and governmental power at both the central and provincial level as to put every Supreme Court decision in this field, whatever it be, into the political mill. Yet it is a role which the court cannot eschew if we believe in constitutional order, any more than can any final court with constitutional jurisdiction in a federal state. There is no other instrument with final authority available for this role. It is of course possible (and indeed there are known examples) for the central and provincial governments to avoid constitutional determinations in the Supreme Court of Canada by entering into co-operative arrangements which do not call for any test of constitutional competence. In this way they may hold some of the tensions in their relations in equilibrium, so long as those arrangements last. The fact that such arrangements exist at all underlines the delicate nature of the Supreme Court's constitutional jurisdiction. Of course, it must proceed with caution in that field but, that having been said, it brings the same independent judgment to bear on constitutional questions as on other matters that are brought before it, fully conscious, however, that there are no more important public issues submitted to its adjudication than those that arise out of alleged conflicts of legislative authority.

The stakes in interpretation and application of ordinary legislation may not be as high because here the courts play not an ascendant role but rather more of a complementary one. The judges, no less than others in society, owe obedience to legislation which they may be called upon to interpret and apply; they have a duty to respect the legislative purpose or policy whatever be their view of its merit. Judges subscribe to this proposition, and then may be seen to proceed to differ on what the purpose or policy is, or to differ on whether the legislation or some part of it is apt to realize the purpose. This is not the time nor the place to enlarge on the variety of approaches to legislative interpretation which in close cases can lead to different results in respect of the same piece of legislation. In the majority of cases where legislation is a factor in the litigation, there is no such difficulty in interpretation as to require the particular expertise of a lawyer or a judge. Where that special competence is necessary, the judges owe it to the enacting legislature as well as to the litigants to expose the legal reasoning which underlies their decisions.

The public expectation is, I suspect, of a somewhat different order. Since so much of the legislation that comes before the courts and before the Supreme Court of Canada involves controls or limitation of the social conduct or business behaviour of persons or classes of persons or corporations, either by direct penal sanction or by supervision of administrative agencies, those affected may look to the courts for some wider exposition than a strict regard for legal issues would warrant. Is the policy a desirable or a workable one? Is the administrative structure fair? Is the procedure fair, are the decisions supported by reasons that are disclosed to the affected persons? There is no invariable stance that a court takes on these questions. Where it has deemed it proper to pronounce on policy (as it has on occasion) it has done so with prudence, and, generally, when prompted by difficulties that reside in the interpretation and application of the legislation. Fairness of administrative procedure is more confidently dealt with by the courts because what is compendiously called "natural justice" has long been regarded as involving legal issues for their consideration.

Natural justice, embracing the right to notice of possibly adverse action, the right to be heard or to make representations before being adversely affected, and the right to be judged by an impartial tribunal, is a central feature of an evolved political and legal tradition which sees the courts as wielders of protective authority against an invasion of the liberty of the individual by government or its agencies. Text books, periodical literature and the everyday press reinforce this tradition, and thus strengthen the public expectation that the courts, and especially the Supreme Court of Canada, will speak out on the matter. The enactment of the Canadian Bill of Rights as a federal measure, and operative only at that level, has fed that expectation. It is well to recall that judges of the Supreme Court spoke strongly on aspects of individual liberty in the *Alberta Press* case, the *Switzman* case, the *Roncarelli* case, and in other cases too, without the back-up or the direction of the Canadian Bill of Rights, which became effective only in 1960. It was able to do so because the avenues for recognizing individual rights or civil liberties had not been closed by competent legislation, nor did any relevant legislation as interpreted by the judges of the Supreme Court preclude them. Legislation may however appear to be preclusive in some areas of civil liberties, and if interpreted with that result the judicial duty of fidelity to legislation as superior law must be acknowledged whatever be the consequences, although the acknowledgment may be accompanied by an expression of regret or even of remonstrance that the legislation went so far.

The Canadian Bill of Rights has now provided a legislative measure and standard of protection of civil liberties but, in the generality of some of its language, it adds to the dilemmas of interpretation which are so often evident in civil liberties cases. Its direction may be clearer in some cases than it is in others, or clearer to some judges in some cases than to others. Each charts his own course here, as in the other roles that he is called upon to play in the discharge of his judicial duties and, indeed, in determining what roles he should take on.

This, however, is simply another aspect of the side discretion opens to a judge of a final appellate court. There may be differences about the scope of the discretion, but there cannot be any dispute about its existence. As I said at the beginning of my remarks, each judge puts his own questions and supplies his own answers and, in yielding ground to institutional considerations, he does so according to his own assessment of what they demand.

3.2

Constitution Act, 1867, Sections 96–101

VII. – Judicature.

96. The Governor General shall appoint the Judges of the Superior, District, and County Courts in each Province, except those of the Courts of Probate in Nova Scotia and New Brunswick.

97. Until the laws relative to Property and Civil Rights in Ontario, Nova Scotia, and New Brunswick, and the Procedure of the Courts in those Provinces, are made uniform, the Judges of the Courts of those Provinces appointed by the Governor General shall be selected from the respective Bars of those Provinces.

98. The Judges of the Courts of Quebec shall be selected from the Bar of that Province.

99. (1) Subject to subsection (2) of this section, the Judges of the Superior Courts shall hold office during good behaviour, but shall be removable by the Governor General on Address of the Senate and House of Commons.

(2)A Judge of a Superior Court, whether appointed before or after the coming into force of this section, shall cease to hold office upon attaining the age of seventy-five years, or upon the coming into force of this section if at that time he has already attained that age.

100. The Salaries, Allowances, and Pensions of the Judges of the Superior, District, and County Courts (except the Courts of Probate in Nova Scotia and New Brunswick), and of the Admiralty Courts in Cases where the Judges thereof are for the Time being paid by Salary, shall be fixed and provided by the Parliament of Canada.

101. The Parliament of Canada may, notwithstanding anything in this Act, from Time to Time provide for the Constitution, Maintenance, and Organization of a General Court of Appeal for Canada, and for the Establishment of any additional Courts for the better Administration of the Laws of Canada.

3.3
The Canadian Judicial System

Figure 1 represents the Canadian judicial system as it exists in Alberta. The names of the "section 92" and "section 96" courts vary from province to province. In Alberta, the section 92 court is called the Provincial Court, while section 96 courts include the Court of Queen's Bench and the Court of Appeal for Alberta, respectively. In British Columbia, the section 92 court is the Provincial Court, while the Supreme Court of British Columbia and the Court of Appeal are section 96 courts. The vertical arrows indicate the paths of appeal. The left-diagonal and right-diagonal hatch-marks indicate section 92 and section 101 courts, respectively. The cross-hatched area represents the section 96 courts and the joint responsibility of the two levels of government.

Figure 1: The Criminal Court Process

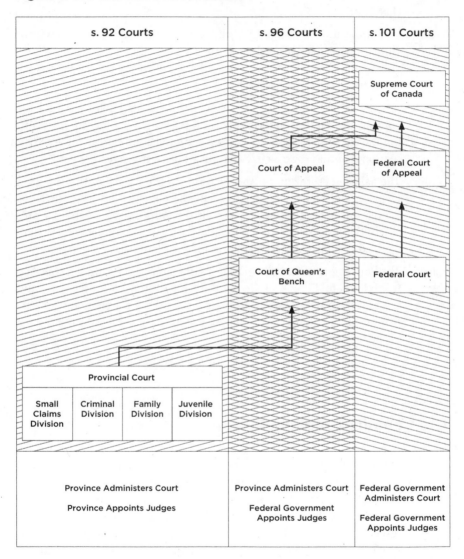

s. 92 Courts	s. 96 Courts	s. 101 Courts

Supreme Court of Canada

Court of Appeal | Federal Court of Appeal

Court of Queen's Bench | Federal Court

Provincial Court

| Small Claims Division | Criminal Division | Family Division | Juvenile Division |

Province Administers Court

Province Appoints Judges

Province Administers Court

Federal Government Appoints Judges

Federal Government Administers Court

Federal Government Appoints Judges

3.4

The Criminal and Civil Court Processes

Figure 1: The Criminal and Civil Court Processes

The Criminal Court Process

Provincial Court

- Trial of all municipal bylaws
- Trial of all provincial offences
- Trial of the following federal offences:
    - Summary conviction offences
    - Hybrid offences when the Crown proceeds by summary conviction
    - Some indictable offices (found in s. 553 of the *Criminal Code*)
    - Preliminary inquiries
    - The *Youth Criminal Justice Act*

Court of Queen's Bench

- Trial of all indictable offences other than those found in s. 553 of the *Criminal Code*
- Hybrid offences when the Crown proceeds by indictment
- Trial of other federal offences after preliminary inquiry in Provincial Court
- Appeals of Summary Conviction matters from Provincial Court

Figure 2: The Court Process

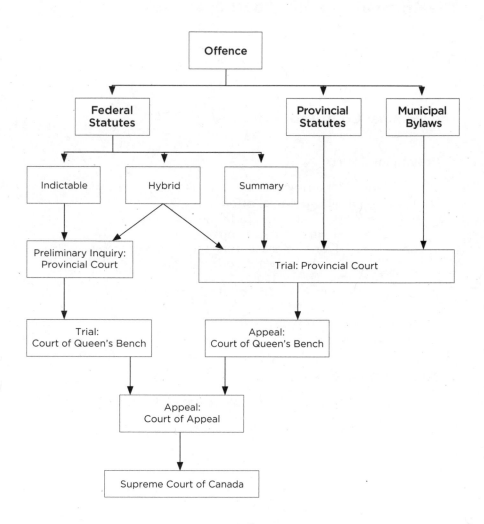

Figure 3: The Civil Court Process

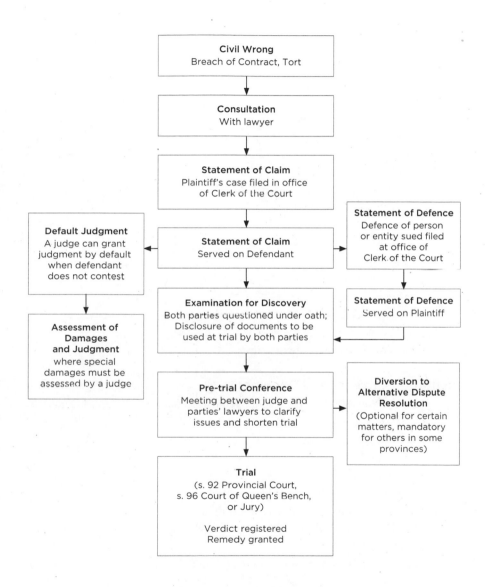

3.5

Key Terms

Concepts

administrative law
appeal "as of right"
civil law
Civil Law system (Quebec)
Common Law system
criminal law
dual court system
indictable offence
leave to appeal
per saltum appeal
preliminary inquiry
public importance test
section 92 courts
section 96 courts
section 101 courts
summary conviction offence
supervisory vs. appellate function

Institutions, Events and Documents

Constitution Act, 1982 (provisions relating to Supreme Court of Canada)
Court of Appeal
Court of Queen's Bench
Exchequer Court (1875–1970)
Federal Court of Appeal (2003)
Federal Court of Canada (1970)
Judicial Committee of the Privy Council
Meech Lake Accord (provisions relating to Supreme Court of Canada)
Provincial Court
Reference re Supreme Court Act, ss. 5 and 6, [2014] 1 S.C.R. 433
Supreme Court of Canada (1875)
Windsor City v. Canadian Transit Co., [2016] 2 S.C.R. 617

4

Judicial Recruitment and Selection

Under the *Constitution Act, 1867*, judicial appointments are made by the two different levels of government to three different levels of courts. Pursuant to section 101, the federal government is responsible for appointing all judges of the Supreme Court of Canada (nine), the Federal Court (thirty-four), the Federal Court of Appeal (twelve), and the Tax Court (nineteen). In addition, the federal government appoints all the judges of the section 96 courts (858), even though these courts are created and maintained by the provinces.[1] This is one of the distinctive features of Canada's unitary judicial system. Vesting the appointment power with the federal government was intended to insure the independence of the provincial superior courts from local politics or prejudice. It is also a legacy of British imperial rule and (some of) the Canadian founders' desire to subordinate provincial governments to Ottawa. As provincial governments have achieved a more equal status in the Canadian federal system, this continuing federal monopoly has become a point of political conflict (see Reading 4.1).[2] Finally, the provincial governments appoint all the judges (1,042 as of 2013) of the provincial lower courts created pursuant to section 92 of the *Constitution Act, 1867*. Not including part-time or supernumerary judges or Justices of the Peace, there are approximately two thousand full-time judges in Canada.[3] Federal judicial appointments are made by the Cabinet on the advice of the Minister of Justice, except for Chief Justices,[4] who are recommended by the Prime Minister. While final responsibility for appointments remains with the Minister of Justice, for provincial superior court judges, the Minister chooses from a list of candidates vetted by the Commissioner for Federal Judicial Affairs and assessed by an independent screening committee. In 2016, an advisory committee was also set up for appointments to the Supreme Court of Canada. Both of these processes are described below.

The procedures for judicial appointments to section 92 courts vary from province to province, but most are based on one of two basic models: a screening committee or a nominating committee. The difference is the stage at which the government uses an independent, non-governmental body to assess potential candidates. A screening committee begins with a list of candidates provided by the Attorney General. It assesses prospective candidates' suitability, provides some form of ranking and sends that list back to the Attorney General. A nominating committee actually conducts the initial recruitment as well as screening, and then presents the government with a list of approved nominees from which it must (in theory) choose.

Another difference between these two approaches is the extent to which they allow political influence. With a nominating committee, governments can only make appointments from a pool of candidates who have already been selected by an independent body; under the screening model, the government is initially unrestricted and only uses the independent committees to confirm choices that the Attorney General has already made. This latter procedure gives the party that forms the government a much freer hand to favour party members and supporters when making appointments to the bench. In recent decades, each province has developed some form of committee, but as Peter McCormick notes, few actually conform to the ideal types of "nominating" and "screening"; in practice, different provinces' committees engage in "some mixture of screening and recommending," thereby enabling patronage to enter the equation to various degrees.[5]

Politics, Professionalism and Patronage

The judicial selection process in all common law nations manifests a tension between judicial expertise and political influence, the most obvious manifestation of which is the long-established practice of appointing rather than electing judges. In theory, the potential for undue political influence is limited by review of nominations by independent screening committees, and reduced still further by nominating committees. In practice, it turns out to be more difficult to reduce political influence in the appointment process. In Ontario, for example, the Conservative government of Premier Mike Harris (1995–2001) became unhappy with the perceived political bias exhibited by the Ontario Judicial Appointments Advisory Committee (JAAC) in its recommendations. The JAAC was created in 1989 by a Liberal government and had Professor Peter Russell as its first chair. Under the preceding NDP government (1991–1995), the chair passed to Judy Rebick, a former president of the National Action Committee on the Status of Women and a well-known feminist advocate. The Harris government requested that the JAAC send its judicial nominations in groups of two or three so that the government would have some choice in making a final appointment.

This emphasis on insulating judicial selection from partisan politics is premised on the assumption that judges and judging are not "political" in the way legislators and legislating are, and therefore that judges need not be politically accountable. (Judges of course are political in the sense that they usually accept and enforce the underlying political principles and beliefs of a society.) Impartiality is an essential ingredient of judicial authority, and the selection process is structured to preserve the perception of judges as impartial arbiters. A non-political selection process assumes a non-political court. According to Weiler's "two models" theory, if the function of a judge is limited to adjudicating disputes, the only prerequisite for appointment is the necessary legal training, accompanied by good moral character and steady work habits (see Reading 2.1).

While the assumptions associated with an adjudicative court were generally true of the common law tradition out of which Canada's legal system has evolved, they became strained with the introduction of written constitutional law and its corollary, judicial review. For reasons discussed in Chapters 1 and 2, courts charged with interpreting constitutionally entrenched restrictions on democratic legislatures affect public policy more directly than courts whose functions are limited to resolving disputes arising under common law and statutes. To the extent that this occurs, the original rationale for excluding political considerations from the selection process is weakened. At the extreme is Weiler's "policy-making court." "Rather than focusing on legal ability and training as the key elements in judicial qualifications," writes Weiler,

> the policy-making model holds that a person's political program and abilities should be most important. In fact, the logic of the system demands that these be evaluated in some manner other than an apolitical appointment process. Instead, judges should either be directly elected, or the various groups whose interests are affected by the judges' decisions should have some more formalized and legitimized form of participation in the making of the selection.[6]

While Weiler's model is theoretical, it reflects a fundamental norm of liberal democracy: that the governors should be accountable to the governed. It also captures what American political scientist V.O. Key has described as "an iron law of politics": "where power rests, there influence will be brought to bear."[7]

Evidence supporting this axiom is most readily seen in the politicization of judicial selection that has developed in the United States, where judicial review was invented and where the fact of judicial "law-making" has long been acknowledged. Under many state constitutions in the United States, judges are selected through public elections. In California, the judges of the state's Supreme Court are initially appointed by the Governor but after twelve years must face a "confirmation vote" in a general election. In 1986, three judges, including the Chief Justice, were rejected by California voters because they were perceived as blocking the majority will on capital punishment. Even though American federal judges are still appointed, strong political forces shape these appointments, especially appointments to the Supreme Court, where potential appointees must appear before the Senate Judiciary Committee and face a confirmation vote by the full Senate. While these practices may seem unacceptable by traditional Canadian standards, they are consistent with a more "political" judicial function.

"Politics" can enter the judicial appointment process in four distinct (albeit sometimes overlapping) ways: patronage, regional representation, group representation and ideological compatibility. Such political appointments tend to reflect the contours of political division and the distribution of influence in the larger society. As such, they vary from country to country, and within the same country over time. In Canada, for example, patronage has declined as a major factor in Supreme Court appointments, while group representation has become more important. Note also that a single judicial appointment can encompass several of these political factors simultaneously. American President George H.W. Bush's 1991 appointment of Clarence Thomas to the U.S. Supreme Court, for example, represented considerations of both ideology (Thomas was a constitutional originalist) and group representation (Thomas, an African-American, replaced Justice Thurgood Marshall, the first and only African-American to serve on the Supreme Court at that point). Similarly, Paul Martin's 2004 appointment of Franco-Ontarian Louise Charron to the Supreme Court of Canada provided symbolic representation for both francophones and women.

Patronage – appointment as a reward for past service to or support of a political party – is the oldest, most common and best-known form of political influence in judicial appointments in all common law nations. In Canada, patronage was a dominant factor in both federal and provincial judicial appointments since before Confederation. While patronage declined significantly after the Second World War, it did not disappear. In 1966, dissatisfaction with the continuing effects of patronage on the quality of federal judicial appointments led the Canadian Bar Association (CBA) to create the Committee on the Judiciary, which sought to provide a non-partisan source of advice to the federal government on judicial appointments. The CBA Committee would receive the names of potential nominees from the Minister of Justice, review the candidates' records, and then rate each candidate as "well qualified, qualified, or not qualified." Under this program, which operated from 1967 until 1988, no candidates receiving an unqualified rating were appointed.

A succession of Liberal ministers of justice during the 1970s is generally credited with improving the quality of federal judicial appointments. Nevertheless, Pierre Trudeau's government continued to use some of its judicial appointments to section 96 courts to reward its members and supporters. In 1982, this practice provoked an angry reaction by the newly elected Progressive Conservative Premier Grant Devine in Saskatchewan. Devine's Attorney General, Gary Lane, accused Ottawa of "stacking the courts with partisan appointees" and declared that he wanted "more consultation on appointments, not just a phone call after the fact."[8] To protest the Liberals' alleged abuse of patronage in judicial appointments in Saskatchewan, the Devine government began reducing the number of section 96 judgeships by eliminating positions as they became vacant through death or retirement, thereby denying Ottawa the opportunity to make appointments. As recounted by Jeffrey Simpson (Reading 4.1), this stalemate, known as the "Saskatchewan Judges Affair," was not resolved until the defeat of the Liberals in the 1984 federal election.

Immediately before the Liberals' 1984 electoral defeat, the patronage issue again became the focus of public attention following a series of judicial appointments occasioned by Pierre Trudeau's resignation as leader of the Liberal Party and Prime Minister in 1984. Before leaving, Trudeau appointed three of his former cabinet ministers to the Federal Court, one without any prior review by the CBA Committee on the Judiciary. Several other Liberal politicians were also appointed to provincial superior courts, the Senate and Crown corporations. Brian Mulroney, the leader of the Progressive Conservative Party, exploited the judicial patronage issue in the 1984 federal election and promised change if elected. In a famous exchange during a televised leader's debate, Mulroney criticized Trudeau's successor, Prime Minister John Turner, for allowing the appointments to go through. Mulroney's famous declaration that "You had an option, sir," was widely seen as the "knockout blow" that helped Mulroney's party win the most seats in Canadian parliamentary history. The newly elected Conservative government informally agreed to consult more closely with the provinces before making superior court appointments.

The incident also led to new studies by the Canadian Association of Law Teachers (CALT) and the Canadian Bar Association. In 1985, both the CALT and CBA issued reports recommending reform, which Mulroney took under consideration. These led to the creation of what has, with some modifications, been the appointment process for section 96 and section 101 courts (except the Supreme Court of Canada) at the federal level since 1988.

The Evolution of Appointment Procedures for Section 96 Courts

A 1989 study by Peter Russell and Jacob Ziegel suggests why the Mulroney government did not rush to embrace the recommendations of the CBA and CALT. Contrary to its promises of reform during the 1984 campaign, it turned out that the Mulroney government did not practise what it preached. Of the 228 federal judges appointed during the first Mulroney government (1984–1988), 48 per cent were found to have associations with the Progressive Conservative Party. While 86 per cent received a good or better rating from the CBA Committee on the Judiciary, of the thirteen who did not, ten had Tory political connections. Russell and Ziegel concluded that there was only "marginal improvement" in the judicial selection process during the Mulroney government's first term; that political patronage remained "pervasive"; and that the 1988 reforms did "little to address the basic flaws in the appointing system."[9]

In 1988, the Mulroney government instituted significant reforms for appointing all section 96 judges and all section 101 judges below the Supreme Court. Under these reforms, the Commissioner for Federal Judicial Affairs screens applications from candidates to ensure they possess the required technical qualifications[10] and then refers their names to the appropriate provincial or territorial screening committee, called Judicial Advisory Committees (JACs). Each provincial (and territorial) JAC initially consisted of five persons (including at least one non-lawyer), but committee membership was soon expanded to include seven members: one each appointed by the provincial Chief Justice, provincial law society, provincial branch of the bar association and provincial Attorney General; and three appointed by the federal Minister of Justice (two of whom must be non-lawyers). The JAC initially ranked candidates as "qualified" or "not qualified." In 1991, this was changed to three categories: highly recommended, recommended or unable to recommend. For section 101 courts below the Supreme Court, the same application form and process applies, and the candidates are screened by the JAC in their province of residence.[11]

Did the new appointment system make a difference? Yes and no. In their study of the JACs' appointments from 1988 to 2003 (Reading 4.2), Hausegger, Riddell, Hennigar and Richez found that fewer judges with major political connections were appointed after the committees were created (41 per cent) than before (48 per cent). Moreover, the vast majority of their respondents found that the JAC system had screened out the poorest candidates and worst "political animals," leading to an overall improvement in judicial quality. However, partisanship and patronage still played a role, particularly in four of the smaller provinces (Prince Edward Island, New Brunswick, Manitoba and

Saskatchewan). By no means had ostensibly "non-political" reforms removed politics from the appointment process.

The JAC system was not changed until Stephen Harper's Conservatives came to power in 2006. The Harper government made three changes to the JAC system. First, the government would appoint a representative from the police community to each JAC. Second, each judicial representative was made a non-voting chair. Finally, the "highly recommended" category was removed in favour of the previous two-level ranking instituted in 1988, by which the screening committee could either recommend or not recommend potential candidates. As Rainer Knopff (Reading 11.2) describes, the legal community was outraged by these changes. Critics, including former Chief Justice Antonio Lamer and then Chief Justice Beverley McLachlin, viewed the changes as politicizing the appointment process and moving away from "merit-based" selections. However, Knopff argues that the false dichotomy between politics and professionalism does not reflect the already politicized nature of courts, which have shifted to a greater policy-making role. The "rhetorical reception" with which the legal community met Harper's JAC changes was "overheated," according to Knopff, and likely motivated by the fact that the changes reduced legal representation on the JACs to a minority position for the first time.

Harper's judicial reforms had a short institutional legacy (see Chapter 11). In 2016, his first full year in power, Prime Minister Justin Trudeau reversed Harper's three changes to the JAC: the police representative was removed, and both the judicial chair's vote and the category of "highly recommended" were reinstated. With these changes, lawyers and judges once again constitute a majority of members on all JACs. The Trudeau changes also require JACs to promote diversity among federally appointed judges: judicial applicants are now asked about their race, gender identity, indigenous status, sexual orientation and physical disability, and this statistical information is collected and distributed to the public. The makeup of JACs is also vetted by the Commissioner for Federal Judicial Affairs; although anyone can apply, committees will be selected with a "view to achieving a gender-balanced Committee that also reflects the diversity of members of each jurisdiction, including Indigenous peoples, persons with disabilities and members of linguistic, ethnic and other minority communities, including those whose members' gender identity or sexual orientation differs from that of the majority." Finally, committee members will receive training in "unconscious bias."[12]

In October, 2017, the Commissioner for Federal Judicial Affairs released data from the first year of appointments under the new system. During that period, 997 applications were received, but JACs were only able to assess 441. Of those assessed, 42 per cent were women, 10 per cent were visible minorities, 32 per cent were completely bilingual and 2.5 per cent were Aboriginal. Of these 441 candidates, 129 were highly recommended, eighty-two were recommended, and 230 were unable to be recommended. Ultimately, seventy-four judges were appointed by the JACs during this period, half of whom were women. While the Commissioner for Federal Judicial Affairs admitted that *some* of the appointed judges were merely "recommended" rather than "highly recommend," neither the Commissioner nor the Justice Minister explained how many.[13]

The Harper and Trudeau changes demonstrate that, even with a screening committee, politics remains an important factor in judicial appointments. Harper's inclusion of the police representative reflected his government's desire to have a judiciary more aligned with a "tough-on-crime" policy perspective, while Trudeau's promotion of group characteristics via diversity criteria reflects the Liberal Party's support for the "identity politics" promoted by the progressive Left. The fact that some "recommended" candidates were appointed above "highly recommended" alternatives portends a desire to have a different kind of bench. Each was an unmistakably political decision, in direct tension with a purely "meritorious" appointment system.

Appointments to the Supreme Court of Canada

Along with its changes to the section 96 appointment process, Justin Trudeau's government also changed the Supreme Court of Canada appointment process in 2016, which had already undergone substantial modification in the preceding decade. Historically, the appointment of Supreme Court justices did not receive much scrutiny, which is not surprising given that until 1949 it was not even the highest court.

Formally, the Governor General selects Supreme Court judges, but in practice this task falls to the Minister of Justice. In our executive-dominated system, this means the Prime Minister plays a major part. The *Supreme Court Act* requires that someone must be a "judge of a superior court of a province" or a lawyer of ten years' standing at a provincial bar to be appointed; it also stipulates that three of the Supreme Court's nine judges must come from "the Court of Appeal or of the Superior Court of the Province of Quebec or from among the advocates of that Province." These relatively minimal requirements meant that, for much of the Supreme Court's first century, patronage played a major role (See Reading 4.1). While the more overt patronage appointments diminished after the Supreme Court became supreme in 1949, criticism of the closed nature of the appointment process mounted after the introduction of the *Charter*. However, reform took some time. In December, 1998, following the appointment of Michel Bastarache, Prime Minister Jean Chrétien defended the existing appointment process. "American-style public confirmation hearings before appointing Supreme Court justices," Chrétien wrote, "would limit the choice of excellent candidates as many would not wish to undergo the ordeal of public and partisan-motivated attacks."[14] Notwithstanding the fact that Bastarache had been a partner in Chrétien's former law firm, reform was not forthcoming.

It was not until Paul Martin replaced Chrétien as Prime Minister that the appointment process for the Supreme Court finally changed. In the words of Adam Dodek, "The 10-year period between 2004 and the end of 2013 produced more changes to the appointment process for Supreme Court judges than any period since the Court was created in 1875" (and that was before Justin Trudeau changed the system again in 2016!).[15] The reforms began when Liberal Justice Minister Irwin Cotler gave a speech to the House of Commons Justice Committee in 2004, in which he detailed the existing process of informal consultation with the legal community. This process was used to select Rosalie Abella and Louise Charron in 2004, with one twist: Cotler himself appeared before the Justice Committee to explain his choices prior to the formal appointment. While some of the opacity had been lifted, the Justice Minister's appearance before the parliamentary committee went over like a lead balloon with those who sought a more democratic process. It was, in the words of one journalist, "like sending your mother to do your job interview."[16]

In 2005, with the impending retirement of Justice John Major, Paul Martin's Liberal government created an advisory committee, which, after the Justice Minister's initial consultations, was given a list of eight candidates. The advisory committee contained one MP from each of the four official parties in the house; a retired judge; members nominated by an Attorney General and law society in the region; and two people from the region nominated by the Minister of Justice. The committee acted as a nominating committee, albeit one with a severely limited pool: it was tasked with reducing the list of eight candidates produced by the Minister of Justice to three, which it did in 2005. By the time Stephen Harper's Conservative Party won a plurality of seats in the 2006 election, the vacancy remained. Although Harper was not legally bound to follow the advisory committee's recommendations, he did just that when he selected Marshall Rothstein from the list of three recommended candidates. Harper also went one step further by having Rothstein appear before a televised committee and answer questions from MPs and representatives from the legal community. (Unlike Senate nomination hearings for the United States Supreme Court, this hearing was not subject to a formal vote.[17]) The hearing, chaired by Professor Peter Hogg, was polite and cordial, and Rothstein comported himself well. Fears that exposing judges to the media would create a political free-for-all were put to rest.

Yet the *ad hoc* nature of the changes meant that the process was subject to the whim of the Prime Minister of the day. This became clear with the prolonged appointment of Thomas Cromwell. Prior to the dropping of the writ for the federal election of October, 2008, Harper announced Cromwell as his prospective appointment. He initially stated that, like Rothstein, Cromwell would be scrutinized by MPs at a public hearing. However, in December, 2008, in the midst of a political crisis during which it looked as if the Conservatives would be replaced by a Liberal-led coalition, Harper formally appointed Cromwell without parliamentary scrutiny. Harper's stated reason was that the Court "must have its full complement of nine judges in order to execute its vital constitutional mandate effectively."[18] But surely his tenuous grip on power in the wake of his parliamentary prorogation played a role.

For Harper's next four appointments between 2011 and 2013 (Justices Michael Moldaver, Andromache Karakatsanis, Richard Wagner and Marc Nadon), he returned to the process used for Justice Rothstein in 2006. The Minister of Justice informally consulted with members of the legal community and created a longlist of vacancies. For these appointments, this list was given to a nominating committee made up solely of MPs – three Conservatives, one Liberal and one NDP – who narrowed the list to three unranked candidates. The Minister selected the prospective appointee from that list; two days later, the prospective appointee answered questions from an *ad hoc* all-party committee of MPs in a public hearing, and was subsequently appointed.

Compared with the Rothstein appointment, the process for these four appointments relied more on legislators than the legal community: both the nominating committee and the public hearing were composed entirely of MPs (apart from the chair of the public hearing). This reliance on legislative scrutiny over consultation with the legal community undoubtedly made the process more democratic, although the lack of committee veto meant that formal power continued to rest with the Minister of Justice and the Prime Minister. Like Harper's changes to section 96 appointments, this shift away from the formal involvement of legal experts was criticized by prominent lawyers. "The line between a merit-based and a partisan process is a fragile one," wrote Lorne Sossin in the *Globe and Mail*, "and is not helped by privileging the lens of parliamentarians and removing the filter of non-partisan, public-interest expertise."[19] It was not the first time that Harper's institutional changes provoked the wrath of legal experts, nor would it be the last.

At this point, the lack of parliamentary scrutiny for the 2008 appointment of Justice Cromwell looked like a blip on the road to greater parliamentary involvement in Supreme Court appointments under Harper. That all changed following the appointment of Marc Nadon. As Thomas Bateman recounts in Reading 11.6, Nadon's appointment was ultimately rejected by the Supreme Court of Canada for failing to comply with a majority of the Court's interpretation of the provisions regarding appointees from Quebec in the *Supreme Court Act*. While Nadon's failed appointment led to an unprecedented public spat between the Chief Justice and the Prime Minister's Office, it also spelled the end of parliamentary scrutiny of Supreme Court appointments under Harper. Amid allegations that opposition MPs on the nominating committee had leaked details about the appointment to the press, Harper dispensed with the committee and the public hearings for his final three appointments. The pre-2004 process of informal consultation prevailed for the appointments of Clément Gascon (Nadon's replacement), Suzanne Côté and Russell Brown. As Bateman notes, "No one appeared to mind."

No one, that is, except Justin Trudeau. After campaigning on a promise to "restore dignity" to the relationship between the federal government and the Supreme Court in 2015, Trudeau overhauled the Supreme Court appointment process after Thomas Cromwell announced he would retire in 2016. Like the initial Harper reforms, an advisory committee and a public hearing remained two planks of the Trudeau reforms. However, the Trudeau government formalized (though it did not legislate) four other aspects.

First, there is now an official application process for Supreme Court appointments, whereby candidates apply to the Officer of Commissioner for Federal Judicial Affairs when a vacancy arises. Second, the Advisory Board no longer consists of parliamentary representatives, but is instead composed of seven members: a retired judge, two lawyers, a legal scholar and three members appointed by the Minister of Justice (two of whom must be non-lawyers). One of the three government appointees acts as chair; for Trudeau's 2016 and 2017 appointments of Malcolm Rowe and Sheilah Martin, the chair was former Progressive Conservative Prime Minister Kim Campbell. The board's responsibility is to submit three to five candidates to the Prime Minister, although its recommendations are technically non-binding. Third, the government has added a level of transparency by making the assessment criteria and questionnaire public, as well as certain answers from the successful judge's questionnaire (see Reading 4.5). The Minister of Justice and chair of the Advisory Board now discuss the selection process in Parliament, the board issues a public report after the appointment, and the successful applicant has a public hearing with MPs and Senators prior to appointment.

Fourth, and more controversially, the process is infused with diversity and language considerations. The Advisory Board was tasked with recommending "functionally bilingual" candidates who could read, understand oral argument and converse with counsel without translation in French and English. The board was also given instructions to "achieve a Supreme Court of Canada that is gender-balanced and reflects the diversity of members of Canadian society"[20] – another nod to the Liberal Party's embrace of "identity politics." To achieve its diversity mandate, initially there were hints that Trudeau would abandon the convention of regional representation by appointing someone from outside Atlantic Canada to replace Cromwell in 2016. However, Trudeau eventually appointed Malcolm Rowe, a bilingual white male judge from the Newfoundland and Labrador Court of Appeal. To replace Beverley McLachlin's Western seat in 2017, Trudeau appointed Sheilah Martin, a bilingual white female from Western Canada (see Table 1). In the battle of region versus group representation, regional diversity (and bilingualism) won out.

Of the bilingualism and diversity criteria, the Advisory Board has treated bilingualism as far more of a concrete requirement. Justice Rowe and Justice Martin were each fluently bilingual, and in a Justice Committee hearing following the announcement of Martin as the prospective appointee, the chair of the Advisory Board, Kim Campbell, noted that "after the interviews the candidates go and do a French test to assess their functional bilingualism."[22] Given the limited number of French speakers outside of Central Canada and New Brunswick, many have worried that the bilingualism requirement could limit the pool of qualified judges; others suggested that it may be unconstitutional, as it could be read as a change to the "composition" of the Supreme Court of Canada.[23] There is reason to believe that the pool was limited with the 2017 appointment to replace Beverley McLachlin, for which there were only fourteen applicants, eight of whom were interviewed. Although the government had made it known that it would only consider applications from the four Western provinces and three Northern territories, fourteen applicants from a population pool of over eleven million people seems extremely low, especially given the moderate requirements of ten years at the bar or appointment on a superior court. A formalized interview to determine language skills – the only known test prospective Supreme Court justices must take – adds further evidence that the bilingualism requirement could be viewed as affecting the Court's "composition."

Overall, the appointments of Justices Rowe and Martin in 2016 and 2017 were relatively uncontroversial. Most interesting were Rowe's answers to his application questionnaire, which were made public upon the announcement of his appointment. Reproduced here as Reading 4.5, Rowe dispenses with any notion that the Court is primarily an adjudicative body: "Supreme Court judges," he says, "ordinarily make law, rather than simply applying it." Rowe

Table 1: Supreme Court Appointments, 2004–2017[21]

Prime Minister	Year	Judge	Region	Advisory Committee?	Public Hearing
Martin (LIB)	2004	Rosalie Abella	Ontario	No	No*
	2004	Louise Charron	Ontario	No	No*
Harper (CON)	2006	Marshall Rothstein	West	Yes (4 MPs + 5 appointed members)	Yes
	2008	Thomas Cromwell	Atlantic	No	No
	2011	Andromache Karakatsanis	Ontario	Yes (5 MPs)	Yes
	2011	Michael Moldaver	Ontario	Yes (5 MPs)	Yes
	2012	Richard Wagner	Quebec	Yes (5 MPs)	Yes
	2013**	Marc Nadon	Quebec	Yes (5 MPs)	Yes
	2014	Clement Gascon	Quebec	No	No
	2014	Suzanne Côté	Quebec	No	No
	2015	Russell Brown	West	No	No
Trudeau (LIB)	2016	Malcolm Rowe	Atlantic	Yes (No MPs, 7 appointees)	Yes
	2017	Sheilah Martin	West	Yes (No MPs, 7 appointees)	Yes

*The Minister of Justice had a public hearing to explain the appointments, but the judges were not present.

**Appointment ultimately rejected by Supreme Court. See Reading 11.6.

was unequivocal that the *Charter* and its increase in judicial power "reflect favourably on our country." And on the question of whether the Court should "lead or mirror a shared sense of justice," Rowe says they should do "both." One might suggest this ambivalence will suit Rowe well when the Court deals with tricky questions like Patriation and Quebec secession. Professor Leonid Sirota (Reading 4.6) is less charitable. Sirota takes Rowe's response about making law to suggest that he "will not feel bound by the constraints that precedent and statutory and constitutional text are thought to impose on judges." Sirota warns that "a judiciary that is no more bound by a sense of modesty than it is by the law itself is a distressing prospect." As Chapter 2 demonstrates, this prospect has become a reality.

Group, Regional and Ideological Representation on Canadian Courts

While overt patronage for judicial appointments to the Supreme Court seems a thing of the past, the other forms of political influence in judicial appointments – regional, group and ideological representation – remain relevant at all levels of Canadian courts. Because these factors tend to reflect the political sociology of a given polity, it is no surprise that Canada's long tradition of regional representation continues to play a prominent role. The *Supreme Court Act's* legal guarantee of three justices from Quebec – effectively constitutionalized by the Court when it ruled Marc Nadon ineligible (see Reading 11.6) – is technically justified by the Court's appellate jurisdiction over Quebec's civil law, but it also symbolizes the "distinct" status of Quebec and francophones in Canadian politics. The French-English dualism of Canadian political experience has also manifested itself in the tradition of alternating the appointment of the Chief Justice between an anglophone and a francophone, as explained in Chapter 3.

Similarly, the convention of *de facto* geographical representation on the Supreme Court testifies to the strong influence of regionalism in Canadian politics. Since the number of Supreme Court judges was raised from seven to nine in 1949, there has been a convention of having three from Ontario, two from the West, and one from Atlantic Canada. While this convention was briefly broken from 1979–1982, when there were three Western judges and only two from Ontario, it has otherwise proven resilient. The appointment of Malcolm Rowe from Newfoundland and Labrador in 2016 is a testament to this, as even the whiff of moving away from regional representation to promote group diversity was abandoned by the Trudeau government. Although he finds little evidence that justices support their "home" region once appointed to the Supreme Court, Professor Robert Schertzer nevertheless argues that "the power and importance of symbolism should not be underestimated" when it comes to regional representation on the Court.[24]

Maintaining the regional convention at all costs, however, creates a tension with growing attempts to imbue the Court with more diverse group representation. Recent decades have seen an increase in ethnic representation among Supreme Court judges; this includes judges from Ukrainian-Canadian (John Sopinka in 1988), Italian-Canadian (Frank Iacobucci in 1991) and Greek-Canadian (Andromache Karakatsanis in 2011) backgrounds, as well as several Jewish judges (Bora Laskin, Morris Fish, Rosalie Abella, Michael Moldaver and Marshall Rothstein). There were growing calls for Justin Trudeau to appoint an Aboriginal justice to replace Thomas Cromwell in 2016 and Beverley McLachlin in 2017, although he ultimately did not. In fact, there has yet to be a visible minority justice appointed to the Supreme Court.

Lower courts have fared better in this regard. Long before Justin Trudeau's recent diversity initiative for federally appointed judges, Canadian lower courts sought to increase ethnic and racial diversity. In Ontario, the Judicial Appointments Advisory Committee was given an explicit "employment equity" mandate at its creation in 1989. From 1989–1995, three of the new judges appointed by the JAAC were Aboriginal, ten from racial minorities, and eight francophones – including Canada's first Aboriginal woman judge, Ontario's first black woman judge and Canada's first East Asian woman judge.[25]

Yet even with such initiatives, the proportion of visible minorities on Canadian courts is lower than the overall population. In Reading 4.3, Andrew Griffith documents this under-representation. As of 2015, there were no judges from visible minorities among the roughly sixty-five judges appointed to the Supreme Court, Federal Court of Appeal or Federal Court. Visible minorities on federally appointed provincial (section 96) courts were also low, ranging between 0.5 and 4.6 per cent depending on the type of court, even though visible minorities made up over 22 per cent of the Canadian population in 2016.[26] Aboriginal judges in particular are under-represented relative to their proportion of the overall population (see Figure 6). Interestingly, while visible minorities are significantly under-represented on all courts, provincial governments have been more likely to appoint visible minorities than the federal government. Griffith argues that courts' legitimacy could suffer as a result of under-representation: "given the over-representation of some groups who are tried in the courts, such as Black people and Indigenous people, a judiciary in which these groups are significantly under-represented risks being viewed as illegitimate to those communities."

One area where the Supreme Court has become far more diverse is gender. Since the 1982 appointment of Bertha Wilson, the first woman ever to serve on the Supreme Court of Canada, there has been a steady increase in the number of women on the Court. Since 2004, four of the nine justices on the Supreme Court (apart from a brief period from 2012–2014) have been women. In Reading 2.3, Justice Wilson argues that women judges' "uniquely feminine perspective" impacts decision-making, and subsequent studies have shown that gender differences do affect voting patterns on the Supreme Court of Canada.[27] This understanding, rooted in judicial realism, has led to a push for more women at all levels of the judiciary, beginning with the Ontario JAAC's diversity mandate mentioned above. During its first six years of operation, 39 per cent of Ontario's 111 judicial appointments were women – increasing the percentage of women provincial judges in Ontario from 3 per cent to 22 per cent.[28]

Across the country, the push for more women judges has been fairly successful. At the beginning of the 1980s, only 3 per cent of federally appointed judges were women. This figure rose to 10 per cent by 1990, 25 per cent by 2002 and was up to 38 per cent by 2017. Yet as Andrew Griffith shows in Reading 4.3, women remain unrepresented on federally and provincially appointed courts relative to their population and their proportion of the legal profession. As of 2015, only 30 per cent of federally appointed judges were women. Provincially appointed judges also vary by province: roughly one-quarter of Alberta's lower court judges are women, compared with over 40 per cent in Manitoba and Quebec. Those dissatisfied with the under-representation of women on the bench can take some heart in the demographic shifts that have occurred within the legal profession. In 1980, only 11 per cent of lawyers with at least ten years' experience were women; today that figure is 44 per cent. Men still make up a significant share of the more experienced lawyers today: only 29 per cent of lawyers aged fifty to sixty-five are women. However, in 2011, women made up roughly 54 per cent of lawyers under forty.[29]

Professors Erin Crandall and Andrea Lawlor (Reading 4.4) caution that demographic change among lawyers alone will not lead to an increase in women judges. While the number of women appointed to federal courts increased throughout the 1980s and 1990s, the trend line had been fairly flat for a period thereafter. Crandall and Lawlor attribute part of this change to differences in the party of appointment, as 35 per cent of judges appointed by the Chrétien/ Martin Liberals from 1997–2005 were women, compared with just 23 per cent appointed by the Harper Conservatives from 2006–2013. The Conservatives were also more likely to appoint someone who had donated to the party in the past, and as Crandall and Lawlor's data show, "as the number of appointees with connections to the government rises, the number of women appointees falls." Crandall and Lawlor argue that two changes are necessary to get more women on the bench: first, prioritizing diversity in the appointment process;

and second, reforming the appointment system to a nominating committee, along the lines of Ontario's JAAC. While a federal nominating committee for non–Supreme Court appointments has not been forthcoming, the number of women appointed under the Trudeau government by Justice Minister Jody Wilson-Raybould confirms that prioritizing diversity in the selection process can make an impact: as of October, 2017, just over 50 per cent the eighty-six judicial appointments to superior courts under Minister Wilson-Raybould have been women, even though they made up only 42 per cent of applicants.[30]

The final form of political influence in judicial appointments is political ideology. The entrenchment of the *Charter of Rights* in 1982 clearly enhanced the potential for Supreme Court judges to influence public policy and elicited growing interest in the ideological orientation of appointments to the Court, especially from interest groups with a policy stake in *Charter* interpretation. For example, during the 1981–1982 period, in anticipation of the enactment of the *Charter*, the National Action Committee on the Status of Women began to lobby for the appointment to the Supreme Court of a woman "acceptable to our purposes."[31] This campaign bore fruit in March, 1982, when Prime Minister Trudeau appointed Bertha Wilson as the first woman justice on the Supreme Court. After the 1988 *Morgentaler* decision that struck down Canada's abortion legislation for violating the *Charter*, pro-life interest groups and MPs openly mused about the need to influence appointments in a conservative direction.[32]

It is generally recognized that ideological compatibility has been a dominant factor in presidential appointments to the U.S. Supreme Court since its origins, with Presidents dating back to Abraham Lincoln using their power of appointment to "pack the court" with judges who support their political program. Recent appointments from Presidents Barack Obama (Elia Kagan and Sonia Sotomayor) and Donald Trump (Neil Gorsuch) show that ideology remains important to this day. While "court packing" in its more dramatic form is mainly an American phenomenon, some appointments to the Supreme Court of Canada have clearly reflected the ideological proclivities of the Prime Ministers who have appointed them. Prior to his appointment in 1970, Bora Laskin had published extensively as a civil libertarian and critic of the decentralization of the Judicial Committee of the Privy Council. On the bench, he was a leading civil libertarian advocate and proponent of greater federal authority. Louise Arbour, appointed by Jean Chrétien in 1999, was a high-profile progressive activist who had worked for the Canadian Civil Liberties Association before her first judicial appointment. Rosalie Abella, appointed by Paul Martin in 2004, had been a leading advocate on "employment equity" prior to her time on the bench. More recently, Russell Brown had publically shown his conservative views while blogging as a law professor prior to his appointment by Stephen

Harper in 2015 (see Reading 11.1), while Sheila Martin, Justin Trudeau's 2017 appointee, had worked *pro bono* for the Women's Legal Education and Action Fund (LEAF) in the 1990s.

While Harper's appointment of Russell Brown was viewed with suspicion by some legal scholars,[33] Emmett Macfarlane (Reading 11.4) argues that his appointment simply adds ideological diversity to a bench in need of it. "Ideological diversity," Macfarlane argues, "is just as important for an institution like the Court as diversity along other representational grounds like gender or race." The idea that appointing a judge with conservative policy preferences is somehow a threat to judicial neutrality ignores both the appointment of progressive judges such as Abella and Martin, and the fact that judicial decision-making is necessarily political. Quantitative studies have shown that judicial ideology plays an important role on the Supreme Court of Canada, particularly in cases involving criminal law and economic disputes. While not as clear-cut as in the United States, these studies nevertheless highlight that certain justices demonstrate liberal or conservative policy preferences depending on the policy issue.[34] And while this "attitudinal" model has been criticized for ignoring other institutional factors (see Reading 8.3), it certainly dispels the notion that judicial ideology has no role to play in Supreme Court decision-making.

To conclude, there have been somewhat contradictory trends in judicial selection in Canada. The desire for a merit-based approach governed by legal expertise remains strong, though some parliamentary scrutiny over Supreme Court candidates has made the process marginally more democratic. Region is important, while an emphasis on group diversity and "identity politics" is growing at the federal and provincial levels. And while ideology is not as prominent in Canada as it is in the United States, Canadian appointments remain political.

Writing about the United States in the late 1980s, Michael Foley noted how "an integral part of the politics of Supreme Court appointments is that they should not be seen as political at all."[35] The Americans may have dropped this pretense in recent years, but it remains a staple of Canadian legal discourse. Yet it is a fiction: even supposedly "non-political" reforms reliant on legal expertise lead to the appointment of a certain type of judge. In Canada, the legal profession's dominance on screening and nominating committees has produced judges that reinforce that profession's preference for *Charter* activism over restraint, even during the Harper era. And moves to increase diversity reflect what Bertha Wilson (Reading 2.3) posited years ago, and what studies of judicial behaviour have been telling us for decades: group characteristics and ideology influence judicial outcomes. Thomas Bateman argues that the great deception of the *Charter* project has been to depoliticize its goals, to conceal the fact that "what appears as a legal project is really a political project."[36] Suffice it to observe that just as the Harper government would never have appointed Sheilah Martin to the Supreme Court, the Trudeau government would never have appointed Russell Brown. As judicial influence grows in post-*Charter* Canada, competition over who gets to appoint judges will remain political.

NOTES

1   Office of the Commissioner for Federal Judicial Affairs Canada, "Number of Federally Appointed Judges in Canada," October 1, 2017, http://www.fja-cmf.gc.ca/appointments-nominations/judges-juges-eng.aspx. This number does not include vacancies, or supernumerary (semi-retired) judges. Including supernumerary judges, there are 1,151 federally appointed judges in Canada.

2   There have been recurrent suggestions that the Constitution be amended to give provincial governments some say in appointments to section 96 courts and the Supreme Court of Canada. Since the *Victoria Charter* of 1971, a majority of the provinces lobbied for increased provincial participation in the appointment process and constitutional entrenchment of the convention of regional representation. The 1987 Meech Lake Accord proposed that the federal government be required to appoint Supreme Court judges from lists submitted by the provinces. However, after the death of the Accord in 1990, the provincial role in federal appointments has been limited to a single nominee on the judicial advisory committees for section 96 courts.

3   Commissioner for Federal Judicial Affairs Canada, "Federally Appointed Judges," October 1, 2017; Lori Hausegger, Matthew Hennigar and Troy Riddell, *Canadian Courts*. 2nd ed. (Don Mills, ON: Oxford University Press, 2015), p. 138.

4   In addition to the Chief Justice of the Supreme Court of Canada and the Federal Court of Appeal, the Prime Minister appoints the Chief Justice for section 96 superior courts in each province.

5   Peter McCormick, "Judging Selection: Appointing Canadian Judges," *Windsor Yearbook of Access to Justice* 30 (2012), p. 48. Hausegger, Hennigar and Riddell summarize the provinces as follows: Seven provinces have nominating commissions (with Alberta's having a "double hurdle"); two (Saskatchewan and Prince Edward Island) have screening committees; and New Brunswick has a body that exercises a veto function. See *Canadian Courts*, pp. 143–145.

6   Paul Weiler, "Two Models of Judicial Decision-Making," *Canadian Bar Review* 46 (1968), p. 406.

7   V.O. Key, *Politics, Parties and Pressure Groups* (New York: Thomas Y. Crowell, 1958), p. 154.

8   *Calgary Herald*, April 11, 1984, p. A5.

9   Peter H. Russell and Jacob S. Ziegel, "Mulroney's Judicial Appointments and the New Judicial Advisory Committees," in F.L. Morton, ed., *Law, Politics and the Judicial Process in Canada*. 3rd ed. (Calgary: University of Calgary Press, 2002), pp. 143–146.

10 These include that the person is a member of a provincial or territorial bar association and has a minimum of ten years' experience as a practising lawyer and/or judge.

11 Hausegger, Hennigar and Riddell, *Canadian Courts*, pp. 150–157. This procedure applies only to new appointments to the federal bench. The government's decision to elevate a sitting judge to a higher judicial office is not subject to review by a provincial screening committee.

12 Office of the Commissioner for Federal Judicial Affairs Canada, "Guide for Candidates," October, 2016, http://www.fja.gc.ca/appointments-nominations/guideCandidates-eng.html.

13 Sean Fine, "Liberals' choice of judges under scrutiny," *Globe and Mail*, October 31, 2017, p. A3. Twelve additional judges were appointed or elevated to other courts, seven of whom were women, making the total number of appointments eighty-six (forty-four of whom were women). Office of the Commissioner for Federal Judicial Affairs Canada, "Statistics regarding Judicial Applicants and Appointees (October 21, 2016–October 27, 2017)," October 27, 2017, http://www.fja.gc.ca/appointments-nominations/StatisticsCandidate-StatistiquesCandidat-eng.html.

14 Jean Chrétien, "A question of merit: ensuring quality and commitment in High Court appointments," *National* (Canadian Bar Association) (December, 1998), p. 15; see also F.L. Morton, "To Bring Judicial Appointments Out of the Closet," *Law, Politics and the Judicial Process in Canada*. 3rd ed., pp. 154–156; William Thorsell, "What to Look For, and Guard Against, in a Supreme Court Judge," *Law, Politics and the Judicial Process in Canada*. 3rd ed., pp. 157–158.

15 Adam M. Dodek, "Reforming the Supreme Court Appointment Process, 2004–2014: A 20-Year Democratic Audit," *Osgoode Hall Law Journal* 67, no. 1 (2014), p. 118.

16 Hausegger, Hennigar and Riddell, *Canadian Courts*, p. 160.

17 Dodek, "Democratic Audit," pp. 124–125. Dodek notes that it is wrong to describe the committee as a "parliamentary hearing," as it was not governed by the rules of Parliament. It is better described as an *ad hoc* televised hearing involving parliamentarians.

18 Kirk Makin, "Top-court appointment bypasses review process," *Globe and Mail*, December 23, 2008, p. A4.

19 Lorne Sossin, "Picking judges injudiciously," *Globe and Mail*, October 18, 2011, p. A15.

20 Prime Minister's Office, "New process for judicial appointments to the Supreme Court of Canada," August 2, 2016, https://pm.gc.ca/eng/news/2016/08/02/new-process-judicial-appointments-supreme-court-canada.

21 Information up to 2013 from Dodek, "Democratic Audit," p. 130.

22 Standing Committee on Justice and Human Rights, House of Commons, 42nd Parliament, 1st Session. Meeting 79 (December 4, 2017), at 1545.

23 Leonid Sirota, "Unconstitutional," *Double Aspect*, August 15, 2016, https://doubleaspect.blog/2016/08/15/unconstitutional/; Lauren Heuser, "Best, not (necessarily) bilingual," *National Post*, June 9, 2016, p. A9; *Maclean's*, "Legal eagles: A roundtable about the Supreme Court appointment process," August 3, 2016, http://www.macleans.ca/news/canada/legal-eagles-a-roundtable-about-the-supreme-court-appointment-process/.

24 Robert Schertzer, "Why regional representation on the Supreme Court does (and doesn't) matter," *Policy Options*, August 17, 2016, http://policyoptions.irpp.org/magazines/august-2016/why-regional-representation-on-the-supreme-court-does-and-doesnt-matter/.

25 Justice Maryka Omatsu, "On Judicial Appointments: Does Gender Make a Difference?", in Joseph F. Fletcher, ed., *Ideas in Action: Essays on Politics and Law in Honour of Peter Russell* (Toronto: University of Toronto Press, 1999), p. 177.

26   "New census data reveals one-fifth of Canadians are immigrants," *National Post,* October 25, 2017, http://nationalpost.com/news/canada/newsalert-ranks-of-indigenous-peoples-boom-ing-in-canada-census-shows.

27   Donald R. Songer, *The Transformation of the Supreme Court of Canada* (Toronto: University of Toronto Press, 2008), p. 209; Cynthia L. Ostberg and Matthew E. Wetstein, *Attitudinal Decision Making in the Supreme Court of Canada* (Vancouver: UBC Press, 2007), p. 22; Donald R. Songer, Susan W. Johnston, Cynthia L. Ostberg and Matthew E. Wetstein, *Law, Ideology, Collegiality: Judicial Behaviour in the Supreme Court of Canada* (Montreal/Kingston: McGill-Queen's University Press, 2012), pp. 144–145.

28   Omatsu, "Does Gender Make a Difference?"

29   Hausegger, Hennigar and Riddell, *Canadian Courts,* pp. 154. See also Cristin Schmitz, "Updated: Women get to bench on 'merit alone' not 'quotas' Wilson-Raybould insists," *Lawyer's Daily,* May 19, 2017, https://www.thelawyersdaily.ca/articles/3774/updated-women-get-to-bench-on-merit-alone-not-quotas-wilson-raybould-insists.

30   Commissioner for Federal Judicial Affairs Canada, "Statistics regarding Judicial Applicants and Appointees."

31   "NAC Memo," Committee Report, September, 1981, Justice Committee, pp. 4–5.

32   "Public to Demand Say in Court Appointments," *Lawyers Weekly,* February 12, 1988, p. 1; "Reduced Role for Politicians Urged in Naming of Judges," *Globe and Mail,* May 16, 1988, p. A1.

33   John Whyte, "Russell Brown doesn't belong on the Supreme Court," *Toronto Star,* August 19, 2015, p. A15.

34   Ostberg and Wetstein, *Attitudinal Decision-Making;* Songer et al., *Law, Ideological, and Collegiality.*

35   Michael Foley, *The Silence of Constitutions: Gaps, "Abeyances," and Political Temperament in the Maintenance of Government* (Oxford: Routledge, 1989), p. 125.

36   Thomas Bateman, "The Charter Revolution and the Efficient Part of Canada's Constitution," *Voegelin View,* June 20, 2017, https://voegelinview.com/charter-revolution-efficient-part-canadas-constitution/.

4.1

Patronage in Judicial Appointments

Jeffrey Simpson

The Spoils of Power: The Politics of Patronage (Toronto: Collins, 1988), 300–310. Reprinted with permission.

... Broadly speaking, the further down the judicial hierarchy, the more obvious the evidence of patronage. The Supreme Court of Canada, for example, is now completely devoid of patronage, or even of the tinge of partisan appointments.... Supreme Court appointments were not always so pure. A scholarly history of the Supreme Court makes clear that partisanship joined religion and region – and merit, when available – as indispensable criteria for Supreme Court appointments until the immediate post-war years. When Louis St. Laurent became prime minister in 1949, the court contained seven justices, four of whom had had extensive political ties to the Liberal party. St. Laurent himself appointed justices from a mixture of non-political and political backgrounds, the most obvious being long-time Liberal cabinet minister Douglas Abbott. But partisanship appeared to wane throughout subsequent years as prime ministers increasingly sought advice from the legal fraternity before making Supreme Court appointments. Twenty-two of forty Supreme Court judges appointed before 1949 had previously been politicians; since then, only two of twenty-two justices had entered politics.

That sharp decline in previous political experience of Supreme Court justices is partly – but only partly – reflected further down the hierarchy. The Canadian Bar Association said as recently as 1985 that "there is ample scope for the functioning of a political patronage system without applying it to judicial appointments." The association declared itself satisfied that patronage had been rooted out of the Supreme Court, but it worried about patronage elsewhere in the judiciary, especially in the Federal Court, whose members are appointed by Ottawa. Writing after Prime Minister Pierre Trudeau sent three former ministers (Mark MacGuigan, Bud Cullen and Yvon Pinard) to the Federal Court as part of his 1984 orgy of patronage appointments, the association remarked, "at present, this court is perceived by many, rightly or wrongly, as a government-oriented court because so many former politicians and federal officials have been appointed to it." The association added, "as to appointments to the Federal Court of Canada, political favouritism has been a dominant, though not sole, consideration; many appointees have been active supporters of the party in power."

Trudeau's parting gesture also featured the appointment of two other Liberal MPs and a defeated Liberal candidate to lower courts. These appointments fitted a familiar Trudeau pattern for patronage. A professor of law before entering politics, Trudeau took considerable care in his early years in office to temper patronage in making senior judicial appointments. This was consistent with other intermittent efforts to change traditional assumptions about patronage. But such efforts declined in intensity as his years in office wore on, so that by the end of his sixteen years as prime minister Trudeau was practising patronage as relentlessly as his predecessors.

The association also analysed federal appointments to higher courts in the provinces – so-called section 96 courts – and concluded that political favouritism still existed in Alberta, Manitoba, Newfoundland, and Ontario, and that it remained a "dominant" but not exclusive consideration in New Brunswick, Nova Scotia, Prince Edward Island, and Saskatchewan. That the three Maritime provinces appeared on the association's list was not surprising; there the traditions of political patronage have persisted longer than almost anywhere else in Canada. But Saskatchewan's inclusion might raise a few eyebrows, until one remembers that Saskatchewan was the fiefdom of Otto Lang, Trudeau's minister of justice and a former dean of the University of Saskatchewan law school.

Lang and his successor Mark MacGuigan scattered prominent or low-profile Liberals throughout the Saskatchewan judiciary, including former party leaders, MLAs, defeated candidates and loyal party workers. This propensity for appointing Liberals to Saskatchewan courts led directly to a *contretemps* with the Conservative government of Premier Grant Devine. The provincial Conservatives, eager dispensers of patronage themselves, became sufficiently riled by Liberal appointments to the bench, and by Ottawa's refusal to consult the provincial government before making appointments, that they tried to restrict Liberal opportunities for patronage. In 1982 the provincial government passed an order-in-council reducing the number of judges on the Saskatchewan Court of Appeal from seven to five.

For the next two years, open warfare raged between the provincial Conservative government and the Trudeau Liberals. The provincial cabinet passed another order-in-council closing down each vacancy on the Court of Queen's Bench, so that its strength fell from thirty to twenty-four. Only the election of the Mulroney Conservatives ended the impasse. With Conservatives in Regina and Ottawa, the provincial party quickly restored the judicial positions, and filled some of them with prominent supporters such as George Hill and Irving Goldenberg, former presidents of the Saskatchewan Conservative party. The Saskatchewan experience of the 1980s mirrored that of Newfoundland in 1960 when Liberal premier Joey Smallwood, rebuffed by the federal

Conservatives in his demand for control of judicial appointments, refused to proclaim legislation creating a new position on the provincial Supreme Court.

The Bar Association's 1985 review of judicial appointments gave provincial governments better marks than it gave the federal government. In five provinces – Alberta, British Columbia, Newfoundland, Quebec, and Saskatchewan – the association thought "political favouritism has played no part in appointments." In Manitoba, favouritism played "some part" in appointments, whereas in those hardy patronage perennials – New Brunswick, Prince Edward Island and Nova Scotia – the association found that "most appointees have been active supporters of the party in power."

That 1985 review, sparked by Trudeau's parting orgy of patronage and his failure to consult the bar before making Yvon Pinard's appointment, flowed from the association's decades-long campaign to squeeze patronage from the process of selecting judges. Moral suasion was about the association's only weapon for many years, although it helped the association's case when its president, R.B. Bennett, became prime minister in 1930 and tried to set a better example in selecting Supreme Court justices. But the concept of formal consultation with the legal community had to await the arrival of Trudeau as minister of justice in 1967.

Trudeau became the first minister of justice to seek an opinion of the Canadian Bar Association's National Council on the Judiciary before appointing a judge. This practice continued when John Turner became minister of justice in the first Trudeau government, and Turner is fairly credited with having improved the quality of judicial appointments across the country. In 1972, a special adviser on judicial appointments was named in the minister's office. These reforms sprang both from Trudeau's own convictions as a professor of law and from intermittent attempts to change some traditional conventions of patronage in his early years in office. In five provinces – Alberta, British Columbia, Newfoundland, Ontario, and Saskatchewan – attorneys-general now formally consult provincial judicial councils before making appointments, while in Quebec the attorney-general consults a nominating committee. British Columbia's *Provincial Court Act* even requires the cabinet to appoint only persons recommended by the judicial council.

Pressure from the bar, then, has been among those restricting the incidence of political patronage on judicial appointments. Some numbers illustrate the point. Will Klein studied federally appointed judges in Manitoba, Ontario, and Quebec from 1905 to 1970. He found that nearly ninety-five percent of former politicians appointed to Ontario courts by Liberal governments were Liberals, and eighty-one percent appointed by Conservative governments were Conservatives. But he also discovered that although forty-three percent of all Laurier's appointments had contested elections, only twenty-one percent of Trudeau's (up to 1970) had done so. Klein concluded that "political activities prior to appointment to the bench have been common to about a third of the judges appointed in Manitoba, Ontario, and Quebec between 1905 and 1970 but that ... proportion of judges with electoral experience has diminished through these years."

What Klein could not measure was the partisanship of appointees who had participated in politics other than by running in elections or serving in legislatures. It was a key omission, since many judicial appointees have been active party supporters without ever having entered electoral politics. His general conclusion that political considerations in judicial appointments have waned over this century was supported by Guy Bouthillier, who examined the careers of appointees to the Quebec Court of Appeal from 1867 to 1972. Bouthillier found that the proportion involved in politics had dropped from over seventy-eight percent between Confederation and World War I to twenty-two percent since World War II. But remember that these sorts of studies undoubtedly underestimate, often considerably, the partisan factor in appointments. They trace only electoral careers, and forget that many judges with the proper political credentials never ran for office. For example, one study in the early 1950s found that in six provinces all judges were supporters of the party in power at the time of their appointment. In the four other provinces, the percentage of party supporters ranged from seventy percent to eighty-seven percent. And a survey for the Association of Canadian Law Teachers in 1966 concluded, "All but a few of the judges appointed during the period were affiliated with the party in power at the time of their appointment, and most were actively engaged in politics.

The practice still continues. For example, Prime Minister Joe Clark appointed five judges to the Superior Court for the Montreal district. All had Conservative credentials: Claude Gérin, who ran unsuccessfully against Liberal kingpin Marc Lalonde; Gérard Trudel, a Conservative organizer; Maurice Mercure, a former Union Nationale candidate and Conservative organizer; Bernard Flynn, who worked for Clark and his predecessor Robert Stanfield; and Claude Nolin, former president of the Conservative party in Quebec.

4.2

Exploring the Links between Party and Appointment: Canadian Federal Judicial Appointments from 1989 to 2003

Lori Hausegger, Troy Riddell, Matthew Hennigar and Emmanuelle Richez

Canadian Journal of Political Science 43, no. 3 (2010), 633–659. Reprinted with permission.

In their study of federal judicial appointments in Canada from 1984 to 1988, Peter Russell and Jacob Ziegel indicated that one of the purposes of their study was to "establish the basis for a future comparison between the judicial appointments made before the introduction of the ... judicial advisory committees and the appointments made after them." Before the establishment of these screening committees, Russell and Ziegel found significant patronage existed in judicial appointments. Indeed, despite the Mulroney government's election pledge to reduce patronage, nearly half of the federal judicial appointments made between 1984 and 1988 had some connection to the governing Progressive Conservative party. Russell and Ziegel found, moreover, that the appointees for whom they discovered partisan connections also tended to be rated as lower quality appointments than appointees with no known political affiliation. However, Russell and Ziegel's data end in 1988 and a full comparison has yet to be made between the pre-committee appointments they studied and those made after the screening committees were introduced.

This article undertakes the comparison envisioned by Russell and Ziegel by examining the political backgrounds of appointees from 1989 to 2003 ... while also, more generally, assessing the impact of the changes to federal judicial appointments announced in 1988.... We conclude that political connections continued to play an important role in who was selected for a judicial appointment after the introduction of the screening committees in 1988, though the new process may have worked to prevent (for the most part) the politically motivated appointment of completely unqualified individuals. Our findings also suggest that the relevance of patronage varied by region and interacted with other "political" factors, such as group representation on the bench....

Background

Historically, patronage played a very significant role in federal judicial appointments. The Canadian Bar Association, in an effort to improve the appointment process, established the National Committee on the Judiciary in 1967 to screen the names of judicial candidates forwarded by the minister of justice. In the early 1970s, ministers of justice began to use special advisors to accumulate information about prospective candidates from judges, members of the law profession and provincial attorneys general.

The system, however, still allowed for patronage to play a considerable role in the appointment process.... In 1991, Russell and Ziegel published their study of the Mulroney government's judicial appointments from 1984 to 1988, based on questionnaire responses from individuals in law, politics, academia and the media who might have been familiar with the appointees. The results indicated that 24.1 per cent of appointees had "major" involvement with the Conservative party (as a party official, as an active participant in an election or leadership campaign or as a candidate for elected office) and 23.2 per cent had "minor" involvement with the Conservative party (minor constituency work, financial contributions or close personal or professional associations with party leaders). Involvement with an opposition party was ascribed to 7.1 per cent of appointees (5.3 per cent "major" and 1.8 per cent "minor")....

Following the re-election of the Mulroney government in 1988, Justice Minister Ray Hnatyshyn introduced a new system for appointments to the s.96 courts and the Federal Court. The responsibilities of the Office of the Commissioner for Federal Judicial Affairs were expanded to include soliciting applications from those interested in a federal judicial position and, after checking to see if they met the technical qualifications for the post, referring those names to the advisory committees established in each province and territory to screen the candidates. After a committee rates the candidates referred to it, the commissioner is responsible for reporting the assessments back to the minister so that appointments can be made from the list on an ongoing basis. [*Ed. Note*: See Introduction to this Chapter.] ...

When the committee system was established originally, candidates were rated as "qualified" or "not qualified," but in 1991 this was changed to "highly recommended," "recommended" and "unable to recommend" and, at that time, committees were also asked to attach a précis about the candidate. Over the first ten years of the committee system, 1892 applications were "recommended" or "highly recommended" while 2477 applications were rated as "not qualified" or "unable to recommend". ...

Data Collection

... [W]e collected the names and brief biographical details of judges appointed by the federal government between 1989 and 2003 to the s.96 courts (trial and appeal) in the provinces, as well as to the Federal Court (trial and appeal) and the Tax Court. There were 856 individuals who received such federal appointments.... To ascertain the political connections (if any) of the appointees we enlisted the help of senior lawyers and law professors in each province to act as informants.... Email requests for participation were sent to potential informants in each province asking them to participate in a web-based survey.

The web survey asked respondents to choose an appointee from their province from a drop-down menu.... For each appointee, our informants were asked first to provide an assessment of their quality prior to their appointment. The informants were then asked whether the appointee had some association with a political party, including minor constituency work, fundraising, being a senior campaign activist, sitting as a party executive or running for office.... The survey then asked informants whether the appointee had any close social [or professional] connections with a federal cabinet minister, member of parliament, executive member of the governing party or other social [or professional] connections.... In addition to providing information about appointees with whom they were familiar, informants were encouraged to provide their general impressions about the judicial appointment process. They were asked to rank how important "political connections" and "social and professional connections" were in the federal appointment process along a five-point scale from Unimportant (1) to Very Important (5). Respondents were then asked how the federal judicial appointments system worked in practice and a text box was available for responses.... The survey concluded by asking informants if they would be willing to participate in a confidential telephone conversation to talk about the appointment process in more depth. A total of 173 individuals participated in the survey in ten provinces and we conducted 35 follow-up interviews....

Findings

... Comparing our results with the earlier study ... we find that, for all but two provinces (PEI and Quebec), the percentage of judges with major connections being appointed is lower after the introduction of the screening committees. In some provinces the difference is quite impressive. Nova Scotia, for example, went from 41.7 per cent with major political connections to only 22.9 per cent, and Newfoundland dropped from 33.3 per cent to 18.5 per cent. In total, we discovered that 17.2 per cent of judges appointed from 1989 to 2003 had major connections to the party that appointed them, a number noticeably lower than

Table 1:

Per Cent of Appointees Having Political Connections by Province, 1989–2003

	Party in Power Involvement		No Known Affiliation	Opposition Involvement	
	Major	Minor		Major	Minor
BC	5.0% (6)	9.1% (11)	76.9% (93)	2.5% (3)	6.6% (8)
AB	20.5% (18)	33.0% (29)	37.5% (33)	4.5% (4)	4.5% (4)
SK	44.7% (17)	23.7% (9)	28.9% (11)	2.6% (1)	0% (0)
MB	42.9% (18)	26.2% (11)	26.2% (11)	2.4% (1)	2.4% (1)
ON	9.5% (27)	32.3% (92)	55.4% (158)	0.7% (2)	2.1% (6)
QC	10.8% (18)	13.2% (22)	75.4% (126)	0.6% (1)	0% (0)
NB	60.0% (18)	26.7% (8)	10.0% (3)	3.3% (1)	0% (0)
NS	22.9% (11)	29.2% (14)	47.9% (23)	0% (0)	0% (0)
PE	90.0% (9)	0% (0)	10% (1)	0% (0)	0% (0)
NF	18.5% (5)	22.2% (6)	44.4% (12)	3.7% (1)	11.1% (3)
Totals	17.2% (147)	23.6% (202)	55.0% (471)	1.6% (14)	2.6% (22)

the 24.2 per cent found by Russell and Ziegel for appointments made between 1984 and 1988. Interestingly, the appointments Prime Minister Mulroney made in his second term, after the introduction of the screening committees (1989 to 1993), demonstrate fewer major political connections than those he made before the committees.… These findings suggest the possibility that the screening committees may indeed have had some impact on the process, at least at this high level of connection.

... [A]dding major and minor connections together, Russell and Ziegel found that before the introduction of committees, 47.5 per cent of judicial appointees (excluding the territories) had some connection to the party that appointed them, while, using comparable measures, we find that 40.8 per cent had connections after the establishment of committees. Although this means that a considerable number of appointees continued to have connections with the party in power, the data also reflect the observation made by a number of our respondents who argued that the committee system has curtailed the appointment of some hard-core partisans who lacked the background to be recommended for appointment.

Overall, the pattern of political connections across provinces is relatively similar in each time period. In both studies, some Maritime provinces, Saskatchewan and Manitoba tend to have the highest level of major political connections and the lowest level of "no known affiliation." In our study, PEI demonstrates the highest level of major connections followed by New Brunswick, Saskatchewan and Manitoba, whereas in the Russell and Ziegel study Nova Scotia was in the top four and PEI was not....

Specific Findings using HHR Measures

Table 2 presents results using our different measures of political connection.... We not only made a distinction between major and minor connections, we also attempted to distinguish the type of those connections. Therefore, we have a category for major direct political activities (such as fundraising, running a candidate's campaign or being a member of the party executive), and a category for major social or professional connections (such as being the spouse, room-mate or law partner of a major political player or even the minister of justice). While appointees falling in the first category definitely qualify as political, those falling in the latter category are not necessarily political themselves – and yet most observers would classify their appointment as a political one. By our measures, 22.4 per cent of appointees from 1989 to 2003 had backgrounds that suggested major political activities, major social or professional connections, or both. Of these, 5.3 per cent had only major social or professional connections. However, as reported in the last column of Table 2, when we examined those appointees more closely we discovered that several had some minor politics in their background (usually donating to a political party). In the end, only 2.3 per cent of judges appointed between 1989 and 2003 could arguably be classified as a major political appointment without being political themselves.

The number of judicial appointees with major and minor connections varied, of course, by province. Prince Edward Island had the lowest number of

Table 2:

<table>
<tr><td></td><td colspan="5" align="center">Province by Political Affiliation, 1989–2003
(% of appointees within province falling in each political affiliation)</td></tr>
<tr>
<td></td>
<td>No Politics</td>
<td>Minor Direct Activities</td>
<td>Major Connections and/or Major Direct Activities</td>
<td>Major Connections Only</td>
<td>Major Connections with Minor Direct Activities</td>
</tr>
<tr><td>BC (n = 121)</td><td>16.5%
(20)</td><td>9.1%
(11)</td><td>5.8%
(7)</td><td>0.8%
(1)</td><td>0.8%
(1)</td></tr>
<tr><td>AB (n = 88)</td><td>10.2%
(9)</td><td>28.4%
(25)</td><td>26.1%
(23)</td><td>5.7%
(5)</td><td>1.1%
(1)</td></tr>
<tr><td>SK (n = 38)</td><td>13.2%
(5)</td><td>21.1%
(8)</td><td>55.3%
(21)</td><td>10.5%
(4)</td><td>7.9%
(3)</td></tr>
<tr><td>MB (n = 42)</td><td>7.1%
(3)</td><td>19.0%
(8)</td><td>52.4%
(22)</td><td>9.5%
(4)</td><td>2.4%
(1)</td></tr>
<tr><td>ON (n = 285)</td><td>6.0%
(17)</td><td>29.8%
(85)</td><td>14.0%
(40)</td><td>4.6%
(13)</td><td>2.1%
(6)</td></tr>
<tr><td>QC (n = 167)</td><td>1.8%
(3)</td><td>12.0%
(20)</td><td>12.6%
(21)</td><td>1.8%
(3)</td><td>0.6%
(1)</td></tr>
<tr><td>NB (n = 30)</td><td>3.3%
(1)</td><td>23.3%
(7)</td><td>76.7%
(23)</td><td>16.7%
(5)</td><td>13.3%
(4)</td></tr>
<tr><td>NS (n = 48)</td><td>22.9%
(11)</td><td>20.8%
(10)</td><td>35.4%
(17)</td><td>12.5%
(6)</td><td>4.2%
(2)</td></tr>
<tr><td>PE (n = 10)</td><td>10.0%
(1)</td><td>0%
(0)</td><td>90.0%
(9)</td><td>0%
(0)</td><td>0%
(0)</td></tr>
<tr><td>NF (n = 27)</td><td>29.6%
(8)</td><td>11.1%
(3)</td><td>33.3%
(9)</td><td>14.8%
(4)</td><td>3.7%
(1)</td></tr>
<tr><td>**Totals
(n = 856)**</td><td>9.1%
(78)</td><td>20.7%
(177)</td><td>22.4%
(192)</td><td>5.3%
(45)</td><td>2.3%
(20)</td></tr>
</table>

judges appointed (10) during our time period, but 90 per cent of those appointees had some major direct political activity in their background, the highest percentage of any province. New Brunswick was also very high with 76.7 per cent of its federal judicial appointments having some kind of major activity or connection in their background. New Brunswick differed from PEI, however, in that 16.7 per cent of its appointees had major social or professional connections without also having been involved in major political activity themselves (whereas PEI had none). Saskatchewan and Manitoba were the next highest provinces, each with over half of their appointees (55.3 per cent and 52.4 per cent respectively) having a history of major political activity, major social or professional connections or both. British Columbia is the province with the lowest number of appointees falling in the major political categories. Only 5.8 per cent of British Columbia appointees had these types of connections. Although we believe Table 2 allows for a more nuanced look at the type of connections between judges and the government appointing them, the overall provincial patterns mirror those using the Russell and Ziegel measures in terms of the provinces demonstrating the highest and lowest levels of major political associations.

The provincial patterns for minor direct political activities demonstrate some differences from those of the major ones. Ontario and Alberta have the highest levels of appointees with minor direct political activities in their background (perhaps reflecting the importance of political donations to the measure) while British Columbia and PEI have the lowest (PEI had little room for this type of connection with nine of its ten appointees having major political activities in their background).

More interesting, perhaps, is the "no politics" category. The numbers in this category are low as we only counted a judge as having no political background if it was definitively stated by respondents and not contradicted by any other respondent (we also did not put anyone in this category who provoked only an "unsure" from respondents). Despite our strict definition, Newfoundland had 29.6 per cent and Nova Scotia had 22.9 per cent of their appointees fall in this category. More surprisingly, 13.2 per cent of Saskatchewan judges appointed between 1989 and 2003 fell into this category. Thus, while Saskatchewan rates as the third highest province in terms of major connections and political activities, it falls as the fourth highest province in terms of appointees with "no politics" in their background. This may reflect the smaller size of the province (as with Nova Scotia and Newfoundland), which allows respondents to be more definitive in their answers. Thus we may be capturing the measure better in that province. Manitoba and New Brunswick present a more expected picture, scoring high in terms of major connections and low in terms of no politics....

Perceptions versus Reality

The perception exists in the media and among much of the legal community that politics plays a significant, if not predominant, role in federal judicial appointments.... However, in undertaking this project, we wondered whether stories of obvious political patronage were reflective of the norm, or whether they were high profile outliers, colouring peoples' view and confusing the issue. Our findings suggest the answer to this may depend on the province. The respondents from PEI are probably in touch with the way their federal judicial appointments are done, as 90 per cent of its appointees in our time period did indeed have some kind of major political connection to the governing party. However, in provinces like Newfoundland, the perception seems to be out of step with the extent of political connections we actually discovered. Respondents from Newfoundland suggested political connections were very important ... and comments were made about how politics is "dominant" in judicial appointments in the province. However, despite these perceptions, Newfoundland placed in the bottom half of provinces in terms of the number of its appointees who had major political connections and, of all the provinces, Newfoundland has the highest number of appointees with "no politics" in their background....

Obviously, however, our data suggest a reality in which differences persist between provinces in the importance of the political backgrounds of those appointed to the bench. Despite the introduction of committees, New Brunswick, for example, still has a large number of appointees with major political connections (often through direct participation), as does Saskatchewan and Manitoba. The appointees in British Columbia, by contrast, demonstrate very few political connections – a low number that has become even smaller since the introduction of the committees....

Group Representation

For judges appointed from 1989 to 2003, another consideration appears to have come to the forefront: group representation. Several respondents mentioned the importance of gender, ethnicity and language to the process, suggesting it was another "card that could be played" and one that could even "trump politics." The Liberal government, in particular, appears to have actively sought out aboriginal lawyers in an effort to encourage them to apply for judicial vacancies. And our data suggest that both the Mulroney and Chrétien governments made conscious efforts to increase the number of women on the federal bench.

Reaction to group representation was mixed, with some respondents suggesting they felt such appointees were of lower quality. This statement was usually directed at female appointees who, in our time period, tended to be appointed at a younger age than their male colleagues. However, when we examined the numbers for gender, female appointees were not rated significantly lower than males. Indeed, a slightly higher number of females were in both the "outstanding" and the "very good" categories of our quality measure.... Interestingly, female appointees were slightly less likely to have major direct political activities in their background, but were slightly more likely to have major social or professional connections to the government appointing them....

Implications

Although the 1990s did see some egregious appointments, and reports from a few provinces suggested there were instances where committees were asked to re-evaluate individuals by the political powers of the day, in general, the vast majority of respondents agreed that the new committee system screened out poor candidates. As one of our respondents stated, "No matter how good your political connections, if you are a crappy lawyer you will not get on the bench." Several respondents suggested that the "real political animals" were now being shut out of the process.... Our replication of the Russell and Ziegel model suggests that the appointment of judges with major political connections is indeed down, and the difference between Prime Minister Mulroney's first and second terms (before and after the introduction of the committees) is particularly suggestive. Given that Russell and Ziegel's data and our own suggest that the appointments of those with strong political connections tended to be rated lower on average than those without major connections, the introduction of the screening committees may have generated at least incremental improvements to the quality of the s.96 and lower s.101 bench. However, our numbers also suggest that partisanship still plays an important role in the process, especially in some provinces, and that this can influence both the perception of the judiciary and its actual functioning if the best candidates are possibly being overlooked because of political considerations. Of course, our data only explicitly measure perceptions of the quality of the appointment to the bench. The next step is to systematically measure the quality of those appointments once they are on the bench, whether they turn out to be good judges. The patterns we have discovered for federal judicial appointments will be a cause for concern if those who are politically connected do in fact make poorer judges....

4.3

Diversity Among Federal and Provincial Judges
Andrew Griffith

Adapted from *Policy Options*, May 4, 2016, http://policyoptions.irpp. org/2016/05/04/diversity-among-federal-provincial-judges/. Reprinted with permission.

With the federal government's general commitment to increased diversity in appointments, and Justice Minister Jody Wilson-Raybould's current review of the judicial appointment process, there needs to be a baseline of information about the current diversity situation in order to measure implementation of these commitments.

Overall, women, visible minorities and Indigenous people are under-represented among the over 1,000 federally appointed judges (65 are in federal courts, the balance are in provincial courts). There is a similar but less pronounced pattern of under-representation among the over 700 provincially appointed judges.

Does this matter given that judges are expected to be objective, impartial and neutral? Their legal education, training and experience prepare them for this end. However, judges are human and, like all of us, they are influenced by their past experiences, influences and backgrounds. We know from Daniel Kahneman (author of *Thinking, Fast and Slow*) and others that no one is completely neutral and bias-free, even if the judicial process does represent "slow" or deliberative thinking, and thus greater objectivity, rather than "fast" or automatic thinking. Diversity of background and experience is another way to improve neutrality in decision-making.

Moreover, given the over-representation of some groups who are tried in the courts, such as Black people and Indigenous people, a judiciary in which these groups are significantly under-represented risks being viewed as illegitimate to those communities. The current debate over murdered and missing Indigenous women and police carding practices exemplify this risk.

Figure 1 highlights the extent of this under-representation: there are no visible minority or Indigenous judges in the Supreme Court and Court of Appeal, no visible minority judges in the Federal Court and no Indigenous judges in the Tax Court. In all the courts except for the Supreme Court, women are significantly under-represented.

Figure 1: Federal Court Diversity

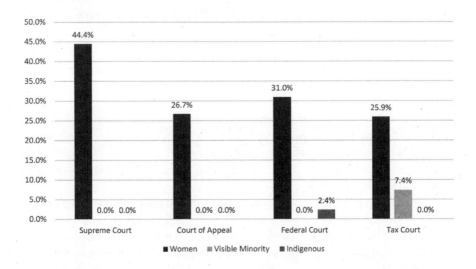

If we look at federally appointed judges to provincial courts (figure 2), the picture is slightly better in terms of both visible minority and Indigenous judges, but in both cases the representation is significantly lower than these groups' population shares. In the superior courts/Queen's Bench women are particularly under-represented, but they are better represented when the representation is compared with that of the federal courts.

Figure 2: Provincial Court Diversity (Provincially Appointed)

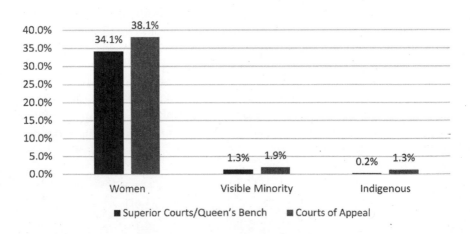

The picture for provincially nominated judges to provincial and territorial courts (figure 3) varies by province, but overall the provinces resemble each other in their under-representation of these groups. The Atlantic provinces, with the exception of Nova Scotia, have no visible minority or Indigenous judges. In the North, despite the large Indigenous population, there are no Indigenous judges. Quebec has relatively few visible minority judges and no Indigenous judges. Saskatchewan and Manitoba, despite their large Indigenous populations, have relatively few Indigenous judges.

Figure 3: Provincial Court Diversity (Provincially Appointed)

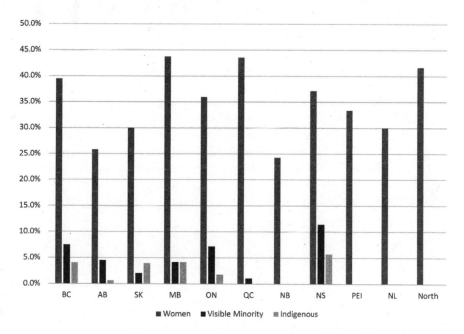

In the next series of charts federally and provincially appointed judges are compared for each under-represented group, by province, starting with women (figure 4). Here there is no overall trend: the federal and provincial appointment of women is similar in British Columbia, Manitoba, Nova Scotia, and Newfoundland and Labrador; in Saskatchewan, Quebec, Prince Edward Island and the North, provincial appointment of women is higher; and in Alberta the appointment of women is significantly lower, given the relatively large share of part-time and supernumerary appointments that are men (about a third of full-time judges are women).

Figure 4: Federal-Provincial Contrast (Women)

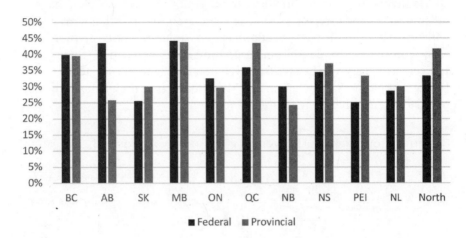

Looking at visible minorities (figure 5), when we compare federal and provincial appointments by province, we see a trend in all provinces except Saskatchewan: provincial judicial appointments are more representative of their populations than federal nominations, although visible minorities are still significantly under-represented.

Figure 5: Federal-Provincial Contrast (Visible Minorities)

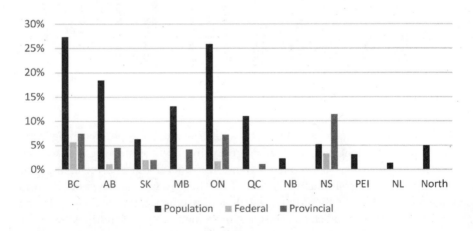

Lastly, with respect to Indigenous appointments (figure 6), we see the same pattern: provincial appointments are more representative of provincial populations than federal appointments in all provinces and territories, except, surprisingly, in the North, where there are no Indigenous territorial judges.

Figure 6: Federal-Provincial Contrast (Indigineous Peoples)

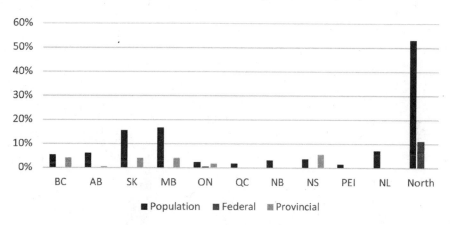

Looking at senior judges (chief and associate-chief justices), there are no federally appointed visible minority or Indigenous judges, and there are only a handful number of provincially appointed senior judges (figure 7).

Figure 7: Chief Justice Diversity (Federal Courts, Federally and Provincially Appointed)

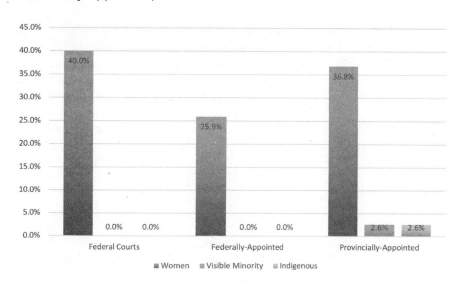

While judicial diversity is low, particularly for visible minorities and Indigenous people, the number of visible minority lawyers continues to increase. Figure 8 presents the proportions of visible minority lawyers aged 25–64 Canada-wide and in the largest provinces, which gives an idea of the size of the pool that can be drawn from. Given that visible minorities are, in general, younger than the general population, visible minority lawyers are also likely to be younger and, therefore, the percentage who would be aged 45 years old or older, the usual age people are considered for these positions, would be lower.

Figure 8: Lawyer-Judges Comparison (Visible Minorities)

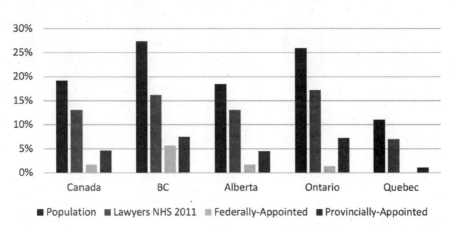

As part of its review of the judicial appointment process, the Office of the Commissioner for Federal Judicial Affairs should expand the existing information on the gender of judges and include visible minorities and Indigenous people. With this information, the government could be held to account for its diversity and inclusion commitments, and it would be easier to track its progress over time.

The provinces and territories that do not already do this should do so, and they should use Ontario's annual reports on appointments as a model, ensuring that the annual reports cover the overall diversity of the entire bench.

A few notes on methodology. The federal government publishes statistics on gender but not on visible minority or Indigenous appointments. All provinces except Alberta and Saskatchewan indicate gender through the use of "Mr." or "Madam" justice (the departments of justice provided the number of women judges). Gender information is thus complete.

To identify visible minority and Indigenous origin name checks, appointment announcements and, when available, photos and biographies were used. All provincial judicial councils or departments of justice were approached (only Ontario reports publicly but Saskatchewan, Quebec and Nova Scotia provided the breakdowns used). The Canadian Bar Association, national and regional branches, and law societies were approached and a number of individual lawyers also helped improve the quality of the data collected. I believe this provides a reasonable assessment of current diversity.

4.4

The Politics of Judicial Appointment: Do Party Connections Impede the Appointment of Women to Canada's Federally Appointed Courts?

Erin Crandall and Andrea Lawlor

Canadian Journal of Political Science 50, no.3 (2017), 823–847. Reprinted with permission.

The influence of party connection on the selection of judges has long been a reality in Canada. While the appointment of blatantly under-qualified party loyalists is no longer a concern in the way it was a few decades ago, recent scholarship has shown that party connection remains a prominent feature among the women and men chosen by the federal government to serve as judges. Participation in a political party is not necessarily a negative attribute for a judicial candidate to possess. Rather, the concern lies in the possibility that political connections may supersede more important considerations used to assess the quality of a judicial candidate, most significantly merit. This, in turn, leads to the worrying question of whether groups that are less likely to have party connections (for example, racialized minorities and women) are more adversely affected by the process of judicial selection than others. Using an original dataset of judicial appointments from 1972 to 2013, this paper takes up this question by examining (1) whether party connection adversely affects the appointment of women judges to federal courts in Canada, and (2) whether a different system of judicial appointment (Ontario's provincial court appointment system) might help to lessen these effects. The findings presented here suggest that party connection (as measured by political party donations) does have a negative effect on the appointment of women to Canada's provincial superior courts, providing evidence that changes to the system of federal judicial appointment are needed....

Judges, Representation, and Judicial Appointment Processes in Canada

In Canada, the desirability of having a judicial branch reflective of the society it serves is now accepted in principle, though the issue continues to stir public debate. For the courts, contentions usually focus on concerns that prioritizing representation will allow less qualified candidates to leap-frog to the bench over the more qualified. Alternatively, some may question whether Canadian courts genuinely struggle with this issue at all. While the underrepresentation of racialized minorities on the bench is undisputed, Canada has performed better than many other advanced democracies at selecting women judges, at least at the peak court level. Nonetheless, while women's representation on the bench has increased in recent decades, the ratio of appointments for women and men has yet to reach parity and as of 2013 women made up only about 33 per cent of superior court judges. More troubling, however, is that in recent years the rate at which women were appointed to Canada's federal courts was actually in decline.

Some might ask, so what? Why should we be concerned with women's representation on the bench? By Erika Rackley's account, arguments in support of diversity in the courts typically fall within three broad categories: (1) those that highlight the importance of diversity as a means of ensuring the legitimacy and authority of the judiciary; (2) those that focus on equity and the importance that all qualified judicial candidates have the same opportunities to become judges; and (3) those that argue that the judiciary will be changed and improved by a greater diversity of decision makers. It is worth noting that none of these positions necessarily undermines the others and it is not uncommon for scholars to endorse combinations of the three....

The current federal appointment system for provincial superior courts has been in place since 1989. As part of the 1989 reforms judicial advisory committees were introduced in each province and territory. These committees are tasked with evaluating judicial applicants as "not recommended," "recommended" or "highly recommended." [*Ed. note*: See Introduction to this Chapter.] ... In practice, the review function of these advisory committees still leaves considerable discretion in the hands of the Minister of Justice in appointing a new judge. For example, of the 300 judicial applications assessed between November 2012 and October 2013, 132 (44 per cent) were recommended by committees, while only fifty-two applicants were appointed to the bench. In fact, the candidate pool is even larger than these numbers indicate as recommended applicants remain on file for two years.

Ontario also reformed its provincial appointment system in 1989 by introducing a judicial nominating committee, known as the Judicial Appointments Advisory Committee (JAAC). Like the federal advisory committees, the JAAC is tasked with evaluating judicial applicants. The committee has developed its own criteria for evaluation, which fall under four major categories: "professional excellence," "community awareness," "personal characteristics" and "demographic profile." For demographic profile, the JAAC explicitly notes that "the provincial judiciary should be reasonably representative of the population it serves. This requires overcoming the serious underrepresentation of women and several ethnic and racial minorities." In comparison to the federal government's judicial advisory committees, the JAAC has considerable control over who is recommended for each judicial vacancy....

The most significant difference between these two systems is certainly the federal minister of justice's broader discretion in selecting judges. For the attorney general of Ontario, such discretion is relatively limited, with the JAAC forwarding only a shortlist of names from which to choose for each judicial vacancy. By comparison, for federal appointments the pool of recommended applicants is not attached to any particular judicial vacancy and in practice is quite large. The large size of the recommended applicant pool means that in comparison to Ontario, the federal government has considerable choice as to whom it will select for judicial office....

Data and Results

... A dataset was compiled of judicial appointments by the federal government to provincial superior courts in all ten provinces and by Ontario's provincial government to its provincial courts. Appointments were coded from 1972 to 2013 for federally appointed courts and from 1999 to 2013 for Ontario's provincial courts. For each judicial appointment, the name of the appointee, the year of appointment, the appointee's gender and the political party making the appointment were collected.... In order to consider how party interests may affect judicial appointments, party donations by judicial appointees are used as a proxy for party connection....

While women made up about 5 per cent of lawyers in 1971, and 29 per cent in 1991, by 2014 about 42 per cent of lawyers in Canada were women. In theory, if no barriers to women's advancement to the courts existed, the likelihood of women being appointed to the bench would increase as the pool of eligible candidates grew over time. However, as Figure 1 shows, this type of trickle up theory – that the diversification of holders of entry level positions will, over time,

Figure 1: Women Appointed to Provincial Superior Courts by Federal Government (1972–2013) (Percentages)

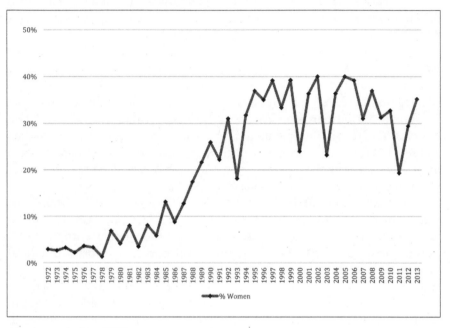

Appointments (N = 2556)

result in the diversification of positions further up the hierarchy – does not tell the full story for superior court appointments by the federal government.

While the reasons why women are not rising to the bench at the same rate as men are multiple and complex, one of the most straightforward explanations is that women are simply not applying for judicial posts. In fact, Minister of Justice Peter MacKay used this argument in 2014 to explain why his Conservative government was not appointing more women to federal courts. Unfortunately, data on the number of women applicants to Canada's federal courts are not available; however, these data have been published for Ontario's provincial courts since 1989. While numbers have fluctuated over this period, overall, there has been a gradual increase in the number of women applicants. In 2012, for example, women made up 58 per cent of applicants to Ontario's provincial courts. Further, a drop in the number of women applicants does not necessarily have to translate into a drop in appointments. Thus, while we cannot be certain, there is reason to believe that recent fluctuations in the number of women appointed to the bench are unlikely to only be a product of a smaller applicant pool.

Into the mid-1980s, women made up less than 10 per cent of federal appointments to provincial superior courts in Canada. Beginning in 1985, this number began to rise (see Figure 1), reaching an impressive 31 per cent by 1992. In 1993, however, the proportion of women appointed decreased dramatically to 18 per cent, before rebounding back to 32 per cent in the following year. This drop came in the same year as the Progressive Conservative government's historic election loss, which had the party fall from 156 to two seats. The remainder of the 1990s saw the appointment of women rest at a fairly even rate, fluctuating between 33 per cent and 39 per cent. We do not see the same type of dramatic dip in the percentage of women appointees in the lead-up to the 1997 federal election, which had the incumbent Liberal party form a majority government for the second time. However, another dramatic dip is observable in 2000, the year of the next federal election, and again in 2003, in the lead-up to the resignation of Prime Minister Jean Chrétien, who was replaced as Liberal leader by Paul Martin in December 2003. The short-lived Martin government saw women appointed to the bench at a relatively high rate (36 per cent in 2004 and 40 per cent in 2005). The 2006 federal election saw Martin's minority government replaced by a Conservative minority government led by Stephen Harper. The 2008 federal election was not accompanied by any sizable dip in the number of women judicial appointees; however, in the year of the 2011 federal election, which saw the Conservatives form a majority government, another dip can be observed. These findings suggest that women are less likely to be appointed in the lead-up to elections (1993, 2000, 2011) and during changes in governing party leadership (2003)....

These fluctuations in the appointment of women judges over time can be better understood when political connections are taken into account. Altogether, donating to a party appears to be disadvantageous for a woman, though the data cannot speak to why this disadvantage may exist. ... Looking at appointments by province helps to further unpack how party connection may adversely affect the likelihood that women will be appointed to the bench. Previous research has found that the number of judges with political connections varies dramatically by province. For example, whereas about 14 per cent of British Columbia's appointees had connections to the party in power between 1989 and 2003, this number was an astounding 90 per cent for Prince Edward Island. [Ed. note: See Reading 4.2.] Consequently, if party connection does affect women appointees differently than men, this difference should be visible by comparing appointments in different provinces.

Table 1: Federal Judicial Appointments in British Columbia by Governing Political Party (1997–2013)

	Liberal (1997–2005)	CPC (2006–2013)
Women appointed	31% (14)	30% (18)
Probable & possible donors	14% (2)	11% (2)
Men appointed	69% (31)	70% (42)
Probable & possible donors	13% (4)	14% (6)

Table 1 looks at federal judicial appointments in British Columbia by Liberal and Conservative governments between 1997 and 2013. Consistent with past research, only a small percentage of judicial appointees, either men or women, made a contribution to the governing party. These low numbers are consistent between the two parties, with the percentage of women donors decreasing only slightly to 11 per cent under the Conservative government and the percentage of men donors rising one percentage point to 14 per cent. The percentage of women appointed in British Columbia also remained stable over this period at about 30 per cent. Altogether, there is little indication that political connection played a large role in federal judicial appointments in British Columbia or that this role was different for men and women over this period.

A very different picture emerges when the lens is turned to other provinces. In their research, Hausegger and colleagues [Reading 4.2] found that Prince Edward Island, New Brunswick, Saskatchewan and Manitoba had the highest number of appointees with connections to the party in power. Because these are smaller provinces, with few judicial appointments year to year, Table 1 combines the appointments for these four provinces (1997 to 2013). From 1997 to 2005, when the Liberals were in power, the donation profiles of women appointees differed considerably from their male counterparts. Whereas 66 per cent of the men appointed during this period were possible or probable donors to the Liberal party, only 25 per cent of women were possible or probable donors. A dramatic shift is visible in both the number of women appointed and their donation profiles with the change to a Conservative government beginning in 2006. Whereas the percentage of men appointees who were possible or probable donors dropped by 7 percentage points to 59 per cent, the proportion of women donors more than doubled from 25 per cent under the Liberals to 58 per cent with the Conservatives. This striking increase in women donors was accompanied by a sizable decrease in the percentage of women appointed: from 1997 to 2005 women made up 35 per cent of appointments in these four provinces, whereas women made up only 23 per cent of appointments under the Conservatives (2006 to 2013).

Table 2: Federal Judicial Appointments in Saskatchewan, Manitoba, New Brunswick and Prince Edward Island by Governing Political Party (1997–2013)

	Liberal (1997–2005)	CPC (2006–2013)
Women appointed	35% (24)	23% (12)
Probable & possible donors	25% (6)	58% (7)
Men appointed	65% (44)	77% (41)
Probable & possible donors	66% (29)	59% (24)

Excludes elevations and promotions. (N) indicates number of appointees.

What do these provincial comparisons tell us about how political connections affect the appointment of women judges? First, the findings appear to corroborate the earlier conclusion made by Hausegger and colleagues that the Liberal government of Jean Chrétien made a conscious effort to increase the number of women on the federal bench. Table 2 in particular illustrates that women appointed during the Liberals' tenure were much less likely to have donated to the party in power than men, indicating that party connection had less influence on the appointment of women judges. By comparison, the data from the first eight years of Harper's Conservative government show little evidence of a similar effort to appoint women. Rather, the dramatic changes seen in the appointments in Prince Edward Island, New Brunswick, Manitoba and Saskatchewan – where the proportion of women appointees who were likely donors more than doubled and the proportion of women appointed decreased by 34 per cent – is consistent with this article's hypothesis that an increase in the proportion of judicial appointees who have donated to the party in power will be accompanied by a decrease in the proportion of women appointed to the bench. These differences between Liberal and Conservative appointments suggest that the Harper Conservatives placed greater priority on the appointment of judges with party connections, a factor more likely to disadvantage women who are less likely to be supporters of the Conservative party....

Conclusion

This article considered whether the influence of party connections adversely affects the appointment of women judges by Canada's federal government. The answer appears to be yes. Using party donations as a proxy for party connection, the data analyzed here suggest that as the number of appointees with connections to the government rises, the number of women appointees falls.

Further, donating to the governing party was found to have a negative impact for the appointment of women judges across both Liberal and Conservative governments. Interestingly, the influence of party connection varies across provinces and time: the disadvantage associated with party connection appears to be most prominent for certain provinces, and though not observed in the lead-up to most of the federal elections and changes to party leaderships analyzed here, there is some evidence that political timing can disadvantage women as well. Further, looking at Ontario's provincial appointment system there is evidence that political connections and timing play a less prominent role in these appointments compared to federal appointments in Ontario.

These are concerning findings and it is worthwhile to think about what steps can be taken to address this apparent weakness of the federal judicial appointment process. First, prioritizing diversity appears to mitigate the effects of political connection. Although not a surprising finding, this research supports the argument made by Sally Kenney that when a representative bench is prioritized by those charged with judicial selection, women are more likely to be appointed. In Canada, this effect is made especially apparent when a governing party appeals to traditional criteria for evaluating judicial candidates, as with the recent tenure of Prime Minister Stephen Harper's Conservative government. The data considered here suggest that this approach is more likely to disadvantage women, not because they are necessarily less meritorious, but because this approach appears to leave greater opportunity for political connections to play a role in appointments. Women are less likely than men to have such connections, particularly with conservative parties, and under these conditions a decrease in the appointment of women appears more likely to follow....

These findings suggest that one of the most effective means for fostering a more representative bench in Canada may simply be to have those in power prioritize diversity. While appealingly straightforward, an appointment system that relies on the benevolence of the party in power is clearly insufficient. The downturn in the number of women appointed under the Harper Conservatives illustrates how progress toward gender parity on the courts is neither steady nor inevitable.

Does this mean that the federal government should reform its appointment system for provincial superior courts? This is a complex question.... A history of political participation is by no means a negative attribute for a future judge to possess. However, if we are to value diversity on the bench, then reforming the appointment process in a way that restrains the influence of political connections makes sense. In this, the nominating committee employed by Ontario may provide a useful model. A nominating committee may help to insulate judicial selection from the influence of political timing (such as elections), or from governments more inclined to take political connections into account when making judicial appointments. Adopting such reforms at the federal level, however, is not a guarantee of success. After all, committees with nominating powers are not necessarily immune to the influence of political connections, especially if the government controls the selection of a majority of its members. On this note, the recent announcement by Justin Trudeau's Liberal government that judicial advisory committees will return to having a minority of their members (three of seven) appointed by the federal government can be seen as a positive development....

No judicial appointment process will be perfect. However, this article provides strong evidence that the system currently employed by the federal government for provincial superior courts is flawed, contributing to a federal bench in which women continue to be underrepresented. Moreover, while the focus of this study has been on how party connections may affect the appointment of women judges, these findings have implications for all persons who aspire to the bench, but who lack political connections. For federal judicial appointments, the status quo facilitates patronage at the apparent cost of diversity.

4.5

The Honourable Malcolm Rowe's Questionnaire
Office of the Commissioner for Federal Judicial Affairs Canada

December 12, 2016, http://www.fja-cmf.gc.ca/scc-csc/nominee-candidat-eng.html. Reprinted with permission.

Under the new Supreme Court of Canada Judicial Appointments Process announced by the Prime Minister on August 2, 2016, any interested and qualified Canadian lawyer or judge could apply for such appointment by completing a questionnaire. The questionnaires were used by the Independent Advisory Board for Supreme Court of Canada Judicial Appointments to review candidates and submit a list of 3 to 5 individuals for consideration by the Prime Minister. Candidates were advised that part of their questionnaire could be made available to the public should they be chosen as the Prime Minister's nominee....

Questionnaire for the Supreme Court of Canada Judicial
Appointment Process

PART 10 – THE ROLE OF THE JUDICIARY IN CANADA'S LEGAL SYSTEM

The Government of Canada needs to appoint judges with a deep understanding of the judicial role in Canada. In order to provide a more complete basis for evaluation, candidates are asked to offer their insight into broader issues concerning the judiciary and Canada's legal system. For each of the following questions, please provide answers of between 750 and 1000 words....

3. Describe the appropriate role of a judge in a constitutional democracy

The role of a judge has common elements at all levels, but there are major differences in what the three levels of courts do in practice. There are also differences as to the roles of the courts depending on the area of the law being dealt with.

First, I will deal with the level of the court. Trial judges are very largely occupied with hearing evidence and finding facts, then applying settled law to the facts as found. Court of appeal judges are mainly occupied in deciding whether errors (of law or principle) have been made by trial judges. In so doing, they seek to maintain consistency in the statement and application of the law in their jurisdiction. From time to time, they also reformulate the law

The Supreme Court is not, primarily, a court of correction. Rather, the role of the Court is to make definitive statements of the law which are then applied by trial judges and courts of appeal. Through the leave to appeal process, the Court chooses areas of the law in which it wishes to make a definitive statement. Thus, the Supreme Court judges ordinarily make law, rather than simply applying it. The Court deals more with constitutional, public law and criminal matters, as well as aboriginal and treaty rights and less with private law. Nonetheless, it remains important for the Court to turn its attention to private law, especially where jurisprudence among the courts of appeal is inconsistent. A further responsibility is to serve as the final court of appeal on matters relating to Quebec's Civil Code. Finally, for issues of over-arching significance for the country, the Court provides an authoritative decision that only it can provide.

I turn now to differences in the role of judges from the perspective of different areas of the law. Judges have a unique role as regards the common law, as it is judge-made. Thus, it is our role to adapt the common law to novel facts and changes in society. This can be contrasted with the role of judges concerning the interpretation of statutes. Applying the proper methodology, the role of judges is to give effect to the will of the legislature, as the making of statute law is the role of elected representatives. The Civil Code does not conform to this common law paradigm and must be dealt with in the structure of analysis of the civilian system.

The role of judges as regards criminal law involves statute law (mainly the Criminal Code), common law (e.g. mens rea) and the Legal Rights guaranteed by sections 7–14 of the Charter. I have addressed common law and statute law. I turn now to the Charter.

The Charter is an affirmation of those rights and liberties that are to be defended against infringement by the state. Judges decide whether such infringement has occurred and, if so, what remedy should follow. This is a profound change in the role of judges. In the past 34 years, Canadians have come to accept and embrace this enhanced role for judges. The wisdom and well-founded principles that have informed this role in the jurisprudence of the Supreme Court reflect favourably on our country. Charter interpretation will always be a work in progress, albeit one in which foundational concepts that have been set out should be maintained.

In addressing the role of judges vis-a-vis aboriginal and treaty rights, one should begin by recognizing that these rights are sui generis. Conceptually, they are distinct, albeit they must be given practical effect in the context of other areas of the law. The historical context should inform decisions related to these rights, as should the realities today of indigenous peoples, both on and off their traditional lands. Concerning foundational issues (e.g. inherent right to self-government), the Supreme Court has chosen to seek to encourage, facilitate and guide governments and indigenous peoples to give full expression to aboriginal and treaty rights, rather than the Court making definitive statements. Doing so prematurely could undermine efforts toward nation to nation resolution of issues directed to the goal of reconciliation. Development of the law, including indigenous law, will be a process with many steps. This does not detract from the need to continue to develop and apply the law relating to such topics as the interpretation and application of treaties, as well as land claims and the protection of aboriginal rights in lands subject to a claim. Thus, in many ways, the role of judges differs as regards aboriginal and treaty rights.

The division of powers between the federal and provincial governments involves issues as old as Confederation. Much of the jurisprudence that still governs is from the period when the Judicial Committee of the Privy Council (JCPC) was the final court of appeal for Canada.

Among the goals of stare decisis are predictability and stability in the law. At the same time, we have embraced the idea (ironically initially stated by the JCPC) that "the constitution is a living tree." Relatively few recent cases deal with the division of powers. (The securities legislation reference is an exception.) Judges have a role in such cases that requires them to be mindful of changes in society (often driven by technology) that can mean that to be effective regulation must be at the federal level. Is what Viscount Haldane wrote a century ago how we should determine whether actions of the federal or provincial governments are within or beyond their jurisdiction? In this regard, judges should have regard to changes in the role of governments relating especially to the economy and technology in dealing with such issues. On occasion, revisiting the division of powers might well induce governments to pursue co-operative federalism, which is often beneficial.

Finally, I would note the role of judges as guardians against the improper use of authority conferred by the legislature on the executive or a regulatory authority. It is fundamental that a citizen can seek redress against the improper use of authority. This is largely a matter of administrative law. In this role the judge should respect the proper exercise authority by the executive, e.g. a Minister, or a regulatory authority, while not hesitating to quash or require remedial action where such authority has not properly been exercised. This is necessary to uphold the rule of law....

5. To what extent does the role of a Supreme Court of Canada Justice allow for the reconciliation of the need to provide guidance on legal questions of importance to the legal system as a whole with the specific facts of a case which might appear to lead to an unjust result for a party?

Most decisions of the Supreme Court serve the dual function of providing a definitive statement of the law and also doing justice according to law in the immediate dispute. (In criminal appeals as of right, often the purpose is limited to doing justice in the immediate dispute.) The dispute between the parties offers a platform for the Court to speak authoritatively as to the law on issues that warrant such a statement. The Court having set out a general statement of relevant law, it then has to apply the law to the facts of the case. One would expect that a just result would follow from the proper application of the law to the facts of a given case. Where the court is giving effect to the Charter or developing the common law, it has considerable leeway in decision-making. The Court's role is more constrained as regards decisions of the legislature and of the executive, e.g. a Minister.

The legislature may have enacted provisions of a statute that give rise in a given case to a sense of harshness or unfairness. The Supreme Court, like any court, looks to the rules of statutory interpretation. As well, where circumstances indicate, the Court will consider whether the statutory provisions are constitutional, having regard to the Charter. Beyond this, it is the duty of the Court to give effect to the decision of the legislature. Similarly, concerning a decision of the executive, if it is accordance with law, then the Court has no role to substitute its view of the public good for that, for example, of a Minister. Each branch of government has a role that should be respected by the others, under the rule of law.

In its role as the ultimate guardian of the rule of law, the Court is required to give authoritative answers to questions like the following: What authority appertains to the federal government and what to provincial governments? When can one level of government legally exercise its jurisdiction notwithstanding that in so doing it encroaches on the jurisdiction of the other? What are the limits of state conduct established by the Charter? Seen another way, what rights are held by individuals or groups that, ordinarily, cannot be derogated from by government? In what circumstances would such derogation be warranted, under Section 1 of the Charter? Where issues arise critical to the country that require legal clarification, what guides exist for governments to act, examples being the *Patriation Reference* (1982) and *Secession Reference* (1995)?

A separate body of jurisprudence has arisen in the context of s.35 of the *Constitution Act, 1982*. Aboriginal and treaty rights, protected by s.35(1), are sui generis. They are being recognized and affirmed in ways that are not yet fully defined. On issues such as the inherent right to self-government and indigenous law, the Court has a unique role with a different dynamic, less engaged in formulating definitive statements, more in setting out guide posts for on-going negotiations between governments and indigenous peoples. The Court's role will almost certainly evolve as part of a broad effort to achieve reconciliation. This will occur while the law relating to treaties, as well as aboriginal title will continue to develop with the jurisprudence.

The Supreme Court maintains and develops the structure of law in Canada. Stability and predictability are important to maintain that structure. But, adaptation to changes in society, including changes in shared goals, is critical to the law's development. It is important to operate from first principles, while also considering practical results. It is no less important to eschew ideological positions. Should the Court lead or mirror a shared sense of justice? The answer is, of course, both. Generally, it should lead when the time is ripe to do so, having regard to the needs and aspirations of Canadians.

4.6

A Judge Unbound

Leonid Sirota

Double Aspect, October 16, 2016, https://doubleaspect.blog/2016/10/17/12167/. Reprinted with permission.

The Prime Minister has at last named his choice to fill the vacancy left on the Supreme Court by the retirement of Justice Thomas Cromwell. It is Justice Malcolm Rowe, now at the Newfoundland and Labrador Court of Appeal. For all the concern – of the Prime Minister's and his government's own making – about whether he would be prepared to breach the convention of regional representation on the Supreme Court in the service of an identitarian quest to appoint, say, an aboriginal woman, Justice Rowe's appointment will, on the surface, be an unremarkable one. The convention stands undisturbed – and perhaps stronger thanks to having been affirmed by a unanimous resolution of the House of Commons – and the Court gets yet another successful and well-connected white male member. (Justice Rowe will be the first Newfoundlander to sit on the Supreme Court, however, so his appointment is groundbreaking in that way – a step forward for old-fashioned regional diversity, if not for the contemporary demographic sort. Justice Rowe, who was born in 1953, is also relatively old – among his new colleagues, only Justice Moldaver was older when he was appointed to the Supreme Court; many were substantially younger.)

Justice Rowe's appointment is noteworthy, however, because of his views on his new job – disclosed by the government as part of a questionnaire that he, as well as others who applied, had to complete in order to be considered. There are other interesting nuggets there, which others have highlighted. There's Justice Rowe's assertion that he was in fact the author of an opinion ostensibly signed by his court [*Ed. note*: Omitted from Reading 4.5; refer to full questionnaire online.]; there's the fact, highlighted by Dave Snow, that he took a French immersion course just before applying, suggesting that his French might be rather rusty, at best; there's a rather turgid writing style, though it is perhaps unfair to judge a man's prose by the way in which he filled out a form. But let me focus on Justice Rowe's ideas about judging and, especially, the Supreme Court. These ideas are, to me, concerning if not disqualifying.

Justice Rowe states that "[t]he Supreme Court is not, primarily, a court of correction," which is certainly true, so far as it goes. He is right to say that "[t]hrough the leave to appeal process, the Court chooses areas of the law in which it wishes to make a definitive statement." But his conclusion – that "the

Supreme Court judges ordinarily make law, rather than simply applying it" – is still remarkable. It is worth recalling, though admittedly Justice Rowe is not the only person who does not, that as John Austin pointed out in *The Province of Jurisprudence Determined*, the phrase "judge made law" was itself made up, by Jeremy Bentham, and was intended as "disrespectful and therefore," Austin thought, "injudicious." More importantly, the idea that judges – those of the Supreme Court anyway – usually "make law rather than simply applying it" suggests that Justice Rowe will not feel bound by the constraints that precedent and statutory and constitutional text are thought to impose on judges, including those of the highest courts. The view is not exactly original – Chief Justice McLachlin has expressed her own sympathy for it, at least extra-judicially – but it is disconcerting nonetheless. For the Rule of Law to exist, courts, like other government institutions, ought to be bound by the law. If judges feel that they can simply make the law up, indeed that this is what they are expected to do, the Rule of Law is not long for this world.

Now, in the very next paragraph, Justice Rowe says that – unlike in common law adjudication – "the role of judges concerning the interpretation of statutes ... is to give effect to the will of the legislature." But of course a substantial part of the Supreme Court's work does in fact involve interpretation of statutes – whether of the Criminal Code, the Income Tax Act, or of other legislation. At best, then, Justice Rowe's previous statement about judges as law-makers is thoughtless, or reflects a certain confusion about what it is that the Supreme Court does. (It may well be that this is what's going on here: as prof. Snow has observed, Justice Rowe is simply wrong to claim that "[r]elatively few recent cases deal with the division of powers.") At worst, he is deliberately saying one thing and its opposite, the better to justify any approach he might be pleased to take in a given case. As Benjamin Oliphant has pointed out, this is indeed something of a tendency in Justice Rowe's answers – and also in the jurisprudence of the Court which he is about to join.

Justice Rowe's view of the Supreme Court's place in the Canadian constitutional framework is, ultimately, the smugly self-assured one that is prevalent in the Canadian legal community. Judges make law – especially, it would seem, constitutional law, where Justice Rowe sees room for reviewing the Privy Council's division of powers jurisprudence (though he does not explain on what issues), while the plebs (including, presumably, its representatives in Parliament) gladly and wisely accepts the pronouncements of the *patres iudices*: "Canadians," Justice Rowe informs us, "have come to accept and embrace this enhanced role for judges. The wisdom and well-founded principles that have informed this role in the jurisprudence of the Supreme Court reflect favourably on our country." Some might even find Justice Rowe's frankness in stating these views refreshing in comparison with the balls-and-strikes boilerplate future members of the U.S. Supreme Court are now generally expected to spout. Yet to me, a judiciary that is no more bound by a sense of modesty than it is by the law itself is a distressing prospect. Considering that the Prime Minister and his advisers seem to be comfortable with it, I may have to get used to it too.

4.7
Key Terms

Concepts

accountability
gender representation
group representation
ideological judicial appointments
impartiality
judicial education
judicial independence
merit
nominating committee
parliamentary scrutiny
patronage
regional representation
screening committee
transparency
"unconscious bias"
V.O. Key's "iron law of politics"

Institutions, Events and Documents

Advisory Board for Supreme Court of Canada Judicial Appointments (2016)
Commissioner for Federal Judicial Affairs (1977)
Judicial Advisory Committees (JACs)
Meech Lake Accord (1987)
National Committee on the Judiciary (1966)
Ontario Judicial Appointments Advisory Committee (1989)
Reference re Supreme Court Act, ss. 5 and 6, [2014] 1 S.C.R. 433
Saskatchewan Judges Affair (1982)
Supreme Court Act (1875)

5

Judicial Independence, Ethics and Discipline

Disputes are a fact of life in political communities. In the course of their personal and commercial interactions, individuals become involved in disputes over what happened (questions of fact) and what the rule is that governs their situation (questions of law). Typically, neither party is willing to allow the other to unilaterally answer these questions for fear that an adversary will exploit any ambiguity of fact or law to his or her own advantage. The self-interest of both parties prevents either from serving as arbiter of the dispute. What is needed is an outside third party who is independent of both disputants and thus can be expected to render an impartial inquiry and resolution of the dispute.

While the need for a mechanism of dispute resolution is common to all societies, different cultures have met this need in different ways. Canada's legal system evolved from the distinctive British common law tradition,[1] which means that Canada has been fortunate enough to inherit the British institutional practices and safeguards of judicial independence that for centuries have made Great Britain an exemplary model for the protection of individual freedom.[2] While the tradition of judicial independence is much older, it became an official part of Britain's "unwritten constitution" with the *Act of Settlement* in 1701. During the seventeenth century, the Stuart kings had flagrantly violated the independence of the British courts. After James II was deposed in the Glorious Revolution of 1688, Parliament and the English bar were eager to provide more certain guarantees for judicial independence in the future. As part of the *Act of Settlement*, they forced the new king, William III, to agree to legal provisions securing the independence of the judiciary. Judicial tenure of office was established on the principle of *quamdiu se bene gesserint* – "during good behaviour" – and henceforth judges could be removed only by address of both houses of Parliament. In addition, judicial salaries had to be ascertained and established by law and were no longer set by royal decree.

Having established judicial independence at home, the British Parliament was somewhat reluctant to introduce it in British North America. Originally, colonial judges served only "at pleasure." This practice inevitably led to abuses by colonial governors, and these abuses were one of the grievances enumerated in the Declaration of Independence by the American revolutionaries in 1776. Significantly, no sooner had the Americans successfully thrown off British political rule than they entrenched the British provisions for judicial independence in their new state and federal constitutions. It was not until the 1830s and 1840s that similar provisions for judicial independence were made for the rest of British North America.[3]

At Confederation in 1867, the now familiar terms of judicial independence were written into the *Constitution Act*. Section 99 of the *Act* provides that "judges of the superior courts shall hold office during good behaviour, but shall be removable by the Governor General on address of the Senate and House of Commons." In 1960, this was amended to require mandatory retirement at the age of seventy-five. Section 100 requires that the "salaries, allowances and pensions of the judges of the Superior, District, and County Courts ... be fixed and provided by the Parliament of Canada" (see Reading 3.2).

These tenure provisions apply explicitly only to the superior courts created pursuant to section 96. This has raised the question of whether the judges of the Supreme Court and Federal Court of Canada, County and District Court judges, and the judges of the section 92 provincial courts, enjoy less independence than their superior court counterparts. Writing in 1976, Professor Lederman argues that, although the independence of these courts is not constitutionally entrenched in explicit, written provisions, it remains part of Canada's "unwritten constitution." While tenure of office in these courts is provided for only by ordinary statute, Lederman declares that these provisions are "'ordinary' in form only, because they are declaratory of basic constitutional principles and traditions" (Reading 5.1). The constitutional reforms of 1982 appear to further reinforce the independence of the Supreme Court of Canada by entrenching its present size and composition.

Historically, the concept of judicial independence extends beyond these formal, institutional guarantees. It also stands for the convention of non-interference in the judicial process by members of the executive and legislative branches of government, as well as the non-interference of judges in the political process. The former branch of the non-interference doctrine was illustrated in the "1976 Judges Affair," when it came to light that several different members of Pierre Trudeau's Cabinet had personally telephoned judges to inquire about cases they were in the process of deciding. While none of these ministers ultimately resigned, the government issued a policy guideline stating that members of the Cabinet could not communicate with the members of judiciary regarding matters before them. Since then, this policy has been strictly observed, and when federal cabinet ministers break it, they typically resign.

In recent decades, increased attention has been given to a new dimension of the old issue of judicial independence: the judges' collective administrative independence from the executive branch of government. Historically, the Departments of Justice at both the federal and provincial levels have been responsible for administering their respective judicial systems. This has resulted in multiple roles for the respective Attorneys General and Ministers of Justice, who are also responsible for arguing the Crown's position in cases before these same courts. An increased sense of the potential for conflict of interest in this situation resulted in a series of reforms. In 1977, the federal government created the Commissioner for Federal Judicial Affairs to administer federal judicial business independently of the Minister of Justice. The Commissioner is responsible for the administration of the salaries, benefits and programs of all federally appointed judges, for most of the judicial recruitment process, and for the staff and budget for the Canadian Judicial Council (see below). Several provinces, including British Columbia, Manitoba, New Brunswick and Ontario, have also created professional court administrators.

The issue of judicial independence reappeared shortly after the adoption of the *Charter*. Section 11(*d*) of the *Charter* provides that "any person charged with an offence has the right [to] ... a fair and public hearing by an independent and impartial tribunal." A provincial court judge in Ontario argued that the executive branch's discretion to set judicial salaries without enactment by the Legislature undermined his independence and thus violated the *Charter*. In *Valente v. The Queen* (1985),[4] the Supreme Court ruled that the section 11(*d*) requirement of an "independent and impartial tribunal" does include "financial security" (as well as "security of tenure" and "administrative independence"), but found that it was not violated in this instance. The following year, the Court rejected a similar claim by a federally appointed judge in *The Queen v. Beauregard* (1986).[5]

However, the issue soon returned to the Court. Responding to the public deficit/debt crisis of the 1990s, several provincial governments imposed across-the-board salary reductions on all public servants – including judges. Provincial judges in Alberta, Manitoba and Prince Edward Island responded by challenging their salary reductions as a violation of section 11(*d*) of the *Charter*. While there were factual differences in each province, the Supreme Court consolidated the three cases and decided them together in its 1997 decision *Reference re Remuneration of Judges of the Provincial Court (PEI)* (Reading 5.5).

This time, the Court accepted the judges' claim. The Court's reasoning and remedy were both novel and controversial. Writing for the majority, Chief Justice Lamer argued that, not only did section 11(*d*) guarantee financial security as part of the independence of provincial (section 92) judges, but that judicial independence is also an "unwritten constitutional principle" implied by the preamble to the *Constitution Act, 1867*. As for a remedy, Lamer ruled that this "unwritten constitutional principle" requires all provinces to create independent judicial compensation commissions to set judges' salaries. In a scathing dissent, Justice La Forest denounced the majority judgment as contrary to "reason and common sense [and as] subvert[ing] the democratic foundations of judicial review." The reference to judicial independence in the *Charter*, La Forest emphasized, appears in a section intended to benefit those accused of crimes, not judges. In the absence of any credible textual basis for the majority's ruling, Justice La Forest characterized it as "tantamount to enacting a new constitutional provision" and ordering the creation of "what in some respects is a virtual fourth branch of government." Notwithstanding considerable unhappiness in provincial capitals, all ten provinces complied with this ruling by creating new judicial compensation commissions, as specified by Chief Justice Lamer. Indeed, even the federal government amended the *Judges Act* to create a new judicial compensation commission for section 96 court judges. Predictably, judicial salaries increased dramatically in the wake of the *Provincial Judges Reference*.[6]

No matter is more critical to the maintenance of judicial independence than the procedure for removing judges guilty of serious misconduct or gross incompetence. While such exigencies must be provided for, the removal procedure must be structured so as to minimize the potential for political abuse. Section 99 of the *Constitution Act, 1867* puts in writing the British convention of requiring address by both houses of Parliament in order to remove a judge for violating the norm of "good behaviour." In the first one hundred years after Confederation, there were only five petitions filed with Parliament for removal of a judge, four of which were in the nineteenth century, and several of which involved alcoholism. For various reasons (including the death of one judge and the resignation of another), Parliament did not vote to remove any of the judges involved. However, in 1967, Parliament was preparing to vote on a motion to remove Ontario Supreme Court Judge Leo Landreville when he resigned instead. Landreville had been the mayor of Sudbury before his appointment to the bench, and it was alleged that as mayor he had accepted bribes in the form of stock. The investigation of the charges against Landreville had been carried out by a one-judge commission authorized by Parliament. This process became the subject of controversy and eventually a successful lawsuit by Landreville.[7]

In 1971, dissatisfaction with the way in which the Landreville investigation had been handled led Pierre Trudeau's government to create the Canadian Judicial Council (CJC). The CJC has thirty-nine members, and consists of the Chief Justices, Associate Chief Justices and other senior members of all the superior courts. It is chaired by the Chief Justice of the Supreme Court of Canada. The CJC investigates complaints about federally appointed judges, and can ultimately recommend their removal to Parliament. Similar councils have been created for provincially appointed judges in all provinces except Prince Edward Island, which only has three provincially appointed judges. Often these councils have the ability to recommend more punishment short of removal, as when the Ontario Judicial Council suspended Ontario Justice Berna Zabel for thirty days for wearing a "Make America Great Again" hat to court the day after the Donald Trump won the 2016 U.S. Presidential election.[8] The transfer of the responsibility to investigate allegations of judicial misconduct from the executive branch to the judges themselves was intended to reduce the potential for political abuse and to enhance the independence of the judiciary. In recent years, the CJC has also become something of an advocate for federally appointed judges, often calling for greater administrative autonomy for section 96 courts.

The CJC came close to exercising its new powers of removal in 1982 at the conclusion of its investigation into allegations of misconduct by then Justice Thomas Berger of the British Columbia Court of Appeal. On November 5, 1981, the federal government and all the provinces except Quebec reached a compromise agreement on the constitutional reforms proposed by the Trudeau government. One of the compromises was the federal government's agreement to delete those sections that dealt with the protection of "aboriginal rights." In the weeks following, Justice Berger publicly criticized Canadian political leaders for this action on at least two occasions (although those rights were subsequently added to the final text of the *Constitution Act, 1982*; see Chapter 10). These criticisms were reported in the press, and a justice of the Federal Court, upon reading these reports, lodged a complaint of judicial misconduct with the CJC. The CJC appointed a committee of investigation and invited Justice Berger to testify in his own defence. He refused but sent two letters defending his actions as a matter of conscience and a question of principle (Reading 5.2). The committee members' final report concluded that Justice Berger was guilty of judicial misconduct and stated that they would have recommended removal from office had it not been for the unique circumstances of the incident (Reading 5.2). The CJC modified the investigation committee's report. Its final report to the Minister of Justice declared that Justice Berger's actions had been "indiscrete" but that they did not constitute grounds for removal from office.

Justice Berger announced his intention to resign anyhow and did so several months later.

The Canadian press gave the "Berger Affair" considerable publicity, and some editorials criticized the CJC for trying to censor or punish Justice Berger for exercising his "freedom of speech." The late Chief Justice Bora Laskin was sufficiently upset with what he considered to be a gross misunderstanding of these events that he publicly addressed the issue in a speech to the Canadian Bar Association in September, 1982 (Reading 5.3). The late Chief Justice's remarks are important because they demonstrate that judicial independence cuts both ways. Not only does it prohibit politicians from interfering in the judicial process, but it also prohibits judges from interfering in the political process. In response to Berger's appeal to individual conscience, Laskin argued that a judge's "abstention from political involvement is one of the guarantees of his impartiality, his integrity, his independence."

The 1990s witnessed more, not less, controversy over allegations of judicial misconduct. In 1996, for the first time in its history, the CJC voted (twenty-seven to two) to recommend to Parliament to remove Judge Jean Bienvenue from the Quebec Superior Court. In the process of sentencing a woman who had been convicted of murder for slitting her husband's throat with a razor, Judge Bienvenue made several disparaging comments about women and Jews killed in the Holocaust. The CJC found that "the public can no longer reasonably have confidence" in him. However, Bienvenue resigned before Parliament was able to vote on the recommendation.

The most publicized incident of the decade was the 1999 "McClung Affair" (Reading 5.4). This incident arose out of a sexual assault case known as *R. v. Ewanchuk* (1999)[9] and turned on the issue of "implied consent." The accused, Ewanchuk, admitted that he had sexually touched the complainant but said that he thought she did not object. When she did, on several occasions, he stopped. This defence of "honest but mistaken belief" raised a nest of prickly issues that had been a source of controversy and conflict between feminists and criminal defence lawyers for decades. When does a sexual advance become a sexual assault? Is any unsolicited advance an assault? Or must woman signal that a sexual advance is or is not welcome? Can this signal be non-verbal and/or implied? How is the partner supposed to know?

The trial judge acquitted Ewanchuk of sexual assault by relying on the defence of implied consent. The Alberta Court of Appeal, in a judgment written by Justice John McClung, upheld that acquittal. The Supreme Court reversed both the trial court and McClung and ruled that there is no defence of "implied consent" in Canadian law. This ruling was warmly praised by feminists but harshly criticized by criminal defence lawyers. The latter claimed that it took away the defence of "honest but mistaken belief" and thus violated the requirement of *mens rea*.

In a concurring opinion, Supreme Court Justice L'Heureux-Dubé undertook a caustic, point-by-point repudiation of McClung's judgment from the Alberta Court of Appeal. Angered by what he considered a personal attack, McClung responded in a letter to the *National Post* and a subsequent interview. McClung's public response was immediately and strongly condemned. McClung then apologized privately to L'Heureux-Dubé and publicly via a letter in the *National Post*. The apologies notwithstanding, women's and other rights advocacy groups filed complaints against McClung with the CJC alleging misconduct and demanding his removal. Complaints were also filed against McClung for *obiter dicta* he had written in a 1996 judgment in the widely publicized gay rights case of *Vriend v. Alberta*, a ruling that also was subsequently reversed by the Supreme Court. McClung's judgment in *Vriend* had already gained notoriety for its outspoken denunciation of "crusading, ideologically determined judges [and] the creeping barrage of special interest constituencies that now seem to have conscripted the *Charter*."[10] In this respect, the gauntlet had been thrown down several years earlier. The whole affair was given added poignancy by the fact that Judge McClung is the grandson of Nellie McClung, one of Canada's best-known suffragettes and early advocates of women's rights.

For a week straight, national and metropolitan newspapers were filled with editorials, guest columns and letters to the editor denouncing and defending both the Court's decision and the two feuding judges. There has been nothing quite like this before or since. In the end, the CJC ruled that McClung's public retort to L'Heureux-Dubé and his remarks about homosexuality in *Vriend* were "inappropriate" and "detract from respect for equality rights." However, the Council stopped at this reprimand and did not recommend removal. The McClung Affair is the subject of the public documents presented in Reading 5.4.

In the last decade, the CJC has made national headlines in complaints involving three judges: Justice Paul Cosgrove of the Ontario Superior Court of Justice, Manitoba Court of Queen's Bench Justice Lori Douglas and Federal Court Justice Robin Camp. In 2009, after a long legal battle, the CJC recommended the removal of Cosgrove, who it found to have engaged in misconduct when he abused his power and gave an apprehension of bias towards the defence in a murder trial. Like Bienvenue, Cosgrove resigned before Parliament could remove him.

In 2010, Alex Chapman brought an allegation of sexual harassment against Justice Lori Douglas in front of the CJC. At the time of the complaint, Lori Douglas was the Associate Chief Justice of the Court of Queen's Bench for Manitoba (Family Division), having originally been appointed to the Court of Queen's Bench in 2005. The complaint dated back to 2003, when Douglas was still a lawyer. Chapman alleged that Douglas' husband, lawyer Jack King, tried to convince Chapman (then King's client) to have sex with Douglas. King had also directed Chapman to a website with thirty sexually explicit photos of Douglas. In testimony before the CJC, King later admitted he had done this, but both he and Douglas claimed it was all done without her knowledge. Chapman argued that Douglas was herself aware, and that he had met her, with King, on two occasions. Chapman's complaint to the CJC alleged inappropriate touching and sexual harassment from Douglas at these meetings.

A CJC inquiry into Justice Lori Douglas began in 2012. Ultimately, the inquiry did not concern the allegations of sexual harassment, which a Review Panel had previously decided did not warrant further consideration. This is because Douglas' husband claimed to have posted the photos and propositioned Chapman without her knowledge (Chapman's own testimony and personal history with the law made his credibility highly questionable).[11] Instead, the inquiry primarily concerned Douglas' knowledge of the existence of the photos in the first place. Prior to appointment, federally appointed judges are asked, "Is there anything in your past or present which could reflect negatively on yourself or the judiciary, and which should be disclosed?" Douglas knew the photos existed in her husband's personal possession, but did not know he had distributed them. She answered "no" on the questionnaire. Did her knowledge of explicit photos mean she should have answered yes, even though the photos were taken before she was a judge?

Ultimately, the CJC Inquiry Committee never completed its investigation. It was initially delayed by Douglas's call for judicial review on account of perceived bias against her, which led the entire five-person committee to resign in 2013. When a new Inquiry Committee was struck in 2014, its proceedings were dominated by battles over whether its members needed to see the photographs of Douglas (they eventually did). In late 2014, an agreement was reached whereby Douglas would retire as a judge in May, 2015 – ten years after her initial appointment, enabling her to receive a reduced pension – and the CJC would suspend its inquiry. In Reading 5.6, R. Lee Akazaki, past President of the Ontario Bar Association, criticizes the CJC for its actions, describing Douglas as "the victim of her late husband's malfeasance." For Akazaki, the CJC's actions have increased the "vulnerability of the independence and integrity of the Canadian judiciary," and could ultimately erode public confidence in the courts. That the CJC would be responsible for such actions is indeed ironic.

The most recent public experience involving judicial discipline at the CJC concerns Justice Robin Camp. While a justice at the Alberta Provincial Court, Camp presided over *R v. Wagar*, in which a man was accused of sexually assaulting a nineteen-year-old homeless woman. Camp acquitted Wagar, but during the trial, he made a number of comments that would later receive scrutiny. He repeatedly referred to the complainant as "the accused," called her "unsavoury" and, in a line reminiscent of Justice McClung two decades earlier, said the complainant "had the ability, perhaps learnt from her experience on the streets, to tell [Wagar] to fuck off." Most infamously, Camp asked the complainant, "why couldn't you just keep your knees together?" The Alberta Court of Appeal ordered a new trial because of Justice Camp's comments (although Wagar was subsequently acquitted in the new trial), and four law professors subsequently launched a complaint against Camp. Because Camp was now a member of the Federal Court, that complaint was sent to the CJC. Although Camp appeared repentant and described his comments at trial as "unforgiveable," in February, 2017, the CJC recommended to the federal Minister of Justice that Camp be removed as a judge.[12] Along with Justices Cosgrove and Bienvenue, Camp was only the third judge whose removal the CJC recommended. Before Parliament could vote, Camp resigned. Excerpts from the initial letter of complaint and the CJC's letter are reproduced here as Reading 5.7.

While all involved, including Camp himself, agreed that his views were repugnant and inconsistent with the law, a debate remains over whether the CJC's recommendation of removal was just, particularly after Camp had undertaken a course on sexism and sexual assault law in Canada following the complaint. Brenda Cossman, a law professor who was tasked with educating Justice Camp, testified at his inquiry that he should not be removed. In Reading 5.8, she describes Camp as a man who was "not like the misogynist monster I had read about," but instead "earnestly apologetic, open-minded and eager to learn." Camp's repentance and honesty shows that he is not beyond redemption, Cossman argues. Those who "believe in the power of education" should not be so quick to punish. Lauren Heuser (Reading 5.9) disagrees. She argues that Camp "exceeded all bounds of judicial propriety by making personal pronouncements on the complainant's character." For Heuser, Camp's inability to empathize meant removal was the proper punishment.

The Justice Camp ordeal has reopened a debate over the need for judicial education seminars on topics such as sexism and "unconscious bias." This debate dates back to the late 1980s and early 1990s. After the McClung Affair, feminist law professors such as Kathleen Mahoney argued that "the federal government should not appoint or promote judges unless they have taken gender sensitivity courses to root out anti-female bias in the courts."[13] Conservative commentators such as Gwen Landolt of REAL Women countered that such education seminars, even when voluntary, had become "an indoctrination centre for feminist thought."[14] In the wake of Camp's resignation, in 2017 former federal Conservative interim leader Rona Ambrose sponsored a bill in the House of Commons that would require federally appointed judges to undergo sexual assault training, which would be developed by sexual assault survivors and support organizations. The bill, which as of this writing is stalled in the Senate, would also require the CJC to report on the number of sexual assault cases heard by judges without training. CJC spokesperson Joanna Smith noted that the Council supported some aspects of the bill, but claimed the reporting requirements "may infringe on judicial independence" by "opening the door for special interest groups dictating the kinds of education judges should adopt."[15] With Conservative legislators pushing for mandatory judicial education, and the CJC condemning "special interest groups," times have certainly changed. The debate over judicial education and its effect on judicial independence, however, remains as vigorous as ever.

Supreme Court judges themselves have been the subject of complaints to the CJC for comments outside the courtroom, though none have resulted in official censure. Conservative advocacy group REAL Women filed complaints against Justice Bertha Wilson (in 1990) and then Justice McLachlin (in 1991) for speeches that advanced feminist interpretations of the law. In 1999, a complaint was made against Justice L'Heureux-Dubé for engaging in advocacy on behalf of gay rights in public comments, during a period in which the Court was hearing several high-profile cases about same-sex partnerships.[16] And in 2001, a complaint was launched after Justice Michel Bastarache gave a candid interview with *Lawyers Weekly* in which he criticized the Supreme Court's expansive approach to the rights of the criminally accused and to Aboriginal rights.[17] In each instance, the CJC rejected the complaint. With the expanded political involvement of judges under the *Charter of Rights*, the Council clearly has adopted a more lenient policy for off-the-bench speeches by sitting judges, while the judges themselves see no need to recuse themselves on cases involving policy issues on which they have spoken publicly. Chief Justice McLachlin's 2015 speech, wherein she claimed Canada attempted to commit "cultural genocide" against Aboriginal peoples,[18] reflects this new normal.

Canadian judges already are nevertheless experiencing unprecedented pressures on traditional norms of judicial independence (Reading 5.7). Ian Greene and colleagues[19] interviewed 101 appellate court judges in the early 1990s, and found that two-thirds reported some form of threat to judicial independence. The most common threat reported was pressure from interest groups for "politically correct" decisions – an indirect rebuff of the "identity politics" that has motivated rights-advocacy organizations' use of *Charter* litigation to advance their policy goals. Criticism by politicians and the media was a concern for judges as well. Interestingly, seven judges complained that the CJC itself was a threat to their judicial independence because it gave Chief Justices too much influence over the careers and working conditions of the other judges.

Greene and his colleagues concluded that there is no doubt that this upsurge in perceived threats to judicial independence is almost completely *Charter*-driven. As the Court has moved toward Paul Weiler's "policy-making" model (Reading 2.1), the desire for greater public accountability has increased, just as Weiler would predict. However, Weiler's analysis is completely at odds with the view advanced by former Chief Justice Dickson in the *Beauregard* (1986) decision and quoted by then Justice McLachlin in the 1989 case *Mackeigan v. Hickman*:

> The rationale for this two-pronged modern understanding of judicial independence is recognition that the courts are not charged solely with the adjudication of individual cases. That is, of course, one role. It is also the context for a second, different, and equally important role, namely as protector of the Constitution and the fundamental values embodied in it.... In other words, judicial independence is essential for fair and just dispute-resolution in individual cases. It is also the lifeblood of constitutionalism in democratic societies.[20]

According to two former Chief Justices of the Supreme Court of Canada, the need for judicial independence becomes even greater when the courts assume the additional role of "protector of the Constitution." According to Weiler's model, appellate courts exercising the function of judicial review (with constitutional veto power) will be subject to more, not fewer, demands for institutional accountability. Much of the current controversy in Canada over the Supreme Court's role under the *Charter* stems from these two conflicting understandings. It also speaks to Thomas Bateman's assessment that the great deception of the *Charter* project has been to conceal how "what appears as a legal project is really a political project."[21]

How can we reach a perfect balance between judicial independence and accountability? This is the $64,000 question (though if set by a judicial compensation commission, it might be higher). Greater democratization and transparency with respect to judicial appointments is one suggestion, although that does nothing for judicial accountability once appointed. Term limits, confirmation votes or even judicial elections – alternatively used by American and European constitutional and high courts – will increase accountability, though at the price of independence. These comparative examples may seem repugnant to Canadians long accustomed to Professor Lederman's assumption that judicial independence is a prerequisite of the "rule of law." But they help us to "think the unthinkable," in Weiler's words; that is, the institutional implications of increasing the policy-making role of courts for the tradition of judicial independence. These examples encourage us to assess the potential costs (and not just the potential benefits) of the greater policy-making role for Canadian courts made possible by the *Canadian Charter of Rights and Freedoms*.

NOTES

1   Except for Quebec, whose civil law originated in France. However, since criminal law and procedure are matters of federal jurisdiction, the criminal law process in Quebec is based on the same common law practices as the rest of Canada.

2   Note that there was no national judiciary under the first United States Constitution, the Articles of Confederation. The more centralist Constitution of 1787 created a national Supreme Court and provided for judicial independence in essentially the same terms as the *Act of Settlement*. The practice of electing judges in some American states, referred to in Chapter 4, dates from a later period in American history.

3   A more detailed account of this matter may be found in Peter H. Russell, *The Judiciary in Canada: The Third Branch of Government* (Scarborough, ON: McGraw-Hill Ryerson, 1987), pp. 78–87.

4   *Valente v. The Queen*, [1985] 2 S.C.R. 673.

5   *The Queen v. Beauregard*, [1986] 2 S.C.R. 56.

6   See Morton and Knopff, *The Charter Revolution and the Court Party* (Toronto: Broadview, 2000), pp. 108–109. Today, judicial salaries for provincial lower courts range from $216,000 (Newfoundland and Labrador) to $294,000 (Alberta). Federally appointed judges range from $315,300 to a high of $405,400 for the Chief Justice of the Supreme Court of Canada (Office of the Commissioner for Federal Judicial Affairs Canada, "Guide for Candidates," October, 2016, http://www.fja-cmf.gc.ca/appointments-nominations/guideCandidates-eng.html). Battles over judicial salaries between governments and judicial compensation commissions have continued in recent years, particularly in the Atlantic provinces. See Sue Bailey, "N.L. mulls $32,000 pay hike for judges amid fiscal crunch," *CBC News*, May 8, 2016, http://www.cbc.ca/news/canada/newfoundland-labrador/judges-raise-newfoundland-deficit-budget-1.3572491.

7   For a fuller account of these matters, see Martin L. Friedland, *A Place Apart: Judicial Independence and Accountability in Canada* (Canadian Judicial Council, 1995), pp. 82–90.

8   Sean Fine, "Judge who wore Trump hat suspended," *Globe and Mail*, September 13, 2017, p. A9. "Make America Great Again" was Trump's slogan during the campaign. Zabel also announced in court that he had "voted" for Trump, which he later explained at his disciplinary hearing referred to the fact that he had predicted Trump would win.

9   *R. v. Ewanchuk*, [1999] 1 S.C.R. 330.

10   *Vriend v. Alberta*, [1998] 1 S.C.R. 493; see also F.L. Morton, "Canada's Judge Bork: Has the Counter-Revolution Begun?" *Constitutional Forum* 7, no. 4 (1996), pp. 121–126.

11 See "Accuser agreed to sex payment, Manitoba judge inquiry told," CBC News, July 18, 2012, http://www.cbc.ca/news/canada/manitoba/accuser-agreed-to-sex-payment-manito-ba-judge-inquiry-told-1.1252551; Christie Blatchford, "Douglas case full of dishonourables," *National Post,* November 30, 2013, p. A15.

12 Prior to the Council's report, a five-person CJC Inquiry Committee also recommended his removal. Of the twenty-three judges on the Council who made Coram, four dissented regarding Camp's removal.

13 "McClung reprimanded for critical remarks made at L'Heureux-Dubé," *National Post,* May 22, 1999, p. A4.

14 "Political Correctness Undermines Judicial System: Reader," Letter to the editor from C. Gwendolyn Landolt, *Lawyer's Weekly,* August 2, 1991, p. 5.

15 Joanna Smith, "Judicial council fears 'special interest groups' shaping sexual assault training," *Canadian Press,* May 16, 2017.

16 F.L. Morton, "L'Heureux-Dubé Crosses the Line," *Law, Politics and the Judicial Process in Canada,* 3rd ed. (Calgary: University of Calgary Press, 2002), pp. 206–211.

17 Cristin Schmitz, "Supreme Court goes 'too far': judge," *National Post,* Jan. 13, 2001; Schmitz, "The Bastarache interview: reasoning to results at SCC," *Lawyers Weekly,* Jan. 26, 2001, p. 19.

18 Sean Fine, "McLachlin: A history of 'cultural genocide'," *Globe and Mail,* May 29, 2015, p. A1.

19 Ian Greene, Carl Baar, Peter McCormick, George Szablowski and Martin Thomas, *Final Appeal: Decision-Making in Canadian Courts of Appeal* (Toronto: James Lorimer, 1998), pp. 183–191.

20 *Mackeigan v. Hickman* [1989], 2 S.C.R. 796. Hickman was the Chief Justice of Nova Scotia who refused to testify before the Royal Commission investigating the Donald Marshall affair. Hickman represented the Royal Commission.

21 Thomas Bateman, "The Charter Revolution and the Efficient Part of Canada's Constitution," *Voegelin View,* June 20, 2017, https://voegelinview.com/charter-revolution-efficient-part-can-adas-constitution/.

5.1

The Independence of the Judiciary
W.R. Lederman

From Allen M. Linden, ed., *The Canadian Judiciary* (Toronto: Osgoode Hall, 1976), 1–12. Reprinted with permission.

Introduction

An independent judiciary has long been an established feature of our Constitution in Canada, coming to us as a primary part of our great inheritance of English public law and governmental institutions. My purpose here is an ambitious one – to explain the essential *positive* functions of an independent judiciary as an integral part of our total constitutional system. This involves examining the relations between the judiciary on the one hand, and parliaments and cabinets on the other, as they play their respective parts in making and applying laws for our country, at both the provincial and the federal levels. Also, of course, this task requires some examination of the institutional arrangements that are the basis of judicial independence, and some assessment of the relevance of such independence to the needs of our time for good government under law.… What I have to say falls under three main headings:

1.   Our English Constitutional Inheritance,
2.   Essential Operational Elements of Judicial Independence, and
3.   Judicial Independence, Democracy, and the Rule of Law.

1. Our English Constitutional Inheritance

Sir Arthur Goodhart has told us, in his distinguished lectures on "English Law and the Moral Law," that the English are not as much without a constitution as they frequently profess to be. He gives four principles which he maintains are equally basic as first or original principles of the English constitution. They are briefly as follows: (1) "That no man is above the law" (among other things, this means that all official persons, the Queen, the judges and members of Parliament included, must look to the law for the definition of their respective positions and powers). (2) "That those who govern Great Britain do so in a representative capacity and are subject to change.… The Free election of the members of the House of Commons is a basic principle of English constitutional law." (3) That there shall be freedom of speech, of thought and of assembly. (4) That there shall be an independent judiciary.

The fourth and final principle which is a basic part of the English constitution is the independence of the judiciary. It would be inconceivable that Parliament should today regard itself as free to abolish the principle which has been accepted as a cornerstone of freedom ever since the Act of Settlement in 1701. It has been recognized as axiomatic that if the judiciary are placed under the authority of either the legislative or the executive branches of the Government then the administration of the law might no longer have that impartiality which is essential if justice is to prevail.

Sir William Holdsworth expressed a very similar view on the status of the judiciary. He said:

The judges hold an office to which is annexed the function of guarding the supremacy of the law. It is because they are the holders of an office to which the guardianship of this fundamental constitutional principle is entrusted, that the judiciary forms one of the three great divisions into which the power of the State is divided. The Judiciary has separate and autonomous powers just as truly as the King or Parliament; and, in the exercise of those powers, its members are no more in the position of servants than the King or Parliament in the exercise of their powers ... it is quite beside the mark to say that modern legislation often bestows undivided executive, legislative and judicial powers on the same person or body of persons. The separation of powers in the British Constitution has never been complete. But some of the powers in the constitution were, and still are, so separated that their holders have autonomous powers, that is, powers which they can exercise independently, subject only to the law enacted or unenacted. The judges have powers of this nature because, being entrusted with the maintenance of the supremacy of the law, they are and always have been regarded as a separate and independent part of the constitution. It is true that this view of the law was contested by the Stuart kings; but the result of the Great Rebellion and the Revolution was to affirm it.

... For present purposes, two things are noteworthy about the Canadian judicial system. First, while it is true that the guarantee of removal from office only by joint address of the Parliament of Canada is explicitly specified by the *B.N.A. Act* just for the Superior courts of the Provinces, this most emphatically does not mean that there is no constitutional protection for the security of tenure in office of other judges in the total judicial system just described. The same point applies concerning the explicit guarantee of salaries in the *B.N.A. Act*, which mentions only the Superior, District and County courts of the Provinces. The position in my view is that the Superior Courts, by virtue of the explicit provisions for them in the *B.N.A. Act* afford the prototype – the model – which should be followed for all other Canadian courts.

In other words, I am saying that security of tenure and salary for judges in Canada, as a matter of basic constitutional law and tradition, is not limited to the strictly literal reach of sections 99 and 100 of the *B.N.A. Act*. I remind you of the words of Goodhart and Holdsworth. They make it clear that essential provision for the independence of the judiciary generally has long been deeply rooted as an original principle in the basic customary law of the constitution. In Britain herself, the explicit provisions about judicial security are in the ordinary statutes – but these ordinary statutes, including the *Act of Settlement* itself, manifest the more fundamental unwritten constitutional principle I have described, as Goodhart and Holdsworth insist. The same point can and should be made about the status of Canadian judges. In Canadian Federal statutes we have provisions ensuring the independence of the County and District Court judges, the judges of the Federal Court of Canada and the judges of the Supreme Court of Canada itself. In various Provincial statutes, security is likewise provided for provincially-appointed judges, for example the Provincial Criminal Court judges in Ontario. My point is that though these are ordinary statutory provisions, they are "ordinary" in form only because they are declaratory of basic constitutional principles and traditions.

Now of course, for the judges who depend on ordinary statute in this respect, there is room for variations in just how their basic constitutional independence is to be implemented. But, provided they are guaranteed security of tenure in office until a reasonable retirement age, subject only to earlier removal for grave misconduct or infirmity, after full due process by way of inquiry, then the basic constitutional mandate for their independence is satisfied. I am not arguing that all judges are, or have to be, under the parliamentary joint address procedure in order to be secure and independent. Adequate due process leading to removal for cause may take several forms. In this respect, we should note the recent advent of the Canadian Judicial Council, under which the federally-appointed judges as a group themselves apply due process and self-discipline concerning any of their own members against whom complaints may have been entered. This is a progressive step in safeguarding the independence of the judiciary that is quite in harmony with the concept of independence....

2. Essential Operational Elements of Judicial Independence

What I have said so far implies that the elements of judicial independence fall into two groups, individual elements and collective ones.

The individual elements may be stated in these terms. A judge is not a civil servant, rather he is a primary autonomous officer of state in the judicial realm, just as cabinet ministers and members of parliament are the primary official persons in the executive and legislative realms respectively. No minister of the Crown, federal or provincial, and no parliament, federal or provincial, has any power to instruct a judge how to decide any one of the cases that comes before him. If a parliamentary body does not like the judicial interpretation of one of its statutes in a particular case, then it can amend the statute, use different words, and hope that this will cause a different judicial interpretation when next the statute is before a court. But that is all a parliamentary body can do or should attempt to do under the constitution. As for ministers of the Crown, when the government is an interested party in litigation or prosecution before the courts, then the minister can instruct counsel to appear and argue in court for the result the executive government would prefer, but that is all a minister can do or should attempt to do under the constitution. The judge remains autonomous, both as to his determinations of fact and his interpretations of the applicable law. As Chief Justice Laskin said recently, the judge must supply his own answers from his own resources, and thus there is something of the loneliness of the long distance runner in every judge. Long term security of tenure in office with the corresponding guarantee of salary ensures that the judge can maintain this position, especially as he is not allowed to hold any other office concurrently with his judicial office.

The reason for this individual independence of judges is best explained in the words of the late Robert MacGregor Dawson, as follows:

> The judge must he made independent of most of the restraints, checks and punishments which are usually called into play against other public officials.... He is thus protected against some of the most potent weapons which a democracy has at its command: he receives almost complete protection against criticism; he is given civil and criminal immunity for acts committed in the discharge of his duties; he cannot be removed from office for any ordinary offence, but only for misbehaviour of a flagrant kind; and he can never be removed simply because his decisions happen to be disliked by the Cabinet, the Parliament, or the people. Such independence is unquestionably dangerous, and if this freedom and power were indiscriminately granted the results would certainly

prove to be disastrous. The desired protection is found by picking with especial care the men who are to be entrusted with these responsibilities, and then paradoxically heaping more privileges upon them to stimulate their sense of moral responsibility, which is called in as a substitute for the political responsibility which has been removed. The judge is placed in a position where he has nothing to lose by doing what is right and little to gain by doing what is wrong; and there is therefore every reason to hope that his best efforts will be devoted to the conscientious performance of his duty....

... But, assuming the appointment of able people to judicial office, this is not in itself enough to ensure that the judicial system functions well as a whole and in all its parts. There are problems of the whole system of courts that have an important bearing on the independence of the judiciary....

... First, my outline of the many parts that make up the unitary Canadian judicial system shows that responsibility for necessary appointments and legislation is shared between the federal and provincial levels of government. Accordingly, for the solution of these system problems, there must be a great deal of federal-provincial consultation and collaboration at the cabinet and parliamentary levels. This applies also to the provision of adequate financial support for the judicial system. Generally speaking, the administration of justice in Canada has been seriously under-financed, and both levels of government are to blame for this.

In the second place, in certain vital respects, collective responsibility for the effective operation of the judicial system should be invested in the judges themselves. Here the role of the Chief Justices and the Chief Judges is very important, as spokesmen for themselves and their brother judges. This refers particularly to the assignment of judges to case lists, and to determination of priorities for the grouping and hearing of cases. In my view, to safeguard the basic independence of the judiciary, the Chief Justices and the Chief Judges should be in operational control of these matters for their respective courts, with adequate administrative staff responding to their directions.

I have now spoken of the individual and the collective elements that go to make up an independent judiciary. But there is a final question that remains to be answered. What, in the end, is the main purpose of maintaining an independent judiciary? Sir William Holdsworth said, "The judges hold an office to which is annexed the function of guarding the supremacy of the law." My third and final topic is an attempt to explain why he said this.

3. Judicial Independence, Democracy, and the Rule of Law

At this point I return with particular emphasis to the special importance of our superior courts of general jurisdiction. We say that we have the rule of laws rather than of men, but this has a special dependence on the men who are the superior court judges. Constitutionally they have the last word on what the laws mean, so, does this not really mean the personal supremacy of superior court judges? I deny this for the following reasons. It is basic to the rule of law that doctrines, ideas and principles are supreme, not persons. The great case of *Roncarelli v. Duplessis* confirmed this as the position in Canada. In aid of this supremacy, we find that the superior courts possess under the constitution a final supervisory review function over lesser courts, and over officials, boards and tribunals of all kinds, to ensure that they stay within the limits of the powers respectively given them by the constitution, or by statute, or by common law. The superior courts have power to nullify decisions of other officials and tribunals for excess of jurisdiction or breach of natural justice in procedure. But here we encounter that basic constitutional dilemma – Who watches the watchman? Who checks the superior courts themselves for excess of jurisdiction or breach of natural justice in procedure? The answer is that, at this primary level of constitutional responsibility, the superior court judges must be trusted to obey the laws defining their own functions, and to check themselves. Believing in the supremacy of law, they must themselves scrupulously obey it. They must be all the more careful about this precisely because there is no one to review their powers, as they review the powers of others. Judicial restraint on these terms at the superior court level is the ultimate safeguard of the supremacy of the law, enacted and unenacted, to use Holdsworth's terms. Remember too that at the intermediate and final levels of judicial appeal you have a plural bench, so that a majority of several judges is necessary to reach a decision. Several heads are better than one, and in the process purely personal peculiarities are likely to be cancelled out. It seems to me that this is as close as we can get to the rule of laws rather than of men.

There are further reasons for confidence in the independent judiciary, and I am speaking now of all judges, both provincially-appointed and federally-appointed. The conditions on which they hold office mean that they have a personal career interest to be served by the way they go in deciding cases that come before them. The laws to be interpreted and applied must be expressed in words, and words are not perfect vehicles of meaning. Hence there is frequently room for partisan interpretation, and that is precisely what you would get if one of the interested parties was in a position to make his interpretation prevail. At least the judges have no such personal interest in biased interpretation one way or the other, hence, in the words of Sir Arthur Goodhart, they are able to bring to the administration of the law that impartiality which is essential if justice is to prevail.

Finally, I assert that the power of the independent appointed judiciary is neither undemocratic nor anti-democratic. The statutes of our popularly elected legislatures do have priority, and will be made to prevail by the courts, if the parliamentarians speak plainly enough. [*Ed. note*: This was written in 1976, before the adoption of the *Charter of Rights* in 1982.] But often their statutes speak only in general terms that must be further particularized by someone else, or they speak in ambiguities that must be resolved by someone else. These tasks fall to interpretative tribunals, especially the courts at all levels of the judicial system. Judicial procedure respects the individual by giving him a fair hearing and allowing him and his counsel to argue that the reason of the law is in their favour. This is as much a feature of democracy as it is to give the same citizen a vote, as a means of influencing his own fate. As for judicial law making, the judicial tasks just referred to do involve discretions that are at times legislative in character. But I must stop here, for the judge as lawmaker is another large subject, with its own place later in this book.

5.2

The Berger Affair
Berger Blasts "Mean-Spirited" Ministers
Ottawa Citizen, November 10, 1981, A4. Reprinted with permission.

Justice Tom Berger said Monday the decision of all Canadian first ministers to abandon native rights as one of the prices for agreement on the constitution was "mean-spirited and unbelievable."

The B.C. Supreme Court justice also said the compromise provincial override clauses on major parts of the *Charter of Rights* is a cause for grave concern in the light of the treatment of minorities by all Canadian governments.

Berger was head of the Royal commission on the MacKenzie Valley pipeline, which heard the concerns of native people about industrial development in the North.

"Last week our leaders felt it was in the national interest to sacrifice the rights because they felt they were serving the greater good in reaching an agreement."

"It was mean-spirited. There are a million and more natives in Canada: Indians, Inuit and Métis and for the most part they are poor and powerless. They were the people who were sacrificed in this deal."

"That is the whole point of minority rights, that they should not be taken away for any reason."

Berger said "I can still hardly believe that it has happened. We have had 10 years of increasing consciousness of native rights and land claims."

"It has had an impact on many people but not on Canadian statesmen. It passed right by them."

Berger said the blame lies with all first ministers including René Lévesque since he did not point to the denial of native rights as a reason for his refusal to sign the agreement.

Berger said Canadians, concerned about the protection of unpopular minorities, can take little comfort from the fact that the federal government insisted on a five-year renewal of every action to override the fundamental, legal and equality rights in the *Charter of Rights*.

Berger said the problem is always "the first time when an inflamed majority wants to strike at a defenceless minority, not five years later when it is irrelevant."

Report of the Committee of Investigation to the Canadian Judicial Council
May 31, 1982

From the material annexed it can be seen that Mr. Justice Berger intervened in a matter of serious political concern and division when that division or controversy was at its height. His office and his experience as a Royal Commissioner (appointments made because of his office and his competence), obviously made his comments newsworthy. He described the decision of the first ministers to "abandon" native rights to be "mean-spirited and unbelievable." In his article he criticized the loss of Quebec's veto and argued for one amending formula in preference to another. He again attacked the first ministers for "repudiating" native rights and argued for the restoration of s.34 "for the recognition and confirmation of aboriginal and treaty rights of Indians, Inuit and Métis."

Justice Berger, while agreeing that what he did may be unconventional, argues that the issues he discussed transcended partisan politics. Because the resolution of the issues in his opinion bore directly on how we were to be governed for the next 100 years, he felt obliged to speak out publicly. He refers to the late Mr. Justice Thorson and Chief Justice Freedman speaking on public issues. We do not have the facts with relation to those matters and are not in a position to comment on them.

Justice Berger also notes that no complaint was made to the Judicial Council about his address to the Canadian Bar Association. It is true that it appears that judges, in speaking to legal bodies, are accorded somewhat greater leeway in expressing their views than they are in speaking to the general public. However, it should be noted that a great part of the address seems to be a thoughtful philosophical discussion of the nature of Canada and its parts and the importance of its preservation. It may be, on reflection, that some of the statements made in this address, although not of as strident a nature as the material complained of, were inappropriate for a judge. It may also be that because he was speaking to an audience of lawyers and judges, the media and others took no notice of his remarks.

Justice Berger's views, which he eloquently defends in his letter to Chief Justice Laskin, are not in issue. What is in issue is his use of his office as a platform from which to express those views publicly on a matter of great political sensitivity. It is possible that other members of the judiciary held opposing views, as obviously elected representatives did, with equal conviction. Justice Berger makes reference to the Honourable Mr. Martland's statements with regard to the *Charter of Rights* after he retired from the bench. The analogy is not a helpful one except to underline the principle that judges do not speak out on political issues while holding office. Mr. Martland at the time he gave his interview was no longer a judge. His franchise had been restored and there was no longer any possibility that he would be called on to determine issues as an impartial judge. In our view, Justice Berger completely misses the mark when he says "does it make all the difference that nothing was said until he (Mr. Martland) retired?" It makes the greatest of difference. Politically controversial statements by a citizen who is no longer a judge and who can never again be called on to be a judge, do not destroy the necessary public confidence in the impartiality of judges.

Not only must judges be impartial, the appearance of impartiality, as Lord Devlin pointed out, must be maintained for the fair and proper administration of justice. If a judge feels compelled by his conscience to enter the political arena, he has, of course, the option of removing himself from office. By doing so, he is no longer in a position to abuse that office by using it as a political platform. One would not have expected Justice Berger's views to have been given the media attention they were given if he had not been a judge but merely a politician expressing his views in opposition to other politicians.

Judges, of necessity, must be divorced from all politics. That does not prevent them from holding strong views on matters of great national importance but they are gagged by the very nature of their independent office, difficult as that may seem. It can be argued that the separation of powers is even more emphatic here than in England. In England, High Court judges have the right to vote. Here, federally appointed judges are denied the right to vote in federal elections and in a number of provinces they have been deprived by statute of a right to vote in provincial elections, and in some cases, even in municipal elections.

It is apparent that some of the native peoples are unhappy with s.35 of the Canadian *Charter of Rights and Freedoms*. If Justice Berger should be called on to interpret that section, for example, the meaning to be given to the word "existing" in the phrase "the existing aboriginal and treaty rights of the aboriginal peoples of Canada," would the general public have confidence now in his impartiality? After Justice Berger spoke publicly on the necessity for Quebec retaining a veto, his brother judges in Quebec were called on to determine whether such a right existed.

Conclusion

In our view it was unwise and inappropriate for Justice Berger to embroil himself in a matter of great political controversy in the manner and at the time he did. We are prepared to accept that he had the best interests of Canada in mind when he spoke, but a judge's conscience is not an acceptable excuse for contravening a fundamental rule so important to the existence of a parliamentary democracy and judicial independence. To say that not all judges are cast in the same mould, as does Justice Berger, is only to state the obvious. On every great matter of political concern it would be probable that judges would hold opposing views privately and, if Justice Berger's view is acceptable, it would be possible to have judges speaking out in conflict one with the other because they hold those opposing views from a sense of deep conviction.

We say again if a judge becomes so moved by conscience to speak out on a matter of great importance, on which there are opposing and conflicting political views, then he should not speak with the trappings and from the platform of a judge but rather resign and enter the arena where he, and not the judiciary, becomes not only the exponent of those views but also the target of those who oppose them.

This is not a question, as Mr. Justice Berger suggests, which each judge must decide for himself. That question has been answered for him from the moment he accepts the Queen's Patent as a judge.

So far as the material before us reveals, Justice Berger's impropriety has been an isolated instance. Chief Justice McEachern also advised us in his Submission that Justice Berger had disengaged himself from the constitutional debate as soon as the Chief Justice spoke to him. Nevertheless, we view his conduct seriously and are of the view that it would support a recommendation for removal from office. There are, however, in addition to those already noted, special circumstances which make this case unique. As far as we are aware, this is the first time this issue has arisen for determination in Canada. It is certainly the first time the Council has been called on to deal with it. It is possible that Justice Berger, and other judges too, have been under a misapprehension as to the nature of the constraints imposed upon judges. That should not be so in the future. We do not, however, think it would be fair to set standards *ex post facto* to support a recommendation for removal in this case.

The judicial office is one which confers important privileges, obligations and protections necessary to the carrying out of the duties of one of Her Majesty's judges. A judge must accept the duty to protect that office, his fellow judges and the public from political controversy as the best way of maintaining "the historic personal independence" of judges.

We conclude that the complaint *non se bene gesserit* is well founded but, for the reasons stated, we do not make a recommendation that Justice Berger be removed from office.

A Matter of Conscience
Justice Thomas R. Berger

Letter to Canadian Judicial Council, December 3, 1981.

CONFIDENTIAL   3rd December, 1981.
The Honourable Chief Justice Bora Laskin,
c/o Canadian Judicial Council
130 Albert Street
Ottawa, Ontario, K1A 0W8
Dear Chief Justice:

I understand that you and your colleagues on the Judicial Council are concerned by my intervention in the constitutional debate. I spoke at Guelph University on November 10th. The following week the *Globe and Mail* published an article of mine on the constitutional accord of November 5th. I enclose copies of both the speech and the article. The Prime Minister has accused me of making a foray into politics.

What I have done may be unconventional. But it was not a venture into politics in any ordinary sense. It is not as if I had discussed the ordinary stuff of political debate – inflation, interest rates, the budget, or the nationalization of the Asbestos Corporation. The issues which I discussed transcended partisan politics. In fact, when the vote on the constitutional resolution was taken this week, there were dissenting votes by members of all parties in the House.

This was, after all, a moment of constitutional renewal, unique in our country's history. The First Ministers (except Premier Lévesque) had signed a constitutional accord. I felt a sense of great dismay about the accord. My remarks were directed not to the Prime Minister or any one of the premiers, nor to any political party, but to our leaders collectively.

While these are questions that rise above narrow partisanship, they are nevertheless political questions in the broad sense. Indeed, they bear directly on the question of how we are to be governed for the next 100 years. It was for this reason that I felt obliged to speak out publicly.

What I did is not without precedent. Mr. Justice Thorson used to participate in the campaign for nuclear disarmament. Chief Justice Freedman went on television in October, 1970, to declare his support for the invoking of the *War Measures Act*. On the occasion of his visit to Vancouver to open the new Court House in September, 1979, Lord Denning told us that the trade unions in England were a threat to the freedom of that country. No doubt each of these judges felt compelled to speak out. It may be said that it would undermine the independence of the judiciary if judges were constantly engaged in such activity. But they are not. These interventions by judges are infrequent, even rare.

I enclose a copy of the Prime Minister's remarks made here in B.C. He taxes me for not supporting him at an earlier stage of the debate (he had also done this at a press conference a week earlier) and then goes on to urge that my conduct has been offensive. In fact, I did support his *Charter* before he abandoned it. I enclose a speech I made to the annual meeting of the Canadian Bar Association in Vancouver in September, to an audience of 1,000 or more lawyers and judges, presenting the case for the *Charter*.

(I remind you that Lord Scarman is one of the leading figures in England who has publicly urged the adoption of a *Charter of Rights* in that country.) I was, I am afraid, outspoken. Yet none of the lawyers, judges or politicians there present complained. I do not understand why what was opportune before November 5th became "inopportune" after November 5th. The views I expressed had not changed (though couched, perhaps, in more forceful language after November 5th).

What I did was done after considering carefully what I should do, and with the best interests of my country in mind. I do not believe that anything I have done has impaired the independence of the judiciary.

The Prime Minister has, with respect to my intervention, urged the judges to "do something about it." I believe it is a mistake to think it is possible to place fences around a judge's conscience. These are matters that no tidy scheme of rules and regulations can encompass, for all judges are not cast from the same mould.

Mr. Justice Addy's letters have arrived. I do not think anything that he has said calls for a reply beyond what I have already written in this letter. It is a question of principle. Should the Judicial Council issue edicts on matters of conscience? If you and your colleagues agree with Mr. Justice Addy, there is nothing more to be said. I believe, however, that these are matters that individual judges must decide for themselves.

Yours sincerely,
Thomas R. Berger
cc: The Hon. Chief Justice McEachern

Outspoken B.C. Judge Resigning
Calgary Herald, May 15, 1982.

VANCOUVER (CP) – Justice Thomas Berger, an outspoken champion of minority rights who refused to accept that his judicial robes include a gag, will be stepping down from the B.C. Supreme Court this summer.

And when he departs on August 27, he will leave an imprint that, flouting tradition, endorses the concept of judges defending minorities against parliamentary incursions.

"I believe a judge has the right, a duty, in fact, to speak out on an appropriate occasion on questions of human rights and fundamental freedoms," Berger said last year.

On Wednesday, Berger resigned from the bench, citing differences between himself and Supreme Court of Canada Chief Justice Bora Laskin and the Canadian Judicial Council over constraints imposed on public speaking by judges.

Starting in September, Berger will teach constitutional law and civil liberties at the University of B.C. two days a week and resume a limited law practice....

... In a letter addressed to Justice Minister Mark MacGuigan, he said his differences with Laskin and the Judicial Council are well known.

He said this extended beyond the dispute over his intervention in a constitutional debate in November, 1981, when he said that on rare occasions a judge may have an obligation to speak out on human rights. Berger said his departure also concerns Laskin's views on judicial involvement in royal commissions.

MacGuigan said Thursday he has no qualms about accepting Berger's resignation, but he was unhappy that Berger made public his letter of resignation now when he plans to remain a judge until August 27.

MacGuigan said judges should avoid public controversies.

5.3

The Meaning and Scope of Judicial Independence
Chief Justice Bora Laskin

From an address to the Annual Meeting of the Canadian Bar Association, September 2, 1982. Reprinted with permission.

... I hope I do not abuse this privilege if I strike a serious note in this address. It would please me better if I could banter and amuse, which I may assure you is not beyond my capacity. But special reasons, to which I will come shortly, impel me to speak more soberly on a subject of fundamental importance to the judicial office. That subject is the meaning and scope of judicial independence. I would have thought that its meaning would have been well understood over the years in which the Judges have exercised their judicial roles. I would have thought that there was a clear public understanding that Judges cannot be measured in the same way as other holders of public office or any members of the public. In my understanding, and in that of most of the members of the legal profession and members of the Bench, Judges are expected to abstain from participation in political controversy. Obviously, considering the storm that has brewed early this year on the Berger affair, I was somewhat mistaken. The limited public role of the Judge, one perfectly clear to me, seems to have been misunderstood or forgotten, even by lawyers, let alone by members of the press and of the public.

A fundamental principle has pervaded the judicial role since it took root in the reign of Queen Anne. It was established – not without fits and starts – that Judges would no longer hold office at the pleasure of the Crown, at the pleasure of the government. They would have security of tenure, once assigned to their position, and would hold office during good behaviour to the age of retirement. Their duration in judicial office would no longer depend on governmental whim, and they could be removed only for judicial misbehaviour.

What this imported, as it evolved over the years, was the separation of the executive and the judiciary; no admixture of the one with the other; no mixture of the judiciary in politics or political controversy; correspondingly, no intermeddling of the executive with the judiciary; each branch was to be independent of the other, left alone to carry on its separate duties. For the Judges, they had utmost freedom of speech in the discharge of their judicial functions. Unbelievably, some members of the press and some in public office in this country, seem to think that freedom of speech for the Judges gave them the full scope of participation and comment on current political controversies, on current social and political issues. Was there ever such ignorance of history and of principle?

A Judge, upon appointment – and I am speaking here of appointments which cover all members of our provincial and federal superior courts as well as the Supreme Court of Canada – takes a prescribed oath of office. It is a short oath which is common to all superior court Judges, being as follows:

> I do solemnly and sincerely promise and swear that I will duly and faithfully, and to the best of my skill and knowledge, execute the powers and trust reposed in me as....
>
> So help me God.

But it is invested with all the authority and surrounded by all the limitations that are imported by the principle of judicial independence and that are spelled out in the *Judges Act*, the federal statute which defines the judicial office.

What does the *Judges Act* say about the judicial office? It says quite clearly that a Judge may not, directly or indirectly, engage in any occupation or business other than his judicial duties. There is a limited exception for him or her to act as commissioner or arbitrator or adjudicator or referee or conciliator or mediator, if so appointed in respect of a federal matter by the federal Government; and similarly, if so appointed by the provincial government in respect of a provincial matter. These are short-term, temporary assignments not intended to give a Judge a regular assignment to carry out a non-judicial role. Two recent illustrations of the distinction may be mentioned. A few years ago, the Government of Canada wished to appoint a Judge as a Deputy Minister of an executive department. He was unwilling to accept the position unless he retained his security as Judge. The Government was prepared to go along. I felt it my duty as Chief Justice to protest and did so vigorously, pointing out that it was either the one position or the other, but not both.

A Judge who wishes to accept an executive appointment could not remain Judge at the same time. In the case I mentioned, the Judge put more store on his judicial position than on the proposed executive position. The matter was accordingly dropped. The same thing happened a little later in Ontario when the provincial government wished to appoint an Ontario Supreme Court Judge as Chairman of the provincial Workmen's Compensation Board. Again, I protested; if the Judge wished to accept the provincial appointment, he should resign from the Bench; he could not be both Judge and non-judicial or executive functionary. The principle was accepted and the matter was abandoned.

These instances concerned permanent appointments to governmental positions. The authorized exceptions to allow governments to appoint Judges to special assignments as, for example, by order-in-council or by a limited inquiry, do not involve Judges in executive government or in governmental operations. They are asked to perform a particular service, with generally a short-term duration, although some inquiries like the MacKenzie Valley Pipeline and the McDonald Inquiry into the RCMP did go on for some years.

I am myself not a great supporter of the use of Judges to carry out short term assignments at the behest of a government, federal or provincial. Apart from anything else, it is not always convenient to spare a particular Judge, given the ever increasing workload of all Courts. Moreover, there is always the likelihood that the Judge will be required to pass on policy, which is not within the scope of the regular judicial function. But I recognize that governments will continue to ask Judges (generally with the consent of their Chief Justice) to perform these limited tasks. The important thing to remember is that these short-term assignments are not intended to establish a career for the Judge in the work he or she carried out. The Judge is expected to make his or her report to the particular government and to regard the assignment as completed without any supplementary comment. Any comment or action is for the government; the Judge himself or herself is *functus*, done with the matter. This has been the general behaviour of Judges who have accepted and carried out special or particular governmental assignments. Whatever has been the value of the inquiry must rest in what it says – the Judge is certainly not intended to be a protagonist, however enamoured he or she may become of the work. Nor is the Judge intended to make a career of the special assignment.

There has been a large increase in the number of federally-appointed Judges in the last decade. Indeed, there are now 466 superior court Judges throughout Canada and 232 county and district court Judges. I do not take account of provincial court Judges who are appointed by provincial governments. The increase in the number of federally-appointed Judges increased the burden of judicial administration, the need to monitor complaints (which are inevitable, even if in most cases misconceived) and the need also to provide outlets for judicial conferences. It was beyond the capacity of Parliament to provide for these matters and they also raised sensitive matters engaging the independent position of the Judges.

In 1971, a new policy was introduced by Parliament to govern supervision of judicial behaviour or, I should say, alleged misbehaviour....

... The Canadian Judicial Council came into being in October, 1971 and has had a considerable amount of business in the past decade. It has exercised its powers of inquiry and investigation with great care, seeking on the one hand to satisfy complaints against alleged judicial misbehaviour and on the other hand to protect the reputation of the Judge against unfounded allegations. The most common type of complaint received against Judges has to do with objections to their judgments. Laymen have misconceived the role of the Council: it is not a court of appeal to rectify decisions alleged to be in error; for that there are established appeal courts, and the Council repeatedly has to tell complainants that the recourse is an appeal, not an invocation of the powers of the Canadian Judicial Council.

Since the Canadian Judicial Council has a statutory mandate to conduct inquiries into alleged judicial misbehaviour, it can hardly ignore a responsible complaint. In the Berger case, the complaint was made by a long-serving superior court Judge. Was the Canadian Judicial Council to ignore it? At least, it had the obligation to consider whether the complaint merited investigation, that it was not merely frivolous. Those members of the press who became engaged with the complaint in Justice Berger's support seemed entirely ignorant of the mandate of the Canadian Judicial Council. They appeared to be of the view that a Judge's behaviour was for him to measure, that it was not open to the Canadian Judicial Council to investigate, let alone admonish a Judge in respect of a complaint against objectionable behaviour. This was clearly wrong and could have been established by some modest inquiry.

My mention of the Berger case is not to reopen an issue which is closed. It is only to set the record straight on the statutory function and duty of the Canadian Judicial Council, whoever be the subject of a complaint to it. In view of the obvious misunderstanding to which the Berger incident gave rise, it seemed important to me that I, as Chairman, should underline the role and duty of the Canadian Judicial Council, however distasteful it may be to assess the behaviour of a fellow Judge. I would have welcomed, as I always do, the balance provided by the media, by the press, and I regret that it was unfortunate that they did not discharge that responsibility on this occasion.

There was one respect in which members of the press, and indeed some public "bodies" and members of Parliament, showed their ignorance of judicial propriety. It was said that pursuit of the complaint against Justice Berger was an interference with his freedom of speech. Plain nonsense! A Judge has no freedom of speech to address political issues which have nothing to do with his judicial duties. His abstention from political involvement is one of the guarantees of his impartiality, his integrity, his independence. Does it matter that his political intervention supports what many, including the press, think is a desirable stance? Would the same support be offered to a Judge who intervenes in a political matter in an opposite way? Surely there must be one standard, and that is absolute abstention, except possibly where the role of a Court is itself brought into question. Otherwise, a Judge who feels so strongly on political issues that he must speak out is best advised to resign from the Bench. He cannot be allowed to speak from the shelter of a Judgeship.

In the Berger case, the Judge's intervention was on critical political and constitutional issues then under examination by the entire Canadian ministerial establishment. No Judge had a warrant to interfere, in a public way, and his conviction, however well intended, could not justify political intervention simply because he felt himself impelled to speak. To a large degree, Judge Berger was reactivating his McKenzie Valley Pipeline inquiry, a matter which was years behind him and should properly be left dormant for a political decision, if any, and not for his initiative in the midst of a sensitive political controversy.

The Canadian Judicial Council – one member of Parliament accused us of being engaged in a witch hunt – was badly served by those who, obviously, did no homework on the Council's role and on its obligation. There was another matter which seemed rather shabby, also the result of failure to do any homework. It was indicated, quite explicitly in some news quarters, that the Canadian Judicial Council acted because the Prime Minister had complained of the Judge's intrusion into the political sphere when the Prime Minister was giving a press interview in Vancouver. The record on this matter is quite clear. The written complaint against Justice Berger was addressed to me under dates of November 18 and 19, 1981 and delivered to me, from Ottawa, on those days. The next day, November 20, 1981, I sent a memorandum to the Executive Secretary of Council asking that the complaints – there were two successive ones – be referred for consideration by the Executive Committee. So far as the Canadian Judicial Council was concerned, the complaint had become part of our agenda. The interview of the Prime Minister did not take place until November 24, 1981. It is therefore mere mischief making to suggest that the Canadian Judicial Council was moved to action by the Prime Minister.

The Berger inquiry, as I have said, is behind us, and I regret that I found it necessary to say as much as I did about it. However, the Canadian Judicial Council, which does not and cannot reach out publicly to the media, deserves to have its record cleared. This would not have been necessary if we had been better served by the press throughout the whole affair. A matter like the Berger case is not likely to recur; the Canadian Judicial Council has signalled the danger of recommended removal from office if it should recur. As it was, the Council took a placating view and administered an admonishment in the following terms:

1. The Judicial Council is of the opinion that it was an indiscretion on the part of Mr. Justice Berger to express his views as to matters of a political nature, when such matters were in controversy.

2. While the Judicial Council is of the opinion that Mr. Justice Berger's actions were indiscreet, they constitute no basis for a recommendation that he be removed from office.

3. The Judicial Council is of the opinion that members of the judiciary should avoid taking part in controversial political discussions except only in respect of matters that directly affect the operation of the Courts.

In view of the obfuscation that surrounded the Berger case, there are a number of propositions that must be plainly stated. First, however personally compelled a Judge may feel to speak on a political issue, however knowledgeable the Judge may be or think he or she may be on such an issue, it is forbidden territory. The Judge must remain and be seen to remain impartial. Compromise which would impair judicial independence and integrity is out, if the Judge is to remain in judicial office. Second, no federally-appointed Judge can claim immunity from the examination by the Canadian Judicial Council of complaints (unless obviously frivolous) lodged against the Judge; nor against the decision of the Canadian Judicial Council to investigate the complaints through a formal inquiry. Third, the Canadian Judicial Council is not limited to recommending removal or dismissal; it may attach a reprimand or admonishment without either recommending removal or abandoning the complaint. Only if it gets to removal does it become necessary, in the case of a superior court Judge, to engage the Minister of Justice and Parliament, whose approval on a recommended removal must be sought. Fourth, Judges who are objects or subjects of a complaint are entitled to a fair hearing, to appear before the Council or before an appointed committee or to refuse to appear (as Justice Berger did refuse). Refusal to appear does not paralyze the Council, and did not in the Case under discussion....

5.4

The McClung Affair
He Said, She Said
National Post, February 26, 1999, A3.

Justice Claire L'Heureux-Dubé of the Supreme Court issued a point-by-point rebuke yesterday to Justice John McClung of the Alberta Court of Appeal, for comments he made in a sexual-assault ruling last year in which he acquitted Steve Ewanchuk:

Judge McClung said: "It must be pointed out the complainant did not present herself (to the accused) in a bonnet and crinolines."
Judge L'Heureux-Dubé countered: "These comments made by an appellate judge help reinforce the myth that under such circumstances, either the complainant is less worthy of belief, she invited the sexual assault, or her sexual experience signals probable consent to further sexual activity."

Judge McClung said: "She told Ewanchuk that she was the mother of a six-month-old baby and that, along with her boyfriend she shared an apartment with another couple."

Judge L'Heureux-Dubé countered: "One must wonder why he felt necessary to point out these aspects of the trial record. Could it be to express that the complainant is not a virgin?"

Judge McClung said: "There was no room to suggest that Ewanchuk knew, yet disregarded, her underlying state of mind as he furthered his romantic intentions."

Judge L'Heureux-Dubé countered: "These were two strangers, a young 17-year-old woman attracted by a job offer trapped in a trailer with a man approximately twice her age and size. This is hardly a scenario that one would characterize as reflective of romantic 'intentions.' It was nothing more than an effort by Ewanchuk to engage the complainant sexually, not romantically."

Judge McClung said: "During each of these three clumsy passes by Ewanchuk, when she said no, he promptly backed off."

Judge L'Heureux-Dubé countered: "The expressions used by (Justice) McClung to describe the accused's sexual assault, such as 'clumsy passes,' are plainly inappropriate in that context as they minimize the importance of the accused's conduct and the reality of sexual aggression against women."

Judge McClung said: "The sum of the evidence indicates that Ewanchuk's advances to the complainant were far less criminal than hormonal."

Judge L'Heureux-Dubé countered: "According to this analysis, a man would be free from criminal responsibility for having non-consensual sexual activity whenever he cannot control his sexual urges."

Judge McClung said: "In a less litigious age, going too far in the boyfriend's car was better dealt with on site, a well chosen explicative, a slap in the face, or, if necessary, a well directed knee."

Judge L'Heureux-Dubé countered: "According to this stereotype, women should use physical force, not resort to the courts to 'deal with' sexual assaults and it is not the perpetrator's responsibility to ascertain consent ... but the women's not only to express an unequivocal 'no' but also to fight her way out of a situation."

Box 1: McClung's Letter to the *National Post*

Mr. Kenneth Whyte
Editor in Chief
National Post
Don Mills, ON

Dear Sir:

Madam Justice Claire L'Heureux-Dubé's graceless slide into personal invective in Thursday's judgment in the *Ewanchuk* case allows some response. It is issued with "the added bitterness of an old friend."

Whether the *Ewanchuk* case will promote the fundamental right of every accused Canadian to a fair trial will have to be left to the academics. Yet there may be one immediate benefit. The personal convictions of the judge, delivered again from her judicial chair, could provide a plausible explanation for the disparate (and growing) number of male suicides being reported in the province of Quebec.

Yours truly,

(signed)
J.W. McClung
Justice of Appeal

Box 2: McClung's Public Letter of Apology

Issued on March 1, 1999

For 40 years I have served the Courts of Alberta at four different levels and to the best of my ability. But last week I made an overwhelming error. When I read the Supplementary Reasons for Judgment of Madam Justice L'Heureux-Dubé in the Ewanchuk case, I allowed myself to be provoked into writing to the National Post. It was published on Feb 26. The letter has been widely quoted and condemned.

I wish to acknowledge that there was no justification for my doing so. I regret my reaction and appreciate that no circumstance could justify the media as the avenue for the expression of my disappointment.

My letter made reference to curtain suicide statistics in the Province of Quebec and was only included as a facetious chide to the judge. I thought it would be so understood. What compounded my indiscretion was the fact, unknown to me, that Justice L'Heureux-Dubé had undergone a suicide bereavement in her own family. I immediately conveyed my explanation and apology to her later the same day. I sincerely regret what happened and have so advised her. It was cruel coincidence to which she ought not have been subjected. But it is a coincidence for which I am answerable.

On Saturday Feb. 27, the *National Post* attributed to me further remarks about the Ewanchuk case. Any remarks were not designed to call into question the authority or finality of the Supreme Court of Canada resolution of the case, nor were they designed to impugn the complainant involved in the Ewanchuk assault. The discussion I had with Mr. Ohler, the reporter, was held as background to the issues in the case. I thought it was an off-the-record discussion, as were discussion the previous day. Obviously Mr. Ohler did not. That, in hindsight, was also my mistake.

To be clear I recognize the overriding authority of the Supreme Court of Canada and any suggestion to the contrary is incorrect. The Canadian system of justice could not function in the absence of a hierarchy of courts.

I deeply regret that what has happened has ignited a debate which could place the administration of justice in an unfortunate light. If so, it was unintentional as I have the highest regard for the justice system in which I serve.

(signed)
John W. McClung
Justice of Appeal

The Canadian Judicial Council Ruling
News Release: "Panel expresses strong disapproval of McClung conduct," Ottawa, May 21, 1999.

A three-member Panel of the Canadian Judicial Council has expressed strong disapproval of the conduct of Mr. Justice John W. McClung of the Alberta Court of Appeal following reversal of his court decision in the *Ewanchuk* case.

The Panel was critical of Mr. Justice McClung's letter to the *National Post* published February 26, 1999 and comments subsequently quoted by the newspaper after the Supreme Court of Canada reversed the *Ewanchuk* decision.

The Council released a letter to Mr. Justice McClung signed by the Panel Chairperson, Nova Scotia Chief Justice Constance R. Glube, setting out the Panel's response to 24 complaints from individuals and organizations. Other members of the Panel were the Quebec Chief Justice Pierre Michaud and Ontario Chief Justice R. Roy McMurtry.

The Panel concluded that the file should be closed with an expression of disapproval of the conduct of Mr. Justice McClung, but that there was no requirement for a formal investigation by an Inquiry Committee under ss. 63(2) of the *Judges Act* for the purpose of deciding whether or not to recommend that the judge be removed from office.

The Panel disagreed with Mr. Justice McClung's characterization of Madam Justice Claire L'Heureux-Dubé's reasons for judgment in the *Ewanchuk* appeal as an attack on him or "unfair and unearned" criticism.

The Panel noted Mr. Justice McClung's apology for his letter to the newspaper and his unequivocal recognition that the letter and its tone were entirely inappropriate.

"In the circumstances, the Panel considers it to be an impetuous and isolated incident which does not warrant further consideration by the Council," said the Panel's letter.

But Mr. Justice McClung's comments on the *Ewanchuk* case in the *National Post* interview were entirely inappropriate, and "can only cause distress to the victim and reflect negatively on the judiciary."

The Panel's letter also addressed complaints about passages in Mr. Justice McClung's reasons for judgment in *Ewanchuk* and in the 1996 *Vriend* [gay rights] case.

It was "simply unacceptable conduct for a judge" to imply in the *Ewanchuk* judgment that the complainant was not a "nice girl" or that she could have resolved any difficulties with a "slap in the face" or a "well-placed knee," the Panel said.

Moreover, Mr. Justice McClung's "gratuitous observations" about gays and lesbians in his reasons for judgment in *Vriend* "constitute inappropriate conduct for a judge," the Panel said. The passages could be interpreted as an assertion that gay people are inherently immoral and as categorizing gays and lesbians as sexual deviants who prey on children, said the Panel's letter.

"The Panel has concluded that your comments cross beyond the boundary of even the wide latitude given to judges in expressing their reasons. They have no logical connection to the issues in the case and detract from respect for equality rights. They constitute inappropriate conduct for a judge."

Mr. Justice McClung's comments in both *Vriend* and *Ewanchuk* were "flippant, unnecessary and unfortunate," said the Panel's letter. But the comments in *Vriend* did not demonstrate underlying homophobia and the comments in *Ewanchuk* did not reflect an underlying bias against women. These comments would not preclude Mr. Justice McClung from treating all litigants fairly and impartially in future.

"In reaching its conclusions, the Panel has taken into account that the two judgments in which your inappropriate comments were made were reversed by the Supreme Court of Canada," the letter said. "The Panel also gave consideration to your long and distinguished career as a lawyer and judge in the years preceding these complaints. In sum, the Panel has found your conduct to be inappropriate but not malicious or reflecting oblique motive. The Panel expects that you will learn from this experience in dealing with future cases."

5.5

Reference re Remuneration of Judges of the Provincial Court (P.E.I.)

Supreme Court of Canada (1997)

The Chief Justice –

The four appeals handed down today ... raise a range of issues relating to the independence of provincial courts, but are united by a single issue: whether and how the guarantee of judicial independence in s.11(*d*) of the *Canadian Charter of Rights and Freedoms* restricts the manner by and the extent to which provincial governments and legislatures can reduce the salaries of provincial court judges....

Financial Security

... Notwithstanding the presence of s.11(*d*) of the *Charter*, and ss.96-100 of the *Constitution Act, 1867*, I am of the view that judicial independence is at root an *unwritten* constitutional principle, in the sense that it is exterior to the particular sections of the *Constitution Acts*. The existence of that principle, whose origins can be traced to the *Act of Settlement* of 1701, is recognized and affirmed by the preamble to the *Constitution Act, 1867*. The specific provisions of the *Constitution Acts, 1867 to 1982*, merely "elaborate that principle in the institutional apparatus which they create or contemplate": *Switzman v. Elbling*, [1957]....

In my opinion, the existence of many of the unwritten rules of the Canadian Constitution can be explained by reference to the preamble of the *Constitution Act, 1867*. The relevant paragraph states in full:

> Whereas the Provinces of Canada, Nova Scotia, and New Brunswick have expressed their Desire to be federally united into One Dominion under the Crown of the United Kingdom of Great Britain and Ireland, with a Constitution similar in Principle to that of the United Kingdom....

Although the preamble has been cited by this Court on many occasions, its legal effect has never been fully explained. On the one hand, although the preamble is clearly part of the Constitution, it is equally clear that it "has no enacting force": *Reference re Resolution to Amend the Constitution*, [1981]. In other words, strictly speaking, it is not a source of positive law, in contrast to the provisions which follow it.

But the preamble does have important legal effects.... The preamble is not only a key to construing the express provisions of the *Constitution Act, 1867*, but also invites the use of those organizing principles to fill out gaps in the express terms of the constitutional scheme. It is the means by which the underlying logic of the Act can be given the force of law.

... The preamble identifies the organizing principles of the *Constitution Act, 1867*, and invites the courts to turn those principles into the premises of a constitutional argument that culminates in the filling of gaps in the express terms of the constitutional text.

The same approach applies to the protection of judicial independence. In fact, this point was already decided in *Beauregard*, and, unless and until it is reversed, we are governed by that decision today. In that case (at p. 72), a unanimous Court held that the preamble of the *Constitution Act, 1867*, and in particular, its reference to "a Constitution similar in Principle to that of the United Kingdom," was "textual recognition" of the principle of judicial independence. Although in that case, it fell to us to interpret s.100 of the *Constitution Act, 1867*, the comments I have just reiterated were not limited by reference to that provision, and the courts which it protects.

... In the same way that our understanding of rights and freedoms has grown, such that they have now been expressly entrenched through the enactment of the *Constitution Act, 1982*, so too has judicial independence grown into a principle that now extends to all courts, not just the superior courts of this country....

... The starting point for my discussion is *Valente*, where in a unanimous judgment this Court laid down the interpretive framework for s.11(*d*)'s guarantee of judicial independence and impartiality.... In *Valente*, Le Dain J. drew a distinction between two dimensions of judicial independence, the *individual independence* of a judge and the *institutional or collective independence* of the court or tribunal of which that judge is a member. In other words, while individual independence attaches to individual judges, institutional or collective independence attaches to the court or tribunal as an institutional entity.... What I do propose, however, is that financial security has *both* an individual and an institutional or collective dimension....

... The institutional role demanded of the judiciary under our Constitution is a role which we now expect of provincial court judges. I am well aware that provincial courts are creatures of statute, and that their existence is not required by the Constitution. However, there is no doubt that these statutory courts play a critical role in enforcing the provisions and protecting the values of the Constitution. Inasmuch as that role has grown over the last few years, it is clear therefore that provincial courts must be granted some institutional independence....

... To my mind, financial security for the courts as an institution has three components, which all flow from the constitutional imperative that, to the extent possible, the relationship between the judiciary and the other branches of government be *depoliticized*....

First, as a general constitutional principle, the salaries of provincial court judges can be reduced, increased, or frozen, either as part of an overall economic measure which affects the salaries of all or some persons who are remunerated from public funds, or as part of a measure which is directed at provincial court judges as a class. However, any changes to or freezes in judicial remuneration require prior recourse to a special process, which is independent, effective, and objective, for determining judicial remuneration, to avoid the possibility of, or the appearance of, political interference through economic manipulation.... *Second*, under no circumstances is it permissible for the judiciary – not only collectively through representative organizations, but also as individuals – to engage in negotiations over remuneration with the executive or representatives of the legislature.... *Third*, and finally, any reductions to judicial remuneration, including *de facto* reductions through the erosion of judicial salaries by inflation, cannot take those salaries....

The Components of Institutional or Collective Financial Security

(a)   *Judicial Salaries Can Be Reduced, Increased, or Frozen, but not Without Recourse to an Independent, Effective and Objective Commission....*

Although provincial executives and legislatures, as the case may be, are constitutionally permitted to change or freeze judicial remuneration, those decisions have the potential to jeopardize judicial independence. The imperative of protecting the courts from political interference through economic manipulation is served by *interposing* an independent body – a judicial compensation commission – between the judiciary and the other branches of government. The constitutional function of this body is to depoliticize the process of determining changes or freezes to judicial remuneration. This objective would be achieved by setting that body the specific task of issuing a report on the salaries and benefits of judges to the executive and the legislature, responding to the particular proposals made by the government to increase, reduce, or freeze judges' salaries.

The commissions charged with the responsibility of dealing with the issue of judicial remuneration must meet three general criteria.... First and foremost, these commissions must be *independent*. The rationale for independence flows from the constitutional function performed by these commissions – they serve as an institutional sieve, to prevent the setting or freezing of judicial remuneration from being used as a means to exert political pressure through the economic manipulation of the judiciary. It would undermine that goal if the independent commissions were under the control of the executive or the legislature....

What s.11(*d*) requires instead is that the appointments not be entirely controlled by any one of the branches of government. The commission should have members appointed by the judiciary, on the one hand, and the legislature and the executive, on the other. The judiciary's nominees may, for example, be chosen either by the provincial judges' association, as is the case in Ontario, or by the Chief Judge of the Provincial Court in consultation with the provincial judges' association, as in British Columbia. The exact mechanism is for provincial governments to determine. Likewise, the nominees of the executive and the legislature may be chosen by the Lieutenant Governor in Council, although appointments by the Attorney General as in British Columbia (*Provincial Court Act*, s.7.1(2)), or conceivably by the legislature itself, are entirely permissible.

In addition to being independent, the salary commissions must be *objective*. They must make recommendations on judges' remuneration by reference to objective criteria, not political expediencies....

Finally, and most importantly, the commission must also be *effective*. The effectiveness of these bodies must be guaranteed in a number of ways. First, there is a constitutional obligation for governments not to change (either by reducing or increasing) or freeze judicial remuneration until they have received the report of the salary commission. Changes or freezes of this nature secured without going through the commission process are unconstitutional. The commission must convene to consider and report on the proposed change or freeze. Second, in order to guard against the possibility that government inaction might lead to a reduction in judges' real salaries because of inflation, and that inaction could therefore be used as a means of economic manipulation, the commission must convene if a fixed period of time has elapsed since its last report, in order to consider the adequacy of judges' salaries in light of the cost of living and other relevant factors, and issue a recommendation in its report. Although the exact length of the period is for provincial governments to determine, I would suggest a period of three to five years.

Third, the reports of the commission must have a meaningful effect on the determination of judicial salaries. Provinces which have created salary commissions have adopted three different ways of giving such effect to these reports. One is to make a report of the commission binding, so that the government is bound by the commission's decision....

What judicial independence requires is that the executive or the legislature, whichever is vested with the authority to set judicial remuneration under provincial legislation, must formally respond to the contents of the commission's report within a specified amount of time. Before it can set judges' salaries, the executive must issue a report in which it outlines its response to the commission's recommendations. If the legislature is involved in the process, the report of the commission must be laid before the legislature, when it is in session, with due diligence. If the legislature is not in session, the government may wait until a new sitting commences. The legislature should deal with the report directly, with due diligence and reasonable dispatch.

Furthermore, if after turning its mind to the report of the commission, the executive or the legislature, as applicable, chooses not to accept one or more of the recommendations in that report, it must be prepared to justify this decision, if necessary in a court of law. The reasons for this decision would be found either in the report of the executive responding to the contents of the commission's report, or in the recitals to the resolution of the legislature on the matter. An unjustified decision could potentially lead to a finding of unconstitutionality. The need for public justification, to my mind, emerges from one of the purposes of s.11(d)'s guarantee of judicial independence – to ensure public confidence in the justice system. A decision by the executive or the legislature, to change or freeze judges' salaries, and then to disagree with a recommendation not to act on that decision made by a constitutionally mandated body whose existence is premised on the need to preserve the independence of the judiciary, will only be legitimate and not be viewed as being indifferent or hostile to judicial independence, if it is supported by reasons....

By laying down a set of guidelines to assist provincial legislatures in designing judicial compensation commissions, I do not intend to lay down a particular institutional framework in constitutional stone. What s.11(d) requires is an institutional sieve between the judiciary and the other branches of government. Commissions are merely a means to that end. In the future, governments may create new institutional arrangements which can serve the same end, but in a different way. As long as those institutions meet the three cardinal requirements of independence, effectiveness, and objectivity, s.11(d) will be complied with.

(b) No Negotiations on Judicial Remuneration Between the Judiciary and the Executive and Legislature

Negotiations over remuneration are a central feature of the landscape of public sector labour relations. The evidence before this Court (anecdotal and otherwise) suggests that salary negotiations have been occurring between provincial court judges and provincial governments in a number of provinces. However, from a constitutional standpoint, this is inappropriate, for two related reasons. First, as I have argued above, negotiations for remuneration from the public purse are indelibly political. For the judiciary to engage in salary negotiations would undermine public confidence in the impartiality and independence of the judiciary, and thereby frustrate a major purpose of s.11(*d*)....

Second, negotiations are deeply problematic because the Crown is almost always a party to criminal prosecutions in provincial courts. Negotiations by the judges who try those cases put them in a conflict of interest, because they would be negotiating with a litigant. The appearance of independence would be lost, because salary negotiations bring with them a whole set of expectations about the behaviour of the parties to those negotiations which are inimical to judicial independence....

(c) Judicial Salaries May Not Fall Below a Minimum Level

... I have no doubt that the Constitution protects judicial salaries from falling below an acceptable minimum level. The reason it does is for financial security to protect the judiciary from political interference through economic manipulation, and to thereby ensure public confidence in the administration of justice. If salaries are too low, there is always the danger, however speculative, that members of the judiciary could be tempted to adjudicate cases in a particular way in order to secure a higher salary from the executive or the legislature or to receive benefits from one of the litigants....

I want to make it very clear that the guarantee of a minimum salary is not meant for the benefit of the judiciary. Rather, financial security is a means to the end of judicial independence, and is therefore for the benefit of the public.... I do not address the question of what the minimum acceptable level of judicial remuneration is. We shall answer that question if and when the need arises....

La Forest J. (dissenting in part) –

... I have had the advantage of reading the reasons of the Chief Justice who sets forth the facts and history of the litigation. Although I agree with substantial portions of his reasons, I cannot concur with his conclusion that s.11(*d*) forbids governments from changing judges' salaries without first having recourse to the "judicial compensation commissions" he describes. Furthermore, I do not believe that s.11(*d*) prohibits salary discussions between governments and judges. In my view, reading these requirements into s.11(*d*) represents both an unjustified departure from established precedents and a partial usurpation of the provinces' power to set the salaries of inferior court judges pursuant to ss.92(4) and 92(14) of the *Constitution Act, 1867*. In addition to these issues, the Chief Justice deals with a number of other questions respecting the independence of provincial court judges that were raised by the parties to these appeals. I agree with his disposition of these issues....

Even if it is accepted that judicial independence had become a "constitutional" principle in Britain by 1867, it is important to understand the precise meaning of that term in British law. Unlike Canada, Great Britain does not have a written constitution. Under accepted British legal theory, Parliament is supreme. By this I mean that there are no limitations upon its legislative competence. As Dicey explains, Parliament has "under the English constitution, the right to make or unmake any law whatever; and, further, that no person or body is recognised by the law of England as having a right to override or set aside the legislation of Parliament." This principle has been modified somewhat in recent decades to take into account the effect of Great Britain's membership in the European Community, but ultimately, the British Parliament remains supreme....

The idea that there were enforceable limits on the power of the British Parliament to interfere with the judiciary at the time of Confederation, then, is an historical fallacy. By expressing a desire to have a Constitution "similar in Principle to that of the United Kingdom," the framers of the *Constitution Act, 1867* did not give courts the power to strike down legislation violating the principle of judicial independence. The framers *did*, however, entrench the fundamental components of judicial independence set out in the *Act of Settlement* such that violations could be struck down by the courts. This was accomplished, however, by ss.99-100 of the *Constitution Act, 1867*, not the preamble.

... The ability to nullify the laws of democratically elected representatives derives its legitimacy from a super-legislative source: the text of the Constitution. This foundational document (in Canada, a series of documents) expresses the desire of the people to limit the power of legislatures in certain specified ways. Because our Constitution is entrenched, those limitations cannot be changed by recourse to the usual democratic process. They are not cast in stone, however, and can be modified in accordance with a further expression of democratic will: constitutional amendment.

Judicial review, therefore, is politically legitimate only insofar as it involves the interpretation of an authoritative constitutional instrument. In this sense, it is akin to statutory interpretation. In each case, the court's role is to divine the intent or purpose of the text as it has been expressed by the people through the mechanism of the democratic process. Of course, many (but not all) constitutional provisions are cast in broad and abstract language. Courts have the often arduous task of explicating the effect of this language in a myriad of factual circumstances, many of which may not have been contemplated by the framers of the Constitution. While there are inevitable disputes about the manner in which courts should perform this duty, for example by according more or less deference to legislative decisions, there is general agreement that the task itself is legitimate.

This legitimacy is imperiled, however, when courts attempt to limit the power of legislatures without recourse to express textual authority. From time to time, members of this Court have suggested that our Constitution comprehends implied rights that circumscribe legislative competence. On the theory that the efficacy of parliamentary democracy requires free political expression, it has been asserted that the curtailment of such expression is *ultra vires* both provincial legislatures and the federal Parliament....

... To the extent that courts in Canada have the power to enforce the principle of judicial independence, this power derives from the structure of *Canadian*, and not British, constitutionalism. Our Constitution expressly contemplates both the power of judicial review (in s.52 of the *Constitution Act, 1982*) and guarantees of judicial independence (in ss.96-100 of the *Constitution Act, 1867* and s.11(*d*) of the *Charter*). While these provisions have been interpreted to provide guarantees of independence that are not immediately manifest in their language, this has been accomplished through the usual mechanisms of constitutional interpretation, not through recourse to the preamble. The legitimacy of this interpretive exercise stems from its grounding in an expression of democratic will, not from a dubious theory of an implicit constitutional structure. The express provisions of the Constitution are not, as the Chief Justice contends, "elaborations of the underlying, unwritten, and organizing principles found in the preamble to the *Constitution Act, 1867*" (para. 107). On the contrary, they *are* the Constitution. To assert otherwise is to subvert the democratic foundation of judicial review....

These are some of the issues that have persuaded me that this Court should not precipitously, and without the benefit of argument of any real relevance to the case before us, venture forth on this uncharted sea. It is not as if the law as it stands is devoid of devices to ensure independent and impartial courts and tribunals. Quite the contrary, I would emphasize that the express protections for judicial independence set out in the Constitution are broad and powerful. They apply to all superior court and other judges specified in s.96 of the *Constitution Act, 1867* as well as to inferior (provincial) courts exercising criminal jurisdiction. Nothing presented in these appeals suggests that these guarantees are not sufficient to ensure the independence of the judiciary as a whole. The superior courts have significant appellate and supervisory jurisdiction over inferior courts. If the impartiality of decisions from inferior courts is threatened by a lack of independence, any ensuing injustice may be rectified by the superior courts....

I turn now to the main issue in these appeals: whether the governments of Prince Edward Island, Alberta and Manitoba violated s.11(*d*) of the *Charter* by compromising the financial security of provincial court judges....

The Chief Justice also finds, as a general principle, that s.11(*d*) of the *Charter* permits governments to reduce, increase or freeze the salaries of provincial court judges, either as part of an overall economic measure which affects the salaries of all persons paid from the public purse, or as part of a measure directed at judges as a class. I agree. He goes on to hold, however, that before such changes can be made, governments must consider and respond to the recommendations of an independent "judicial compensation commission." He further concludes that s.11(*d*) forbids, under any circumstances, discussions about remuneration between the judiciary and the government.

I am unable to agree with these conclusions. While both salary commissions and a concomitant policy to avoid discussing remuneration other than through the making of representations to commissions may be desirable as matters of legislative policy, they are not mandated by s.11(*d*) of the *Charter*....

By its express terms, s.11(*d*) grants the right to an independent tribunal to persons "charged with an offence." The guarantee of judicial independence inhering in s.11(*d*) redounds to the benefit of the judged, not the judges. Section 11(*d*), therefore, does not grant judges a level of independence to which they feel they are entitled. Rather, it guarantees only that degree of independence necessary to ensure that accused persons receive fair trials....

From the foregoing, it can be stated that the "essential objective conditions" of judicial independence for the purposes of s.11(*d*) consist of those minimum guarantees that are necessary to ensure that tribunals exercising criminal jurisdiction act, and are perceived to act, in an impartial manner. Section 11(*d*) does not empower this or any other court to compel governments to enact "model" legislation affording the utmost protection for judicial independence. This is a task for the legislatures, not the courts.

With this general principle in mind, I turn to the first question at hand: does s.11(d) require governments to establish judicial compensation commissions and consider and respond to their recommendations before changing the salaries of provincial court judges?...

In my view, it is abundantly clear that a reasonable, informed person would not perceive that, in the absence of a commission process, all changes to the remuneration of provincial court judges threaten their independence. I reach this conclusion by considering the type of change to judicial salaries that is at issue in the present appeals. It is simply not reasonable to think that a decrease to judicial salaries that is part of an overall economic measure which affects the salaries of substantially all persons paid from public funds imperils the independence of the judiciary. To hold otherwise is to assume that judges could be influenced or manipulated by such a reduction. A reasonable person, I submit, would believe judges are made of sturdier stuff than this....

The threat to judicial independence that arises from the government's power to set salaries consists in the prospect that judges will be influenced by the possibility that the government will punish or reward them financially for their decisions. Protection against this potentiality is the *raison d'être* of the financial security component of judicial independence. There is virtually no possibility that such economic manipulation will arise where the government makes equivalent changes to the remuneration of all persons paid from public funds. The fact that such a procedure might leave *some* members of the public with the impression that provincial court judges are public servants is thus irrelevant. A reasonable, *informed* person would not perceive any infringement of the judges' financial security.

... Under the reasonable perception test, however, commissions are not a necessary condition of independence. Of course, the existence of such a process may go a long way toward showing that a given change to judges' salaries does not threaten their independence. Requiring commissions *a priori*, however, is tantamount to enacting a new constitutional provision to extend the protection provided by s.11(d). Section 11(d) requires only that tribunals exercising criminal jurisdiction be independent and impartial. To that end, it prohibits governments from acting in ways that threaten that independence and impartiality. It does not require legislatures, however, to establish what in some respects is a virtual fourth branch of government to police the interaction between the political branches and the judiciary. Judges, in my opinion, are capable of ensuring their own independence by an appropriate application of the Constitution. By employing the reasonable perception test, judges are able to distinguish between changes to their remuneration effected for a valid public purpose and those designed to influence their decisions....

I now turn to the question of discussions between the judiciary and the government over salaries. In the absence of a commission process, the only manner in which judges may have a say in the setting of their salaries is through direct dialogue with the executive. The Chief Justice terms these discussions "negotiations" and would prohibit them, in all circumstances, as violations of the financial security component of judicial independence. According to him, negotiations threaten independence because a "reasonable person might conclude that judges would alter the manner in which they adjudicate cases in order to curry favour with the executive."

In my view, this position seriously mischaracterizes the manner in which judicial salaries are set. *Valente* establishes that the fixing of provincial court judges' remuneration is entirely within the discretion of the government, subject, of course, to the conditions that the right to a salary be established by law and that the government not change salaries in a manner that raises a reasonable apprehension of interference. There is no constitutional requirement that the executive discuss, consult or "negotiate" with provincial court judges.... Provincial judges associations are not unions, and the government and the judges are not involved in a statutorily compelled collective bargaining relationship.... The atmosphere of negotiation the Chief Justice describes, which fosters expectations of "give and take" and encourages "subtle accommodations," does not therefore apply to salary discussions between government and the judiciary. The danger that is alleged to arise from such discussions – that judges will barter their independence for financial gain – is thus illusory....

5.6

A Self-Harming of Judicial Independence: The Legacy of the Inquiry into Lori Douglas
R. Lee Akazaki, Past President, Ontario Bar Association

An Open Mind: About Law & Ethics, December 8, 2014, https://leeakazaki. com/2014/12/08/a-self-harming-of-judicial-independence-the-legacy- of-the-inquiry-into-loridouglas/. Adapted from original and reprinted with permission.

The Canadian Judicial Council Inquiry Committee regarding the Honourable Lori Douglas is now over. The embattled Manitoba judge, whose late husband allegedly posted nude photographs of her online and encouraged his former client to sleep with her, decided to settle for early retirement after the committee's November 4, 2014, *Ruling on Preliminary Motions*, in which the tribunal insisted on viewing the photographs. Douglas did obtain a temporary stay of the ruling from the Federal Court, but this step effectively bought her time to bring a halt to the proceedings.

Despite the stay and the settlement of the complaint, the CJC's ruling has damaged the independence of the Canadian judiciary at a time when our lawmakers seek to protect fellow citizens from cyber-stalking and other offences based on privacy breaches.

The two allegations against Justice Douglas to which the photos were held to be relevant and admissible, were:

1. Whether Douglas ought to have disclosed the existence of the photographs at the time of applying to be a judge, because they "could reflect negatively on yourself or the judiciary, and which should be disclosed." Candidate Douglas had answered "No" on the application questionnaire.

2. Whether the photos could be seen as inherently contrary to the image and concept of integrity of the judiciary, such that the confidence of individuals appearing before the judge, or of the public in its justice system, could be undermined.

These counts were cited under s. 65(2) of the *Judges Act*, and the committee's jurisdiction was to decide whether Douglas has become incapacitated or disabled from the due execution of the judicial office by reason of clause (d) of that provision, by "having been placed, by ... her conduct or otherwise, in a position incompatible with the due execution of that office."

The subordinate phrase, *or otherwise*, is problematic especially in conjunction with the principal clause, *having been placed*, expressed in the passive voice. Since it was of public record that Douglas' husband had published the photos to the adult site, the underlying subject matter of both allegations involved Douglas as the victim of a spousal betrayal: i.e., the two counts were about a thing that had been done to her. Blaming a victim of an offence and making him or her an offender is unconstitutional in Canada, and offends justice at even a visceral level.

From a strict application of the law of evidence, the decision to admit and view the photographs was not defensible, and resembled the rough justice employed in minor rulings during the course of a trial. This type of ruling, often defensible in minor matters, had no place in a matter where the accused was battling to save her professional existence against charges of dubious validity and the notoriety brought by the images themselves. Had this been a law school Evidence examination, members of the committee should have received a failing grade.

Quite apart from the abysmal legal skills in the committee's decision, the committee's compass seemed very much to be off kilter. What, indeed, were its statutory role and functions? Did s. 65 of the *Judges Act* require the panel to turn the capacity hearing into an obscenity trial? Was the issue going to be that Douglas could stay on the Bench if the photos were artful, and should be removed if the photos were lewd? When one runs to ground the committee's analysis, the Kafkaesque emptiness of juridical purpose is the only lasting impression with which one is left.

According to reports of Douglas' rationale for giving up the fight, this ruling was the straw that broke the camel's back. She was justifiably tormented by the idea that her inquisitors, colleagues on the bench and at the bar, had insisted on viewing the photos. In Canada, our law is replete with judicial pronouncements against interim rulings denying a party's day in court. How then did this happen? Given the tenuous grounds upon which the complaint was registered in the first place, it would have been important to circumscribe the factors for admissibility of the photographs based on necessity. Was it *really* necessary to view the photos? Should the panel have predicted an outcome in which Douglas forfeited her day in court?

The history of the women's movement in the 20th century, from the Suffragettes campaigning for the vote in Britain, to the Sartre-Beauvoir alliance in France, has been marked by women's ambitions of equality with men. In Canada, the recognition of women as "persons" came with a landmark constitutional law decision of our Supreme Court. In the hierarchy of things, self-determination depends on one's place in the grammatical structure, *who* is acting and *what* is on the receiving end of the act. Accountability and responsibility is about what one has done. Historically, women and children were considered to be of diminished responsibility in the eyes of the law, because of the paucity of acts they were legally empowered to do. Self-determination and one's place in the common phrase are inextricably part of the narrative.

In the Douglas inquiry, it has always been hard to see what she has done, and to see her as anything other than the victim of her late husband's malfeasance. At that level, without an *actus reus* and *mens rea*, many have wondered how she could have become the subject of the inquiry. If she could not be the subject of the inquiry, then how could the tribunal proceed to review her conduct?

Any undergraduate gender studies major can spot the Inquiry Committee's legal blunder. By making the photographs the subject of investigation, Douglas has been made an object of the inquiry. The reason why second-wave feminists protested the entry into the mainstream of sexualized depictions of women but did not call for the removal of Masters' paintings from art galleries, was the difference between the woman's body as object and the woman as subject. (This is the distinction which the Taliban and other gynophobes fail to make, when censoring or destroying depictions of female nudity.)

Whatever the photographs actually depicted, it was not disputed that they showed the judge, a lawyer at the time they were taken, in a state of undress. Whatever one's views about the propriety of allowing such photographs to be taken, allowing them to have been taken and whether Douglas knew her husband had uploaded them to an internet site (which she denied) which were the subject of inquiry. The actual photographs, in this context, were immaterial. The proof of this logic is that the hearing, had it any merit, ought to have proceeded whether or not the photographs continued to exist. The *subject* of the inquiry was Douglas and her conduct, and whether the conduct merited disclosure in an application for judicial office. Focusing the inquiry on *what* was depicted in the photographs, rather than *who* or *in what circumstances*, the jurists standing in judgment over Douglas objectified her body and therefore threatened her dignity. Suddenly, a person who had put up with years of personal upheaval and was ready to defend the charges gave up and offered to leave office.

Blackmail was the threat, not the naughty pictures

The Inquiry Committee thus showed itself out of its depth on the gender dynamics of a proceeding whose very pith and substance was gender dynamics. While one might offer excuses for the committee having skipped the Gloria Steinem book tours, it is harder to forgive the failure to recognize the legal policy consequences of its unnecessary ruling that the images be admitted into evidence.

If the consequences of disclosing the existence of personal secrets is unceremonious removal from public life, the secret as object has value only to one person or class of persons: criminals seeking to exploit public officials. In an age when people with ill intentions can find out just about anything about anyone by hacking into databases, and when governments are taking measures to outlaw "revenge-porn", the Douglas Inquiry was the opportunity to combat all forms of cyber-blackmail as an instrument of control over judicial officers. Instead of removing this weapon from those who would seek to compromise a judicial officer, the committee has made the weapon more lethal. Can this have been consistent with the committee's mandate under s. 60(1) of the *Judges Act*, to "promote efficiency and uniformity, and to improve the quality of judicial service, in superior courts"?

By insisting on viewing the photographs and making them relevant to the question of the capacity of a judge to sit on a Canadian court, the CJC Inquiry Committee has itself made them an issue. The Committee has thus rendered our judges blackmail targets, not because of what such photographs might depict, but rather because a ruling and precedent that the photographs can precipitate a capacity inquiry leading to removal from office. By increasing the value to a blackmailer of information of the photographs, the legacy of the Lori Douglas Inquiry is obvious:

- increased vulnerability of the independence and integrity of the Canadian judiciary

- discouragement of qualified candidates from applying for judicial office, not only among those who may have been victimized as Douglas was by her late husband, but also anyone with an unconventional but lawful private activity

Making any lawful activity unlawful, or creating an offender out of the victim of an act, is overstepping judicial authority. Judges make poor legislators because of the undue risk of unexpected consequences. Such risks are usually detected by parliamentarians with support from committees, policy staff and public consultations. If parliamentarians get it wrong, they can pass amendments. Judges and tribunals have to wait for the next similar case to come along, and the interim the bad law from the bad case remains the law of the land.

How should judges judge the judges? What was exposed in this narrative was not Douglas' body but the human frailty of those who occupy trusted offices. As people become more complex, so will judges, politicians and law enforcement officers. To expect such officials to lead monastic lives, separated from the rest of Canadian society, will only lead to harsh, sharp-edged law such as the ruling on evidence that precipitated Douglas' downfall. Such an approach to law can only lead to unqualified people seeking office, the encouragement of those unable to draw the line between lawful and unlawful private diversions and thus immune to the extortionist's craft.

Clearly, we need better and clearer articulation of the circumstances in which judges can be removed from office. We cannot make this the end of the debate over this troubled case. To ensure that Lori Douglas' case means something, we need clearer guidelines to triage the actual threat to judicial integrity and independence. That way, if another Lori Douglas comes along and it is clear he or she did nothing wrong, the complaint can be summarily dismissed; and the public can be confident that judges can preside over their own discipline.

5.7

The Inquiry into Justice Robin Camp
Complaint to the Canadian Judicial Council
Alice Woolley, Jennifer Koshan, Elaine Craig and Jocelyn Downie.
Reprinted with Permission

November 9, 2015
Canadian Judicial Council
Ottawa, ON K1A 0W8

Dear Sir or Madam,

By way of this letter we submit a complaint to the Canadian Judicial Council about Justice Robin Camp, currently of the Federal Court Trial Division. The events that form the basis for this complaint occurred when Justice Camp was a judge at the Alberta Provincial Court; however, those events undermine public confidence in the fair administration of justice, both in general and in relation to Justice Camp's current capacity for independence, integrity and impartiality, and his ability to respect the equality and dignity of all persons appearing before him. As a consequence, only the Canadian Judicial Council can provide a remedy appropriate to restore public confidence in the fair administration of justice.

On September 9, 2014 then Judge Camp acquitted Alexander Scott Wagar of sexual assault. That result was overturned by the Alberta Court of Appeal in a judgment dated October 15, 2015 (R v Wagar 2015 ABCA 327).… Justice Camp's decision to acquit is not part of the grounds for this complaint. Indeed, we take no position on whether or not Mr. Wagar could or should have been convicted based on a proper application of the law to the evidence before Justice Camp.

Our complaint arises instead from Justice Camp's sexist and disrespectful treatment of the complainant in the case and his disregard for the law applicable to sexual assault. This was not a case of mere judicial error. Mistakes by judges as to the law, even egregious mistakes, are not properly the subject of a complaint to the Canadian Judicial Council. Complaints are warranted only in exceptional cases where the judge's disregard for legality is such as to undermine the rule of law and, consequently, to bring the administration of justice into disrepute. In our view, Justice Camp's treatment of the law is in that category....

[*Ed. Note*: The letter's discussion of the law governing complaints about judicial conduct has been omitted.]

A. Justice Camp Showed Disregard for the Law on the Basis of Stereotypical Thinking

At numerous points during the proceeding, Justice Camp was dismissive of, if not contemptuous towards, the substantive law of sexual assault and the rules of evidence. In particular, he showed disregard, if not disdain, for the rape shield provisions under the Criminal Code, the legal definition of consent to sexual touching, and the Criminal Code provision and case law regarding the doctrine of recent complaint. His articulated disrespect for these legal rules was, in some instances, combined with a refusal to apply them. Consistently, the legal rules that Justice Camp took issue with were those aimed at removing from the law outdated and discredited stereotypes about women and sexual violence. In a dismissive manner, Justice Camp repeatedly referred to the legal rules requiring that these stereotypes not be relied upon as "contemporary thinking." He was frequently sarcastic and disrespectful to Crown counsel when she attempted to explain to him how these rules work and why they are important.

i. The Use of Evidence of Other Sexual Activity

Justice Camp characterized Canada's rape shield provisions as unfair and incursive. He suggested that the limits to admitting evidence of the complainant's sexual history "hamstring the defence" and arose from "very, very incursive legislation" (Transcript 58:39). He stated that "I don't think anybody, least of all Ms. Mograbee [Crown counsel], would – would – would argue that the rape shield law always worked fair – fairly. But it exists."

He challenged the Crown's assertion that the objective of Canada's rape shield provisions is to avoid the kind of twin myth reasoning that evidence of the complainant's other sexual activity can engender: "Well, surely we're – we're not talking about dangerous thinking, Ms. Mograbee. We're talking about the law.... The law doesn't stop people thinking." Indeed, the objective of the categorical preclusion of twin myth reasoning under section 276(1) is most certainly aimed at stopping triers of fact from a particular line of thinking.

Having made these comments about the rape shield provisions, he then proceeded to allow cross-examination in this regard without complying with the requirements for a hearing under section 276(2) and section 276.1 of the Criminal Code (Transcript 64:26). His refusal to comply with section 276 of the Criminal Code should be considered in light of his personal characterization of these provisions as unfair and overly incursive.

ii. The Definition of Consent to Sexual Touching

In both his comments throughout the proceeding, and his reasons for decision, Justice Camp demonstrated absolute disregard and disdain for the affirmative definition of consent to sexual touching established by Supreme Court of Canada in R v Ewanchuk, [1999] 1 SCR 330 and sections 273.1 and 273.2 of the Criminal Code. He asked the complainant questions such as "why didn't you just sink your bottom down into the basin so he couldn't penetrate you?" and "why couldn't you just keep your knees together?" He also indicated that she had not explained "why she allowed the sex to happen if she didn't want it" and noted that when she asked the accused if he had a condom that was "an inescapable conclusion [that] if you have one I'm happy to have sex with you" (Transcript 392:4)....

When the Crown attempted to explain to Justice Camp that a sexual assault victim's request that her attacker wear a condom does not establish that she has consented to the sexual activity up to that point he responded "please, Ms. Mograbee, we're grown-ups here." (392-27).

The definition of consent in Ewanchuk and sections 273.1 and 273.2 of the Criminal Code reflect an important legal approach to the issue of nonconsensual sex aimed at protecting the equality interests of vulnerable segments of Canadian society. This definition of consent is well settled in Canadian law. The open mockery of this legal definition by a judge presiding over a sexual assault trial in 2014 is likely to bring the administration of justice into disrepute ... [and] must also be viewed in light of his ultimate failure or refusal to apply the legal definition of consent to sexual touching....

iii. The Doctrine of Recent Complaint

Justice Camp also criticized the Canadian legal position that a judge ought not to draw an adverse inference as to credibility based solely on the complainant's failure to report the sexual assault immediately. During the Crown's preliminary submissions, he commented that the Complainant "abused the first opportunity to report" before conceding this was "no longer contemporarily relevant." During the Crown's final submissions, he commented that the recent complaint doctrine was "followed by every civilized legal system in the world for thousands of years" and "had its reasons" although "[a]t the moment it's not the law" (Transcript 394:35). When the Crown submitted that that kind of antiquated thinking had been set aside for a reason, he replied "I hope you don't live too long, Ms. Mograbee" (Transcript 395:6)....

Justice Camp's comments reveal that he was aware of the legal rule regarding delayed disclosure, but dismissive of its validity given its departure from the historical practices of what he described as "every civilized legal system." ...

In his reasons for judgment he made statements such as:

- "She certainly had the ability, perhaps learnt from her experience on the streets, to tell [him] to fuck off." (Transcript 450:29)

- "She certainly had the ability to swear at men. For a person who didn't want have sex, she spends a long time in the shower with the accused and went through a variety of sexual activities." (Transcript 451:2)

Justice Camp's reasons for judgment, when considered in light of his criticisms of the law, and his responses to Crown counsel when she attempted to explain these legal rules, demonstrates that the failures in his legal analysis arose not from a mistake, but because he did not like the law as it exists. He simply would not accept the parameters the law imposes on judging allegations of sexual assault. As a result, he assessed the case through his personal judgment (informed by stereotypical thinking about women and sexual violence), not the legal judgment that law requires. Simply put, he refused to apply these three legal rules aimed at eliminating from the law a set of discriminatory stereotypes that the Supreme Court of Canada and Parliament have deemed baseless. ...

B. Justice Camp's Conduct Was Disrespectful Towards The Complainant

Justice Camp's statements and reasoning in Wagar demonstrate a pervasive inability or refusal to account for the perspective of the complainant. The complainant was a homeless, 19-year-old woman who was marginalized by her socio-economic status and active battle with addictions. It is unclear from the transcript, but she may also have been marginalized by race, Aboriginality or disability.

Justice Camp made numerous statements that suggest that, from his perspective, it was the complainant who was on trial. He referred to her as "unsavoury" repeatedly (353: 31; 407:25; 435:23.). Synonyms for the label unsavoury in the context he used it include: unpleasant, undesirable, disagreeable and degenerate. He stated that "certainly the complainant and the accused are amoral people" and that "the complainant and the accused's morality, their sense of values, leaves a lot to be desired."

Tellingly, he referred to her as "the accused" throughout the entire proceeding, even after he was corrected by the Crown. For example, "the accused hasn't explained why she allowed the sex to happen if she didn't want it" (Transcript 437:9).

He drew conclusions about her credibility based on his stereotypical assumptions about the "kind of person" she is (Transcript 179:41) and about "the kind of thing that young women will talk about" (Transcript 351:39).

He also made light of both the issue of sexual violence and the testimony of the complainant by commenting: "she got really drunk in the laundry room and in the washroom of the basement suite because she was drinking what she called abstinence, ironically, but was absinthe and white rum" (Transcript 433:2).

C. Justice Camp's Comments and Reasoning Perpetuate Discriminatory Stereotypes

… Justice Camp's statements throughout the proceeding and in his reasons for judgment include numerous statements that perpetuate other discriminatory rape myths that have been categorically rejected at law. Indeed, the entire proceeding is threaded through with statements and questions by Justice Camp based on harmful stereotypes about women and sexual assault. The following list of examples is demonstrative and not inclusive of every instance in which this occurred:

- Myth: Women Who Behave A Certain Way Are More Likely To Have Consented.…

- Myth: Women Who Allege Rape Are Often to Blame for Their Sexual Victimization

- Myth: Women Who Allege Rape Are Simply Spiteful.…

- Myth: Women Who Actually Do Not Want to Be Raped Will Fight Their Attacker Off.…

[*Ed. Note*: The original letter provided transcript examples to support the allegation that each myth had been employed.]

Conclusion

In every case in which a judge has been removed from the bench, the behaviours considered by the Judicial Council arose from a single proceeding, but were serious enough to bring the administration of justice into disrepute. The judges in those instances displayed contempt or disregard for the people appearing before the court, disregard for the law, and attitudes grotesquely out of keeping with Canadian values. Justice Camp's behaviours in this case are of a similar quality. That any modern judge could ask a complainant if she kept her knees together, couple that with numerous other sexist and degrading comments, and then go on to ignore much of the law incumbent upon him to apply, eliminates confidence in that judge's commitment to independence, integrity, impartiality, and commitment to equality, brings the administration of justice into disrepute, and undermines the rule of law.

Before closing, we note that Justice Camp is now sitting on the Federal Court. As a result, he will be asked to consider cases involving issues of race, gender, and disadvantage (at times connected with sexualized violence), most obviously in immigration cases but also in matters involving federal human rights. His capacity to do so consistent with the Canadian Judicial Council's "Ethical Principles for Judges" and with the law has been shown to be profoundly compromised, and we call for his removal as a Justice of the Federal Court.

Report of the Canadian Judicial Council to the Minister of Justice

Presented in Ottawa, March 8, 2017. Reprinted with Permission

INTRODUCTION

From the time they are considered for appointment to the Bench, and every day thereafter, superior court judges in Canada are expected to be knowledgeable jurists. They are also expected to demonstrate a number of personal attributes including knowledge of social issues, an awareness of changes in social values, humility, fairness, empathy, tolerance, consideration and respect for others.

In short, Canadians expect their judges to know the law but also to possess empathy and to recognize and question any past personal attitudes and sympathies that might prevent them from acting fairly. Those qualities sustain public confidence in the judiciary.

For the reasons that follow, we find that Justice Robin Camp failed to meet those high standards and acted in a manner that seriously undermined public confidence in the judiciary. Accordingly, we recommend that Justice Camp be removed from office.

BACKGROUND

Further to a request from the Attorney General of Alberta, an Inquiry Committee ("Committee") was constituted by the Canadian Judicial Council ("Council"), pursuant to s. 63(3) of the *Judges Act*, R.S.C., 1985, c. J-1 ("the *Act*"), to conduct an investigation into the conduct of the Honourable Robin Camp ("the Judge")....

The Committee issued a 112-page report on 29 November 2016.... The Committee found that of the 21 specific allegations of misconduct made against the Judge, 17 are fully made out and two are partly made out.

The Committee found that throughout the *Wagar* trial ("the trial"), the Judge made comments or asked questions evidencing an antipathytoward laws designed to protect vulnerable witnesses, promote equality, and bring integrity to sexual assault trials. It also found that the Judge relied on discredited myths and stereotypes about women and victim-blaming during the trial and in his Reasons forJudgment.

The Committee concluded that the Judge committed misconduct and placed himself in a position incompatible with the due execution of the office of a judge within the meaning of paragraphs 65(2)(*b*) and (*d*) of the *Act*....

The Committee concluded that the Judge's conduct in the trial was so manifestly and profoundly destructive of the concept of impartiality, integrity and independence of the judicial role that public confidence is sufficiently undermined to render the Judge incapable of executing the judicial office. It expressed the unanimous view that a recommendation by the Council for the Judge's removal is warranted....

COUNCIL DELIBERATIONS

Council has considered the Committee report, as well as the record in this matter and the Judge's written submissions.

Council agrees with the Committee that the Judge committed serious misconduct and placed himself, by his conduct, in a position incompatible with the due execution of the office of a judge within the meaning of ss. 65(2)(*b*) and (*d*) of the *Act*.

That conduct included asking the complainant, a vulnerable 19 year old woman, "why didn't [she] just sink [her] bottom down into the basin so he couldn'tpenetrate [her]" and "why couldn't [she] just keep [her] knees together," that "sex and pain sometimes go together [...] – that's not necessarily a bad thing" and suggesting to Crown Counsel "if she [the complainant] skews her pelvis slightly she can avoid him."

While there is disagreement from the Judge about the effect and consequences of his conduct, he has readily acknowledged misconduct.... Given the

Judge's acknowledgement, the key issue before us is not whether there was misconduct, but whether the gravity of the misconduct warrants removal from office.

In his written submissions, the Judge argues that his removal is not warranted for four main reasons.

Unconscious bias or ignorance

First, while he admits his misconduct, the Judge renews his argument that his misconduct was the product of unconscious bias or ignorance, and not animus (which might be defined as hostility or ill feeling). He says this is relevant because unconscious bias and ignorance are inherently more remediable. Had the Committee properly characterized his misconduct, he argues, it would or should have concluded that the sanction of removal was not warranted. He argues that removing him would mean that sincere apologies and extensive education are incapable of restoring public confidence in a judge who displayed unconscious bias.

In this last sense, the Judge is correct. Apologies and education may not be sufficient in certain instances. We accept the Committee's characterization of the Judge's misconduct.

The Judge's questions to the alleged victim in this case were not simply attempts at clarification. He spoke in a manner that was at times condescending, humiliating and disrespectful.

The Judge's misconduct was manifestly serious and reflected a sustained pattern of beliefs of a particularly deplorable kind, regardless of whether he was conscious of it or not. As the Committee wrote at para. 293, one consequence of the Judge's misconduct in the trial is that it:

> ... adds to the public perception that the justice system is fuelled by systemic bias and it therefore courts the risk that in other sexual assault cases, unpopular decisions will be unfairly viewed as animated by that bias, rather than by the application of legal principles and sound reasoning and analysis.

Sincere apologies and extensive education may be capable of restoring public confidence in a judge whose misconduct consists of comments made and questions asked during a trial. However, all relevant circumstances must be taken into account. A single, highly prejudicial or offensive, comment might be sufficiently grave to seriously undermine public confidence in a judge and the judiciary. An important consideration is whether a judge's conduct after the fact is sufficient to restore public confidence....

Reasonableness of legal decisions

Second, the Judge asks Council to find that he made reasonable legal decisions at trial regarding the application of s. 276 of the *Criminal Code*. That section, commonly referred to as the "rape shield" provision, offers protection against the questioning of complainants regarding past sexual activity in trials for sexual offences.

The Judge submits that he applied the provision reasonably and that this should mitigate the gravity of his misconduct.

The Judge's acquittal of the accused was overturned by the Alberta Court of Appeal, which found several errors of law. On 31 January 2017, the accused was found not guilty after a new trial before the Alberta Provincial Court (*Wagar 2017*). As a result of this decision, Council accepted to receive further written representations from the Judge with respect to Mr. Wagar's second acquittal.

In his submissions, the Judge argues essentially that because his questions were legally relevant to the issues before him, they were therefore permissible. The remarks, he argues, were "based on unconscious bias and insensitive wording as opposed to hostility toward the law or the values inspiring it." In conclusion, the Judge argues that "*Wagar (2017)* shows that the IC's inferences are not necessarily correct. It proves that Justice Camp was right on the law and right on the facts, despite his admitted ignorance."

We find that the Committee's inferences are entirely reasonable and supported by the facts. We agree with the Committee that it is not appropriate for Council to interpret or second-guess the decision of the Court of Appeal. We find that the legal *outcome* of both the first trial and the new trial is of limited relevance to the issues before Council.

The respective roles of courts of appeal and Council are quite different: courts remedy legal errors while Council addresses issues of conduct. A judge may render an impeccable legal decision and still engage in misconduct. We reject the suggestion that there is an inconsistency in the Committee's reasoning in that the Committee "did not think Justice Camp's questions were legitimate. It thought his questions reflected disdain for the values underlying sexual assault law." (Judge's submissions of 23 February 2017)....

The Judge spoke of "contemporary thinking" during the trial, showing that he possessed more awareness of the issues than he later professed. He showed obvious disdain for some of the characteristics of the regime enacted by Parliament in respect of sexual assault issues.

We are mindful that any criticism Council levels against a judge must not have a chilling effect on the ability of judges, generally, to pursue relevant inquiries on the facts or law and to call attention to deficiencies in the law in appropriate cases. Indeed, judges have a duty to be critical of existing legislation in specific circumstances, for example where a judge forms a view that a specific provision contravenes our Constitution or otherwise operates in a deficient manner. We do not in any way intend to deter judges from asking the hard questions and taking the difficult positions that are sometimes necessary to discharge their judicial responsibilities.

However, some of the Judge's comments in this case were not in the nature of legitimate legal inquiries or comment. In this regard, we agree with the Committee that several of the Judge's comments "had little or nothing to do with the issues facing the Judge in the Trial" and were not of the type that could justifiably stray beyond matters directly connected to legitimate legal reasoning and result. *Wagar 2017* changes nothing in this respect.

Evidence of remediation

Third, the Judge says Council should reject the Committee's doubt that he was fully remediated through the education he had undertaken about the history of sexual assault law and reforms of his beliefs in the area of sexual assault and victims of violence after the complaint was made. He argues that Council should accept that he is remorseful, educated and rehabilitated and that removal is therefore not warranted....

Like the Committee, we recognize that the Judge engaged in serious remedial efforts after Council initiated a complaint against him, many months after the trial. He readily apologized for his actions and sought educational opportunities to address what he saw as shortcomings.

We also accept that experts in gender equality expressed the view that Justice Camp better understands the reasons behind the evolution of the law of sexual assault in Canada and the hurtful effect of his comments. However, this misses the most serious point....

Whether or not the Judge is sincerely remorseful or personally rehabilitated is not determinative of the matter. Even if we were to agree that the Judge is fully rehabilitated, we agree with the Committee that, in all the circumstances, the Judge's efforts at remediation must yield to a result that more resolutely pursues the goal of restoring public confidence in the integrity of the justice system....

In our view, the statements made by Justice Camp during the trial and in his decision, the values implicit in those statements and the way in which he conducted himself are so antithetical to the contemporary values of our judicial system with respect to the manner in which complainants in sexual assault case should be treated that, in our view, confidence in the system cannot be maintained unless the system disassociates itself from the image which the Judge, by his statements and approach, represents in the mind of a reasonable member of the public. In this case, that can only be accomplished by his removal from the system which, if he were not removed, he would continue to represent.

Proportionality of sanction

Fourth, the Judge argues that, assessed in the context of the outcomes of other judicial conduct cases, a recommendation for his removal would be disproportionate and unfit.

We disagree. As noted earlier, there are instances where a single, highly prejudicial or offensive, comment might be sufficiently grave to seriously undermine public confidence in a judge to the extent that removal is the only acceptable outcome. In such instances, remediation is of little assistance in coming to a final conclusion, which must be based on objective criteria that include trust, confidence and respect....

In this instance, the Judge's misconduct was evidenced over a continued period during the trial. Some of the Judge's most egregious comments were repeated in his reasons for decision, issued much later. The reasonable person's confidence in the Judge's ability to discharge the duties of office is seriously undermined.

Considering all the circumstances of this case, we reject the notion that removal is a disproportionate sanction.

CONCLUSION

Council has carefully considered the Committee's report and all of the Judge's submissions in this matter.

We find that the Judge's conduct, viewed in its totality and in light of all of its consequences, was so manifestly and profoundly destructive of the concept of impartiality, integrity and independence of the judicial role that public confidence is sufficiently undermined to render the Judge incapable of executing the judicial office.

Accordingly, Council recommends that Justice Camp be removed from office.

5.8

For Judge 'knees together' Camp: Education is power
Brenda Cossman

The Globe and Mail, December 3, 2016, F10. Reprinted with permission.

I admit that I was skeptical when I first got the phone call about the possibility of working with Justice Robin Camp. I had of course read all the media reports about the "why didn't you keep your knees together" judge. I had read the complaint to the Canadian Judicial Council, highlighting all of the other sexist remarks made during the course of the trial. It would have been easy to turn away.

But, I told myself that I believe in the power of education, and I should at least meet him.

The man that I met was not like the misogynist monster I had read about in the press. The man I met was earnestly apologetic, open-minded and eager to learn. And because I believe in the power of education, I decided to work with Justice Camp. I knew it wouldn't be a popular decision with my feminist colleagues, but popularity is not how I make decisions.

So, Justice Camp and I embarked on an intensive course in the history of sexism in sexual assault law. My assessment was that he understood the law as it was currently written, but not the decades of legal campaigns to rid the law of sexist rape myths. He knew what the law was, but not why it was this way, or the way it had been before. By the time we were done, I believe that he understood this history, and in turn, had a more robust grasp not only on why the law says what it says, but also why his comments were so egregious in light of this history.

Some may say, legitimately, that Justice Camp should have known all this before. Some may say that he was only open to learning because his job was on the line. Some may say it was too little too late. Some say the damage to the justice system was already done. These are all fair comments. The Inquiry Committee of the Canadian Judicial Council has adopted a version of them.

But, I worry that we are swift to punish. I worry that we prefer punishment to education. Because I believe in the power of education, and I am rather more skeptical of the power of punishment. History shows that education has a better pedigree of success than punishment.

I worry even more about the impulse to punish in light of the recent rise of a powerful backlash against any and all equality-seeking groups. We have moved into a new post-empathy era, where more people are prepared to stand defiantly and unapologetically in favour of discrimination, sexism, and racism. I worry that we dismiss the possibility of education and move to punish those who are genuinely remorseful.

I also worry, in the new post-truth era, that we dismiss facts that we simply do not like. Justice Camp's most frequently cited comments – the infamous "why didn't you keep your knees together" – was an attempt, albeit a dreadfully worded one – to get at issues that both the defence counsel and the Crown had put into play. There was a real legal issue, though you wouldn't know it from any of the press coverage.

While it is understandable that the Inquiry Committee felt compelled to draw a line on sexist comments, and condemn Justice Camp for having crossed it, I wonder about the precedent. Feminist lawyers and advocates recognize the pervasive nature of sexism in the judiciary. Are we going to fire each and every judge who has uttered sexist comments in the course of a trial? Or, are we going to try to educate them? Preferably before the sexual assault trials, but what about after?

I leave open the possibility that some judges are beyond redemption. I am not convinced that Robin Camp was one of these. But that is because my default is not punishment. It is education.

5.9

Bad People Make Bad Judges
Lauren Heuser

The Walrus, March 16, 2017, https://thewalrus.ca/bad-people-make-bad-judges/. Reprinted with permission.

Robin Camp, the federal court judge who recently resigned, seemed to be heading places. After immigrating to Canada from South Africa in 1998, he'd had a successful career as a litigator and lecturer at the University of Calgary law faculty before being appointed to Alberta's provincial court in 2012, and elevated to the federal court in 2015.

It's anyone's guess where he might have gone from there had a fateful sexual assault trial not landed on his docket in 2014. On trial was a Calgary man accused of sexually assaulting a woman in a bathroom at a house party. The case turned on whether the complainant's sexual activity with the accused, Alex Wagar, was consensual, or, if not, whether Wagar had honestly but mistakenly believed she had consented.

Following a three-day trial, Camp acquitted Wagar. As his comments throughout the hearing revealed, Camp's thinking was informed by stereotypes and myths about sexual assault victims – stereotypes and myths that Canada's courts have clearly said are forbidden in judicial reasoning.

Among other legal errors, Camp harboured serious misunderstandings about consent: what can be considered in determining whether the complainant gave it, and what an accused must show to establish he thought he'd obtained it. Camp suggested that the complainant was more likely to have consented because she "abused the first opportunity to report"; she "foolishly" took her chances by not reacting when Wagar came in and locked the bathroom door ("If she sees the door being locked, she's not a complete idiot, she knows what's coming next"); or noting that if she'd been truly "frightened, you'd think she'd … shout."

While these legal mistakes were serious, they were not what led to the Canadian Judicial Council (CJC) recommending, last week, that Camp be removed from the judiciary. Rather, the errors that made Camp's conduct inexcusable were of a more contextual nature – revealed less by his most incendiary legal questions than by the totality of his disrespectful commentary. It's rare that words seem worse in context than outside of it, but such was the case here.

While our society tends to put judges on a pedestal, they are not actually held to a standard of perfection. There is good reason for this. For one, judges are human and prone to err like the rest of us. As University of Calgary law professor Alice Woolley has written: "Making a mistake when applying the law does not make a judgment wrongful, even in a serious criminal case. Judges make mistakes all the time and that they do is an understandable product of their humanity."

Second, our justice system is structured to account for legal errors and, when necessary, to correct for them – either through legal appeals or increased education. In Camp's case, we have seen both. The *Wagar* decision was appealed and a new trial was ordered. At the same time, in the House of Commons, Conservative Party leader Rona Ambrose has pushed to pass Bill C-337, a bill that would require lawyers to undergo sexual assault education before being eligible for judicial appointment.

Thus, the fact that Camp's reasoning was rife with legal errors was not the reason he was ousted. Even some of his most infamous remarks – the ones that most scandalized the public – may have been honest, if egregiously worded, legal mistakes. As Brenda Cossman, a law professor at the University of Toronto, argued in a *Globe and Mail* editorial [*Ed. note*: See Reading 5.8]: "Camp's most frequently cited comments – the infamous 'why didn't you keep your knees together' – was an attempt, albeit a dreadfully worded one, to get at issues that both the defence counsel and the Crown had put into play. There was a real legal issue, though you wouldn't know it from any of the press coverage."

Cossman, one of the experts brought on to assist with Camp's rehabilitation, took the position that Camp's genuine efforts to educate himself in the wake of the CJC's investigation weighed in favour of giving him a second chance. Camp, she suggested, was not a judge who is "beyond redemption."

There would be much to this argument had the sum of Camp's errors been his misunderstandings about our sexual assault laws, or even his misunderstandings about sexual assault victims. It is certainly possible to condemn ignorance while committing to educate the ignorant.

But gross legal errors weren't the worst of Camp's mistakes. As the full record makes clear, Camp often exceeded all bounds of judicial propriety by making personal pronouncements on the complainant's character. Despite her circumstances being altogether heartbreaking—at the time of the alleged assault, she was only 19 years old, homeless, unemployed, a drug abuser, and without a support network – Camp seemed to view her with something bordering disdain. At points, his comments read like something out of *Bleak House*:

> I record that all the witnesses were, in a sense, unsavoury.... The complainant ... had spent the day in question sneaking into the movies without paying.... She'd also spent a considerable amount of time stealing clothes.... It didn't cross her mind that she should work to earn money to buy those things.

> After they had been to steal liquor, she got really drunk ... in the washroom of the basement suite because she was drinking what she called abstinence, ironically, but was absinthe and white rum....

> In her first version of what happened in the washroom ... she said she went to the washroom to throw up. And I pause to make the point that it would be surprising if her evidence was perfect.... She was, of course, drunk at the time....

As one gets a flavour of here, the odiousness of Camp's conduct in many ways has little to do with sexual assault. The problem, rather, is an attitudinal one: a seeming inability to empathize with an individual whose life circumstances have plainly been difficult. "What is troubling ... is not that this occurred in relation to a sexual assault complainant," Woolley writes. "What is disturbing is that this occurred in relation to anyone at all whose conduct the judge is assessing." Judges must have the capacity to see the individuals who come before them as human.

More than we might like to admit, the proper administration of justice hangs on the integrity of the individuals tasked with applying the law. If we cannot trust them to regard all individuals as persons of dignity who are equal before them and the law, it is difficult to trust their ability to apply the law fairly. As the CJC recognized, "Fundamentally, Justice Camp's misconduct is rooted in a profound lack of impartiality and failure to respect equality before the law."

Misconduct of this nature is not something you could trust education to correct for – particularly for a professional of Camp's years. In time, experience may, however. Having now found himself the target of so many people's disgust, Camp may come to understand first-hand why his conduct towards the complainant was so problematic. It's painful to be treated as an object of disdain.

5.10

Key Terms

Concepts

administrative independence

financial security

"good behaviour"

impartiality

judicial accountability

judicial compensation commissions

judicial education

judicial independence

security of tenure

sexual assault law

Institutions, Events and Documents

Act of Settlement (1701)

Bastarache interview (2001)

Berger Affair (1981)

Constitution Act, 1867, ss. 96–100

Canadian Charter of Rights and Freedoms, s. 11(d)

Canadian Judicial Council (1971)

Inquiry Committee into Justice Lori Douglas (2010–2014)

Inquiry Committee into Justice Robin Camp (2016–2017)

Judges Affair (1976)

McClung Affair (1999)

R. v. Ewanchuk, [1999] 1 S.C.R. 330

Ref re Remuneration of Judges of the Prov. Court of P.E.I.; Ref re Independence and Impartiality of Judges of the Prov. Court of P.E.I., [1997] 3 S.C.R. 3

The Queen v. Beauregard, [1986] 2 S.C.R. 56.

Valente v. The Queen, [1985] 2 S.C.R. 673

Vriend v. Alberta, [1998] 1 S.C.R. 493

6

Interest Groups and Access to Judicial Power

Traditionally, access to the courts has been strictly limited to individuals who meet the threshold requirements of "standing" - the right to bring a case before a court. In order to establish standing, a would-be litigant must usually prove the existence of a *lis*, or legal dispute. Not all disputes raise legal issues, and not all legal issues arise in the context of real-life disputes. In the realm of constitutional law, mere distaste for or opposition to a particular statute or government policy does not constitute a dispute. A legally recognizable dispute requires the existence of a specific legal interest and an injury or a demonstrable threat of injury to that interest. Finally, a case must not become "moot" during the course of litigation. If the original dispute that gave rise to the case ceases to exist, a judge will normally refuse to answer the legal issues raised and terminate the judicial hearing.

Like other aspects of the judicial process, these restrictions on access to the courts can be traced back to the original purpose of common law courts as adjudicators of real-life disputes between individuals. As the celebrated American jurist Felix Frankfurter once observed, "the mechanisms of law - what courts are to deal with, which causes, and subject to what conditions - cannot be dissociated from the ends that the law serves."[1] As with other human tools and institutions, the ends influence the means, the "what" shapes the "how."

These traditional restrictions on access to the courts ably serve their original adjudicatory purposes but are subject to criticism in modern public law cases, which often have a policy dimension that transcends the immediate dispute. As Weiler has pointed out, other policy-making institutions are not restricted in these ways. If final appeal courts are essentially policy-makers, why should an interest group have to wait for a dispute involving one of its members in order to bring its policy issue into court? These rules not only frustrate groups' ability to get their issues before a court; they also restrict judges' ability to act in a timely fashion.

Given Canadian judges' historical attachment to the more British, adjudicatory view of the judicial process, it was not surprising that until quite recently the rules governing standing and mootness in Canadian constitutional law were stricter than their American counterparts. For example, in 1953 in the celebrated *Saumur* case,[2] the Supreme Court struck down the Quebec City bylaw used to prosecute Jehovah's Witnesses for distributing their pamphlets. The fifth and deciding vote for the Supreme Court majority ruled that the bylaw violated Quebec's own *Freedom of Worship Act*. The government of Quebec Premier Maurice Duplessis promptly responded to this decision by amending the *Act* to exclude the Jehovah's Witnesses' pamphleteering from its protection. When Saumur initiated a new legal action to have this amendment declared invalid, the Supreme Court (affirming the judgment of the Quebec courts) ruled that, since the amended legislation had not actually been applied against any Witnesses, there was no real *lis* (dispute). Thus, the Court refused to rule on the validity of the amended *Act*.

The rules on standing remained restrictive until the mid-1970s. The governing precedent was the 1924 ruling in *Smith* that, "An individual ... has no status to maintain an action restraining a wrongful violation of a public right unless he is exceptionally prejudiced by the wrongful act."[3] In 1975, the Supreme Court overruled this precedent by granting standing to Thorson, a federal civil servant seeking a declaratory judgment that the Trudeau government's new bilingualism legislation was invalid even though he was not personally affected by it. Three judges led by Justice Judson dissented, arguing that "the action was an attempt to get an opinion which the Court had no right to give." But the other six judges granted Thorson standing, based on what Chief Justice Laskin declared was "the right of the citizenry to constitutional behaviour by Parliament."[4] Justice Judson's dissent shows that Laskin's decision to eliminate the requirement of a *lis* served not just to broaden access for litigants, but also expanded the Court's jurisdiction and thus its ability to intervene in the policy process.

The rules governing standing were further relaxed the following year in *Nova Scotia Board of Censors v. McNeil*.[5] Even though the Censor Board's ruling applied only to theatre owners, not the viewing public, the Court granted standing to a reporter to challenge the Board's ruling to ban the film *Last Tango in Paris*. This trend reached its peak in the Court's 1981 ruling in *Minister of Justice (Canada) v. Borowski*, when the Court ruled that, even though pro-life crusader Joe Borowski was not personally harmed or even affected by the abortion law, he could still challenge its constitutional validity. The majority decision certainly seemed consistent with its precedents of *Thorson* and *McNeil*, but this time it was Chief Justice Laskin who dissented, warning that "the result would be to set up a battle between parties who do not have a direct interest [and] to wage it in a judicial arena."[6] (How to reconcile this argument with Laskin's earlier declaration of "the right of the citizenry to constitutional behaviour by Parliament" is an interesting question.) The *Borowski* decision removed the traditional requirement that a would-be litigant demonstrate a concrete personal interest that is affected by the legal issue raised, and created instead a very broad right for all citizens to go to the courts and demand that the judges force the government to "behave constitutionally."

In 1992, the Court placed some restrictions on standing when it ruled that an interest group (the Canadian Council of Churches) did not have standing to challenge new amendments to the *Immigration Act* because the same challenge could have been brought by a private individual. But while the Court was saying "no" to the Canadian Council of Churches, it reaffirmed its very broad discretion to grant standing in *Charter* cases:

> By its terms the *Charter* indicates that a generous and liberal approach should be taken to the issue of standing. If that were not done, *Charter* rights might be unenforced and *Charter* freedoms shackled. The *Constitution Act, 1982* does not of course affect the discretion the Court possesses to grant standing to public litigants. What it does is entrench the fundamental right of the public to government in accordance with the law.[7]

The Supreme Court's rules for standing were liberalized even further in *Canada (Attorney General) v. Downtown Eastside Sex Workers United Against Violence Society* in 2012. The Court confirmed that a group could bring a constitutional challenge to Canada's prostitution laws in a British Columbia court even though a similar challenge was underway in Ontario, insofar as the B.C. group's challenge was "a reasonable and effective means to bring the challenge to court."[8]

The Supreme Court has also weakened the doctrine of mootness as a barrier to engaging the courts in constitutional politics. In October, 1988, Borowski returned to the Supreme Court, this time to challenge the abortion law on its merits. However, eight months earlier in its second *Morgentaler* decision,[9] the Supreme Court had struck down the abortion law, although for the very opposite reasons argued by Borowski. The Court now ruled that, with no law left to challenge, Borowski's case had become moot and dismissed it, again without ruling on the merits. But even as it dismissed Borowski's claim as moot, the Supreme Court elaborated a new mootness doctrine that allowed otherwise moot cases to be decided if they can meet certain criteria.[10] This relaxed stance on mootness continued in the Court's most far-reaching LGBTQ rights decision, *M v. H* (1999),[11] a case the Court heard even though the dispute over property division between the two lesbian partners had already been resolved in an out-of-court settlement. Mootness is no longer a meaningful barrier to hearing a case that the Court wants to decide for legal or policy reasons.

Likewise, the Supreme Court rejected a "political questions" doctrine from precluding judicial review of government decisions involving foreign policy or national defence. The political questions doctrine is a convention developed by the United States Supreme Court that prevents courts from hearing constitutional challenges to foreign policy or national defence decisions of the government. It is based on the judges' view of the proper role of the courts: that responsibility for such decisions is explicitly allocated to other branches of government (i.e., separation of powers); that judges lack the expertise and facts necessary to make such decisions; and that foreign-policy decisions are based on practical judgment and thus are not susceptible to judicial decision based on "neutral principles." In its 1985 decision in *Operation Dismantle*,[12] the Supreme Court of Canada avoided dealing with the political questions doctrine while dismissing an anti-nuclear group's claim because it was based on alleged facts that could not be proven. In a concurring opinion, however, Justice Wilson boldly stated that Crown prerogative did not shield the government's foreign-policy decisions from *Charter* challenges, nor did any political questions doctrine. The political questions doctrine has since played no role in the Court's post-*Charter* jurisprudence.

Getting into court is one thing; getting to the Supreme Court of Canada is another. As noted in Chapter 3, Parliament amended the *Supreme Court Act* in 1975 to abolish most appeals "as of right." Since then, the Court has only granted "leave to appeal" in those cases that it deems to raise legal issues of "public importance." Since "public importance" is not defined in the *Supreme Court Act*, the Court has virtually complete discretion in deciding which appeals to hear and which not to. How does the Supreme Court decide if a case raises an issue of sufficient "public importance"? The late Justice John Sopinka (along with his colleague Mark Gelowitz) identified five important considerations: a novel constitutional issue; a significant federal statute of general application; a provincial statute similar to legislation in other provinces; conflicting decisions in the provincial courts of appeal; and the need to revisit an important question of law.[13] Applying these legal criteria, however, is an art rather than a science, and they do not impose any significant restrictions on the judges' discretion to hear only those cases they want to hear.

Another important exception to the traditional requirement of a *lis* is the reference procedure (Reading 6.1). Starting with the original *Supreme Court Act* of 1875, the federal government has given itself the authority to "refer" questions of law to the Supreme Court of Canada for answering, and provincial governments soon followed suit for their own courts of appeal. A reference procedure is not really a case in the true sense, as there is no real dispute and no real litigants, but only a request for an advisory opinion on a hypothetical legal issue. This distinctive characteristic of the Canadian judicial process is not found in American jurisprudence. Article III of the American Constitution spells out the requirement of a *lis* by limiting the federal courts to hearing only "cases or controversies."

The fact that reference cases are technically "advisory opinions" on hypothetical questions of law should not lead one to underestimate their importance. Even though judicial decisions in references are not technically binding on anyone (since there are no real parties), they are still regarded as authoritative. As Professor Kate Puddister (Reading 6.1) shows, there have been over two hundred references heard at Canadian appellate courts since Confederation. Predictably, governments almost never refer questions to the courts in a political vacuum. References tend to be politically timely, either anticipating a political problem that is on the horizon or, in some cases, already being litigated in a lower court. For example, Puddister shows how the reference power was used most frequently in the 1930s and 1980s, periods defined, respectively, by the Great Depression and "mega constitutional" politics. Yet even in the post-*Charter* era, governments have been more likely to use their reference power to ask courts about the boundaries of government power rather than the boundaries of *Charter* rights. The *Patriation Reference, Secession Reference* and *Senate Reference* (Readings 2.4, 2.5 and 2.6), arguably three of the most important Supreme Court references of all time, provide proof of this.

Including the reference power, there would appear to be few remaining legal barriers to prevent the litigation of the constitutionality of most government decisions or policies. If a majority of the judges on the Supreme Court decide they want to become involved, they are no longer restrained by the doctrines of mootness, standing or political questions. Accordingly, groups that "lose" in the legislative arena are inclined to take advantage of this new forum to challenge government policy that they oppose.

Interest Groups and the Courts
For both governments and interest groups, there is an alternative to participating directly as a party in public law litigation: the legal device of the intervenor or *amicus curiae* ("friend of the court"). Under this form of "third-party" participation, a court may grant permission to an individual, group or government to present a written factum, participate in oral argument or both. Historically, there was considerable reluctance to allow such third-party participation because it violates the logic of the adversarial process. If the principal function of

the court is to resolve the dispute before it, the judges can and should rely on the self-interests of the disputants to develop the legal arguments and facts. If one party fails to do this adequately, only the individual litigant suffers the consequences. However, this argument is less persuasive in public law cases, where the policy dimension of the dispute means that parties beyond the disputants will also be affected. If a constitutional ruling is going to affect other governments or groups, why should they not be allowed to present legal arguments and facts to the court?

Canadian courts were not traditionally receptive to allowing non-government parties to intervene. This policy changed slightly in the 1970s, when, under the leadership of Chief Justice Laskin, non-government parties were allowed to participate as intervenors in cases involving the controversial issues of abortion and sex discrimination against status Indian women. Nevertheless, in 1975, Kenneth McNaught, one of Canada's leading historians, concluded that "our judges and lawyers, supported by the press and public opinion, reject any concept of the courts as positive instruments in the political process ... political action outside the party-parliamentary structure tends automatically to be suspect – and not the least because it smacks of Americanism."[14] Seven years later, the *Charter of Rights and Freedoms* was adopted. Since then, there has been a veritable surge in interest-group litigation.

With the adoption of the *Constitution Act, 1982*, there was a widespread expectation amongst the advocacy groups that had lobbied for the *Charter* that the Supreme Court would continue to welcome non-government intervenors. To these groups' chagrin, this did not happen. From 1983 to 1986, the Court rejected more than half the interest-group requests for intervenor status. The Supreme Court's "closed-door" policy provoked a chorus of protests from interest groups. One of the most influential actors in the campaign to persuade the Court to change its ways was Alan Borovoy, General Counsel of the Canadian Civil Liberties Association (CCLA). In an unusual "open letter" to the Supreme Court of Canada (Reading 6.2), Borovoy forcefully argued that it was both unfair and unwise to allow governments but not rights-advocacy groups to intervene in the scores of *Charter* appeals that were beginning to filter their way up to the Court. In such a novel document as the *Charter*, the Court was essentially working on a "blank slate." The Court's first interpretation of each right would become an instant "landmark" precedent, shaping the course of subsequent development. Borovoy predicted (correctly) that most governments would instinctively oppose broad interpretations of rights because these would result in more limitations on governments' choice of policy goals and means. It was important for the country, Borovoy argued, for the Court to hear "countervailing long-term theories for interpreting the *Charter*." Allowing non-government intervenors would mean a better-informed Court, which in turn would produce a better *Charter* jurisprudence.

The protests worked. In 1987, the Supreme Court issued new rules for intervenors (factums limited to twenty pages; no oral argument except for special circumstances) and also began a new "open-door" policy. Encouraged by the Court's new policy, the number of interest-group requests to participate as intervenors also soared. From 1987 to 2001, the Court accepted more than 80 per cent of requests to intervene; by 2008, that number had risen to over 90 per cent. From 2000 to 2008, nearly 50 per cent of cases at the Supreme Court had intervenors, and that number was on an upward trend (for *Charter* cases, the number was closer to 90 per cent).[15] Although provincial Attorneys General are the most frequent type of intervenor, the routine presence of non-government interest groups in the Court's proceedings marks a radical departure from the pre-*Charter* era, and is another indicator of its increased policy-making role.

While there are persuasive legal reasons for allowing non-government intervenors, the policy also encourages and supports interest-group litigation as a political tactic. What Borovoy did not state in his open letter to the Court was that the CCLA and other *Charter* groups also have a vested interest in "theories for interpreting the *Charter*." Most *Charter*-oriented groups want to encourage judges to give a broad judicial reading of the rights that most directly concern them. The largest, best-organized and best-financed use of *Charter* litigation has been mounted by Canadian feminists. Feminists gained a head-start on other interest groups by successfully lobbying Parliament for a favourable wording of section 15 equality rights while the *Charter* was still in draft stage. Soon after the *Charter* was proclaimed, the Canadian Advisory Council on the Status of Women commissioned a study that recommended the creation of a single, nationwide "legal action fund" to coordinate and pay for a policy of systematic litigation of strategic "test cases."[16] On April 13, 1985, only days before the equality rights section of the *Charter* came into effect, the Women's Legal and Education Action Fund (LEAF) was launched.

Sherene Razack's account of LEAF's early activities and strategies (Reading 6.3) discloses some of the subterranean aspects of *Charter* politics. In addition to creating a single national fund to take test cases to court as part of a plan of systematic litigation, LEAF also conducted a behind-the-scenes campaign of "influencing the influencers." This campaign was based on the belief that "Rights on paper mean nothing unless the courts correctly interpret their scope and application." By "correct interpretation," LEAF meant a theory of equality that stressed equality of results or "adverse impact," not just equal application of equal laws. To ensure that the theory of equality adopted by the courts was the right one, LEAF undertook a broad range of activities in addition to the traditional techniques of lobbying legislators and top bureaucrats. These included encouraging and even sponsoring legal scholarship that supported an "adverse impact" interpretation of section 15, participating in judicial training programs, participating in the relevant committees of the Canadian Bar Association and provincial legal societies, encouraging the appointment of feminist judges and cultivating contacts in the media.

The first two decades of LEAF's organizational efforts were certainly rewarded. In a study of forty-seven appeal court decisions between 1982 and 1996, the authors found that the feminist party or interest won 72 per cent of the disputes and changed public policy in a desired direction in seventeen of those cases. The study noted that, in addition to the immediate legal outcomes, interest-group litigation can serve a number of other valuable political purposes: agenda-setting, mobilization of public support, problem-definition, and legitimating and consolidating earlier legal victories.[17] In Reading 6.4, Christopher Manfredi shows that LEAF's interventions at the Supreme Court of Canada produced policy impact that goes beyond mere judicial wins and losses. In the fields of abortion, sexual assault, family policy and sexual orientation, LEAF's interventions preceded substantial policy change – and often societal change – in a feminist direction. Even when the LEAF position "lost" in court, LEAF "raised issues to a position on the policy agenda that they might not have reached, or reached as quickly, without the visibility of Supreme Court decisions."

Feminists, of course, are not the only ones to use the *Charter* to influence policy. In a study of over twenty-five hundred Supreme Court and Federal Court decisions (during the 1988–1998 period), Gregory Hein found 819 organizations involved as litigants or intervenors (Reading 6.5). These organizations came from across the political spectrum: Aboriginal groups, civil libertarians, corporate interests, labour interests, professionals, social conservatives, victims of crime, *Charter* Canadians and New Left activists (Table 1). By far the most frequent participants before these courts were corporate interests – representing 56 per cent ($n=468$) of the total (Figure 1). Hein argues that such diversity, plus the heavy corporate involvement, disproves the criticism that interest-group litigation is primarily a tool of interests on the political Left. To the contrary, Hein claims that his data show the *Charter* has had a democratizing effect on the Canadian political system by opening up the courts to interests that in the past were typically excluded. However, most corporate involvement was in civil cases against other corporations or private parties (not challenges to government laws and policies). In addition, the corporate propensity to litigate was lower than that of the various social justice groups (Table 3). Corporations thus had a less direct effect on public policy.

Hein also presents a theory as to why such diverse groups end up in the courts. Sometimes, they are "pushed" by the necessity of responding to adverse new laws or a new legal challenge to a policy or legal precedent they support. Sometimes, they are "pulled" by organizational characteristics such as strong legal resources, rights-based identities and "normative visions that demand judicial activism." These are the "judicial democrats" who believe that judicial activism in defence of the rights of minorities is good because it remedies a structural defect in Canada's parliamentary democracy – its tendency to under-represent the politically disadvantaged. In response to *Charter* critics, Hein counters that "We now have a judicial system that responds to a diverse range of interests."

Hein's "judicial democrats" thesis is challenged by Ian Brodie (Reading 6.6), who points out that judges are even less "representative" of Canadian society than legislatures. Brodie claims that, if these groups were truly "disadvantaged," they could not afford to use systematic litigation strategies. Rather than being the "grass-roots, bottom-up" movement described by Hein, Brodie notes that lawyers are hardly a "disadvantaged" group, and points to substantial government funding as the real explanation for judicial democrats' extensive and successful litigation efforts. The most controversial source of such funding comes in the form of the Court Challenges Program (CCP).

There can be little doubt that the CCP, initiated by the federal government in September, 1985, encouraged *Charter* litigation. Indeed, the government's initial allocation of $9 million over five years was for the express purpose of funding litigation arising under the equality rights, language rights and multiculturalism provisions of the *Charter*. Applications for financial support were screened according to the criteria of "substantial importance ... legal merit [and] consequences for a number of people." The administrators of the program stated that they would "emphasize the setting of social justice priorities." Selected cases were eligible for $35,000 at each stage of litigation – trial, provincial appeal court and the Supreme Court of Canada. The CCP was cancelled by Conservative Prime Minister Brian Mulroney in February, 1992, but was reinstated by Jean Chrétien's Liberals in 1994 as an independently incorporated body.

Critics of the CCP complained that its directors were mostly drawn from the membership of the same rights-advocacy groups that receive money from the CCP. The CCP's 2001 announcement that it would no longer publish an annual list of grant recipients because of lawyer-client confidentiality only further angered those who saw it as promoting an unfair playing field. In 2006, Conservative Prime Minister Stephen Harper cancelled the CCP, although following litigation from minority language groups, his government restored the language rights component of the program in 2008. The full CCP was reinstated by Justin Trudeau's Liberal government following its 2015 election victory.

The program is now allocated $5 million per year, with $1.5 million of that guaranteed for official language minority rights. The reformed program is now split into a Language Rights Panel and an Equality Rights Panel, each of which determines what cases will be funded.

The revival of the CCP has also revived the debate over the utility of having the state fund groups to challenge state policy. Carissima Mathen and Kyle Kirkup (Reading 6.7) reject the argument that it is "illogical for the government to fund Canadians to sue it." They claim this rests on a simplistic view of rights, and that the government's role in protecting and promoting constitutional rights need not be "merely defensive." Mathen and Kirkup concur with Gregory Hein's assessment that funding court challenges has made the process more inclusive, and that allowing those who "lack political power" to hold the government to account enriches democracy.

Ian Brodie, whose book *Friends of the Court*[18] documented the history of the CCP, was one of its most prominent critics. In Reading 6.8, he explains that the program has become a "political football" – tossed between cancellation and revival – due to its narrow ideological focus on funding progressive, equality-seeking groups. There is no inherent reason, Brodie argues, that the CCP should not fund litigants associated with conservative causes, such as free-speech advocates and religious organizations. In short, for the new CCP to move above the partisan fray, it "should benefit more than just social-reform and minority-language groups." One way to do this would be to "make the CCP broader and less partisan than it has been in the past."

An additional critique of the CCP, not taken up in the following readings, is that the program has a centralist bias. The CCP is not simply a matter of the state funding groups to challenge state policies. In almost all cases, it is the *federal* government funding rights-advocacy groups to challenge *provincial* policies. This is explicitly the case in language rights cases. From Pierre Trudeau onwards, federal governments of both parties have sought to protect the Quebec anglophone community against *Bill 101* and other language policies of Parti Québécois governments in Quebec. Federal Liberal governments have been equally supportive of litigation by francophone minorities outside of Quebec against unilingual provincial policies. When the Supreme Court strikes down an offending provincial law, the CCP allows Ottawa to do indirectly what it lacks the jurisdiction to achieve directly, except through the now discredited federal powers of reservation and disallowance. As Brodie notes, in the area of section 15 equality rights litigation, most of the groups that have received funding have been partisans of the identity politics of the progressive Left, which explains why Stephen Harper's Conservative government cancelled the CCP and Justin Trudeau's Liberal government restored it. In both the language rights and equality rights cases, federal funding of interest-group litigation against recalcitrant provincial governments echoes much earlier criticisms of the first *Supreme Court Act* as a form of "disallowance in disguise" (See Reading 9.1). It is also consistent with earlier comparative studies that found that in federal states, final national courts of appeal tend to "serve upper class and nationalizing interests rather than dominant local interests and thus [are] more satisfactory to persons trying to break through the web of local interests."[19] (See the introduction to Chapter 9.)

The funding of organized interests is central to Charles Epp's widely cited theory of the causes of Canada's "rights revolution" (Reading 6.9). Epp rejects as too legalistic the explanation that the adoption of the *Charter* in 1982 was the cause. Citing examples of nations with rights documents without much judicial enforcement of those rights, Epp argues that forces outside a bill of rights matter for rights protection. In response to the question, "Do Bills of Rights Matter?" Epp replies: yes, but only if there is a "support structure for legal mobilization." The three key elements of such a structure are: (1) rights advocacy organizations that (2) enjoy substantial support among skilled lawyers and (3) that have non-member funding – private foundations (United States) or governments (Canada). Epp provides empirical evidence that many of the effects attributed to the *Charter of Rights* actually precede its adoption in 1982, and better coincide with the growth of a support structure for mobilization in Canada during the 1970s.

Epp's thesis has been challenged, however. In Reading 6.10, Donald Songer uses longitudinal data from the Supreme Court of Canada to argue that the *Charter* was a more significant factor in Canada's rights revolution than Epp suggests. Writing in 2008, Songer agrees with Epp that constitutional rights protection is not "self-executing." However, Songer argues that when one disaggregates criminal from other civil liberties cases, examines rights challenges to executive action and "takes a more comprehensive view of constitutional lawmaking," the *Charter*'s effect on the Supreme Court is far more pronounced. Using year-over-year data from the *Charter*'s first two decades, Songer argues that the *Charter* produced a "dramatic increase in rights litigation in the Supreme Court of Canada."

Both Epp and Songer share a recognition that myriad factors have led to the growth of judicial power in Canada. These include the Court's docket control; its relaxed requirements for standing and mootness; its reluctance to adopt a political questions doctrine; the continued availability of reference opinions; a support structure for legal mobilization (including funding by the Court Challenges Program); and the entrenchment of the *Charter of Rights*. Collectively, they have had the net effect of increasing judicial policy-making. Well-funded interest groups – a crucial aspect of the support structure for legal mobilization Epp describes – remain a central part of *Charter* politics as well.

And while debates about "judicial democrats," the "Court Party" and a "level playing field" persist, it is hard to deny the strength and scope of judicial power are at their highest points in Canadian history.

NOTES

1   Felix Frankfurter and James Landis, *The Business of the Supreme Court* (New York: Macmillan, 1928), p. 2.

2   *Saumur v. City of Quebec*, [1953] 2 S.C.R. 29.

3   *Smith v. Attorney-General of Ontario*, [1924] S.C.R. 331, pp. 337–338.

4   *Thorson v. Attorney-General of Canada*, [1975] 1 S.C.R. 138, pp. 142, 163.

5   [1976] 2 S.C.R. 265.

6   [1981] 2 S.C.R. 575, p. 587.

7   *Canadian Council of Churches v. Minister of Employment and Immigration*, [1992] 1 S.C.R. 236, p. 250.

8   *Canada (Attorney General) v. Downtown Eastside Sex Workers United Against Violence Society*, [2012] 2 S.C.R. 524, para. 52.

9   *R. v. Morgentaler*, [1988] 1 S.C.R. 30.

10   *Borowski v. Canada (Attorney General)*, [1989] 1 S.C.R. 342.

11   *M v. H.*, [1999] 2 S.C.R. 3.

12   *Operation Dismantle v. The Queen*, [1985] 1 S.C.R. 441.

13   John Sopinka and Mark A. Gelowitz, *The Conduct of An Appeal* (Toronto: Butterworths, 1993), p. 167.

14   Kenneth McNaught, "Political Trials and the Canadian Political Tradition," in M.L. Friedland, ed., *Courts and Trials: A Multidisciplinary Approach* (Toronto: University of Toronto Press, 1975), p. 137.

15   Ian Brodie, "Intervenors and the *Charter*," in F.L. Morton, ed., *Law, Politics and the Judicial Process in Canada*. 3rd ed. (Calgary: University of Calgary Press, 2002), pp. 295–297; Benjamin R.D. Alarie and Andrew J. Green, "Interventions at the Supreme Court of Canada: Accuracy, Affiliation, and Acceptance," *Osgoode Hall Law Journal* 48, no. 3/4 (Fall/Winter, 2010), pp. 295–400.

16   M. Elizabeth Atcheson et al., "Equality Rights and Legal Action," in F.L. Morton, ed., *Law, Politics and the Judicial Process in Canada*. 3rd ed. (Calgary: University of Calgary Press, 2002), pp. 309–315.

17   F.L. Morton and Avril Allen, "Feminists and the Courts: Measuring Success in Interest Group Litigation in Canada," *Canadian Journal of Political Science* 29, no. 1 (March, 2001), pp. 55–84.

18   Ian Brodie, *Friends of the Court: The Privileging of Interest Group Litigants in Canada* (Albany: SUNY Press, 2002).

19   Martin Shapiro, *Courts: A Comparative and Political Analysis* (Chicago: University of Chicago Press, 1981), p. 24.

6.1

The Canadian Reference Power
Kate Puddister
Political Science, University of Guelph

The Canadian reference power allows the executive (Cabinet) to ask the courts for an advisory opinion on any legal question. This stands in contrast to the more routine court case where one party takes another party to court over a perceived wrong. Provincial governments can ask reference questions at provincial courts of appeal, which can be further appealed (by right) to the Supreme Court of Canada, while the federal government can ask questions directly to the Supreme Court. References are a distinct type of case because they require courts to engage in *abstract* review, or the adjudication of an issue or controversy without a live dispute or facts. In an abstract case, a court can be asked to rule on the constitutionality or legality of government policy that may be in force or a policy that has simply been proposed. The reference power is provided to provincial governments through each province's judicature statute and to the federal government through section 53 of the *Supreme Court Act*. Importantly, the reference power (both federally and provincially) is wide-ranging, allowing governments to ask the courts for advice on virtually any issue. Essentially, the reference power allows a government obtain a judicial decision on a matter it deems important without having to wait for a live case to materialize, sidestepping the normal litigation route to the Supreme Court or provincial courts of appeal. References give governments privileged access to the courts that is denied to citizens, interest groups, or opposing political parties. Furthermore, those involved in reference cases abide by the decisions made, making references more binding than advisory in nature.[1]

The types of questions asked in reference cases are not confined to technical legal issues. The reference procedure allows governments to insert the courts into policy debates that can be contentious and partisan. Governments have used the reference power to ask for advice on issues relating to political institutions, like the reform of the Senate, the patriation of the constitution, or the unilateral secession of a province [*Ed. note*: See Readings 2.4, 2.5 and 2.6]. References have also been used to address contentious issues (sometimes with moral implications) such as the constitutionality of same-sex marriage, the regulation of firearms, assisted human reproduction [Reading 9.6], and the criminalization of prostitution [Reading 7.5]. Additionally, references have played an important role in settling federalism related disputes between

255

governments over constitutional jurisdiction in a variety of policy areas like agriculture, regulation of the economy and natural resources. In sum, governments throughout Canada's history have used references to address a diverse range of issues, relying on this power over two hundred times since the federal government first created its reference power in 1875. At the time of writing, 209 reference cases have been heard at Canadian appellate courts, including the provincial courts of appeal, the Supreme Court of Canada and the Judicial Committee of the Privy Council, by the author's count.

Canadian Reference Cases 1875 to 2017

Although there are few statutory restrictions on what governments can ask courts in reference cases, the majority (almost 70 percent) of reference questions asked by governments concern the constitution, including the *Constitution Act, 1867* and *Constitution Act, 1982*. Of the constitutional questions asked, the majority (approximately 56 percent) ask the courts to interpret the division of powers set out in sections 91 and 92 of the *Constitution Act, 1867*. Division of powers references are often born out of disputes between a provincial government and the federal government over constitutional jurisdiction. For example, in the *Securities Reference*, the federal government asked the Supreme Court if its proposed *Securities Act* fell within the constitutional jurisdiction of the Parliament of Canada. In contrast to division of powers issues, the reference power has been used sparingly by governments to address *Charter* related issues, which comprise less than 8 percent of all references. The *Same-Sex Marriage Reference* (2004) is an example of a *Charter*-based reference, as this case asked the Supreme Court if extending the right to marry to same-sex couples was consistent with the *Charter of Rights and Freedoms*.[2]

Almost 30 percent (28.2) of all reference cases from 1875 to 2017 concern statutory interpretation. A statutory interpretation case is not concerned with the constitution, but instead asks a court to interpret whether one piece of legislation conflicts with related and existing statutes. The *Nadon Reference* is an example of a statutory interpretation reference. The federal government asked the Supreme Court to interpret sections in the *Supreme Court Act* regarding the eligibility requirements for appointment to the Supreme Court, after the suitability of the government's nominee to fill one of the Quebec seats on the Court was challenged [See Reading 11.6].

These data demonstrate that while *Charter* cases routinely comprise a majority[3] of the Supreme Court's constitutional law decisions, the reference power is used more often to ask the courts to interpret the boundaries of government power, rather than extending rights to a particular group. The limited number of *Charter*-related references reflects the fact that many of the issues that arise concerning the compatibility of government action with the *Charter* will more naturally arise in concrete or routine cases. The availability of concrete review for *Charter* issues can be contrasted with references that concern the interpretation of constitutional jurisdiction. In *Charter*-related cases, there may be a number of interested societal groups who seek to challenge government action in the courts, whereas in reference cases, there may not be a litigant that is able to bring the matter into court for judicial review.[4]

Governments can and do use the reference power to submit the legislation of other governments to the courts for review, also known as a cross-governmental reference. Table 1 below demonstrates that almost 22 percent (21.8) of all references are cross-governmental, with the federal government referring provincial legislation to the Supreme Court in approximately 9 percent of all references, and provincial governments referring federal legislation to a provincial appellate court in over 12 percent of cases.

Table 1: Cross-Governmental References 1875 to 2017

		Reference initiating government		
		Provinces	Federal	Total
	Provincial	85 (40.6%)	19 (9.2%)	104 (49.8%)
Statute or action under consideration[5]	Federal	27 (12.6%)	60 (29%)	87 (41.6%)
	Other	6 (2.9%)	8 (3.9%)	14 (6.7%)
	Both	2 (1%)	2 (1%)	4 (1.9%)
	Total	120 (57%)	89 (43%)	209 (100%)

An example of a provincially initiated cross-governmental reference is the *Quebec Senate Reform Reference* (2013) where the Quebec government referred the federal government's proposal for reforming the Senate to the Quebec Court of Appeal for review. The most recent example of a federally initiated cross-governmental reference is *Reference re Quebec Sales Tax* (1994), where the federal government submitted Quebec's legislation providing for a provincial sales tax to the Supreme Court of Canada for review. In both cross-government reference examples, the courts sided with Quebec, with the Quebec Court of Appeal finding the federal government's plans for Senate reform unconstitutional and the Supreme Court of Canada holding Quebec's tax policy as a valid exercise of provincial constitutional jurisdiction.

Figure 1: Provincial and Federal Reference Cases 1875 to 2017

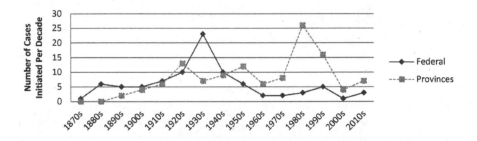

Figure 1 illustrates that the use of the reference power has ebbed and flowed over time, with reference use peaking in the 1930s and the 1980s. Why did reference cases spike during these periods? The 1930s and 1980s characterize periods of substantial transition, with the 1930s marking the economic crisis of the Great Depression and the 1980s marking an era in Canadian politics often referred to as mega constitutional politics. A brief examination of the political dynamics and some of the reference cases of the 1930s and the 1980s can illuminate why governments relied on the reference power at a greater rate in the 1930s and the 1980s compared other decades in Canadian political history.

The 1930s: The Great Depression

In the 1930s, governments in Canada struggled to deal with the economic crisis of the Great Depression within the confines of the division of powers set out in the constitution, leading governments to use the reference power at a rate greater than all other decades. During this period, political conflicts were often translated into legal conflicts – conflicts which found their way into the courts through reference cases. Many of the conflicts concerned a suite of legislative initiatives aimed at ameliorating some of the effects of the Depression on Canadians, often referred to as the Bennett New Deal (named for Prime Minister R.B. Bennett). The Bennett New Deal consisted of eight pieces of legislation that attempted to introduce a series of labour reforms, economic regulation and specific policies that attempted address the needs of agricultural producers. Importantly, the Bennett New Deal raised concerns regarding constitutionality, as many aspects of the legislative program appeared to infringe on provincial constitutional jurisdiction and were arguably enacted *ultra vires* (or outside) the authority of the Parliament of Canada.[6]

When the New Deal was introduced, Mackenzie King and the Liberal Party struggled with how to frame its opposition. The Liberals opposed the New Deal as a matter of partisanship and because there were genuine concerns regarding constitutionality of the legislative reform. However, King and the Liberals were concerned that their opposition to the New Deal could lead to criticisms of being out touch with the struggles of Canadians during the Depression. In the 1935 national election campaign, King and the Liberal Party promised to send the New Deal legislation to the courts for review through the reference power. After winning 1935 election, Prime Minister King followed through on his promise and promptly referred all eight statues to the Supreme Court in six different reference cases. In response to the reference questions, the Supreme Court of Canada and the Judicial Committee of the Privy Council (JCPC) found five of the eight New Deal statutes to be *ultra vires* the Parliament of Canada.

It is worth noting that the King government's use of the reference power was largely a product of political strategy, as it allowed King to achieve his goal of eliminating the Bennett New Deal without being exposed to criticisms for being anti-labour or out of touch.[7] In using the reference power, King could simply blame the courts for hindering the government's response to the Depression, resulting in a narrative that fueled public criticism of the courts, and the movement to abolish appeals to the JCPC.[8] Relying on the courts through the reference power to respond to the New Deal was not the only option available to the King government. Instead, because the legislation was thought to infringe on provincial constitutional jurisdiction, King could have waited for a provincial government to challenge the legislation itself, or alternatively, the King government could have repealed or amended the legislation in Parliament. However, using the reference power to respond to the Bennett New Deal was a more optimal political strategy because it provided the King government the power to create the reference questions, allowing it to frame the dispute and advance its preferred narrative. If the King government had simply repealed the New Deal, it would not only expose itself to public criticism, it would also have the responsibility of filling the void left by the repealed legislation and would have to advance its own response to the Great Depression. The use of the reference power by the King government not only delegated decision-making to the courts, it provided the government with more time to craft its own response to the economic crisis.

The 1980s: Mega Constitutional Politics

The 1930s had the highest rate of governments seeking judicial review through the reference power. The 1980s comes in at second place. This decade (and the one that follows) corresponds to a period in Canadian politics often referred to as mega constitutional politics. As Peter Russell explains, mega constitutional politics refers to a period where the central concerns of governance are aimed at the very foundation of the political community and are centered on issues that are highly emotional and intense, like questions relating to the stability of the state and political identity.[9] The era of mega constitutional politics concerned large normative questions such as Quebec nationalism and separatism, indigenous self-government, regionalism, and Canadian nationalism. Examples of mega-constitutional politics can be found in the 1981 constitutional negotiations, the Meech Lake and Charlottetown Accords, the sovereignty referendums in Quebec in 1980 and 1995, the breakthrough election of the Reform Party in 1993, and the growth of indigenous rights movements, including the Oka crisis in Quebec.

Many of the political episodes of mega constitutional politics percolate into the courts through references cases. Indeed, fifty references took place in the 1980s and the 1990s, which totals almost a quarter of all reference cases since 1875. During this era, references were used by both the federal and provincial governments to respond to stalemates in negotiations. This is best demonstrated in the *Patriation Reference*, which asked the Supreme Court if the Parliament of Canada could unilaterally amend the constitution without the participation of the provinces. In a complex and highly criticised decision [see Reading 2.4], six Supreme Court justices found that a 'substantial degree' of provincial consent was necessary, without specifying what constituted a substantial degree. A majority of the judges also found that the federal government could legally ask the UK Parliament to amend the *British North America Act*, but that doing so would offend a political convention that required significant provincial consent. The *Patriation Reference* gave some support to each side of the dispute and ultimately helped to bring the parties back to the negotiation table, leading to the *Constitution Act, 1982*.

References were also used by governments to respond to failed intergovernmental negotiations. For example, the absence of Quebec support for the 1981 agreement that led to the *Constitution Act, 1982*, prompted the *Quebec Veto Reference* (1982), which asked the Quebec Court of Appeal and the Supreme Court if the consent of Quebec was necessary for constitutional reform. The Supreme Court decisively ruled that Quebec did not hold a veto over constitutional amendments. During the era of mega constitutional politics, references were also used to ask the courts to rule on disputes over constitutional jurisdiction. During the 1980s, reference opinions were sought in six instances to address disputes between the federal and provincial governments over the ownership and regulation of natural resources. This was the case in the

Newfoundland Continental Shelf Reference (1984), which asked the Supreme Court to determine if the federal or provincial government held control over the continental shelf (the seabed that surrounds the coastline). Although the Supreme Court ruled in favour of the federal government, this ruling eventually led to the Atlantic Accord agreement between the federal government and Newfoundland and Labrador. Overall, the effect of references on intergovernmental negotiations is mixed. References have been used to bring parties back to negotiation, but have also resulted in the further entrenchment of conflict between governments.

Conclusion

This chapter has described some of the important trends of the Canadian reference power. The two decades examined mark periods of exceptional challenge and transition for Canadian governments. Politics in the 1930s was consumed by alleviating the effects of the Depression, while the desire for a new constitutional order and national unity were top priorities in the 1980s. These two moments of political consternation resulted in an increased use of the reference power, as governments have found it advantageous to seek a reference opinion from the courts to respond to a variety of issues. This highlights the political utility of the reference power and demonstrates that governments are quite willing to delegate decision-making to the courts and rely on judicial review as a means of political strategy. This reliance on the courts to deal with difficult political questions through reference cases has the potential to embroil the courts into political and partisan controversy, raising concerns for judicial independence. As a result, the reference power highlights that courts are important political institutions and speaks to the critical role that judicial power can play in shaping Canadian politics and public policy.

NOTES

1   Gerald Rubin, "The Nature, Use and Effect of Reference Cases in Canadian Constitutional Law," *McGill Law Journal* 6 (1960), pp. 168–190; Peter W. Hogg, *Constitutional Law of Canada*, Student edition (Toronto: Carswell, 2010), pp. 8–18.

2   The *Same-Sex Marriage Reference* also asked the Supreme Court a question regarding the division of powers and Parliament's authority to legislate with respect to same-sex marriage.

3   Lori Hausegger, Matthew Hennigar, and Troy Riddell, *Canadian Courts*, 2nd edition (Don Mills, ON: Oxford University Press, 2015), pp. 60–61

4   Barry L. Strayer, *The Canadian Constitution and the Courts: The Function and Scope of Judicial Review*, 3rd edition (Toronto: Butterworths, 1988), p. 319.

5   The *Secession Reference* is an example of a case coded as 'other,' as the Supreme Court was
     asked to assess if a province could unilaterally secede from the federation, in the abstract,
     rather than in reference to a specific piece of legislation. Another example is *Reference re
     Mineral and Other Natural Resources of the Continental Shelf* [1983] 145 D.L.R. (3d) 9, where
     the Court of Appeal for Newfoundland was asked to decide if the Province held the authority
     over particular lands off the coast of Newfoundland. Cases coded as 'both' include cases
     where a court was referred a series of questions that asked it to consider both provincial and
     federal legislation, as was the case in *Reference re Agricultural Products Marketing* [1978] 2
     S.C.R. 1198.

6   W.H. McConnell, "The Judicial Review of Prime Minister Bennett's New Deal," *Osgoode Hall
     Law Journal* 6, no. 1 (1968), pp. 39–86

7   James G. Snell and Frederick Vaughan, *The Supreme Court of Canada: History of the Institu-
     tion* (Toronto: University of Toronto Press, 1985), p. 165.

8   Alan Cairns, "The Judicial Committee and Its Critics," *Canadian Journal of Political Science*
     4, no.3 (1971), pp. 301–345.

9   Peter H. Russell, *Constitutional Odyssey: Can Canadians Become a Sovereign People?* 3rd
     edition (Toronto: University of Toronto Press, 2004), pp. 74–75.

6.2

Interventions and the Public Interest

Alan Borovoy

Reprinted with permission.

July 17, 1984

> TO: Supreme Court of Canada
> RE: Interventions in Public Interest Litigation
> FROM: Canadian Civil Liberties Association
>   per A. Alan Borovoy (General Counsel)

In the era of the *Charter of Rights and Freedoms*, the issue of participation in the
cases before the Supreme Court of Canada has acquired a new significance. It is
likely that a great many *Charter* cases will be determining issues of fundamental principle affecting the very nature of Canadian democracy. Moreover, the
impact of the Court's judgments will be far less vulnerable than ever to abridgement or amendment at the hands of the political authorities. It is significant
that in the more than 200 years of American history, the political authorities
in that country have enacted fewer than 25 amendments to their Constitution.

In many ways, the new Canadian Constitution will be even harder than its American counterpart to amend at the political level.

While it is possible, of course, for Parliament and the provincial legislatures to invoke the override in section 33 against the application of key *Charter* provisions, that is likely to be a relatively rare event outside the Province of Quebec. As a result of the widespread public participation in the Joint Parliamentary hearings and their aftermath, the *Charter* has acquired enormous prestige throughout much of the country. In every jurisdiction apart from Quebec, the ousting of *Charter* protections will entail a substantial political price. During all the years that such overrides have existed in both the federal *Bill of Rights* and a number of its provincial counterparts, they have been invoked in a relatively infinitesimal number of cases – and, so far, not once to overcome the impact of a judicial decision.

The effective transfer of so much power to the judiciary raises issues of fundamental fairness. Since the entire community will be increasingly affected for substantially longer periods by the decisions of the Court, larger sectors of the community should be able to participate in the process which produces those decisions. It is simply not fair to limit such participation on the basis of the coincidence of which parties litigate first. Public respect for both the *Charter* and the Court will require a more inclusive process.

The peculiar position of government serves to strengthen these considerations. In many cases, government will be a party. In criminal matters, for example, the federal or a provincial government will be prosecuting. But, even when they have not been parties, governments seeking to intervene have usually been allowed to do so. The frequency of such involvement in *Charter* cases will enable governments in a systematic way to put before the Court their various theories of what the *Charter* provisions mean. This gives the governments a special advantage over every other interest in the community. The party against which a government is litigating in any particular case might well not have any interest in addressing the long-term implications of whatever interpretation may be at issue. Indeed, the limited interest of a particular party might be better served by making certain tactical concessions to the government's long-term point of view. If no one else but the immediate parties regularly participate, the Court and the community will likely be deprived of countervailing long-term theories for interpreting the *Charter*.

Suppose, for example, section 7 were to become an issue in the context of a criminal case. It may well be in the interest of the prosecuting government to argue for the narrowest interpretation possible. The accused, on the other hand, might wish to argue that the concluding words in the section must have a substantive as well as a procedural impact. He might consider it tactically wise, therefore, to concede to the government that the word "liberty" is restricted to *physical* freedom. But there may be a number of free enterprise groups which would agree with the substantive interpretation of the concluding words but would argue that "liberty" includes freedom of contract. There may also be some social democratic groups which would argue that "liberty" means something more than physical freedom and something less than contractual freedom but would urge nevertheless that the concluding words should receive a procedural construction only.

Or, suppose the leaders of a pressure group were charged with a breach of the *Election Expenses Act*. The accused might believe that it is in their interest to argue that no such restriction on interest group advocacy is compatible with the *Charter*'s protections for "freedom of expression." On the other hand, it might be in the interests of the prosecuting government to argue that its goal of financial equity during election campaigns constitutes a reasonable limit on *Charter* freedoms and the restriction at issue is the only way to achieve such a goal. But there may be other groups in the community which differ with both litigants. They may believe that the government's goal is legitimate but not its means. They may wish to demonstrate to the Court how a less restrictive means could adequately achieve the same goal.

The examples go on and on. Suffice it, for present purposes, to acknowledge how both the quality of jurisprudence and the appearance of fairness can be undermined by restricting participation in court to the principal litigants.

In this regard, it would be helpful to consult the experience of the common law democracy which has developed the most sophisticated adjudication in the area of constitutional rights – the United States. Both at the appellate level and in the U.S. Supreme Court, there has been a growing receptivity to the participation of third parties. While *amicus* counsel are rarely heard during the course of oral argument, they are frequently permitted to file written briefs. In the Supreme Court, the inclusion of an amicus brief is virtually automatic on the written consent of the principal parties. And, if such consent is not forthcoming, there are special provisions for obtaining leave directly from the Court itself.

What is most significant about the American situation, however, is not simply the rules but also the actual experience. With the passage of time, the rules have been applied in an increasingly liberal fashion. Indeed, in cases of crucial public importance, the principal parties rarely object to amicus participation. There is reason to believe that the attitude of the Court itself paved the way for this development.

As long ago as 1952, the late Mr. Justice Felix Frankfurter criticized the U.S. Solicitor-General for refusing too often to grant such consent.

For the Solicitor-General to withhold consent automatically in order to enable this Court to determine for itself the propriety of each application is to throw upon the Court a responsibility that the Court has put upon all litigants, including the government....

Two years later, a similar observation was made by the late Mr. Justice Hugo Black.

Most of the cases before this Court involve matters that affect far more people than the immediate record parties. I think the public interest and judicial administration would be better served by relaxing rather than tightening the rule against *amicus curiae* briefs.

A recent survey illustrates the growing liberalism of the American practice. During the period from 1941 until 1952, fewer than 19 percent of the cases in the U.S. Supreme Court involved the participation of *amicus curiae*. From 1953 until 1966, this participation rose to 23.8 percent. And, during the period 1970 until 1980, *amicus* involvement had increased to more than 53 percent of all cases in the U.S. Supreme Court. These statistics produced the following remark in a journal of legal scholarship.

It seems fair enough to conclude ... that *amicus curiae* participation by private groups is now the norm rather than the exception.

When the kinds of cases are examined, the statistics acquire an even greater significance. During the period between 1970 and 1980, there was *amicus* participation in more than 62 percent of the cases involving church-state issues. The free press cases recorded more than 66 percent *amicus* participation and in race discrimination matters, such involvement had climbed to more than 67 percent. Union cases revealed a remarkable 87.2 percent participation by *amicus curiae*. Moreover, there is also a growing number of cases in which there is *multiple amicus* participation. In those cases during the 1970–1980 period which featured the involvement of at least one *amicus* brief, as many as 26.7 percent included the participation of four or more such interventions. In the famous *Bakke* case involving affirmative action for Blacks in university enrollment, there were more than 50 *amicus* briefs.

The American experience suggests also that these *amicus* briefs have played a vital role in a number of important cases. Consider, for example, the brief of the American Civil Liberties Union in the famous case of *Miranda v. Arizona*. Samuel Dash, counsel to the Senate Watergate Committee and Director of the Institute of Criminal Law and Procedure at Georgetown University Law Centre, made the following comment.

> Perhaps the most striking lesson to learn from these materials is the role an *amicus* brief can play in shaping a majority opinion, even without oral argument. Undoubtedly, the most effective presentation to the Court was the *amicus* brief of the American Civil Liberties Union.... It is clear that it presented a conceptual legal and structural formulation that is practically identical to the majority opinion – even as to use of language in various passages of the opinion. Also, it is from this brief and its appendix that the Court apparently draws its lengthy discussion of the contents of leading and popular police interrogation manuals. Both the ACLU brief and the Court explain that resort to the manuals is necessary because of the absence of information on what actually goes on in the privacy of police interrogation rooms.

In the case of *Mapp v. Ohio*, the issue was whether unlawfully seized evidence could be introduced against an accused in a state trial. Although such evidence had for some years been rendered inadmissible in federal prosecutions, the 1949 case of *Wolf v. Colorado* had held that this principle did not extend to state prosecutions. Although counsel for the accused in *Mapp* attempted to distinguish the *Wolf* case, an *amicus* brief filed by the ACLU urged the court to over-rule the earlier case. The majority of the court accepted the ACLU argument and over-ruled *Wolf*. As lawyer Ernest Angel commented in a subsequent law journal article, "the *amicu* scored an important victory."

In *Poe v. Ullmann*, a majority of the U.S. Supreme Court held that a prohibition on the distribution of birth control information was not justiciable. But the dissent of Mr. Justice Douglas argued that the law was unconstitutional on a ground raised by the *amicus* brief of the ACLU – the right to privacy. Four years later, in *Griswold v. Connecticut*, the Court majority adopted a position closer to that of Justice Douglas and the ACLU. According to Ernest Angel,

> The case is noteworthy for the … invalidation of of the statute … *for the part played by the amicus* and for the formulation of a right of privacy doctrine. (Emphasis ours)

There is some suggestion that the *amicus* brief of the National Association for Advancement of Coloured People played an important role in the case of *Furman v. Georgia* where the U.S. Supreme Court held that the death penalty constituted "cruel and unusual punishment" in the circumstances at issue. In the famous *Bakke* case, the Court included as an appendix to its judgment the joint *amicus* brief which had been filed by Columbia, Harvard, Standford, and Pennsylvania Universities.

While such non-party interventions have not arisen often in Canada, they are nevertheless rooted in our legal history. Apart from those few cases where it may have been considered equitable to accommodate certain private interests, most of the interventions in recent Canadian history have been prompted by broad and fundamental issues of public policy. As far back as 1945, for example, in the case of *Re Drummond Wren*, the Supreme Court of Ontario permitted the Canadian Jewish Congress to argue, *amicus curiae*, that racially restrictive covenants were not legally enforceable. During the last decade, however, the number of such interventions has increased significantly. On at least a dozen occasions during this period, Canadian tribunals have permitted the involvement of strangers to the litigation. In a good number of these cases, the matter at issue concerned an interpretation of our quasi-constitutional statute, the *Canadian Bill of Rights*. Whatever considerations have motivated this and other courts to permit such interventions in cases involving the *Bill of Rights*, the argument will be even stronger when the document at issue is the new *Canadian Charter*.

It is our view, therefore, that the Supreme Court of Canada should develop a rule on interventions which broadens the effective right of constituencies other than the immediate parties to participate in important public interest litigation. We recognize, of course, that these considerations must be balanced against the concerns of efficiency. Among the consequences accompanying the advent of the *Charter* is an increased workload for the Supreme Court of Canada. Understandably, therefore, the Court will feel obliged to avoid, where possible, the prospect of unduly long and repetitive hearings. We believe, however, that the valid interests of efficiency can coexist with an expanded role for intervenors.

This objective can be accomplished by permitting a wide latitude for partial interventions, i.e., interventions primarily through written briefs rather than oral argument. A liberal rule for the inclusion of such briefs would broaden the right to participate and permit the judges to obtain an ever expanding amount of assistance without in any way increasing the amount of time allocated for the Court's hearings.

While the practice in the U.S. Supreme Court is a possible model, we believe that some reasonable modifications are in order. Instead of foreclosing almost automatically on the oral participation of intervenors, our Court might adopt the practice of selectively inviting their counsel to appear for the purpose of speaking to whatever limited issues would assist in the disposition of the cases at Bar. From their advance reading of the briefs and factums, the judges could decide which, if any, of the intervenors' counsel they may wish to hear and on what issues. Such invitations to counsel could range from involvement on one or more limited points to virtually full-scale participation in certain special cases. Even at that, the presentations of such counsel could be subject to abridgement at the hearing itself to whatever extent it became evident that they were not contributing significantly beyond what had already been advanced on behalf of the parties. In all of these ways, the Court could still control its processes and prevent any undue prolongation of the oral hearings.

The adoption of this approach should also help to overcome some of the concerns that have been expressed about interventions in criminal cases. To whatever extent there were several interventions on the side of the Crown, it has been said that the situation might look like a "ganging up" on the accused. It will be appreciated, however, that such an appearance is rendered far less likely when the interventions are handled primarily through written briefs rather than oral argument. In any event, such interventions would be addressed, not to the guilt or innocence of a particular accused, but rather to the resolution of a question of law or the interpretation of a section of the *Charter*. All of these considerations should militate against prohibiting interventions in criminal cases.

Moreover, there is no reason why this approach should not apply equally to the proposed interventions of the various attorneys general. Governmental intervenors are no more likely (and may well be less likely) than non-government intervenors to adopt arguments which are significantly different from those of the immediate parties. Upon meeting whatever liberal threshold test is adopted, government intervenors, like their non-government counterparts, should be able to participate. But they too should do so subject to the rules applying to everyone – usually through partial rather than full intervention.

In the submission of the Canadian Civil Liberties Association, it is essential to continue and expand the role of intervenors before the Supreme Court of Canada. The *Charter of Rights and Freedoms* has launched a new era in the relationship between the judicial and political processes of this country. Ever since the Joint Parliamentary hearings on the Constitution, there has been a heightened public awareness and concern about *Charter* developments in particular and public interest law in general. Indeed, one of the consequences of the constitutional deliberations has been a raised public consciousness with respect to a wide spectrum of public law issues. Many of the processes of the Court, therefore, will be the subject of increased scrutiny. Thus, it is more important than ever that those processes conform to public perceptions and expectations of fairness. On the basis of all these considerations, the Canadian Civil Liberties Association respectfully urges the adoption of an approach which is hospitable to non-party interventions in public interest litigation.

6.3

The Women's Legal Education and Action Fund
Sherene Razack

Canadian Feminism and the Law: The Women's Legal Education and Action Fund and the Pursuit of Equality (Toronto: Second Story Press, 1991), 36–63. Reprinted with permission.

Rights on paper mean nothing unless the courts correctly interpret their scope and application. *Charter* activists began trying to influence judicial interpretation through charterwatching, an all-consuming activity. It entailed having national consultations, planning conferences, writing books and articles, making speeches, doing audits of statutes, offering workshops; in short, attempting to inform the decision-makers, women, and the Canadian public (in that order) exactly what the new equality guarantees should mean in law.

The frenzy of activities began, as though by a starter's gun, when the government included in its constitution bill a three-year moratorium on section 15's equality rights. Ostensibly giving governments sufficient time to bring their legislation into conformity with the law, the delay inspired women to plan for the day when they could take their unresolved equality claims to court, armed with the hard-won guarantees of sections 15 and 28.

Not surprisingly, the women most compelled to plan for litigation and to charterwatch were those legally-trained or connected to the women's organizations active on the lobby.... In May, 1982 ... several of the women connected to the issue applied for funding and organized a national think tank which was held in Toronto. They invited well-known constitutional experts Peter Hogg and Walter Tarnopolsky because, not only were they trying to secure answers to their questions about what the constitutional equality guarantees meant, they were beginning to adopt what they described as a process of "influencing the influencers," an approach fuelled by their increasing awareness that "things were being written that we didn't exactly agree with." A number of ideas surfaced at this time about how best to promote women's interests in law: the idea of a defence fund was already on the table and to this was added the idea of a legal text book and a symposium, all based on the belief that "it was very important to get in at the academic level."

In their own educational session, billed as a workshop on the *Charter* and held in the same month as the think tank, the women proceeded to determine what their position was on the new law.... Again, the rationale was the same: if women could convey their point of view to those in "responsible positions," they could influence how equality rights were ultimately understood in the courts.

Energetic in their efforts to promote women's constitutional interests, a core of women in Toronto, who were active on constitutional issues, created a trust fund known as the Charter of Rights Educational Fund (CREF), a Charter of Rights Coalition (CORC), and called together 30 women in the area who launched several educational activities. The minutes of the meeting held on November 25, 1982, at the large and prestigious law firm of Tory, Tory (where Mary Eberts worked) indicated a general consensus on the need to publicize the issues and further educate women on the specifics of the equality guarantees. Under the auspices of CREF, two study days were planned and, at a later meeting, a committee was struck to coordinate the massive undertaking of an audit of federal and provincial statutes not in compliance with the *Charter*. The idea of a legal defence fund, supported very strongly by the group's only independently wealthy member, Nancy Jackman, is described in the minutes as the "least formalized" of all the projects....

The CORC group received government funding to plan a national conference on *Charter* issues that would complement the symposium then being planned "for legal types." Nancy Jackman, who led the CORC team, remembered that they then began to build a series of "mini-coalitions" across the country, using the institutionalized women's groups as a base. The function of these coalitions was to "bug" their governments about the moratorium and educate women about the *Charter*. CORC prepared a slide tape show and an educational kit which optimistically declared:

> There is potential in the *Charter of Rights* to support whatever change women want. It's like a magic wand one could wave to bring about things like fair labour legislation, better protection for women in areas such as sexual assault and enactment of affirmative action programs. *Women can get what we want if we lobby now and do our research and help judges understand what equality means.* (Emphasis in original)

In August of 1984, nine months before section 15 of the *Charter of Rights and Freedoms* came into effect, specific planning began for the birth of the Women's Legal Education and Action Fund. The small group that met at 21 McGill, a private Toronto women's club, on August 9, 1984, began the organizing of the fund with characteristic energy and a shared sense of what needed to be done. Besides the authors of the forthcoming *Women and Legal Action*, the planning group for LEAF initially included Marilou McPhedran, two well-known professional women Shelagh Day and Kathleen O'Neil, and Nancy Jackman whose importance as a potential financial contributor to the fund would become evident over the next few months.

Events moved quickly. In September the group considered who might form the board of LEAF, which was scheduled for birth immediately after section 15 came into force; by October, they had received for their use $100,000 from the Jackman Foundation. The release of *Women and Legal Action* that month made it clear that a litigation fund could not succeed without a great deal of money, a requirement that made funding for LEAF the greatest priority. High profile professional women, typically lawyers and human rights professionals, were drawn into the organizing, and fundraising began in earnest. Kathleen O'Neil was asked to go to her organization, the Federation of Women Teachers of Ontario; endorsements were sought from the YWCA; and every conceivable network was activated in the interest of finding the financial support for LEAF.

Kasia Seydegart was hired to plan the fundraising and suggested that the group cultivate well-known human rights advocates such as the Canadian Human Rights Commission's Gordon Fairweather ... and Judge Rosalie Abella, who wrote the *Report of the Royal Commission on Equality in Employment* published in October 1984. By November, animated by "the dream ... to make the promise of equality contained in section 15 a reality for all Canadian women," the group could record in the minutes their finances to date: $117,000 from the Federation of Women Teachers of Ontario ($70,000 in funds and the rest in services); an initial $50,000 from the Jackman Foundation; and $700 in smaller donations. Appeals to wealthy women and grant applications consumed the rest of 1984.

In the frenzy of organizing, LEAF women relied heavily on their traditional networks. Thus, although the minutes of January 11, 1985, contained a passing reference to the need to involve immigrant women and women of colour, and Magda Seydegart recalled pressing for community involvement, the composition of both the working committee and the board remained homogeneous in character. Seventeen professional white women made up the working committee struck on December 18, 1984; eleven of them were either lawyers or human rights professionals. On April 13 and 14, 1984, when LEAF officially came into being with an elected board and an executive committee, the composition did not change.

LEAF embodied the three main features recommended in *Women and Legal Action*: the establishment of a single national fund, the direct sponsorship of (preferably winnable) cases, and a complementary strategy of education and lobbying. As the epicentre of this strategy LEAF, Mary Eberts wrote, had a good chance of occupying the field of equality rights in the courtroom, but

> expertise can be applied in ways other than this case-by-case approach. Counsel and volunteers from the organization can become involved in legal writing, legal education, and continuing education of bench and bar. In this fashion, they may come to influence how decision-makers view the legal issues involved. Just as important, however, they may influence how lawyers prepare and present cases they bring forward.

"Occupying the field" on equality issues in court, doing proactive litigation, influencing the influencers, were components of LEAF's vision. The criteria for selecting cases, as adopted at the founding meeting, reflected their ambitious intent. Cases taken had to concern equality rights; arise under the *Charter of Rights and Freedoms* or under Quebec's *Charter*; present strong facts; and be of importance to women. Finally, LEAF declared itself particularly interested in cases in which women were doubly disadvantaged, that is, subjected to sex discrimination as well discrimination on the basis of race, disability, etc.

A decision was made early on to begin immediately in the courtroom. On April 17, 1985, in a blaze of publicity, LEAF announced its first two cases – one concerned the right of married women to keep their own names, and the other attacked the requirement that welfare recipients, the majority of whom are women, live as single persons in order to qualify for assistance. Beth Symes described the day:

> [Counsel] Eloise Spitzer's name change case involved the Yukon, a Francophone [Suzanne Bertrand, a French Canadian living in the Yukon who wished to retain her maiden name because it reflected her French-Canadian ancestry] and a blatant case we could win. The second case, the spouse-in-the-house case, was chosen [because] it was for disadvantaged women and because it was a symbol of the state oppressiveness [toward] women. April 17 was

a wonderful spectacle on the hill. We raised $20,000 that day in Ottawa and $25,000 in Toronto.

It was an auspicious beginning, full of hope and confidence and undeterred by the enormity of the task at hand....

***

When the Women's Legal Education and Action Fund officially came into being on April 17, 1985, its founders intended its structure to replicate the best features of American litigation funds and to avoid their worst short-comings. Impressed by the record of the American organization the National Association for the Advancement of Colored People (NAACP), in particular their strategy of pursuing incremental gains in specific areas, LEAF's founders concluded that Canadian women would best secure their legal rights in a similar way. In American terminology, the NAACP approach was to "occupy" a particular area of law and become known as the expert litigators in that field, and by selecting winnable issues and controlling the development of case law, judges could be asked to take small steps at any one time. Such a long-term strategy of staged litigation requires considerable funding, preferably from a broad, non-governmental base. The intention is for the litigating organization to act as the sponsor of a party to the case, financially a more onerous role than that of intervenor where an organization acts as a "friend of the court" and limits its participation to offering a written and oral opinion on how the case affects the interests it promotes. In the United States, the vision of a proactive legal fund usually involves lobbying and public education, activities that mandate a close relationship with feminist communities.

LEAF's founders intended to pursue a proactive strategy involving the building of test cases. Accordingly, they developed five criteria for case selection, and, following Karen O'Connor's recommendations in her book on American women's legal organizations, they erected a structure to complement the strategy of seeking out important cases nationally, researching them, and having the financial resources to shepherd cases through the lengthy and costly court process. O'Connor also emphasized the importance of strong national headquarters and highly-skilled legal volunteers, the value of publicity both for funders and for credibility in the legal community, the value of local affiliates in keeping the organization in touch with its constituency, and the importance of both legal and public education. Conspicuously absent was any mechanism for ensuring the legal fund's accountability to feminist communities....

LEAF's first litigation report recognized that "selecting the right test cases for litigation involves a careful process of winnowing, investigation and research." Typically (and LEAF, as I show below, has not been typical in this respect), someone brings a possible test case or, more commonly, a legal problem women have experienced to the organization's attention. The staff then proceeds to research the issue involved, meeting with a variety of legal consultants before it reaches the legal committee for consideration. Unless one or more of the consultants contacted have a strong community orientation, and unless there are sufficient time and resources to seek consultation further afield, only the legal aspects of the issue are considered. For LEAF, then, as a feminist organization seeking to protect and improve women's legal rights essentially through the telling of women's stories in court, the first challenge is to accommodate a variety of women's voices to a process that fundamentally negates consultation and difference....

Attracting the large sums of money that litigation requires also places a women's legal defence fund under greater than usual pressure to respond to funders' desires. LEAF's founders knew from the beginning that a broad funding base was desirable, but in actively pursuing it those involved in funding gained a keen appreciation of the compromises in image that would be required. To Marilou McPhedran, the group's chief fundraiser at several points in its history, fundraising meant "breaking into those echelons where feminists have never been very comfortable" and presenting an appropriate image for corporate and government funders that spoke of LEAF women's credibility as members of the legal, not the feminist, community. To another LEAF founder, Beth Atcheson, LEAF had to appear to be an elite corps because this was the only way to garner sufficient financial support from those most able to give it. This left LEAF, however, in the position of being attractive to its funders but alienated from the feminist communities it served and needed. When LEAF hosted a $100-a-plate dinner, it raised funds from the middle and upper classes but strengthened its image as an organization with few ties to women in the community. Moreover, as the beneficiaries of relatively large government grants, LEAF was vulnerable to the rancour of some segments of the community who felt that litigation activities attracted more governmental support than grass-roots activities – rape crisis centres, for example.

Perhaps because of who in Canadian society are legally trained and the necessity of attracting large sums of money (and therefore being "credible" to potential corporate and government funders), LEAF's founders and its main activists, as we have seen, were a remarkably homogeneous group who for the most part chose to remain professionally anchored in the corporate legal world. LEAF women themselves have noted that one way of coming to terms with the contradiction of a feminist challenge from within the corporate world is to capitalize on this insider status. LEAF certainly reflected this approach: it used the resources of large law firms, the status of well-known litigators, and its own credibility as a legal organization with elite connections (when lobbying governments, for example) to contribute to its success. In both its internal and external activities, however, an organization that operates in this fashion runs the risk of losing the self-critical edge that comes with diversity of races, classes, and occupations....

In what was to become a trend of disturbing significance, men began to use the *Charter* soon after its promulgation to protest against the few protections women enjoyed in law. In one of these cases, *Seaboyer/Gayme*, two men accused of rape protested that their right to a fair trial as guaranteed in the *Charter* was infringed upon because of provisions in the Criminal Code that prohibited using as evidence a victim's previous sexual history (except in three specific instances). LEAF applied for and was granted intervenor status whereupon it had 30 days to submit its legal argument concerning why these "rape shield" provisions should continue to stand. In what was intended to be a strategic move, LEAF hired a well-known male criminal lawyer who prepared a somewhat scant brief for the court; it included some examples of possible infringements on the right to a fair trial that might result from the rape shield provisions of the Criminal Code. Further, the approach taken was a rather conservative one where no mention was made of the relationship between these provisions in the Code and women's right to equality under section 15 of the *Charter*. A group of feminists working on the possibility of civil remedies for women harmed by pornography were highly critical of the LEAF brief, pointing out the lack of equality arguments and noting particularly the ill-advised examples that conceded there may be times when a women's previous sexual history may be relevant to a determination of whether or not she was raped.

For LEAF, the *Seaboyer/Gayme* case was its first reminder of the perils of not seeking consultation within the wider feminist community. To its credit, the organization then responded constructively to criticism and developed a process of "workshopping" cases with working groups of feminists who had specific expertise on the issues under consideration. Indeed, the working group formed to discuss what had gone wrong in *Seaboyer/Gayme* remained active for subsequent cases, and workshopping has continued to be the approach taken, the cost of such consultation notwithstanding. According to Mary Eberts, a working group is formed for cases where there is enough lead time, consisting of a member of the national legal committee and/or LEAF's executive director, volunteer lawyers, and representatives from the local LEAF chapter. Each working group develops its own links with the women's community. As the report on the second year of LEAF litigation commented: "Developing case strategy requires a sure vision about the meaning of equality and how that theory should be made concrete in this particular instance, a vision that cannot be arrived at in isolation." ...

∗∗∗

While the progress made in winning acceptance of the principle of adverse impact was heartening, LEAF had no sooner begun its litigation activities when it became clear that, the favourable judicial climate of the 1980s notwithstanding, it would not be able to maintain the type of control over equality litigation it had originally anticipated. More was at stake than judicial recognition of unintentional discrimination. As Beth Symes ruefully reflected at the round table discussion in 1988, in which LEAF's founders discussed their achievements and common history:

> If you're going to build law with respect to equality, you want to build it your way. So therefore, you flood the courts with your cases and your issues in the order in which you want the court to hear them. We have not occupied the field. Men have. We have been involved in damage control ... men have been popping up all over Canada in various courts challenging things that we as women fought to get, such as maternity benefits, such as the rape shield provisions. Resources have gone into these interventions.

LEAF's careful building of feminist jurisprudence based on precedent and their planning the court's progress toward acceptance of key concepts fell by the wayside when proactive quickly turned to reactive and LEAF found itself acting as a third party, as an intervenor in cases brought by men. They were thereby forced to abandon their agenda and respond to one set by men's claims for equality....

In its first three years of litigation, LEAF opened over 300 files. Of these, it adopted 64 cases for consideration by the legal committee, pursuing over 30 in some detail. Its caseload far exceeded capacity, and in 1989 LEAF had to limit its acceptance of intake calls to one day of the week. While there were cases where LEAF took a proactive approach, initiating court action and seeking to build on acceptance of such concepts as adverse impact (and these naturally had a longer gestation time than others), most of its cases to date were those in which LEAF acted as an intervenor, defending women's interests in cases brought by men....

6.4

The Policy Consequences of LEAF's Legal Mobilization

Christopher P. Manfredi

Feminist Activism in the Supreme Court: Legal Mobilization and the Women's Legal Education and Action Fund (University of British Columbia Press, 2004), 149–192. Reprinted with permission from the publisher.

In her introduction to the 1996 compendium of LEAF's Supreme Court factums, Carissima Mathen identified three principles underlying the organization's litigation activity:

1. Women as a group, compared with men as a group, experience widespread and pervasive discrimination.

2. Women who are oppressed on the basis of, for example, their race, class,

3. sexual orientation, religion or disability, experience inequality different in degree and/or kind, in various contexts.

4. Law can be an effective tool for egalitarian social change.

The first two of these principles are abundantly evident in LEAF's factums themselves. LEAF continually stressed the social, economic, and political inequalities between men and women. In addition, especially in later cases when LEAF joined coalitions with other equality-seeking groups, its factums highlighted the multiple disadvantages experienced by certain women. That LEAF invested the resources necessary to intervene in almost forty Supreme Court cases is also evidence of at least its belief in the third principle. By engaging in litigation to bring the first two principles to the Court's attention, LEAF expected to affect the law in ways that would reduce women's inequality. In essence, by fully realizing the third principle, LEAF hoped to render the first two principles moot.

I focus my attention on LEAF's third principle by examining whether legal mobilization has been an effective strategy for the Canadian feminist movement. Although LEAF's principles understand effectiveness in terms of policy consequences (law generating egalitarian social change), at least two other measures of effectiveness should not be ignored. One measure is the effect on legal rules: Did legal mobilization change (or preserve) legal rules in the manner desired? The second measure is the organizational effect on social movements:

Did legal mobilization strengthen the movement? ... Superimposed over all these considerations is whether any particular group's activity makes a difference. In other words, would law and policy have developed as they did even in the absence of legal mobilization by a social movement? ...

The LEAF Difference

In a comparative study of the impact of women's groups on judicial decision making in Canada and the United States, Lori Hausegger used multi-variate regression analysis to measure the difference these groups made in litigation. The results, at least with respect to LEAF, were mixed. According to Hausegger, LEAF's presence did matter in terms of outcome, increasing the likelihood of a favourable outcome by 33 percentage points and leading Hausegger to conclude that LEAF was "a very valuable ally" in litigation. Indeed, Justice L'Heureux-Dubé was likely the swing vote in the Court's four-to-three decision to uphold the *Criminal Code's* hate propaganda provisions in *Keegstra*, and she may have been persuaded by LEAF's arguments.

By contrast, Hausegger found that LEAF's interventions did not necessarily increase the likelihood of generating favourable doctrine. Although Hausegger found that LEAF had a significant influence on doctrine in the areas of general equality principles and pornography, its influence was less evident in the areas of abortion, family law, and sexual assault. In fact, she found that legal considerations had a more significant impact in all five issue areas than any other variable, including women's interest-group participation.

In broader terms, however, one might argue that LEAF made a difference through the type of evidence it brought to the Court's attention. The use of legal scholarship and other extralegal documents to communicate new legal theories and policy information to courts came of age in the United States in the 1940s, when US Supreme Court justices such as Felix Frankfurter, Charles Evans Hughes, and Robert Jackson explicitly acknowledged their utility and legitimacy as sources of information. Historically rooted in the sociological and economic studies first introduced into American constitutional jurisprudence by Louis Brandeis, the strategic and tactical use of law review and other non-legal publications was perfected by the NAACP in its constitutional struggle against racially restrictive covenants and segregated education.

While the US Court began to consider extrinsic evidence early in the twentieth century, the Canadian Supreme Court remained hostile to its use until the 1970s.... The use of extrinsic evidence is unavoidable, however, under section 1 of the *Charter* and the criteria established for its application in Oakes. Indeed, it is precisely the "expediency or likely success of a particular policy" that is reviewed under the proportionality element of the Oakes test.

... The use of extrinsic evidence in the form of legal scholarship, government reports, and other documents was a central feature of LEAF's factums.... LEAF's opportunity to introduce new types of evidence and arguments concerning a wide range of issues never before dealt with by the Court, as well as the "percolation" of that evidence and those arguments through citations in subsequent decisions and the legal literature, represents an important accomplishment of legal mobilization. In some sense, LEAF's interventions have affected the legal culture in which *Charter* litigation is embedded. While this might not always translate into obvious doctrinal or policy change, it must nevertheless be seen as a positive consequence by the movement.

Consequences: Rule Changes, Movement Dynamics, and Social Conditions

Abortion

In 1988, without LEAF's participation, the Supreme Court of Canada removed national-level rules governing access to legal abortions. As Flanagan argues, the judicial nullification of section 251 of the *Criminal Code* created a new policy status quo, favourable to feminist interests, which LEAF was in a position to defend. The likely necessity of defensive action was the result of three factors. First, the Court did not declare a constitutional right to abortion, which left the future development of access rules squarely in the hands of legislatures. Second, the *Morgentaler 2* Court expressly invited Parliament to make another attempt at abortion regulation in light of its judgment. Finally, pro-choice advocates faced an active pro-life counter movement, symbolized by Joe Borowski, which actually predated the 1988 judgment. The existence of this counter movement, in combination with the Court's reluctance to declare a constitutional right to abortion and its invitation to enact new federal legislation, placed the post-1988 status quo at risk....

For LEAF, therefore, post-1988 legal mobilization in the abortion field consisted of opposition to proposed legal rules that would have changed the status of fetuses in a manner threatening to abortion access. It mobilized in *Borowski* to block the establishment of a constitutionally entrenched right to fetal life, and in *Daigle* to oppose civil and common law rules giving fathers input into the abortion decision. In *Winnipeg Child and Family Services*, LEAF mobilized against a common law (*parens patriae*) rule allowing state interference with maternal liberty in the name of fetal interests, and in *Sullivan* it fought the interpretation of a criminal law rule that would extend personhood to fetuses. In sum, although feminist legal mobilization itself was not directly responsible for changing the legal framework governing abortion policy, it played a role in preserving the post-1988 status quo. At the level of legal rules, the cases in which LEAF participated achieved the feminist movement's objective of protecting the gain represented by *Morgentaler 2*.

But did the post-1988 legal framework, which LEAF mobilized to preserve, have its intended policy impact? Policy impact was certainly at the heart of the Supreme Court's nullification of the *Criminal Code's* abortion provisions in *Morgentaler 2*. Indeed, the Court relied extensively on the Report of the Committee on the Operation of the Abortion Law (the Badgley Report) in determining whether the structure and decision-making criteria of section 251 of the *Criminal Code* violated the security of the person of women in a manner contrary to the principles of fundamental justice. Among the committee's several findings, the Court found two especially relevant to its evaluation of section 251 under section 7 of the *Charter*. One finding was that, under the existing therapeutic abortion regulations, there was an average interval of eight weeks between a woman's first medical consultation and the performance of an induced abortion.… In the view of the majority, therefore, the decision-making delays attributable to section 251 posed a real risk to the physical health of women seeking therapeutic abortions. This led the Court to find an infringement of security of the person.

The second important finding of the Badgley Report on which the Court relied concerned the committee's investigation of the impact of provincial requirements and hospital practices on the distribution and availability of therapeutic abortions. The committee found that 271 hospitals in Canada had established therapeutic abortion committees by 1976. This represented only one-fifth of all hospitals, and less than half of all the hospitals that met the basic provincial standards necessary for establishing a committee. As a result, according to the report, 45 percent of the Canadian population was not served by hospitals with therapeutic abortion committees. Moreover, access to "committee hospitals" varied among provinces and regions.

… The data available from Statistics Canada on therapeutic abortions suggest that this changed in the post-1988 policy world. Although the total number and rate of therapeutic abortions per thousand women aged between fifteen and forty-four years increased by 5.0 and 2.7 percent respectively from 1985 to 1988, there was a significant increase in both measures after 1988. Between 1988 and 1989, the number of abortions increased by 9.1 percent (from 72,693 to 79,315), while the rate per thousand women increased by 8.6 percent (from 11.6 to 12.6). In the first full year of decriminalization (1989-90), the number of abortions increased by 17.1 percent (from 79,315 to 92,901), and the rate per thousand women increased by 15.9 percent (12.6 to 14.6). Indeed, from 1988 to 1998, which covers the entire period of LEAF's Supreme Court activity in this policy field, the number of therapeutic abortions increased by 52.0 percent (72,693 to 110,520), and the rate per thousand women increased by 35.3 percent (11.6 to 15.7). [*Ed. Note*: According to the Canadian Institute for Health Information and calculations made by the Abortion Rights Coalition of Canada, in 2015 these numbers were 100,104 reported abortions and 14 per 1,000 women of childbearing age.[1]]

The growth in the number of abortions is primarily a function of an increase in the number of abortions performed in clinics rather than hospitals, a development directly traceable to *Morgentaler 2*. Prior to 1988, abortion clinics operated only in Quebec, but within six years of the decision, every jurisdiction except Prince Edward Island, Saskatchewan, and the two territories had private abortion clinics. While the number of abortions performed in hospitals increased by only 387 from 1989 to 1990, the number performed in clinics increased by 13,177. Indeed, the number of abortions performed in hospitals was actually less in 1995 (70,549) than in 1989 (70,705), while the number performed in clinics increased by 405 percent. Between 1978 and 1989, clinics performed only 5.8 percent of all abortions, but between 1990 and 1995 they accounted for 35.4 percent.

In this sense the removal of a legal rule – that therapeutic abortions must be performed in accredited hospitals – affected access by legitimating a new venue for the procedure.... It is not entirely clear whether decriminalization and greater access to private clinics solved the second problem identified by the Court in 1988 – unequal access across provinces. In retrospect, a simple change in legal rules should not have been expected to resolve this issue. As the Badgley Report itself noted, it was not the law itself that produced operational disparities in obtaining therapeutic abortions but rather "the Canadian people, their health institutions and the medical profession." ...

These policy developments are consistent with Rosenberg's argument regarding the conditions under which courts can bring about social change. According to him, one such condition is the emergence of parallel institutions willing to implement the policy change ordered or implied by a judicial decision. In this case, the removal of barriers to the establishment of private abortion clinics, and the willingness of key actors to establish such clinics, compensated for the absence of change in the behaviour of hospitals. In essence, hospitals became largely irrelevant to the implementation of judicially mandated social change.

Reducing Violence: Sexual Assault and Pornography

In 1983 the federal government redesigned the law of sexual assault both procedurally and substantively. These changes were "complainant friendly" in the sense that they removed key elements of the old crime of rape and sought to protect complainants from certain lines of defence questioning. Not surprisingly, these changes came under attack from defence lawyers and rights organizations such as the Canadian Civil Liberties Association. The main line of attack was that the changes violated the legal rights entrenched contemporaneously in the *Charter*. LEAF intervened to support the government's defence of its rules, largely by arguing that an emphasis on procedural concerns without considering equality issues would undermine efforts to reduce violence against women.

... The success of feminist legal mobilization at this level is mixed. From 1991 to 1995, LEAF found itself on the losing side of three key judgments involving the balance between legal rights and equality concerns. However, the federal government did not accept these losses as final, and worked with the feminist movement – led by LEAF – to construct legislative responses to the judgments.... Tracing the actual policy consequences of these various legislative and judicial reforms is exceedingly difficult. The theory underlying LEAF's arguments throughout its sexual assault interventions was that any dilution of the protective measures found in the 1983 reforms would discourage women from reporting sexual assaults, reduce conviction rates, and ultimately, increase the incidence of sexual assault. Unfortunately, the readily available data on crime in Canada do not lend themselves easily to measuring changes in these variables.... The rate [of reported sexual assaults] increased steadily from 1983 to 1993, and then began to drop until stabilizing from 1999 to 2001. Interestingly, rates peaked just after *Seaboyer* in 1991, but continued to drop even after *O'Connor* in 1995....

The General Social Survey (GSS), conducted by Statistics Canada, offers additional insights into the incidence of sexual assault. In 1988, 1993, and 1999, the GSS surveyed Canadians (approximately 26,000 in 1999) about their crime victimization experiences and perceptions of crime and the justice system. Among the eight offence types included in the survey of Canadians over the age of fifteen is sexual assault. Perhaps the most striking result of the survey is the generally low rate at which Canadians report any criminal victimization to the police. In 1999, for example, the overall reporting rate for Canada was 37 percent, with break and enter (62 percent) and motor vehicle theft (60 percent) having the highest reporting rates, likely because of insurance requirements. Personal crimes, including theft of personal property, sexual assault, robbery, and general assault had a combined reporting rate of 32 percent. Significantly, the number of sexual assaults that victims said they reported to the police was too small to be expressed in 1999.... Whether because or in spite of the various rule changes throughout the 1990s, by the end of the decade sexual assault remained an infrequently reported crime. Nevertheless, the GSS suggests relative stability in the incidence of sexual assault over time....

Whatever its actual policy consequences, LEAF's sexual assault dialogue with the Supreme Court and the federal government generated organizational benefits for the feminist movement. In particular, according to Sheila McIntyre, "the coalition formed to circumvent *Seaboyer* remained intact and expanded in the succeeding five years." The coalition was an important participant in consultations by the Department of Justice on violence against women, held annually from 1994 to 1997. Funded by the government, these consultations had broad representation from various constituencies within the women's movement. Most importantly, according to McIntyre, non-lawyers outnumbered lawyers by about a six-to-one ratio. Legal mobilization around sexual assault law provided both the necessity and opportunity for building an effective coalition that was far more inclusive than LEAF alone.

The same cannot be said for LEAF's interventions in cases involving government regulation of pornography.... The decision to support the federal government's defence of the *Criminal Code's* obscenity provisions [in *Butler*] exacerbated, to the breaking point, existing tensions within the feminist movement. According to Lise Gotell, LEAF's unequivocal position that pornography is inherently violent and degrading to women "produced an intensification of the feminist porn wars in Canada as artists, academics, writers, lesbians, bookstore and media workers, and sex trade workers, reacted with outrage to the presentation of anti-pornography feminism as feminist orthodoxy." Beyond the procedural issue of LEAF's lack of consultation with movement stakeholders, critics objected in particular to LEAF's singular portrayal of women as "passive, silent victim[s]" rather than "agents with voice." ...

This result might have been acceptable if the practical consequences of pornography regulation were less ambiguous. Statistics Canada provides data only on "offences against public morals," which is the category in which the *Criminal Code's* anti-obscenity provisions (section 163) fall. Very few charges are laid under this category – a total of only 607 from 1997 to 2000, or about 150 per year. Even if all these charges were laid under section 163, they would still represent a tiny fraction of *Criminal Code* charges. Moreover, given the small annual variation in the number of charges – from a low of 138 in 1999 to a high of 166 in 1998 – these data do not suggest a "crackdown" on such activity in the wake of *Butler*. The absence of strong enforcement raises questions about the impact of section 163 on the supply of pornography and hence its impact on what LEAF deemed to be an important factor contributing to violence against women (and women's equality more generally).

Family Policy

... On two issues – child support and maternity and parental leave – significant policy change occurred despite LEAF's failure to persuade the Supreme Court to change the relevant legal rules. In the first issue, a majority of the Court in *Thibaudeau* rejected the claim supported by LEAF that the existing income inclusion and deduction rules in the *Income Tax Act* infringed section 15. Although the federal government prevailed in court on this issue, the constitutional challenge inspired the development of a new approach to child support....

The same characterization applies to changes in the maternity and parental leave regime following the defeat in *Schachter*. Even before the Court's decision, the federal government had extended parental leave benefits (first introduced in 1990) to natural fathers. Consequently, natural parents had access to a total of twenty-five weeks of benefits: fifteen weeks of maternity benefits and ten weeks of parental benefits (which could be claimed entirely by one parent or shared by both parents). By 1998, 93 percent of women who took maternity leave from paid employment received monetary compensation (up from 77 percent in 1980), mostly in the form of employment insurance benefits....

In short, there can be little doubt that the current child support and maternity and parental leave benefits schemes are more generous now than they were when LEAF intervened in *Schachter* and *Thibaudeau*. Thus, even without directly affecting rules through litigation, legal mobilization appears to have had an effect in these areas of public policy. At a minimum, it raised issues to a position on the policy agenda that they might not have reached, or reached as quickly, without the visibility of Supreme Court decisions.

Sexual Orientation

There is little doubt that the sexual orientation cases in which LEAF intervened resulted in favourable rule changes. By imposing a constitutional obligation on provinces to include sexual orientation in their human rights statutes, *Vriend* essentially nationalized a policy that seven provinces had already adopted legislatively. More dramatically, *M. v. H.* established a new, more inclusive definition of spouse that effectively changed public policy in every province and territory, as well as at the federal level. ... In June 2000, the federal government's Bill C-23, *An Act to Modernize the Statutes of Canada in Relation to Benefits and Obligations*, received royal assent. This Act amended sixty-eight federal laws by extending benefits and obligations to all couples who have been cohabiting in a conjugal relationship for at least one year. ... Clearly, legal mobilization in this policy area, partly supported by LEAF, has initiated a process that may have broad social consequences.

[*Ed. note*: Following victories at lower courts, in the 2004 *Reference re Same-Sex Marriage*, a unanimous Supreme Court of Canada held that same-sex marriage "flows from" the *Charter*, although it did not answer the question of whether the opposite-sex definition of marriage was constitutional. In 2005, the federal Parliament passed same-sex marriage legislation.]

Conclusion

The cases in which LEAF has intervened changed legal rules either directly – as in *Gordon, Eldridge, Vriend, M. v. H.*, and *G.(J.)* – or indirectly – as in *Thibaudeau* and *Schachter*. In other cases, particularly in the area of sexual assault, LEAF's interventions were part of a broader policy debate about the proper balance between collective interests and individual rights. In these cases LEAF brought the perspective of feminist theory to bear on the debate and affected both legislative responses to judicial decisions and the judicial response to those legislative adjustments. At times, however, these achievements came at the cost of dividing the feminist movement, especially in the area of pornography. Indeed, LEAF's attempt to repair that division in *Little Sisters* may have had some impact on its credibility with the Court, at least in the short term.

As the literature on legal mobilization stresses, however, there is often a great distance between changes in legal rules and practical achievements. By far the most successful area for feminist legal mobilization has been abortion. The number of legal abortions performed in Canada increased significantly after 1988. Moreover, almost all of that increase can be traced to the elimination of the legal rule that only hospitals may perform abortions. Although LEAF did not participate directly in the removal of that rule, it has participated in litigation to help prevent its reestablishment. LEAF also helped in ushering in new maternity and parental leave policies and a new federal child support regime through its attack on existing rules. While those attacks failed in the Court, they resonated with the public and policy makers, resulting in political victories in the aftermath of legal defeat. Finally, to the extent that LEAF has contributed to the normalization of same-sex relationships, it has influenced the implementation of rule changes that will undoubtedly have a far-reaching effect on Canadian society.

NOTE

1   Abortion Rights Coalition of Canada, "Statistics - Abortion in Canada," April 5, 2017: http://www.arcc-cdac.ca/backrounders/statistics-abortion-in-canada.pdf

6.5

Interest Group Litigation and Canadian Democracy

Gregory Hein

Adapted from *Choices: Courts and Legislatures* (Montreal: IRPP 6:2 (2000)). Reprinted with permission.

Anyone who wants to understand judicial politics in Canada has to consider the efforts of organized interests. Groups are at the centre of most policy debates, trying to persuade an audience of elected officials, bureaucrats, editorialists and ordinary citizens to accept rival positions. The stakes are higher when they enter the courtroom.

Canadians can no longer ignore interest group litigation because it affects the style and substance of our political life. It has become an important strategy for interests trying to shape public policy. Stories about court challenges are reported in the media every week and interest groups participate in most of the cases: civil libertarians guard free expression with vigilance, even if their efforts help men who produce and consume child pornography; disabled people refuse to accept laws that ignore their needs; feminists take on defence lawyers who attack Criminal Code measures designed to counter sexual assault; pro-choice activists and pro-life groups return to court to argue about the presence or absence of fetal rights; gays and lesbians pursue an ambitious campaign to stop discrimination based on sexual orientation; First Nations assert Aboriginal treaty rights; hunters enter the courtroom to oppose measures that restrict the use of guns; groups that promote law and order denounce judges for paying too much attention to the rights of the criminally accused and too little attention to the victims of violent crimes. Unions enter the judicial system to help workers and corporations challenge regulations that frustrate their ability to maximize profits. Their adversaries also litigate. Environmentalists and economic nationalists try to enforce laws that discipline the free market.

Canadians who find these efforts unsettling identify several concerns. Organizations raise difficult moral, economic and political questions, but courts are not designed to sustain public discussions on complex issues. The most controversial claims pit courts against legislatures by asking judges to reject choices made by elected officials. Political life is pulled into our judicial system by groups that generate a steady stream of cases, but without confirmation hearings we know little about the men and women elevated to the Supreme Court. We know even less about superior court judges who also exercise broad powers. These fears are expressed by those who think that litigation can undermine the struggle for a better society and by those who insist that democracy is threatened by organizations that encourage judicial activism.

The debate in the 1980s was initiated by critical legal scholars and neo-Marxists who refused to believe that courts would be transformed into brash agencies of social change. The debate in the 1990s has been dominated by scholars and politicians on the right. According to their account, activists on the left have been wildly successful because so many judges are "removed from reality." These interests flood the courts because they cannot win the support of legislative majorities: most voters find their demands radical and dogmatic. We are told that gays and lesbians want to impose values that will undermine the traditional family. Aboriginal Peoples are determined to establish title over huge tracts of land and secure access to lucrative resources just by presenting flimsy oral histories. Feminists promote an interpretation of equality that leads to "reverse discrimination." Civil libertarians, by guarding the rights of alleged criminals, make it more difficult for police and prosecutors to secure law and order. For critics on the right, these "special interests" belong to a coalition which could be called the "court party." They bring the claims that fuel the growth of judicial power. Instead of trying to build public support for their ideas, these activists urge the Supreme Court to expand social services and benefits, alter the meaning of Aboriginal treaties written centuries ago, bolster regulatory regimes or repair legislative omissions. This use of litigation diminishes Canadian democracy, we are told, because it allows members of the court party to circumvent the legislative process.

This study offers an alternative argument by marshalling a large body of empirical data. The account advanced by conservative critics is incomplete and misleading. While warning us about "zealous" activists who invite judicial activism, they never tell us that courts are filled with a broad range of interests that express a wide array of values. Litigants talk to judges about child custody, labour disputes, income tax policy, advertising laws, medical procedures that cause harm, and the dangers of hazardous substances. This diversity exists because successive generations of Canadians have asked courts and governments to create new opportunities to participate in the judicial system and the legislative arena. We will see that critics on the right are correct when they argue that social activists are eager to pursue legal strategies. However, their interpretation ignores the economic interests that also appreciate the benefits of litigation. Corporations exert a surprising degree of pressure by asking judges to scrutinize the work of elected officials.

The evidence suggests that Aboriginal Peoples, *Charter* Canadians, civil libertarians, and new left activists have the greatest potential to influence public policy through litigation because they are pulled and pushed into the courtroom by the stable characteristics and the changing circumstances. These interests can be called *judicial democrats* because a provocative idea is embedded in their legal arguments and political appeals – judicial review can enhance democracy. Finding deficiencies that weaken our system of government, they believe that the courts should listen to groups that lack political power, protect vulnerable minorities and guard fundamental values, from basic civil liberties forged by the common law tradition to ecological principles that have emerged in the past century.

This study also reveals that corporations do not have the stable characteristics that elevate the propensity to litigate. However, they do confront the changing circumstances that make legal action a compelling strategic manoeuvre. Businesses counter hostile actions, to block investigating government agencies and to go to court when their political resources have been depleted.

The Study

In vibrant liberal democracies, we find a dizzying array of interests that take different shapes. Nine categories were identified that are both coherent and salient. Examples appear in Table 1.

1. Aboriginal Peoples have a unique claim to land and resources as the first inhabitants of the continent now called North America. They are nations struggling to win recognition of land, treaty and self-government rights.

2. Civil libertarians are determined to stop the state from undermining traditional guarantees that many individuals prize. Students, journalists, writers, church activists and defence lawyers challenge laws that violate freedom of expression, freedom of religion and rights that protect the criminally accused.

3. Corporate interests are businesses that compete in a range of sectors: financial, retail, manufacturing, construction, pharmaceutical, agricultural, communications and natural resources. Their advocacy groups demand low levels of taxation, flexible regulatory regimes and trade liberalization.

4. Labour interests are organized into unions and advocacy groups that represent miners, loggers, civil servants, teachers, nurses, police officers, auto-makers and technicians. Eager to improve the lives of workers, they defend the welfare state and oppose trade policies that produce unemployment.

5.   Professionals have the credentials to practice as lawyers, judges, accountants, academics, pharmacists, doctors, architects and engineers. Most work in the private sector as entrepreneurs, but some are employed by large public institutions. They pursue collective action to promote their interests and to protect the integrity of their respective professions.

6.   Social conservatives want to preserve traditional values sustained for centuries by church and family. They oppose open access to abortion services, homosexuals who demand "special rights," gun regulations that punish citizens without reducing crime, feminists who want to marginalize fathers, and a popular culture that encourages promiscuity.

7.   Groups that represent victims want to help individuals hurt by cancer, AIDS, drug addiction, smoking, intoxicated drivers, violent crimes, mining tragedies, silicone breast implants, the transmission of infected blood and sexual abuse in schools.

8.   *Charter* Canadians believe that state intervention is required to solve pressing social problems. They derive inspiration and impressive legal resources from the 1982 Constitution. Groups representing ethnic, religious and linguistic minorities, women and the disabled can base their claims on guarantees designed to protect their interests.

9.   New left activists also believe that state intervention is needed to address grave social problems, but they do not enjoy constitutional rights that were explicitly designed to protect their interests. Environmentalists, gays and lesbians, anti-poverty advocates and economic nationalists can invoke the *Charter* to stop military tests, fight discrimination, preserve wild spaces and stop governments from dismantling the welfare state, but they have to hope that judges will use their discretion to extend the scope of existing guarantees.

Table 1: Categories of Organized Interests

Aboriginal Peoples
Assembly of First Nations
Assembly of Manitoba Chiefs
Congress of Aboriginal Peoples
Dene Nation
Native Council of Canada
Union of New Brunswick Indians

Civil Libertarians
Amnesty International
Canadian Civil Liberties Association
Canadian Council of Churches
Canadian Federation of Students
Centre for Investigative Journalism
Criminal Lawyers' Association

Corporate Interests
Canadian Bankers' Association
Canadian Manufacturers' Association
Canadian Telecommunications Alliance
Merck Frosst Canada
Thomson Newspapers
R.J.R. MacDonald

Labour Interests
Canadian Labour Congress
International Longshoremen's and
     Warehousemen's Union
National Federation of Nurses' Unions
Public Service Alliance of Canada
Union des employés de service
United Fishermen and Allied Worker's Union

Professionals
Association provinciale des assureurs-vie du Québec
Association québécoise des pharmaciens propriétaires
Canadian Association of University Teachers
Canadian Bar Association
Canadian Institute of Chartered Accountants
Canadian Medical Association

Social Conservatives
Alliance for Life
Evangelical Fellowship of Canada
Human Life International
Inter-Faith Coalition on Marriage and the Family
National Firearms Association
REAL Women

Victims
Canadian Cancer Society
Canadian Council on Smoking and Health
Canadian HIV/AIDS Legal Network
Canadian Resource Centre for Victims of Crime
Central Ontario Hemophilia Society
Westray Families

Charter Canadians
Canadian Council of Refugees
Canadian Disability Rights Council
Canadian Jewish Congress Fédération
     des francophones hors Québec
Native Women's Association of Canada
Women's Legal Education and Action Fund

New Left Activists
Canadian Peace Alliance
Council of Canadians
Equality for Gays and Lesbians Everywhere
National Anti-Poverty Association
Sierra Legal Defence Fund
Société pour vaincre la pollution

To understand the legal strategies that groups pursue every decision appearing in the Federal Court Reports (1,259) and the Supreme Court Reports (1,329) from 1988 to 1998 was reviewed. Organizations appear as *parties* when they have a direct stake in a case. If groups are allowed to participate as *intervenors*, they can present oral arguments and written submissions to address issues raised in a dispute. To understand the purpose of litigation, six possible targets were identified.

1. Groups can achieve their objectives by confronting *private parties*. They counter individuals, unions, professional associations and corporations.

2. Litigants also take aim at *constrained officials* who exercise limited statutory powers. Some work for line departments, but most have positions on boards, tribunals, commissions and inquiries.

3. Organizations can bring claims against *Cabinet ministers* to block unfavourable decisions or to make governments act. By seeking writs of mandamus, they can ask courts to enforce mandatory duties.

4. The stakes are higher when groups mobilize the law to overturn the *statutes and regulations* that are introduced by governments.

5. To improve their chances of winning future contests, litigants can try to shape *judicial interpretations*. The primary goal of this strategy is to direct judges when they define the meaning, purpose and scope of common law rules, ordinary statutes and constitutional guarantees.

6. Groups also enter the courtroom to defend favourable policies when their adversaries launch *hostile actions*.

Interest Group Litigation Before the *Charter*

Courts played an important role before the *Charter* was entrenched by protecting property, hearing administrative actions, enforcing the criminal law and resolving disputes between both levels of government. Courts were also asked to defend civil liberties, even in the nineteenth century. Most cases were initiated by individuals facing charges or governments fighting jurisdictional battles, but organizations supported some challenges at a distance.

These efforts were exceptional. For more than a century, few organizations entered the courtroom to affect public policy and it was possible to have a complete understanding of Canadian politics without ever thinking about interest group litigation. The labour movement concentrated on the party system because courts did little to help workers. Activists who wanted to solve social problems pressured legislators and devised novel strategies in order to change public attitudes. While achieving some of their objectives in court, corporations lobbied Cabinet ministers and senior officials because they appreciated the importance of elite accommodation and the power of bureaucracies.

Interest Group Litigation After the *Charter*

This study reveals that a transformation has occurred. Interest group litigation is now an established form of collective action. Organizations present 819 claims between 1988 and 1998. They appear as parties or intervenors in

30 percent of the disputes considered by the Federal Court and the Supreme Court. Figure 1 records the frequency of participation.

Groups from every category pursue legal strategies. This single finding is remarkable – we now find the same mix of political players trying to influence courts and governments. We find elements of continuity and change. Court dockets are still laden with corporations. They bring 468 legal actions, far more than the other interests. Companies engage in civil litigation against private parties, and challenge regulations governing banking, federal elections, international trade, environmental protection and the pharmaceutical industry. Groups representing professionals participate in 32 cases. As employees, they try to win higher salaries and as experts, they talk to judges about a range of issues, including the principles that guide child custody disputes and criminal investigations. Very few of their challenges try to alter major public policies. The unions and advocacy groups that represent labour interests bring 58 claims. They back members alleging gender discrimination, fight for higher salaries, counter measures that undermine collective bargaining, try to escape criminal contempt charges and assert the right to strike.

The big change is that courts now hear from interests that struggled for decades to win access. For more than a century, courts and governments in Canada maintained barriers that discouraged or even prevented litigation.

Graph 1 reveals that litigation is now an important strategy for groups that once confronted these obstacles:

- Aboriginal Peoples launch 77 claims between 1988–98. First Nations take on the federal government when it fails to act in their best interests; they secure title to lands by asserting Aboriginal rights and challenge laws that fail to respect treaty rights.

- *Charter* Canadians are just as active: 80 legal arguments are presented to oppose measures restricting abortion services, to chastise provincial governments for breaching language rights, to reveal racism in the criminal justice system, and to overturn election laws that discriminate against the mentally ill.

- Civil libertarians participate in 40 cases that attack policies impairing democratic rights, fundamental freedoms and guarantees that protect the criminally accused.

- New left activists bring 37 claims. The activists enter the courtroom in order to protect delicate ecosystems, help poor people facing arrest, overturn policies that exclude homosexuals, and counter measures that limit demonstrations.

- Social conservatives bring fewer claims, only 18. The most controversial claims try to persuade courts to recognize fetal rights. Unlike their American allies and their Canadian adversaries, social conservatives have not formed any legal advocacy groups; these are specialized organizations designed to fight legal campaigns. In the early 1990s, the Canadian Rights Coalition was established to take on doctors who dared to perform abortions, but it soon disappeared.

- Organizations that represent victims bring even fewer court challenges, only nine. They usually participate outside the courtroom. Most legal claims are brought by individuals who allege negligence or breach of trust to win compensation. Class actions are also orchestrated to counter threats that harm hundreds of victims.

Figure 1: Organized Interests in Court, 1988–1998

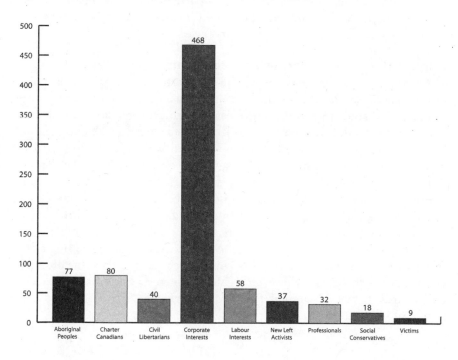

We find this diverse range of interests because governments and courts have created new opportunities to participate. The *Charter* was entrenched by federal politicians who wanted to strengthen the national community and weaken regional identities. Since the patriation round in 1982, governments have introduced funding programs and statutory rights to make administrative regimes, the regulatory process and the judicial system more accessible.

The Supreme Court has also introduced changes that have encouraged interest group litigation. The law of standing has been liberalized in stages. The old common law rule favoured property owners and corporations trying to protect private rights and filtered out citizens who wanted to address public problems. Under the new rule, applicants who ask a serious legal question and demonstrate a "genuine interest" can win access if certain conditions are satisfied. The Supreme Court has also relaxed the requirements for intervening. Groups with a record of advocacy displaying expertise in a particular area usually receive permission to appear as friends of the court.

The Legal Status of Participants

[*Ed. note*: Hein's database indicates that groups seeking "private" benefits (e.g., corporations, unions, professionals) usually participate as actual parties, while groups seeking "public goods" (e.g., *Charter* Canadians, civil libertarians, new left activists) typically participate as interveners.]

Confronting Private Parties and Constrained Officials

The debate over judicial activism gives us a distorted picture of interest group litigation because it *focusses* on the contentious cases that pit courts against legislatures. This study reveals that organizations achieve some of their objectives without asking judges to review the work of elected officials. Half of the actions initiated by corporations are civil claims against private parties and are driven by one of the great engines of capitalism – the desire to accumulate profits. Businesses enter the courtroom to stop trademark, copyright and patent infringement. They also seek damages for negligence and breach of contract. It is important to acknowledge this body of litigation to understand why companies enter the courtroom, but these cases rarely affect public policy.

Groups from every category target constrained officials exercising statutory powers. Some of these claims are ignored because they lack the drama of constitutional challenges. However, organized interests know that bureaucracies, boards, tribunals, commissions and inquiries make thousands of decisions that implicate major public policies.

Shaping the Interpretive Process

Courts define the meaning, purpose and scope of common law rules, ordinary statutes and constitutional guarantees. Organizations aware of this central fact know that precedents are building blocks. Over time they can persuade judges to jettison old standards, reject threatening arguments advanced by adversaries and improve their chances of winning future contests.

Charter Canadians and civil libertarians pursue this strategy more than other interests. A full quarter of their claims target judicial interpretations.

Challenging Elected Officials

The other claims are more captivating because the stakes are higher. When litigants target Cabinet decisions and public policies they ask appointed judges to reject choices made by politicians who have won the support of citizens in general elections. Decisions can rearrange legislative agendas that reflect public concerns, strain regulatory regimes already burdened by onerous responsibilities, alter spending priorities when governments are striving to trim deficits and spark violent reactions that divide communities. The evidence presented in Table 2 cuts to the very heart of the debate over judicial activism. It demonstrates which interests exert pressure on the federal state by challenging laws and political executives.

Table 2: Targeting Elected Officials, 1988–1998

Organized Interests	Cabinet Ministers		Statutes and Regulations		Total	
	No. of Claims	(%)	No. of Claims	(%)	No. of Claims	(%)
Corporate Interests	48	42	45	34	93	38
Aboriginal Peoples	33	29	18	14	51	21
Charter Canadians	10	9	19	14	29	12
New Left Activists	15	13	9	7	24	10
Civil Libertarians	2	2	20	15	22	9
Labour Interests	3	3	9	7	12	5
Social Conservatives	1	1	6	5	7	3
Professionals	1	1	5	4	6	2
Victims	0	0	0	0	0	0
Totals	113	100	131	100	244	100

Source: Court Challenges Database

Professionals oppose mandatory retirement, social conservatives attack laws that fail to protect the fetus, and unions question measures that restrict collective bargaining and the right to strike, but these are the exceptions. Overall, these groups bring only 10 percent of the claims that target elected officials and most cases try to knock down minor provisions. Groups supporting victims never pursue this strategy.

Far more pressure is generated by the interests that worry critics on the right. Aboriginal Peoples, *Charter* Canadians, civil libertarians and new left activists bring 52 percent of the claims that attack Cabinet decisions and public policies. To win, these litigants have to persuade judges to accept controversial roles – they have to be full partners in the legislative process. Aboriginal Peoples and new left activists question laws passed by both levels of government, but they often target Cabinet ministers.

Charter Canadians and civil libertarians also pursue this strategy, but they tend to target statutes and regulations.

The big surprise is that corporate interests are so active. Table 2 reveals that they present 38 percent of the claims that challenge laws and Cabinet decisions. Requesting writs of mandamus, businesses try to enforce rules governing international trade. Invoking the federal division of powers, they attack laws that address competition, new drugs, environmental protection and tax policy. The *Charter* is also mobilized by corporate litigants.

Propensity to Litigate

This study demonstrates that hundreds of businesses enter the judicial system to advance their interests and a significant proportion ask courts to confront governments. However, the evidence does not suggest that they are inclined to litigate. To understand strategic preferences, we have to consider the entire universe of associations – those that choose legal action and those that stay outside the judicial system. A ratio indicating litigation propensity can be formulated if we estimate the number of associations and the number of court challenges they mount.

What do we find? On the one hand, there are at least 180,000 businesses generating more than 500,000 dollars in revenue annually. They bring 468 claims. On the other hand, Aboriginal Peoples, *Charter* Canadians, civil libertarians and new left activists are represented by only 1,600 organizations. They participate in 234 cases. This comparison suggests that corporations do not display a propensity to litigate. Table 3 confirms what many already suspect. The interests that conservative critics blame for the expansion of judicial power are far more inclined to litigate.

Table 3: Propensity to Litigate

Organized Interests	Population	No. of Claims	Ratio
Corporations	180,000	468	1:385
Aboriginal Peoples, Charter Canadians Civil Libertarians, New Left Activists	1,600	234	1:7

Source: Court Challenges Database

[*Ed. note*: The section "Understanding Interest Group Litigation" has been deleted for space reasons except for the subsection on "judicial democrats."]

Entering the Courtroom to Enhance Democracy

Aboriginal Peoples, *Charter* Canadians, civil libertarians and new left activists believe that litigation has the potential to make our public institutions more accessible, transparent and responsive, if courts hear from a diverse range of interests, guard fundamental social values and protect disadvantaged minorities. We know that some activists agree with the neo-Marxists and critical legal scholars who warned social movements to resist the lure of constitutional litigation. They doubt that lawyers and judges are the real champions of democracy. We also know that Aboriginal Peoples, *Charter* Canadians, civil libertarians and new left activists make shrewd strategic calculations to improve their chances of success. However, the normative assertion that is embedded in their legal claims and political appeals is a crucial distinguishing feature. These interests display a greater propensity to litigate because the architects who design campaigns and the allies who work outside the courtroom believe that judicial review can enhance democracy. They are moved by this conviction.

Judicial democrats emphasize a structural defect that all liberal democracies confront. Without courts enforcing constitutional guarantees, governments can make choices that harm minorities, especially if they are vulnerable or unpopular. This threat is serious, they argue, because our representative institutions do not reflect the diversity of Canadian society. For example, a growing number of women sit in Parliament and the provincial legislatures, but men still dominate these chambers; we see few visible minorities and even fewer Aboriginal Peoples. This deficiency raises the possibility that policies will not reflect the interests of "weaker voices" that struggle for recognition. Moved by public sentiments, ideological preoccupations or financial pressures, governments might be tempted to impose limits on the rights that minorities assert. This problem exists, we are told, even when politicians do not intend to discriminate. The men who dominate our representative institutions often fail to appreciate the deleterious effects of laws that appear to be fair.

Judicial democrats who believe that courts should protect minorities suggest that majorities are more apparent than real. They identify faults acknowledged by political scientists and disenchanted voters. Elections are blunt instruments for registering preferences. During campaigns, personality is more important than policy and debates lack substance. Parties usually win control of the state by securing the support of pluralities not majorities. After taking office, a new government with only a general mandate can decide to pursue a disruptive legislative agenda that most citizens oppose. Because party discipline is so strong, it is difficult to know how many representatives actually support a proposed policy.

The activists who offer this critical assessment also tell us that democracy is weakened by a persistent bias. Interests trying to shape public policy do not enjoy the same opportunities. Some have access to the Cabinet ministers and bureaucrats who exercise real power. Others are excluded or ignored because they question deeply held attitudes and practices that have been accepted for generations. Corporations are privileged because of their role in the economy. Worse, their influence has been bolstered by the pressures of globalization. Groups concerned about public problems are often dismissed when they demand expensive social programs and strict regulations that penalize important industries. The judicial democrats who see this bias do not believe that our institutions are open and transparent. Elite accommodation leaves little room for public deliberation and bureaucrats draft thousands of regulations away from the scrutiny that shapes the legislative process – they write "secret laws."

Aboriginal Peoples, *Charter* Canadians, civil libertarians and new left activists who want courts to enforce fundamental values find cautionary narratives in our past. They tell us that federal officials undermined Aboriginal culture and suspended basic human rights. Adults did not enjoy the privileges of citizenship and children were sent away to residential schools, wrenched from their families and communities. Voters could have objected to these practices in general elections, but they did not. In Manitoba, the Protestant Anglophone majority failed for more than a century to respect rights designed to protect the Catholic Francophone minority. During the 1940s, Japanese Canadians were taken to detention camps. Civil libertarians also remember the 1950s, when religious minorities in Quebec were subjected to a campaign of harassment, orchestrated by the Premier and carried out by the police. In several provinces, mentally disabled women were forced into sterilization programs. During the 1960s, the RCMP investigated thousands of civil servants to root out homosexuals. Feminists were still fighting blatant forms of discrimination in the

1970s, opposing social policies that stopped pregnant women from receiving unemployment benefits, provisions in the Indian Act that stripped Aboriginal women of their status and a family law regime that hurt women by discounting their contributions.

Judicial democrats display a propensity to litigate because still believe that courts have to counter grave threats. Civil libertarians have to be vigilant because police officers who resent the *Charter* and politicians who promise law and order are tempted to limit fundamental guarantees. Aboriginal women who want to advance their interests have to litigate to win access to constitutional conferences. Legal action is still an essential strategy for environmental groups; provincial officials eager to promote economic growth still leave pollution laws unenforced; federal officials are still tempted to circumvent the requirements for environmental assessments, especially when lucrative projects could be jeopardized. Disabled men and women have to fight for services they deem to be essential. Coalitions of anti-poverty activists feel compelled to litigate when governments pass laws that stigmatize and harass homeless people. Francophones in English Canada and Anglophones in Quebec have to invoke education rights to secure good facilities and autonomous school boards; they have to ask judges to supervise provincial officials who are reluctant to redistribute revenue and authority. Feminists must go to court to help women who are victims of sexual violence. Governments are willing to draft comprehensive agreements, Aboriginal leaders tell us, because courts continue to enforce Aboriginal rights.

Unlike these judicial democrats, the executives and lobbyists who represent corporations and entire industries do not believe that active courts should try to enhance democracy. In certain contexts, they say the very opposite. When litigation has hampered their ability to generate profits, businesses espouse an argument that is also made by conservative critics. They admire the virtues of majoritarian democracy and lament the loss of legislative supremacy. This defence becomes apparent when governments try to improve access to legal remedies. In Ontario, coalitions organized to stop the Class Proceedings Act during the late 1980s and the Environmental Bill of Rights during the early 1990s. To oppose these threatening measures, businesses questioned the legitimacy of judicial review, criticized the institutional capacity of courts and emphasized the disruptive effects of litigation. What did they fear? Mischievous activists would "flood" the judicial system with "frivolous" claims. Because courts would become partners in the regulatory process, it would become less flexible and more cumbersome. Favourable decisions made by politicians who appreciate the central role that corporations play would be overturned by judges who are shielded from the realities of a competitive global economy.

Countering Immediate Threats

Judicial democrats and corporate interests are also pushed into the courtroom by immediate threats that can only be stopped through litigation. Table 4 reveals an inescapable strategic problem. Organizations have to target hostile actions to defend public policies, Criminal Code provisions, common law standards, judicial interpretations and administrative orders that favour their interests. It is startling to see that 34 percent of the claims brought by *Charter* Canadians are intended to counter these threatening claims. Critical legal scholars and neo-Marxists predicted this trend. After the patriation round, they warned social reformers who were dazzled by the possibilities of constitutional litigation that time and money would have to be spent reacting to claims brought by their enemies. Feminists intervene to protect Criminal Code provisions governing sexual assault, hate speech and pornography. Groups representing the disabled support policies that mandate special education. A growing number of issues pull competing organizations into the courtroom: cases that implicate the fetus attract pro-choice activists and pro-life groups; fishing companies and Aboriginal Peoples fight over valuable natural resources; some Aboriginal bands oppose Aboriginal women who challenge residency requirements; rival drug manufacturers try to secure and block the notices that allow companies to produce pharmaceuticals; and new left activists and businesses defend or attack measures designed to protect the natural environment.

Table 4: Hostile Actions

Organized Interests	No. of Claims	Percentage of Total Claims Brought by Groups in Each Category
Charter Canadians	27	34
New Left Activists	7	19
Civil Libertarians	6	15
Aboriginal Peoples	10	13
Corporate Interests	25	5

Source: Court Challenges Database

Corporations face another threat that can only be countered through litigation. Governments conduct inspections, initiate civil actions and bring criminal charges to enforce a range of laws. We already know that businesses raise the Constitution as a sword to cut away policies that constrain their activities. Corporate litigants also hold up the Constitution as a shield to block the state from scrutinizing their affairs. Businesses can devise a wide array of legal arguments because the Supreme Court has decided that any *Charter* guarantee can be invoked as a defence. To advance their interests, businesses attack procedures allowing authorities to conduct searches and seizures, general inquiry powers, regulatory offences and measures that restrict the right to counsel in the old Combines Investigation Act, the new Competition Act, the Income Tax Act and laws governing the banking industry. This desire to obstruct scrutiny will always be an important source of litigation.

Diminished Political Resources

Organizations also enter the courtroom when contextual changes diminish the level or value of their political resources. Their fortunes can be affected by the rate of economic growth, unemployment, environmental disasters, the appointment of new Cabinet ministers and international conflicts. Because influence is not a fixed characteristic, all interests can be placed at a disadvantage – even huge industries that employ thousands of workers and generate billions of dollars in revenue. We know that tobacco companies have been hurt by compelling scientific evidence and adverse public opinion for more than a decade. Governments have introduced a number of measures to restrict the use of their product. Jurisdictions in Canada and the United States have initiated civil claims to recover health-care costs. This hostility makes litigation an attractive strategy. For example, R.J.R. Macdonald won an impressive victory in a decision that has been denounced by health-care advocates, groups representing victims and new left activists who feel that corporations wield too much power. Invoking the guarantee of free expression, it persuaded the Supreme Court to remove an advertising ban. The other cases are less dramatic. Fishing companies on both coasts have been hit hard because federal officials have taken remedial steps that restrict commercial enterprises to halt the decline of stocks. Businesses unable to secure favourable policies have responded by pressing their claims in court.

Only ideologues believe that corporations are invincible. Still, in a world shaped by the pressures of globalization, businesses that can survive in the international economy enjoy an advantage. Governments determined to eliminate annual deficits and tackle accumulated debts now support policies that favour competitive corporations. They are promoting the benefits of trade liberalization, deregulation, and tax reduction. This shift has undermined other interests. Politicians trying reduce the size of the state are less willing to agree with activists who demand expensive national programs and onerous regulatory regimes. In this climate, judicial democrats find litigation even more compelling, especially when they encounter indifference and hostility. After failing to win in the legislative arena, *Charter* Canadians can mount legal challenges to reform the Income Tax Act and expand the scope of social services. When federal officials fail to implement the core recommendations of a royal commission that examines the plight of Aboriginal Peoples, First Nations can ask judges to hear their concerns. New left activists ignored by political elites can knock down policies that exclude homosexuals and demand the strict enforcement of environmental laws. Governments that have achieved a budget surplus have more room to consider policy options, but judicial democrats have learned an important lesson during the past decade: litigation is indispensable when the country is toiling through tough times.

Interest Group Litigation and Canadian Democracy

This study tells us what we need to know to contemplate the effects and implications of interest group litigation.

- The central insight is that Aboriginal Peoples, *Charter* Canadians, civil libertarians, and new left activists are drawn into court by the stable characteristics that elevate the propensity to litigate and by the changing circumstances that make legal strategies seem compelling. These are the judicial democrats. They will continue to generate a steady stream of controversial claims because they believe that democracy can be enhanced by judicial review.

- Judicial democrats are not in court alone. The judicial system is filled with a wide array of groups that express a broad range of values. This diversity is a triumph for citizens who struggled for decades to win new opportunities to participate in our public institutions.

- Some organized interests are reluctant litigants. Professionals, social conservatives and victims mobilize the law sporadically. Although groups that represent workers are more willing to bring legal claims, they usually attack constrained officials, leaving major public policies unscathed.

- Corporations do not display a propensity to litigate, but they do encounter the changing circumstances that push interests into the courtroom. They ask judges to overturn cabinet decisions and laws passed by both levels of government, often to resist state intervention.

The purpose of this study is to understand a controversial form of collective action, but it can also help us assess the current relationship between citizens, legislators, and judges. In the current debate over judicial activism, most commentators exaggerate the hazards and underestimate the rewards.

Courts interpreting cryptic constitutional declarations and treaties signed centuries ago do make decisions that cause turmoil. They can disrupt legislative agendas, strain regulatory regimes already burdened by arduous responsibilities and force governments to adjust the allocation of resources. Our political life might be less tranquil and more uncertain today. However, we now have a judicial system that responds to a diverse range of interests. This is an accomplishment that Canadians should celebrate. Judges hear from professionals advancing pecuniary claims, Aboriginal Peoples who want their treaty rights respected, and environmentalists who monitor the erosion of important. Courts enforcing the *Charter* help businesses trying to protect commercial expression, homosexuals who want the family law remedies that heterosexuals expect and linguistic minorities struggling to preserve their culture.

Critics troubled by active courts want to restore the relative calm we once enjoyed by resurrecting "traditional judicial review." What do they propose? The Supreme Court has to bring back the old standing requirements, discourage interests from intervening, consider only narrow legal questions raised by live controversies and question the value of extrinsic evidence. They resent judges who allow political adversaries to clutter the courtroom, evaluate policy alternatives with misplaced confidence and try to settle future disputes in a single decision. Conservative critics believe that prudence should replace arrogance. It is too easy for judges to advance their personal preferences, they insist, if the "living tree metaphor" can be invoked as a *licence* to alter the meaning and scope of enumerated guarantees. The Supreme Court has to remember the primary purpose of a liberal democratic constitution: to protect individuals by placing limits on the state. Legal remedies should not increase the presence of the state. Judges should never punish governments for failing to act by filling perceived omissions. They should also resist the temptation to expand services, benefits, regulatory regimes and Aboriginal treaties.

This argument can sound appealing, especially when the Supreme Court delivers a decision that divides the country. Still, the measures that conservative critics propose have a distinct bias that Canadians should know about. Resurrecting traditional judicial review would filter out certain interests and values. Returning to the old rules governing standing and intervenor status would hurt public interests unable to demonstrate a direct stake in a dispute. Excluding extrinsic evidence would make it more difficult for litigants who want to trace the adverse effects of a law. Freezing the meaning and scope of constitutional guarantees would leave judges unable to address new social problems that create discrimination. If courts only placed limits on the state, litigation would be a poor strategy for citizens who want to bolster regulatory regimes or expand social services. Taken together, these obstacles would hinder interests concerned about racism, homophobia, gender inequality, environmental degradation, poverty, the lives of the disabled and the plight of Aboriginal Peoples. Traditional judicial review would not, however, frustrate litigants advancing conventional pecuniary claims and legal action would still be an effective strategy for interests that want to resist state intervention.

Although constrained courts would cause fewer disruptions, we would pay a price. Litigation would help corporations but not groups trying to address public problems. Critics of judicial activism stumble here. They want to stop social reformers from seeking the legal remedies that businesses have always requested. Seen from this perspective, the current relationship between citizens, legislators, and judges is attractive because it meets a basic requirement of democracy that many Canadians embrace. Nations composed of diverse interests should not have institutions that respond to some and ignore others.

6.6

Response to Gregory Hein
Ian Brodie
Political Science, University of Calgary. Written for the 3rd edition (2002).

Gregory Hein writes that interest group litigation is now an established part of Canadian political life, and he is right. His defence of interest group litigation's influence on Canadian politics is a bit harder to accept.

Many people criticize the judicialization of politics. Hein acknowledges the most common criticisms. It undermines the influence of elected officials. It brings political issues to courts, and courts are poorly equipped to deal with these issues. It turns important decisions over to judges who are appointed through a secretive process. In response, he argues that the courts attract the same kinds of interests as other political institutions. Both "progressive" groups and corporations use litigation to achieve their goals. He also argues that for years Canadians have demanded more ways to participate in the judicial and political processes.

Up to this point, Hein is arguing that interest group litigation does little to change the overall thrust of Canadian politics. The same kinds of interests are being pursued in the political process as in the courts. More interest group litigation is all about increasing participation in politics, and the more participation the better.

Hein then goes on to look at the views of "judicial democrats." These groups (and, I suspect, Hein himself) think the judicialization of politics improves Canadian politics. How? Because Canada's elected institutions do not represent the full diversity of Canadian society. They often overlook the weaker voices in society and tend to favour corporations over public interest groups. According to this argument, interest groups use the courts to protect disadvantaged minorities and even the political score.

These arguments are not persuasive. First, the argument that Canada's elected institutions do not represent all the diversity of Canadian society. Which groups are underrepresented? Does parliament need more women? More poor people? More farmers? More factory workers? More transgendered persons? The alternative the judicial democrats propose is to have more decisions by judges. Judges are all lawyers. They are also wealthier, whiter, and older than the rest of the population. The courts are much less diverse than parliament or most provincial legislatures. Do judicial democrats think that having judges make more political decisions will improve the "representativeness" of Canadian government?

Second, Hein's judicial democrats say that interest group litigation protects disadvantaged minorities. The political process is biased against interests that lack the resources to be heard in parliament, cabinet, or the bureaucracy. Certainly, groups with money, a stable staff, solid political strategies, and expertise tend to get access to political decision-makers. However, the judicial process also has biases, as Hein points out. Groups must have money, experienced lawyers, and expertise to win in court. Do these kinds of groups have trouble getting a meeting with a senior bureaucrat, a cabinet minister, or a political aide? Would a group that was truly shut out of the political process be able to mount a single court case, let alone long-term litigation campaigns?

This point hints at a deeper problem in Hein's argument. He portrays interest group litigation as a grassroots phenomenon, a ground-up process. He writes as if groups of Canadians band together spontaneously to challenge government actions in court. However, this is hardly accurate. Governments often support the "judicial democrats" through programs like the Court Challenges Program [*Ed. note*: see Readings 6.7 and 6.8]. If a group has government support for its litigation, is it really "disadvantaged"?

6.7

Defending the Court Challenges Program
Carissima Mathen and Kyle Kirkup

Policy Options, February 22, 2017, http://policyoptions.irpp.org/magazines/february-2017/defending-the-court-challenges-program/. Reprinted with permission.

After much anticipation, the federal government has announced the reinstatement of the Court Challenges Program. Set to cost $12 million over five years, the CCP will assist Canadians with legal challenges to advance and protect their Charter rights. The decision is a welcome one.

The program's history spans some 40 years. It was introduced in skeletal form in 1978, applying only to minority language rights. In 1985, Prime Minister Brian Mulroney extended it to equality rights challenges to federal laws. Mulroney ended the Program in 1992, but the Liberals under Jean Chrétien resurrected it two years later.

After coming to power in 2006, Prime Minister Stephen Harper could not end the Program fast enough. Given that his government was skeptical of the Charter, the move was unsurprising.

Some critics have claimed that it is illogical for the government to fund Canadians to sue it. That argument rests on a simplistic view of constitutional rights: that they represent an infringement on the government which it generally resists. Of course, any government is entitled to advance its policy goals, and is likely to vigorously defend its choices in court. But that hardly precludes government recognition of, and support for, the broader principle of judicial review. Recent events in the United States have demonstrated how critical that function is. We applaud the government's recognition that its role vis-à-vis the constitution is not purely defensive. Such recognition also counters the notion that taxpayers are unfairly footing the bill. Constitutional challenges are primarily directed to the public interest, and the government is right to support this initiative.

At least some of the earlier criticism of the Program can be traced to suspicion of so-called "judicial activism." On that count, the program eroded traditional democratic processes. Vulnerable groups used it to achieve social change by evading the appropriate venue for such change: the legislature. The legalization of same-sex marriage in 2005, for example, is viewed as the direct consequence of funding that was granted to LGBTQ organizations to pursue Charter challenges on the issue. This critique overlooks the fact that in a constitutional democracy, parliamentary sovereignty is necessarily limited.

Democratic values are enriched, not threatened, when all members of society, especially those who lack political power, can hold the government to account.

One might also wonder why a government would admit the need for a Court Challenges Program at all. Shouldn't constitutional flaws be caught earlier in the process? We strongly support advance scrutiny of laws and policies. But it can be difficult to anticipate a law's effects. Or, a government may press ahead with a controversial law that it believes it can later defend. In such situations, Canadians should not be forced to depend on the pro bono services of lawyers and experts in order to vindicate their constitutional rights. The program has never funded anything close to the full cost of litigation. But it can provide crucial support in an environment where constitutional challenges are increasingly complex and expensive.

The program will face controversial choices, including possible applications related to medical aid in dying; the practice of solitary confinement in Canada's federal prisons; and religious freedom. This is, in part, because the government has decided to expand the program's funding from language and equality rights to include the Charter's fundamental freedoms, democratic rights, and life, liberty, and security of the person. That should diminish the charge that the program is "tilted" towards some Charter rights at the expense of others. It is true that expanding the program's scope may pose a challenge in cases featuring distinct, and competing, constitutional rights. Such decisions will require care, but in principle, there is no reason to deny funding simply because a case engages multiple Charter rights. Performed correctly, such an approach is likely to enhance the program's credibility.

In announcing the reinstatement, Justice Minister Jody Wilson-Raybould said that the government was seeking to give voice to Canadians. The program does just that. It demonstrates the value of a robust constitutional culture. Inclusive and optimistic, the Court Challenges Program is a powerful symbol of Canadians' commitment to our Constitution, and to each other.

6.8

The Court Challenges Program Rises Once Again
Ian Brodie

Policy Options, April 21, 2016, http://policyoptions.irpp.org/magazines/
april-2016/the-court-challenges-program-rises-once-again/. Reprinted with
permission.

Here we go again.

The oft-cancelled Court Challenges Program (CCP) is to be resurrected. The program, which sees the federal government subsidize activists and interest groups to sue it and other governments using the Charter of Rights, has been established and cancelled several times throughout its controversial 40-year history. This year's federal budget set aside an annual $5 million budget to start up the program once again. Why has this little program become a political football? Can the Trudeau government give it a more stable life?

Prime Minister Pierre Trudeau created the CCP in 1978. It was part of a broader Liberal effort to undermine the Parti Québécois (PQ) government, in this case by paying activists to challenge the PQ's Bill 101 and, for good measure, the unilingualism legislation of other provinces, in court. The elder Trudeau used the Charter of Rights to create new language rights in the area of education, so in 1982 his government expanded the CCP to cover these new rights. And when the Mulroney government was looking for a low-cost way to prove its "progressive" bona fides, it expanded the CCP again to support litigation by feminist, gay and disability rights groups. Pretty soon, CCP-funded cases were forcing a broad-scale social reform agenda on governments from coast to coast.

The political agenda of the CCP and the idea of the federal government funding only one side in contentious litigation soon sapped the program's political support. In 1992, the Mulroney government was looking for ways to reduce government spending and closed it. But the Liberals promised to re-establish the program during the 1993 election, turning it into a political football. The resurrected program was even more firmly married to progressive social reform groups, and it therefore ended up back on the scrap heap when the Stephen Harper Conservatives took office. During last fall's campaign, Justin Trudeau promised to re-resurrect the program, and discussions are now underway about how to design it.

Before the details of the new CCP are ironed out, Trudeau's ministers should ask some fundamental questions. Will it just be cancelled again by the next Conservative government? Is it fated to be a political football? Or could the Trudeau government do the country a service and set it up to survive future changes of government? After all, the protection of human rights is supposed to be above partisan politics. Shouldn't a program to fund human rights litigation also be above partisan politics?

The new government's challenge is to make the CCP broader and less partisan than it has been in the past. The new CCP will certainly subsidize the equality rights litigation of social reform groups. It will fund a new generation of test cases about equality rights, drawing the courts into issues around the rights of transgender Canadians. And it will continue to finance cases about minority language rights. But the Charter covers more than equality and language rights. The new CCP should benefit more than just social-reform and minority-language groups.

Why not let the CCP finance free speech litigation by journalists like Ezra Levant and Mark Steyn? After all, they have both paid a high price to highlight the oppressive provisions of federal and provincial human rights codes. Why not let the CCP help traditional religious groups protect the rights of religious minorities in court? Going beyond Charter issues, why not let the program finance challenges to interprovincial trade barriers? If the CCP 3.0 had a board of directors and management team with a broader view of rights litigation, it should be able to survive a future change of government.

Whatever the Trudeau government decides about the scope of the program, it should be careful to keep it out of cases that pit one Charter right against another. In the 21st century, human rights issues are not always as clear cut as they were in the early years after the Charter. Back then, most rights litigation was trying to roll back oppressive government policies. These days, the courts are often called upon to decide between two competing Charter claims in a single case. The federal government should not be weighing in to finance one side or the other in cases like that.

Just such a case will likely come before the CCP as soon as it opens for business. Trinity Western University, a private, evangelical university in British Columbia, is suing three provincial law societies over its right to have a law school. Trinity Western, as befits a religious institution, expects its students to abide by traditional religious rules regarding marriage and sexuality. Some law societies are refusing to recognize the credentials of its graduates, because they cannot tolerate an institution that does not embrace same-sex marriage. In 2001, when ruling on a similar case about Trinity Western's teacher training program, the Supreme Court said that neither freedom of religion nor equality on the basis of sexual orientation is absolute. Since then, same-sex marriage became the law of the land. The issue is therefore being litigated over again.

The new cases are on the way to the Supreme Court. Will the resurrected CCP fund the equality rights side or the freedom of religion side? Better to instruct the CCP to avoid this kind of case altogether. Since the Supreme Court has recognized that in a conflict between equality rights and freedom of religion, neither side can make an absolute claim. That, along with a broader set of directors and mandate, could relaunch the CCP without making it a political football again.

6.9

Do Bills of Rights Matter?
Charles Epp

American Political Science Review 90, no. 4 (1996), 765–779. Reprinted with permission.

Constitutionalism and the Conditions for Application of a Bill of Rights

Constitutions, the most basic of political institutions, affect ordinary politics by prescribing the rules of the political game. Liberal constitutions typically employ two very different kinds of rules to constrain arbitrary power: a) some rules structure governing institutions in such a way that decision making is channeled and thereby limited (this is the purpose of the separation of powers and federalism), and b) other rules define particular issues as outside the authority of the ordinary democratic process (this is the purpose of bills of rights). Both types of rules, it may appear, produce similarly profound and direct effects on politics. But not all rules are created equal: *federalism and the separation of powers are self-activating; bills of rights are not.*

Bills of rights are not self-activating because, unlike the separation of powers, they provide individuals with no direct control over institutional resources. In other words, although bills of rights create legal interests (rights), they create no corresponding institutional resources to actualize those interests. Thus, in Madison's evocative metaphor, constitutional rights guarantees are mere "parchment barriers." Nonetheless, remarkably profound effects are often attributed to bills of rights. I survey those hypothesized effects and then turn to the conditions – judicial attitudes, discretionary docket control, and external support for legal mobilization – that are likely to influence the application of bills of rights in practice.

Bills of Rights

Bills of rights are often thought to affect politics in several ways. First, observers commonly suggest that they promote an emphasis on rights in political culture. Similarly, some scholars argue that rights guarantees shape the development of political and social movements. Second, observers commonly suggest that bills of rights increase the level of intervention by courts in the policy-making processes of other governmental institutions. Similarly, contemporary scholars often trace the extraordinary vibrancy of judicial review, judicial attention to rights, and judicial policy-making on rights in the United States to the presence of a bill of rights in the U.S. Constitution. Third, contemporary writers have suggested that the presence of a bill of rights, by encouraging a broader policy-making role for the judiciary, opens the political opportunity structure and thereby encourages a fragmentation of broad coalitions and parties into numerous competing interest groups as groups abandon collective solutions in the legislature for more individualized solutions in the courts.

There are reasons to be skeptical, however, that the mere presence of a bill of rights will have much effect. Madison, for instance, wrote to Jefferson that "experience proves the inefficacy of a bill of rights on those occasions when its control is most needed.... I have seen the bill of rights violated in every instance where it has been opposed to a popular current."

The Support Structure for Legal Mobilization

The most important weakness of a bill of rights, as I previewed above, is that, unlike the self-enforcing structure embodied in federalism and the separation of powers, a bill of rights creates no automatic institutional resources for its own enforcement. Although bills of rights commonly empower at least some courts to redress violations of rights, there remain several weaknesses to the machinery of enforcement. Some scholars emphasize what they believe to be courts' relatively weak enforcement powers. Perhaps as important, however, is that rights guarantees rarely provide potential litigants with the resources necessary to mobilize the law. The legal system functions as an entrepreneurial market in which development of law is affected by individuals' decisions to mobilize the law; and decisions to mobilize the law depend on individuals' capacity to do so, which depends partly on their access to resources. At the level of national supreme courts, in particular, cost is an important barrier to access. The cost of taking any particular case to a supreme court is substantial. The total cost of getting an issue onto such a court's agenda is not limited only to the cost of the particular case that eventually reaches that agenda, but includes also the cost of the various lower court cases that create the legal conditions that encourage a supreme court to resolve the issue. Those who hope to place a particular issue on the Supreme Court's agenda must have sufficient financial resources to support extensive litigation in lower courts, or must be able to rely on the resources of a broader class of litigants....

Three types of resources – organized group support, financing, and the structure of the legal profession – appear to be important conditions shaping access to the judiciary. Together these resources constitute the support structure for legal mobilization. First, a wide range of scholarship identifies organized group litigants as important influences on judicial agendas. Galanter suggested that "repeat players," typically organizations, fare significantly better in court, and influence legal change and agenda-setting significantly more, than do "one shot" litigants. In recent decades, the number and diversity of organized groups providing support for rights litigation has grown significantly in a number of countries. In the United States, organized support for civil liberties and civil rights grew after about 1910 with the development of a number of rights-advocacy organizations. The organizations contributed significantly to the judicial rights agenda. The NAACP Legal Defense Fund, for example, organized, financed, and provided legal counsel for many of the most important civil rights cases to reach the U.S. Supreme Court.

Another factor contributing to access to the higher judiciary is financing, particularly governmental sources of financing. Governmental sources of financing appear to be necessary conditions for the presence on the agenda of claims by criminal defendants and the poor. In the United States, legal aid in civil cases and the most important forms of aid for criminal defendants are relatively new developments, growing only in the last sixty years.

Finally, access to lawyers and the structure of the legal profession influence access to the judicial agenda. With some exceptions, the assistance of a lawyer is necessary to take a case to a supreme court. Lawyers contribute to legal strategy and they provide much of the network through which information about rights litigation travels. Additionally, the degree of diversity of the legal profession appears to influence access to the judicial agenda....

[*Ed. note*: The author then describes how judicial attitudes and discretion over the Court's docket also contribute to the expansion of a public law agenda.]

Study Design and Data

... I have derived several indicators of the Supreme Court's agenda that may be expected to reveal the *Charter*'s influence especially clearly. They are 1) the proportion of the issue agenda devoted to civil rights and civil liberties; 2) the frequency of exercise of judicial review; 3) the level of support for civil rights and liberties; 4) the extent of reliance on constitutional foundations for decisions (which I expand to include all "higher law" foundations, namely the common law standard of natural justice, the 1960 statutory *Bill of Rights*, constitutional law other than the *Charter*, and the *Charter*); 5) the extent of participation in cases by interest groups and other third parties; and 6) the size of the docket.

Although Canadian observers nearly universally attribute profound effects to the *Charter*, Morton and Knopff recently have argued that the effects often attributed to the *Charter* alone are, instead, the result of active political pressure by the "Court Party," an informal coalition of rights-advocacy groups, lawyers, and judges [*Ed. note*: See Reading 12.4]. As Morton states, "the *Charter* itself is not so much the cause of the revolution as the means through which it is carried out." That analysis is consistent with the support structure hypothesis.

Canada's Support Structure for Legal Mobilization

Canada also affords a test of the support structure hypothesis because the Canadian support structure for legal mobilization grew dramatically between 1965 and 1990, with much of the growth preceding adoption of the *Charter*. I briefly survey developments in the three components of Canada's support structure.

Rights Advocacy Organizations. The development of private rights-advocacy organizations in Canada occurred in a relatively short space of time, roughly between the late 1960s and the early 1980s. Prior to 1970, business and agricultural groups dominated the Canadian interest group system, but after that year the number of non-producer advocacy organizations virtually exploded. Interest groups focusing on civil liberties and civil rights, in particular, did not exist before the mid-1960s, and their prominence in Canadian politics grew substantially by the early 1980s. The two principal civil liberties organizations, the British Columbia Civil Liberties Association and the Canadian Civil Liberties Association, were founded in 1962 and 1964, respectively, but only became relatively active after about 1970.

Advocacy organizations supporting civil rights also began to form in the years following the mid-1960s. In the area of women's rights, the National Action Committee on the Status of Women was formed in 1971; the Canadian Advisory Council on the Status of Women, a quasi-state organization, in 1973; the National Association of Women and the Law, in 1977; and the Women's Legal Education and Action Fund, in 1985. The major aboriginal rights organizations also formed in the late 1960s and early 1970s. Of 239 major aboriginal political organizations existing in 1993, 43 formed in the 1960s, 92 in the 1970s, and 28 in the 1980s. The Advocacy Resource Centre for the Handicapped, a leading organization advocating expanded rights for the handicapped, was formed in 1980.... [Federal and provincial] human rights commissions and the law reform commissions [also] became institutional sites for liberal rights advocacy, and there has been a fluid interchange of talent and legal resources between these governmental agencies, the law schools, and private rights advocacy organizations.

Canadian rights advocacy organizations are primarily liberal or left-liberal in orientation. To a significant extent, this reflects deliberate policies by the national government to cultivate liberal advocacy organizations. The Canadian Department of the Secretary of State, under the direction of Trudeau's Liberal Government in the late 1960s, developed an aggressive program to finance citizens' advocacy organizations focusing on such issues as women's rights, language rights, and multiculturalism. Nonetheless, several conservative organizations support litigation, among them the National Citizens' Coalition and REAL Women, but they have enjoyed much less success than liberal groups because, as Morton and Knopff observe, "they are decidedly swimming against the ideological tide."

Government Sources of Financing. The national and provincial governments have developed a variety of programs that finance rights litigation and advocacy. In the decade after 1965, in a major policy revolution, the Canadian provinces created legal aid programs that finance both civil and criminal cases. Spending on court cases by the new legal aid organizations increased dramatically in the 1970s.

The Court Challenges Program, a set of funds created specifically for financing test cases on language rights and equality rights, is another government-sponsored legal program that began prior to passage of the *Charter*. The Program was established in 1978 to finance court cases on language rights protected under the *Constitution Act, 1867*; since then, it has "supported almost every major language law case at the [Supreme] Court." The government added an equality rights component to the Program in 1985 to finance cases under the equality provisions in the *Charter of Rights*. Between 1985 and 1992, the equality component of the Program provided financing for 178 court cases at all levels of the system, including 24 cases in the Supreme Court. [*Ed. note*: See Readings 6.7 and 6.8 for an update on the Court Challenges Program]....

The Legal Profession. Several highly significant changes in the legal profession have occurred since 1945, with the most important developments occurring between the mid-1960s and the early 1980s. First, Canada's system of legal education changed dramatically as the importance and autonomy of law schools increased. In Canada, as in the U.S., training for the practice of law has shifted from apprenticeship, a system in which legal education is dominated by the relatively conservative interests of the practising bar, to law schools. Ten of Canada's 20 law schools were created after World War II, and the number of full-time law professors increased dramatically, almost doubling between 1971 and 1982 alone. As the importance and autonomy of the law schools increased, legal training increasingly emphasized theoretical and constitutional issues. By 1982, the year of the *Charter*'s adoption, Canadian law professors were remarkably young (the median age was 38) and generally supportive of a growing policy-making role for the judiciary on civil liberties and civil rights. The growth of law schools also provided an institutional base for critical scholarship and advocacy on constitutional issues....

Additionally, in the decade after 1970, Canada's lawyer population grew dramatically and began to diversify, and lawyers increasingly engaged in advocacy activities. The most significant growth of the Canadian lawyer population occurred between 1971 and 1981, when the number more than doubled. The lawyer population grew at a faster pace prior to 1981 than after that year; thus the *Charter* induced no unprecedented growth in the number of lawyers.

The Canadian legal profession also began to diversify by ethnic origin and sex in the decade following 1970. [*Ed. note*: See introduction to Chapter 4]....
Taken together, these changes in Canada's interest group system, governmental financing of litigation, and the legal profession fundamentally transformed the Canadian support structure for legal mobilization *prior to adoption of the* Charter *in 1982*....

Patterns in the Canadian Supreme Court's Agenda
In light of these various changes in Canada's constitution, its support structure for legal mobilization, the Supreme Court's attitudinal composition, and the Court's docket control, what changes have occurred in the Court's agenda and when did they begin? I pursue here a data triangulation strategy, using a variety of alternative measures of the Canadian Supreme Court's agenda and workload from 1960 through 1990. The data generally tell much the same story: significant changes in the Canadian Supreme Court's agenda, on a number of dimensions, began in the early 1970s and continued at rates that remained largely unchanged by adoption of the *Charter* in 1982....

The issue agenda. First, the Supreme Court's issue-agenda changed dramatically between 1960 and 1990 (see Figure 1). The proportion of the agenda devoted to civil liberties and civil rights grew dramatically, and the proportion devoted to tax cases and ordinary economic disputes declined dramatically. Both developments began prior to adoption of the *Charter* in 1982. Civil rights and civil liberties cases constituted 13% or less of the Court's agenda prior to 1975, and by 1990 they claimed about 60% – but the growth rate between 1980 and 1985, 86%, was only marginally faster than the 78% growth rate between 1975 and 1980. Similarly, the proportion of the Court's agenda devoted to tax and ordinary economic issues abruptly began to decline after 1975 but prior to adoption of the *Charter* in 1982.

Figure 1: Issue Agenda of the Supreme Court

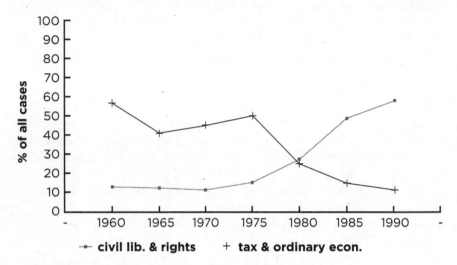

Source: Author's coding of Supreme Court decisions.
N = 1960, 77; 1965, 73; 1970, 80; 1975, 119; 1980, 119; 1985, 68; 1990, 110.

Figure 2: Judicial Review by the Supreme Court

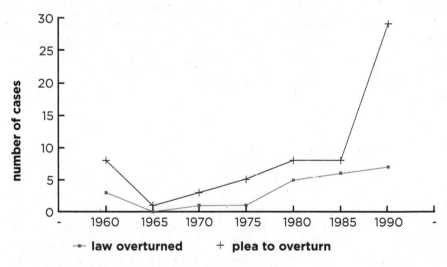

Source: Author's coding of Supreme Court decisions.

Judicial Review. The Canadian Supreme Court's exercise of judicial review increased between 1960 and 1990 too, but again, the growth appears to have been unaffected by passage of the *Charter.* Figure 2 presents two summary measures, the number of cases in which the Court has considered whether to overturn a law, and the number of cases in which it did overturn a law. The Court's use of judicial review increased moderately between 1960 and 1990, but the largest increase occurred between 1975, when the Court struck down a law in only one case, and 1980, when it struck down laws in five cases. After 1980, although the number of laws struck down increased, the rate of growth appears to have declined. The number of cases in which litigants asked the Court to exercise judicial review, on the other hand, significantly grew after passage of the *Charter.* Although the growth apparently originated in the late 1960s or early 1970s, between 1985 and 1990, the number of requests for judicial review increased dramatically. In 1985, the Court decided eight cases centering on a request for the exercise of judicial review; in 1990, it decided almost thirty such cases.

Support for rights claims. Adoption of the *Charter* may have affected the Court's level of support for rights claims but, if so, the effect was neither clear nor dramatic (see Figure 3). In the early period of the study, changes in the level of support are an artifact of the small number of rights cases, and so most of our attention should focus on the years after 1970. At the aggregate level, the Court's level of support for rights claims grew significantly between 1980 and 1985, but dropped again by 1990. Contrary to expectations, the *Charter* had no sustained effect on the Court's level of support for the rights claims on its agenda. These aggregate-level results, however, do not control for changes over time in the nature of the rights-claims being decided. Additionally, the aggregate-level results do not reveal a growing dispute on the Court in the late 1980s over which rights-claims should be supported: in broad terms, some justices favored criminal due process and negative liberties, while others favored egalitarian claims. Nonetheless, the results in Figure 3 suggest that the *Charter*'s effects have been more subtle than is generally believed.

Figure 3: Support for Rights Claims by Supreme Court

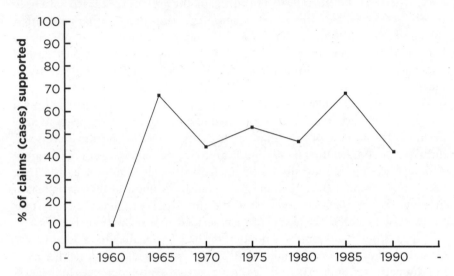

Source: Author's coding of Supreme Court decisions.
N = 1960, 10; 1965, 9; 1970, 9; 1975, 17; 1980, 30; 1985, 31; 1990, 60.

Figure 4: Non-Charter Rights Cases in Supreme Court

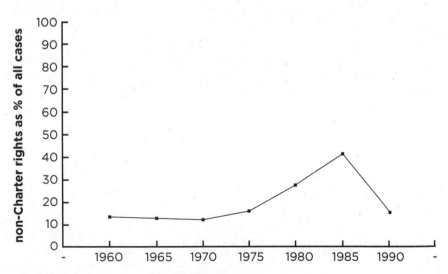

Source: Author's coding of Supreme Court decisions.
N = 1960, 77; 1965, 73; 1970, 80; 1975, 119; 1980, 119; 1985, 68; 1990, 110.

Basis for decisions. Trends in several indicators of the basis for Supreme Court decisions reveal another dimension of the Court's agenda. First, even after passage of the *Charter,* the proportion of cases involving rights claims *not* founded on that document continued to expand (see Figure 4). There was a substantial increase in non-*Charter* rights cases in 1985 over 1980; in fact, a surprisingly small proportion of the cases in 1985 were decided on *Charter* grounds, probably in part because of the time lag in bringing *Charter* cases through several levels of the judicial system. The drop in the number of non-*Charter* cases in 1990 resulted either from *Charter* cases squeezing non-*Charter* cases off the agenda or from a translation of what previously would have been non-*Charter* cases into *Charter* language. These data cannot answer that question. But it is clear that *Charter* cases themselves were only a small proportion of rights claims in 1985 and that, for much of the period prior to the late 1980s, rights claims developed in formal independence of the *Charter.*

Second, trends in the Court's use of all higher law foundations – including non-*Charter* constitutional law (primarily federalism), the 1960 *Bill of Rights,* the common law standard of natural justice, and after 1982, of course, the *Charter of Rights* – are presented in Figure 5. The proportion of cases decided on all higher law grounds began to increase prior to 1982. Part of that growth reflects an increase in the number of federalism cases decided by the Supreme Court. After 1982, the proportion of cases in each of the non-*Charter* categories declined as the proportion of cases involving the *Charter* increased. By 1990, *Charter* cases began to replace non-*Charter* cases on the agenda, although even in 1990 a significant portion of higher-law cases were not based on the *Charter.* Because the use of higher law foundations for decisions began increasing as early as 1975 and, because the most important changes after 1982 consisted not of an acceleration in the rate of growth for *all* higher law cases but a shift toward *Charter* foundations from other higher law foundations, it is possible that passage of the *Charter* simply changed the foundation on which claimants based their challenges....

Figure 5: Higher Law Foundations for Decisions in the Supreme Court

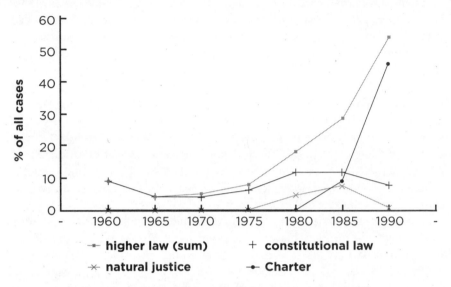

Source: Author's coding of Supreme Court decisions.
N = 1960, 77; 1965, 73; 1970, 80; 1975, 119; 1980, 119; 1985, 68; 1990, 110.

[*Ed. note*: The author then describes how two other trends – the increase in individual litigants rather than businesses, and a growing caseload – preceded the *Charter*. He finds that third-party intervention also increased prior to the *Charter*, though non-governmental intervention by third parties increased after 1980.]

Discussion

The Canadian Supreme Court's agenda indeed has been transformed in the last several decades. The Court is now a major constitutional policy-maker, focuses much of its attention on civil rights and liberties, increasingly decides cases brought by individuals who are supported by interest groups and government financing, increasingly faces complex disputes involving large numbers of parties, increasingly relies on higher-law foundations for its decisions, increasingly entertains requests to strike down laws, and increasingly does strike down laws.

Most observers have attributed this broadly based transformation to Canada's recent adoption of the *Charter of Rights and Freedoms* or, secondarily, to the efforts of left-liberal justices on the Supreme Court. The evidence presented here, however, suggests that the *Charter*'s influence is overrated and that judicial liberals gained control of the Court too late to have done more than encourage already-existing developments. Instead, changes in the Court's agenda appear to have resulted from the combined influence of two developments: the shift to a discretionary docket in 1975 and the development of a support structure for legal mobilization.

The shift to a largely discretionary docket in 1975 significantly contributed to the agenda transformation. When the Court gained discretion over its docket, it abruptly began moving private disputes from its agenda, making way for a growth in the agenda on public law in general and civil liberties and rights in particular. This shift occurred even though judicial liberals were in the minority on the Court at the time and remained so until after the mid-1980s....

The growth of the support structure for legal mobilization also contributed to the agenda transformation. The various components of the support structure began growing and diversifying just prior to the start of the Court's agenda transformation, and the support structure continued growing as that transformation unfolded. Temporal priority and correlation alone cannot prove causation but the weakness of the primary alternative explanations, those focusing on judicial attitudes and adoption of the *Charter*, lends credibility to the support structure hypothesis.

Moreover, there is direct evidence of causal links between the support structure and the Supreme Court's agenda. Government financial aid has supported a range of important rights cases that have reached the Supreme Court. Legal aid, for instance, directly contributed to the growth of the Court's agenda on criminal procedure. In interviews conducted for this study, lawyers who were active in criminal defense and human rights work in the 1970s identified the growth of legal aid as the principal source of financing for criminal cases in the Supreme Court. Governmental sources of case financing also supported other types of rights cases. The government's Court Challenges Program financed virtually all of the language rights cases to reach the Supreme Court and many of the equality cases. Financing provided by the Department of Indian Affairs and Northern Development has supported nearly all of the aboriginal rights cases to reach the Supreme Court.

Additionally, both the diversification of the Canadian legal profession and the growth of large law firms influenced the Supreme Court's agenda. In the 1980s, large Toronto firms allowed a number of their women lawyers to divert time and resources to the development of a legal strategy and funding for women's rights litigation. Those lawyers created the Women's Legal Education and Action Fund (LEAF) in 1985, which has financed virtually all of the women's rights cases since 1985 in the Supreme Court.

Even the *Charter* itself may be understood as a product of the changes in the Canadian support structure that transformed the Supreme Court's agenda. A number of rights advocacy organizations directly influenced the language of the *Charter* in highly significant ways by participating in the drafting process or by putting pressure on the national government's negotiators in that process. For instance, the Canadian Civil Liberties Association, along with several other groups, successfully lobbied for significant changes in the *Charter*'s procedural rights provisions.

Although both the *Charter* and the Supreme Court's agenda transformation reflect changes in the support structure for legal mobilization, the *Charter* nonetheless has exerted an independent influence on some aspects of the Supreme Court's decision-making. In particular, the Court's level of support for liberal rights claims grew, albeit temporarily, after passage of the *Charter*. Furthermore, this growing support apparently encouraged litigants to bring more such cases, as evidenced by the dramatic growth between 1985 and 1990 in the number of requests for judicial review....

Conclusion

In recent decades, constitutional engineers have relied heavily on bills of rights as a means for protecting rights. However, bills of rights are not self-activating. Interpreting and developing the often ambiguous provisions of a bill of rights depends on mobilization of the law by individuals, but individuals by themselves typically lack the capacity to take cases to a country's highest court. The effects of a bill of rights, therefore, depend on the extent of organized support for mobilization of the law. Admittedly, a bill of rights may affect judges' willingness to strike down legislation or to check official action but, in the absence of adequate resources for legal mobilization, few non-economic cases are likely to reach the judicial agenda, and judges will have few occasions to use their constitutional authority. Thus constitutional reform alone, in the absence of resources in civil society for legal mobilization, is likely to produce only empty promises. None of this indicates that bills of rights are irrelevant to politics. Bills of rights matter, but only if civil societies have the capacity to support and develop them.

6.10

Do Constitutions Matter?

Donald Songer

The Transformation of the Supreme Court of Canada: An Empirical Examination (Toronto: University of Toronto Press, 2008), 70–76. Reprinted with permission.

... Since the early 1970s the agenda of the Supreme Court of Canada has been profoundly transformed. The aspect of that transformation that has received the most attention in the media and in scholarly analyses has been the increasing attention to constitutional conflicts in general and especially to civil rights and liberties. The ramifications of this increasingly political role of the Court has been noted by many observers, and the normative effects of this new involvement in critical aspects of public policy have been subject to heated debate. Virtually all scholars who have joined the debate over this new policy-making role of the Court seem to have assumed (at least implicitly) that the *Charter* of Rights was the critical event that enabled the Court (or in the eyes of some, required the Court) to adopt a more overtly political role. In stark contrast, Epp [see Reading 6.9] argues that 'the *Charter*'s influence is overrated.' Epp admits that a 'dramatic rights revolution has occurred in Canada in the last several decades' and that the *Charter* served as a useful legal foundation for rights advocates. But he also contends that the *Charter* was not the primary event that made this 'rights revolution' possible. Instead, he argues that the agenda changes on the Court 'appear to have resulted from the combined influence of two developments, the shift to a discretionary docket in 1975 and the development of a support structure for legal mobilization.'

To bolster his arguments, Epp presents a series of line graphs that trace developments in the Supreme Court's agenda from 1960 to 1990. Unfortunately, several of his methodological choices raise serious questions about the validity of his conclusions. Most significantly, he examines the Court's agenda every five years (e.g., in 1960, 1965, 1970) and for that reason cannot establish precisely when agenda changes took place. Furthermore, his examination of trends includes only two data points (1985 and 1990) after the adoption of the *Charter*. Moreover, his definition of 'civil rights and liberties' combines all criminal appeals – whether or not the appellant raised a specific rights claim – with traditional categories of civil liberties such as religious liberty, privacy, equality rights, and freedom of expression. Finally, when focusing on constitutional decision making, Epp concerns himself solely with constitutional challenges to statutes and ignores constitutional challenges to administrative action. When one examines the changing agenda of the Court on a year-by-year basis, disaggregates criminal and other civil liberties issues, and takes a more comprehensive view of constitutional lawmaking, a picture emerges that is somewhat different from the one Epp describes. This examination is undertaken below.…

[In Figure 1], the *Charter* period is defined as starting in 1984, the year the first case raising a *Charter* issue reached the Court (represented by the vertical line in Figure 1). Two data trends are presented. The solid line indicates the proportion of all of the cases in which a civil rights or liberties issue was raised during a non-criminal appeal. The broken line reflects Epp's definition of civil rights; that is, it combines criminal appeals with more traditional concepts of civil liberties.

Figure 1: Do Constitutions Matter? Change Over Time on the Supreme Court: Civil Liberties Cases Before and After the Charter

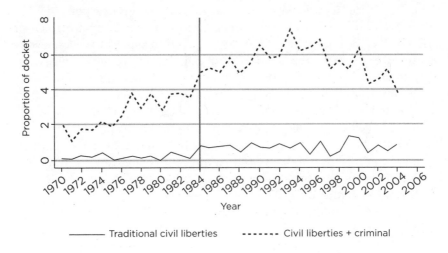

Looking first at the more limited, traditional concept of civil rights, it is obvious that before 1984, civil liberties issues appeared on the Court's agenda. The highest number of cases heard by the Court in any of these fourteen pre-*Charter* years was six, and there were only two years during which five or more civil liberties cases were on the agenda. As a proportion of the docket, those two years were the only two years during which civil liberties cases made up 5 per cent of the docket.… There was no trend towards increasing attention to civil liberties as the 'support structure' for civil liberties (which Epp saw as the crucial influence on the rights agenda) gradually increased.

In sharp contrast, the number and proportion of rights cases increased dramatically after the *Charter* was adopted. For every one of the first eleven years of the post-*Charter* period, the number of rights cases on the Court's agenda equalled or exceeded the highest number of rights cases heard in any pre-*Charter* year. In ten of these same eleven years, the proportion of the docket devoted to rights cases exceeded the highest proportion of rights cases in all fourteen pre-*Charter* years examined.

Turning to the combined total of criminal appeals with other rights issues, there does seem to be some support for Epp's argument that docket control had a significant impact on the Court's rights agenda. From 1970-1975, there were fewer than thirty rights cases on the docket every year and the proportion of the docket devoted to his definition of rights cases stayed below 30 per cent every year. There was no noticeable change in the first year after the Court gained docket control; but starting in 1977, there were forty or more cases involving rights in five of the seven years. Also, the proportion of the docket devoted to criminal appeals and other rights cases fluctuated between 30 and 40 per cent in six of the seven years.

Nevertheless, even using Epp's own measure of 'rights' cases, the *Charter* seems to have had immediate and persistent effects. Prior to the *Charter*, there had not been a single year in which criminal and other rights cases made up as much as 40 per cent of the Court's docket. Yet in the single year between 1983 and 1984, the proportion of rights cases jumped 15 per cent, becoming more than 50 per cent of the docket for the first time. Moreover, the proportion of the docket devoted to this expanded definition of rights cases did not dip below 50 per cent for seventeen consecutive years and has never dropped to the level of the pre-*Charter* high point.

In summary, there seem to have been two sharp break points in the increasing tendency of the Court to hear rights cases using Epp's expanded definition of rights cases and only one sharp break point using a more limited, traditional understanding of what constitutes a rights case. The *Charter*'s adoption was a crucial turning point for both agenda changes. The trends in agenda change do not reveal the more gradual or linear increase in the attention to rights cases that would be expected if the gradual increase in 'the development of a support structure for legal mobilization' posited by Epp were the critical cause of the increasing rights agenda of the Court.

A second piece of evidence used by Epp to support the argument that the impact of the *Charter* is 'overrated' relates to trends in the proportion of cases on the Court's docket either seeking or receiving judicial review.... Epp's analysis is limited to data points positioned five years apart and, as noted earlier, is limited to challenges to the constitutionality of statutes. In the analysis below, year-by-year data are provided both for challenges to the constitutionality of statutes and for a more inclusive category: all requests for judicial review (i.e., including challenges to the constitutionality of executive actions as well as to statutes).

Prior to 1984, statutes could only be challenged under the *Constitution Act of 1867*. Most challenges involved questions of federalism. The trends shown in Figure 2 suggest that in this pre-*Charter* period there was considerable fluctuation in the number of such constitutional challenges, from a high of twelve cases in 1981 to a low of just one in 1970 and 1983. Significantly for Epp's thesis, there was no linear trend toward increasing use of judicial review over time as the support structure for rights litigation grew. Perhaps even more damaging to Epp's thesis, few of these cases involved civil liberties. Only 9 per cent of the pre-*Charter* challenges to statutes involved traditional questions of civil liberties, and another 9 per cent involved challenges to criminal statutes. In contrast, more than half the constitutional challenges were raised against the exercise of economic regulation by federal or provincial governments.

Even a casual examination of the trend data in Figure 2 suggests that the *Charter* has had a dramatic effect on the Supreme Court's exercise of judicial review. In the final two pre-*Charter* years, the Court considered only five cases raising constitutional challenges to statutes; that number then tripled during the first two years of *Charter* litigation. Pre-*Charter*, there had been only three years during which the Court considered six or more requests for judicial review; post-*Charter*, the Court has considered at least that many constitutional challenges in every year, and the median number of constitutional challenges considered by the Court in a year has been twelve (i.e., the post-*Charter* median has equalled the pre-*Charter* maximum). Moreover, while most pre-*Charter* constitutional challenges involved government economic regulation, 64 per cent of post-*Charter* challenges have involved civil liberties issues.

The effect of the *Charter* on judicial review is even more dramatic when one considers all constitutional challenges rather than just challenges to the constitutionality of statutes. Figure 2 indicates that prior to the *Charter*, the number of constitutional challenges to either legislative or executive actions fluctuated widely over the years without any clear trend. The year 1981 was the high point for constitutional litigation, with 15 per cent of the Court's docket involving constitutional challenges. Yet in each of the next two years, constitutional challenges made up less than 5 per cent of the Court's docket. There was a dramatic increase in constitutional litigation as soon as the first *Charter* cases reached the Court. In the very first year of *Charter* litigation, the proportion of the docket devoted to constitutional challenges was three times as great as in the previous two years, and in every year after that the docket space devoted to constitutional challenges was greater than the proportion of litigation asking for judicial review in any of the fourteen years of pre-*Charter* litigation examined in the current study.

Figure 2: Do Constitutions matter? Change Over Time on the Supreme Court: Judicial Review Before and After the Charter

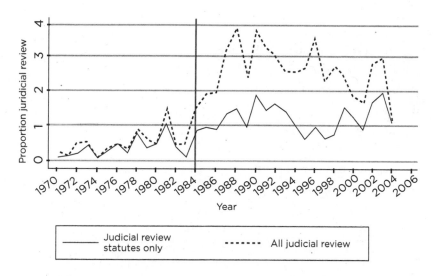

In summary, the answer to the question posed at the beginning of this section is 'yes' – at least in the Canadian experience, constitutions *do* matter. This is not to suggest that constitutional protection of rights is self-executing or that the actions of well-resourced groups determined to push for the expansion of rights are unimportant. The world has seen many examples of paper guarantees of rights with little practical significance. Yet the timing of the dramatic increase in rights litigation in the Supreme Court of Canada suggests that the formal constitutional protection of rights is vital to any rights revolution....

6.11
Key Terms

Concepts

advisory opinion

agenda setting

amicus curiae

direct sponsorship vs. intervenor

Great Depression

"influencing the influencers"

intervenor

judicial democrats

lis

mega-constitutional politics

minority language groups (MLGs)

mootness

offensive vs. defensive rights protection

political questions doctrine

rights advocacy organizations

standing

support structure for legal mobilization (SSLM)

systematic litigation

test case

Institutions, Events and Documents

American Civil Liberties Union (ACLU)

Borowski v. Canada (Attorney General), [1989] 1 S.C.R. 342

Canada (Attorney General) v. Downtown Eastside Sex Workers United Against Violence Society, [2012] 2 S.C.R. 524

Canadian Council of Churches v. Minister of Employment and Immigration, [1992] 1 S.C.R. 236

Minister of Justice (Canada) v. Borowski, [1981] 2 S.C.R. 575

Court Challenges Program (CCP)

National Association for the Advancement of Colored People (NAACP)

Operation Dismantle v. The Queen, [1985] 1 S.C.R. 441

R. v. Morgentaler, [1988] 1 S.C.R. 30

Re: Resolution to amend the Constitution, [1981] 1 S.C.R. 753 (*Patriation Reference*)

Reference re Secession of Quebec, [1998] 2 S.C.R. 217

Saumur v. City of Quebec, [1953] 2 S.C.R. 29

Supreme Court Act (1875)

Thorson v. Attorney-General of Canada, [1975] 1 S.C.R. 138

Women's Legal Education and Action Fund (LEAF)

7

Precedents, Statutes and Legal Reasoning

One of the most distinctive characteristics of the judicial process is its formalized method of reasoning. Because their authority flows from the public perception that they are "merely" applying pre-existing rules to resolve new disputes, judges are not permitted the broad prerogative enjoyed by the legislative and the executive branches. Unlike the latter, courts are not supposed to create new policies to deal with new problems. In their oral or written judgments, judges must explain where and how they derived the "rule" used to settle a case. There are three principal sources for these "rules": a written constitution, legislative statutes (including administrative regulations) and prior judicial decisions, known as precedents. This chapter is primarily concerned with the role of precedent and statutory interpretation in judicial reasoning, though constitutional precedent is considered as well.

Until the middle of the nineteenth century, most internal or domestic law in English-speaking societies was common law. Common law originated in the judicial recognition and enforcement of traditional usages and customs of the Anglo-Saxon and later Norman peoples in the British Isles. As these judicial decisions were made, they in turn became part of the common law. The common law in contemporary Canadian society consists of all previous judicial decisions by Canadian and British courts, as they are recorded in the case reports of these nations. The common law system is distinguished from the civil law system by its basis in precedent rather than legislative enactment. The civil law system originated in ancient Roman law, developed on the European continent, and was imported into Quebec by the French. It is based on a single, comprehensive code, and enacted by the legislature.

The law of precedent, or *stare decisis*, is a self-imposed judicial rule that "like cases be decided alike." As Gordon Post explains, the law of precedent is essentially a formalization of the common-sense use of past experience as a guide to present conduct (Reading 7.1). The value of judicial adherence to *stare decisis* is twofold. First, continuity and certainty in the law is a prerequisite of civilized human activity. If there is no reasonable guarantee that what is valid law today will still be valid law tomorrow, personal, economic and political intercourse would grind to a halt. In each of these spheres of human activity, present-day decisions and activities are predicated on expectations about the future. Ensuring a high degree of predictability and continuity between the present and the future is one of the primary purposes of a political regime. As the institutions charged with interpreting and adapting the laws over time, the courts are responsible for maintaining continuity and certainty. As the famous British jurist A.V. Dicey said:

> The duty of the court ... is not to remedy a particular grievance but to determine whether an alleged grievance is one for which the law supplies a remedy.... If Parliament changes the law, the action of Parliament is known to every man and Parliament tries in general to respect acquired rights. If the Courts were to apply to the decision of substantially the same case, one principle today and another principle tomorrow, men would lose rights which they already possessed; a law which was not certain would in reality be no law at all.[1]

The rule of precedent also contributes to guaranteeing the "rule of law, not of men." One of the ideals of the Western tradition's conception of justice is that the laws be applied equally and impartially to all persons. This ideal precludes any *ad hoc* application of the law and demands instead that laws be applied uniformly or that any deviation from the rule be justified on principle, that is, by another rule. The idiosyncrasies or personal preferences of a judge are not permissible grounds for judicial decisions. This would reintroduce the "rule of men" rather than the "rule of law." By minimizing the discretion or freedom of individual judges, *stare decisis* preserves the "rule of law."

Stare decisis minimizes but does not eliminate the element of judicial discretion or creativity. While legal reasoning presents itself as a deductive process, in reality it is a more subtle blend of both inductive and deductive reasoning. Legal reasoning is accurately described as "reasoning by example."[2] The judges are essentially asking "[w]hether the present case resembles the plain case 'sufficiently' and in the 'relevant' aspects."[3] In determining what is "sufficient" and what is "relevant," the judge must ultimately make certain choices. Because of this element of choice, a judge is responsible for striking the balance between continuity and innovation. The central thrust of the theory of legal realism (discussed in Chapter 2) has been to emphasize this element of choice and judicial discretion and the ensuing responsibility of the judge for his choice.

Weiler's analysis of the Supreme Court's responsibility for the development of tort law is based on this legal realist perspective (see Reading 7.2). Weiler argues that judges can no longer claim that precedent "dictates" nonsensical or patently unfair legal conclusions. Judges must be critical in their use of precedent and go beyond the surface "rule" to discover the animating "principle." The proper function of the common law judge, according to Weiler, is to derive specific rules from more general principles, as the situation demands. Since situations change, rules must change also. While the "cattle trespass" exemption to normal tort law responsibility may have been appropriate to the rural, agricultural society of eighteenth-century England, it had become a dangerous anachronism in twentieth-century Canada. Similarly in *Boucher v. the King*, the Supreme Court of Canada was faced with a conflict between the definition of "seditious libel" developed in nineteenth-century, homogeneous, Protestant Britain, and the norms of freedom of religion and speech in twentieth-century, pluralistic Canada (see Reading 7.3). Appeal court judges have a duty, says Weiler, to adapt the common law to the changing needs and circumstances of contemporary society.

Strict adherence to *stare decisis* is yet another aspect of courts' "adjudication of disputes" function that poses problems for judicial policy-making. Refusal to disavow or change past decisions plays no constructive role in a policy-making institution, as the examples of legislative and executive practice make clear. While certainty and continuity are legal virtues, adaptability and innovation are more important in the policy-making process. The case for abandoning a strict adherence to precedent is especially strong in constitutional law. Not only is policy impact more probable, but constitutional law lacks the flexibility of common law and statutes. If the courts make a "mistake" in these areas, it can be corrected by remedial legislation. But if the Supreme Court makes a constitutional decision with undesirable policy consequences, the only direct way to correct the damage is through formal constitutional amendment, an extremely cumbersome and difficult process.[4] Predictably, the U.S. Supreme Court was the first court of appeal in a common law nation to abandon *stare decisis* as an absolute requirement. The demotion of *stare decisis* from a binding rule to a guiding principle is another index of a court's evolution toward a greater policy-making role.

The recent advent of judicial realism in Canadian jurisprudence has brought with it a decline in the status of the rule of *stare decisis*. Long after the U.S. Supreme Court had abandoned absolute adherence to precedent, the Supreme Court of Canada continued to perceive itself as bound to adhere not only to its own previous decisions but to those of the British House of Lords as well. (Ironically, the Judicial Committee of the Privy Council, which served as Canada's final court of appeal until 1949, did not consider itself bound by its previous decisions, since, technically, it was not a court of law but an advisory board to the Imperial Crown.) Ten years after the abolition of that role, the Court declared its independence from British precedents as well. In 1966, the British House of Lords officially declared that, when appropriate, it would no longer follow its own prior decisions. However, the Supreme Court of Canada continued to profess strict adherence to its prior decisions until the 1970s, under the leadership of Bora Laskin. In 1972, before his appointment as Chief Justice, Laskin had written that *stare decisis* was "no longer an article of faith in the Supreme Court of Canada, but it still remains a cogent principle."[5] Speaking as the new Chief Justice at the Centennial Symposium of the Supreme Court in 1975, Laskin repeated that *stare decisis* was no longer "an inexorable rule," but rather "simply an important element of the judicial process, a necessary consideration which should give pause to any but the most sober conclusion that a previous decision or line of authority is wrong and ought to be changed" (Reading 3.1).

Practising what he preached, Laskin led the Supreme Court to overturn three precedents during the next three years, including an old Privy Council decision dealing with the federal division of powers.[6] This abandoning of strict adherence to *stare decisis* is yet another indicator of the Supreme Court's institutional evolution toward more of a policy-making role.

The second principal source of law is legislative statutes. Beginning in the nineteenth century, legislatures in Great Britain, Canada and the United States began to codify large portions of the common law. In large part, this was a democratic reaction against the perceived elitism of the "judge-made" character of the common law. By reducing the confusing maze of common law precedent to clearly worded legislative statutes, it was thought that the law would be made easier for "the people" to understand, and that the democratic authority of "government by consent" would be enhanced.

The influential nineteenth-century British philosopher Jeremy Bentham was a leading critic of the common law ("customary law") and an advocate of codification. According to Bentham, common law was uncertain and unpredictable:

> The customary law, you say, punishes theft with hanging: be it so. But by what law is this done? Who made it? When was it made? Where is it to be found? What are the parts that it contains? By what words is it expressed? Theft, you say, is taking under certain

circumstances: but taking by whom? Taking of what? Under what circumstances? Taking by a person of such a sort, taking a thing of such a sort, taking under such and such circumstances. But how know you this? Because so it has been adjudged. What then? Not if it be a taking by any other person, nor if of any other thing, nor if under any other circumstances. O yes, in many other cases....

It appears then, that the customary law is a fiction from beginning to end.

Bentham also criticized the common law because it gave too much political power to lawyers and judges. Of lawyers, he said:

By this means two monopolies establish themselves, one within another: a monopoly by the profession itself against the rest of the people; and a monopoly of the illustrious in the profession itself against the obscure.

Bentham's view of judges was even less charitable:

Caligula published his laws in small characters: but still he published them: he hung them up high, but still he hung them up. English judges neither hang up their laws, nor publish them.[7]

The codification reform movement became widely influential by the end of the nineteenth century. In 1892, Canada replaced criminal offences at common law with a comprehensive statute, the *Criminal Code*. In so doing, Parliament hoped to reap the alleged advantages of codification mentioned above, including restricting judicial discretion in the criminal law. Since crimes were now clearly and authoritatively defined, judges would simply apply the law as Parliament had written it. It would no longer be necessary to refer to a vast and confusing system of precedent to apply the criminal law, or so it was hoped.

In fact, precedent and *stare decisis* quickly found their way back into the criminal law. Perhaps, as Graham Parker has suggested, it was (and still is) impossible for judges and lawyers trained in the common law tradition to properly construe a code of law.[8] More likely the common law "habit" simply compounds a more serious problem – the ultimate ambiguity of statutory terminology itself. Try as they might, legislators will never be able to draft statutes that anticipate and encompass all possible future situations. This is due in part to the inherent tension between the generality of words and the specificity of reality, and in part to human ignorance of the future. As new situations inevitably arise, the applicability of the original wording of statutes becomes increasingly questionable. The only practical way to bridge this gap is through judicial discretion; and the traditional (if not the only) way to discipline the exercise of judicial discretion is through adherence to *stare decisis* – to decide like cases alike. In the final analysis, judicial interpretation of statutes is similar to the "reasoning by example" method of the common law.

The preceding argument notwithstanding, judicial discretion in interpreting statutes, including the *Criminal Code*, is much more circumscribed than in interpreting the common law. As Weiler says, judges can develop new torts, but not new crimes, and there are sound reasons for preferring this arrangement. As issues of tort law are rarely the subject of partisan political controversy, an innovative court cannot be accused of usurping the legislative function. The controversies over capital punishment and abortion show that the same is not true of the criminal law. In the area of tort law, judicial expertise is very high, relative to other policy-making institutions. Finally, judicial initiatives in substantive criminal law would pose the threat of punishing innocent persons. No comparable problem of "due process" arises in tort law.

A secondary but important influence on judicial reasoning is legal scholarship – commentary on judicial decisions and legal problems that is published in law reviews and academic books. Legal commentaries summarize, clarify and critique individual judicial decisions or a series of related precedents having to do with a particular issue of law. A lawyer arguing a point of law before a court may cite a law review article to support the interpretation he or she is trying to persuade the judges to adopt. Likewise, judges may cite legal commentary to bolster the authority of their interpretive choice on a given point of law.

Today most of this commentary is written by university law professors, and most law reviews are published by university-based law schools. Legal commentaries have a long history in the English common law. Some of the most respected jurists of the common law – William Blackstone (1723–1780), for example – are famous precisely because of their published commentaries. Notwithstanding such longevity, the practice in the Supreme Court of Canada until quite recently was not to consider or cite commentaries by *living* authors. At the end of the 1960s, the Supreme Court Reports contained "barely a dozen references a year to academic texts, and virtually none to legal journals."[9] By the 1990s, by contrast, the Supreme Court cited hundreds of books and articles a year, most written by living authors. Although most references were to Canadian authors, U.S. writers accounted for about one-half as many citations as Canadians.[10] In Reading 8.2, Peter McCormick shows that the Supreme Court continues to rely on academic material, citing between two hundred and three hundred articles a year. This is down, however, from a high of four hundred to six hundred in the 1990s and early 2000s.

Legal commentary has taken on added significance in the case of the *Charter*. In 1982, the *Charter* represented something of a fresh start in Canadian law. There were few past precedents that were unambiguously applicable to *Charter* interpretation. As the Deputy Minister of Justice told a conference in 1991, "Imagine the difficulty of advising the government what the *Charter* means when there have been no decisions."[11] This left a legal vacuum that was quickly filled by an avalanche of *Charter* scholarship.

The academic commentary that followed the adoption of the *Charter* was not simply spontaneous. It was in part a calculated component of the strategy of rights-advocacy groups to maximize the political utility of *Charter* litigation. The 1984 report that led to the creation of the Women's Legal Education and Action Fund (LEAF) declared that a "critical component" of a systematic litigation would be "to build a theory of equality which is accepted by academics, lawyers and the judiciary. Legal writing in respected law journals, presentations of papers at legal seminars, and participation in judges' training sessions are all means of disseminating and legitimating such theories of equality."[12] Once LEAF was established, it adopted a self-styled campaign of "influencing the influencers" that included fostering supportive legal scholarship (See Reading 6.3). As Christopher Manfredi (Reading 6.4) shows, the Supreme Court, and the country's legislators, were duly influenced. LEAF's position in high-profile cases involving abortion, sexual assault and sexual orientation frequently had a marked effect on public policy, even in cases where it lost in court.

Professor Martin Shapiro's observation about American legal scholarship is even truer in the post-1982 Canadian context: "[T]he study of law and courts [is] part of the process of making the [law]; that is, [part of] the public discourse that continuously constitutes and reconstitutes constitutional and other law."[13] Legal scholars follow and comment on what the courts are saying, and the judges take note of what the law professors write. The authors of legal commentary have become important partners in the development of Canadian law. Perhaps the most prominent example is "dialogue theory," a concept created by legal scholars Peter Hogg and Allison Bushell that the Supreme Court subsequently used to justify a number of important *Charter* decisions (see Readings 12.7 and 12.8). Advocacy literature has played a similarly important role in LGBTQ and feminist litigation. One notable example is the Women's Court of Canada, a "virtual court" composed of feminist academics who "reconsider" leading Supreme Court of Canada decisions on equality rights, and have published them in the *Canadian Journal of Women and the Law*.

The growth of advocacy research in the field of legal scholarship is a predictable consequence of the *Charter*'s empowerment of judges. One of the iron laws of politics is that "where power rests, there influence will be brought to bear."[14] Patrick Monahan and Marie Finkelstein have identified the incentives that encourage advocacy scholarship: "Because of the political potency of *Charter* arguments, there is a tremendous incentive to try to shape perceptions of the *Charter*'s meaning so as to advance one's political goals."[15]

American political scientist Martin Shapiro has more bluntly described constitutional scholarship in his own country as a form of "lobbying the courts."[16] "The distinction between scholarship and advocacy," Shapiro writes,

> ... has always been uncertain or nonexistent in most of the legal scholarship produced in law schools. Much of that scholarship consists of doctrinal analysis that purports to yield the correct or a good, better or best statement of the law. The central strategy is a massive and deliberate confusion of is and ought. The previous cases are examined to show that, properly interpreted, the body of existing law really adds up to the law as the author thinks it ought to be. In short, most such writing consists of expanded and embroidered legal briefs. The key question in understanding such work is, "Who's the client?"[17]

A further reason for the importance of legal scholarship in Canada's post-*Charter* era is the growing emphasis on extrinsic evidence to help guide judicial decision-making. Historically, in order to determine guilt or innocence – "what really happened" (or "historical facts") – common law courts developed special rules to guard against biased or false evidence. The judge assumed a neutral and passive role. The parties to the dispute were responsible for developing all the relevant facts and legal arguments as part of the rules and procedures known collectively as the adversarial process.

Precisely because it is well suited to its original purpose, the adversarial process is much less adept at collecting the kind of facts relevant to public policy-making decisions. Policy-makers want to know about general patterns of human behaviour – what Horowitz calls "social facts" – in order to formulate public policy (Reading 7.4). To get these facts, legislators and administrators may consult past studies of the problem, commission new studies to provide current socio-economic information, and conduct extensive hearings to gather additional information, including indications of political support and opposition. Under the traditional rules of the adversarial process, judges can do none of this.

The advent of written constitutional law and judicial review placed serious strains on common law courts' fact-finding procedures. While the inevitable policy impact of constitutional law decisions created a felt need among judges for additional factual information, their procedures were inadequate and even hostile toward such information. There was also a strong sense that it was inconsistent with the adjudicatory function of courts to base a decision on "social facts." This was perceived as more a legislative than a judicial activity. In some cases the relevant "historical facts" and the "social facts" may actually suggest conflicting solutions. When it comes to collecting and using facts, there are serious and real tensions between the adjudicatory and policy-making functions of courts. Horowitz describes this tension as the problem of institutional capacity, as distinct from the problem of institutional legitimacy. The latter questions the legitimacy of unelected, unaccountable judges making policy in a democracy. The question of institutional capacity is whether courts are institutionally equipped to make informed and effective policy choices.

Historically, Canadian judges used social facts very sparingly. The adjudicatory view of the judicial function, the influence of the decisions and style of the Judicial Committee of the Privy Council, and a deference to the tradition of parliamentary supremacy all led Canadian judges to use a textually oriented form of judicial reasoning. However, since the 1982 *Charter of Rights*, Canadian courts have made extensive use of social facts. Major *Charter* cases often involve dozens of interest groups who submit factums as intervenors, as the Supreme Court cites from social science evidence with great frequency (see Chapter 6). As the Supreme Court has transitioned to a policy-making Court, the role of social facts in the courtroom play an increasingly relevant role in high-stakes constitutional litigation.

The trends highlighted in this chapter – a diminishing reliance on precedent, an increasing reliance on social facts and concerns about institutional capacity – have been mutually reinforcing. This is demonstrated by two of the most prominent Supreme Court cases in recent years. In *Canada v. Bedford* (2013),[18] the Supreme Court struck down three *Criminal Code* provisions that prohibited activities related to prostitution. Two years later, in *Carter v. Canada* (2015),[19] the Court struck down Canada's criminal prohibition against assisted suicide. In each case, a unanimous Supreme Court relied heavily on the trial judge's extensive use of social facts to overturn its own precedent from the 1990s.

Chelsea Ogilvie (Reading 7.5) examines these cases in the context of precedent reversal (or, as the Court prefers to call it, "revisiting" precedent). In permitting the trial court to overturn its precedent, the Supreme Court risked abandoning the principle of vertical *stare decisis* that supports its own position at the top of the judicial hierarchy. However, the Court created two rules that it claimed would limit the possibilities for such reversal. As Chief Justice McLachlin wrote in *Bedford*, "the matter may be revisited if new legal issues are raised as a consequence of significant developments in the law, or if there is a change in the circumstances or evidence that fundamentally shifts the parameters of the debate."[20]

With respect to prostitution and assisted dying, the Court unanimously held that both conditions had been met. While the statutory prohibitions and constitutional text had not changed, the Supreme Court's own jurisprudence on the section 7 *Charter* right to life, liberty and security of the person had changed substantially. In particular, the development of new "principles of fundamental justice" constituted a change in law. Moreover, the Court claimed that the new social facts presented at each trial, particularly evidence of policy changes in other jurisdictions, showed that the social facts had changed as well. Changes to Supreme Court doctrine and new social science evidence thus created a "perfect storm of winning conditions," in Ogilvie's words, for advocates of policy change in *Bedford* and *Carter*.

Some commentators remain unconvinced by the Court's two-part test. Journalist Andrew Coyne said the assisted suicide ruling marked the "death of judicial restraint," and that the erosion of precedent marked the end of "the fading notion that the courts, in interpreting the law, should be bound by … something."[21] Ogilvie is less critical of the Court, but does note that the Court's rationale for changing precedent has shifted. In the past, Canadian courts were likely to overturn precedent in three instances: when it was obviously outdated, unworkable or confusing. *Bedford* and *Carter* represent a change not just to two specific Supreme Court precedents, but also to rules regarding precedent itself. In theory, at least, these decisions have removed yet another adjudicative shackle and propelled the Court ever further towards the policy-making model.

NOTES

1   A.V. Dicey, *Lectures on the Relation between Law and Public Opinion in England during the Nineteenth Century.* 2nd ed. (London: MacMillan, 1914), pp. 365, 367.

2   Edward H. Levi, *An Introduction to Legal Reasoning* (Chicago: University of Chicago Press, 1949), p. 1.

3   H.L.A. Hart, *The Concept of Law* (Oxford: Oxford University Press, 1961), p. 124.

4   This is not true of judicial decisions based on sections 2 and 7 through 15 of the *Canadian Charter of Rights and Freedoms*, which are subject to the section 33 "notwithstanding clause."

5   "The Institutional Character of the Judge," *Israel Law Review,* 7 (1972), p. 341.

6   *R. v. Paquette,* [1977] 2 S.C.R. 189; *McNamara Const. Western Ltd. v. The Queen,* [1977] 2 S.C.R. 654; and *Reference re Agricultural Products Marketing Act,* [1978] 2 S.C.R. 1198.

7   Excerpts are from Chapter 15, "No Customary Law Complete," in *The Collected Works of Jeremy Bentham: Of Laws in General,* edited by H.L.A. Hart (London: Athlone Press, 1970), pp. 184–195.

8   Graham Parker, *An Introduction to Criminal Law.* 2nd ed. (Toronto: Metheun, 1983), p. 43.

9   Ian Greene, Carl Baar, Peter McCormick, George Szablowski and Martin Thomas, *Final Appeal: Decision-Making in Canadian Courts of Appeal* (Toronto: James Lorimer, 1998), 150.

10 Greene et al., *Final Appeal,* p. 150.

11 Mary Dawson, Justice Department, Human Rights Division. "Oral remarks," (Roundtable Conference on the Impact of the Charter on the Public Policy Process, Centre for Public Law and Policy: York University, 15–16 Nov. 1991) [unpublished].

12 M. Elizabeth Atcheson et al., "Equality Rights and Legal Action," *Law, Politics and the Judicial Process in Canada.* 3rd ed. (Calgary: University of Calgary Press, 2002), pp. 309–315.

13 Martin Shapiro, "Public Law and Judicial Politics," in Ada W. Finifter ed., *Political Science: The State of the Discipline II* (Washington, D.C.: APSA, 1993), pp. 365–381 at 373.

14 V.O. Key, *Politics, Parties and Pressure Groups* (New York: Thomas Y. Crowell, 1958), p. 154.

15 Patrick J. Monahan and Marie Finkelstein, "The Charter of Rights and Public Policy in Canada," Osgoode Hall Law Journal 30, no. 3 (1992), p. 543.

16 Shapiro, "Public Law and Judicial Politics," p. 374.

17 Ibid.

18 *Canada (Attorney General) v. Bedford,* [2013] 3 S.C.R. 1101.

19 *Carter v. Canada (Attorney General),* [2015] 1 S.C.R. 331.

20 *Bedford,* at para. 42.

21 Andrew Coyne, "Activist Supreme Court's rulings alarming," *Regina Leader-Post,* February 14, 2015, p. D5.

7.1

Stare Decisis: **The Use of Precedents**
C. Gordon Post

Introduction to Law (Englewood Cliffs: Prentice Hall, 1963), 80–83.
Reprinted with permission.

In the resolution of conflicts a court invokes and applies rules of law to proven facts. A question arises: Just where does a court find these rules?

There are two *chief* sources of law: *statutes* and *precedents*. The former, of course, come from the legislature which consists of the elected representatives of the people. The latter come from the courts; precedents are the products of earlier decisions. To the latter, we should add the decisions of an increasing number of administrative bodies and the precedents established thereby, but of this matter we shall speak later.

Most everybody knows what a statute is, but what is a precedent? In a general, non-legal way, precedent plays an important role in our lives. Often, we do things as our parents did them and cite their experience as precedent for what we do now; out of some continuing or repetitive situation there comes a rough rule of thumb. When a father is questioned as to why he spanked his son for some infraction of the household rules, he might reply that as a boy in like circumstances he had been spanked as had his father before him. He might go on to explain that such treatment was an application of the rule of experience, "Spare the rod and spoil the child." …

… In all of these instances, there is the application of a rule of experience to a given situation. These are homely examples. Clubs, business organizations, boards of trustees, student groups all have their rules, some written, some unwritten, which are often invoked as precedent for doing, or not doing, one thing or another. And a precedent here is defined by Webster as "something done or said that may serve as an example or rule to authorize or justify a subsequent act of the same or analogous kind."

Judicial Precedent
A judicial precedent is defined in the same dictionary as "a judicial decision, a form of proceeding, or course of action that serves as a rule for future determinations in similar or analogous cases."

The driver of a wagon loaded with buckskin goods stopped for the night at a certain inn. He was received as a guest and the innkeeper took charge of his property. During the night a fire broke out which resulted in the destruction of horses, wagon and goods. The owner of the property thus destroyed sued the innkeeper for damages.

Let us suppose that this was a case of first impression, that is, a situation which is before a [Canadian] court for the first time. After hearing the evidence from both sides, the judge does not simply say "I decide for the plaintiff," or "I decide for the defendant." He decides for one or the other and gives his reasons. He will speak as follows: "An innkeeper is responsible for the safe keeping of property committed to his custody by a guest. He is an insurer against loss, unless caused by the negligence or fraud of the guest, or by the act of God or the public enemy." The judge looks to the English common law and finds that the liability of innkeepers was expressed tersely in *Cross v. Andrews*: "The defendant, if he will keep an inn, ought, *at his peril*, to keep safely his guests' goods," and at greater length by Coke in *Calye's Case*: "If one brings a bag or chest, etc., of evidences into the inn as obligations, deeds, or other specialties, and by default of the innkeeper they are taken away, the innkeeper shall answer for them."

The judge will go on to explain the reason for the rule. He will say that the rule has its origins in public policy.

> Every facility should be furnished for secure and convenient intercourse between different portions of the kingdom. The safeguards, of which the law gave assurance to the wayfarer, were akin to those which invested each English home with the legal security of a castle. The traveller was peculiarly exposed to depredation and fraud....

Stare Decisis

Let us suppose that a year or so later, another driver with a wagon load of hides spends the night at an inn. Again, the horses, the wagon, and the hides, are turned over to the innkeeper; and again, a fire occurs during the night and the property of the guest is burned up. The owner of the property then sues the innkeeper for damages. The situation here is exactly the same as in the earlier case.

The judge in the second case, according to the theory, will apply the rule or principle (which is the precedent) and decide in favour of the plaintiff. The precedent or authority of the first case is precise and fits the facts of the second case very nicely. This application by courts of rules announced in earlier decisions is spoken of as *stare decisis*, which means "let the decision stand." This has been, and is, a fundamental characteristic of the common law, although … it is the practice upon occasion for a high court to overrule its own precedents.

Obviously, a legal system in which judges could decide cases any which way, manifesting prejudice, whimsy, ignorance and venality, each decision being an entity in itself unconnected with the theory, practices and precedents of the whole, would be a sorry system, or, one might say, no system at all, and a source of little comfort either to attorneys or litigants. Speaking of *stare decisis* many years ago, Judge Maxwell said: "In the application of the principles of the common law, where the precedents are unanimous in the support of a proposition, there is no safety but in a strict adherence to such precedents. If the court will not follow established rules, rights are sacrificed, and lawyers and litigants are left in doubt and uncertainty, while there is no certainty in regard to what, upon a given state of facts, the decision of the court will be."

One concludes, after a little thought, that *stare decisis* is "the instrument of *stability* in a legal system," that it "furnishes a legal system with *certainty* and *predictability*," and "clothes a legal system with reliability"; in addition, it "assures all persons of *equality and uniformity of treatment*" and judges with "an instrument of *convenience and expediency*." In short, "*Stare decisis* preserves the judicial experience of the past."

After a little more thought, however, one also sees that stare decisis is an instrument of conservatism, of immobility, of eyes-in-the-back-of-the head, of stultification. The application of the same rule, decade after decade, long after changed conditions have robbed the rule of its validity, makes the rule a troublesome fiction.

But, American high courts do not hesitate to overrule their own precedents when social, economic, or political change demand a corresponding change in the law. Cardozo has said that,

> If we figure stability and progress as opposite poles, then at one pole we have the maxim of *stare decisis* and the method of decision by the tool of a deductive logic; at the other we have the method which subordinates origins to ends. The one emphasizes considerations of uniformity and symmetry, and follows fundamental conceptions to ultimate conclusions. The other gives freer play to considerations of equity and justice, and the value to society of the interests affected. The one searches for the analogy that is nearest in point of similarity, and adheres to it inflexibly. The other, in its choice of the analogy that shall govern, finds community of spirit more significant than resemblance in externals.

"Much of the administration of justice," says Pound, "is a compromise between the tendency to treat each case as one of a generalized type of case, and the tendency to treat each case as unique." "Each method," concludes Cardozo, "has its value, and for each in the changes of litigation there will come the hour for use. A wise eclecticism employs them both."

7.2

Architect of the Common Law

Paul Weiler

In the Last Resort: A Critical Study of the Supreme Court of Canada (Toronto: Carswell-Methuen, 1974), 57–65. Reprinted with permission.

I shall begin my analysis of the role and performance of the Supreme Court of Canada by reviewing some of its decisions in the area of tort liability for personal injuries. Perhaps some students of the judicial process will ask why bother with these rather insignificant cases? Let's get on to the attention-getting constitutional or civil liberties decisions. However, there are several reasons why I think tort law is a good starting point. First, we can fully understand much of the contemporary character of the judicial process only if we see how it is directed at the adjudication of private law disputes between one individual and another. Moreover, most of this area of law is almost totally judge-made, the *common law*. Our Supreme Court is a useful vehicle for reflecting on the true range and complexity of the judicial function precisely because of the breadth of its jurisdiction. The Court regularly handles the garden variety tort case as well as the newsworthy public law dispute. We must not miss the opportunity to appraise the exercise of judicial creativity in a private law area where the Court is not distracted by the involvement of other institutions, whether legislative or administrative. Finally, as I shall try to demonstrate, these attitudes concerning the private law role of the Supreme Court of Canada are wrong. Tort cases do raise important issues of public policy, and it is critical that they be settled intelligently. Let us start with a typical motor vehicles action which reached the Court, and produced a not-so-typical response.

The Curious Doctrine of Cattle Trespass

One sunny summer afternoon, Floyd Atkinson was driving a jeep along a gravelled country road in a farming district in Ontario. Suddenly, upon reaching the brow of a hill, he was confronted with a herd of cows belonging to a farmer named Leo Fleming. Although he applied his brakes and steered past some of the cows, Atkinson's jeep eventually struck three of the animals, killing two, and causing serious injuries to his own knee. The driver sued the farmer for his personal injuries and the latter responded with a claim for his two dead cows. Apparently Fleming took the attitude that he could let his cows wander where they wanted and they customarily pastured on the highway, strolling back and forth across the road. The trial judge found this to be negligence on his part and, given a certain lack of due care on the driver's part also, apportioned the relative responsibility 60 percent to the farmer and 40 percent to Atkinson.

This would seem to be a relatively straightforward case and easy to resolve in terms of the ordinary doctrines of negligence law. Unfortunately, hidden away in the nooks and crannies of the common law was a legal rule which absolved the farmer of any duty to prevent his cattle from straying on the highway and endangering its users. This rule owed its origin to two factors: (1) when highways were first created at the end of the medieval period in England, land was dedicated by the adjoining landowners subject to their own right of passage for their animals; (2) for a very long time this created no risk of danger from domestic animals such as cattle because traffic was so slow moving that the animals could easily be avoided. With the advent of automobiles, this factual situation was radically changed. However, the House of Lords, in its 1947 decision in *Searle v. Wallbank*, declined an invitation to revise the legal duties of the farmer to bring them into line with modern needs, and the Ontario Court of Appeal felt compelled to respect the authority of this common law precedent in its 1952 decision in *Noble v. Calder*. The true wishes of the Ontario judges were expressed in these concluding passages from their own opinion in *Fleming v. Atkinson*.

> I do not want to part with this case without expressing the hope that it may draw attention to the present unsatisfactory state of the law in this province as to civil liability for injuries sustained due to the presence on our public highways of straying domestic animals. *The Courts cannot change the law; the legislation can.* The common law as applied by the House of Lords in England to the highways there is not adequate here, and yet the Courts of this province must follow those decisions. (Emphasis added) ...

... When the case reached the Supreme Court of Canada, one judge, Mr. Justice Cartwright, agreed that the English common law, as reflected in *Searle*, defined the duties of the cattle owner until and unless they were changed by legislation. In his view it was not the function of the judges to alter a legal doctrine when it no longer reflected reasonable social policies. Fortunately for Canadian law, and for Floyd Atkinson, Mr. Justice Judson for the majority took a wider view of the judicial mission. He did not consider himself bound by an English doctrine which originated in features which are not part of Canadian society and which was reiterated in a heavily-criticized House of Lords decision. The decision of the Supreme Court in *Fleming v. Atkinson* is important because it clearly expressed our judicial independence of the House of Lords, especially when that body adheres to such an irrational legal anomaly. It is even more important as an example of the style of legal reasoning which a truly independent Supreme Court, at the top of our judicial hierarchy, must exhibit.

> A rule of law has, therefore been stated in *Searle v. Wallbank* and followed in *Noble v. Calder* which has little or no relation to the facts or needs of the situation and which ignores any theory of responsibility to the public for conduct which involves foreseeable consequences of harm. I can think of no logical basis for this immunity and it can only be based upon a rigid determination to adhere to the rules of the past in spite of changed conditions which call for the application of rules of responsibility which have been worked out to meet modern needs. It has always been assumed that one of the virtues of the common law system is its flexibility, that it is capable of changing with the times and adapting its principles to new conditions. There has been conspicuous failure to do this in this branch of the law and the failure has not passed unnoticed. It has been criticized in judicial decisions (including the one under appeal), in the texts and by the commentators.... My conclusion is that it is open to this Court to apply the ordinary rules of negligence to the case of straying animals and that principles enunciated in *Searle v. Wallbank*, dependent as they are upon historical reasons, which have no relevancy here, and upon a refusal to recognize a duty now because there had been previously no need of one, offer no obstacle.

Judson's opinion is almost a textbook illustration of the conception of legal reasoning I proposed in the preceding chapter. Judges should not just blindly follow a legal rule because it has been recognized in the law for a long time. If the rule appears to require unjust results in the immediate situation, the judge must ask why. He should have a sense of unease when asked to use a rule that does not fit comfortably into the basic principles of tort responsibility which condition a lawyer's perception of the area. Perhaps there will be good reasons for this exceptional doctrine: on investigation of the cattle trespass rule, its only support turns out to be ancient history. In such a situation the legal obligation of a judge is clearly the forthright elimination of the legal anomaly which produces that kind of injustice.

The Need for Judicial Renovation

What are the lessons we can draw from *Fleming v. Atkinson* about when and how the Court should respond in the common law? The case is certainly an unprepossessing factual situation with which to lead off a detailed assessment of the work of the Supreme Court across the spectrum of Canadian law. The question of whether the farmer or the motorist should bear the losses caused by a cow does seem to be of a somewhat lesser order of importance than constitutional disputes, issues of civil liberties and due process, problems of administrative regulation of the economy, and other such issues which regularly appear before the Supreme Court. The legal situation in the *Fleming* case is typical of the private law disputes which still constitute the bulk of the Court's work and which many now advocate deleting from its jurisdiction. [*Ed. note*: This is no longer true, as right of appeal in civil cases was abolished in 1975.] I will leave my assessment of these proposals for later when we have a more detailed view of the kinds of problems involved in these cases. For the moment we must recognize that there was an issue of general law to be resolved in the case and that the Supreme Court of Canada still has final judicial authority in this area. As is typical of a great many private law doctrines, tort liability for escaping cattle will not affect very many people but when it does arise, the question of whether damages can be collected will be of vital importance to the person involved. There are many legal doctrines with precisely this impact and the cumulative quality of their policies tells a lot about the justice afforded to the individual in our society. Up to now, the judiciary has been primarily responsible for their development in Canada. It behooves us then to enquire into the Court's performance in this area and to suggest the standards by which it should govern itself.

As Mr. Justice Judson stated in *Fleming v. Atkinson*, there is a general *principle* of law firmly established in this area. A person is required to take reasonable care in his behaviour when it creates the risk of physical injuries to another. If he does not take care and his faulty behaviour causes losses to another, the law requires that he assume responsibility for payment of damages to make whole the innocent victim. This legal principle had been clearly and authoritatively established in the general law of torts in the case of *Donoghue v. Stevenson*, but had become embedded in the motor vehicle area some time earlier. Appraised in the light of this theory of liability, the special immunity for "cattle trespass" was an historical anomaly. As Judson J. showed in his opinion, there may have been some rationale for its original adoption in England several hundred years ago but there certainly was no valid argument which could be made for its retention in contemporary Canada.

Mr. Justice Cartwright's dissent did raise some doubt whether the Court should leave it to the legislature to administer the *coup de grace* to the doctrine. To adopt the framework of analysis I sketched earlier, assuming there are good policy reasons for tort liability in this situation, are there countervailing legal values which should make a court wary of itself abolishing the immunity? In my view, the *Fleming* case is significant because when we assess in a realistic way the arguments against judicial innovation, they seem largely inapplicable here. In this respect *Fleming* is typical of tort law and, indeed, of much of the private law area.

What about the argument of predictability in the law and the possibility that judicial elimination of the immunity will defeat the expectations of those who relied on it being the law? Did the farmer rely on his immunity from tort liability when he failed to take reasonable care to control his cattle? If he did, is this the kind of expectation the legal system should be concerned to satisfy? Simply to ask these questions is to answer them. In tort law, at least as regards accidental injuries, the reliance on interest of possible defendants enters primarily at the point of insurance planning against liability for the risk. Studies have indicated that special rules of tort immunity such as this one, especially when they are hedged in by equally anomalous exceptions, are irrelevant to insurance decisions. Indeed, if there are any reasonable expectations which will be frustrated in a situation similar to that of the *Fleming* case they will be those of the injured motorist when he consults his lawyer and finds that the farmer is protected by a special rule dating back to medieval England. If the farmer's lawyer (or that of his insurer) has any understanding of this whole area of tort law and the rationale for its evolution, he can estimate the shakiness of the farmer's immunity and anticipate its probable removal. For these reasons, the Supreme Court in *Fleming v. Atkinson* could quite confidently ignore the argument about the damage to the predictability of the law.

What about the competence of the Court to make an intelligent change in the law? The possible defects in judicial law reform seem irrelevant to this actual problem. There is no need for lengthy investigations, social science research, expert testimony, and so on, to decide about change. The issue is basically one of esoteric "lawyer's law" which can be resolved by careful analysis of the implications of the basic legal principles underlying the area. If the legislature were moved to reform in this area, it would have to rely on the same sort of appraisal and it would find it in the textbooks and law review articles which are equally available to the Courts.

In fact, the "cattle trespass" rule is one in which the resources of the judicial forum are especially valuable. The issue is narrow in compass, occurs infrequently, and is only one of a very large number of such relatively independent tort problems. Yet there are a lot of judges in a lot of courts hearing such cases all the time. Each judge sees the human implications of the issue vividly portrayed in the concrete dispute before him. On the basis of the research and arguments prepared for him by opposing counsel, he can work out the solution which seems most rational in the light of the basic policies in the area. This proposed rule, when reported, can become a piecemeal addition to the evolving common law of torts. The legislature seems much too bulky and unwieldy an instrument to solve the problem of cattle trespass. It operates at the wholesale level while so much of our private law requires retail treatment.

But at least the legislature is elected, one may suggest. Should not changes in the law be made by a representative body, rather than the appointed and tenured court? We must turn to the reasons for our qualms about judicial innovation and take a realistic view of their relevance to particular cases. The problem in *Fleming v. Atkinson* is not one which will figure in an election campaign. It is inconsistent with democratic values (though not always illegitimate for this reason) for a court to intervene and impose its own policies in an area where the popular will has been expressed in the political arena. If the legislature were moved to reform in this esoteric problem area, it would merely be ratifying a proposal worked out by an equally unrepresentative Law Reform Commission at as invisible a level as would be a judicial innovation.

Once more we find that not only is there no real argument against a judicial initiative, but there are positive reasons in favour of such an active role. Private law doctrines such as this often lead to a distortion of the legislative process. Pressure for reform is very diffuse and unorganized. There is no lobby of accident victims petitioning the government. Instead, there is usually only an academic who has shown how some legal relic is working a real injustice on the very few people who run afoul of it. However, there is often a narrow interest group which might be somewhat harmed by the change. The farmer's insurance premiums will go up a bit and he may have to answer for his negligence in a lawsuit. A politician might be a little worried about the farmers' votes if their organizations object, especially if there is no countervailing lobby pressing for the reform. It is extremely unlikely he would be moved to *create* the cattle trespass immunity, but he might be loath to come out in the open and remove it entirely. The safest course in his eyes is to "let sleeping dogs lie," allow the proposal to die on the legislative order paper, and rationalize this inaction on the grounds (often valid) that he is busy on too many other problems.

By contrast, the Supreme Court was duty-bound to reach a positive conclusion about this legal problem in order to resolve the concrete dispute between Fleming and Atkinson. It had to hear the arguments from both sides, decide which position was most persuasive, and justify its conclusion in a written opinion which is reported for others to see and criticize. If judges within such an institution are willing to exercise their power to develop our law in a rational way, then we can provide the individual litigant who has been hurt with a forum to which he can come as a one-man lobby looking for legal justice. There is something to be said in a democracy of an institution which will resolve such disputes on the basis of the quality of the arguments presented, rather than the number of votes represented.

On just about every dimension then, these legal or institutional values seem to favour *judicial* initiative in this area, and they certainly do not warn against it. In order to complete this picture, let me give an example of a tort law reform I do not think a court is entitled to make, even though the judges may be convinced of its substantive desirability. The basic principle underlying our current law of torts, the one appealed to in *Fleming v. Atkinson*, is that negligent fault is the basis of liability. More and more voices contend that this is too narrow a criterion. Especially in the motor vehicle accident area, we hear proposals for a market deterrence, etc. I think we are going to see some such doctrine adopted in Canada shortly but this reform should be the work of the legislature, not the Court. Why is this so?

In the first place, this will introduce a very substantial change in the incidence of legal liability and it may require substantial increases in the premium level. To the extent that insurance companies have charged lower premiums in reliance on the fault doctrine, they can claim that this justifiable expectation should not be frustrated by retrospective judicial alteration of the law. I am not sure myself how compelling this argument is. It depends on the degree of increased recovery in the new system and the ability of the insurance industry to finance the extra payments for past losses out of future premiums.

The real point is that the Court could not likely estimate this either, which brings us to a second and major objection against judicial adoption of strict liability. The Court simply is not competent to set up a complete new scheme for compensating automobile accident victims. This is not a simple matter of eliminating an irrational anomaly like the cattle trespass doctrine and applying the established principle of fault. The objectives of a strict liability scheme require a complex series of adjustments in the kinds and level of damages recoverable, the relationship of tort liability to various other forms of liability compensation, the nature of the insurance which is to be used, and even the forum in which claims are to be made. To perform this job, we want royal commissions, legislative committees and research by a battery of experts. We cannot rely on the efforts of a few Supreme Court judges sitting in their chambers in Ottawa.

Finally, the Court does not have the authority to adopt such a scheme into law. Let us suppose that a Royal Commission had been appointed, had laboured for several years examining the issues and the various alternatives, and then worked out a detailed scheme. The expert work has been done but the legislature, for various reasons, has not gotten around to acting on it. Should the Court decide to implement this new scheme in substitution for the common law of fault-based tort liability on the assumption that it is indeed a better system? In my view, the answer is still no! As anyone who reads Canadian newspapers will realize, the desirability of compensation without fault is a matter of sharp political controversy in several Canadian provinces. It has figured prominently in several election campaigns and governments have teetered on the edge of defeat in trying to get schemes enacted. The various plans present important and ambiguous value judgments about such matters as social welfare, compulsory government insurance, administrative agencies, and the responsibility of the dangerous driver. The place where these controversial issues should be aired and inevitable compromises worked out is the public legislative arena where the participants can be held responsible for their judgments. The last place in which we would want the decision made is the sheltered, closed world of the judges who are in the process of resolving a private lawsuit....

7.3

Boucher v. The King

Supreme Court of Canada, [1951] S.C.R. 265

Rand J.: For the reasons given by me following the first argument, I would allow the appeal, set aside the verdict and conviction and enter judgment of not guilty.

[*Ed. note*: The reasons given by Mr. Justice Rand, following the first argument, read as follows.]

This appeal arises out of features of what, in substance, is religious controversy, and it is necessary that the facts be clearly appreciated. The appellant, a farmer, living near the town of St. Joseph de Beauce, Quebec, was convicted of uttering a seditious libel. The libel was contained in a four page document published apparently at Toronto by the Watch Tower Bible & Tract Society, which I take to be the name of the official publishers of the religious group known as the Witnesses of Jehovah. The document was headed "Quebec's Burning Hate for God and Christ and Freedom Is the Shame of all Canada": it consisted first of an invocation to calmness and reason in appraising the matters to be dealt with in support of the heading; then of general references to vindictive persecution accorded in Quebec to the Witnesses as brethren in Christ; a detailed narrative of specific incidents of persecution; and a concluding appeal to the people of the province, in protest against mob rule and Gestapo tactics, that through the study of God's Word and obedience to its commands, there might be brought about a "bounteous crop of the good fruits of love for Him and Christ and human freedom." At the foot of the document is an advertisement of two books entitled "Let God Be True" and "Be Glad, Ye Nations," the former revealing, in the light of God's Word, the truth concerning the Trinity, Sabbath, prayer, etc., and the latter, the facts of the endurance of Witnesses in the crucible of "fiery persecution."

The incidents, as described, are of peaceable Canadians who seem not to be lacking in meekness, but who, for distributing apparently without permits, bibles and tracts on Christian doctrine; for conducting religious services in private homes or on private lands in Christian fellowship; for holding public lecture meetings to teach religious truth as they believe it of the Christian religion; who, for this exercise of what has been taken for granted to be the unchallengeable rights of Canadians, have been assaulted and beaten and their bibles and publications torn up and destroyed, by individuals and by mobs; who have had their homes invaded and their property taken; and in hundreds have been charged with public offences and held to exorbitant bail. The police are declared to have exhibited an attitude of animosity toward them and to have treated them as criminals in provoking, by their action of Christian profession and teaching, the violence to which they have been subjected; and public officials and members of the Roman Catholic clergy are said not only to have witnessed these outrages but to have been privy to some of the prosecutions. The document charged that the Roman Catholic Church in Quebec was in some objectionable relation to the administration of justice and that the force behind the prosecutions was that of the priests of that Church.

The conduct of the accused appears to have been unexceptionable; so far as disclosed, he is an exemplary citizen who is at least sympathetic to doctrines of the Christian religion which are, evidently, different from either the Protestant or the Roman Catholic versions: but the foundation in all is the same, Christ and his relation to God and humanity.

The crime of seditious libel is well known to the Common Law. Its history has been thoroughly examined and traced by Stephen, Holdsworth and other eminent legal scholars and they are in agreement both in what it originally consisted and in the social assumptions underlying it. Up to the end of the 18th century it was, in essence, a contempt in words of political authority or the action of authority. If we conceive of the governors of society as superior beings, exercising a divine mandate, by whom laws, institutions and administrations are given to men to be obeyed, who are, in short, beyond criticism, reflection or censor upon them or what they do implies either an equality with them or an accountability by them, both equally offensive. In that lay sedition by words and the libel was its written form.

But constitutional conceptions of a different order making rapid progress in the 19th century have necessitated a modification of the legal view of public criticism; and the administrators of what we call democratic government have come to be looked upon as servants, bound to carry out their duties accountably to the public. The basic nature of the Common Law lies in its flexible process of traditional reasoning upon significant social and political matter; and just as in the 17th century the crime of seditious libel was a deduction from fundamental conceptions of government, the substitution of new conceptions, under the same principle of reasoning, called for new jural conclusions....

... The definition of seditious intention as formulated by Stephen, summarized, is, (1) to bring into hatred or contempt, or to excite disaffection against, the King or the Government and Constitution of the United Kingdom, or either House of Parliament, or the administration of justice; or (2) to excite the King's subjects to attempt, otherwise than by lawful means, the alteration of any matter in Church or State by law established; or (3) to incite persons to commit any crime in general disturbance of the peace; or (4) to raise discontent or disaffection amongst His Majesty's subjects; or (5) to promote feelings of ill-will and hostility between different classes of such subjects. The only items of this definition that could be drawn into question here are that relating to the administration of justice in (1) and those of (4) and (5). It was the latter which were brought most prominently to the notice of the jury, and it is with an examination of what in these days their language must be taken to mean that I will chiefly concern myself.

There is no modern authority which holds that the mere effect of tending to create discontent or disaffection among His Majesty's subjects or ill-will or hostility between groups of them but not tending to issue in illegal conduct, constitutes the crime, and this for obvious reasons. Freedom in thought and speech and disagreement in ideas and beliefs, on every conceivable subject, are of the essence of our life. The clash of critical discussion on political, social and religious subjects has too deeply become the stuff of daily experience to suggest that mere ill-will as a product of controversy can strike down the latter with illegality. A superficial examination of the word shows its insufficiency: what is the degree necessary to criminality? Can it ever, as mere subjective condition, be so? Controversial fury is aroused constantly by differences in abstract conceptions; heresy in some fields is again a mortal sin; there can be fanatical puritanism in ideas as well as in mortals; but our compact of free society accepts and absorbs these differences and they are exercised at large within the framework of freedom and order on broader and deeper uniformities as bases of social stability. Similarly in discontent, affection and hostility: as subjective incidents of controversy, they and the ideas which arouse them are part of our living which ultimately serve us in stimulation, in the clarification of thought and, as we believe, in the search for the constitution and truth of things generally.

Although Stephen's definition was adopted substantially as it is by the Criminal Code Commission of England in 1880, the latter's report, in this respect, was not acted on by the Imperial Parliament, and the *Criminal Code* of this country, enacted in 1891, did not incorporate its provisions. The latter omits any reference to definition except in section 133 to declare that the intention includes the advocacy of the use of force as a means of bringing about a change of government and by section 133A, that certain actions are not included. What the words in (4) and (5) must in the present day be taken to signify is the use of language which, by inflaming the minds of people into hatred, ill-will, discontent, disaffection, is intended, or is so likely to do so as to be deemed to be intended, to disorder community life, but directly or indirectly in relation to government in the broadest sense: Phillimore, J. in *R. v. Antonelli* "seditious libels are such as tend to disturb the government of this country...." That may be through tumult or violence, in resistance to public authority, in defiance of law. The conception lies behind the association which the word is given in section 1 of chapter 10, C.S. Lower Canada (1860) dealing with illegal oaths:

"To engage in any seditious, rebellious or treasonable purpose"; and the corresponding section 130 of the *Criminal Code*: "To engage in any mutinous or seditious purpose."

The baiting or denouncing of one group by another or others without an aim directly or indirectly at government, is in the nature of public mischief: *R. v. Leese & Whitehead*; and incitement to unlawful acts is itself an offence.

This result must be distinguished from an undesired reaction provoked by the exercise of common rights, such as the violent opposition to the early services of the Salvation Army. In that situation it was the hoodlums who were held to be the lawless and not the members of the Army: *Beatty v. Gillbanks*. On the allegations in the document here, had the Salvationists been arrested for bringing about by unlawful assembly a breach of the peace and fined, had they then made an impassioned protest against such treatment of law abiding citizens, and had they thereupon been charged with seditious words, their plight would have been that of the accused in this case.

These considerations are confirmed by section 133A of the *Code*, which is as follows:

> what is not sedition – No one shall be deemed to have a seditious intention only because he intends in good faith, –
>
> (a)   to show that His Majesty has been misled or mistaken in his measures; or,
>
> (b)   to point out errors or defects in the government or constitution of the United Kingdom, or of any part of it, or of Canada or any province thereof, or in either House of Parliament of the United Kingdom or of Canada, or in any legislature, or in the administration of justice; or to excite His Majesty's subjects to attempt to procure, by lawful means, the alteration of any matters in the state; or,
>
> (c)   to point out, in order to their removal, matters which are producing or have a tendency to produce feelings of hatred and ill-will between different classes of His Majesty's subjects.

This, as is seen, is a fundamental provision which, with its background of free criticism as a constituent of modern democratic government, protects the widest range of public discussion and controversy, so long as it is done in good faith and for the purposes mentioned. Its effect is to eviscerate the older concept of its anachronistic elements. But a motive or ultimate purpose, whether good or believed to be good, is unavailing if the means employed is bad; disturbance or corrosion may be ends in themselves, but whether means or ends, their character stamps them and intention behind them as illegal.

The condemned intention lies then in a residue of criticism of government, the negative touchstone of which is the test of good faith by legitimate means toward legitimate ends. That claim was the real defence in the proceedings here but it was virtually ignored by the trial judge. On that failure, as well as others, the Chief Justice of the King's Bench and Galipeault, J. have rested their dissent, and with them I am in agreement.

7.4

Fact Finding in Adjudication

Donald L. Horowitz

The Courts and Social Policy (Washington: The Brookings Institute, 1977),
45–51. Reprinted with permission.

The fact that judges function at some distance from the social milieu from which their cases spring puts them at an initial disadvantage in understanding the dimensions of social policy problems. The focused, piecemeal quality of adjudication implies that judicial decisions tend to be abstracted from social contexts broader than the immediate setting in which the litigation arises, and, as already indicated, the potentially unrepresentative character of the litigants makes it hazardous to generalize from their situation to the wider context.

The judicial fact-finding process carries forward this abstraction of the case from its more general social context. To make this clear, it is necessary to distinguish between two kinds of facts: historical facts and social facts. Historical facts are the events that have transpired between the parties to a lawsuit. Social facts are the recurrent patterns of behavior on which policy must be based. Historical facts, as I use the term, have occasionally been called "adjudicative facts" by lawyers, and social facts have also been called "legislative facts." I avoid these terms because of the preconceptions they carry and the division of labor they imply. Nonetheless, by whatever designation they are known, these are two distinct kinds of facts, and a process set up to establish the one is not necessarily adequate to ascertain the other.

Social facts are nothing new in litigation. Courts have always had to make assumptions or inferences about general conditions that would guide their decisions. The broader the issue, the more such imponderables there are. The breadth of the issues in constitutional law has always made it a fertile field for empirical speculation. Does a civil service law barring alleged subversives from public employment have a "chilling effect" on free speech? Is the use of third-degree methods by the police sufficiently widespread to justify a prophylactic rule that would exclude from evidence even some confessions that are not coerced? Does pornography stimulate the commission of sex crimes, or does it provide cathartic release for those who might otherwise commit such crimes?

Constitutional law is a fertile field, but it is not the only field in which such questions arise. If a court refuses to enforce against a bankrupt corporation an "unconscionable contract" for the repayment of borrowed money, will that make it more difficult for firms needing credit to obtain it and perhaps precipitate more such bankruptcies? Does it encourage carelessness and thus undercut a prime purpose of the law of negligence if an automobile driver, a shopkeeper, or a theater owner is permitted to insure himself against liability inflicted as a result of his own fault?

These are, all of them, behavioral questions. They share an important characteristic: no amount of proof about the conduct of the individual litigants involved in a civil service, confession, obscenity, bankruptcy, or negligence case can provide answers to these probabilistic questions about the behavior of whole categories of people. As a matter of fact, proof of one kind of fact can be misleading about the other. What is true in the individual case may be false in the generality of cases, and vice versa. The judicial process, however, makes it much easier to learn reliably about the individual case than about the run of cases.

The increasing involvement of the courts in social policy questions has increased the number and importance of social fact questions in litigation. As the courts move into new, specialized, unfamiliar policy areas, they are confronted by a plethora of questions about human behavior that are beyond their ability to answer on the basis of common experience or the usual modicum of expert testimony. A few examples, drawn from a social science manual for lawyers, will make the point:

> Do the attrition rates for different racial groups applying for admission to a union apprenticeship program suggest a pattern of racial discrimination?

> How would the elimination of a local bus system through bankruptcy affect low income people and the elderly poor in particular?

> How are different income groups and communities of varying sizes differentially affected by the formula allocation of General Revenue Sharing funds?

Obtaining answers to such behavioral questions has become exigent, and not only because the interstices in which courts make fresh policy keep expanding. If a judge or a jury makes a mistake of fact relating only to the case before it, "the effects of the mistake are quarantined." But if the factual materials form the foundation for a general policy, the consequences cannot be so confined.

Traditionally, the courts have been modest about their competence to ascertain social facts and have tried to leave this function primarily to other agencies. They have shielded themselves by applying doctrines that have the effect of deferring to the fact-finding abilities of legislatures and administrative bodies, to avoid having to establish social facts in the course of litigation.

The reasons for this general modesty are well grounded. There is tension between two different judicial responsibilities: deciding the particular case and formulating a general policy. Two different kinds of fact-finding processes are required for these two different functions. The adversary system of presentation and the rules of evidence were both developed for the former, and they leave much to be desired for the latter.

In general, the parties can be depended upon to elicit all of the relevant historical facts, through the ordinary use of testimony and documentary evidence, and the judge or jury can be presumed competent to evaluate that evidence. Social facts, on the other hand, may not be elicited at all by the parties, almost surely not fully, and the competence of the decision-maker in this field cannot be taken for granted.

These deficiencies of the adversary process have led to proposals for the employment of outside experts as consultants to the courts. So far, relatively few impartial experts have been appointed, and the proof of social facts has largely been left to the traditional adversary method.

Expert testimony is the conventional way for the litigants to prove social facts, but its deficiencies are considerable. The experts are usually partisans, employed by the parties, and their conclusions tend to reflect that status. If the parties provide a skewed picture of the problem they purport to represent, their expert witness may do the same. Finally, reliance on expert witnesses hired by the parties makes the judge the prisoner of the parties' definition of the issues of social facts that are involved.

The rules of evidence are equally inapt for the verification of social facts. They are geared to the search for truth between the parties, not to the search for truth in general. Understandably, there is a prohibition on the introduction of hearsay evidence. Courts must act on what happened, not on what someone said happened. The emphasis in judicial fact-finding on choosing between conflicting versions of events by assessing the credibility of witnesses also places a premium on requiring witness to have firsthand knowledge of the events about which they testify. Sensible though the hearsay rule may be, however, it makes the ascertainment of scientific facts of all kinds including social science, very difficult. Books and articles constitute inadmissible hearsay; they are not alive and cannot be cross-examined. Consequently, when behavioral materials are introduced into evidence, it is usually pursuant to some exception to the hearsay rule....

... The use of expert testimony involves another kind of exception. Duly qualified experts, unlike ordinary witnesses, need not confine themselves to testifying about facts. They may also state their opinion, which may be nothing more than a guess or a bias. Yet the studies on which their opinion may be based remain inadmissible as hearsay (though they may be introduced to impeach an expert's opinion).

All of these cumbersome devices tend to make the judge dependent on secondary interpretations of the relevant empirical material and to discourage him from going directly to the material itself. As we shall see in later chapters, filtered knowledge has its problems.

If new rules and mechanisms do develop to aid in informing the courts about social facts, further problems will arise. The courts may have to administer a dual system of evidence – one part for historical facts, another for social facts – and there is the problem of what might be called contamination. Evidence introduced for one purpose may, as it often does, spill over to infect the other set of issues. Compartmentalization to prevent contamination is one of the hardest jobs a judge must perform. This particular problem suggests again the underlying tension between deciding the litigants' case and making general policy.

How have social fact issues been handled by the courts in practice? They have been handled in much the same way that the rules of evidence and the adversary system have been adapted to accommodate social facts: by neglect or by improvisation.

A first, quite common way is to ignore them or to assume, sometimes rightly, sometimes wrongly, that the litigants' case is representative. This is patently inadequate....

... A third way of dealing with social facts is to go outside the record of the case in search of information. This is what Mr. Justice Murphy did when he sent questionnaires to police forces in thirty-eight cities in order to determine the relationship between the admissibility of illegally obtained evidence and police training in the law of search and seizure. The same impulse has sometimes moved other judges, restless in their ignorance of behavioral fact, to consult experts of their acquaintance, as Judge Charles Clark, then former Dean of the Yale Law School, consulted the Yale University organist about a music copyright case that was pending before him. These attempts, primitive as they are, show the existence of a deeply felt need rather than a method of satisfying it.

What these examples also suggest is that the need for empirical data is often not even sensed until the case is on appeal. The traditional formulation of causes of action rarely incorporates social facts as an element of proof. When behavioral facts are implicitly incorporated (for example, "reasonable care of a prudent man under the circumstances"), these standards are often not met by evidence but left to the decision-maker to judge from his own experience.

The law thus tends to slight the need for behavioral material in a number of ways. In practice, this means that the option of utilizing such material falls on counsel. Generally, public-interest lawyers have been much more assiduous about introducing evidence of social facts than have other lawyers, and it is they who have often compiled voluminous records of expert testimony and memoranda....

That the process of adjudication places the emphasis heavily on the accurate ascertainment of historical facts, while it neglects and renders it difficult to prove social facts, is, of course, exactly what might be expected from its traditional responsibilities. This is to say, the fact-finding capability of the courts is likely to lag behind the functions they are increasingly required to perform.

To argue that this problem of capability exists is still to say nothing of the materials on which proof of social facts might be based. The problems here are considerable. There may be no studies that cast light on the issue in litigation. If there are, the behavioral issue may be framed in a way quite inappropriate for litigation. Studies may, of course, be specially commissioned for the purposes of the lawsuit. Even if the potential bias of such studies is overcome, the constraints of time and resources may dictate research methods much less than satisfying. On large issues, existing data are likely to be fragmentary. Then the question becomes one of generalization from partial or tentative findings, or one of drawing inferences from proxies. This is no place for a full-scale consideration of the imperfect fit between law and social science. It is enough to say here that the problems of social science do not disappear in litigation, but are instead compounded by the litigation setting, the different ways in which lawyers and social scientists ask questions, and the time constraint.

This last point needs to be underscored. As I have said earlier, litigation is, for the most part, a mandatory decision process. Courts do not choose their cases; cases choose their courts. With certain exceptions, a case properly brought must be decided. Whereas a legislator or administrator has some freedom to shy away from issues on which his quantum of ignorance is too great to give him confidence that he can act sensibly, courts are not afforded quite the same latitude. Courts have difficulty finding and absorbing social facts in the context of a largely mandatory decision process that puts them at a comparative disadvantage in social policymaking.

7.5

Stare Decisis and Social Facts in the *Charter* Era

Chelsea Ogilvie

This reading is excerpted from Chelsea Ogilvie's M.A. thesis, "Winning Conditions for *Charter* Reconsideration: Assisted Suicide and the Supreme Court of Canada" (University of Calgary, 2015).

Stare decisis, or "standing by a decision," is a fundamental doctrine in the common law legal tradition. Treating like cases alike, or adhering to precedent, "promotes the evenhanded, predictable, and consistent development of legal principles" (*Payne* 1991). With *stare decisis*, the law becomes more transparent and individuals can confidently conduct their affairs in line with the law, knowing that what was decided in one case will inform how a similar case will be treated. To achieve this transparency, judges must remain impartial and apply precedent evenly across all cases.

But how does *stare decisis* achieve equality before the law in a system of many judges, in multiple courts, at different levels, and (in federal systems) across jurisdictions? Is every judicial ruling an immediately binding precedent for every other judge in the system? Not quite. For the Supreme Court in particular there must be some freedom within the "prudential" doctrine of *stare decisis* for judges to justifiably abandon a precedent. Even though judges are hesitant to openly reverse precedent, a series of justifications has evolved over the decades to allow such reversals when they are necessary. Very rarely will judges step outside of the accepted reasons for precedent reversal when openly abandoning *stare decisis*.

Among the reasons for precedent reversal, there are three that are particularly well-established, and therefore relatively uncontroversial: that a precedent is obviously outdated, that it is unworkable, and that it is confusing. The least controversial reason for relaxing *stare decisis* and departing from precedent is that the precedential decision is simply outdated. The law in Canada pre-dates even Confederation; as a Commonwealth country, Canada inherited hundreds of years of British case law along with the common law system. Precedential decisions could therefore be quite old [*Ed. note*: See reading 7.2].

Another justification for departing from precedent is that the original decision is unworkable in practice. *R. v. Askov* is arguably the most famous example of this legal dilemma in Canada. The 1990 decision involved the *Charter* right to a "trial within a reasonable time" (s.11(b)). The Supreme Court decided that "institutional delay" would constitute a breach of s.11(b), and argued that six to eight months was the reasonable limit for an accused person to wait for a trial. As a direct result of the *Askov* decision, more than 40,000 criminal charges were dropped (mostly in Ontario) because the "reasonable time" for a trial had expired. Amidst criticism from law-enforcement agencies and the public, the Court "corrected" its mistake 16 months later in *R. v. Morin* (1992).

[*Ed. note:* The Court once again revisited the issue of trial delay in *R. v. Jordan* (2016), when it controversially created a "presumptive ceiling" of 18 months for cases in provincial (s.92) courts or 30 months for cases in superior courts (or in provincial courts after a preliminary inquiry).]

More recently, Justice Rothstein raised a similar problem in *Ontario (Attorney General) v. Fraser* (2011). Rothstein justified his (dissenting) opinion to reverse the recent *Health Services* decision on labour rights – in part – because of the practical difficulties it caused through conflicts with other legislative regimes. Arguing that the approach to collective bargaining articulated in *Health Services* raised "significant problems relating to workability" and disrupted the long-standing model of dealing with labour relations in Canada, Rothstein voted to relax *stare decisis* and reverse the four-year old *Health Services* precedent. Rothstein wrote in dissent, however. The Court's majority formally maintained the *Health Services* precedent.

Apart from being unworkable in a very practical sense, court decisions can also cause confusion by conflicting with established legal principles. Thomas Bateman outlines one example of this problem in Canada in his study of the evolution of s.15 interpretation, which deals with equality and discrimination (2011). In what Bateman considered a "collective effort" the Supreme Court justices wrote a unanimous decision in *Law v. Canada* (1999), which outlined a new, complicated test for s.15. The new test attempted to uphold the older *Andrews* test developed in 1989, while adding a subjective component of human dignity. Dignity became a core element of s.15, not merely an underlying value (*Law v. Canada* 1999). The vague and very subjective nature of "feeling digni-fied" led to a myriad of decisions that created a "teeter-totter" effect between the subjective aspects of the *Law* test and the more objective *Andrews* test. The academic community heaped heavy criticism on the *Law* test for "muddying" the already complicated approach to s.15.

Almost a decade later, the Supreme Court once again attempted to set down a unified approach to s.15. In *R. v. Kapp*, the court backtracked through almost twenty years of jurisprudential development to return to a s.15 test that was almost identical to the *Andrews* test. In doing this, they effectively aban-doned the precedent set in *Law*. The justification for ignoring *stare decisis* was grounded in the admission that "several difficulties [had] arisen from the attempt in Law to employ human dignity as a legal test."

Reversal in Constitutional Cases

The criteria for precedent reversal in constitutional cases need to take into account that constitutional precedents can be particularly rigid, thus posing special challenges to legislatures that do not find them socially or politically desirable. If a decision revising the common law or interpreting a statute proves unworkable or confusing, legislators can simply change the problematic law. However, cases dealing with constitutional law are much more difficult to circumvent and therefore carry much more weight.

In light of the difficulties associated with both section 33 and constitutional amendment, the only realistic way around undesirable constitutional decisions is often judicial reconsideration. Indeed, both scholars and judges argue that for this reason the principle of *stare decisis* should "operate more flexibly" in constitutional cases to allow for legal change as society progresses. However, even if we accept that departing from precedent might be easier in *Charter* cases, we should keep in mind that it was in a *Charter* case, *Fraser* (2011), that Justice McLachlin emphasized the "high threshold" for "reversing a precedent," and in another *Charter* case, *Bedford*, that she insisted "the threshold for revisiting a matter is not an easy one to reach." The difference between "reversing" and "revisiting" may be significant for McLachlin. In *Fraser*, McLachlin rejected Justice Rothstein's attempt to "reverse" *Health Services*, whereas in *Bedford* (and subsequently in *Carter*) she "revisits" – and clearly departs from – precedents set two decades earlier. In neither of the latter two cases does the language of "reversing" precedent appear; the softer language of "revisiting" is always used instead.

McLachlin's linguistic distinction between reversing and revisiting precedent reflects the difference, much discussed in the literature, between overruling and "distinguishing" precedents. However, just because judges do not admit to reversing a precedent does not mean that it is not happening. David Muttart argues that a precedent has effectively been changed if future cases would be decided differently as a direct result of the new decision, or if the decision "clearly effects a modification in the law." This kind of change certainly occurred in *Bedford* (at all judicial levels) and in *Carter* in the trial court and at the Supreme Court of Canada.

The *Charter* and Criteria for "Revisiting" Constitutional Precedent

How, then, do the courts decide when the difficult threshold for reversing or (more commonly) "revisiting" a precedent has been met in *Charter* cases? What are the relevant criteria? Justice McLachlin provided much of the answer in *Bedford*.

Both *Bedford* and its precedent, *Reference re ss.193 and 195* (1990, hereafter referred to as the *Prostitution Reference*), dealt with the constitutionality of legislation that criminalized aspects of prostitution, particularly running bawdy houses and soliciting for the purposes of prostitution. While the *Prostitution Reference* determined that the bawdy-house provision did not infringe the *Charter*, it did find that the ban on soliciting infringed the freedom-of-expression rights of prostitutes under s.2(b) of the *Charter* and their right to "liberty" under section 7. The Court's majority, however, found that the infringement of freedom of expression was a "reasonable limit" under section 1 of the *Charter*, while the infringement of s.7 liberty was in accord with the "principles of fundamental justice." This precedent held for over 20 years, until Terri Jean Bedford and other sex workers challenged the same *Criminal Code* provisions on the grounds that their s.7 rights to life, liberty, and security of the person were infringed by laws that made a legal profession unnecessarily dangerous. The *Bedford* challenge succeeded at all levels of the judicial process (trial, provincial court of appeal, and Supreme Court). Clearly, *Bedford* got over the difficult "threshold" for revisiting a precedent. How?

Writing for a unanimous Supreme Court in *Bedford* (2013) Chief Justice McLachlin outlined two criteria for reconsidering precedent: 1) that a new legal issue has been presented, and 2) that there has been "a change in the circumstances or evidence that fundamentally shifts the parameters of the debate."

New Legal Issues

While any area of law can grow and evolve, developments in jurisprudence and interpretation have been much more pronounced in *Charter* law than any other legal arena. The rate of growth of *Charter* jurisprudence – a result of being a relatively young body of law combined with the intentional "living tree" approach to interpretation – means that "new legal issues" will often arise in *Charter* cases, even with respect to policy issues, such as prostitution or euthanasia, where precedents already exist.

However, Justice McLachlin's *Bedford* opinion made it clear that legal issues settled in the precedential *Prostitution Reference* could not be recast as "new" legal issues and revisited by trial judges in subsequent litigation. In particular, trial judges were bound by the clear decision in the *Prostitution Reference* that the soliciting ban was a "justified limit on freedom of expression." That was not a "new legal issue." New issues did, however, arise with respect to section 7 of the *Charter*. These were of two kinds. First, substantive s.7 rights that did not play a significant role in the 1990 *Prostitution Reference* were emphasized in *Bedford*. Whereas the 1990 *Prostitution Reference* found only an infringement of s.7 liberty rights, the plaintiffs in *Bedford* successfully asked the Court to find infringements of rights to life and security of the person – issues that were not considered in 1990. This effectively made the safety of prostitutes much more central than it had been in the *Prostitution Reference*, a point we will return to.

Second, the s.7 "principles of fundamental justice" had undergone considerable interpretive development since 1990. Just as the new s.7 legal issue of "security of the person" highlighted the safety of prostitutes, so the new principles of fundamental justice – particularly arbitrariness, overbreadth, and gross disproportionality – would make it more difficult to justify ways in which the Criminal Code prohibitions of prostitution-related activities might endanger the otherwise legal activity of sex work. Together, these new legal developments provided the basis for distinguishing *Bedford* from the *Prostitution Reference*. Ultimately, of course, a different outcome would depend on evidence regarding the connection between the Criminal Code provisions and the actual safety (or lack thereof) experienced by prostitutes.

Social Facts

In addressing the shift in evidence or circumstances, Justice McLachlin used a well-established distinction in the literature between "adjudicative" (or "historical") facts on the one hand, and "social" or "legislative" facts on the other [*Ed. note*: See Reading 7.4]. Historical facts are well suited to the adversarial process of determining which party to a dispute is in line with the law, or whether or not a law has been broken. However, they are less helpful in *Charter* cases, where the law itself is on trial. As Maioni and Manfredi put it, determining whether an impugned policy unjustifiably infringes the *Charter* entails understanding the varied and far-reaching effects of complex policies that involve "multiple stakeholders, constantly changing facts and evidence, and predictive assessments of future implications." The factual circumstances of the immediate parties to the case will not suffice. The same is true when courts consider such section 7 "fundamental justice" issues as "arbitrariness," "overbreadth," and "gross disproportionality," which are *roughly* analogous to the section 1 tests of rational connection, minimal impairment, and proportionate effects, respectively. In this respect, the development of "new legal issues" under the s.7

fundamental justice standard enhance and shape the role of social facts in the s.7 context.

It is changing social facts (or changing knowledge of social facts) that can justify a departure from precedent in *Charter* cases. While historical facts are provable (and falsifiable) through cross-examination and expert testimony, social facts are more difficult to nail down. New, previously unknown (or under-appreciated) evidence may come to light. Moreover, new social-science studies are constantly refuting the "truth" of previous work, and similar data can produce contradictory conclusions. This implies that the evolution of factual understanding might justify different legal outcomes with respect to a particular policy over time.

Bedford and the Interaction of "New Legal Issues" and "Social Facts"

The Court in *Bedford* made use of both new legal issues and developments in social evidence to revisit, and depart from, the *Prostitution Reference*. The Supreme Court originally determined that a law prohibiting communication for the purpose of prostitution was in violation of s.2(d) freedom of expression rights, but was justifiable as a reasonable limit under s.1. This claim was therefore off limits to the judges in *Bedford*. However, other new claims were accepted and were assessed in light of both new legal issues (particularly new principles of fundamental justice) and developments in social evidence.

Sex workers Terri Jean Bedford, Amy Lebovitch and Valerie Scott claimed that the communication and bawdy-house provisions, as well as a law that banned living off the avails of prostitution, violated their s.7 security of the person rights (a new legal issue) and were not in accord with the new principles of fundamental justice – arbitrariness, overbreadth and gross disproportionality. This new approach to s.7 raised safety concerns that were not considered in the *Prostitution Reference,* necessitated an examination of the dangers of prostitution, and relied on extensive social facts that were "not available in 1990." With over 25,000 pages of evidence, the plaintiffs demonstrated that the dangers of prostitution – a legal activity – were heightened, if not caused, by effective criminalization of "in-call" sex work. The new social facts showed that sex work was safest when conducted from a fixed location, with clear communication prior to engagement in order to screen potential clients, and/or with the help of support staff like bodyguards and receptionists. None of these safety precautions were legal under the Criminal Code provisions.

Given the dangerous and potentially fatal nature of street prostitution, Chief Justice McLachlin found that the bawdy-house provision violated the s.7 rights of sex workers. She argued that the real harms facing sex workers on the street were "grossly disproportionate" to the purpose of the bawdy-house law, which was to "prevent community harms in the nature of nuisance." McLachlin struck down the "living off the avails of prostitution" provision for similar reasons. Using the principle of "overbreadth," she found that the legislation went beyond what was necessary to protect sex workers from pimps, and instead caught "non-exploitive" individuals who might contribute to the prostitutes' safety (such as bodyguards or drivers). The new principles of fundamental justice, combined with new social facts about both the dangers of prostitution and ways to make the practice safer, led to a different outcome in *Bedford* than the *Prostitution Reference* twenty years earlier.

This combination of new legal issues and developments in social evidence was essential to the *Bedford* decision. The relationship between these two criteria for revisiting precedent is also central to *Carter*.

Winning Conditions for Physician-Assisted Suicide in Court

Even before Chief Justice McLachlin articulated her two criteria for reconsidering precedent in *Bedford*, the plaintiffs in *Carter* (2015) were hopeful that both new legal issues and social-fact developments in the decades since *Rodriguez* – the 1993 case in which a 5-4 Supreme Court majority upheld the ban on physician-assisted suicide (PAS) – would be substantial enough to encourage a reconsideration of the PAS issue. Regarding new legal questions, the plaintiffs followed the same strategy that would later be successful in *Bedford*: they emphasized substantive section 7 rights that had not received much attention in *Rodriguez*, as well as the emergence of "overbreadth" and "gross disproportionality" as new principles of fundamental justice. As a further argument, they also highlighted the "proportionate effects" component of the section 1 *Oakes* test, which roughly corresponds to section 7 "gross disproportionality."

In terms of social facts, the plaintiffs claimed that the evidence presented in *Rodriguez* "simply bears no comparison" to newly available evidence. In particular, they pointed out that Justice Sopinka's majority decision in *Rodriguez* had been based on the fact that it was impossible to determine a societal consensus on the divisive issue, that a ban on PAS was the international norm, and that there was no guarantee a liberalized regime could prevent abuse and protect vulnerable persons. The plaintiffs argued that none of these assumptions held up in the face of new social-fact evidence. To use McLachlin's terminology in *Bedford*, the *Carter* plaintiffs essentially argued that "change[s] in the circumstances or evidence [had] fundamentally shift[ed] the parameters of the debate."

Despite dissenting and critical reports on the effectiveness of PAS regulatory regimes, the plaintiffs in *Carter* had extensive social evidence from numerous jurisdictions to draw from that supported their position that safeguards were working, and that the slippery slope argument was unfounded. These studies in favour of legalized PAS were not available to Rodriguez and her legal team in 1993, leading to Sopinka's conclusions that there was no evidence to support the proposition that anything other than a complete prohibition of PAS would protect vulnerable population groups. As a result, justification balances under ss.7 and 1 of the *Charter* tipped in favour of the ban.

Applying the new social facts to the new legal issue of overbreadth, both the trial and Supreme Court concluded that the complete prohibition went too far, and was not necessary to protect vulnerable persons. As such, the ban was in accord with neither the s.7 principles of fundamental justice nor s.1 reasonable limits. The emergence of (arguably) successful regulatory regimes provided critical evidence to demonstrate that there were other *Charter*-compliant policy options available to Parliamentarians who were concerned with protecting vulnerable persons and preventing abuses. Because of this, both Justice Smith at the trial court and the Supreme Court concluded that since it is possible, with carefully designed safeguards, to "establish a regime that addresses the risks associated with physician-assisted death," the blanket prohibition could not pass the minimal impairment part of the s.1 analysis, making Canada the first jurisdiction to legalize PAS through a constitutional rights challenge.

Going up against the hurdle of *stare decisis*, the plaintiffs successfully gauged that the time was right for a renewed legal challenge. Not only was public support strongly in favour of legalizing PAS, but evidence from permissive regimes spoke to the effectiveness of safeguards at protecting vulnerable persons. From a legal standpoint, developments in s.7 jurisprudence leaned in favour of precedent reversal, and allowed the plaintiffs to use the less-controversial strategy of distinguishing. While the Appeal Court overturned the trial-level win for the *Carter* plaintiffs, the Supreme Court in *Bedford* laid out the criteria for revisitation that paved the way a high court success in *Carter*. The *Carter* plaintiffs could not have asked for a more perfect storm of winning conditions to see their case to victory.

7.6

Key Terms

Concepts

adversarial process

advocacy scholarship

civil law system

codification

common law system

extrinsic evidence

historical/adjudicative facts

institutional capacity

institutional legitimacy

legal commentary

precedent

precedent reversal

predictability

social/legislative facts

stare decisis

statute

Institutions, Events and Documents

Boucher v. The King, [1951] S.C.R. 265 (Seditious Libel Case)

Canada (Attorney General) v. Bedford, [2013] 3 S.C.R. 1101

Carter v. Canada (Attorney General), [2015] 1 S.C.R. 331

Criminal Code of Canada (1892)

Fleming v. Atkinson, [1959] S.C.R. 513 (Cattle Trespass Case)

Jeremy Bentham

R. v. Askov, [1990] 2 S.C.R. 1199

R. v. Jordan, [2016] 1 S.C.R. 631

R. v. Morin, [1992] 1 S.C.R. 771

R. v. Oakes, [1986] 1 S.C.R. 103

8

Judicial Decision-Making

The subject of this chapter is the decision-making process of appeal courts, specifically the Supreme Court of Canada. The practising bar and the general public are typically interested only in the practical "product" of courts – the final judgment and opinion. However, the character and even the quality of the final "product" are influenced by the internal procedures and jurisdiction of a court – how a court goes about its business. To better understand the judicial process, we must go behind the institutional facade of courts and examine how appeal court judges actually decide cases and write opinions.

Courts, like other institutions, have a particular institutional logic, one formed by and around their purpose. The traditional adjudicative function of courts has molded their internal decision-making procedures in all common law countries. Yet high courts, particularly the Supreme Court of Canada, have undergone considerable institutional change. Some change was external, such as amendments to the *Supreme Court Act* granting docket control and the constitutional entrenchment of the *Charter of Rights and Freedoms*. Other change has been internal, as different chief justices' leadership style and vision for the Court contributed to new norms and rules. Although it is still composed of nine judges sitting at the top of Canada's judicial hierarchy, the Supreme Court of Canada functions very differently today than it did half a century ago.

To simplify, the judicial decision-making process can be broken down into the following steps: granting leave, reading factums, oral argument, the conference and opinion writing. First, for those cases that are not appealed to the Court "as of right," the Court must grant leave to appeal. As noted in Chapter 6, when Parliament amended the *Supreme Court Act* in 1975 to abolish appeals as of right in certain civil cases, the Supreme Court gained significant control over its own docket. The impact of this change has been dramatic. Between 1970 and 1975, 72 per cent of the Supreme Court's docket came from appeals as of right, and only 23 per cent by its own decision to grant leave to appeal. This situation was reversed after 1975. From 2010–2016, only 23 per cent of the Supreme Court's cases were "as of right," which means that over three-quarters of cases were those the Court chose to hear using its "public importance" test.[1] The contrast between the old and new Supreme Court was captured by Ian Bushnell's observation that prior to the 1975 reform, "it [was] the litigant who [was] afforded access and he [brought] the legal issue with him," while now "it is the legal problem that determines access, and the litigant is brought along with it."[2]

To consider an application for leave, the Court sits in three panels of three judges, appointed by the Chief Justice and changed every year. Leave applications were traditionally done orally, but due to a backlog, the *Supreme Court Act* was amended in 1987 to allow written submissions, which are now the norm. Since 1995, staff lawyers act as a filter between the application and the three-judge panels by summarizing leave applications and providing a recommendation for the panel to consider. The vast majority of leave decisions made by these panels are unanimous. Although in the past the full Court would occasionally reverse the panel's decision to grant or deny leave, this seems extremely rare today.[3] Collectively, the Court typically receives between five and six hundred applications for leave each year, and grants leave to appeal to roughly 10 per cent of these applicants.[4]

Once leave has been granted, the Chief Justice decides the panel personnel for the case itself. Panel sizes are typically five, seven or nine judges (by contrast, the U.S. Court sits as a full panel of nine judges for leave hearings and for the case itself). As with many other internal changes to the Court, changes to the structure of judicial panels can be traced to Chief Justice Bora Laskin, who in the 1970s initiated a number of procedural reforms designed to increase the Court's collegiality and to reduce the number of separate opinions. One such change concerned his preference for the Supreme Court to sit as a full nine-judge bench rather than in panels of five. Before his appointment as Chief Justice, Laskin had publicly disapproved of the practice of having five-judge panels for important cases, and he quickly exercised his new administrative prerogatives to implement his preferred policy of nine-judge panels. The results were significant. In the three terms preceding his appointment, nine-judge panels heard only 10 per cent of the cases argued before the Supreme Court. In the eight years following Laskin's elevation to the chief justiceship, the average increased to 36 per cent.[5] The number of nine-judge panels has increased to such an extent that, in the early years of the McLachlin Court, they constituted over 50 per cent of its workload.[6] The cumulative effect of this trend has been to increase the authority of the Supreme Court's pronouncements on constitutional issues and so to make it a more influential participant in the political process.

After panel personnel has been decided, the justices receive factums (written arguments) from the parties. They read these, along with the previous rulings, transcripts and possible intervenor factums (see Chapter 6), in advance of oral argument. Then comes the oral hearing itself, which typically takes place eight months after the appeal is filed with the Court. The Court used to allow unlimited time for parties to present oral arguments, but changed this policy in 1987; since then, oral argument for normal appeals has been limited to two hours, one for each side (intervenors who have been granted oral access are typically given twenty minutes each). During oral argument, Supreme Court justices can be quite active, interrupting counsel and asking questions.[7] While the closed-door nature of Supreme Court decision-making makes it impossible to quantify with complete precision, there is no doubt that oral argument can be extremely important in shaping judicial decision-making: in interviews, former justices have indicated that oral argument can cause them to change their minds in anywhere between 10 and 20 per cent of the cases they hear.[8]

After oral argument comes the judicial conference, the modern variant of which, once again, was institutionalized by Bora Laskin. One of Laskin's goals was to move away from the practice of *seriatim* opinion-writing, in which each judge gives his or her own "findings" or reasons for judgment. *Seriatim* opinions reflected and reinforced the tradition of judicial independence, but are not particularly helpful for judicial decisions with policy implications: a decision that gives five different "rules" for the majority decision is not as helpful as a single authoritative opinion, which enables the Court to "speak with one voice." A judicial conference can facilitate the accommodation of these different perspectives into one statement.

Although holding a judges' conference after oral argument was introduced by Laskin's predecessor, Chief Justice Cartwright, it was formalized by Laskin. Conferencing was calculated to enhance the efficiency and coherence of the Supreme Court's opinion-writing. During a conference, judges can discover those with whom they agree and disagree, and responsibility to draft a single opinion (and a dissent, if necessary) can be assigned by the Chief Justice. Conferencing also facilitates strategic coordination among judges and innovation in the law. If judges are writing their reasons independently in isolation, there are incentives for each judge to try to "follow precedent" as faithfully as possible. Caution is the best policy. By contrast, when judges conference before any opinion writing begins, new directions can be identified, discussed and even adopted.

Justice Bertha Wilson (Reading 8.1) provides a fascinating look at the inner workings of the modern Supreme Court conference. Although Justice Wilson was writing over thirty years ago, contemporary research confirms that many aspects she describes remain the same. Conferences occur immediately after the oral hearing, and justices state their views in reverse order of seniority, with the most junior member speaking first (in the United States Supreme Court, they go in order of seniority). In his research, Emmett Macfarlane found that the tone of the conference was highly dependent on the Chief Justice at the time, with Brian Dickson noted for fostering greater collegiality than Bora Laskin. Under the McLachlin Court, conferences tended to be thorough and collegial. However, the majority of conferences were under twenty minutes in length, with some as short as five minutes. For especially difficult cases, such as the *Secession Reference*, the Court will sometimes reconvene for additional conferences.[9]

The most immediate effect of the institutionalization of conferences was felt in the final step of judicial decision-making: the drafting of opinions. After initial agreement and disagreement is determined at the conference, individual justices will either volunteer or be assigned by the Chief Justice to draft opinions (including dissenting opinions if necessary). These drafts are eventually circulated, at which point the justices give feedback – most commonly in writing, but sometimes through informal face-to-face discussion. Justice Wilson's account of her time on the Supreme Court in Reading 8.1 confirms the attempt to build consensus and judges' tendency to concur – often after some bargaining – with the written opinion of another judge. The fewer the number of voices, the greater the authoritative thrust of the decision.

Of course, the most important way in which the Supreme Court can authoritatively "speak with one voice" is through unanimous decisions. As Peter McCormick (Reading 8.2) notes, the Supreme Court's unanimity rate has seen peaks and troughs. For non-*Charter* cases, the 1980s saw unanimity in roughly 75–80 per cent of cases; since the 1990s, that number has hovered around 70 per cent. *Charter* cases traditionally saw more dissents, with a heavily divided Court rendering unanimous judgments in only half of its *Charter* cases throughout the 1990s. By 2010, however, both *Charter* and non-*Charter* cases were unanimous between 60 and 70 per cent of the time. Unanimity during the McLachlin Court was 73 per cent, an impressive number considering that her Court was more likely to hear cases with nine-judge panels.[10]

Conferencing also seems to have facilitated another trend: a small but growing number of decisions delivered simply as unsigned opinions of "The Court." Aware of the political sensitivity of issues raised in certain high-profile cases, the Supreme Court has increasingly adopted a "united front" strategy for controversial decisions, such as those involving Quebec secession (Reading 2.5), assisted suicide (Reading 7.5) and Senate reform (Reading 2.6). Yet as Macfarlane notes, unanimity can have "the effect of both narrowing and broadening the Court's written reasons."[11] Compromise and consensus can lead to unclear opinions that avoid the core issues and limit guidance for lower courts. The Supreme Court's infamous unanimous decision *Law v. Canada* (1999), which tried to incorporate "human dignity" into a test for measuring discrimination in *Charter* equality claims but was abandoned after a decade, is one such example of the Court achieving unanimity at the expense of clarity.[12]

However, an institutional change that may curb the Court's quest for greater collegiality and consensus is the parallel development of the increasing use of law clerks. A law clerk is typically a recent law school graduate individually selected by a justice to aid in his or her work. The Supreme Court of Canada did not hire its first law clerk until the late 1960s, but today, each justice has three clerks, as well as an assistant and a court attendant. In addition to providing administrative aid, clerks play an important role in synthesizing factums for the justices and bringing contemporary legal and social-science scholarship before the Court. By acting as a "filter" for each justice, and by introducing them to the latest academic research, Supreme Court clerks wield tremendous power.[13]

A final change in the way the Supreme Court decides cases is what "authorities" it cites. Appeal court judges are obliged to support their decisions with precedents. Peter McCormick (Reading 8.2) shows that the Court has abandoned its early reliance on JCPC and English court precedents, to such an extent that during the McLachlin Court, 89 per cent of Supreme Court citations are to Canadian courts, and 59 per cent to the Supreme Court itself. Citations to all other foreign courts are down, including English courts (6 per cent), American courts (3.5 per cent) and other countries (1.5 per cent). McCormick concludes that Canada's *Charter* Revolution has given way to its own process of "consolidation and normalization" as the Supreme Court more frequently cites itself, demonstrating "an inward rather than an outward focus."

A second important trend in citation practices is the increasing reference to legal academic literature. Historically, precedents, not academic commentary, served as the primary source of authority. Four decades ago, the Supreme Court had an unwritten presumption against using contemporary academic sources. At the end of the 1960s, the Supreme Court Reports contained "barely a dozen references a year to academic texts, and virtually none to legal journals."[14] In the 1990s, by contrast, the Supreme Court cited hundreds of books and articles a year. While the Court has not abandoned academic citations (and still cites between two and three hundred articles a year), McCormick shows that that number has dropped considerably from the 1990s and early 2000s, when the Court was often citing four to six hundred academic pieces per year. The decreasing reliance on academic material reflects, for McCormick, "a judiciary that no longer needs the input of the academic profession to develop judicial doctrine." Like a student moving from a first-year course to a graduate seminar, the Supreme Court is increasingly confident to create its own ideas rather than rely on the authority of others.

As the Supreme Court has grown in prominence, political scientists have provided increased scrutiny of the norms and rules that govern judicial decision-making. In Reading 8.3, Emmett Macfarlane explores the origins and applicability of the three dominant theories of judicial decision-making: the legal view, the attitudinal model and the strategic model. The legal view, which sees law as distinct from politics or morality, constitutes "conventional wisdom" among lawyers, law professors and judges. However, like the adjudicative model described in Chapter 2, it can overstate the importance of precedent and understate the policy-making desires of judges. The attitudinal model – dominant among American political scientists – flips the legal view on its head, and argues that judges are "largely free to decide cases based on their ideological preferences." The strategic model builds on attitudinal assumptions but incorporates aspects of rational choice theory to determine how judges, based on their colleagues' votes and the reaction of other branches of government and the public, "modulate their choices accordingly."

While the attitudinal model and (to a lesser extent) the strategic model have been applied to the Supreme Court of Canada, Macfarlane shows how they have been critiqued for being reductionist and placing a narrow focus on self-interest. Judges are neither slaves to doctrine nor utility-maximizers seeking to strategically impose their policy preferences on an unsuspecting public. Instead, Macfarlane argues that students of high courts should pay closer attention to how institutional factors affect judicial decision-making, including norms of collegiality and how judges themselves conceive of their overall role vis-à-vis other political actors. A richer conception of how judges understand their role can help future scholars learn more about which factors affect Supreme Court decision-making.

Dave Snow and Mark Harding (Reading 8.4) explore precisely how scholars have changed their approach to judicial decision-making since the introduction of the *Charter*. They identify three distinct "waves" of scholarship. Whereas the first two largely concerned normative debates about legitimacy and "dialogue" (see Chapter 12), recent research has shifted to situating Canada within a broader comparative research project. Judged against those that preceded them, today's studies of judicial decision-making in Canada are more likely to be quantitative, methodologically rigorous and comparative. They have contributed to a far greater understanding of the inner workings and outputs of the Supreme Court of Canada. However, Snow and Harding worry that this empirical focus has led scholars to abandon important normative questions about the legitimacy of judicial review and the place of an empowered Supreme Court in Canadian democracy. "Far from being sterile," Snow and Harding conclude, these normative debates "remain especially fertile ground for scholarly exploration." These debates are taken up in Chapter 12.

NOTES

1   Supreme Court of Canada, "Statistics 2006–2016 – Category 3: Appeals Heard," 2017, http://www.scc-csc.ca/case-dossier/stat/cat3-eng.aspx. Calculations done by editors.

2   S.I. Bushnell, "Leave to Appeal Applications to the Supreme Court of Canada: A Matter of Public Importance," *Supreme Court Law Review* 3 (1982), p. 488.

3   Emmett Macfarlane, *Governing from the Bench: The Supreme Court of Canada and the Judicial Role* (Vancouver: UBC Press, 2000), p. 79; Lori Hausegger, Matthew Hennigar and Troy Riddell, *Canadian Courts*. 2nd ed. (Don Mills, ON: Oxford University Press, 2015), p. 102; Roy B. Flemming, *Tournament of Appeals: Granting Judicial Review in Canada* (Vancouver: UBC Press, 2004); Supreme Court of Canada, "Statistics 2006–2016."

4   Supreme Court of Canada, "Statistics 2006–2016."

5   S.I. Bushnell, "Leave to Appeal Applications to the Supreme Court of Canada," p. 479.

6   Donald R. Songer, *The Transformation of the Supreme Court of Canada: An Empirical Examination* (Toronto: University of Toronto Press, 2008), p. 116.

7   Hausegger, Hennigar and Riddell, *Canadian Courts*, p. 107; Macfarlane, *Governing from the Bench*, p. 93.

8   Ian Greene, Carl Baar, Peter McCormick, George Szablowski and Martin Thomas, *Final Appeal: Decision-Making in Canadian Courts of Appeal* (Toronto: Lorimer, 1998), p. 123; Macfarlane, *Governing from the Bench*, p. 93.

9   Macfarlane, *Governing from the Bench*, pp. 102–105, 121.

10   Cristin Schmitz, "Supreme Court heard fewer cases, was more divided, in past year," *Lawyer's Daily*, February 16, 2017, https://www.thelawyersdaily.ca/articles/3346/supreme-court-heard-fewer-cases-was-more-divided-in-past-year. Data are from 2000–2016, so they do not include McLachlin's last year on the bench. From 200 to 2009, the unanimity rate was 63 per cent. See Songer, *Transformation*, p. 116.

11   Macfarlane, *Governing from the Bench*, pp. 126, 123.

12   *Law v. Canada (Minister of Employment and Immigration)*, [1999] 1 S.C.R. 497. See also Thomas M.J. Bateman, "Human Dignity's False Start in the Supreme Court of Canada: Equality Rights and the Canadian Charter of Rights and Freedoms," *International Journal of Human Rights* 16, no. 4 (2012), pp. 577–597.

13   F.L. Morton and Rainer Knopff, *The Charter Revolution and the Court Party* (Peterborough: Broadview, 2000), p.110; Macfarlane, *Governing from the Bench*, pp. 106–107.

14   Greene et al., *Final Appeal*, p. 150.

8.1

Decision-Making in the Supreme Court
Justice Bertha Wilson

University of Toronto Law Journal 36, no.3 (1986), 227–248.
Reprinted with permission.

This tension [between the judge as an individual member of the Court versus the Court as an institution] is in a rather different category from the others I have mentioned. Some judges think that the best way for an appellate court to operate is for each judge to perform his or her judicial function independently – ideally with each member of the Court writing a separate judgment. Lord Reid was a great advocate of this approach. He believed that the diversity of views expressed, although admittedly making it more difficult to identify the *ratio decidendi* of the case, had the advantage of providing greater flexibility in the development of the law. Lower courts could pick and choose from among a variety of different judicial approaches the one that seemed most appropriate to changing social conditions; the others would simply wither away. Indeed, the majority of the Law Lords, when interviewed by Alan Paterson for his book, *The Law Lords,* expressed the view that between the 1940s and the 1970s the Court's attitude to dissenting judgments had changed radically. The pressure to present a united front had gone, and the right and duty of individual expression had become central to Their Lordships' perception of their role. On the other hand, the Judicial Committee of the Privy Council for many years published only one opinion, apparently on the theory that dissenting views would weaken the authority of the tribunal which, notionally at least, was only advising the sovereign on the resolution of the dispute.

Present practice in the Supreme Court of Canada lies somewhere between these two extremes. Different members of the Court hold differing views on the extent to which it is important to develop a consensus on particular legal issues. Is public confidence in the institution enhanced by unanimous judgments? Some think so. Or do strong dissents and separate concurring reasons reflect the potential for growth and change in the system? Is there any merit in "watering down" a judgment in the interests of unanimity? To what extent should judges try to persuade their colleagues to their point of view? And why do some judges find this process of judicial "lobbying" repugnant?

The answers one gives to these questions will depend, I think, on one's concept of what a collegial court is and how it should function. For some reason very little has been said or written on this very fascinating subject. Yet no consideration of the decision-making process of an appellate tribunal is complete without it. If there is, indeed, an obligation on a collegial court to strive for a consensus, or at least to submerge individuality in the interests of fewer sets of reasons, then the dynamics of the Court's process would seem to be extremely important. So let us take a brief look at what happens following the hearing of an appeal.

After argument is concluded the judges retire to a conference room to express their tentative views on the case. It is our practice for each judge to state his or her views in reverse order of seniority, beginning with the most junior judge and concluding with the most senior. The thinking behind this tradition was to avoid the more junior members of the Court simply adopting the views of their elders and betters. I may say that whatever may have been the case in the past, there is very little risk of this happening today; the members of the Court are, as the Chief Justice euphemistically puts it, "fiercely independent." It is interesting to note that the United States Supreme Court does it the other way round, proceeding on the basis of seniority, with the Chief Justice expressing his views first.

The first tentative expression of views at our conference will usually disclose whether there is any prospect of unanimity or whether there is clearly going to be more than one judgment. We decide at this conference who is going to prepare the first draft. This will be a member of the group which appears likely to form the majority. One of that group will normally volunteer or, if there is no volunteer, the Chief Justice will ask one of the group to take it on. The other judges then set aside their record in the case until a draft is circulated. Depending on the complexity of the case and the number of other judgments which a particular judge is working on, it may take several weeks or, regrettably, even months before a judgment is circulated. When this happens the judges on the panel get their papers out again, review their bench notes and any memoranda they may have dictated immediately following the hearing, study the draft, and decide whether or not they are going to be able to concur. They may at this point ask their law clerks to do some additional research.

Sometimes members of the panel will make suggestions for amendment which the author of the draft may accept or reject. Sometimes these suggested amendments are proffered in terms that that judge's concurrence is premised on their adoption. More often than not they are put forward on the basis that the judge views them as an improvement or clarification or as additional support for the result but would be willing to concur in any event. If amendments are made, the draft is recirculated and approval sought for the changes from those proposing to concur. The changes may be dropped at this point or, if not, they may spark concurring reasons.

A member of the Court may find the draft reasons totally unacceptable and will memo his or her colleagues that he or she proposes to dissent. This grinds the process of concurring to a halt since it is viewed as "bad form" to concur with the original reasons until you have seen the dissent. The same process of suggested amendment may take place with respect to the dissenting reasons. Two and maybe three sets of draft reasons are now in circulation. It is agreed at the next court conference that this is an appeal on which judgment should be released soon, on the next judgment day, if possible. The pressure is on. At this point, if not before, the individual judge's approach to decision-making becomes very important. This is particularly so in a court with a very heavy caseload. The ideal would, of course, be if all the judges could spend as much time on the cases assigned to their colleagues as they spend on the ones they are writing themselves. This is simply not possible. As the late Chief Justice Laskin put it: "If the case load is heavy, the tendency will be for judges to concentrate their limited time and their energy on opinions that have been assigned to them; and to show generous institutional faith in opinions in other cases prepared by others." Laskin concluded, therefore, that on a busy court "there is an institutional preference to support a majority result by reasons acceptable to a majority." I have no doubt that this is correct, and it should, of course, be the focal point of our concern about overworked courts. Under the pressure of a heavy caseload the delicate balance which should exist between judicial independence and collegiality may be displaced and collegiality may give way to expediency. This is an extremely serious matter for an appellate tribunal because the integrity of the process itself is threatened. The only answer is to grant fewer leaves and make sure that the balance between the Court's sitting time and its non-sitting time is appropriate and correct, one that allows adequate time for research and reflection, for conferring with one's colleagues, and for the drafting and redrafting of reasons for judgment.

First drafts have a way of developing a life of their own as they pass through a number of different hands. This is hardly surprising in view of the tensions in the decision-making process which I have been discussing. Nor is it surprising that there are multiple judgments on a court of nine people. Consciously or subconsciously, judges bring their philosophy of judging to bear on their judgments. Yet scant attention has been paid to the pre-suppositions about the role of the judge on which our different philosophies are based, and to the process by which decisions are reached. I believe this is changing. I think the advent of the *Charter* is bringing the role of the courts into sharper focus and that one of the benefits may be a more sophisticated appreciation by both lawyers and judges of what we do. Perhaps with that more sophisticated appreciation will go an enhanced sense of responsibility and dedication to our task.

8.2

The *Charter* by the Numbers

Peter McCormick

The End of the Charter Revolution: Looking Back from the New Normal
(University of Toronto Press, 2015), 169–225. Reprinted with permission.

I have told a story about an end to the Charter revolution – about a major disruption to the status quo that was gradually contained and absorbed and turned into a new normal.… My contention is that the Supreme Court of Canada's decisions transmit implicit information beyond their content, and I will identify eight objective indicators that all send the signal that the time of the really big changes is over, and that the Supreme Court has gone "steady state." My indicators are:

1. Caseload size & components
2. The frequency of dissents and separate concurrences
3. Citations to the jurisprudence other countries
4. Citations to academic authority

[*Ed. note*: In his book, McCormick examines four additional indicators: the size and content of decisions; the phenomenon of "swing" and "contest" judgments; judicial citations, age, and precedential replacement; and citations to minority reasons.]

1. Caseload Size and Components

Theoretically, any judicial decision in Canada can be appealed to the Supreme Court of Canada, but in practice only a vanishingly small percentage of Canadian cases actually get that far. 100 cases per year is a little high for current practice, but it sets a reasonable frame.

Most Supreme Court decisions are reserved judgments – after oral argument, the Court "reserves judgment," delivering its decision (outcome plus reasons) several months later. Some decisions (the proportion was as high as 30% in some years) are delivered as oral "from the bench" decisions on the same day as the oral argument. These tend to very abrupt dismissals, often the single formulaic sentence, "The appeal is dismissed for the reasons given in the court below." This "reserved for judgment" hurdle is important, and all the comments that follow are based on reserved judgments only.

The first measure of Charter importance is obvious – how many Charter cases are decided per year? But it isn't quite that simple, because the Court's total caseload has been shrinking fairly steadily for the last two decades. "Ten cases in 1990" is actually much less impressive, as a proportion of the Court's time and attention, than "ten cases in 2015." A more accurate measure is the proportion of the total caseload per year that involves Charter issues.

Figure 1: Charter cases as a proportion of all reserved decisions

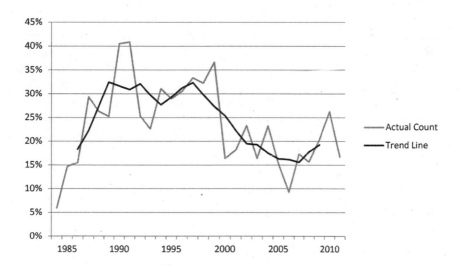

Figure 1 shows Charter cases as a proportion of the total caseload; the jagged line is the precise figure for each calendar year, the smoother line reflects five-year running averages (the two before and the two after as well as the specific year) to soften the lines and reveal the longer-term trends. These trends are clear: Charter cases as a proportion of total caseload rose from the obvious standing start, hovered just over 30% of the total caseload for about a decade, and then began a steady decline to their current level of something below 20%. Charter cases make up a steadily decreasing share of a gradually declining total caseload. 2006 was the first time since 1985 that the count for Charter cases was in single digits. In the single year of 1990, the Court handed down five Charter decisions every month; for the last dozen years, it has averaged barely one. These are the caseload figures of a Court that has moved on, a Court for whom the Charter is no longer the pre-emptive focus of its attention.

2. Frequency of Disagreement: Minority Reasons in Charter Cases

Most Supreme Court decisions of the last twenty-five years have been unanimous, with a single set of reasons joined by every member of the panel. However, there have also been a considerable number of decisions that included one or more dissenting opinions, meaning that one or more judges think that the majority got the decision wrong and they want to tell a wider world about this error....

The standard way of measuring the frequency of disagreement is to count the number of those cases that include a dissent. Figure 2 considers the year-by-year caseload of the Supreme Court in these terms, dividing the cases into Charter and non-Charter categories for the purpose. The figure works with five-year running averages to allow more general patterns to emerge from the year-on-year fluctuations. It is clear that Charter decisions have been much more dissensual than the other parts of the caseload, to such an extent that for the first decade, almost half of all Charter cases involved one or more dissents. Disagreement rates for other cases have generally been lower. After the middle of the 1990s, both Charter dissent fall significantly and dissent frequencies for the two types of cases converge....

Figure 2: Percentage of Cases with Dissent, Charter and Non-Charter

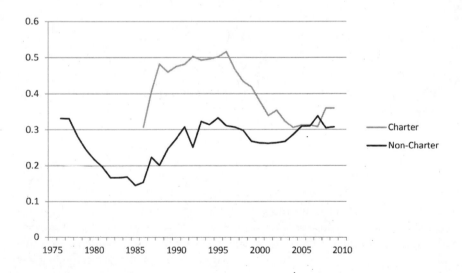

Dissents are not the only form of judicial disagreement; judges can also write separate concurrences, agreeing with the outcome but not agreeing (or at least not agreeing completely) with the reasons. Separate concurrences are easily undervalued because they do not challenge the outcome – indeed, the Supreme Court itself keeps its statistics in terms of whether or not decisions are "unanimous as to outcome," which carries the clear message that dissents do, but concurrences do not, undermine the solid unanimity of the decision.

This practice prematurely relegates the concurrences to an inappropriately low status. As former USSC Justice Scalia said, a decision that gets the reasons wrong gets everything wrong that it is the business of a judicial decision to accomplish. For appellate courts the reasons matter more than the outcome, because it is the reasons that constitute precedent and constrain the future decisions of its own and lower courts. Many separate concurrences involve serious disagreement, often signalled by the deceptively innocuous self-description of reaching the same outcome "but by a different route." It is tempting to think of dissents as "big disagreement" and concurrences as "little disagreement," but this is a mistake.

Figure 3: Participation in Separate Concurring Reasons, as % of Panel Appearances

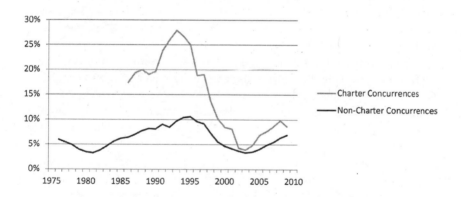

Figure 3 traces separate concurrences by calculating wrote-or-joined concurrence behavior in reserved judgments as a percentage of all opportunities, and running separate graph lines for Charter and non-Charter cases (again with five-year running averages).... Again, concurrences are much more frequent for Charter cases than they are for the rest of the caseload. Again, the pronounced surge through the Charter decade trails off sharply in the second half of the 1990s, although this too is much more exaggerated – instead of falling from 18% to 12%, it falls from almost 30% to less than 5%. And again the last decade has shown a considerable convergence of the frequency of concurring behavior.

For separate concurrences as for dissents, then, the clear pattern is a period of a prolific blossoming of ideas through separate opinions that flourishes briefly and then, after some point toward the middle of the 1990s, begins to fade. Since the critical change point in the middle, not at the end, of the 1990s, this is not the "McLachlin factor" promoting greater collegiality, as some accounts have it, but rather a change driven by something other than changes in personnel; my suggestion is that it represents the gradual establishment of a new constitutional orthodoxy and the end of a period of rapid change....

3. "Foreign" Citations

The entrenchment of a Charter of rights was a new adventure for Canada, but it is not unique in the world. Most obviously the United States has had an entrenched Bill of Rights for two hundred years, and an Americanization of Canadian constitutional law was one possible consequence. More generally, the judicialization of rights has a globally pervasive phenomenon, and it was to be expected that the Canadian Court might draw on the experiences of other countries to make up for the paucity of relevant domestic jurisprudence on which to draw. That is to say: we might anticipate a Charter-era rise in foreign citations, which my "revolution is over" thesis anticipates would be a largely transient phenomenon.

A first complication is that although the "American/not American" dichotomy frames the debate in the United States, it is much less useful for Canada, where citations to English courts have in a double sense not been citations to "foreign" courts. For one thing, an English quasi-court, the Judicial Committee of the Privy Council, served as Canada's highest court of appeal until 1949 – not a Supreme Court "of" Canada, to be sure, but effectively a Supreme Court "for" Canada. For another, the English high courts long held (and to a lesser extent still hold) a special status and authority within the common law; for some time even after 1949 the House of Lords was still arguably the "highest court" for the English common law (even if Canadian cases could not be appealed to it). I have been treating the Charter as part of a "big story" in the operations of the Supreme Court of Canada, but there is no question that another big story has been the steady waning of this English influence. For present purposes, it is therefore more useful to shift the focus from "non-Canadian" judicial citation to "foreign" judicial citation, using this last term in such a way as to exclude English judicial authority.

Table 1: Frequency of English, American and "Other" Citations

Chief Justice	SCC	Other Cdn	English	U.S.	Other
Rinfret	21.7%	16.7%	59.8%	0.8%	1.0%
Kerwin	28.7%	21.4%	46.9%	1.5%	1.5%
T/C/F	38.8%	24.3%	32.8%	3.1%	1.1%
Laskin	38.4%	29.4%	27.0%	3.3%	1.9%
Dickson	38.9%	35.3%	16.6%	7.2%	2.0%
Lamer	55.8%	27.5%	9.4%	5.6%	1.8%
McLachlin	58.7%	30.1%	6.1%	3.5%	1.6%

To support my argument, the figures for both elements of non-Canadian and non-English citation should exhibit two features: first, a noticeable increase around the time of the entrenchment of the Charter, and second, a steady decline from that initial jump. This double pattern reflects an initial judicial revolution that was unusually open to the exploration of alternative ideas or formulations, but this proved to be a window that gradually closed as domestic sources, and especially domestic judicial decisions, became available in sufficiently numbers. Table 1 hints at this in that the Dickson Court shows the highest relative frequency for both categories, although the modest increase in American citations starts earlier than might have been expected, in the 1960s, and the increase in "other" citations is so modest as to be almost invisible. Let me unfold the data from the Chief Justiceships into a year by year pattern in one of my by-now-familiar graphs.

Figure 4: Frequency of US and "Other" Citations, by Year

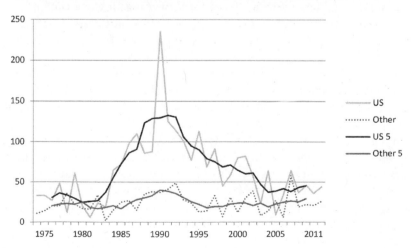

The picture for the citation frequency of American cases is quite spectacular. The pre-1980 figures reflect a long-standing practice for Canadian courts not to cite American authority outside of a few very specific areas of law (such as insurance law). But the upward trend is strong, with 1979 being the first time that the single-year count went above 50, and 1987 the first time that it went above 100. The count for 1990 almost makes the case in itself. The smoother curve within these dramatic fluctuations is the five-year running average for American citations. Having trended strongly upward through the Dickson years, and holding steady over the early part of the Lamer Chief Justiceship, the count then moves relentlessly down: 1995 is the last calendar year for which the American citation count for the full year is over 100, and 2005 is the first time since 1981 that it fell to single figures. American citation frequency again reflects the same trajectory of a new or altered behavior that is not sustained over time, signalling a judicial transformation that gives way to consolidation and normalization.

Much the same can be said, at a more modest level and less dramatically, of citations to "other" (that is: anything other than Canadian or English or American) judicial citations. Only once (2007) has the single year count exceeded fifty, and on only one other occasion (1992) did it approach this level. The smooth line reflects the five year running averages for other citations. Expressed this way, there is a (modest) surge for these citations, a bulge that peaks in 1990 with a couple of lower "waves" since. Even at this, much of the citation can be explained without making any use of such grand labels as "judicial globalisation" and without talking about legal and constitutional reasoning "going global" – it is instead a reflection of the common law that Canada shares with a number of other countries, such as Australia (and more recently New Zealand). In terms of judicial citations, we are indeed still "waiting for globalization."

There was some thought at the time of entrenchment that the citation of American case-law would become a strong component at least of our Charter jurisprudence, and possibly (with this as the beach-head) gradually of other areas of law instead. This has not happened. Similarly, the more recent academic literature has reverberated with the idea of a global community of judges, organized primarily around human rights law and especially entrenched human rights law, and driven by new forums and structures for interaction between national high court judges. There is no sign in the citation patterns of this having happened either. After an initial and Charter-prompted surge of interest in "other" and especially American case-law, such citations have sagged to (or even below) pre-Charter levels; the flip-side of less frequent citation of English sources has been more frequent citation of the Supreme Court itself, an inward rather than an outward focus.

4. Academic Citations

The Canadian Supreme Court also sometimes cites academic sources, although this development is more recent, and was initially more controversial, than one might expect. As recently as the 1950s, our Supreme Court had a firm practice of not allowing academic books or journals to be cited in arguments presented to the Court. Only in 1985 did CJ Dickson include a listing of "authors noted" to parallel the longstanding list of "cases noted," in the standard decision-reporting format.

Academic citations matter because they are a way of expanding the universe from which judges draw their cues and their ideas, and a way of involving a broader set of legal and academic professionals in the exploration of alternatives. Presumably the novelty of the Charter, and the doctrinal void it created, would make this source of ideas more attractive, a tendency is enhanced by the fact that recently judges are much more likely to have taught full- or part-time. But by a parallel logic, as the void is filled by new judicial decisions, the academic material would become less useful, less necessary.

Figure 5: Count of "Academic" Citations, by Year

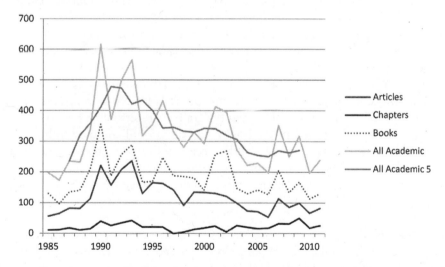

The second-from-the-bottom line represents articles in legal journals (this being the only type of academic articles that the court ever cites), and the third-from-the-bottom line represents citations to books (almost always legal texts, and typically the long-standing law school reference texts that have gone through a steady string of revised editions). The bottom line is labelled "chapters" and the reference is to articles in edited collections of some kind, sometimes the result of a specific conference, and including published proceedings of conferences. The oscillating line of the top pair is the year-by-year total of the three lower lines; and the smoother line that runs through its oscillations is the five-year running average of the total count.

This figure, too, follows the usual shape, both overall and for both books and articles (although not for the smaller count of chapters). There is a sharp rise through the late 1980s, peaking some time during the 1990s (although this peak is much earlier than the others), and then a slow slide back to the initial levels from which the jump began. This reflects a judiciary that no longer needs the input of the academic profession to develop judicial doctrine that responds to the revolutionary challenge, and is increasingly content to work off the more traditional source of judicial citation, especially its own.

Conclusion

Some of these signals are stronger and clearer than others. Perhaps no one of them is completely convincing on its own, but they reinforce each other by following a similar pattern and they all point to the same double story: first, something very significant and destabilizing happened to the Supreme Court of Canada in the late 1980s and the early 1990s; and second, that destabilization has more recently been contained. If we didn't already know about the entrenchment of the Canadian Charter of Rights and Freedoms, these patterns would send us looking for something of the sort.

My argument is that the new constitutional revolution is over. The ground-breaking mission of the Supreme Court is largely accomplished because the ground has been broken, and the trails that were being blazed in the 1980s are now been paved roads. Interesting things will continue to happen from time to time, and there may be the occasional surprise, but basically the Court from now on will be working within the framework that it has spent the last 25 years constructing. Dealing with legal disputes against the background of settled law is what courts do all the time; in this sense, the Charter has become business as usual.

This really should not be a surprise; we should all have known that this would happen at some point. What I have provided is the demonstration that there are solid and objective statistical measures, drawn from the Supreme Court's own performance and behavior and utterances, that confirm the fulfilment of those expectations.

8.3

Studying Judicial Behaviour

Emmett Macfarlane

Governing from the Bench: The Supreme Court of Canada and the Judicial Role (University of British Columbia Press, 2013), 15–38. Reprinted with permission from the publisher.

What are the sources of judicial decisions? Does "the law" matter? What conditions foster unanimous outcomes or divided ones? How do judges interpret the broadly worded, often ambiguous concepts enumerated in the *Charter*? Why does the Court sometimes exhibit "activist" behaviour and at other times appear deferential to legislative choices? Is the Court a legal institution or a political one?

Scholars have developed theories that purport to explain judicial motivations and decision making. Legal explanations of how judges make their decisions generally view questions of precedent, the language of constitutional and statutory provisions, and the application of legal rules to the facts of a given case as being essential to understanding case outcomes.... Political science explanations of judicial behaviour tend to view judicial decision making as a primarily political and value-laden exercise, where case outcomes are determined largely by the justices' personal policy preferences (that is, their different ideologies or "attitudes").... This chapter develops an approach ... that accounts for these various perspectives but that provides a more comprehensive and institutionally grounded appreciation of how the Court works.

The Legal View

The classic legal or formalist conception of judicial decision making envisions judging as a mechanical process in which the law is applied in an objective fashion. The emergence of legal realism in the 1920s is often said to have called this view into question by advancing the notion that, rather than discovering or merely interpreting the law, judges create it and are influenced by their personal backgrounds and ideological predilections. Although legal formalism in its purest form has long been cast in doubt (if it ever existed), this traditional view of judging often appears influential in contemporary political rhetoric. The controversy that erupted in 2009 over the fact that then nominee of the Supreme Court of the United States (US Supreme Court) Sonia Sotomayor dared to connect "empathy" to her vision for the role of a judge is illustrative. In order to secure her appointment, Sotomayor avoided defending her previous use of the term during her appearance before the Senate Judiciary Committee as well as not expressing disagreement when its members repeatedly invoked the rhetoric of judge as "neutral umpire," a description Chief Justice John Roberts used at his own committee hearing in 2005. Such rhetoric is surprising, if not completely absurd, given the partisan and openly ideological debates that surround appointments to the American court.

While few contemporary legal theorists would invoke the umpire analogy to describe a judge's role, they generally maintain that the law is substantially autonomous from politics. The modern legal view, broadly speaking, acknowledges that judges (especially at the appellate level) have a degree of discretion, but it maintains that they are constrained by precedent, the text of the constitution and the relevant statutes, and a host of long-held rules. Put simply, legal scholars argue that the law remains an important and independent factor in judicial decision making, even if it does not preordain the outcome of cases in the absolute fashion the pre-realist conception of legal theory may have once asserted.

This is not to say that all legal theorists hold homogenous views on what the law is and how judges ought to decide. The dominant perspective in both the United States and Canada is legal positivism, which conceives of the law as a system of rules that are generally distinct from politics or morality. This view constitutes conventional wisdom within the law profession, legal academic community, and, of course, among most judges....

Critics of the legal approach contend that legal rules provide little to no real constraint on judicial discretion. The harshest detractors have argued that there is no evidence to support the legal model's influence because factors such as precedent or textual analysis have not been (and could not be) subject to empirical falsification. Since justices on both sides of a given decision can cite precedents in their favour, it is not possible to gauge the impact of precedent in any systematic or meaningful way. In making this assertion, these scholars discount important, albeit qualitative, case study research that purports to demonstrate the influence of legal variables – particularly the arguments put forward by the parties to cases – on decision making at the US Supreme Court....

It does not help the credibility of the legalist approach that judges are usually less than forthright about the role that values and policy choices often play in their work. When Roberts US CJ talks about a judge as an umpire it simply rings untrue. Similarly, former Supreme Court of Canada Justice Claire L'Heureux-Dubé declared to a parliamentary committee examining reform of the appointments process in 2004: "We talk about ideology, but very few of us have any. You may not perceive that, but we look at a case by first reading and knowing the facts and then reading the briefs, and then we make up our minds." Statements such as these promote the belief among some political scientists that judicial reasoning serves only to mask political preferences and that, consciously or subconsciously, judges have constructed a smokescreen of legal verbiage to maintain authority and that they continue to exert policy influence.

The Attitudinal Model

Political scientists have studied judicial behaviour with respect to the US Supreme Court since the early twentieth century. C. Herman Pritchett, who is credited as one of the first political scientists to draw on legal realism to examine Supreme Court decision making, examined dissents, concurrences, voting blocs, and the ideological configurations of the Court's non-unanimous decisions to conclude that judicial differences of opinion were a result of the conscious or unconscious preferences and prejudices of the justices. Building on such work, and influenced by the "behavioural revolution" in political science, other scholars developed a full attitudinal model of judicial decision making. With lifelong judicial tenure and significant control of the docket, attitudinalists see Supreme Court judges as particularly free to decide cases based on their ideological preferences. Segal and Spaeth, the leading proponents of the modern attitudinal model, write:

> The attitudinal model represents a melding together of key concepts from legal realism, political science, psychology, and economics. This model holds that the Supreme Court decides disputes in light of the facts of the case vis-à-vis the ideological attitudes and values of the justices. Simply put, Rehnquist votes the way he does because he is extremely conservative; Marshall voted the way he did because he was extremely liberal....

The full attitudinal model has only recently been applied to the Supreme Court of Canada by C.L. Ostberg and Matthew Wetstein. Their 2007 book, which measures the justices' attitudes by performing a content analysis of newspaper editorials, finds that ideology plays a significant role in the justices' decisions. They explain that the role of these attitudes, however, is less definitive and more subtle than in the US context, and they acknowledge "that other factors, such as the cultural and historical legacy of parliamentary supremacy, the institutional norm of collegiality, and recent criticism of activist rulings, to name a few, help suppress attitudinal decision making by the post-*Charter* justices." Finally, despite confirming the major premise of the attitudinal model, Ostberg and Wetstein note that not all judges can be labelled attitudinalists, strategists, or legal pragmatists, adding that more research is needed that sheds light on the inner workings of the Court.

The most fundamental criticism of the attitudinal model is that it paints an extremely reductionist and instrumentalist portrait of decision making. For decades, this view prompted many legal scholars to ignore or dismiss the assertions of political scientists and their evidence. Attitudinal scholars espouse a narrow and simplistic conception of ideology. Despite the controls put in place to gauge the impact of attitudes relative to variables such as the justices' gender or relevant case facts, too much of the decision-making context is left out to provide a realistic portrayal of how judges make up their minds. Yet, for the proponents of the attitudinal model, its simplicity is a virtue. Modelling is not meant to provide a comprehensive depiction of the real world. Rather, by focusing on crucial aspects of reality, a model is said to "explain" a high percentage of behaviour through prediction.

In both the leading American and Canadian applications of this model, however, scholars are able to predict, on average, fewer than three out of every four judicial votes. Even this statistic only applies to sets of cases in areas of law to which the attitudinal model is successful – in some areas, even those where one might expect political attitudes to be salient, the model fails. This means that a significant portion of the justices' decisions are left unexplained by mere reference to attitudes....

However thin the attitudinal model is from a conceptual standpoint, and regardless of any arguments about the strength of the existing findings, the most damaging aspects of the approach stem from fatal methodological problems inherent in the way attitudinalists model judicial behaviour. First, problems pertaining to measuring judicial ideologies make the model inherently circular. Even ideological measures based on newspaper editorials about judicial nominees are not, contrary to the attitudinalists' claim, fully "exogenous" or independent, as they are no doubt often based on the judge's past voting records or views that journalists may label conservative or liberal but which could be premised on legal or other considerations of the nominee. As a result, the attitudinal model confirms its premise because the measures it derives for ideology are based on the very outcomes that it seeks to demonstrate are influenced by ideology in the first place....

The attitudinal model has long been the leading conception of judicial decision making in American political science literature. Given its underlying intuitive appeal, this is not surprising. A careful reading of either the American or Canadian Supreme Court's most prominent decisions makes clear that judges do not rely solely on objective legal rules or standards. Political values play at least some part in judicial reasoning. It is understandable that behaviouralists would want to develop an approach that finds systematic evidence of the role ideology plays in decisions. Unfortunately, as the preceding discussion makes clear, the attitudinal model does not present a complete picture of how courts and judges operate....

The Strategic Model

The strategic model is closely related to the attitudinal conception in that it also assumes that judges pursue their policy preferences, but it draws on rational choice theory to argue that in order to secure the majority decision on a multi-member court, judges must make strategic choices. Thus, judges may not vote according to their "sincere preferences" if they are not convinced the outcome of a case will be decided in their favour. In making decisions, they must consider the likely votes of their colleagues on the bench and the potential reaction of other actors in the system, including the legislative or executive branches of government, and modulate their choices accordingly....

Strategic scholars argue that their results show that the legal reasoning in written opinions, rather than just the votes on the case, is important and that justices prefer legal rules that reflect their policy preferences.... More importantly, strategic scholars acknowledge that their approach is complementary to attitudinal theory but argue that their model is more complete because it takes a more comprehensive view by accounting for the various processes and structures beyond attitudes that shape decision behaviour.... [Yet] the strategic model remains susceptible to many of the same critiques as the attitudinal approach. Many of the strategic studies conceive of institutions in the narrow sense of seeing them as a set of rules within which the game of maximizing self-interest takes place. Further, like the behaviouralist approach, the strategic model holds largely instrumentalist and reductionist assumptions about judicial decision making.

Critics suggest that rational choice models recognize "at best a narrow subset of possible human standards." While any number of goals could conceivably be examined under a rational choice model, most strategic scholars see implementing policy preferences as the goal of judges. Noting that policy goals are not the only inspiration for judges' decisions, Richard Posner's economic analysis suggests that other factors might include seeking prestige or popularity or seeking more leisure time. Posner, himself a judge on the Seventh Circuit of the US Court of Appeals, maintains that "judges are rational, and they pursue instrumental and consumption goals of the same general kind and in the same general way that private persons do." Without a more robust consideration of the ways in which the institutional environment helps to shape and even produce these different motivations, the strategic model cannot identify the circumstances under which the justices' strategic goals might change.

Insight into strategic behaviour on the Supreme Court of Canada is limited by a lack of available data. Only a handful of studies have examined strategic decision making, and those that have done so focus on particular aspects of the Court's work or on specific case examples. Scholars in Canada do not have access to docket sheets, internal memoranda, and private notes of the justices that have made the approach more comprehensive in the US context. Systematic analysis of any strategic behaviour at the Court may not be possible until researchers have access to such papers, which are currently restricted in the national archives....

More recently, Wetstein and Ostberg have examined strategic leadership on the Court, finding that the voting behaviour of each of the three most recent chief justices changed significantly on becoming chief, leading them to write more majority opinions and fewer dissenting opinions. They found that Chief Justices Brian Dickson and Antonio Lamer emerged as "task leaders" who were able to guide the Court through control of majority coalitions, whereas, in her first few years as chief justice, Beverley McLachlin has been a pre-eminent "social leader" through an effort to increase the level of consensus on the Court. The ability of the chief justice to strike panels and assign decisions is an important institutional feature in the Canadian context....

Historical Institutionalism

Historical institutionalists consider the broader structural and institutional factors that shape judicial decisions. These scholars challenge the instrumentalist view of judicial decisions as merely the aggregate effect of individual behaviour. Historical institutionalism considers norms, values, and ideas to be an integral part of the analysis, going beyond the strategic model's consideration of institutional rules and the actions of other political actors. Central to the approach adopted here is a focus on judicial "role perceptions" – the institutional actors' sense of duty, obligation, or recognition that their actions are inherently meaningful – which inform the justices' behaviour in complex ways that intersect with ideological, strategic, and legal considerations....

Just as the historical institutionalists are guided by a much broader, more porous conception of institutions, I argue that judicial scholars should incorporate into theories of decision making a more expansive notion of the judicial role.... An interpretivist, institutionally grounded vision of the judicial role would necessarily account for institutional culture, collegiality, and a judge's broader perspective on her – and her institution's – place in the rest of the political system and wider society. This sense of the primacy an actor's role perceptions can have on behaviour requires an historical institutionalist account....

Critics of historical institutionalism do not see it as providing sufficient analytic clarity or evidentiary rigor to accomplish these goals. Referring to the approach as post-positivist, Segal and Spaeth complain that by relying on justices' sense of obligation, post-positivist scholars reduce the legal approach to something that could never be proven because virtually any decision can be consistent with it if all that is required is for justices to convince themselves that their decisions are legally appropriate. The authors claim that "by accepted standards of scientific research" the post-positivist brand of neo-institutionalism simply cannot generate a valid explanation of judicial decision making because it is not falsifiable....

Historical institutionalists are aware of the potential problems implicit in their approach, particularly the threat of raising a structure versus agency debate. If scholars blur the distinction between the institutional context and the actors' motives or ideas too far, then it becomes impossible to develop a reasonable picture of the influences on decision making. As Clayton writes, "if ideas and institutions are inseparable, if everything is connected to everything else, then it is unclear where new institutional analysis leads." Historical institutionalism clearly stands as more of an "approach" than a full-fledged theory of judicial decision making. The utility of its premises, however, is that rather than attempting to explain decisions through prediction, the approach seeks to impart a more comprehensive understanding of the complex processes at play. As a result, historical institutionalists can take a diverse, cosmopolitan path to examining judicial behaviour, one that draws on, and builds bridges between, legal, attitudinal, and strategic theory....

The historical institutionalist account can also seek to accommodate a more realistic understanding of the justices' motivations. Lawrence Baum suggests that in many ways the strategic approach looks unrealistic, given that individual justices have little capacity to affect outcomes nor do they gain much in the way of tangible benefits from advancing favoured policies. He argues that the evidence amassed by behaviouralists and rational choice scholars tells us very little about the motivations at play, as they really only demonstrate that the different outcomes judges reach accord to differences in policy preferences.... By examining judges' "audiences," Baum contends that we can understand the "motivational basis for patterns of judgments that are incorporated into the dominant models" as well as those patterns that go beyond them. His basic point is that, like any professionals, judges care about what people think about them. For this reason, the esteem of their colleagues, the wider legal community, and even the media and the public at large matter. Attention to the reaction of these various audiences can consciously or subconsciously rein in attitudinal or strategic behaviour....

A Focus on the Judicial Role

The criticism laid out in this chapter of these dominant approaches should not be mistaken for a dismissal of their underlying premises. Just as many political scientists consider legal factors important to understanding how courts work, many legal scholars now acknowledge that judicial attitudes play at least some part in Supreme Court of Canada decisions. In fact, if legalists were to completely discount the role of judges' values in decision making, then they themselves risk adopting the straw man conception of the legal model that has been erected by some attitudinalists. Yet, a reliance on the attitudinal model leaves us with an impoverished view of judicial decision making, no matter how reasonable its foundation....

Integrating judicial role conceptions into the analysis allows this study to extend beyond describing each of the important stages of the Court's decision-making process. It provides a consideration of the institutional forces at play that may be independent from, or otherwise constrain or shape, attitudinal, strategic, or legal motivations. As a result, this approach is also conducive to building bridges between the competing theories of judicial behaviour. There can be little doubt that a justice's background, ideology, personal values, or life and educational experiences influence her decision making. Some of the justices themselves have acknowledged as much in speeches or writing. Yet, there can also be little doubt that different justices allow those values to come into play to varying degrees and in varying ways. Conceived of in this way, role perceptions might be broadly understood as the judge's "world view," overlapping with, but extending beyond, mere political ideology.

8.4

The Three Waves of Post-*Charter* Supreme Court Scholarship

Dave Snow and Mark S. Harding

American Review of Canadian Studies 45, no.4 (2015), 451–466. Reprinted with permission.

Within political science, the comparative study of law and politics has evolved considerably over the past half-century. Studies of judicial decision-making have grown in methodological sophistication, while qualitative approaches have provided greater insight into how courts work. Contemporaneously, several countries introduced institutional reforms that increased judicial power, most notably through constitutional or legislative bills of rights. In this article, we examine the interaction of these factors in the Canadian context, particularly how the 1982 constitutional entrenchment of the Canadian Charter of Rights and Freedoms affected the scholarly study of the Supreme Court of Canada. The Court quickly grew in political influence and became a focal point for political scientists, as scholars sought both to explain how it functioned and to assess the effects of its newfound policy-making role.

Below, we identify three "waves" of post-Charter Supreme Court scholarship, each of which has been marked by distinct goals, methods, and debates. The first wave, from the introduction of the Charter until roughly 1997, involved prospective theoretical debates over national unity, institutional change, and the potential of the Court to create social transformation. The second wave, from 1997–2004, drew more conclusively from decades of jurisprudence. Scholars focused extensively on the "dialogue" and "legitimacy" debates, and began to probe how the Charter had produced other institutional changes such as interest group litigation and legislative "Charter-proofing." While there was a growth in empirical data, these data were often used to bolster normative arguments concerning the implications of judicial review for Canadian democracy.

Although such debates still persist, we argue that the dominant discourse has shifted to such a degree that there now exists a third wave of post-Charter Supreme Court literature. Stemming from seminal works on the Canadian Court by American political scientists in the mid-to-late 2000s, the third wave has been less normative, more explicitly comparative, and committed to methodological rigor. In contrast to first- and second-wave philosophical and ideological debates, it is characterized by the use of established quantitative and qualitative methods based in the comparative political science literature. Moreover, third-wave scholars have the explicit goal of situating the Canadian Court within a larger global research project; no longer is Canada treated as *sui generis*....

The First Wave: National Unity, Legalized Politics, and Social Change

As recently as 1987, Paul Fox wrote that Canadian political scientists had "neglected the judiciary" compared to the other branches of government. The constitutional entrenchment of the Canadian Charter of Rights and Freedoms in 1982 marked a dramatic change, as Canadian political science was suddenly preoccupied with prospective speculation about the Charter's impact on

Canadian democracy. During this first wave of post-Charter literature – from roughly 1982 to 1997 – scholars were primarily concerned with the national unity, institutional change, and normative questions about liberal democracy.

Compared with later periods, the first wave of post-Charter scholarship focused on federalism and national unity.... Along these lines, Peter H. Russell predicted the protection of mobility rights (section 6) and minority language rights (sections 16–23) would overcome the "balkanization" of provincial protectionist policies. Although the issues subject to Charter scrutiny – such as affirmative action, abortion, and censorship – would be politically controversial, they would be litigated by national interest groups that would transcend once-dominant regional cleavages. First-wave scholars also predicted that, because the Supreme Court hears appeals from both provincial and federal courts, the Charter would be a unifying document insofar as it would act to equalize (and hence, centralize) provincial policies across the country....

First-wave scholarship was also characterized by normative ideological disagreement. As summarized by Richard Sigurdson, early Charter scholarship was characterized by "left- and right-wing Charterphobia." Progressive critics, more prominent in the first wave than later waves, largely consisted of law professors. They shared three assumptions: first, they agreed that the Charter had legalized politics, but held that, because judges and lawyers were part of Canada's socioeconomic elite, legalized politics meant conservative politics. Second, they claimed a bill of rights was inherently antistatist, and that it would constrain other branches of government from advancing the welfare state. Finally, progressive critics feared the Charter undermined Canadian identity by moving Canada away from its collectivist roots and toward American individualism.

By contrast, conservative Charter critics – almost exclusively political scientists – emphasized framers' intent, limited government, and individual rather than group rights. These scholars tended to fuse institutional and ideological criticisms. Institutionally, they claimed that the Charter was antidemocratic, as it moved the unelected judiciary from an adjudicative to a policy-making role. Ideologically, they argued that the biggest beneficiaries of the Charter had been a cadre of left-wing interest groups, referred to as the "Court Party." ...

Not every political scientist studying the Charter shared the view of either progressive or conservative critics; Sigurdson, for example, called both sides "unnecessarily alarmist." However, when compared with second-wave debates below, first-wave scholarship comes across as tentative, speculative, and even tame.... Methodologically, the first wave of post-Charter scholarship mostly adopted a traditional institutional approach, characterized by the centrality of law, the impact of institutions on political behavior, and a holistic view of political regimes. Moreover, the academic debates were quite insular, analyzing Canada as *sui generis*. Small-N case analyses typically focused on the Charter itself and Supreme Court decisions; there was little direct study of how other political actors had responded to the Charter....

The Second Wave: The Results Are In

By the late 1990s, the Supreme Court's influence on public policy had become undeniable, and large-N empirical studies of Charter cases enabled scholars to draw broad conclusions about jurisprudential trends and the growth of judicial power.... These studies were not characterized by advanced quantitative methods such as regression techniques, they nevertheless bore out the fact that the Supreme Court's influence on public policy was undeniable, as many first-wave scholars had predicted....

The second wave, which occurred from roughly 1997–2004, was unquestionably characterized by two inter-related normative debates: the legitimacy debate and the dialogue debate. The legitimacy debate, supplementing first-wave arguments with new evidence from over a decade of judicial review of the Charter, concerned the institutional and democratic consequences of increased judicial power. On one side were Charter critics, who believed the judiciary had overstepped its bounds and that the implications were negative for Canadian democracy. The most prominent critics were Morton and Knopff, who claimed in *The Charter Revolution and the Court Party* that 15 years of Charter jurisprudence had transformed Canadian politics to a regime that verged on judicial supremacy. [*Ed. note*: See Reading 12.4] ...

Interestingly, the first-wave left-wing opposition to the Charter had largely eroded, as most progressive scholars supported the Charter. Progressive scholars applauded rather than derided the growing influence of interest groups; because of judicial independence, they believed courts were the best venue to protect the rights of the politically disadvantaged minorities that lacked a voice in legislatures. For both sides in the legitimacy debate, two decades of evidence led to different conclusions about the Charter's benefits to Canadian democracy. The legitimacy debate occurred in tandem with the "dialogue" debate, the beginning of which set the stage for much second-wave scholarship. [*Ed. note*: See Readings 12.7 and 12.8] ...

Scholarly disagreement over the dialogue metaphor sparked a third feature of second-wave scholarship: exploration of the extent to which the Supreme Court's Charter decisions influenced other political institutions. Janet Hiebert was the first scholar to systematically examine the capacity of Parliament to respond to Charter decisions. She argued that although Parliament could and should engage in coordinate constitutional interpretation, in many cases it had shirked this responsibility. In a more optimistic study, James B. Kelly claimed judicial activism had been increasingly displaced by "legislative activism." Because the federal cabinet and Department of Justice vetted legislation for Charter violations to ensure Charter compliance prior to judicial review, Kelly found the Court often deferred to Cabinet choices – although the increased role for the Department of Justice gave some credence to first-wave predictions about the legalization of politics. These studies reflected the second-wave movement to explore how the Supreme Court's Charter decisions affected the other branches of government.

Like the first wave, second-wave debates were largely Canada-centric. However, they centered on new scholarly ideas contained in seminal works – particularly by Hogg and Bushell (1997) and Morton and Knopff (2000) – that transformed the literature. And although some new empirical studies analyzing nearly two decades of jurisprudence shed light on the Court's enhanced institutional role, the main debates remained primarily normative, with empirical studies often cited to buttress normative arguments....

The Third Wave: Comparative Politics and Methodological Rigor
The scholarly debates of the second wave were by no means settled by the time third-wave scholarship began to penetrate the political science literature in Canada.... [Yet] they have taken a back seat to empirical studies of Supreme Court outputs that build on and seek to replicate methodologies and theories from scholarship on the US Supreme Court.

Like the second wave, the shift to third-wave scholarship, which we define here as taking place from 2004 to present, was driven largely by new scholarly works that shifted the dominant ideas and paradigms within the subfield. An early example was Roy B. Flemming's *Tournament of Appeals*. Flemming, an American political scientist, drew explicitly from American scholarship on the US Supreme Court to examine the Supreme Court of Canada's selection process for hearing appeals.... Subsequently, C.L. Ostberg and Matthew E. Wetstein's *Attitudinal Decision Making in the Supreme Court of Canada*, published in 2007, was a more expansive example of American scholars applying methods that had been used to explain judicial decision-making in the US Supreme Court....

... Ostberg and Wetstein's objectives, methods, and conclusions marked substantive differences from the first and second waves. Whereas first- and second-wave research was largely qualitative, the sheer number of cases analyzed meant Ostberg and Wetstein were interested primarily in quantitative results, and their manuscript made heavy use of formal modeling and advanced quantitative methods. Moreover, although the authors recognized that their findings could have implications for ongoing normative debates – such as the fact that conservative justices were as likely as liberal justices to engage in activism, and that the appearance of the Women's Legal Education and Action Fund (LEAF) had a positive effect in equality cases – they were not particularly concerned with whether the presence of attitudinal conflict was positive or negative for the legitimacy of the court or for Canadian democracy as a whole. These issues were relegated to the sideline in favor of methodological rigor and theory-testing.

These third-wave themes – normative disinterest, methodological rigor, and comparative replicability – also animated Donald Songer's 2008 book, *The Transformation of the Supreme Court of Canada* [Ed. note: See Reading 6.10]. The book was a major empirical study of virtually every aspect of the Court, from individual justices' demographic characteristics to the changing nature of the types of cases they heard. Songer sought to move away from normative debates and examine the Court objectively, using quantitative statistical methods whenever possible. He claimed, with some justification, that the existing political science literature on the post-Charter Court had hitherto been dominated either by "doctrinal" accounts that traced the evolution of jurisprudence or "normative" critiques of the Court's growing influence....

Although some of his findings were at odds with the attitudinal model, Songer, along with American political scientist Susan Johnson, joined Ostberg and Wetstein for a 2012 manuscript, *Law, Ideology, and Collegiality*.... Building on the two previous works, it found religion, region, and gender were statistically significant explanations of judicial decision-making, and confirmed that attitudinalism could not explain unanimous decisions.... These findings led empirical weight to assumptions that many post-Charter scholars had intuitively held about the Court for years, from the mundane (small panels and shorter judgments are more likely to produce unanimity) to the substantial (constitutional issues and interest group participation are more likely to produce divisions).

... The elements that defined these studies – rejecting normative debates, committing to comparative methods and theories, and using Canada to test comparative theories of decision-making – were also prominent in the most recent empirical study of the Supreme Court, Canadian scholar Emmett Macfarlane's *Governing from the Bench* [Ed. note: See Reading 8.3]. Like other third-wave scholars, Macfarlane criticized Canadian law and politics research as descriptive, atheoretical, and insufficiently empirical. Macfarlane saw his study, which drew from 28 interviews with clerks and former justices, as a qualitative complement to Songer's primarily quantitative analysis.... Whereas Songer highlighted a number of factors that have changed within the Court,

Macfarlane's institutional analysis provided an explanation for why those factors have changed. He found both exogenous and endogenous institutional changes have acted as independent variables, and that the changes endogenous to the Court – such as relaxed justiciability rules, increased workload for clerks and staff, more permissive use of social science evidence and intervenors, and increasing norms of collegiality and consensus-building – were especially instructive. Macfarlane describes a Court infused with agency, composed of justices who have willingly moved it to its growing position of importance, explicitly deciding cases to strengthen the legitimacy of the institution itself at the expense of personal ideology.

Although Macfarlane took issue with many of the assumptions inherent in the attitudinal literature, his work nevertheless represents third-wave scholarship for a number of reasons. *Governing from the Bench* continues the commitment to methodological rigor and engagement with dominant comparative (and primarily American) political theories. Like the third wave as a whole, it is more comparative politics than political philosophy; its debates concern the relative utility of different approaches (institutionalism vs. behavioralism) rather than the desirability of regime characteristics or different theories about how to address inequality in society....

The Third Wave in Comparative Perspective

Our analysis of the three waves demonstrates the formative power of ideas in influencing scholarship and changing the terms of debate. Just as new data and new ideas in the late 1990s shifted the debate away from first-wave speculation to second-wave debates about democratic legitimacy and inter-institutional dialogue, several particularly influential studies brought forward new ideas that have systematically restructured the major debates in the Canadian law and politics scholarship. These studies have ushered in a new era of scholarship that is far more concerned with understanding how the Supreme Court comes to its decisions than whether those decisions are good or bad.

This is a welcome development for scholars of law and politics both inside and outside of Canada. At the broadest level, third-wave studies have provided a wealth of information about how the Supreme Court of Canada works, the types of decisions it hears, and the different factors affecting its decision-making. More specifically, the third wave takes seriously the comparative literature on judicial decision-making and presents Canada as a case study to be evaluated according to criteria that have been tested in other jurisdictions. The third-wave commitment to comparative methods and approaches surely represents a maturing on the part of Canadian law and politics scholarship....

While the commitment to comparative theory should be commended, we do not necessarily believe that it ought to be accompanied by the concomitant retreat from normativism that has characterized much of the third wave.... This understandable desire to avoid normative questions could lead to the unfortunate conclusion that Canadian scholars ought to leave normative debate to the philosophers or, even worse, that first-and second-wave debates have been settled.... As the third wave continues, the major question will be whether its methodological rigor and empirical findings are used to enrich or replace the normative questions from earlier waves of post-Charter scholarship....

Recent events in Canada further emphasize that normative questions related to the dialogue and legitimacy debates ought not to be abandoned. The Harper government era (2006–2015) in particular featured several important clashes with the courts, and the Supreme Court specifically, over a number of key planks of its legislative agenda, including safe injection sites, youth criminal justice, mandatory minimum sentences, and prostitution. These cases and their corresponding legislative sequels demonstrate the utility of the dialogue metaphor and the continued relevance of the debate over the appropriate role of courts and legislatures. Similarly, recent controversy over the Harper government's failed attempt to appoint Justice Marc Nadon to the Supreme Court, in addition to its propensity to appoint former prosecutors and conservative legal academics to the bench, illuminates the persistence of the legitimacy debate [*Ed. note*: See Chapter 11].

As the Supreme Court of Canada continues to adjudicate cases that push the boundaries of judicial policy-making, both methodological and normative rigor will remain as important as ever to understanding and continuing these debates. Third-wave empirical surveys of the Supreme Court of Canada can thus provide for intellectual cross-fertilization by contributing to this global research project, producing empirical evidence to enrich the normative debates in Canada and elsewhere. Far from being sterile, debates over the legitimacy of judicial review and the place of the Supreme Court in Canadian democracy remain especially fertile ground for scholarly exploration, particularly given third-wave contributions.

8.5
Key Terms

Concepts

appeals "as of right"

attitudinal decision-making

Charter revolution

collegiality

concurring opinion

conference

dissenting opinion

factums

law clerks

leave to appeal

legal model of decision-making

majority opinion

normative vs. empirical

oral argument

panel size

public importance test

role conceptions

seriatim opinion writing

strategic model of decision-making

unanimity

Institutions, Events and Documents

Canadian Charter of Rights and Freedoms (1982)

Law v. Canada (Minister of Employment and Immigration), [1999] 1 S.C.R. 497

Reference re Secession of Quebec, [1998] 2 S.C.R. 217

Supreme Court Act, R.S.C., 1985, c. s-26

9

Judicial Review and Federalism

Constitutional Origins

The *Constitution Act, 1867* united on a federal basis the separate colonies that had until that time constituted British North America. The federal form was essential to the act of union. None of the provinces, particularly Quebec, was willing to relinquish the degree of political autonomy and self-government to which they aspired and to be subsumed under a single unitary state. At the same time, the most influential leaders of the Confederation movement, men like John A. Macdonald and George Brown, desired a strong central government based on "legislative union" in order to avoid what they considered to have been the near fatal weakness of the central government in American federalism.[1]

The *Constitution Act, 1867* represented an uneasy compromise between these conflicting goals. Provincial demands for preserving local autonomy and self-government were accommodated through a distribution of legislative powers between the newly created federal Parliament and the provincial legislatures, primarily in sections 91 and 92 of the *Act*. The centralists' goals were recognized by a very broad wording of Parliament's section 91 law-making powers, and by the unilateral power to strike down provincial laws through the devices of disallowance and reservation in sections 55–57 and 90 of the *Constitution Act, 1867*. The result was a written constitutional document establishing a highly centralized form of federalism. As it turned out, this original design was modified considerably by subsequent political developments in which judicial review played a major role.

It is now accepted that judicial review is a corollary to a federal form of government based on a written distribution of powers between two levels of government. For a federal division of legislative powers to be effective, there must be a mutually acceptable process for settling the inevitable disputes over where one government's jurisdiction ends and the other's begins. Neither level of government can be permitted to define unilaterally (and thus to redefine) the boundaries of federal-provincial jurisdiction, as this would violate the equal status of both levels of government, a central principle of federalism.[2] In practice, the need for a "neutral umpire" of federal systems has been met through judicial review by a final court of appeal.

Historical Origins

Originally, judicial review of the Constitution came easily and without controversy in Canada. The *Constitution Act* took the form of an Imperial statute, and section 129 mandated the continuation of the existing legal regime. This meant that the *Constitution Act* was subject to the already existing *Colonial Laws Validity Act*, which required consistency of colonial law with British Imperial statutes. The Judicial Committee of the Privy Council was charged with the responsibility of enforcing this policy. The Judicial Committee had served as the final court of appeal for British North America prior to Confederation, and it simply continued in this capacity after 1867. Any alleged violation of the federal division of powers set out in the *Constitution Act* could be challenged in the existing superior courts of the provinces and appealed from a provincial court of appeal directly to the Judicial Committee in London.

This explained the founders' lack of urgency in creating a Supreme Court of Canada. The absence of a national court of appeal also made the introduction of judicial review in Canada easier. When the federal government moved to exercise its section 101 authority to create such a court, controversy quickly erupted. As Professor Jennifer Smith explains, the attempt to create the Supreme Court of Canada became entangled in the already robust politics of federal-provincial competition (Reading 9.1). This controversy was engendered in large part by the inclusion of the reference procedure as part of the *Supreme Court Act*. Some "provincial rights" advocates perceived the creation of a "federal" court of appeal and the simultaneous creation of a reference authority vested exclusively with the federal government as an ill-disguised attempt to refurbish the already controversial disallowance power by cloaking it with judicial legitimacy. This suspicion of "disallowance in disguise" was supported by the original form of the reference procedure and the comments of John A. Macdonald.

Provincial fears of a centralizing Supreme Court notwithstanding, the *Supreme Court Act* was finally adopted in 1875. The newly created Supreme Court of Canada immediately began to exercise the power of judicial review and did so without controversy. However, its decisions could be appealed to the Privy Council, and it could be avoided altogether by *per saltum* appeals directly from a provincial court of appeal to the Privy Council. Both of these routes of appeal were abolished by amendments to the *Supreme Court Act* in

1949, which established the Supreme Court of Canada as the final and exclusive court of appeal for Canada. Until 1949, however, the Supreme Court was decidedly the junior partner in overseeing the judicial aspects of Canada's constitutional development. Its early decisions were frequently overturned by the Privy Council, and the doctrine of *stare decisis* meant that it was bound to follow the Privy Council's lead. This meant that until 1949, the Supreme Court of Canada was functionally more like a middle-tier British appeal court. The habits and procedures associated with such a court – such as trying to follow the "right" precedent rather than creating a new precedent – lingered on for almost another generation.

Constitutional Interpretation

Constitutional interpretation raises problems that do not occur in common law or statutory interpretation. Because constitutional law regulates the powers of governments (rather than the private rights of individuals or corporations), it inevitably affects the making of public policy. Judicial review thus injects into the judicial process a political dimension that previously did not exist. Common law judges were reluctant to acknowledge the policy-making function conferred on them by judicial review, as it seems to contradict and undermine so many of the traditional aspects of the judicial process. As a result, Canadian, British and Australian judges tended to transfer the techniques of statutory interpretation to constitutional interpretation.

This was especially true of the Privy Council's approach to the *Constitution Act*. While this is easily explained by British judges' unfamiliarity with the practice of a "written constitution" (indeed, to them it was just another Imperial statute), it had the unfortunate effect of establishing this mode of constitutional interpretation as the standard for Canadian judges to follow. Discontent with the substance of the Privy Council's constitutional decisions (discussed below) led in turn to criticisms of its technique of interpretation. These critics called for an approach to constitutional interpretation that acknowledged the inherent policy dimensions of constitutional law and reflected the need to adapt a written constitution to the changing needs and circumstances of the society it governs. The late Professor William Lederman summarized this issue as follows:

> There are principally two types of interpretation – literal or grammatical emphasizing of the words found in statutes and constitutional documents; and sociological, which insists that constitutional words and statutory words must be carefully linked by

judicially noticed knowledge and by evidence to the ongoing life of society.[3]

Examples of these two different approaches to constitutional interpretation are found in the excerpts from the Privy Council opinions of Lord Sankey (Reading 9.2) and Lord Atkin (Reading 9.3). Lord Sankey articulated his now famous "living tree" approach in his opinion in the well-known "Persons Case."[4] Henrietta Muir Edwards, a leader of the women's suffrage movement in the West, had been proposed for an appointment to the Senate from Alberta. At issue was whether any woman could be appointed to the Senate. Legally, the case boiled down to whether the term used in section 24 of the *Constitution Act*, "qualified persons," included women. The Supreme Court of Canada ruled that it did not, basing its decision on internal evidence of the *Constitution Act* itself and the indisputable fact that, at the time of Confederation, women did not have the right to vote, much less to hold public office. While this decision was arguably correct in a narrowly technical sense, it was overturned on appeal by the Privy Council. Lord Sankey stressed the necessity of interpreting constitutional language in light of society's changing beliefs and needs and not just internal grammatical constructions and the original intent of the framers.

Lord Atkin's very different approach to constitutional interpretation occurred in the 1937 *Labour Conventions Case*.[5] This case raised the issue of Parliament's authority to enact legislation implementing Canada's treaty obligations when the legislation involved matters that would normally have fallen under the provinces' section 92 jurisdiction. Despite the recent *Statute of Westminster* (1931), which had affirmed the sovereignty of Canada in the conduct of her foreign affairs, Lord Atkin ruled that the federal government's treaty-making power did not allow it to trench upon matters of provincial jurisdiction when implementing a treaty. This decision was widely perceived as a serious blow to the effective conduct of Canadian foreign policy and was blamed on Lord Atkin's "watertight compartments" view of Canadian federalism. This view was widely condemned as being out of touch with the economic and political realities of twentieth-century Canada.

Constitutional Politics

The Privy Council's decision in the *Labour Conventions Case* is only one in a long series of constitutional cases that progressively narrowed the scope of the federal Parliament's section 91 powers while expanding the section 92 jurisdiction of the provinces. Parliament's broad residual power to make laws for the "Peace, Order and Good Government of Canada" was whittled away to almost nothing by the Privy Council's "emergency doctrine" test. The unrestricted power to make laws for the "Regulation of Trade and Commerce" was soon reduced by judicial interpretation to the narrow ambit of "interprovincial trade." At the same time, the Privy Council's decisions expanded what originally appeared to be the rather meagre provincial powers to make laws in relation to "Property and Civil Rights in the Province" and "all matters of a merely local or private Nature in the Province." Throughout all of these decisions, the Privy Council adhered to the textually oriented, legalistic method of interpretation described above.

Mounting dissatisfaction with the Privy Council's performance as final constitutional arbiter for Canada manifested itself in the "judicial nationalism" discussed in Chapter 2. Following the recommendations of the 1939 *O'Connor Report*, Parliament abolished all appeals to the Privy Council in 1949. While Canadian critics of the Judicial Committee were unanimous in condemning the provincial bias of its decisions, they were far from agreeing on a diagnosis of the problem or a prescription for an acceptable "made in Canada" jurisprudence after 1949. One school of thought criticized the Judicial Committee of the Privy Council for being too textual and literal in its interpretation of the Constitution, and thereby failing to make it a "living constitution," in accord with the changing times. The other principal group of critics accused the Judicial Committee of not following the text's centralist orientation closely enough.[6] The inability of Canadian scholars, judges and political leaders to agree on an appropriate constitutional jurisprudence has carried over into the post-1949 era. The latent pro-Ottawa attitudes of the old Judicial Committee critics have not been acceptable to Quebec leaders or other "provincial rights" advocates. The result has been a continuing credibility problem for the Supreme Court whenever it acts as final arbiter in jurisdictional disputes between Ottawa and the provinces.

One of the most important post-1949 federalism cases was the 1976 *Anti-inflation Reference* (Reading 9.4).[7] As Peter Russell recounts, this case seemed to present a perfect opportunity for the Supreme Court, led by its new Chief Justice, Bora Laskin, a known centralist, to repudiate once and for all the moribund "emergency doctrine" of the Privy Council. Several post-1949 decisions of the Supreme Court had silently ignored the old "emergency doctrine" and spoke instead of an "inherent national importance" test (also known as "national concern"). Centralists anticipated that the time was ripe to institute this new and much broader basis for the exercise of the federal government's residual power. The public policy significance of the case was underscored by the large number of intervenors, consisting of both provincial governments and private groups. The Supreme Court itself tacitly acknowledged the policy dimensions of the case by devising new procedures to allow for the introduction of very untraditional, socio-economic evidence by both sides.[8] While the Supreme Court's final decision modestly increased the "Peace, Order and Good Government" authority of the federal government, it did not repudiate the work of the Privy Council. The "emergency doctrine" was preserved and even extended to peacetime situations. This compromise result may appear somewhat anticlimactic, but it illustrated the Supreme Court's sensitivity to conflicting elite views of federalism and its instinct for the middle ground when this occurs.

As it turned out, the *Anti-Inflation Reference* was the first in a series of Supreme Court decisions during the late 1970s that dealt with federalism issues – all of which were won by Ottawa.[9] These decisions contributed to federal-provincial tensions on other fronts and led to growing provincial suspicions about the dependence of the Supreme Court on the Liberal government in Ottawa. Following quickly on several of these cases, an article appeared in the press suggesting that "the image of Chief Justice Laskin and his eight 'sober, grey men' acting as spear-carriers for the federal prime minister fails to add anything to one's hopes for improved national unity."[10]

The implications of these remarks so upset Chief Justice Laskin that he purposely went out of his way to respond publicly. At a hastily arranged "Seminar for Journalists" the same month, the late Chief Justice declared:

> I have to be more sad than angry to read of an insinuation that we are "acting as spear carriers for the federal prime minister" or to read of a statement attributed to a highly respected member of the academic community that "the provinces must have a role in the appointment of members of the Supreme Court in order to ensure that they have confidence that it can fairly represent the interests of the provincial governments as well as of any federal government." ...
>
> ... The allegation is reckless in its implication that we have considerable freedom to give voice to our personal predilections, and thus to political preferences.... We have no such freedom, and it is a disservice to this Court and to the work of those who have gone before us to suggest a federal bias because of federal appointment.[11]

There is no doubting the sincerity of the late Chief Justice's remarks, and he was subsequently supported by Professor Peter Hogg in an article that argued persuasively against a federal bias in recent Supreme Court decisions.[12]

But in politics, perceptions, not facts, often carry the day, and this 1978 incident betrayed a continuing lack of confidence in the Supreme Court among provincial elites.[13] This problem took on heightened significance in the 1980s, as the Supreme Court began to interpret and enforce the 1982 *Charter of Rights and Freedoms*. It was not a coincidence that less than a decade after the clash between former Chief Justice Laskin and Professor Black, the Meech Lake Accord (1987) proposed to amend the Constitution to ensure all new Supreme Court appointments would be made from lists submitted by the provinces. While the Meech Lake Accord was eventually defeated, the judicial nominations provision demonstrated continuing tensions between the Court and defenders of provincial rights.

Professor Peter Russell has argued that the Supreme Court is so sensitive to maintaining its image as a "neutral umpire" that it is willing to sacrifice the consistent application of legal principle and precedent in order to achieve "politically balanced" results.[14] The *Anti-Inflation Reference* (Reading 9.4), the *Patriation Reference* (Reading 2.4) and the *Secession Reference* (Reading 2.5) each illustrate Russell's thesis. In *Anti-Inflation*, the Court escaped an apparent "no win" situation by upholding the wage and price restraint legislation but on the very novel – and narrower – grounds of a "peacetime emergency." Similarly, the Court's ruling in the *Patriation Reference* has been described as "bold statecraft ... [but] questionable jurisprudence" (See Readings 2.4 and 2.6). The Court's ruling that federal unilateralism was "legal but unconstitutional" represented a political compromise designed to induce both sides to resume negotiating (which they did). As Mandel (Reading 2.4) and others have noted, however, it took an unprecedented legal ruling on constitutional conventions to reach this result.

In the *Secession Reference*,[15] the Court once again gave something to both sides, but at the expense of legal clarity. The Court ruled that a "unilateral declaration of independence" (UDI) by Quebec would be unconstitutional. However, the Court went on to say that if the separatist option were to win a "clear majority on a clear question," then there would be a constitutional duty for Ottawa and the rest of Canada to negotiate the terms of separation with the Quebec government. If the governments of English Canada failed to negotiate "in good faith," then Quebec would be justified in proceeding alone. As in the 1981 *Patriation Reference*, both sides claimed victory. By recognizing and accommodating the legitimacy of multiple "models" of the federation, Robert Schertzer (Reading 2.5) argues the decision enhanced the Court's own legitimacy as an arbiter of federalism disputes.

The Court's decision in the *Secession Reference* reignited the debate over the "impartiality" of the Supreme Court in federal-provincial relations. Critics of the decision in Quebec and the West charged that the Court had acted in a partisan manner both in agreeing to hear the Liberal government's reference and in the specifics of its ruling.[16] While these criticisms are themselves argu-ably partisan (to varying degrees), they connect with a broader theoretical literature that judicial review has an intrinsic centralist bias. Drawing upon a comparative perspective, André Bzdera has marshalled persuasive evidence that judicial review has had a centralizing effect in each of the nine federal states studied.[17] Bzdera explains the "net centralist/nationalist bias of federal high courts" by their institutional linkages to the central government: creation, administration, budget, internal procedures and especially the appointment of judges. Bzdera's findings are supported by American political scientist Martin Shapiro. Shapiro's comparative study of centralized court systems – those with a final national court of appeal – found that they tend to "serve upper class and nationalizing interests rather than dominant local interests and thus [are] more satisfactory to persons trying to break through the web of local interests."[18] Bzdera's and Shapiro's findings are consistent with the centralizing effect of the Court Challenges Program noted in the introduction to Chapter 6. These arguments help explain the provincial governments' persistent attempts to gain an agency in the appointment of judges to the Supreme Court of Canada, as witnessed in the 1987 Meech Lake Accord.

In the last two decades, the Supreme Court's federalism jurisprudence has shifted. On the one hand, during the 1990s and 2000s, the federal government won most federalism disputes with the provinces in the Supreme Court, cer-tainly the most prominent ones. On the other hand, a series of federal victories came at a cost: the Supreme Court's downgrading of the "national concern" branch of Parliament's authority to make laws for "Peace, Order and Good Government" (POGG). From 1995 to 2003, in a series of cases involving to-bacco advertising, environmental regulation, the gun registry and marijuana legislation, Supreme Court majorities avoided POGG analysis entirely, often claiming it was "unnecessary."[19] It was unnecessary because the Supreme Court upheld the federal legislation in each case under the federal government's nar-rower power to make criminal law under section 91(27) of the *Constitution Act, 1867*. While the federal government rode its winning streak, it had to do so without the use of its strongest player, the national concern branch of POGG.

Commentators recognized that federal criminal law power was a less pow-erful constitutional instrument than POGG, particularly when the criminal dimension of a federal law is only tangentially connected to the regulatory as-pect that intrudes on provincial jurisdiction.[20] In the 2010 *Reference re Assisted Human Reproduction Act*,[21] the limits of the criminal law power were finally exposed. As Dave Snow (Reading 9.6) recounts, in 2004 the federal government created sweeping federal legislation to govern assisted human reproduction. The law, initially justified by a Royal Commission as justifiable under POGG's "national concern" branch, consisted of criminal prohibitions and a national regulatory framework meant to address everything from human cloning to the governance of private fertility clinics. In 2006, the Quebec government put a reference question to its Court of Appeal asking whether the legislation violated the provincial jurisdiction over health.

Quebec won, first at the Court of Appeal, and then in a narrow 5–4 decision at the Supreme Court of Canada. While the federal prohibitions were upheld (most were not even challenged), the vast regulatory framework contemplated by the federal government was deemed unconstitutional. Two decades of sustained efforts to create a national assisted human reproduction regime were shuttered. The Court did not even address POGG's national concern branch; more tellingly, the federal government did not even offer it as a defence of the legislation. Snow suggests that the national concern branch of POGG "may be well and truly dead," while "punishment and penalties must be at the forefront of [future] criminal legislation that could potentially impugn on health policy." In the following years, the Harper government suffered a number of high-profile losses regarding its own authority vis-à-vis the provinces, including its attempt to create a national securities regulator (the 2011 *Securities Reference*),[22] and its attempts to unilaterally reform the Senate and amend the *Supreme Court Act* (see Readings 2.6 and 11.6). If there ever was a federal winning streak at the Supreme Court of Canada, it has certainly come to an end.

Notwithstanding these important victories for the provinces, questions about the Supreme Court's "balance" remain. While the perception of the Supreme Court as "neutral umpire" may endure in English Canada, some Quebec scholars continue to see a centralist bias in its rulings.[23] This debate must also be placed in the real world of Canadian politics. Patrick Monahan's contribution (see Reading 9.5) demonstrates that, in Canada's ongoing federal-provincial tug-of-war, a loss in court does not necessarily mean a policy loss. His case studies show how the availability of alternative policy instruments often permit a government to achieve indirectly what the courts have forbidden it from doing so directly. These alternative means include the enactment of the same policy by the other level of government; delegation of the disputed jurisdiction from the "winner" to the "loser"; substitution of an alternative regulatory instrument; and even constitutional amendment. More recently, Gerald Baier has argued that a greater emphasis on intergovernmental collaboration has diminished the importance of the judiciary in federalism disputes, particularly during the twenty-first century.[24] Several recent high-profile cases show that we cannot discount the Court's role; the *Securities Reference*, *Reference re Assisted Human Reproduction Act*, the *Senate Reference* and a divided case concerning the destruction of federal gun registry data[25] show that the Supreme Court's role as the final arbiter remains important.

NOTES

1   This skepticism toward federalism appeared quite justified at the time. The Confederation process took place during and after the bloody American Civil War, which had pitted the "states' rights" advocates of the Southern slave-holding states against the national government.

2   The disallowance and reservation powers violate the principle of parity, and for that reason it has been argued that Canada is not a "true" federal state. However, Ottawa has not used disallowance or reservation since 1943 and 1961, respectively. Although both powers still exist *legally*, it is generally accepted that a convention of non-use has been established, and that it is politically unacceptable for the federal government to reactivate either of these powers. For example, in 1989, when the Quebec government invoked the section 33 notwithstanding clause to reinstate its "French-only" public signs law (which had been struck down by the Supreme Court a month earlier), some MPs called on Prime Minister Mulroney to use disallowance to protect the rights of the anglophone minority in Quebec. With much of his Cabinet from Quebec and Alberta, two of the most vocal advocates of provincial rights, it was not surprising that the Prime Minister did not consider disallowance a viable option.

3   W.R. Lederman, "Thoughts on Reform of the Supreme Court of Canada," *The Confederation Challenge*, Ontario Advisory Committee on Confederation, Vol. II (Toronto: Queen's Printer, 1970), p. 295.

4   *Edwards v. A.G. Canada,* [1930] A.C. 123, 1 DLR 98 (PC). The case was decided October 18, 1929.

5   *Canada (Attorney General) v. Ontario (Attorney General)*, [1937] UKPC 6, [1937] A.C. 326.

6   See Alan C. Cairns, "The Judicial Committee and its Critics," *Canadian Journal of Political Science*, 4 (September, 1971), p. 301.

7   [1976] 2 S.C.R. 373.

8   See introduction to Chapter 6.

9   The principal cases were two cases dealing with provincial regulation of broadcasting, *Capital Cities Communications v. C.R.T.C.*, [1978] 2 S.C.R. 141, and *Public Service Board v. Dionne*, [1978] 2 S.C.R. 191; and two cases dealing with provincial authority to tax and regulate the production of natural resources, *CIGOL v. Government of Saskatchewan*, [1978] 2 S.C.R. 545, and *Central Canada Potash v. Government of Saskatchewan*, [1979] 1 S.C.R. 42.

10 Edwin R. Black, "Supreme Court Judges as Spear-Carriers for Ottawa: They need watching," *Report on Confederation* (February, 1973), p. 12.

11 Bora Laskin, "Judicial Integrity and the Supreme Court of Canada," *Law Society Gazette* (1978), pp. 118, 120.

12 P.W. Hogg, "Is the Supreme Court of Canada Biased in Constitutional Cases?" *The Canadian Bar Review* (1979), p. 722.

13 A telling example of Western-Canadian skepticism toward the Supreme Court was the front cover of an issue of *Alberta Report*, an influential regional weekly news magazine. Referring to the federal Cabinet's decision to refer the legal issues of the French language dispute in Manitoba to the Supreme Court, the cover headlines read: "FRENCH ROULETTE – Manitoba is hauled into Ottawa's court over provincial language rights" (April 23, 1984).

14 Peter H. Russell, "The Supreme Court and Federal-Provincial Relations: The Political Use of Legal Resources," *Canadian Public Policy* 11, no. 2 (1985), pp. 161–170.

15   *Reference re Secession of Quebec*, [1998] 2 S.C.R. 217.

16   See the essays by Josée Legault, Jacques Yvan Morin, Ted Morton and Alan Cairns in David Schneiderman, ed., *The Quebec Decision: Perspectives on the Supreme Court Ruling on Secession* (Toronto: James Lorimer, 1999).

17   André Bzdera, "Comparative Analysis of Federal High Courts: A Political Theory of Judicial Review," *Canadian Journal of Political Science* 25, no. 1 (1993), pp. 3–30.

18   Martin Shapiro, *Courts: A Comparative and Political Analysis* (Chicago: University of Chicago Press, 1981), p. 24.

19   *RJR-MacDonald Inc. v. Canada (A.G.)* [1995] 3 S.C.R 199; *R. v. Hydro-Québec* [1997] 3 S.C.R. 213.; *Reference re Firearms Act*, [2000] 1 S.C.R. 783; *R. v. Malmo-Levine*; *R. v. Caine* [2003] 3 S.C.R. 571, 2003 SCC 74.

20   Gerald Baier, *Courts and Federalism: Judicial Doctrine in the United States, Australia, and Canada* (Vancouver: UBC Press, 2006), pp. 140–142.

21   [2010] 3 S.C.R. 457.

22   *Reference re Securities Act*, [2011] 3 S.C.R. 837.

23   See Jean Leclair, "The Supreme Court of Canada's Understanding of Federalism: Efficiency at the Expense of Diversity," *Queen's Law Journal*, 28, no. 2 (1993), pp. 411–453; Eugénie Brouillet, "Canadian Federalism and the Principle of Subsidiarity: Should We Open Pandora's Box?," *Supreme Court Law Review* 54 (2011), pp. 601–632. Gerald Baier, however, supports Russell's thesis that the Court has been largely balanced. See Baier, *Courts and Federalism*.

24   Gerald Baier, "The Courts, the Constitution, and Dispute Resolution," in Herman Bakvis and Grace Skogstad, eds., *Canadian Federalism: Performance, Effectiveness, and Legitimacy*. 3rd ed. (Toronto: Oxford University Press, 2012).

25   *Quebec (Attorney General) v. Canada (Attorney General)*, [2015] 1 S.C.R. 693. A majority of justices (5-4) allowed the federal government to destroy the information, which Quebec wanted to retain. All three Quebec justices wrote the dissent (with Justice Abella concurring).

9.1

The Origins of Judicial Review in Canada
Jennifer Smith

Canadian Journal of Political Science, 16 (1983), 115–134. Reprinted with permission.

For many years students have been taught that the practice of judicial review in Canada is less important than it is in the United States. This is because it has had less scope, and it has had less scope because until recently Canada's written constitution, unlike the American Constitution, included no bill of rights. Whereas in both countries the courts, acting as "umpires" of their respective federal forms of government, have had the power to declare laws beyond the competence of the jurisdiction enacting them, the American courts have had the additional and, to many, fascinating power to enforce against governments the guarantees of the rights of citizens contained in the *Bill of Rights*. Obviously this line of comparison is outmoded now. After a prolonged and at times bitter debate, the federal government and nine of the ten provincial governments reached agreement last year on a set of amendments to the *British North America Act*, among them a *Charter of Rights and Freedoms*. As a result, the breadth of the courts' power of judicial review more closely approximates that possessed by their American counterparts. Is this development consistent with the nature of Canada's constitutional arrangements? Does the *Charter* provide the basis of the completion of an initially limited power? ...

As early as the fifteenth century, it was customary for the King's Privy Council rather than English domestic courts to hear appeals arising out of colonial matters. This practice was regulated by the *Privy Council Acts* of 1833 and 1844, which established the Judicial Committee of the Privy Council, specified its membership and authorized it to hear appeals from colonial courts. Thus the Judicial Committee acted as the highest appellate court for the colonies. As [B.L.] Strayer points out [in *Judicial Review of Legislation in Canada*], it showed no inclination to question its authority to review the validity of colonial legislation, undoubtedly because the colonies themselves possessed only limited or subordinate legislative powers. He attributes considerable importance to the precedent it set throughout the Empire for the exercise of a similar power by colonial courts. According to Strayer, we must look to the British colonial system, and especially its doctrine of judicial review of colonial legislation, for the origin of judicial review in Canada: "The constitutional law of the Empire in 1867 apparently embraced the convention that where legislative powers were granted subject to limitations the courts would enforce those limitations. The *BNA Act* was drafted and enacted in this context.".…

Strayer's search for an explanation of judicial review arises out of his insistence that it is not "absolute," that is, not fully guaranteed in the *BNA Act*. In his opinion, the relevant clauses of the *Act* gave Parliament and the local legislatures too much regulatory power over the courts to support such a view, power more in keeping with the principle of parliamentary as opposed to judicial supremacy. Indeed, according to W.R. Lederman, Strayer implies that an "element of judicial usurpation" figures in its establishment, an implication Lederman cannot accept. By contrast, Lederman reads into sections 96 to 100 of the *Act* an "intention to reproduce superior courts in the image of the English central royal courts." If he can demonstrate that these English courts had acquired a "basic independence" enabling them to withstand even the undoubted supremacy of the British Parliament, then courts deliberately modelled after them in Canada would assume a similar status. In "The Independence of the Judiciary," Lederman undertakes such a demonstration. [*Ed. note:* See Reading 5.1] …

Yet a closer examination of the framers' views may throw some light on this debate.… [Their] clearly worded statements indicated a view of federalism rather more in line with the American example than that set out in the Quebec scheme. Taken together with the views expressed at the Quebec Conference and in the debate in the Parliament of Canada, they also suggest that no one had any illusions about the significance of judicial review, particularly as it related to the distribution of legislative powers between Parliament and the local legislatures. The point at issue was whether the type of federalism set out in the Quebec Resolutions required it. Under the Resolutions, the central government possessed the power to disallow local laws just as the British government retained the power to disallow Parliament's enactments, a parallel feature not unnoticed by critics of the scheme like Christopher Dunkin. Disallowance not only undermined the need for judicial arbitration, whether by the Judicial Committee or a national court, it also suited partisans of parliamentary supremacy like Jonathan McCully, who clearly understood the threat to this supremacy posed by a tribunal patterned after the American Supreme Court.

The question of whether to establish a final appellate court was settled eight years after Confederation when Parliament finally used the power it possessed under section 101 of the *BNA Act*. The debate at the time is illuminating, since in picking up the threads of the earlier arguments it does so in the light of some years' experience of union. It also reveals an attitude towards the new court and its power of judicial review somewhat at variance with that held today.…

… While the constitutionality of the bill was generally accepted, there remained the question of members' understanding of the Court's position in relation to the central government. Here opinions varied. In introducing the bill, Fournier stressed the need for a court to settle disputes arising out of conflicting jurisdictional claims, particularly when the extent of provincial powers was in question. In this sense he portrayed the proposed court as the completion of the "young construction" established at Confederation, citing earlier remarks by Cartier and Macdonald in support of this view. Along side the notion of the court as an impartial arbiter, however, there is present in his speech the rather different view of it as a substitute for the failing remedy of disallowance. As he explained, the government was required daily to "interfere" with provincial legislation considered *ultra vires* the provinces' jurisdiction, and it was falling behind in the task. The result was that the statute books were filled with an "enormous mass of legislation" of dubious constitutionality, leaving citizens uncertain about what was and was not law. In light of this definition of the problem, namely, the excesses of provincial legislatures, the suggestion that the new court could resolve it more speedily than the central government's power of disallowance must have struck his listeners as doubtful. Indeed, it quickly became clear he was seeking legitimacy, not speed. The Governor-General, he pointed out, could disallow provincial laws only on the advice of the federal cabinet, in turn advised by law officers of the Department of Justice, and this state of affairs, predictably, was "not satisfactory." What was needed was a tribunal whose decisions – especially those adverse to the provinces – were acceptable to all parties. Apparently Fournier viewed his "independent, neutral and impartial court" as an instrument of the central government. He contended that Ottawa needed "an institution of its own" in order to ensure proper execution of its laws because, however contrary to the spirit of Confederation, the time might come when "it would not be very safe for the Federal Government to be at the mercy of the tribunals of the provinces."

Some members feared that the powers conferred on the court would conflict with the principle of parliamentary supremacy. An Ontario member, Moss, excused the length of his speech by emphasizing the gravity of establishing a tribunal whose power to determine jurisdictional disputes finally rendered it "paramount" to Parliament itself. Rejecting this view, Macdonald interpreted the Court's role under the "Special Jurisdiction" clauses as one of informing the "conscience" of the government. It would function simply as an adviser to the government in much the same way as the Judicial Committee did when asked for advice by the British Crown. Macdonald's view was consistent with Fournier's exposition of these clauses for, as noted earlier, the Minister of Justice had stated that the Court's decisions in such instances were to have the same effect as its decisions in reference questions, namely, a kind of "moral weight." Since moral weight undoubtedly influences but does not command, it would appear that for both men the supremacy of Parliament remained unimpaired. Their position seemed well grounded for neither the reference case provision nor the special jurisdiction clauses gave the new court's opinions the status of legal judgments. Yet many of their colleagues assumed that it did, especially Robert Haythorne, a Liberal senator from Prince Edward Island, who warned members that "their power of interpretation [on constitutional matters] ceased when the bill passed." ...

Yet while both the constitution and practical necessity apparently pointed in the same direction, members of parliament clearly entertained two different views of the role of the proposed court in the very area that was thought to stand most in need of its services, namely, jurisdictional conflicts. As is evident from the above, some saw in the court an instrument of the federal government that would enable it to deal more satisfactorily with provincial pretensions. How else to interpret Senator Scott's contention?: "The fact that so many of the Acts in the different Provinces were *ultra vires* showed that a bill of this kind was necessary." The raft of suspect provincial statutes, for Scott, posed a problem for which the central government was inadequately equipped. But why was it ill equipped when it possessed the power of disallowance? As noted earlier, for Fournier the central government's problem was its inescapable partisanship. Only a court and its long-standing reputation of nonpartisanship could tame the aggression of the provinces without provoking bitter controversy. Left unstated was the assumption that the central government, by contrast, was unlikely to experience the embarrassment of an adverse ruling in its exercise of legislative power. Thus the view of the court as a tribunal whose very impartiality would serve the federal cause ignored the obvious tension between that impartiality and the central government's partisanship. The opinion of men like Macdonald that the proposed bill must not and, indeed, did not affect the principle of parliamentary supremacy simply overlooked it in favour of the central government. Had he not said that the special jurisdiction clauses were "principally for the purpose of informing the conscience of the Government"? Despite his interest in setting up the court, he was obviously unwilling to relinquish ultimate determination of the constitution to it.

At the same time, as we have seen, many supposed that the new court did signal a shift from the central government's control over the distribution of legislative powers to judicial determination of disputes arising out of it. It might be objected that this view was as incorrect as Macdonald's on the grounds that the executive's control in this respect was only partial to begin with, limited to supervision of provincial enactments through its power of disallowance, and that Parliament's own enactments in turn were subject to disallowance by the British government. Moreover, the Judicial Committee, representing the judicial mode of constitutional arbitration, had retained its position as the highest court of appeal for the new colony at the outset of Confederation. Nevertheless, it is clear that for many participants in the debate, the Court's institution spelled a retreat from the executive fiat of disallowance in favour of the judicial remedy. And they assumed, contrary to Macdonald's supposition, that its jurisdiction would extend to impugned federal as well as provincial enactments. Indeed, opponents of the court, such as Senator Kaulbach of Nova Scotia, criticized it precisely because it would "take from this Parliament the right to decide constitutional questions." ...

... In the event it appears that those who subscribed to the second view were closer to the mark. Certainly the new Supreme Court agreed with them. As Strayer points out, in its first reported constitutional decision, *Severn v. the Queen* (1878), the court, "without showing any hesitation concerning its right to do so," found an Ontario licensing statute invalid on the ground that it interfered with Parliament's jurisdiction over trade and commerce. The following year, in *Valin v. Langlois*, it reviewed and upheld the *Dominion Controverted Elections Act, 1874* as a valid exercise of Parliament's legislative power. In the latter case, Chief Justice Ritchie set out the Court's power of judicial review with unmistakable clarity:

> In view of the great diversity of judicial opinion that has characterized the decisions of the provincial tribunals in some provinces, and the judges in all, while it would seem to justify the wisdom of the Dominion Parliament, in providing for the establishment of a Court of Appeal such as this, where such diversity shall be considered and an authoritative declaration of the law be enunciated, so it enhances the responsibility of those called on in the midst of such conflict of opinion to declare authoritatively the principles by which both federal and local legislation are governed....

Although the Chief Justice's generous conception of the court's role in constitutional matters reaffirmed both the hopes and fears of those who supposed its decisions would be as authoritative as he claimed they were, the notion of the court as an instrument of the central government was not wholly eliminated. There remained the reference case provision of the *Supreme Court Act* which obliged the court to advise the executive on any question referred to it. To the extent that this obligation is understood as an executive advisory function as opposed to a judicial one, it recalls Macdonald's view of the court as an aid to the government, or the "conscience" of the government. If so, it is hardly surprising that the provinces were uncomfortable with the comprehensiveness of the reference case provision, especially since it enabled the government to refer provincial laws to the courts for a ruling on their validity. In the event, Parliament's competence to enact it was tested before the Judicial Committee in *Attorney-General for Ontario v. Attorney-General for Canada* (1912). The provinces choosing to intervene argued that it imposed an executive function on the court and thereby violated section 101 of the *BNA Act* which permitted Parliament to establish a tribunal possessed of judicial powers only. In his judgment delivered on behalf of the Judicial Committee, Earl Loreburn, L.C., appeared to accept their contention that the Court's task in the reference case was in essence merely advisory and therefore nonjudicial, but he did not consider this fatal to its judicial character as a whole.

The competing views of the court apparent at its inception have left their mark on it. For example, those who approve its role as umpire of the federal system are critical of the fact that its establishment was permitted rather than required under the terms of the *BNA Act*, that its members are appointed formally by one level of government rather than both, and that the reference case procedure remains. On the other hand, partisans of parliamentary supremacy, understandably less enamoured of the American Supreme Court whose example inspired the criticisms just mentioned, prize these very features as symbols of the Court's ultimate dependence on the will of Parliament....

Viewed in the light of the older controversy about the Court, the debate culminating in the recent set of amendments contained in the *Constitution Act, 1982* took a familiar turn. In the earlier contest, both opponents and partisans of judicial review focussed attention on its implications for the distribution of legislative powers so critical to the shape of the country's federalism. While some saw in it a solution to conflicts arising out of competing jurisdictional claims, others interpreted it as a direct challenge to their presumption in favour of Parliament's control of the constitution. Over a century later, the issue of judicial versus parliamentary supremacy surfaced again in connection with the proposed *Charter of Rights and Freedoms*. Prime Minister Pierre Trudeau, a determined champion of the notion of a charter, often defended his cause without even referring to the task it necessarily imposes on the courts. Instead, he claimed that it would "confer power on the people of Canada, power to protect themselves from abuses by public authorities." A charter would liberate people by preventing governments from denying specified freedoms. On the other hand, opponents of the idea, like the then Premier of Saskatchewan, Allan Blakeney, attempted to counter the undeniable appeal of this claim by drawing attention to the role of the courts that it implied. According to Blakeney, including rights in a written constitution means transferring responsibility for them from duly elected legislatures, the democratic seat of governments, to nonelected tribunals. It amounts to requiring the courts to make "social judgments" in the course of interpreting a charter's clauses, judgments which, in his view, properly belong to "the voters and their representatives." In the event, a *Charter of Rights and Freedoms* now forms part of Canada's newly amended constitution. Are we entitled to conclude, then, that acceptance of the *Charter*, and the increased scope for judicial review that it entails, signals a resolution of the issue of parliamentary versus judicial supremacy in favour of the latter? The answer is not quite.

It is true, as Peter Russell points out, that section 52 of the *Constitution Act, 1982*, by declaring the Constitution of Canada to be the "supreme law" and any law inconsistent with its provisions to be of "no force or effect," gives the courts' power to invalidate unconstitutional laws an explicit constitutional footing for the first time. Further, under the provisions of the new amending formula, the composition of the Supreme Court is protected from easy change by the stringent requirement of unanimity on the part of the Senate, the House of Commons and provincial legislative assemblies. The Court is also listed under section 42(1) as an item that can be amended only in accordance with the general formula set out in section 38(1). Thus the court is constitutionally entrenched. However, neither the federal government's power to appoint Supreme Court justices nor the nonjudicial advisory task required by the reference mechanism is affected. More important still is the fact that the *Charter* itself, to the disappointment of its partisans, contains a provision enabling the legislative bodies of both levels of government to override some of its guarantees, namely, those dealing with fundamental freedoms, legal rights and equality rights. The provision is qualified to the extent that legislatures choosing to avail themselves of it are required to declare expressly their intention and reconsider the matter every five years, and there has been speculation about the likely effect of these qualifications on politicians' willingness to resort to the "override." Nevertheless, its very appearance in the context of the *Charter* strikes an incongruous note and is testimony to the strength of the lingering tradition of parliamentary supremacy. Finally, there is the first clause of the *Charter* which subjects its guarantees to "such reasonable limits prescribed by law as can be demonstrably justified in a free and democratic society." Ultimately it is up to the Supreme Court to stake out the "reasonable limits." In the meantime, we do know that they are held to exist, that there is thought to be something higher than, or beyond the *Charter*'s guarantees to which appeal can be made in order to justify their denial or restriction. And the initiative in this regard is secured to governments. While the courts' power of judicial review has undoubtedly surmounted the rather narrow, partisan function envisaged for the new Supreme Court in 1875 by Macdonald, the principle of parliamentary supremacy persists.

9.2

The "Living Tree" Approach to Interpreting the *BNA Act*

Lord Sankey, *The "Persons" Case*, Judicial Committee of the Privy Council.

Edwards v. A.G. Canada, [1930] A.C. 123, 1 DLR 98 (PC).

... The *British North America Act* planted in Canada a living tree capable of growth and expansion within its natural limits. The object of the *Act* was to grant a Constitution to Canada. "Like all written constitutions it has been subject to development through usage and convention."

    Their Lordships do not conceive it to be the duty of this Board – it is certainly not their desire – to cut down the provisions of the *Act* by a narrow and technical construction, but rather to give it a large and liberal interpretation so that the Dominion to a great extent, but within certain fixed limits, may be mistress in her own house, as the Provinces to a great extent, but within certain fixed limits, are mistresses in theirs.

9.3

The "Watertight Compartments" Approach to Interpreting the *BNA Act*

Lord Atkin, *Labour Conventions Case*, Judicial Committee of the Privy Council.

Canada (Attorney General) v. Ontario (Attorney General), [1937] UKPC 6, [1937] A.C. 326.

... It must not be thought that the result of this decision is that Canada is incompetent to legislate in performance of treaty obligations. In totality of legislative powers, Dominion and Provincial together, she is fully equipped. But the legislative powers remain distributed, and if in the exercise of her new functions derived from her new international status Canada incurs obligations they must, so far as legislation be concerned, when they deal with Provincial classes of subjects, be dealt with by the totality of powers, in other words by cooperation between the Dominion and the Provinces. While the ship of state now sails on larger ventures and into foreign waters she still retains the watertight compartments which are an essential part of her original structure. The Supreme Court was equally divided and therefore the formal judgment could only state the opinions of the three judges on either side. Their Lordships are of opinion that the answer to the three questions should be that the *Act* in each case is *ultra vires* of the Parliament of Canada, and they will humbly advise His Majesty accordingly.

9.4

The *Anti-Inflation* Case: The Anatomy of a Constitutional Decision

Peter H. Russell

Canadian Public Administration, 20 (1977), 632–665. Reprinted with permission.

The Supreme Court of Canada's decision in July, 1976 on the constitutional validity of the federal *Anti-Inflation Act* was probably the Court's most heralded decision since it became Canada's final court of appeal in 1949. For the first time since 1949 a major national policy, upon which the federal government placed the highest priority, was challenged before the Court. Also, this was the first clear test of whether the Supreme Court would "liberate" the federal Parliament's general power to make laws for the "peace, order and good government of Canada" from the shackles placed upon it by the Privy Council's jurisprudence and thereby provide the constitutional underpinning for a revolutionary readjustment of the balance of power in Canadian federalism. And it was the first major constitutional case for a Supreme Court headed by Chief Justice Bora Laskin, who during his academic career had earned a reputation as Canada's leading authority on constitutional law and as an articulate critic of the Privy Council. All in all, the case appeared to be a showdown....

The Constitutional Stakes

On October 14, 1975 the federal government unveiled the new anti-inflation program. The program had four main prongs, only one of which was highly controversial and required new legislation. This was a scheme to control prices and wages in certain key sectors of the economy. The Liberal party had vigorously opposed a Conservative party proposal for wage and price controls in the federal election fifteen months earlier. But now Mr. Trudeau's government was apparently convinced that this was a policy whose time had come. Legal authority for the wage and price control policy was contained in the *Anti-Inflation Act* which became law December 15, 1975 (with retroactive effect to October 14, 1975) and in the detailed regulations or "guidelines" promulgated on December 22, 1975.

It was clear from the start that there was a good deal at stake constitutionally in the enactment of this legislation. The *Anti-Inflation Act* purported to give the federal government regulatory authority over prices, profit margins and wages in selected areas of the private sector: construction firms with twenty or more employees, other firms with five hundred or more employees, and professionals. The *Act* applied directly to the federal public sector, and it authorized the government to enter into agreements with the provinces to apply the program to the provincial public sectors. Normally most of the economic relations which the federal *Act* purported to regulate in the private sector are under exclusive provincial jurisdiction. Since the *Snider* case in 1925, labour relations has been treated as a field of divided jurisdiction, with federal authority confined to the limited number of activities which can be brought under specific heads of federal power. A long series of judicial decisions, beginning with the *Parsons* case in 1881, gave the provinces the lion's share of regulatory power over business and commercial transactions in the province. The only earlier peacetime attempt to control prices and profit levels on a national basis had been ruled unconstitutional by the Judicial Committee of the Privy Council of the *Board of Commerce* case [1922].

On what constitutional basis then could the federal government hope to rest the *Anti-Inflation Act*? ... [I]t was the federal Parliament's general power "to make laws for the peace, order and good government of Canada" which appeared to be the only constitutional basis for the *Act*, and it was in the possibility of successfully invoking the general power for this purpose that a revolution in constitutional doctrine was in the making.

Constitutional case-law had produced two rival conceptions of what could sufficiently magnify legislative matter normally subject to provincial jurisdiction to bring them under the general or residual power of the national Parliament: the emergency doctrine and the test of inherent national importance. The emergency doctrine was authored by Viscount Haldane of the Judicial Committee of the Privy Council in the 1920s, and, with but one clear exception, consistently followed by that tribunal until the end of its regime as Canada's highest court. The doctrine's only positive application was to justify the virtually unlimited scope of national power in time of war and postwar transition. Beyond war, the Judicial Committee's vision of emergencies serious enough to set aside the normal distribution of powers and invoke the general power had been limited to such possibilities as "famines," "epidemics of pestilence" or a drastic outbreak of the "evil of intemperance." Economic crisis – even the need for a national scheme of unemployment insurance during the Depression – failed to meet the Judicial Committee's standard of necessity. Further, it appeared that the presumption of constitutionality which attached to war-related legislation did not apply to *permanent* peacetime measures....

In 1946 Viscount Simon in the *Canada Temperance Federation* case wrote an opinion which offered a much wider conception of peace, order and good government than Haldane's emergency test. In dismissing Ontario's attempt to have the Privy Council overrule *Russell v. The Queen* (the Privy Council's earliest decision finding federal legislation constitutional on the basis of peace, order and good government), Viscount Simon held that the Dominion Parliament could not legislate in matters which are exclusively within the competence of the provincial legislature "merely because of the existence of an emergency." The "true test" for determining whether the national legislature may assume jurisdiction over matters which are normally provincial "... must be found in the real subject matter of the legislation: if it is such that it goes beyond local or provincial concern or interest and must from its inherent nature be the concern of the Dominion as a whole ... then it will fall within the competence of the Dominion Parliament as a matter affecting the peace, order and good government of Canada...." This holding seemed to return the interpretation of peace, order and good government to the pre-Haldane formula of national dimensions of concern enunciated by Lord Watson in 1896, namely "... that some matters, in their origin local and provincial, might attain such dimensions as to affect the body politic of the Dominion, and to justify the Canadian Parliament in passing laws for their regulation or abolition in the interest of the Dominion." On its face this inherent national importance or national dimensions conception of peace, order and good government appeared to offer the federal government a much wider opportunity to exercise regulatory power in peacetime on more than a temporary basis in areas normally reserved to the provinces....

Thus, as the federal government in the fall of 1975 moved toward the implementation of a fairly comprehensive scheme of price and wage controls, the question in constitutional law of whether the peace, order and good government clause would provide a basis for national regulation of broad areas of economic and social activity took on more than academic importance.

Political and Legal Strategies of the Parties
... Nowhere did the *Act* speak the language of national emergency. Instead, the preamble referred to inflation as "a matter of serious national concern," language clearly suggesting Viscount Simon's approach to peace, order and

good government in the *Canada Temperance Federation* case. The only mark of emergency or crisis legislation on the face of the *Act* was its penultimate section limiting its duration to three years unless Parliament agreed to an extension. Statements by government spokesmen in Parliament made it clear that the omission of any reference to a state of emergency was deliberate....

Now, with the federal government playing something of a double game, how did the provinces respond to the constitutional issue? Briefly, because they saw that it was not in their political interests at the time to oppose the federal program, they agreed not to raise the constitutional issue. However, because they wished to avoid conceding constitutional power to Ottawa, they were careful not to commit themselves to any particular view of the *Act's* constitutional validity. At this stage it was in the interests of both levels of government to suppress the constitutional issue....

The provinces kept their word. They did not exercise the right which all of them have to refer the question of the *Act's* constitutionality directly to the courts. All, in varying ways, took steps to bring their public sectors into the program. But, nonetheless, they kept their constitutional options open and, as we shall see, when the constitutional issue was forced before the Supreme Court, a number of them attacked the broad grounds upon which the federal government tried to defend this legislation....

If the federal and provincial governments were the only agencies for initiating judicial review, there would probably not have been an *Anti-Inflation* case. In Canada, only the federal and provincial governments have access to the most direct means of bringing questions before the courts – the reference procedure. Private litigants can raise constitutional issues in the courts only when they are plaintiff or defendant in normal litigation, and Canadian courts have tended to be relatively stringent in granting "standing" to raise such issues. [*Ed. note*: This is no longer accurate. See Chapter 6.] One of the interesting features of the *Anti-Inflation* case is that it was the persistence of private interest groups, namely a number of trade unions, in trying to challenge the constitutional validity of the anti-inflation program through normal litigation which eventually persuaded the federal government to resort to the reference device and bring the issue directly before the Supreme Court.

It is particularly interesting that organized labour rather than business interests were responsible for initiating the constitutional challenge to the anti-inflation program. Traditionally, organized labour has favoured strengthening rather than weakening the capacity of the federal government to deal with national and international economic forces. But once labour representatives perceived what in their view was the unjust character of the federal program, they began to oppose it vigorously, and soon after its introduction officials of the Canadian Labour Congress announced their intention to challenge the program in the courts. There is no indication that union leaders had any qualms about the long-run constitutional consequences if their court action was successful. The attack through the courts was adopted as simply one of the means for conducting the anti-control campaign. However, it should be noted that the grounds upon which the CLC initially proposed to base its challenge were that the controls program was too selective to meet the national dimensions test and that provinces could not turn over their legislative jurisdiction to the federal authority by order-in-council. While these arguments did not so clearly threaten the scope of federal authority, those which union counsel subsequently used before the Supreme Court were much more anti-centralist....

[*Ed. note*: The author then describes how, after the Anti-Inflation Board reduced an arbitration award that had been granted to the Renfrew County branch of the Ontario Secondary School Teachers Federation (Agreement Between the Government of Canada and the Government of the Province of Ontario), the Ontario Secondary School Teachers Federation brought forward an action to challenge the *Anti-Inflation Act* as *ultra vires* the federal Parliament. The federal Minister of Justice then referred "the question of the federal *Act*'s constitutional validity and of the Ontario Agreement's validity to the Supreme Court of Canada."]

The Reference: The Parties and their Submissions
... [T]he questions submitted to the court by the Reference Order were presented in the barest possible way:

    1.   Is the *Anti-Inflation Act ultra vires* the Parliament of Canada either in whole or in part, and, if so, in what particulars and to what extent?

    2.   If the *Anti-Inflation Act* is in *ultra vires* the Parliament of Canada, is the Agreement entitled "Between the Government of Canada and the Government of the Province of Ontario," entered into on January 13, 1976 effective under the *Anti-Inflation Act* to render that *Act* binding on, and the Anti-Inflation Guidelines made thereunder applicable to, the provincial public sector in Ontario as defined in the Agreement?

The reference itself was not accompanied by any factual material describing the situation which gave rise to the legislation or details concerning the implementation of the Anti-Inflation program. However, procedures were soon set in motion to provide the basic ingredients of a law case – adversaries and their submissions – and make the decision-making process less like an academic seminar and more like the adjudication of a concrete dispute.

There was no difficulty in obtaining parties to argue all sides of both questions. The federal government, of course, would appear in support of the legislation. All the provinces were notified of the hearing but only five decided to participate: Ontario, Quebec, British Columbia and Saskatchewan in support of the legislation (although for the latter three this "support" turned out to be qualified indeed) and Alberta in direct opposition. Alberta would be joined by five unions (or groups of unions) who were considered to have distinct interests at stake in the proceedings. This labour representation included the Ontario teachers and public service unions which had been attempting to litigate the constitutional issues in Ontario courts, the Canadian Labour Congress which had been pressing for judicial review since the introduction of the *Act* and one major international union, the United Steel Workers of America. Thus, the reference procedure, compensating for the relatively cautious policy of Canadian courts in granting access to the judicial process, enabled the major political contestants to do battle in the judicial arena. But the Supreme Court was not prepared to go all the way in the "politicization" of its process and drew the line at political parties, declining to give permission to the Ontario NDP to appear as an interested party....

The Court's Decision

Five weeks after the conclusion of the hearing the Supreme Court pronounced its judgment. The Court unanimously found that the Ontario Agreement did not render the Anti-Inflation program binding on the provincial public sector. On the question of the *Anti-Inflation Act*'s constitutional validity, the Court split seven to two: seven judges found that it was constitutional on emergency grounds, but Justices Beetz and de Grandpré, both from Quebec and the most recently appointed judges, dissented. That is the bare bones of the decision, but, as is always the case with appellate decisions, the reasons of the judges are more important than their votes....

The Court's decision on the primary question concerning the constitutional validity of the *Anti-Inflation Act* can be analyzed by breaking the question into two components: (1) the interpretation of the peace, order and good government clause and (2) the judgment as to whether the *Anti-Inflation Act* could be upheld as emergency legislation. The court split in quite different ways on these two aspects of the question. Three opinions were written: Chief Justice Laskin's reasons were supported by three Justices, Judson, Spence and Dickson; Mr. Justice Ritchie's were concurred in by Justices Martland and Pigeon; Mr.

Justice de Grandpré concurred in Mr. Justice Beetz's opinion. On the second aspect of the question, Chief Justice Laskin's group of four and Justice Ritchie's group of three formed the majority which found the *Act intra vires*. But on the first issue – the fundamental question of constitutional doctrine – the reasoning of Mr. Justice Beetz's dissenting opinion was adopted by the Ritchie threesome and so became, in effect, the majority position of the Court.

The short five-page opinion of Mr. Justice Ritchie at least has the merit of highlighting the Court's division on the meaning of peace, order and good government. Ritchie rejects broad considerations of national concern or inherent national importance as the framework within which to test whether Parliament can exercise its peace, order and good government power in areas normally under provincial jurisdiction. For him the relevant precedent is not Viscount Simon's judgment in the *Canada Temperance Federation* case, but the decisions following it, especially the *Japanese Canadians* case, in which the Privy Council returned to the emergency doctrine. Since then, Justice Ritchie takes it to be established "that unless such concern [i.e., national concern] is made manifest by circumstances amounting to a national emergency, Parliament is not endowed under the cloak of the 'peace, order and good government' clause with the authority to legislate in relation to matters reserved to the Provinces under s.92." For more elaborate jurisprudential reasons he refers to Mr. Justice Beetz with whose reasons he is "in full agreement."

Justice Beetz provided a re-interpretation of previous judicial decisions on this constitutional issue. This re-interpretation followed the main line of argument submitted to the Court by Mr. Lysyk and Professor Lederman. The essence of this approach is to draw a radical distinction between the "normal" and the "abnormal" uses of peace, order and good government. The normal use of the clause is as a national residual power to cover "… clear instances of distinct subject-matters which do not fall within any of the enumerated heads of s.92 and which, by nature, are of national concern." Thus, it has been invoked successfully in the past to support such fields as radio, aeronautics, the incorporation of Dominion companies and the national capital, all of which in Justice Beetz's view display the requisite "degree of unity," "distinct identity" or "specificity." But the containment and reduction of inflation fails to meet this test of specificity: "It is so pervasive that it knows no bounds. Its recognition as a federal head of power would render most provincial powers nugatory." The normal application of peace, order and good government has the effect of adding, by judicial process, new subject matters of legislation to the list of exclusive federal powers in Section 91 of the *BNA Act*. National concern, national dimensions are still relevant in determining whether such unforeseen, discrete, new subject matters should be brought under the federal residual power or under its counterpart on the provincial side, Section 92(16) – "Matters of a merely local or private nature in the province." But the only constitutional basis for federal legislation cast in such broad terms as the *Anti-Inflation Act* is the abnormal use of peace, order and good government – the emergency doctrine. It is abnormal precisely because it "operates as a partial and temporary alteration of the distribution of power between Parliament and the provincial Legislatures." Once the Court agrees to apply this doctrine no longer is the power of Parliament limited by the identity of subject matters but solely "by the nature of the crisis."

This then was the new constitutional doctrine fashioned by Justice Beetz and supported by a bare majority of the Court. Against it – but by no means in total opposition to it – was Chief Justice Laskin's opinion supported by three other judges. The Chief Justice wrote a long review of all the major cases bearing upon peace, order and good government. While it is not always clear just where this review is going, it contains one basic point of contrast with the majority position. Instead of driving a wedge between the normal and abnormal use of the general power, Chief Justice Laskin tries to weave a single piece of cloth out of all the strands to be found in previous decisions. The key to this approach, the central idea which gives the multi-coloured fabric some shape and pattern, is Lord Watson's proposition in the *Local Prohibition* case that "… matters in origin local or provincial … might attain national dimensions." Since then Laskin sees the jurisprudence moving in two directions – under Viscount Haldane narrowing to the hint of "studiously ignoring" Lord Watson's "national dimensions," but then returning to it, at first cautiously in judgments written by Lord Atkin and Chief Justice Duff followed by the more expansive views of Viscount Simon. The Chief Justice's response to this legacy of competing emphases is not to pick his own favourite strand and discard the others but to identify the extremes which clearly lie beyond the main body of jurisprudence. Thus, at one extreme, basing the use of peace, order and good government on the mere desirability or convenience of national regulation (a possible interpretation of the first Privy Council decision on this issue, *Russell v. The Queen*) is ruled out. But at the other extreme, a pure Haldane approach which ignores "national dimensions" and confines the use of peace, order and good government to war-related emergencies is equally beyond the pale. In between these extremes there are many possibilities, and the Chief Justice warns against fixing constitutional doctrine so tightly as to prevent the constitution from serving "… as a resilient instrument capable of adaptation to changing circumstances."

In the case at hand, because all of the parties accepted as constitutional doctrine the use of peace, order and good government to deal with a national emergency, "… it becomes unnecessary to consider the broader ground advanced in its support.…" So the Chief Justice was willing to rest his decision on the narrow ground of emergency (semantically softened to "crisis"). But unlike the majority he did not rule out the broader ground advanced by the federal government.…

Given the clear consensus both on the Court and among the litigants concerning the power of Parliament in a national emergency (or crisis) to override the normal division of powers, the second dimension of the constitutional question – whether in fact the *Anti-Inflation Act* was emergency legislation – may become more important than the general doctrinal issue of the meaning of peace, order and good government. The Supreme Court's handling of this issue indicates a significant shift to a more deferential attitude to the exercise of emergency powers in peacetime by the national government.

The Court's split on the issue – Chief Justice Laskin's group of four plus Justice Ritchie's group of three versus Justices Beetz and de Grandpré in dissent – did not turn on the empirical question of whether in fact there was an emergency. It concerned the prior question of whether emergency legislation must be clearly identified as such by Parliament. The dissenters took the position that a necessary but by no means sufficient test of valid emergency legislation is a clear, unambiguous indication by Parliament that it is enacting the legislation on an emergency basis. Justice Beetz emphasized that responsibility for declaring an emergency must lie with the "politically responsible body," not the courts. The court's responsibility begins after the affirmation by Parliament that an emergency exists. In this case not only was there no acknowledgment on the face of the federal *Act* (as there had been with other recent exercises of the emergency power), but there was clear evidence to show that this was no accidental oversight. Breaking the convention which precludes Canadian judges from considering parliamentary history, Justice Beetz referred to the numerous passages in Hansard where government spokesmen refused to be pinned down on the constitutional basis of the legislation and refused to preface the Bill with a declaration of an emergency. Further, the large gaps in the *Act*'s coverage – the omission of farmers and small businesses, the optional nature of the provincial public sector's inclusion – were, in Justice Beetz's view, not easily reconciled with an emergency characterization of the *Act*. He was also impressed by the lack of provincial support for the view that it was emergency legislation.

For the majority, Parliament's failure to declare an emergency or stamp "emergency" on the face of the *Act* was not fatal. The reference in the *Act*'s preamble to a level of inflation "contrary to the interests of all Canadians" which had become "a matter of serious national concern," combined with similar statements in the government's White Paper, were enough to indicate how serious the situation must have appeared to Parliament. The omissions from the *Act*'s coverage and the opting-in approach to the provincial public sector, in

Chief Justice Laskin's view, could be accounted for in terms of administrative convenience and need not be regarded as indicating a lack of any sense of crisis. Since there were no formal deficiencies in the federal *Act*, the only grounds upon which its validity as emergency or crisis legislation could be impugned was the factual question: did an emergency exist? Here, for at least three of the justices, the onus of proof was placed squarely on the *Act*'s opponents....

Chief Justice Laskin approached the issue in terms of assessing the rationality of Parliament's judgment. The Court would be justified in overruling the *Act* as emergency legislation only if it found that:

> ... The Parliament of Canada did not have a rational basis for regarding the *Anti-Inflation Act* as a measure which, in its judgment, was temporarily necessary to meet a situation of economic crisis imperilling the well-being of the people of Canada as a whole and requiring Parliament's stern intervention in the interests of the country as a whole.

... [T]he Chief Justice concluded that the Court would be unjustified in finding Parliament lacked a rational basis for its judgment that the legislation was needed to meet an urgent crisis. But we should note how in this part of his opinion he attempted to retain as close a link as possible between the emergency use of peace, order and good government and broad consideration of national dimensions or national aspects. With severe inflation impinging so heavily on areas of federal responsibility, the subject matter of the *Anti-Inflation Act* – the regulation of prices and wages – loses its ordinary parochial or local character and becomes a matter sufficiently urgent for the well-being of all Canadians as to require national action.

The Significance of the Decision

... As for the meaning of the peace, order and good government clause in the *BNA Act*, the decision did not yield the particular benefit sought by federal legal strategists. The legislation was not sustained on broad grounds of inherent national importance or concern. Viscount Haldane was not put away in mothballs. The jurisprudence of Viscount Simon and the *Johannesson* case, which Mr. Macdonald said his government was counting upon, was not accepted by the Court's majority as the key to interpreting peace, order and good government. But the federal government did not come away from the decision empty-handed. To begin with, what I shall call the "Lederman doctrine" on peace, order and good government, adopted by Justice Beetz and supported by a majority of the judges, means that when new matters of legislation are considered distinct and specific enough to justify the residual or "normal" use of the peace, order and good government, they are added to the list of *exclusive* federal powers. The exclusiveness of federal jurisdiction in areas such as aeronautics and radio communications, which are cited as instances of this normal use, was not clear in the past. The Lederman doctrine, while apparently not as favourable to federal power as Viscount Simon's dictum, still is not necessarily unfavourable....

But the Court's handling of the emergency question constitutes a more distinct gain for the federal authorities. The majority's ruling that Parliament does not have to proclaim an emergency or crisis in order to be able to defend legislation successfully in court as emergency legislation increases the maneuverability of federal government leaders. This is especially important with regard to crisis situations related to peacetime economic management when the open admission in Parliament that an emergency or urgent crisis exists might be politically embarrassing to the government. The majority's position means that the federal government does not have to pay the price of that embarrassment in order to secure the emergency argument as the basis for an Act's constitutional validity. To put the matter bluntly, temporary federal legislation may be upheld on emergency grounds if federal lawyers can persuade the Court that there is not enough evidence to conclude that it would have been unreasonable for Parliament to have regarded a matter as an urgent national crisis at the time it passed the legislation. Given the probable deference of most Supreme Court Justices to the judgment of Parliament, this is at least a small gain for federal authority.

It may, however, be a significant loss to those Canadians who care about maintaining parliamentary democracy and constitutionalism. For it must be remembered that all of the judicial decisions upholding federal legislation on emergency grounds (as well as those denying it on these grounds) indicate that "the rule of law as to the distribution of powers" is set aside for the duration of the emergency. One can understand the need for an overriding emergency power to protect the state against threats to its very survival, as well as the reluctance of judges to question a clear determination by Parliament that such an emergency exists. But the constitution as a limit on governmental authority will come to mean very little if it is set aside too easily. At the very least, the better constitutional policy might be to insist, with Justice Beetz, that it should be the responsibility of Parliament rather than the courts to proclaim an emergency.

Finally, what does the *Anti-Inflation* case indicate about the future of judicial review in Canada? First, I think it is likely that the frequency with which constitutional issues are brought before the court will increase rather than decrease. The Supreme Court's almost perfect record in upholding federal laws

will not be a serious deterrent to those who wish to challenge federal legislation. For provincial governments, and even more, for private interest groups,
constitutional litigation is just one weapon that can be used to fight a larger
campaign. Even the Parti Québécois, for instance, although it has no respect
for the Supreme Court as an institution of national government, contemplates
constitutional litigation as a tactic in its larger constitutional warfare. If it loses,
it can portray the decision as yet further evidence of the hostility of federal
institutions to Quebec's interests; if it wins this would vindicate the charge that
the federal government is encroaching on areas of provincial jurisdiction. But
private individuals and groups may be even more likely to provoke constitutional litigation. The rapid growth of the legal profession, more generous rules
of standing, the influence of the American example and the new jurisdictional
rules under which the Supreme Court's docket is shaped primarily by judicial
selection of nationally important cases, all of these factors are likely to generate more privately-initiated constitutional cases. And, as labour's approach to
the *Anti-Inflation* case indicates, when these pressure groups litigate constitutional issues they may be inclined to let the constitutional chips fall where
they may for the sake of pursuing some short-run advantage on an immediate
policy issue.

So the Supreme Court's decision in this case will not deter resort to judicial review in the future. Nor, despite the scant attention given Professor
Lipsey's brief, should future litigants in constitutional cases be deterred from
supporting their arguments with this kind of social science evidence. None of
the judges denied that Professor Lipsey's brief was admissible evidence, and the
Chief Justice explicitly acknowledged its relevancy even though he did not find
it completely persuasive. Further, where the question of constitutionality turns
on the reasonableness of regarding a situation as an urgent national crisis requiring national legislation, what other than empirical arguments can lawyers
who wish to challenge the legislation use? I am not suggesting that there will be
a sudden revolution in the Supreme Court's style of jurisprudence, but that we
will likely see more lawyers using this type of material in future constitutional
cases. One leading constitution scholar has suggested that "… the admission of
social science briefs in constitutional cases where legislative facts are in issue …
may prove in the long run to be the most influential point of the case."

On a more fundamental plane, the Court's majority in subscribing to
Professor Lederman's approach to peace, order and good government, rather than Professor Laskin's (as he once was), have opted to maintain a more
traditional style of opinion-writing. The central concern apparent in this style
of reasoning is "distilling the essences" of legal categories and characterizing
the subject matter of legislation. It is basically the old game of sticking the

legislation in the right pigeon-hole. Most of our judges (and probably, still most of our lawyers) find this a more congenial exercise than reasoning about legislative schemes in terms of the necessary requirements of effective national policy-making.

Judicial decisions based on the majority's approach have the *appearance* of being based on narrow, technical, purely legal considerations. But the preference for this style of jurisprudence is based on larger considerations of constitutional policy. Only Justice Beetz gave a clear expression of the underlying policy reason for rejecting the federal government's first submission that the *Anti-Inflation Act* should be sustained under peace, order and good government as a matter of inherent national importance. "It is not difficult to speculate," he wrote "as to where this line of reasoning would lead: a fundamental feature of the Constitution, its federal nature, the distribution of powers between Parliament and the provincial legislatures, would disappear not gradually but rapidly." So, for policy reasons, a jurisprudential style which would make policy reasons more transparent, is rejected. As a result, Canadians cannot expect judicial reasoning to add very much to the country's stock of constitutional wisdom. The question remains whether this masking of judicial power is in itself a kind of constitutional wisdom.

9.5

Does Federalism Review Matter?
Patrick Monahan

Politics and the Constitution: The Charter, Federalism and the Supreme Court of Canada (Toronto: Carswell, 1987), 224–240. Reprinted with permission.

... [T]here appear to be a variety of ways in which governments or individuals can avoid or modify the effect of constraints associated with federalism. Federalism is premised on a theory of the exhaustion of powers; if one government is denied jurisdiction over a particular matter, then the other level of government must necessarily possess such jurisdiction. Accordingly, if the Supreme Court finds that legislation enacted by one level of government is *ultra vires* on federalism grounds, there are a variety of regulatory alternatives still available. First, the other level of government may choose to enact the legislation in substantially the same form. Alternatively, the results of the litigation may be reversed by intergovernmental agreement, in which the "winning" level of government delegates to the "loser" part or all of the disputed jurisdiction. Finally, the "losing" level of government may simply reassert regulation over the activity in question through substituting an alternative policy instrument in place of the one struck down by the Court.

This leads to the following fundamental maxim of Canadian federalism: contrary to repeated judicial pronouncements to the contrary, it is *always* possible to do indirectly what you cannot do directly. The only relevant question is whether the costs of indirection are so high that they outweigh the benefits....

Federal Product Regulation: The Aftermath of *Dominion Stores* and *Labatt Breweries of Canada Ltd.*

In *R. v. Dominion Stores Ltd. (1980) and Labatt Breweries of Canada Ltd. v. A.-G. Canada (1980)* the Supreme Court had limited federal power to provide for national product standards. In *Dominion Stores,* the Court had ruled that a scheme prescribing grade names and standards associated with those names could not be applied to intraprovincial traders. In *Labatt*, the Court had struck down s.6 of the *Food and Drugs Act*, ruling that s.6 was an impermissible attempt to regulate local trade. Both of these decisions were widely criticized by commentators at the time, who saw the rulings as threatening national product standards and thus as promoting increased consumer ignorance and confusion in the market.

Today, close to a decade after the rulings in these cases, the chaos and confusion which these commentators feared has failed to materialize.... How can we account for the negligible impact of the cases, particularly in light of the predictions of dire consequences which were heard in the months immediately following the release of the decisions?

Consider first the aftermath of the *Dominion Stores* case. The key to understanding the limited impact of this case is the long history of constitutional litigation dealing with the regulation of farm products. Federal-provincial attempts to regulate the marketing of farm products date back to the mid-1930s. The Privy Council had determined that the regulation of intraprovincial trade in natural products was a provincial responsibility, while only Parliament could regulate interprovincial and international trade. The two levels of government had overcome this division of responsibility through interprovincial bargaining and agreement. The relevant standards would be set through federal-provincial agreement; each province would then implement the agreement for products traded locally, while the federal government would enact legislation covering interprovincial and international trade. In this way a common set of product standards would apply across the country, notwithstanding the constitutional division of responsibility.

This system of dovetailing legislation was in place long before the litigation involving *Dominion Stores*. Part II of the *Canada Agricultural Products Standards Act* established a compulsory scheme of grade names and standards for products moving in interprovincial and export trade. The same set of grade names and standards applied to local traders in Ontario pursuant to the [Ontario] *Farm Products Grades and Sales Act*. The validity of these provisions was not at issue in the appeal. What was challenged was Part I of the federal legislation, which sought to establish a voluntary system of grade names and standards for products traded locally. It was this voluntary system of grade names which was ruled unconstitutional by the Court.

This legislative background makes it easy to understand why the decision in *Dominion Stores* has had minimal impact on the regulation of natural products. Notwithstanding the Court's ruling, the same set of natural product standards remains validly in force. The only difference is that prosecutions must be brought under Part II of the federal *Act* or the relevant provincial legislation, depending upon the origin of the product in question. The consequence is that it will be necessary for investigators to obtain information on the origin of the product before laying a charge. But there is no reason in principle why such information could not be obtained.

Perhaps the greatest irony of the case is that there was evidence that the apples which were the subject of the charge in *Dominion Stores* had been traded interprovincially. Thus, although the charge was laid under Part I of the federal *Act*, the investigators could have proceeded under Part II, which contained compulsory standards for interprovincial traders. Had this latter option been chosen, there would have been no constitutional defence to the charge and the only issue would have been whether the apples complied with the relevant standard. Thus, the constitutional issue was manufactured by a discretionary decision to proceed under Part I of the legislation.

In short, the *Dominion Stores* case was little more than a footnote to the long history of constitutional litigation involving the marketing of farm products. The federal and provincial governments had previously agreed on a package of dovetailing legislation establishing a common set of regulatory standards. The *Dominion Stores* case did not call into question the validity of that federal-provincial arrangement. The only effect of the case was to prevent the federal government from applying a "voluntary" scheme of regulation to products traded locally. Given the continued consensus between federal and provincial governments over the relevant standards to be applied in this area, the impact of the decision has been minimal.

There was no similar set of dovetailing federal-provincial legislation in the *Labatt Breweries* case. Section 6 of the federal *Food and Drugs Act* purported to set down national standards for all food products, without distinguishing whether they were traded locally or interprovincially. There was no comparable provincial legislation in place. Thus, one might have expected that the Court's ruling that s.6 was *ultra vires* to have had a fairly significant impact on food products standards. Yet this impact has yet to materialize. In general, food products sold in Canada continue to meet the standards set down in the federal legislation. Federal officials responsible for compliance with the so-called "food recipe" standards report very few violations in the wake of the *Labatt Breweries* case....

Given the inability of the federal government to enforce compliance with the standards, why has there not been a dramatic increase in the numbers of sellers seeking to substitute lower quality products in place of higher quality ones?

There are undoubtedly a number of factors which have contributed to the absence of widespread violations of the *Act*. First, the product standards were already in place and had become widely accepted by the industry as being in its own best interest. Thus, it is hardly surprising that the bulk of the industry would continue to support the product standards even after the result in *Labatt Breweries*. Second, the federal government still possesses considerable authority to enforce the product standards. Since the *Labatt Breweries* litigation, federal officials have sought to enforce the product standards through prosecutions under s.5 of the *Food and Drugs Act*, which provides:

> 5. (1) No person shall label, package, treat, process, sell or advertise any food in a manner that is false, misleading or deceptive or is likely to create an erroneous impression regarding its character, value, quantity, composition, merit or safety.

It is arguable that prosecutions under s.5 are somewhat more difficult than prosecutions under s.6. Under s.6, the relevant test was whether an article was "likely to be mistaken" for food for which a standard had been prescribed under the regulations. If it was likely to be mistaken for such food, then it had to comply with the applicable standard. In contrast, s.5(1) makes it an offence to package food in a manner that is "false, misleading or deceptive or is likely to create an erroneous impression regarding its character." ... It is arguable that the standard under s.5 is somewhat higher, since there is an obligation to demonstrate that the labelling of the food is "misleading": it may be, for example, that food has not been labelled in accordance with the regulations, but that it cannot be demonstrated that this improper labelling was "false, misleading or deceptive."

Yet, on further examination, it is apparent that there are also certain broad similarities between the standards established under ss.5 and 6. Section 6 itself did not directly require compliance with the food standards in the regulations. It was also necessary to demonstrate a "misleading" of the public in order to prosecute under s.6; the offence in s.6 was one of packaging, selling or advertising food "in such a manner that it is likely to be mistaken" for food subject to the regulations. Nor was this "misleading" element of the offence a mere *pro forma* requirement. It should be recalled that the trial judge in the *Labatt Breweries* case had found that "the plaintiff's Special Lite beverage ('food') has not been labelled, packaged or advertised in such a manner that it is likely to be mistaken for the beverage 'light beer' ('food')." Thus, even though Labatt's Special Lite did not comply with the standard for "light beer," the trial judge was prepared to grant a declaration that there had not been a violation of s.6 of the *Act*. In short, while s.5 of the *Act* does not permit direct enforcement of the standards in the regulations, neither did s.6. Instead, both sections depend on some demonstration that there has been a misleading of the public.

This leads to the obvious question: is s.5 of the *Act* also vulnerable to a constitutional challenge? While the answer is not altogether free from doubt, it would appear that s.5 of the *Act* could be defended as an exercise of Parliament's jurisdiction over "criminal law." The criminal law power has always included the authority to proscribe trade practices contrary to the interest of the community such as misleading, false or deceptive advertising. There is a strong argument to the effect that s.5 is a valid exercise of that power....

In summary, neither *Dominion Stores* nor *Labatt Breweries* has had any significant impact on the manner in which goods are marketed or on government policy. The impact of the *Dominion Stores* litigation was minimal due to the existence of dovetailing federal and provincial legislation regulating natural products. As for *Labatt Breweries*, the industry has continued to voluntarily comply with the food recipe standards, notwithstanding the outcome of the litigation. Over the longer term, there are a number of alternative regulatory instruments which can be utilized in order to ensure appropriate compliance with the standards. Neither case seems to have made a great deal of difference for the politics of Canadian federalism.

Natural Resource Regulation: The Aftermath of *CIGOL* and *Central Canada*

In the late 1970s, the Supreme Court appeared to have dealt a body blow to provincial attempts to regulate the natural resource industry. In *CIGOL* (1979), the Court struck down a provincial tax designed to capture the dramatic increase in oil prices resulting from the 1973 Middle East war. In *Central Canada*

Potash (1979), the Court ruled invalid a provincial scheme establishing quotas and minimum prices for the production of potash in Saskatchewan. There were howls of protest from the western provinces following these decisions. The provinces complained that fundamental issues of federal-provincial politics were being resolved by an institution "not in the mainstream of the political process." Various premiers claimed that the Supreme Court was "biased" in favour of the federal government and that the method of appointment to the Court had to be changed to allow for provincial participation.

A decade after these controversial decisions, constitutional questions no longer seem to feature in discussions of the energy issue. The public policy agenda has become preoccupied with the global over-supply of oil and the resultant drop in world oil prices. The constraints facing contemporary Canadian governments in the energy field are constraints arising from market forces, rather than from the constitutional jurisprudence of the Supreme Court. Indeed, Quebec, rather than the West, has become the principal advocate of Supreme Court reform. Once again, the obvious question: how did provincial governments, particularly those in the West, manage to overcome the constitutional obstacles which seemed so pressing and problematic less than a decade ago?

Consider first the aftermath and provincial response to the *CIGOL* case. The immediate priority of the province of Saskatchewan was to ensure that it would not have to refund the $500 million collected under the invalid production tax. The government achieved this result by levying an income tax on the oil industry, retroactive to December 31, 1973. This alternative form of tax was constitutionally valid, since income taxes are direct taxes and within the provincial taxing power under s.92(2) of the *BNA Act*. The $500 million previously collected by the government under the invalid production tax was to be set off against the liability arising from the income tax. The legislation also imposed limits on the deductibility of expenses for the purpose of calculating liability for tax.

This income tax allowed the government to achieve its main goal, which was to ensure that the increase in energy rents resulting from the oil crisis remained in Saskatchewan. But income taxes are more complex and costly to administer than production taxes. In order to levy an income tax there must be a calculation of the "profit" that is subject to tax; a production tax can be levied on the more straightforward basis of the bare number of units produced or sold. Moreover, an income tax presents opportunities and incentive for tax avoidance behaviour by those subject to the tax. Tax avoidance is a marginal consideration in the administration of a production tax. This means that, although the income tax was an adequate regulatory substitute for the production tax struck down in *CIGOL*, it was not a perfect substitute. The income tax was more costly to the government, in terms of the additional resources which had to be committed to enforcement. The income tax also carried with it a social cost – the cost of the resources invested in socially unproductive tax avoidance behaviour by the industry.

Having imposed an income tax as an interim measure, the province continued to press for some form of constitutional amendment to remedy fully its difficulty. Fortuitously for Saskatchewan, by 1981 the federal government badly needed western support for its constitutional reform package. In an attempt to gather support, the federal government agreed to amend s.92 of the *BNA. Act* so as to broaden provincial powers over the natural resource sector. The new s.92(a) of the *Act*, enacted as part of the constitutional reform package by Westminster in 1982, granted provinces power to make "laws in relation to the raising of money by any mode or system of taxation in respect of … non-renewable natural resources.…" This amendment eliminated the requirement that a provincial tax be "direct" rather than "indirect."

The constitutional amendment has enabled the province of Saskatchewan to enact the *Freehold Oil and Gas Production Tax Act*, 1982 as well as the *Mineral Taxation Act*, 1983. The first *Act* provides for a production tax on the freehold oil and gas produced in the province; the second *Act* levies a production tax on the production of specified minerals. In short, the province has now fully regained the constitutional ground it lost in *CIGOL*.

What assessment can be offered of the instrumental impact of the Court's decision? First, it is clear that the decision was not nearly as crippling to provincial regulatory power as had been suggested initially. The province was able to replace immediately the invalid production tax with an income tax, thereby avoiding any significant revenue loss. At the same time, there were nontrivial costs associated with the imposition of an income tax in place of a production tax. In short, while the decision was not the disaster which some had feared, neither was it wholly irrelevant to the formulation of provincial energy policy.

Second, the fact that the result in the case was later reversed by constitutional amendment does not mean that the litigation was thereby rendered meaningless. Because the rule announced by the Court had to some extent limited provincial power, the federal government had been provided with an important constitutional bargaining chip. The federal government was able to play that chip when it was faced with widespread opposition to its constitutional proposals. Had the *CIGOL* litigation been decided the other way, the federal government would have had to have offered some other constitutional concession in order to achieve the same result.

There is a final point that needs to be emphasized, relating to the nature of the federal–provincial bargaining surrounding this issue. The energy issue in the late 1970s and early 1980s was framed and understood in explicitly regional terms, with the resource-rich provinces being pitted against consuming provinces. Federal–provincial bargaining on such a regionally-sensitive issue requires the active involvement of the highest political levels of the respective governments. Further, agreement is impossible without each side being seen to offer significant political concessions to the other. In contrast, the issues arising from the *Dominion Stores* and *Labatt Breweries* litigation have not been perceived as explicitly regional issues. Federal–provincial bargaining on food product standards, for example, is understood as an issue which seems to affect all regions of the country in roughly equal fashion. There are a number of consequences which flow from this difference. First, it is possible to achieve federal-provincial consensus on such "technical" issues without the active involvement of the highest political levels. Second, because the negotiations can be framed in technical rather than political terms, there is no necessity for each side to be seen to be offering "concessions" to the other....

[*Ed. note*: The author then describes the *Central Canada* case, where "the ultimate impact on provincial regulatory power was much less severe than had been feared initially."]

Conclusion: The Impact of Constitutional Constraint

What general conclusions can be drawn from these case studies of the impact of constitutional adjudication on Canadian government? The first conclusion is obvious: the outcomes of constitutional cases are much less determinative of public policy than is often supposed by lawyers and legal scholars. In each of the cases examined, the constitutional result was initially seen as a significant setback to the losing government. Yet in each instance, the governments concerned have been able to achieve the same regulatory goals through alternative instruments. It must be conceded that in certain instances this conclusion had resulted largely from market forces rather than from the conscious intervention of government. The point remains that there was no instance in which the constitutional rule announced by the Court determined the eventual behaviour of the parties.

This does not mean that constitutional constraints are wholly illusory. As I have emphasized throughout this chapter, often the only means of overcoming a constitutional constraint is through intergovernmental agreement: in such instances, the constitutional decision fixes the initial bargaining position of the parties. In other instances, the alternative regulatory instrument is an imperfect substitute for the device struck down by the Court. The point is simply that constitutional reasons will rarely constitute conclusive reasons against undertaking particular public policies. Federalism does not create regulatory vacuums. There will inevitably be a variety of regulatory instruments or legal arrangements which could be utilized in order to achieve a given policy goal. Constitutional reasons may operate so as to rule out the use of some of those regulatory instruments or legal arrangements. But constitutional constraints will rarely make all of the possible instruments off limits. In this sense, constitutional constraints must be seen in relativistic terms. They operate so as to increase the costs associated with achieving policy goals, forcing government to employ alternative regulatory instruments or else to coordinate efforts with those of other levels of government. Policy-makers are then faced with a choice: either bear the increased costs associated with the alternative instrument or abandon the goal. Constitutional constraints help to shape the legislative demand curve.

9.6

Criminal Law, Federalism, and Assisted Reproduction

Dave Snow

"Blunting the Edge: Federalism, Criminal Law, and the Importance of Legislative History after the *Reference re Assisted Human Reproduction Act*," *University of British Columbia Law Review* 48, no.2 (2015), 541–592. Reprinted with permission.

The Canadian attempt to make national law for assisted reproductive technologies (ARTs) provides a cautionary tale. After 15 years of concerted policy-making efforts, in 2004 Parliament passed the *Assisted Human Reproduction Act*, a comprehensive piece of legislation containing criminal prohibitions and a framework for national regulation. Just over 6 years later, however, a majority of Supreme Court of Canada justices ruled in *Reference Re Assisted Human Reproduction Act* that most regulatory, administrative, and licensing aspects of the *AHR Act* were *ultra vires* the federal Parliament, as they were in pith and substance related to health rather than criminal law. Dreams of a uniform national policy were dashed, the federal criminal law power was diminished, and the onus was put on provinces to regulate this important field....

In 1989 Prime Minister Brian Mulroney announced the creation of the Royal Commission on New Reproductive Technologies.... After consultation with over 15,000 Canadians, the Commission published its final report, *Proceed with Care*, on 15 November 1993. Its recommendations fell into three general categories: prohibiting certain activities and technologies using the *Criminal Code*, regulating permissible activities, and establishing a federal regulatory and licensing body that would provide "permanent mechanisms" to respond to ARTs....

The Royal Commission clearly envisioned that the federal government would be the key driver of ART policy. It stressed that a national strategy was "the only feasible response" because "the potential for harm to individuals and to society is too serious to allow Canada's response to be delayed, fragmented, or tentative" and strongly advocated national legislation to address all issues falling within the field....

Almost 15 years after the Royal Commission was established, Canada finally passed legislation with respect to new reproductive technologies: the 2004 *Assisted Human Reproduction Act* (*AHR Act*). With the *AHR Act*, Parliament prohibited a number of activities and technologies, including human cloning, payment for surrogacy and gametes, and germ-line genetic manipulation.... It also created a federal regulatory structure for "controlled activities" related to the use and importation of human reproductive material, which were prohibited activities unless carried out in accordance with future regulations and a license. Regulations defining the parameters of such activities would be subsequently created by Health Canada. Finally, Parliament created Assisted Human Reproduction Canada, a federal agency charged with monitoring compliance with and enforcement of the *AHR Act*, creating and administering a licensing framework for the controlled activities, and maintaining a health data registry. Like the Royal Commission, Parliament made it clear that ARTs required, above all else, national leadership....

Federalism Complicates the Matter

In the past, when Parliament has legislated for matters concerning health, it typically has relied on one of two federal heads of power. The first is the authority to make laws for the "Peace, Order, and Good Government" (POGG) of Canada under section 91 of the *Constitution Act, 1867*. Long ago considered a residual power, by the time the Royal Commission reported in 1993, the Supreme Court of Canada (building on jurisprudence from the Judicial Committee of the Privy Council) had limited POGG's application to federal legislation that might otherwise come within provincial jurisdiction to two instances: in order to respond to a "national emergency" or to justify legislation in an area of "national concern." The Royal Commission claimed ARTs qualified as an issue of "national concern," which the Supreme Court had previously described as subject matter containing a "singleness, distinctiveness and indivisibility that clearly distinguishes it from matters of provincial concern," and for which there was "provincial inability" to effectively legislate. At the time of the Royal Commission, it was far from certain that federal ART legislation would fit these criteria under POGG's national concern test. … Comprehensive national policy on ARTs was thus a constitutional gamble the Commission considered worth taking.…

Throughout the 1990s and early 2000s – the exact time the iterations of the *AHR Act* went through Parliament – the Supreme Court began avoiding POGG as a potential support for disputed federal legislation. In its place, the Supreme Court often upheld federal legislation on the basis of the criminal law power under section 91(27) of the Constitution – Parliament's other constitutional authority in cases that implicate health.… Thus, just as Parliament was debating federal legislation concerning ARTs, the Supreme Court was adapting the rules that would permit the government to justify such legislation. On one hand, this meant a diminished role for POGG, which had potentially been the most expansive federal grant of power. On the other, a majority of the justices still upheld federal legislation in each case, leading political scientist Gerald Baier to speculate in 2006 as to whether the criminal law power had merely become a "proxy" for the national concern component of POGG. There was a plausible case to be made that, given the existence of criminal prohibitions in the federal ART legislation, the criminal law justification would withstand judicial scrutiny, even when applied to the regulatory, licensing, and administrative aspects of the *AHR Act*. This is certainly the position Parliament took as it developed its legislation.…

However, the requirement that the criminal law power be used to address a public health "evil" is crucial to understanding how Parliament attempted (and ultimately failed) to justify its authority over ARTs. The language Parliament uses to justify legislation has become, and will continue to be, important for federalism cases involving the criminal law. As such, one might expect that, when justifying legislation under the criminal law power, Parliament would frame the legislation as primarily addressing a public health evil. However, this was not the case. Indeed, there was an inconsistency among Members of Parliament – or more accurately, among members of the governing Liberal Party, which held a majority from 1993–2004 – when articulating the purposes of the *AHR Act*. On the one hand, government officials repeatedly stated that the provisions in the *AHR Act* – both the criminal prohibitions and the regulatory, licensing, and administrative provisions – were constitutionally permissible because of Parliament's authority under the criminal law power. On the other hand, the government's *language* sounded eerily similar to that used by the Royal Commission, which had justified prospective legislation on the basis of the "national concern" branch of POGG.... For example, Minister of Health Allan Rock described ARTs before the Standing Committee on Health in 2001 as "surely an area where federal leadership is needed, where the Government of Canada is uniquely positioned to lead, where a consistent approach is needed to deal with national issues that reflect national values." ...

Given the changes in the Supreme Court's federalism jurisprudence and the already-tenuous application of POGG's national concern doctrine, Parliament was aware that the *AHR Act* would have to be justified on the basis of the criminal law power – indeed, by the time the legislation was referred to the Quebec Court of Appeal in 2008, the Attorney General of Canada did not even bother to defend the legislation on the basis of POGG's "national concern" doctrine....

The *AHR Act* Goes to Court

In 2007, 3 years after the *AHR Act* passed, Quebec launched a reference case in its Court of Appeal, charging that much of the *AHR Act* was *ultra vires* Parliament ... insofar as they intruded on provincial jurisdiction over health and medicine under subsections 92(7), 92(13), 92(16), and section 93 of the *Constitution Act, 1867*. In June 2008, the Quebec Court of Appeal issued its opinion. All three justices unanimously agreed with the Government of Quebec and held that all the impugned provisions were *ultra vires* the federal Parliament. This would have stripped Parliament of most of the regulatory, administrative, and licensing powers the *AHR Act* granted it, which is to say virtually every power that did not relate to an outright criminal prohibition....

In December 2010, a divided (4-4-1) Supreme Court of Canada issued a 127-page decision in *Reference re Assisted Human Reproduction Act*. The arguments were the same as those posed to the Quebec Court of Appeal; once again, the Attorney General of Canada did not attempt to justify the legislation under POGG's "national concern" doctrine, as the Royal Commission had recommended. The two main opinions in the case – one authored by Chief Justice McLachlin and the other by Justices LeBel and Deschamps – were sharply divided over many issues.... However, the main question that ostensibly separated the justices was the overall purpose or "pith and substance" of the impugned provisions within the overall context of the legislation. In the end, a majority of justices largely accepted Quebec's argument, and found most of the *AHR Act*'s controlled activities and regulatory authority to be *ultra vires* the Parliament of Canada insofar as their pith and substance concerned the regulation of medicine and the provision of health care services.

... Chief Justice McLachlin (writing for herself and Justices Binnie, Fish, and Charron) agreed with the Attorney General of Canada's submission and held that the purpose of the *AHR Act* was to create a number of prohibitions supported by a few incidental regulations. The Chief Justice held that the *AHR Act* was primarily designed to "prohibit practices that would undercut moral values, produce public health evils, and threaten the security of donors, donees, and persons conceived by assisted reproduction." "The dominant thrust" of the legislation was prohibitory, as it was "essentially a series of prohibitions, followed by a set of subsidiary provisions for their administration." ... The group of four justices led by McLachlin would have upheld the *AHR Act* in its entirety as a valid exercise of the criminal law power.

Justices LeBel and Deschamps (writing for themselves and Justices Abella and Rothstein), by contrast, held that the impugned provisions were designed to promote beneficial activities such as family-building and scientific research.... They found the pith and substance of these impugned provisions, and indeed one of the fundamental purposes of the legislation, was to set national standards for "a specific type of health services provided in health-care institutions by health-care professionals." Making frequent reference to the Royal Commission and legislative history, they found the legislation's non-criminal components did not concern "an evil needing to be suppressed," but instead "a burgeoning field of medical practices and research that ... brings benefits to many Canadians." Just like the Quebec Court of Appeal, LeBel and Deschamps effectively saw a division of labour between prohibited (harmful) and non-prohibited (beneficial) components of the legislation. The unifying purpose that brought these two aspects together was the national regulation of ARTs. However, this group of justices held that this was not a satisfactory justification under Parliament's criminal law power. The criminal prohibitions did "not depend on the existence of the regulatory scheme," but were able to "stand alone ... regardless of whether a scheme regulating other activities existed" just as "the regulation of activities associated with assisted human reproduction [does] not depend on other activities being prohibited completely." ...

Justice Cromwell, at that time the most junior justice on the Court, cast the decisive vote. He generally agreed with LeBel and Deschamps that most of the impugned provisions fell under the provincial jurisdiction over health, as they "permit[ted] minute regulation of every aspect of research and clinical practice" and were not used to "simply prohibit 'negative practices'." However, he found three impugned provisions – concerning donor consent, the age of consent, and reimbursement for donor- and surrogacy-related expenditures – were sufficiently criminal in nature to qualify as criminal law.... Justice Cromwell's vote effectively invalidated most of the *AHR Act*'s controlled activities, licensing power, and regulatory provisions, leaving a void yet to be filled by most provinces concerning many facets of assisted reproductive technology policy....

Defining the Criminal Law Power's New Limits

The majority opinion in *Re AHRA* represents the clearest limitation on the federal criminal law power in years.... Parliament still has wide authority to create unqualified criminal prohibitions with a penalty, even if those prohibitions concern areas that cover health care – even if they concern ARTs specifically....

Looking back at testimony from legal experts preceding the *AHR Act*, this has produced a curious outcome.... From 1996–2004, most expert witnesses thought Parliament had the authority under the criminal law power to create regulations related to ARTs. However, the same legal (and most medical) experts were largely opposed to the use of unqualified criminal prohibitions as a way to regulate behaviour, precisely because a criminal prohibition is "inflexible" and a "blunt instrument." ... A blunt instrument was the only means by which Parliament could institute national ART policy, and even then, a majority of Supreme Court justices held that the controlled activities contained in the *AHR Act* – prohibitions assigned only after administrative determinations and licensing – were not blunt enough. Controlled activities were too flexible, too tied to the promotion of beneficial health promotion. If in the future Parliament wants to create, by any means necessary, national policy in areas that touch on health care, then it is clear that unqualified prohibitions are the safest route. With respect to Parliament, there is a greater incentive to explicitly emphasize the public health "evil" it is trying to eliminate....

The subsequent amendments to the *AHR Act* provide ample evidence of this increased emphasis. Parliament could not, of course, go back in time and change the language used to justify federal action from 1996–2004 and infuse it all with a criminal purpose. What it could do was amend the legislation in such a way that made the criminal purposes as clear as possible. In 2012, as part of the much-maligned 425-page omnibus budget implementation bill, Parliament amended the *AHR Act* to comply with the Supreme Court ruling. These amendments repealed the provisions the Court had found *ultra vires*, closed down Assisted Human Reproduction Canada, removed the distinction between "controlled" and prohibited activities, and eliminated all licensing requirements. They also repealed section 10 of the *AHR Act*, which had previously made using, altering, and manipulating human reproductive material a "controlled activity," and replaced it with a new qualified prohibition. The new section 10 will, once in force, prohibit the distribution, use, and importation of human gametes, unless tests and quality assurance have been conducted in accordance with regulations.

The most interesting aspect of the amendment, however, is the wording of the new subsection 10(1), which states: "The purpose of this section is to reduce the risks to human health and safety arising from the use of sperm or ova for the purpose of assisted human reproduction, including the risk of the transmission of disease." While legislative purposes are frequently articulated at the beginning of a law through a statement of principles or a statutory declaration, it is unusual for a particular subsection to include such an interpretive statement. Clearly, the government and its legal advisors have taken the Supreme Court ruling in *Re AHRA* under consideration in making this change. The new section explicitly identifies a distinct criminal law purpose – reducing risks to health and safety, such as disease – that is directly connected to the prohibition contained therein. While the prohibition is qualified insofar as it is subject to regulation, the justification is more explicitly connected to a criminal law purpose than were the provisions the Court ruled *ultra vires*. It is, as a result, far more likely to withstand judicial scrutiny. It should also be a harbinger of things to come for federal laws that, while connected in principle to the criminal law, contain some regulatory or administrative aspect....

Conclusion

Over 20 years after the Royal Commission began its work on creating a national framework, the Supreme Court, in the eyes of many, set much of ART policy in Canada back to square one. The dream of national regulation of ARTs is over. Yet the case will likely have implications far beyond the regulation of ARTs, and it should influence future disputes between Parliament and the provinces over the line between health care and the criminal law, particularly regarding legislative history....

Moving forward, Parliament will be more successful if it tailors federal legislation to eliminating an "evil" rather than promoting beneficial activity. The 2012 amendment to the *AHR Act*, which clarified that the purpose of a particular *section* was "to reduce the risks to human health and safety," is a case in point. If more policies that straddle the health care/criminal law divide – such as physician-assisted suicide, sex work, and safe injection sites – face litigation from provincial governments, it will be good strategy for Parliament to emphasize the evil it seeks to eliminate and the way in which its specific regulatory instruments will achieve that goal....

Another perhaps unintentional effect of the majority judgment in *Re AHRA* is to make unqualified prohibitions – condemned by legal and medical experts throughout committee hearings in the build-up to the *AHR Act* as "blunt" and "inflexible" – a safer option for Parliament. The blunt force of absolute criminal prohibitions is now the feature Parliament must emphasize at all phases in order to withstand constitutional challenges on the basis of federalism. Time will tell, but for now it looks as if a bare majority of the Court has taken an already-blunt instrument and further blunted its edge.

Re AHRA also signals another intriguing development: the continued marginalization of the "national concern" branch of POGG. Back in 1993, the Royal Commission emphasized POGG as the main constitutional justification for national ART legislation. As subsequent Supreme Court cases moved even further away from POGG as a justification for national action, Parliament abandoned POGG in favour of the criminal law power when providing a constitutional anchor for the *AHR Act*. However, the language Parliament frequently used to describe the legislation – such as a desire to provide a "consistent approach" to address "national issues that reflect national values" and to avoid "the patchwork situation that exists in the United States" – was far more reflective of POGG's national concern branch than it was of criminal law purposes. The fact that the Attorney General of Canada did not even use the "national concern" defence in Court, coupled with the fact that a majority of Supreme Court justices rejected national concern arguments cloaked in the criminal law power, suggests this branch of POGG may be well and truly dead. No longer can the criminal law power act as a proxy for national concern. National action must now reflect national condemnation.

What does this all mean? To an even greater extent than before *Re AHRA*, unqualified prohibitions are far more likely to be upheld than qualified ones, and in either case it is good constitutional strategy for Parliament to stress the more traditionally negative aspects of its criminal law power. Punishment and penalties must be at the forefront of criminal legislation that could potentially impugn on health policy. Some may feel, as they did with the *AHR Act*, that such a reliance on criminal prohibitions will inevitably produce poor public policy. If so, then poor public policy may be the only route to national authority with respect to health.

9.7

Key Terms

Concepts
criminal law power (s. 91(27))
disallowance
emergency doctrine

federalism

judicial review

living tree doctrine

national concern branch ("inherent national importance")

neutral umpire

Peace, Order and good Government (POGG)

per saltum appeals

property and civil rights (s. 92(13), *Constitution Act, 1867*)

reservation

residual power

stare decisis

unilateral declaration of independence (UDI)

watertight compartments

Institutions, Events and Documents

Anti-Inflation Reference, [1976] 2 S.C.R. 373

Canada (AG) v. Ontario (AG), [1937] UKPC 6, [1937] A.C. 326 ("Labour Conventions case")

Canadian Industrial Gas & Oil Ltd. [CIGOL] v. Government of Saskatchewan et al., [1978] 2 S.C.R. 545

Central Canada Potash Co. Ltd. et al. v. Government of Saskatchewan, [1979] 1 S.C.R. 42

Colonial Laws Validity Act (1865)

Constitution Act, 1867, ss. 91 and 92

Dominion Stores Ltd. v. R., [1980] 1 S.C.R. 844.

Edwards v. A.G. Canada [1930] AC 123, 1 DLR 98 (PC) (the "Persons case")

Judicial Committee of the Privy Council (1833)

Labatt Breweries of Canada Ltd v. Canada (AG), [1980] 1 S.C.R. 914

O'Connor Report (1939)

Reference re Assisted Human Reproduction Act, [2010] 3 S.C.R. 457

Reference re Secession of Quebec, [1998] 2 S.C.R. 217

Reference re Securities Act, [2011] 3 S.C.R. 837

Statute of Westminster (1931)

Supreme Court Act (1875)

10

Aboriginal Law and Judicial Review

Arguably the most contentious aspect of modern Canadian politics is Aboriginal politics. From the failure of the Meech Lake and Charlottetown Accords to the Truth and Reconciliation Commission to the protests that overshadowed Canada's sesquicentennial celebrations in 2017, the rights claims made by Canada's Aboriginal population play an increasing role in our political conversation. Since the passage of the *Constitution Act, 1982*, Aboriginal politics have become inextricably tied up with the politics of rights. And in Canada, the politics of rights inevitably means an increased role for the courts, particularly the Supreme Court of Canada.

For demographic reasons alone, Aboriginal law and politics looks set to increase in salience. The Aboriginal population is young, with a median age of thirty-two years compared to forty-one years for non-Aboriginals. Aboriginal peoples represent the fastest-growing segment of the Canadian population (4.9 per cent in 2016, compared to 3.8 per cent in 2006 and 2.8 per cent in 1996), and are growing at four times the rate of the non-Aboriginal population. While part of this growth has been due to an increase in self-reported identification, high fertility rates and rising life expectancy are also contributing.[1]

There is no homogenous Aboriginal (or Indigenous)[2] identity in Canada. Of the 1.67 million Canadians who identify as Aboriginal, 58 per cent (roughly 977,000) are First Nations (legally, "Indians"); 35 per cent (588,000) are Métis; 4 per cent (65,000) Inuit; and 3 per cent (44,000) report other or multiple Aboriginal identities.[3] In the last generation, "First Nations" has become the term of choice for descendants of those who lived in what is now Canada prior to the arrival of European settlers, although "Indian" is the term used in much of Canadian law. "Métis" refers to those whose mixed ancestry is traced to First Nations and European settlers, while "Inuit" refers to a separate Aboriginal people who trace their ancestry to what is now northern Canada. Under section 35(2) of the *Constitution Act, 1982*, "aboriginal peoples of Canada" collectively includes "the Indian, Inuit and Métis peoples of Canada."[4]

Historically, the 1763 Royal Proclamation was the first document to recognize Aboriginal peoples as distinct political entities. However, they were not treated politically as equals, either by European explorers or by the *British North America Act*. As John Borrows (Reading 10.2) explains, European explorers used the doctrines of "discovery" and *terra nullius* to assert complete sovereignty over lands in the Americas. The justification for taking possession of lands both inhabited and uninhabited, as described by Thomas Flanagan, was that Aboriginal inhabitants "did not possess sovereignty because they were not organized into territorial states with stable governments and thus were not actors under the law of nations."[5]

While the applicability of the doctrine of *terra nullius* (literally, "no one's land") has been disputed by Canadian scholars and by the Supreme Court alike,[6] there can be little doubt that the Fathers of Confederation did not believe Aboriginal peoples had statehood or underlying sovereignty. As Martin Papillon argues, Aboriginals were "absorbed into the dominant political order without their consent."[7] No Aboriginal representatives, for example, were invited to the 1864 Quebec or Charlottetown conferences that gave birth to modern Canada. The *British North America Act* made "Indians, and Land reserved for Indians" the sole purview of the federal Parliament, but Indian reserves were not given anything approximating the status of provincial governments. Historic treaties were negotiated between the Crown and specific First Nations, but as Dwight Newman (Reading 10.3) notes, they simultaneously preserved "traditional harvesting rights" for signatory First Nations, while allowing the Crown to "take up" land for development. For much of Canada's first century, Registered Indians living on reserve were essentially wards of the state, and until 1967 needed to give up their Indian status in order to vote in federal elections. The abuses of Canada's residential schools system, which forcibly removed an estimated 150,000 First Nations children from their homes to be educated and assimilated into the dominant culture, further contributed to political alienation among Aboriginal peoples.

In this political context, Pierre Trudeau's Liberal government published its infamous 1969 White Paper, which proposed to abolish the *Indian Act* and the reserve system, eliminate any differentiated status for Aboriginal peoples and transfer responsibility for Aboriginal peoples to the provinces. Amid opposition from Aboriginal groups, the federal government soon backed away from this policy proposal. Very soon after, the legal landscape for Aboriginal-Crown relations was altered by a divided Supreme Court of Canada in *Calder v. British Columbia* (1973).[8] *Calder* was the first decision in which Supreme Court justices held that Aboriginal peoples held "title," a claim to land that had not been surrendered to the Crown through treaties (see Reading 10.3). This case portended greater judicial involvement in Aboriginal-Crown affairs, particularly given the subsequent passage of the *Constitution Act, 1982*.

Aboriginal rights are mentioned in the text of the *Canadian Charter of Rights and Freedoms* itself, albeit briefly. Section 25 of the *Charter* states that it "shall not be construed so as to abrogate or derogate from any aboriginal, treaty or other rights or freedoms that pertain to the aboriginal peoples of Canada," including the 1763 Royal Proclamation and existing land claims agreements. However, the main articulation of Aboriginal rights in the Canadian Constitution is technically outside the *Charter*. Section 35(1) of the *Constitution Act, 1982* states that "existing aboriginal and treaty rights of the aboriginal peoples of Canada are hereby recognized and affirmed." The fact that Aboriginal and treaty rights are "outside the *Charter* but inside the rights regime"[9] may actually give them greater force, as neither section 1's "reasonable limits" nor the section 33 "notwithstanding clause" can be applied in section 35 cases.

In Reading 10.1, Kirsten Matoy Carlson shows how the growth of Aboriginal rights consciousness has led to substantial legal change. Prior to 1982, the federal government devised policies for settling Aboriginal land claims, but did so in a manner that did not recognize the full scope of title recommended by Aboriginal groups. The hopes for a changed landscape following the inclusion of section 35 were initially dashed during the 1980s and early 1990s. Four constitutional conferences between 1983 and 1987 failed to produce an agreement on the scope and content of section 35, and the 1992 referendum on the Charlottetown Accord – which would have included explicit recognition of an "inherent right to self-government" and a statement that Aboriginal peoples constitute one of the "three orders of government" in Canada – also failed.

Yet Carlson shows how political failure created judicial opportunity. Beginning with *R. v. Sparrow* (1990),[10] a fishing rights case, the Supreme Court has adopted a "generous, liberal interpretation" of the language of section 35, as it has with the language of the *Charter* (see Reading 12.3). The Court in *Sparrow* created a high standard for the extinguishment of Aboriginal rights, as well as a justificatory test for limits on Aboriginal rights. The Court has maintained this liberal approach in subsequent cases involving fishing rights (*R. v. Van der Peet*, 1996; *R. v. Côté*, 1996); historical treaty interpretation (*R. v. Badger*, 1996); Aboriginal title (*Delgamuukw v. British Columbia*, 1997); and Métis hunting rights (*R. v. Powley*, 2003).[11] These cases have placed constitutional limits on provincial and federal governments' abilities to infringe or extinguish Aboriginal rights, have required greater government consultation with potentially affected Aboriginal communities and have led to substantial policy revision.

For Carlson, what is most striking about these cases is that the Court decided them during a period in which there was a "loss of political will to discuss the constitutionality of Aboriginal and treaty rights" (Reading 10.1). It was only in the context of political failure – specifically, the failed constitutional conferences of the mid-1980s and the failure of the Charlottetown Accord – that the Supreme Court "re-entered the policymaking arena" to broaden the language of section 35. Like LGBTQ and feminist groups with the *Charter* (see Readings 6.4 and 12.3), Aboriginal organizations have achieved policy change via the courts after failing to do so in legislatures.

The steady expansion of Aboriginal and treaty rights has forced the Supreme Court to re-evaluate its approach on a number of occasions. And while it has been reticent to defend the doctrines of discovery and *terra nullius*, the Court has been equally unwilling to endorse the other end of the spectrum: that Aboriginal title over land in Canada *supersedes* Crown sovereignty. John Borrows (Reading 10.2) shows how the Supreme Court wrestled with this conception in what some have called its most far-reaching case, *Tsilhqot'in Nation v. British Columbia* (2014).[12] *Tsilhqot'in* involved an application by the Tsilhqot'in people residing in central British Columbia who, because they had never surrendered their land via treaty, argued that the Crown could not allow a private company to cut trees on their territory. In granting a declaration of Aboriginal title over the land, the Supreme Court recognized that the Tsilhqot'in had the right to enjoy, occupy, possess and manage the land, including the right to economically benefit off the land. The decision was groundbreaking; Borrows calls it "exceedingly strong," and "an important step" towards repairing Canadian-Indigenous relationships. "Canada is a better place as a result of its 153 paragraphs," Borrows concludes. "It sets a new world standard."

Yet there is much uncertainty in *Tsilhqot'in*. The decision both "constru[es] Aboriginal title broadly" and "reinforce[es] the province's political authority" (Reading 10.2). This is especially true with respect to the doctrine of *terra nullius*. On the one hand, the Court explicitly says that "[t]he doctrine of *terra nullius* (that no one owned the land prior to European assertion of sovereignty) never applied in Canada."[13] Yet earlier in the same paragraph, the Court held that, "At the time of assertion of European sovereignty, the Crown acquired radical or underlying title to all the land in the province."[14] Borrows argues that both cannot be true: How could the Crown acquire sovereignty over lands "owned by Indigenous peoples" by mere assertion without employing some version of *terra nullius*? It is a question the Court did not answer. The Court's ambivalence on this matter reflects a Canadian judiciary that is as yet unwilling to grapple with the logical consequences of a true assertion of Aboriginal title in "unceded" territory: that most Crown lands would legally belong to

Aboriginal peoples, or more radically, that it could lead to the dismantling of the Canadian state.[15]

As in other decisions with far-reaching implications for the Canadian state, such as the *Patriation Reference* and the *Secession Reference* (Readings 2.4 and 2.5), the Supreme Court's decision in *Tsilhqot'in* left many questions unanswered. This uncertainty in *Tsilhqot'in* is one reason that Dwight Newman (Reading 10.3) cautions against those who believe that the Supreme Court of Canada has been the venue for an "unbroken chain of Aboriginal 'wins'" in the past few decades.[16] Newman points to a number of cases that have produced unexpected negative outcomes for Aboriginal communities, including the affirmation of provincial rights in *Grassy Narrows*.[17] On Aboriginal rights issues, Newman has advice for all sides: private industry should develop a better understanding of Aboriginal issues, courts should avoid ambiguity in their decisions (a tall order) and politicians should strive for greater clarity in discourse (an even taller one). Aboriginal communities, meanwhile, might be better situated to "build on their legal victories through serious negotiations with governments and industry" rather than engage in uncertain litigation.

In addition to jurisprudence on Aboriginal title, a number of Supreme Court cases since 2004 have considered whether the Crown has a "duty to consult" Aboriginal communities when governments make decisions that could have an adverse impact on Aboriginal rights. As Newman (Reading 10.3) points out, the duty to consult arises not in instances when Aboriginal communities hold "well-established traditional harvesting rights," but instead when uncertainty about rights claims abound. Beginning with *Haida Nation v. British Columbia* (2004),[18] the Supreme Court has said that the "honour of the Crown" compels the government to engage in consultations when an Aboriginal community might be impacted. The specific requirements of such consultation vary depending on the strength of the rights claim and the nature of the intended action. Newman notes that the duty-to-consult jurisprudence is an example of the unintended consequences of judicial decisions: while initial judgments were about imposing duties on governments, the main thrust of these decisions has "arguably been to empower some Aboriginal communities in the context of negotiations with the private sector," particularly with respect to resource extraction.

Writing in 2015, Newman was critical of the "unintended consequences" created by the legal ambiguities and uncertainties of the Supreme Court's duty-to-consult decisions. They were creating problematic incentives and potential "flashpoints" – especially around "major infrastructure projects." The references were to new oil and gas pipelines such as Enbridge's Northern Gateway and Kinder Morgan's Trans Mountain, both of which had been approved by the

National Energy Board but which were still being challenged and delayed by legal challenges from affected Aboriginal communities. "The Court," Newman wrote, "arguably needs to measure more carefully the implications of some of its decisions."

This advice appears to have caught the Court's attention. In a pair of decisions released late in 2017, it clarified the meaning and narrowed the scope of the duty to consult. In the *Clyde River*[19] and *Chippewas of the Thames First Nation*[20] decisions, the Court made it clear that there is no Aboriginal "veto" over proposed development, even if the affected community is not satisfied with the mitigations or accommodations offered by the developer or government. The Court wrote that "balance and compromise are inherent in the [consultation] process," which should be "a cooperative one with a view towards reconciliation."[21] The Court repeated this message three months later in its ruling in *Ktunaxa Nation v. British Columbia*: section 35, the Court wrote, "is a right to a process, not to a particular outcome."[22] How these decisions will play out in future section 35 consultations will be important for both Aboriginal and non-Aboriginal Canadians.

In Reading 10.4, Minh Do (writing prior to *Clyde River, Chippewas* and *Ktunaxa*) reads the Court's duty-to-consult jurisprudence in light of broader themes of reconciliation. Since the 2015 report of the Truth and Reconciliation Commission of Canada,[23] a comprehensive investigation into the legacy of Canada's residential schools, "reconciliation" has been the dominant term on the lips of Canada's political elites. Do identifies three different visions of reconciliation adopted by the Supreme Court in its five main "duty-to-consult" cases between 2004 and 2010: Reconciliation as a *relationship*, which accepts Aboriginal difference and prevents unilateral action against Aboriginal peoples; reconciliation as *consistency*, where Aboriginal difference is recognized but rights are "defined within the structures of Crown sovereignty"; and reconciliation as *resignation*, where social harmony takes precedence over Aboriginal rights claims. While Do finds aspects of all three approaches in the Court's jurisprudence, she argues that *consistency* has been most prominent. Such an approach is likely to retain power imbalances between the Crown and Aboriginal peoples, Do argues, as "the Crown's power to structure the terms of Aboriginal participation in consultative settings remains unchallenged." As these different (and perhaps inconsistent) interpretations of reconciliation are advanced by the Court in its decisions, this could lead to an increased uncertainty in the judicial arena.

It is wrong, however, to understand courtroom conflict over Aboriginal rights as a singular battle between the Crown and Aboriginal groups. As Daniel Voth demonstrates in Reading 10.5, the courtroom has been a venue for conflict with respect to "inter-Indigenous politics" as well. Voth shows how courtroom litigation "can promote divisive, exclusionary, zero-sum political relationships between Indigenous peoples." There is no one single Aboriginal identity; indeed, the inscription of difference between Métis, Indians and Inuit in the *Constitution Act, 1982* has actually reinforced divisions, as happened between the Manitoba Métis Federation (MMF) and Treaty 1 First Nations in *Manitoba Métis Federation v. Canada and Manitoba*.[24] Voth analyzes arguments used at the intervention stage at the Manitoba Court of Appeal, where the MMF sought a declaration that the federal Crown had not met its fiduciary obligations in implementing the *Manitoba Act, 1870* because it did not disburse land to Métis families. He shows how the MMF undermined the Treaty 1 peoples' application to intervene (even endorsing "pro-settler interpretations of history"), while First Nations groups demanded they be consulted prior to the Crown's granting of rights or land to the Métis.

Voth's analysis provides a new spin on the argument advanced by Gerald Rosenberg in his famous book *The Hollow Hope*[25] – namely Rosenberg's argument that American courts are not the best avenue to promote social change. Of course, as Chapter 6 shows, many Canadian interest groups – particularly LGBTQ and feminist ones – have had great success in achieving social change using the *Charter* in the Supreme Court. Yet Voth shows how Rosenberg's argument is especially relevant with respect to Aboriginal rights in Canada. Voth argues that there are "structural biases within Canadian courts," such as *stare decisis*, that reflect cultural ethnocentricity and will prevent Aboriginal groups from achieving their goals in the courtroom. Given the primacy of *stare decisis* in the Canadian legal tradition (see Chapter 7), it seems unlikely the courts will jettison the principle any time soon. For these reasons, Voth argues that "[t]he best strategy is not to deploy courts in Indigenous struggles seeking strategic ends."

The readings in this chapter thus leave us with a conundrum. On the one hand, Kirsten Matoy Carlson (Reading 10.1) shows how the Supreme Court of Canada was crucial to "revitalizing" Aboriginal and treaty rights at a time that the expansion of those rights lacked political support. These decisions have led governments to substantially restructure their approach to Aboriginal rights. Yet Aboriginal peoples' foray into the courts is no guarantee of success. John Borrows (Reading 10.2) shows how the Supreme Court strengthened the provincial Crown's underlying title and overriding sovereignty even in important victories for Aboriginal peoples; Dwight Newman (Reading 10.3) shows that claims of an Aboriginal "winning streak" are overwrought, and that certain instances of "overreach" have backfired for Aboriginal groups' negotiating positions; Minh Do (Reading 10.4) shows a Court that has used the duty to consult in a confusing manner that could undermine reconciliation; and Daniel

Voth (Reading 10.5) demonstrates how the judicial process can pit Aboriginal groups against one another and fracture allegiances.

For Aboriginal litigants, Canadian courts have undoubtedly produced legal change. But what about social and economic change? And has this change been in the desired direction? Like so much else in Canadian politics, the answer remains contested. What cannot be doubted is that the judicial process will be central to the development of Aboriginal law for decades to come.

NOTES

1   Statistics Canada, "Aboriginal Peoples in Canada: Key Results from the 2016 Census," October 25, 2017, http://www.statcan.gc.ca/daily-quotidien/171025/dq171025a-eng.pdf.

2   In recent years, the term "Indigenous" has increasingly been adopted to refer to Aboriginal peoples, especially since the 2007 United Nations Declaration of the Rights of Indigenous Peoples. Justin Trudeau's Liberal government in particular has shifted from the use of "Aboriginal" to "Indigenous" in its communications. In Canada, the two terms are effectively used interchangeably, and the readings in this chapter use both terms. Because "Aboriginal" remains the dominant term in Canadian law and jurisprudence, we retain it in this introduction unless quoting directly.

3   Statistics Canada, "Aboriginal Peoples in Canada."

4   Section 91(24) of the *Constitution Act, 1867* (formerly the *British North America Act*) gives the federal government jurisdiction over "Indians, and Land Reserved for Indians"; and section 35(2) of the *Constitution Act, 1982* mentions "Indians" as well. In *Reference whether "Indians" includes "Eskimo"*, [1939] S.C.R. 104, the Supreme Court ruled federal jurisdiction over "Indians" extended to Inuit, and in *Daniels v. Canada (Indian Affairs and Northern Development)* [2016] 1 S.C.R. 99, it extended this to non-status Indians and Métis. Rules governing "Registered Indians" and Indian reserves are governed by the federal *Indian Act*, and the federal department responsible for Aboriginals is formally known as the Department of Indian Affairs and Northern Development. Under the *Indian Act*, Registered (status) Indians retain certain benefits not available to other Aboriginals (including non-status Indians), such as exemptions from federal and provincial taxes, extended hunting seasons, fewer firearms restrictions and rights associated with reserves. There is also an ongoing debate within the Métis community as to whether self-identification and "mixed ancestry" should be sufficient for Métis membership, or whether people should hold connections to "historically rooted Métis communities." See Chris Andersen, "Who Can Call Themselves Métis," *The Walrus*, December 29, 2017, https://thewalrus.ca/who-can-call-themselves-metis/.

5   Thomas Flanagan, *First Nations? Second Thoughts.* 2nd ed. (Montreal: McGill-Queen's University Press), p. 54.

6   Thomas Flanagan, for example, has written that "the European concept of nation does not properly describe Aboriginal communities" pre-Confederation, that they did not possess sovereignty and that "European colonization of North America was inevitable" (Flanagan, *First Nations*, p. 6). By contrast, John Borrows (Reading 10.2) argues that *terra nullius* connotes a "discriminatory denigration of Indigenous peoples' social organization," that Aboriginal sovereignty predated colonization and that it should be recognized in law. As Borrows's analysis demonstrates, the Supreme Court has not yet fully endorsed this view.

7 Martin Papillon, "Canadian Federalism and the Emerging Mosaic of Aboriginal Multilevel Governance," in Herman Bakvis and Grace Skogstad, eds., *Canadian Federalism: Performance, Effectiveness, and Legitimacy.* 3rd ed. (Toronto: Oxford University Press, 2012), p. 285.

8 Ian Greene, *The Charter of Rights and Freedoms: 30+ Years of Decisions that Shape Canadian Life* (Toronto: Lorimer, 2014), p. 353.

9 *Calder v. British Columbia,* [1973] S.C.R. 313.

10 *R. v. Sparrow,* [1990] 1 S.C.R. 1075.

11 *R. v. Van der Peet,* [1996] 2 S.C.R. 507; *R. v. Côté,* [1996] 3 S.C.R. 139; *R. v. Badger,* [1996] 1 S.C.R. 771; *Delgamuukw v. British Columbia,* [1997] 3 S.C.R. 1010; *R. v. Powley,* [2003] 2 S.C.R. 207.

12 *Tsilhqot'in Nation v. British Columbia,* [2014] 2 S.C.R. 257.

13 Ibid., at para. 69.

14 Ibid.

15 See, for example, Eve Tuck and K. Wayne Yang, "Decolonization is Not a Metaphor," *Decolonization: Indigeneity, Education and Society* 1, no. 1 (2012), p. 9.

16 See Bill Gallagher, *Resource Rulers in Canada: Fortune and Folly on Canada's Road to Resources* (Self-Published, 2012).

17 *Grassy Narrows First Nation v. Ontario (Natural Resources),* [2014] 2 S.C.R. 447.

18 *Haida Nation v. British Columbia (Minister of Forests),* [2004] 3 S.C.R. 511.

19 *Clyde River (Hamlet) v. Petroleum GeoServices Inc.,* [2017] 1 S.C.R. 1069.

20 *Chippewas of the Thames First Nation v. Enbridge Pipelines Inc.,* [2017] 1 S.C.R. 1099.

21 Ibid., at para. 60.

22 *Ktunaxa Nation v. British Columbia (Forests, Lands and Natural Resource Operations),* [2017] 2 S.C.R. 386, at para. 83. Chief Justice McLachlin and Justice Rowe co-authored the majority decision for seven justices. While Justices Moldaver and Côté wrote a separate concurring opinion on religious freedom, they agreed with the majority's reasoning on section 35.

23 *Honouring the Truth, Reconciling for the Future: Summary of the Final Report of the Truth and Reconciliation Commission of Canada* (Ottawa: Truth and Reconciliation Commission of Canada, 2015).

24 Voth discusses the case at the Manitoba Court of Appeal and at the Supreme Court of Canada. *Manitoba Métis Federation Inc. v. Canada (Attorney General) and Manitoba (Attorney General),* (2008) MBCA 131; *Manitoba Métis Federation v. Canada (Attorney General) and Manitoba (Attorney General),* [2013] 1 S.C.R. 623. The Supreme Court found in favour of the MMF (6–2), holding that the Crown "failed to implement the land grant provision set out in s. 31 of the *Manitoba Act, 1870* in accordance with the honour of the Crown" (at para. 154).

25 Gerald N. Rosenberg, *The Hollow Hope: Can Courts Bring About Social Change?* (Chicago: University of Chicago Press, 1991).

10.1

Political Failure, Judicial Opportunity: The Supreme Court of Canada and Aboriginal and Treaty Rights

Kirsten Matoy Carlson

American Review of Canadian Studies 44, no.3 (2014), 334–346. Reprinted with permission.

What role do courts play in public policymaking? Fifty years ago, Robert Dahl found that courts largely defer to the political process in national public policymaking.… In contrast, I find that the Supreme Court of Canada succeeded in revitalizing the making of Aboriginal and treaty rights policy in the 1990s even without the support of politicians.… The Court reinvigorated the policymaking process by encouraging politicians to revisit Aboriginal and treaty rights policies. When the political process failed, the Court re-entered the policymaking arena by recognizing and protecting a wide range of Aboriginal and treaty rights from governmental incursion.…

I distinguish Aboriginal peoples and their experiences from interest groups under the Charter. Three factors differentiate Aboriginal peoples. First, the Charter does not include section 35(1) recognizing and protecting existing Aboriginal and treaty rights. Second, while scholars and politicians assumed that the courts would interpret Charter rights, the *Constitution Act* established a political process for the definition of Aboriginal and treaty rights. Thus, court power in this area was not a foregone conclusion. Third, Aboriginal and treaty rights differ from Charter rights because they seek to change the division of powers by adding Aboriginal governments into Canadian federalism as a third order of government.…

My account emphasizes both how politics affect the Court and how the Court affects politics. As in other moments of court power, the Court's rise was the product of complex institutional and political dynamics. The Court emerged as a significant and influential player in policymaking at a specific historical juncture as the political process failed to accommodate Aboriginal and treaty rights, Aboriginal peoples mobilized legally, and the institutional power of the Court grew.…

Aboriginal and Treaty Rights in Canada Before and After 1982

Aboriginal and treaty rights fared poorly both in the courts and politically before 1982. The federal government dominated policymaking regarding Aboriginal peoples under section 91(24) of the *Constitution Act, 1867*. It pursued policies of assimilation, either extinguishing Aboriginal rights through treaties or denying their existence and validity through the *Indian Act*. Provincial governments joined the federal government in rarely recognizing Aboriginal rights. As late as 1969, the federal government issued a policy statement announcing that it had fulfilled its treaty obligations and denying the existence of Aboriginal rights. The government soon retracted this statement. It devised several policies for settling Aboriginal claims from 1969 to 1981, but these policies refused to recognize Aboriginal rights and required their extinguishment in negotiated agreements.... The Supreme Court of Canada heard 20 Aboriginal and treaty rights cases before 1982, but only recognized the claimed right in 25 percent of them. Aboriginal and treaty rights received very little protection as federal and provincial governments could unilaterally abrogate these rights at will through legislation or other action....

The rise of the Supreme Court as a player in Aboriginal and treaty rights policy occurred after a decade of heated political debates among Aboriginal peoples, provincial premiers, and the federal government. Section 35 of the *Constitution Act, 1982* recognized and affirmed the "existing aboriginal and treaty rights" of Indian, Métis, and Inuit peoples. From 1983 to 1987, federal officials, provincial Premiers, and Aboriginal leaders engaged in four widely televised constitutional conferences to define the scope and content of section 35. Aboriginal peoples faced provincial as well as federal opposition to their proposals for constitutional recognition of an inherent right to self-government. As a result, these very public conferences ended without any major agreement on the scope or content of Aboriginal and treaty rights in section 35(1).

A month after the failure of the last conference on constitutional issues relating to Aboriginal peoples, then Prime Minister Brian Mulroney announced the Meech Lake Accord, which would recognize Quebec as a distinct society within Canada and considerably increase provincial powers in exchange for Quebec's formal acceptance of the *Constitution Act, 1982*. Aboriginal peoples found the terms of the Accord, as well as their exclusion from it, shocking. They remained in Quebec's shadow.

Changing the Game: *R. v. Sparrow*

In 1990, the Supreme Court influenced the constitutional discussions over Aboriginal and treaty rights by deciding *R. v. Sparrow*. In *Sparrow*, the defendant, Ron Sparrow, a member of the Musqueam First Nation, claimed that federal fishing regulations violated his Aboriginal right to fish as protected by section 35(1). The lower courts found that Sparrow did not have an existing Aboriginal right, but he prevailed in the Supreme Court. The Court unanimously held that Aboriginal and treaty rights are constitutionally protected rights that cannot be unilaterally extinguished by the federal and provincial governments. Governments cannot interfere with Aboriginal and treaty rights without justifying the infringement with a valid legislative objective.

The Court's initially positive stance towards section 35(1) in *Sparrow* helped create the basic conditions for its later role as a policymaker. The decision strengthened the legal position of Aboriginal peoples and encouraged them to litigate more Aboriginal and treaty rights claims. The Court's holding combined with its instruction for "a generous, liberal interpretation of the words in the constitutional provision" suggested that courts might be more receptive to Aboriginal and treaty rights claims than they had been previously. As a result, Aboriginal peoples sought further recognition and protection of their rights, filing three times as many Aboriginal title claims after 1990 as they did before....

In *Sparrow*, the Court extended its newly defined institutional role under the *Constitution Act, 1982* beyond the Charter of Rights and Freedoms. While the Charter extended judicial review to cases brought under it, the Court distinguished Section 35(1) as "not subject to s. 1 of the Charter, nor to the legislative override under s. 33." Section 35's location outside the Charter, however, did not leave it unenforceable. Rather, the Court commenced its *Sparrow* decision by stating that it was its first opportunity to explore the scope of sec. 35(1) and "indicate its strength as a promise to Aboriginal peoples." It found that even though "there is no explicit language in the provision that authorizes this court or any court to assess the legitimacy of any government legislation that restricts aboriginal rights ... the words 'recognition and affirmation' ... import some restraint on the exercise of sovereign power." ... It established high expectations for governments, reaffirming its responsibility to act as a fiduciary and demanding justification of regulations that infringe on Aboriginal rights.

The Court's language also indicated its awareness of its role in a larger dialogue about Aboriginal and treaty rights. The Court explained, "s. 35(1) of the *Constitution Act, 1982*, represents the culmination of a long and difficult struggle in both the political forum and the courts for the constitutional recognition of aboriginal rights." The Court then implied a preference for political negotiations, stating, "Section 35(1), at the least, provides a solid constitutional base upon which subsequent negotiations can take place." But in lieu of these negotiations, it did not shy away from holding the government to the promise it made in Section 35(1)....

Sparrow's Political Aftermath: Reinvigorating the Constitutional Debate

The *Sparrow* decision signaled to federal and provincial leaders that they should return to the negotiating table if they did not want the Court making Aboriginal and treaty policy. The Mulroney government's review of several policies shortly after the Court decided *Sparrow* suggests it received the Court's message. Generally, the government announced that it would establish a Royal Commission.... Within two years, the Department of Fisheries and Oceans (DFO) had adopted the Aboriginal Fisheries Strategy, which reallocates fishing licenses to Aboriginal peoples and involves them in the design and implementation of fisheries management. Similarly, the government revised its comprehensive land claims policy based on the *Sparrow* decision. Provincial leaders also responded by revisiting their Aboriginal positions....

Two almost contemporaneous bursts of Aboriginal activism created additional incentives for political elites to include Aboriginal and treaty rights in future constitutional negotiations. First, less than a month after the Court handed down *Sparrow*, the Meech Lake Accord died, in part due to Aboriginal protest. Aboriginal peoples, led by the Assembly of First Nations and Elijah Harper, a member of the Manitoba Legislative Assembly and the Red Sucker Lake First Nations, used the Meech Lake Accord ratification process to illustrate the repercussions of leaving Aboriginal peoples out of constitutional negotiations.... Without ratification by all the provinces, the Meech Lake Accord died.

Second, violence erupted in Quebec after the town of Oka sought to extend a golf course onto lands claimed by the Mohawk. Negotiations between the town and the Mohawk failed. Over 200 Mohawk protested and barricaded the location. The situation escalated in July 1990 when Quebec police, trying to tear down the barricade, exchanged gunfire with the protesters. Negotiations resumed and failed. At Quebec's request, more than 2,500 soldiers in full combat gear arrived in tanks at the edge of the disputed territory in September. The 78-day standoff finally ended when the Mohawk suddenly abandoned the barricade. The Oka Crisis demonstrated how badly Canadian politicians had miscalculated the ramifications of ignoring Aboriginal and treaty rights. The *Sparrow* decision, the death of the Meech Lake Accord, and the armed confrontation at Oka pushed Aboriginal and treaty rights into the Canadian political spotlight.

Reconsidering Aboriginal and Treaty Rights

The political branches responded to the *Sparrow* decision, the Meech Lake fiasco, and the Oka Crisis by including Aboriginal issues in a final round of constitutional negotiations. These final constitutional negotiations, known as the

Canada Round ... sought public input into the reform package and then asked for public approval of it.

Political elites negotiated Aboriginal and treaty rights policy in the Canada Round in the shadow of the *Sparrow* decision. First, *Sparrow* reminded governments that the Court could – and would – define Aboriginal and treaty rights and may have influenced the federal government's decision to include them in the negotiations. The political activity following *Sparrow* also loomed in the foreground. Both the newly elected Ontario Premier, Bob Rae, and Premier Gary Filmon of Manitoba knew that they could not afford to marginalize Aboriginal and treaty rights and insisted that Aboriginal peoples participate fully in the Canada Round. For the first time, Aboriginal leaders joined provincial premiers and federal officials in all the constitutional reform discussions. Second, Aboriginal leaders brought *Sparrow* to the table with them as a negotiating tool. The deal they crafted, the Charlottetown Accord, reflected the increased strength of Aboriginal peoples at the negotiating table. It included an explicit recognition of an inherent right to self-government, substantial protections for Aboriginal and treaty rights, and a permanent place for Aboriginal peoples at the constitutional negotiating table. A majority of Canadian voters, however, rejected the Charlottetown Accord in a public referendum on October 26, 1992....

The failure of the Canada Round shifted the institutional dynamics around Aboriginal and treaty rights policymaking. With no future constitutional negotiations on the horizon, the opportunity arose for the Court to continue its role as a constitutional interpreter of Aboriginal and treaty rights....

The Ascension of the Court as Policymaker

The Court heard an unprecedented number – 26 in all – of Aboriginal and treaty rights cases from 1996 to 2005.... Twenty-two of these cases involved section 35(1) claims. The Court applied section 35(1) in 81 percent of these cases, and used them to redefine Aboriginal and treaty rights policy. Within the next ten years, the Court would apply the *Sparrow* test in cases involving treaty rights (*R. v. Badger*), Aboriginal title (*Delgamuukw v. British Columbia*), claims to self-governance (*R. v. Pamajewon*), Métis harvesting rights (*R v. Powley*), and to both federal and provincial actions (*R. v. Côte*).

The Court's widespread application of *Sparrow* in myriad Aboriginal and treaty rights cases translated into the increased recognition and protection of Aboriginal and treaty rights. After 1990, the Court recognized Métis harvesting rights, Mik'maq treaty rights, Aboriginal rights to commercial and subsistence fishing, and treaty hunting, fishing and harvesting rights.

The Court decided these cases despite the loss of political will to discuss the constitutionality of Aboriginal and treaty rights and opposition by governments to the recognition and protection of these rights through litigation. Federal and provincial governments continued to prosecute Aboriginal peoples for exercising their fishing and hunting rights (*Marshall v. Canada*; *R. v. Blais*; *R. v. Powley*), to appeal acquittals of Aboriginal peoples based on these rights (e.g., *R. v. Vanderpeet*), and to argue for their limited interpretations (e.g., *R. v. Sundown*; *Blais*; *Powley*). The Court granted leave to appeal in two cases filed after *Sparrow* was decided – *Marshall* and *Powley* – in which the government denied the existence of the right entirely and refused to offer any kind of justification for its infringement.

Federal and provincial governments did revise some Aboriginal and treaty rights policies from 1992 to 2005. The biggest policy changes came from the Chretien government, which issued its Inherent Right Policy in 1995, and the British Columbia government, which changed its treaty making policy. Both of these policy changes created more opportunities for intergovernmental negotiations between First Nations and governments over the division of powers. The time-consuming nature of these processes, their limited applicability to Inuit and First Nations, and the concessions required of Aboriginal peoples in them has undercut the substance and progress of these policy changes.

In contrast, the Court decided several Aboriginal and treaty rights cases from 1996 to 2005. These cases represented a dramatic shift from the Court's earlier jurisprudence, which sanctioned the Crown's unilateral extinguishment of Aboriginal and treaty rights. The Court reversed lower court opinions refusing to recognize and protect these rights. As a whole, these decisions redefined Aboriginal and treaty rights policy by defining the scope and content of some Aboriginal and treaty rights, constitutionally limiting the ability of federal and provincial governments to infringe on or extinguish these rights, and requiring government consultation with Aboriginal peoples before these rights could be infringed.

Courts, Political Processes, and Policymaking

The history of the constitutional entrenchment of Aboriginal and treaty rights suggests a more complicated narrative about the interactions among courts, politicians, and interest groups than is usually told in Canada. It demonstrates how political failures may present opportunities for court power. Judges interpreted a new constitutional provision to empower and recognize the rights of a historically marginalized population. Aboriginal peoples used the *Sparrow* decision to ensure their representation in subsequent constitutional negotiations, to negotiate a favorable constitutional deal, and to persuade the public of the legitimacy of their claims. When political elites failed to define the scope and content of Aboriginal and treaty rights, the Court redefined and shaped future policies in an area of increasing national significance.

The Court, however, did not act in isolation – its ascendancy in the Aboriginal and treaty rights arena was not simply a cunning power grab at a time when political elites were weak and the Court, itself, was growing in power. The Court's primacy occurred within a specific historical context. It depended not only upon its own decision to act but on the constitutional entrenchment of Aboriginal and treaty rights, Aboriginal legal mobilization, and the judicialization of politics in Canada....

The Court's action indicates its sophistication as a player in the larger series of interactions among courts and politicians. Courts may act strategically as decision-makers. Intentionally or unintentionally, by taking a strong initial stance on Aboriginal rights in *Sparrow*, a fairly uncontroversial subsistence fishing rights case, the Court positioned itself to play a larger role in Aboriginal and treaty rights policy. In interpreting section 35(1), the Court encouraged political definition of Aboriginal and treaty rights but did so in a gradual way that would allow it to step in to preserve its own institutional legitimacy if the political process failed. In this context, political inertia empowered rather than constrained the Court....

My analysis offers insights into the importance of court power for politically marginalized groups. After centuries of legal and political marginalization, Aboriginal peoples bartered their way into the Constitution, but only further definition of their rights could dislodge the binary division of powers and the prevailing myth of Canada's two founding peoples. The constitutional entrenchment of their rights increased the likelihood that the Court could intervene to redefine their rights by creating legally plausible arguments to support more recognition and protection of their rights. But it was not clear that the courts would make decisions favorable to them.

In response, Aboriginal peoples mobilized politically and legally to preserve their enhanced position within the polity. This mobilization elevated them to the constitutional table, challenging both executive federalism and dualism in Canada.... The Court's decision in *Sparrow* helped to keep Aboriginal and treaty rights on the national political agenda at a time when the Meech Lake Accord threatened to eclipse it by resolving the more central and important Quebec issue and thus, ending further constitutional negotiations. Without this judicial support, Aboriginal peoples may have lost political currency in subsequent political negotiations. With it, Aboriginal peoples remained at the table and gained fuller participatory rights in the next round of constitutional negotiations. Moreover, the Court's decision inspired further legal and political mobilization by Aboriginal peoples. Thus, for Aboriginal peoples, the implications of court power here extended beyond the court's decisions to the legal and political advocacy they fueled.

10.2

The Durability of *Terra Nullius*: *Tsilhqot'in v. British Columbia*

John Borrows

University of British Columbia Law Review 48, no.3 (2015), 701–742.
Reprinted with permission.

Indigenous peoples across the world have long critiqued the idea that their lands were legally vacant when Europeans arrived on their shores. Nevertheless, many countries with significant Indigenous populations were subject to legal regimes which confiscated Indigenous lands and destabilized their decision-making powers. Though never perfected, the so-called doctrine of discovery was deployed to justify these actions. It was premised on the notion that Indigenous peoples were inferior to other peoples. Under this doctrine lands were declared to be legally empty, allowing European law to control Indigenous peoples.

The Supreme Court of Canada purported to deny a key aspect of this creed in the case of *Tsilhqot'in Nation v. British Columbia* (2014). It wrote that "[t]he doctrine of *terra nullius* (that no one owned the land prior to European assertion of sovereignty) never applied in Canada." If only this declaration were deeply true. Canadian law still has *terra nullius* written all over it. The same paragraph which purportedly denied *terra nullius* contains the following statement: "At the time of assertion of European sovereignty, the Crown acquired radical or underlying title to all the land in the province." If land was owned by Indigenous peoples prior to the assertion of European sovereignty, one wonders how the Crown acquired title in that same land by merely asserting sovereignty, without a version of *terra nullius* being deployed. The Crown's claim to underlying title on this basis "does not make sense." Some kind of legal vacuum must be imagined to create the Crown's radical title. The emptiness at the heart of the Court's decision is disturbing.

Nevertheless, Canadian law took an important step towards repairing its relationships with Indigenous peoples with the *Tsilhqot'in* decision. It is an exceedingly strong decision. It demonstrates the intelligence, wisdom, honesty, humility and humanity of an extraordinary group of jurists. It illustrates the constitution's recognition of Canada's pre-existing legal systems in Canada, which generate present-day rights through the doctrine of continuity. The case is very significant; it contains ground-shifting implications. Canada is a better place as a result of its 153 paragraphs. It sets a new world standard. I do not believe I am overstating the case's positive implications.

At the same time it must be emphasized that the *Tsilhqot'in* case is only "a" step in the right direction. Reconciliation between Indigenous peoples and the Crown still remains a long distance down the road. One bold stride forward, however strong, does not a journey make. The Crown (and Courts) must shed further baggage to ensure the decision's trajectory continues. The Crown's unilateral claims to land in British Columbia must be further attenuated. Nevertheless, to be balanced and fair, I must re-emphasize that there are many positive elements to the case. It has prompted hope in many Indigenous communities. While euphoria will fade it would be unwise to minimize the decision's potential. *Tsilhqot'in* contains many principles which might take us towards more mutually desirable legal destinations....

Case Context and Decision

The Tsilhqot'in people are one of these Nations who never surrendered their land and independence. They are an Athapaskan speaking people, of approximately 3,000 citizens, organized into 6 bands. They live in what has been labelled central British Columbia, though they have resided there from time immemorial. The Tsilhqot'in people possess distinct systems of law and governance. They have a rich traditional economy and strong social bonds. They are a resilient people with an abiding commitment to sustainable living. They are not afraid to assert their rights and they have constantly fought to retain and protect their land....

In 1864 the Tsilhqot'in eventually blocked the construction of a road through their territory. In retaliation for this and other atrocities against their people, the Tsilhqot'in killed nineteen settlers and expelled every non-native person from their territory. It was war. However, British Columbia colonial officials regarded Tsilhqot'in defence as criminal justice offences. As a result colonial officials hanged four Tsilhqot'in Chiefs under questionable legal proceedings. The denial of due process drove a further wedge between the parties. Deceit and dishonourable conduct have marked British Columbia's relations with First Nations peoples ever since. Nevertheless the Tsilhqot'in continued to live on their territory with minimal external demands on their lands. This was the case until 1983, when the Province of British Columbia granted Carrier Lumber Ltd. a forest licence to cut trees in part of their territory.

Over the next 15 years the Tsilhqot'in resisted the province's actions through blockades, negotiations and legal action. In 1998 they eventually filed for a declaration of Aboriginal title before the courts. They claimed approximately 438,000 ha (4,380 km2) of land under section 35(1) of Canada's Constitution....

[*Ed. note*: The author then describes the trial decision, which was largely "favourable to the Tsilhqot'in people," and the Court of Appeal decision, which overturned the trial court and created a narrowed claim for Aboriginal title.]

On June 26, 2014, the Supreme Court of Canada granted a declaration of Aboriginal title over Tsilhqot'in land. The Tsilhqot'in were recognized as holding "ownership rights similar to those associated with fee simple, including: the right to decide how the land will be used; the right of enjoyment and occupancy of the land; the right to possess the land; the right to the economic benefits of the land; and the right to pro-actively use and manage the land." At the same time, as noted, the provincial Crown's overriding sovereignty and underlying title was strengthened in relation to Indigenous peoples without effectively justifying the reason for this conclusion.

In coming to this conclusion (construing Aboriginal title broadly in favour of the Tsilhqot'in appellants while reinforcing the province's political authority) the Supreme Court of Canada applied well-developed lines of judicial authority. It held that cases such as *Calder, Guerin, Sparrow, Delgaumuukw,* and *Haida Nation* established that:

- The Crown's underlying title was always subject to established Aboriginal land interests;

- Aboriginal title recognized broad rights of land use and control;

- Aboriginal title could only be infringed by governments if they established a compelling and substantial public interest and acted in a manner which upheld their fiduciary duty;

- Consultation with Aboriginal peoples was necessary when resource development was proposed on claimed land;

- Governments had a legal duty to engage in good faith negotiation to resolve Aboriginal title claims.

In making these findings the Court attempted to signal that it was not breaking new legal ground in recognizing Tsilhqot'in title. There is some truth to this view. Many earlier cases (such as the ones cited above) support a large, liberal and generous conception of Aboriginal rights. These cases allowed the Court to hold that Aboriginal title was to be broadly construed.

Nevertheless, while the cited cases support the Court's ultimate decision, the Court also ignored, reinterpreted or downplayed other decisions which would have made it more difficult for the Tsilhqot'in to succeed in establishing title.... The Court could have cited these less favourable opinions to deal with Aboriginal rights on much narrower grounds – but it did not. This choice greatly benefitted the Tsilhqot'in....

Sufficiency of Occupation

Social organization can be seen as a synonym for self-government. When a Nation organizes itself over an entire territory, and controls land, makes decisions about its use, and excludes others in accordance with its laws, we should be clear about what we are saying – such a Nation governs itself.... The main issue before the Supreme Court was a contrasting characterization of Indigenous governance relative to land (i.e. Tsilhqot'in social organization in their territory)....

[In *Tsilhqot'in*], the Supreme Court of Canada found the Tsilhqot'in had proven sufficiency of occupation necessary to establish Aboriginal title.... The Tsilhqot'in exhibited "evidence of a strong presence on or over the land claimed, manifesting itself in acts of occupation that could reasonably be interpreted as demonstrating that the land in question belonged to, was controlled by, or was under the exclusive stewardship of the claimant group." Control and stewardship are hallmarks of effective governance, and the Tsilhqot'in organized themselves ways which secured their lands and resources....

The Court's recognition of the territorial nature of Aboriginal title is a huge victory for the Tsilhqot'in. It shows that Canadian law can recognize and affirm estates in land which pre-date European arrival. It demonstrates that Indigenous land use can be characterized in ways which do not denigrate Aboriginal peoples' social organization. This bodes well for future cases where social organization will figure prominently in claims to governance over these and similar Aboriginal title lands.

Evidence and Indigenous Legal Traditions

... It is worthwhile noting (though the Supreme Court did not explicitly acknowledge this fact) that large portions of the *Tsilhqot'in* case depended upon Tsilhqot'in Elders testimony, who gave evidence on their territory.... Tsilhqot'in Elders spoke volumes about Tsilhqot'in law. They did it in their own language and in accordance with their own legal traditions. Their rules of conduct and legal narratives were very prominent features of the case. Tsilhqot'in invocations and applications of Indigenous law were keys to establishing a sufficiency of Indigenous social organization necessary to prove title. The Trial Judge accepted the fact that the "Tsilhqot'in people were a rule ordered society." The positive receipt of oral tradition demonstrates the absolute centrality of Indigenous law in confirming Aboriginal rights. In this respect Indigenous law and governance is an essential part of Canada's constitutional framework.... In making these statements the Supreme Court implicitly affirmed that Indigenous legal traditions can give rise to enforceable obligations within Canadian law....

Rights Conferred by Aboriginal Title

Having recognized that the Tsilhqot'in people possess Aboriginal title, the Supreme Court subsequently explored the scope of rights conferred through a broader recognition of Aboriginal title. It wrote that the rights which flow from Aboriginal title are very broad. Since Tsilhqot'in title arose prior to European sovereignty the Court called it an independent legal interest (meaning it was not created by the Crown or Courts).... Furthermore, the Supreme Court of Canada held that the Crown does not retain any beneficial interest on Aboriginal title lands. First Nations who have title can use their lands as they choose, subject to two limits: 1) Aboriginal title cannot be alienated except to the Crown, 2) nor can it be encumbered, developed or misused in ways that would prevent future generations of the group from using and enjoying it....

As noted, the breadth of this holding is unparalleled in Canadian law. While Aboriginal title theoretically existed in Canadian law prior to this decision, this is the first time an Indigenous group has actually secured a robust protection of their land rights in Canadian courts. The Tsilhqot'in people possess natural resources, which are likely valued in the billions of dollars. The Tsilhqot'in can protect their lands against environmental degradation, which has been one of their major goals. They can also continue to run horses, hunt, fish, trap and gather if they so choose. They can prioritize these uses over other uses, despite the fact that their lands and resources might have higher market values if leased or licenced for other purposes. All this demonstrates that the Tsilhqot'in now have a measure of control over their land which is largely akin to (though not exactly like) fee simple ownership....

Furthermore, in noting the breadth of Aboriginal title, it needs to be acknowledged that Tsilhqot'in title also imposes significant limits on the Crown's underlying title. In this spirit the Court wrote that "Crown title ... is burdened by the pre-existing legal rights of Aboriginal people who occupied and used the land prior to European arrival." ... These limits substantially reduce the ability of the Crown to control, use or benefit from land subject to Aboriginal title. However, the Crown still has a paramount legal interest in Aboriginal title lands. This is where the judgment becomes more problematic when considering whether the court has really rejected the doctrine of discovery.

Terra Nullius Reproduced

Despite the Supreme Court's purported refutation of *terra nullius* at paragraph 69 of the decision, as noted, in the very same paragraph the Court reproduced and reaffirmed one of the doctrine's most troubling aspects. The Court wrote, citing *Guerin*: "At the time of assertion of European sovereignty, the Crown acquired radical or underlying title to all the land in the province." This problematic claim rests on an empty incantation; it is devoid of self-reflectivity concerning the discriminatory denigration of Indigenous peoples' social organization which it implies.

The declaration that Crown sovereignty can displace Indigenous sovereignty through a bare assertion presumes the land is empty of governance or that Indigenous governance powers are inferior. British words uttered half a world away diminished Tsilhqot'in jurisdiction. As noted, this implies there is some kind of emptiness underlying Aboriginal title which must be filled by Crown-derived law to avoid a legal vacuum. Yet the Tsilhqot'in people were in full possession of the land at the time – as the Court now recognizes. The Tsilhqot'in "historically acted in a way that would communicate to third parties that it held the land for its own purposes." They excluded others from their lands on a territorial basis. They repelled the Crown's citizens during the Tsilhqot'in war. In light of these findings the assertion of Crown sovereignty leading to radical Crown title rests on an *"inanis iustificationem"*: an empty justification. It is a restatement of the doctrine of *terra nullius* despite protestations to the contrary. The assertion of radical title retroactively affirms the Crown's appropriation of Indigenous legal interests without their knowledge or consent. In most other contexts this would be called stealing. But this is not just a dime store robbery; this fraud radically dispossesses each original owner.

We must ask why the Crown and not the Tsilhqot'in, have underlying title to the land in their territories? After all the Tsilhqot'in people are its rightful, prior and present owners, as the Supreme Court now acknowledges. It "does not make sense" to vest rights possessed by Indigenous peoples in other peoples through the mere act of assertion. It requires a discriminatory denigration of Indigenous peoples' laws and life-ways to hold that Indigenous title and governance is subject to non-Indigenous paramount interests as a by-product of European sovereign assertions. There is no Tsilhqot'in authority for such a proposition. There is no persuasive common law authority either – other than the Court saying it is so, and repeating this through the generations. This "bootstrapping" is not persuasive from a common law or Indigenous legal perspective....

Thus, it is apparent that the doctrine of *terra nullius* has not been entirely or even largely expunged from Canadian law, despite the Supreme Court of Canada's protestations to the contrary. Aboriginal title is still a "burden on the underlying title asserted by the Crown at sovereignty." The doctrine of discovery is alive and well in Canada. One wonders how the Supreme Court could bluntly state that it was rejecting *terra nullius* while leaving much of the doctrine intact. The Court's undermining of Indigenous constitutional rights and interests do not accord with its high-sounding statements....

The negative implications of this approach create at least four significant challenges for Indigenous peoples: a) the Crown is empowered to justifiably infringe Aboriginal title, b) the Crown can shift the burden for proving Aboriginal title to Indigenous peoples, c) the Crown can subject Indigenous peoples to provincial jurisdiction, d) the Courts can characterize Aboriginal title as existing within legal vacuum when provincial legislation is not present. The problems with *terra nullius* are not just academic conundrums; they have significant negative effects in the real world. The Crown continues to benefit from the discriminatory denigration of Aboriginal peoples' social organization at the time so-called sovereignty was asserted over their lands....

Conclusion

This brief essay has suggested that Indigenous peoples should not accept the Court's word at face value when it says the doctrine of *terra nullius* does not apply in Canada. Despite the decision's many strengths the *Tsilhqot'in* case is implicitly saturated with the prejudice which marks the doctrine of discovery. While Indigenous peoples now have the possibility of owning and using lands in British Columbia for a wide variety of purposes, the Crown still retains underlying title and paramount sovereign authority over these lands. These propositions are the echo and remnants of *terra nullius*. Crown power can be directly traced to discriminatory assumptions rooted in European sovereign assertions when the Crown "discovered" Canada. These assumptions are repeated and applied in the *Tsilhqot'in* case.

In making this assessment I trust that readers will understand that the Supreme Court of Canada has taken *a* significant step in the road to decolonization by recognizing that Aboriginal title exists in Canada. Its conclusion is very positive for Indigenous peoples in the broader context of the dispossession they have encountered. As was stated at the outset of this paper, the *Tsilhqot'in* case is one of the most important Indigenous rights cases the world has seen. This is cause for celebration and appreciation. Tsilhqot'in people now own and control their land in the claim area and can use it for a wide variety of purposes. If Aboriginal peoples claim title through some "official" process they now have a broader array of remedies to enforce that interest. They can bring Injunctions, claim damages, and secure orders for the Crown to engage if proper consultation and accommodation of Aboriginal title. If Aboriginal peoples establish title they can also bring legal suits to secure all the usual remedies for a breach of land rights, as long as they are adapted to the special nature of Aboriginal peoples' relationship to land. This is all very powerful stuff....

At the same time this brief comment highlights that one powerful step towards a better relationship does not a journey make. The Crown and Courts still have much baggage to jettison in constructing a jurisprudence which clearly rejects that Canada was *terra nullius* when Europeans arrived. The *Tsilhqot'in* decision demonstrates there is still a long distance to travel in this regard. Canadian law will remain problematic for Indigenous peoples as long as it continues to assume away the underlying title and overarching governance powers which First Nations possess. However, a powerful seed has now been planted which could expand the Court's future vision; it now needs to be given room grow much further....

10.3

Is the Sky the Limit? Aboriginal Legal Rights in Resource Development
Dwight Newman

Macdonald-Laurier Institute for Public Policy, June 2015, http://www.macdonaldlaurier.ca/files/pdf/MLIAboriginalResourcesNo7-06-15-WebReady-V3.pdf. Excerpt reprinted with permission.

Over the past three decades, in the cases that have been brought before them, Canadian courts have continued their work in interpreting the entrenched Aboriginal and treaty rights in section 35 of the *Constitution Act, 1982*. Section 35(1) provides: "The existing aboriginal and treaty rights of the aboriginal peoples of Canada are hereby recognized and affirmed." This rather undetailed text clearly presented a significant challenge for the courts in interpreting the effects of that section.

The Supreme Court of Canada, in its 1990 decision in the *Sparrow* fishing rights case, adopted a description of section 35's purpose as that of achieving a "just settlement" with Aboriginal Canadians. Later decisions of the Court have worked out an evolving conceptual framework that sees the section as aspiring to "reconciliation" between Aboriginal and non-Aboriginal Canadians. In the 2005 *Mikisew Cree* decision, Justice Binnie writes that "[t]he fundamental objective of the modern law of aboriginal and treaty rights is the reconciliation of aboriginal peoples and non-aboriginal peoples and their respective claims, interests and ambitions."

The Aboriginal and treaty rights entrenched by section 35 are increasingly recognized as bearing on issues related to natural resource development and management.... The judicial recognition of Aboriginal land rights had actually begun before the 1982 constitutional amendment, commencing with the 1973 *Calder* decision. Although the Nisga'a Nation lost on technical issues in the case, six of the seven justices of the Supreme Court of Canada recognized in principle the existence of Aboriginal title – a continuing claim to land where it had not been surrendered through treaties.

After 1982, such claims had even greater potential impact, since rights, even if ill-defined, were now constitutionally protected [*Ed. note*: See Reading 10.1]. The Supreme Court of Canada gradually had to work out various elements of a jurisprudence, often in the context of claims bearing on resources. Later, in the *Sparrow* case, it established a test for when limits on Aboriginal rights were justified. In the 1996 *Van der Peet* decision, again concerning fishing rights, it worked out a general legal test for the identification of protected Aboriginal rights. In 1997, it applied and modified that test in the context of Aboriginal rights to land, or Aboriginal title, in the well-known *Delgamuukw* decision. Through the same period, it was also working out principles of treaty interpretation, such as in the 1996 *Badger* case on hunting rights under Treaty 8.

However, Aboriginal and treaty rights do not come into play just in the context of a direct government regulation affecting well-established traditional harvesting rights. Resource development projects can have indirect impacts as well, something that has come to the fore in the "duty to consult" jurisprudence that has dominated the last 10 years of case law. In 2004, in the *Haida* decision, the Court elaborated a duty on governments, in situations of uncertainty about rights claims, to consult with potentially affected Aboriginal communities when contemplating a government decision that could impact on their rights. That case has given rise to a massive jurisprudence on the "duty to consult," and many resource projects are affected. [*Ed. note*: See Reading 10.4]

Revisiting the "Winning Streak"

... The legal implications of Aboriginal and treaty rights in the context of natural resources issues are often not well understood. Some Canadians seemingly still do not realize that there are constitutionally entrenched Aboriginal and treaty rights that apply in this area. Others think that Aboriginal and treaty rights potentially put relatively complete legal control in the hands of Aboriginal communities.

The latter view has flourished in part through well-meaning efforts by some to explain to Canadians the real legal weight of Aboriginal and treaty rights. Bill Gallagher's writing and speaking about 200 legal wins by Aboriginal communities in *Resource Rulers in Canada* has been very prominently referenced of late and has been important in waking up Canadians to Aboriginal communities' real legal power. In describing these significant developments, though, Gallagher has used language that suggests that Aboriginal communities are winning, and will win, every case they take before the courts.… These sorts of claims have had a broader influence, with the claim getting gradually transmuted by media commentators.…

While these comments are an important corrective for any Canadians who do not realize the significant impacts of Aboriginal rights, they risk going too far in the other direction and falling into inaccuracy. First, Gallagher's reference to "charter protection" for Aboriginal rights is not correct. The Aboriginal and treaty rights provision in section 35 of the *Constitution Act, 1982* is not part of the *Charter* but is a distinct part of the Constitution, subject to its own interpretive principles in light of its different text and history. Second, many hearing Gallagher's remarks will interpret a "winning streak" to sound like something without exceptions. In reality, Aboriginal communities have won many important cases, but they have also lost numerous times as well.…

Just who can properly describe a particular case as a "win" or "loss" is complicated. Each case has a result for the parties and also has some effects on the law more generally. These do not necessarily match up. In some cases, an Aboriginal litigant has lost on the facts, but the Court has elaborated law that helps future claims. But it is also possible to see the law develop in ways unfavourable to future Aboriginal claims. On any reasonable reading of the case law history, it is simply not accurate to think there is some unbroken chain of Aboriginal "wins." …

The object of the current paper, then, is to try to get behind what is really going on in terms of recent developments on Aboriginal and treaty rights that potentially impact on natural resource development. Considering, in particular, the case law of about the last five years, what is the legal trajectory on these issues? As is often the case in the real world of law, the answer is complex and nuanced.…

Haida Nation

... The duty to consult doctrine has developed in a particular form in the Canadian courts since the *Haida Nation* decision in 2004. The transformative aspect of the *Haida* decision was that the Supreme Court of Canada articulated that governments making administrative decisions that may impact on Aboriginal or treaty rights have a proactive duty to consult with the potentially impacted Aboriginal communities before making the decision. As put by Chief Justice McLachlin in that case, "consultation and accommodation before final claims resolution, while challenging, is not impossible, and indeed is an essential corollary to the honourable process of reconciliation that s. 35 demands. It preserves the Aboriginal interest pending claims resolution and fosters a relationship between the parties that makes possible negotiations, the preferred process for achieving ultimate reconciliation." In the post-*Haida* case law, both the honour of the Crown and the section 35 aspiration to reconciliation demand that governments consult before they cause negative impacts on Aboriginal and treaty rights, even where there remains uncertainty on the scope of the right.

The more specific requirements of consultation depend on the circumstances and are not always easy to determine. But they vary based on the *prima facie* strength of the right at issue and the degree of adverse impact on the right. The requirements may include accommodation (still not well defined) in some circumstances, although the courts have also consistently said that the duty to consult is not to be a legal veto power held by Aboriginal communities.

The duty to consult stands out as an example of the courts not always foreseeing the actual consequences of their decisions. Although the court judgments were all about governments being subject to the duty to consult – and governments responded by developing various policy regimes to carry out consultation – the main impact of the duty to consult has arguably been to empower some Aboriginal communities in the context of negotiations with the private sector....

Recent Case Law on Duty to Consult

There have been a series of key legal developments since 2010 on the duty to consult. Some of this case law has simply seen the Supreme Court of Canada clearing up certain points. The *Rio Tinto* case in 2010, in particular, saw the Court explaining that how governments meet the duty to consult is effectively up to them.... In that decision, the Court also reaffirmed that the duty to consult related to the future impacts of government decisions and did not provide a means of seeking remedies for historical wrongs. However, to complicate matters, the Court almost went out of its way to signal some upcoming issues on the duty to consult, thus generating new uncertainties. First, it affirmed some lower court case law that the duty to consult applies from an early, strategic stage of decision-making, but without offering any explanation on how to identify exactly when the duty is triggered. Second, the Court said that the question of whether there was a duty to consult on legislative action was a question for later, thus undermining some past case law on the point....

The underlying question of whether there is a legal duty to consult in the context of legislative action has remained a key uncertainty that has very significant policy implications. In December 2014, a trial court released an enormously complex judgment suggesting that some phases of the process moving toward legislation cannot trigger the duty to consult, but others can (*Courtoreille v. Canada* 2014). [*Ed. note*: The Federal Court of Appeal reversed this decision in 2016, holding in part that the ruling offended the principle of parliamentary privilege. The Supreme Court has granted leave to appeal.] ... The uncertainty continues, in ways that have some paralysing effects on government policy-making when governments do not know if they can move forward on statutory reforms or not.

Other decisions engaging with aspects of the duty to consult during this time period have arguably also seen the courts generating new uncertainties. In the same year as *Rio Tinto*, the Supreme Court of Canada's complex, divided decision in *Beckman v. Little Salmon* also saw it enunciating the idea that the legal duty to consult continues to exist in some form even when all parties have signed a modern treaty agreement that purported to exhaustively define consultation arrangements between the Yukon government and First Nations....

If the duty to consult doctrine can be used to challenge legislation over whether it provides enough room for consultation, then that altered doctrine has very significant consequences. In 2012, a number of mining legislation amendments came into effect in Ontario so as to require prospectors and developers to engage in consultation and to try to clarify the role of industry in consultation. The statutory amendments rendered moot some litigation that had arisen from the absence of such provisions. However, today some Aboriginal community advocates are looking at the possibility of challenging the constitutionality of the legislation, arguing that it offers inadequate protections....

In several major recent court decisions, Aboriginal communities have lost on major duty to consult issues. Where governments have been responsibly attempting to follow the law on duty to consult and been developing reasonable processes, their efforts are being accepted by courts as meeting their legal responsibilities.... Courts are trying to make the law work in sensible ways, including in the context of projects that have effects on multiple traditional territories....

Historic Treaties

Historic treaties negotiated in the latter part of the 19th century and first part of the 20th century are relatively short agreements that do not contain detailed textual clauses. Many of the Victorian or numbered treaties that reach from Ontario across the prairies and into northeastern British Columbia and parts of the North have, though, a clause that simultaneously preserves traditional harvesting rights for the treaty First Nations and that allows the Crown to "take up" land for agriculture, mining, and other development.

There have been some important recent judicial decisions on the implications of these treaties for resource issues, including one of the more significant "losses" for Aboriginal communities. In July 2014, the Supreme Court of Canada decided the *Grassy Narrows* case. This case arose from special issues raised related to the application of Treaty 3 in the Keewatin area in northwestern Ontario, which was federal land at the time Treaty 3 was signed and only later annexed to Ontario. The case arose from an argument put by the Aboriginal claimants that even today the federal government needed to be involved in any decisions by the province of Ontario to "take up" land for development.

The Court reaffirmed the Court of Appeal's rejection of this argument. In the course of its decision, the Supreme Court also more generally interpreted the "taking up" clause in the Victorian/numbered treaties and affirmed the primary provincial role in resource development decisions and the possibility of provinces justifiably infringing on treaty rights. Several paragraphs of the decision try to develop a careful balance between the protection of traditional harvesting rights, the consultation obligations that arise when there are impacts on these rights, and the ultimate context of possible infringement of these rights. As in much of its section 35 jurisprudence, an optimistic read of the Court's statements would be seen as trying to create conditions for negotiation between the parties, and a more sceptical read would see it as not creating much certainty on some issues....

There may be further complexities ahead. First Nations in many regions have been particularly enthusiastic to pursue resource revenue sharing deals. Where advocacy in the political process has not worked – the Saskatchewan government for one has firmly rejected the notion – they have threatened possible legal action based on oral history accounts of the treaties. There are some oral history accounts to the effect that First Nations in some of these negotiations intended only to share the land to the "depth of a plough," even though this is obviously inconsistent with the treaty text that refers to the Crown taking up land for mining purposes. Based on these accounts, while still Chief of the Federation of Saskatchewan Indian Nations (FSIN), Perry Bellegarde began referring to "unfinished treaty business" and asserting Aboriginal claims to subsurface resources in the regions covered by the numbered treaties in order to seek a resource revenue sharing arrangement. He continued to press these claims after being elected as National Chief of the Assembly of First Nations in December 2014. These claims will be a challenging future issue....

Modern Treaties

Modern treaties, negotiated in recent decades with many First Nations in areas without historic treaties – though not very successfully in British Columbia – are highly detailed agreements hundreds of pages in length. The federal government provides funding to First Nations for the negotiations, which is an advance against a future settlement. Where negotiations have been unsuccessful, there is an emerging issue. In British Columbia, First Nations now have over $500 million in outstanding debt from treaty negotiations.

Even with agreed modern treaties, a number of legal issues have emerged in recent years. In 2010, the Supreme Court of Canada decided two major cases on the principles applying to interpretation of modern treaties (*Beckman v. Little Salmon/Carmacks First Nation* and *Quebec (Attorney General) v. Moses*). One of these in particular, the *Little Salmon* case, saw the Court move away from textual interpretation of these treaties and open up room for further consultation in ongoing relationships going even beyond the treaty terms.... What courts have to say about the interpretation of modern treaties will have major implications for resource development in the years ahead.

The particular uncertainty around treaty rights creates very significant challenges. The negotiation of modern treaties has the potential to resolve outstanding issues and to mark an agreement to new paths forward. From many Aboriginal perspectives, such treaties embody new relationships in sacred ways, and from some perspectives, they must thus be allowed to have an evolving meaning. But governments seeking clarity and certainty may well become less inclined to enter into various kinds of treaty terms if they cannot predict what they will mean....

Common Themes
Legal Overreaches by Aboriginal Communities
In the context of long histories of dispossession, assimilation attempts, and other injustices, Aboriginal communities naturally turn to the courts for

remedies. Important decisions in support of Aboriginal and treaty rights have been welcome responses to past and present wrongs. However, at a policy and strategic level, the pursuit of some claims through the courts can have unexpected – and negative – outcomes.

Aboriginal communities are sometimes subjected to a chorus of suggestions that they can get farther and farther ahead through more spending on lawyers and more litigation. The language suggesting they have attained an unbroken string of wins, discussed in the introduction, may feed into this idea. But there have been losses as well, and a great deal of uncertainty, and the pursuit of further cases in a nonstrategic manner might actually add further losses or, more seriously, adverse legal precedents....

Aboriginal communities have overreached in some cases, sometimes with negative results that have set back their position from what it would have been if they had never litigated. Obviously, parties are free to press for the full extent of their legal rights. But if they push for rights beyond those they can plausibly attain within the legal system, we may say they have overreached in non-strategic ways.

The *Grassy Narrows* decision of the Supreme Court of Canada is a very important example of the point. While the Aboriginal community that pursued the case wanted only to argue some quite particular aspects of Treaty 3 as it bore on parts of northwestern Ontario, the case ended up being a chance for the Supreme Court of Canada to reinforce the provinces' roles in regulating and their ability to impact on treaty rights. In doing so, the Court extended propositions from *Tsilhqot'in* to the treaty rights context, while silently overturning past case law on the point. The effort to use Treaty 3 in highly constraining ways against the Province of Ontario ended with provincial rights affirmed in new ways. A tenuous legal case led to the generation of what other Aboriginal communities may consider a highly adverse precedent....

Although there is not one simple legal trajectory, and there are many things going on at the same time, there is a real possibility that *Tsilhqot'in* should be considered as having marked a sort of peak for Aboriginal rights claims in the courts, at least in the short term. Though time will tell on some claims, there is a real possibility that Aboriginal communities might be better situated right now to build on their legal victories through serious negotiations with governments and industry. Their ability to do so obviously depends on government and industry willingness to come to the table. But the pressure of the case law encourages that as well....

Legal overreaches may arise from genuine misassessments of the likelihood of success of a particular claim, in which case nobody would want to tell a party not to pursue its rights to the fullest extent possible. However, they may also arise from an environment in which it is assumed too readily that cases will succeed, in which there are complex financial incentives on some parties to encourage litigation, and/or in which communities feel like legal claims are their sole option....

The Supreme Court of Canada's Unintended Consequences on the Natural Resource Sector

When matters have gone before the courts, we also see that courts have ended up making decisions that may have unintended consequences on the natural resource sector. That the Supreme Court of Canada can have such unintended consequences has been a reality outside of the section 35 case law in other areas of constitutional law where it has made decisions without considering their implications for resource development. This is quite possibly because unlike in the days of justices like Jack Major or Gérard LaForest, the Court has not in recent years had any justices with extensive pre-judiciary work on resource sector issues. It may also be that industry associations are not necessarily intervening in cases that appear to be more remote from their direct concerns.

In the section 35 jurisprudence of the last five years, we see the specific paragraphs in *Tsilhqot'in* that cause confusion, such as those on consent. We might also add the case's reference to Aboriginal title lands being subject only to uses that are consistent with their use by future generations, something that constrains Aboriginal communities in their own use of their land, but in ways that are challenging to interpret.

We see the duty to consult jurisprudence that has generated major uncertainties on matters like whether legislation is subject to the duty to consult – an uncertainty that paralyses even statutory reforms desired by Aboriginal communities.... We also have seen that diverging possibilities on interpretation have a real potential to undermine the incentives to negotiate modern treaties. The Court arguably needs to measure more carefully the implications of some of its decisions.

Unintended consequences on the resource sector would largely seem to flow from lack of attention to the ways in which cases in this context affect many different parties, only some of whom are before the courts.... Complex policy-making is unavoidable in this area, and we do need to find ways to ensure that courts are responding appropriately. For example, in the judicial appointments process, governments should ensure that courts that will deal with Aboriginal rights issues have judges on them with strong background knowledge of Aboriginal law, natural resources issues, and economic issues generally.

Emerging Flashpoints

A typical year at the Supreme Court of Canada actually features only a handful of section 35 cases, out of the 70 to 100 cases the Court adjudicates. But there is a significant amount of litigation on section 35 issues filed and underway in lower courts. There are real prospects of major issues in the courts in the years ahead. In a March 2014 speech, which she gave three months before the Court released her *Tsilhqot'in* judgment, Chief Justice Beverly McLachlin articulated that section 35 cases, rather than *Charter* cases, will likely be the key challenges for the Court in the coming years.

In the context of natural resources, one of these upcoming issues relates specifically to the meaning of modern treaties, and that is one with huge significance to future negotiation processes.... There are a variety of reasons why there might be emerging flashpoints rather than emerging solutions. The courts have developed some of their Aboriginal rights doctrines that affect resource development in ways that encourage parties to perpetuate or develop uncertainties. In the context of the duty to consult, when their arguments fail in political arenas, Aboriginal communities across the numbered treaty areas can press for better economic opportunities in their often struggling communities. They can argue that there is uncertainty on the historic numbered treaties, and whether they transferred subsurface minerals or only shared land "to the depth of a plough." As noted above, Perry Bellegarde has referred to this as "unfinished treaty business." The creation of new uncertainties has been seen as a way of furthering opportunities for Aboriginal communities, rather than the focus always being on optimal policy approaches.

Another flashpoint: For a variety of reasons, including opposition from non-Aboriginal Canadians with certain perspectives on environmental and other matters, it has become extremely difficult to get major infrastructure projects done in Canada. Amongst others, the impacts of Aboriginal title and of the duty to consult on long linear infrastructure projects are subject to immense lack of clarity. Those trying to get projects done may end up in the years ahead in more confrontational stances with Aboriginal communities if some greater clarity cannot be achieved. New possibilities of direct litigation between Aboriginal communities and industry seem to be emerging....

Recommendations

- Possibly the most important recommendation here is greater clarity in the political discourse, something best achieved by everyone being ready to take some necessary risks. Political actors should be willing to discuss the strength of governments' position and the legal tools available to governments, including their ability to justifiably infringe or override Aboriginal and treaty rights, and should develop policies (ideally in collaboration with Aboriginal communities) around when they will use these tools in the public interest. This approach could be beneficial to all as it would assist in clarifying the possible routes forward. That is a challenging recommendation of course, given all the dynamics in the area. But all sides are going to need to take some courageous steps.

- In the face of calls always pushing for principled stances, Aboriginal communities need to think about what will best move things forward at a practical level. They should take advantage of their considerable new power and consider where negotiation will lead to better results than litigation. They need to advocate for their rights, while being cautious about overreaching in cases that might set back their own position.

- Courts should try to refrain from including ambiguous statements in their Aboriginal rights judgments. When they do, legal scholars and others should critique those court decisions and try to clear up those ambiguities. Governments should consider taking reference cases to the courts to seek faster clarification of some of the ambiguities existing in this case law.

- Industry associations and governments should work to lessen the burdens on smaller companies through providing appropriate forms of assistance to them around duty to consult issues. Permitting the use of flow-through share financing for consultation costs is a positive step, but further steps could include the ongoing development of pooled consultation resources and the development of very clear policies on what is required in the context of early-stage exploration activities.

- Industry should continue to develop its understanding of Aboriginal issues and work to engage proactively with Aboriginal communities and organizations. Industry should also consider whether there are new litigation options available to it or whether it should consider intervening in litigation that is underway.

These recommendations are complex to implement and are directed to different sectors, but the hope is not to drive wedges, rather to bring various interests together. There are no simple solutions. But appropriate action in response to themes that emerge from the past five years of section 35 jurisprudence, especially strong efforts by all sides that promote principled and practical negotiations, can help further work toward positive shared futures for Aboriginal and non-Aboriginal Canadians in a country that has enormous potential as a resource superpower.

10.4

"Aboriginal-Crown Relations and the Duty to Consult in the Supreme Court"

Minh Do

Political Science, University of Toronto

In Canada, the duty to consult constitutes a constitutional obligation requiring the Crown to consult Aboriginal parties when an action may adversely affect their rights. The Supreme Court of Canada (SCC) has elaborated how the duty to consult fits within Canadian constitutionalism by linking the duty to principles of the Crown's fiduciary duty and the goal of reconciliation. However, the literature concerning the SCC's conceptualization of reconciliation has yet to address how the duty, which aims to facilitate reconciliation, may reveal additional advancements in the SCC's understanding of reconciliation. Moreover, the policy prescriptions offered by the SCC when advising actors how to fulfill the duty also reveals the policy consequences of advancing particular understandings of reconciliation.

Drawing from the SCC "duty to consult" cases, I argue that consistency, whereby Aboriginal rights are treated as compatible with Canadian law and Crown authority, is the main vision of reconciliation advanced by the SCC. According to this vision, existing Canadian law and policy processes can adjudicate and protect the rights of Aboriginal peoples. Although the SCC's articulation of the honour of the Crown opens some possibility for Crown representatives to advance a new relationship with Aboriginal peoples, the other policy ideas conforming to consistency, and even "resignation" as reconciliation, can ultimately dissuade Crown actors from this goal.

A Summary of the Duty to Consult Jurisprudence

Generally, in the five "duty to consult" cases analyzed below – *Haida Nation* (2004), *Taku River* (2004), *Mikisew Cree* (2005), *Carrier Sekani* (2010) and *Little Salmon/Carmacks* (2010) – the SCC has held that the duty is a part of the Crown's fiduciary obligation towards Aboriginal peoples, an obligation that can be understood to "temper" the Crown's sovereign power. An extension of this fiduciary obligation is that the Crown must act honourably with the intention of substantially addressing the concerns of Aboriginal peoples whose rights are at stake. Acting honourably includes consulting Aboriginal peoples when Crown actions may adversely impact Aboriginal rights or rights claims. The duty is grounded in the honour of the Crown and good faith dealings to facilitate the goal of reconciliation between the rights of Aboriginal peoples and the sovereignty of the Crown. [*Ed. note:* see Reading 10.3]

The SCC has also steadily articulated the scope and content of the duty. For instance, the adequacy of consultation is determined by a spectrum involving the strength of the rights claim and the potential for infringing rights. Dubious claims with minimal risk of infringement may only involve a duty to give notice of proposed action, while strong rights claims and serious infringements to the rights claims may require more substantive forms of consultation. The Crown proposal under scrutiny only includes specific actions at issue rather than broader projects from which the specific action is a part. In effect, the duty cannot be triggered to address historical grievances. The SCC also clarified that the duty still exists regardless of whether it is explicitly stated in the terms of a modern treaty. Consequently, the duty cannot be bargained away in a modern treaty process because it is a constitutional obligation.

The court has also provided guidelines relating to the processes of fulfilling the duty. The SCC has stated that administrative tribunals can only fulfill the constitutional obligation if they are given an explicit legislative mandate and the necessary resources to provide remedial concessions. However, the judiciary has ruled that tribunals "with the authority to consider questions of law, are likely to have the concomitant jurisdiction to interpret or decide constitutional questions, including those concerning section 35(1)."[1] Therefore, tribunals with specialized experience regarding issues arising from extractive industries are considered to be fit to administer Aboriginal rights.

Reconciliation as Understood by the SCC

Since the duty to consult is meant to facilitate reconciliation between the Crown and Aboriginal peoples, how the SCC defines the duty and promotes certain policy measures in the fulfillment of the duty may help reveal the SCC's understanding of what reconciliation entails and how it should be advanced by policy actors. Over time, the SCC has presented three varying understandings of reconciliation: as a process of *curtailing* federal powers to be consistent with fiduciary responsibilities to Aboriginal peoples, a means to *resolve* pre-existing Aboriginal claims with the Crown's assertion of sovereignty, and as a principle representing the need to *balance* Aboriginal and non-Aboriginal societal interests.

Scholars identify reconciliation as a process of *curtailing* federal powers to respect fiduciary responsibilities to Aboriginal peoples in the *Sparrow* (1990) decision. In this decision, reconciliation is framed as requiring the federal government to exercise its powers in a manner consistent with advancing the rights and interest of Aboriginal peoples, so infringements to Aboriginal rights require justification. D'Arcy Vermette claims this approach to reconciliation attempts to "protect Aboriginal rights from unchecked federal powers" and places the judiciary in a position to re-examine the Crown's sovereign power relative to Aboriginal rights.[2] Therefore, Aboriginal rights are reconciled with the existence of Canadian society and sovereignty in a manner that rejects assimilation and accepts Aboriginal difference.

By contrast, the idea that reconciliation *resolves* pre-existing Aboriginal claims with the Crown's assertion of sovereignty departs from reconciliation as curtailing federal powers, since the courts are less willing to challenge the existence of Crown sovereignty and its territorial control. Under this conceptualization of reconciliation, Aboriginal rights must be defined within the structures of Crown sovereignty and territorial control, which dismisses how Aboriginal rights flow from distinct legal systems that emerge from Aboriginal peoples' territorial occupation and control of land. This understanding of reconciliation emerged in the *Van der Peet* (1996) decision, but did not wholly displace the previous understanding of reconciliation as curtailing federal powers and the *Sparrow* justification test remains.

Finally, reconciliation can also take the form of *balancing* Aboriginal and non-Aboriginal interests to advance social harmony. This approach to reconciliation has been heavily criticized for severely limiting Aboriginal rights and placing most of the burden of reconciliation on Aboriginal communities to reconcile themselves to status quo Canadian societal interests. As a result, social peace is advanced by the necessity of violating Aboriginal rights, which reflects poorly on Canadian society's attempt to reject colonial and assimilatory practices. This additional understanding of reconciliation is identified in the *Gladstone* (1996) case, thus layering a new dimension to reconciliation in Aboriginal law jurisprudence.

Elsewhere, Mark Walters has conceptualized different visions of reconciliation: resignation, consistency, or relationship.[3] Though not identical, Walters' *resignation* is broadly similar to the SCC's "balancing" approach listed above; the very idea of "balancing" interests to advance social harmony means Aboriginal peoples must be resigned to Crown sovereignty as well as the societal interests of non-Aboriginal peoples, rendering Aboriginal rights as less deserving of protection than other interests. Likewise, the idea that reconciliation should "resolve" pre-existing Aboriginal claims within the framework of Crown sovereignty and territorial control is compatible with Walters' *consistency* approach to reconciliation, as Crown sovereignty is not challenged as a precondition to respecting Aboriginal claims. Finally, reconciliation involving the "curtailment" of federal powers to protect Aboriginal rights is most consistent with Walter's *relationship* approach to reconciliation. Since the federal government must curtail its powers over Aboriginal peoples to protect Aboriginal rights, this approach may facilitate the inclusion of Aboriginal legal and political practices in Canada's constitutional order.

My subsequent analysis employs Walter's framework of categorizing reconciliation as resignation, consistency and relationship to the Supreme Court's major "duty to consult" cases. These cases are *Haida Nation* (2004), *Taku River* (2004), *Mikisew Cree* (2005), *Carrier Sekani* (2010) and *Little Salmon/Carmacks* (2010). The first three cases (the "*Haida* trilogy") articulate the major dimensions of the duty, such as when the duty is triggered and its scope; the 2010 cases supplement the *Haida* trilogy by further elaborating the conditions under which the duty is triggered and its scope. Of the three models of reconciliation, the Supreme Court has been most favourable to the "consistency" approach to reconciliation, wherein Aboriginal claims are to be resolved within the framework of crown sovereignty.

Reconciliation as Resignation

The SCC presents ideas that conform to the vision of reconciliation as resignation. For instance, in the *Little Salmon/Carmacks* case, the SCC made a statement that treats certain Aboriginal grievances as characteristics of the past, rather than a real present-day problem grounded in a past legacy of mistreatment by the Crown. Although this statement was only made in one case, it is nevertheless troubling that the SCC in any instance would ignore the ongoing and continuous nature of the relationship between the Crown and Aboriginal peoples: that they have a long legacy of distrust that affects current relations between the two parties. Although the SCC is not directly stating that Aboriginal peoples should be resigned to Crown sovereignty, the Court, in this instance, denies the extent to which the Crown represses Aboriginal peoples. Denying this legacy of repression undermines Aboriginal peoples' own demands to be free from Crown control and jurisdictional authority. Moreover, this denial also represents a distinct narration or account of events that is highly contested by Aboriginal peoples.

A more direct idea that alludes to resignation is how the SCC consistently denies the existence of Aboriginal sovereignty. Although the SCC states in four of the five cases (all but *Carrier-Sekani*) that Aboriginal peoples held prior occupancy of lands before European contact, the political autonomy that accompanies occupancy is not recognized. Only in one instance in the *Haida* case did the SCC use the phrase "Aboriginal sovereignty" to acknowledge pre-existing political autonomy before Crown sovereignty. These allusions to Crown-Aboriginal relations as resignation through the denial of Aboriginal sovereignty are also found when the SCC describes the purpose of reconciliation. In all five cases, the SCC states the purpose of reconciliation concerns harmonizing and balancing interests, so advancing reconciliation encourages both the Crown and Aboriginal peoples to find compromises to avoid confrontation. All five cases demonstrate that the court believes reconciliation between Crown sovereignty and prior Aboriginal occupancy is best achieved when parties are willing to compromise to find consensus, rather than take hard negotiating positions that can only be resolved through formal adjudication processes. However, if the goal of s. 35 is to recognize and affirm Aboriginal rights, it is problematic that defending Aboriginal rights could be interpreted as taking a hard negotiating position.

In another instance, the Supreme Court treats reconciliation, which is the goal of the duty, as an event to "move on" from the past rather than an ongoing process. When the SCC historicizes Aboriginal grievances in *Little Salmon/Carmacks*, it states that the process of reconciliation is a means to settle "ancient grievances" as "the future is more important than the past." However, "moving on" without first addressing the problematic aspects of the past is not accepted by many Aboriginal peoples. When addressing how Aboriginal peoples should behave in the context of the duty to consult, the SCC then states that Aboriginal peoples should not forget that they are also Canadians that need to "fully participate with other Canadians in their collective governance." In each of these five cases, the SCC states that Aboriginal peoples cannot expect certain measures of accommodation in the consultative process. Consequently, the SCC has emphasized that Aboriginal peoples have no veto in the consultative process. Instead, policy outcomes should reflect the result of the consensual relationship between the Crown and Aboriginal peoples.

Reconciliation as Consistency

The SCC most frequently expresses visions of reconciliation as consistent with the broader Canadian constitutional framework. When the SCC asserts the idea that Aboriginal people held occupancy of lands before the Crown asserted its sovereignty, this prior occupancy is understood to give rise to different rights, such as the duty to consult, that can be exercised and respected *within* Crown sovereignty. Although the SCC presents ideas that are problematic from the standpoint of Aboriginal peoples' claims to political sovereignty, there is at least the recognition that Aboriginal peoples have a special place in Canada's constitutional order by virtue of their prior occupancy. But valuing Aboriginal rights is constrained by other norms, such as the norm to respect *de facto* Crown sovereignty.

The Supreme Court also reflects a vision of consistency when describing how the adequacy of the duty can be assessed using existing standards of administrative law and policy responsiveness. The duty is treated as an extension of existing Canadian legal principles, most notably procedural rights. The court rejects the possibility that Aboriginal legal traditions should be incorporated. In the *Little Salmon/Carmacks* (2010) case, the Little Salmon/Carmacks First Nation refuted the idea that administrative law can adequately protect Aboriginal rights, but the SCC remained firm that "administrative law is flexible enough to give full weight to the constitutional interests of the First Nation." Therefore, the SCC recognizes that Aboriginal peoples have distinct constitutional rights, but these rights are articulated using concepts found in Canadian law. In both *Little Salmon* and *Mikisew Cree*, the duty to consult is treated as a right to ensure the Crown's procedural obligations to Aboriginal peoples in the same manner as upholding procedural fairness to other actors.

The SCC also takes the position that consultation must be meaningful to Aboriginal parties for the duty to be fulfilled. Particularly in the cases constituting the *Haida* trilogy, the SCC emphasizes that consultation must involve the *possibility* that the Crown will alter its plans to address the views of the affected Aboriginal party; this possibility necessarily entails the Crown seriously considering the views of the consulted. This standard articulated by the SCC is consistent with regular consultative processes and does not consider Aboriginal understandings or practices of consultation.

While the *Haida* trilogy invoked the principle of "proportionality" to provide guidelines on the content of the duty when it is triggered, the SCC has been less willing to prescribe *how* the duty should be fulfilled. The Court has stated in two cases that the Crown must fulfill the duty and must exercise its powers to create administrative schemes for that purpose. However, the SCC often restricts itself to commenting about policy instruments involved in the specific dispute they must adjudicate. For instance, since *Carrier Sekani* (2010) involved a dispute over regulatory review, the SCC addressed the role of tribunals and found that tribunals often cannot engage in consultation themselves, but can assess whether the duty has been fulfilled. Yet the SCC has remained relatively silent regarding how the Crown can fulfill the duty.

In contrast, the court is more willing to articulate policy problems and offer policy solutions by clarifying the scope and content of the duty for policy actors to act with more certainty. The SCC's aversion to articulate the means by which the duty can be fulfilled most likely reflects the Court's own institutional role and limits. The SCC is willing to intervene to clarify disputes or offer remedies in certain disputes, but prefers political actors to create schemes to fulfill the duty.

Reconciliation as Relationship

Lastly, some of the SCC's policy ideas indicate visions of reconciliation as requiring the need to create a distinct relationship between the Crown and Aboriginal peoples. When framing the purpose of the duty in *Haida*, the SCC holds that Aboriginal peoples were never conquered. In *Mikisew Cree* and *Little Salmon/Carmacks*, the Court finds that the duty prevents indifference that has, in the past, undermined attempts at reconciliation. The SCC's mentioning of the duty as a means to prevent Crown indifference can be interpreted as a positioning of reconciliation as a societal goal with real stakes rather than simply a lofty, distant ambition. In *Mikisew Cree*, the Court even says that infringement of unproven Aboriginal rights could be "as destructive of the process of reconciliation as some of the larger and more explosive controversies." These two ideas frame the purpose of the duty as a means to facilitate a new relationship between the Crown and Aboriginal peoples, both of which are here to stay.

The SCC's articulation of the honour of the Crown as the standard of expected behaviour for Crown representatives is particularly striking. Although the content of honourable actions differs depending on the context, the SCC is completely clear that the Crown is expected to act honourably towards Aboriginal peoples. Nevertheless, this does not mean that the Crown loses its authority. Rather, acting honourably ensures that the Crown exercises its power legitimately and prevents unilateral actions from being taken against Aboriginal peoples. In *Mikisew Cree* and *Little Salmon/Carmacks*, each of which concern treaty interpretation, the SCC also recognizes that the honour of the Crown is a legal requirement that, in some circumstances, comes from Aboriginal peoples' surrender of land. Therefore, a distinct Crown-Aboriginal relationship does not reflect magnanimous actions from the Crown, but represents an obligation grounded in exchanges and promises made between two parties.

Conclusion

Although the five duty to consult cases examined in this paper reveal that all three visions of reconciliation are advanced to some degree, the SCC ultimately interprets and resolves Crown-Aboriginal disputes within a *consistency* framework of reconciliation, revealing an overall preference for respecting the duty within existing structures of Canadian laws and policy practices. Interestingly, the purpose of reconciliation includes ideas that correspond to all three visions: resignation, relationship and consistency. On the one hand, some framing devices allude to Aboriginal peoples being resigned to accept Crown sovereignty, such as the assertion that the goal of reconciliation is to "move on" from the "ancient grievances." Conversely, other frames show the SCC being sympathetic towards the creation of a distinct relationship between Crown and Aboriginal actors such as the recognition of the Crown's role in preventing just reconciliation to occur through Crown indifference. How the SCC frames the purpose of the duty reveals contestation regarding how the Crown and Aboriginal peoples should advance reconciliation. As a result, policy actors are confronted with conflicting visions of what the duty is meant to achieve, as different justifications for the duty correspond to different understandings of reconciliation. These conflicting justifications make it possible for policy actors to have varying understandings of the goals of duty.

There may be important consequences to the SCC's emphasis on consistency to understand reconciliation between the Crown and Aboriginal peoples. For instance, reconciliation under a consistency framework may promote asymmetrical relations between the Crown and Aboriginal peoples, as the Crown's power to structure the terms of Aboriginal participation in consultative settings remains unchallenged. Consequently, policy actors may be ideationally trapped to consider disputes over consultation and decision making in land management issues as problems of procedural fairness within a Canadian legal framework rather than as disputes over how to incorporate Aboriginal understandings of procedural fairness in the policy process. Indeed, Walters states that the resignation and consistency approaches to reconciliation are inadequate, while reconciliation as relationship is the only viable means to advance decolonization.

If this is the case, then the duty to consult only leaves space for decolonization, where the SCC has characterized the honour of the Crown and certain aspects of the purpose of the duty in terms that are amenable to establishing a new Crown-Aboriginal relationship. Specifically, the honour of the Crown could encourage the Crown to proactively include Aboriginal perspectives when formulating policy processes, effectively "indigenizing" consultation processes. Since other forms of reconciliation find some expression in duty to consult jurisprudence, policy actors may be given some discretion regarding how to advance reconciliation when practicing the duty. More conflict between policy actors may result as varying interpretations of reconciliation and the duty may collide in the policy process.

NOTES

1   Sari Graben and Abbey Sinclair, "Tribunal Administration and the Duty to Consult: A Study of the National Energy Board," *University of Toronto Law Journal* (Fall 2015): 389–90.

2   D'Arcy Vermette, "Dizzying Dialogue: Canadian Courts and the Continuing Justification of the Dispossession of Aboriginal Peoples," *Windsor Yearbook of Access to Justice* 29, no. 1 (2011), p.59.

3   Mark Walters, "The Jurisprudence of Reconciliation: Aboriginal Rights in Canada," in *The Politics of Reconciliation in Multinational Societies*, eds. Will Kymlicka and Bashir Bashir (Oxford: University of Oxford Press, 2008), p.177.

10.5

Her Majesty's Justice Be Done: Métis Legal Mobilization and the Pitfalls to Indigenous Political Movement Building

Daniel Voth

Canadian Journal of Political Science 49, no.2 (2016), 243–266. Reprinted with permission.

The movement by Indigenous peoples to litigate their ongoing disputes with Canada has grown sharply since the 1970s. This trend to channel Indigenous-settler conflict into Canadian courts has reached all Indigenous peoples to varying degrees. The Métis, like their kin and allies in other Indigenous nations, have long-standing grievances stemming from the devastating processes of land dispossession, erasure and termination wrought by settler colonization. Specifically for Métis people, legal mobilization is a key tool being deployed in the effort to seek remediation for the failed disbursement of land to Métis families after the passage of the *Manitoba Act 1870*. The Manitoba Métis Federation (MMF), having been made aware of possible failings in the disbursement of their lands as early as 1968, opened a new legal front in the form of the *MMF v.*

Canada (Attorney General) and *Manitoba (Attorney General)* in 1981 to press their grievances.

Important research has been conducted examining when and how governments and activists engage in legal mobilization.... However, it is less clear what effect deploying litigation to achieve strategic goals has on specific relationships between different (but often related) Indigenous peoples.... This paper will argue that the interaction between the MMF and Treaty 1 peoples seeking leave to intervene at the Manitoba Court of Appeal in *MMF v. Canada* illuminates the way litigating Indigenous-settler disputes can promote divisive, exclusionary, zero-sum political relationships between Indigenous peoples.... These divisions are incentivised by the Supreme Court's explication of Aboriginal title whereby it is in the strategic interest of a single Indigenous people to be found by a judge to have title to the exclusion of their kin in shared Indigenous territories....

The Anatomy of *MMF v. Canada*

In April of 1968 a gathering of Indigenous and non-Indigenous people was held in Winnipeg, Manitoba, styled the annual Indian and Métis Conference. This gathering was in the process of disbanding after the incorporation of the Manitoba Métis Federation on December 28, 1967. The delegates to this conference passed the following resolution: "Resolved: that the Manitoba Métis Federation continue its work of investigation into the Manitoba Métis land grant question." With these seemingly bland words the MMF became embroiled in a fight against Métis land dispossession with legal as well as political dimensions before the organization's first birthday. It would not be until March 8, 2013, almost 45 years later that *MMF v. Canada* would finally come to a head at the Supreme Court of Canada....

The case itself focused on the disbursement of land negotiated by Assiniboia's (as Manitoba was known before July 1870) representatives to Canada in 1870. The MMF argued unsuccessfully at trial in 2007 that the land was not expeditiously provided and, as a result, Métis people were unable to access the full value of their land entitlements under the *Manitoba Act 1870*, and their land grant was not handled in a fashion consistent with the legal concept of the honour of the Crown. The MMF sought declaratory relief to aid in their land claim negotiations with Canada and Manitoba.... The Supreme Court ultimately held in 2013 that the Crown did not fulfil its responsibility to act honourably in distributing the land owed to the Métis after 1870.

The MMF argued at the Supreme Court that because the Métis possess an Aboriginal interest in the land, disbursing the land promised in the *Manitoba Act 1870* was a federal fiduciary duty undertaken on behalf of the Métis. The court held "the relationship between the Métis and the Crown, viewed generally, is fiduciary in nature. However, not all dealings between parties in a fiduciary relationship are governed by fiduciary obligations." ... The Court granted a declaration "that the federal Crown failed to implement the land grant provision set out in s. 31 of the Manitoba Act, 1870 in accordance with the honour of the Crown."

Unpacking the Courts and Legal Mobilization

Choosing to use Canadian courts to advance Indigenous resistance is never an easy decision for Indigenous peoples. Both Canada and the United States deploy(ed) deception, armed and forced removal, erasure and genocide in the service of establishing their settler states. Law-making power as well as the adjudication of those laws was and remains an integral part of the project of creating and maintaining a state comprised of settlers. However, there has long been a struggle by Indigenous peoples and others resisting state oppression to use settler legal discourses and institutions in a way that advances Indigenous material interests without reinforcing the structures of Indigenous oppression. Part of the difficulty of developing these strategic engagements has hinged on the question of whether legal mobilization can effect social change. More generally, the position that judges and courts cannot effect social change is articulated in Gerald Rosenberg's book, *The Hollow Hope: Can Courts Bring About Social Change?* Rosenberg has argued cogently that not only can courts not bring about change in society, they also contribute a false hope that encourages activists to pour their limited resources into what he ultimately believes is a pipe dream.

This touched off a polite and generative exchange with Michael McCann who argues that no institution can single-handedly bring about large-scale change in a society. McCann states that Rosenberg's "analysis itself obscures the fact that discrete institutions are almost never solitary organs of change in our political system." McCann ultimately believes Rosenberg's "focus on courts as independent agents of change involves an unrealistic test that every branch would fail." Instead, McCann approaches the question of social change through legal mobilization with an eye to the contingent nature of the task of affecting change through the courts.... In particular, it is McCann's attention to "building a movement" which seems relevant to this article's interest in the inter-Indigenous politics at play in the MMF case....

[*Ed. note*: The author discusses how some scholars, including John Borrows (see Reading 10.2), call for a "reconceptualization of the operation of precedent" with respect to Indigenous litigation, based on the cultural ethnocentricity inherent in *stare decisis*. He argues that the structure of Canadian law "goes to great lengths to find for the settler status quo."]

The Inter-Indigenous Risks of Litigation

… There are structural biases within Canadian courts that limit their legal mobilization utility. But there is a perhaps more insidious reason to reject Indigenous legal mobilization: courts' indirect power to divide Indigenous peoples rather than contribute to Indigenous movement building.… The *MMF v. Canada* case serves as an interesting avenue through which to investigate these dynamics. My analysis will focus on the interaction between the MMF and Treaty 1 peoples that played out in the Manitoba Court of Appeal. Treaty 1 peoples sought but were denied intervener status using shared counsel for their collective representation at the Manitoba Court of Appeal. This group included Brokenhead Ojibway Nation, Fort Alexander (Sagkeen First Nation), Long Plain First Nation, Peguis First Nation, Roseau River Anishinabe First Nation, Sandy Bay First Nation and Swan Lake First Nation. They sought to intervene collectively as the signatory nations to Treaty 1. The application to intervene was the first attempt that Treaty 1 peoples made to intervene in the court case, not having done so at trial before the Court of Queen's Bench. Interveners must satisfy to the Manitoba Court of Appeal that they have an interest in the subject matter under consideration and a reasonable likelihood that they will "make a useful contribution to the resolution of the appeal without causing injustice to the immediate parties." The Manitoba Court of Appeal includes provisions in its practices that demand a prospective intervener show more than the possibility of one's rights being "affected by the precedential value of a case." The Court will not allow an intervention if it is likely to cause an injustice to the parties or undue delay in the progression of the case.…

The [Treaty 1 peoples'] motion to intervene contained several arguments that would have raised considerable indignation among the MMF litigants. Treaty 1 peoples offered that the Crown had no right to grant any land or rights to the Métis in 1870 without full consultation with, and accommodation of, Treaty 1 peoples.… On this point Treaty 1 peoples posited in their brief that "neither the Métis community, nor the federal or provincial government considered the interests of Treaty 1 First Nations in these proceedings" (para 6). This choice of language positions the Métis with the federal and provincial governments in a collective lack of concern for the interests of First Nations peoples. This frames the Métis not as an Indigenous people agitating for their dispossessed land and rights but rather as part of a cadre of settler interests seeking to dispossess First Nations peoples.…

Adding to this, Treaty 1 peoples argued in their notice of motion that the *Manitoba Act 1870* provided 240 acres of land per Métis child, whereas Treaty 1 provided only 160 acres per family of five, working out to be 32 acres per person. They suggested that these smaller land allotments were unfair.... As James M. Pitsula has argued, Indigenous political organizations have long used differentials in government financial allocations between Métis and First Nations as leverage to extract additional resources from the state. These differentials and the attempt to parlay them into additional resources have also frustrated Indigenous political movement building. However, in the *MMF* case this dynamic is formalized within legal argumentation to position the Métis as competitors for finite resources rather than as subjects of the same programme of dispossession....

However, by seeking to discard parts of the trial judge's findings, Treaty 1 peoples were offering something the MMF should have wanted. The trial judge created a judicial history in his reasons that set up the context of the 1870 Red River Resistance. The trial judge stated that after 1763 "Britain gained sovereignty over all of Canada which would have included the area not covered by the grant, but which ultimately became Manitoba." The trial judge also found that Lord Selkirk had extinguished the Indian title two miles back from either side of the Red River in 1817 (2008a).... Treaty 1 peoples and the Métis have an obvious interest in challenging such an ethnocentric historical narrative. Both First Nations' and Métis' interests are implicated in the trial judge's pro-state view of northern plains history. But counsel for the MMF argued that no court would ever look on the trial judge's historical narrative as binding on future cases. The MMF argued in their response "those comments are a mere recounting of the historical narrative, or of the conventional understanding at the time. The comments are *obiter dicta*, and they are plainly not binding on anyone."

It does not help the MMF to have such blatantly pro-settler interpretations of history connected, even as background, to their claims. As the preceding section has pointed out, such interpretations of the past are patently ethnocentric in their construction of Indigenous peoples, and serve as feats of judicial-historical magic in the service of Crown sovereignty.... In a troubling fashion the MMF's decision to defend the recounting as inconsequential and/or "the conventional understanding at the time" positions the Métis as defenders of the ethnocentric history that serves to dispossess them and their relations in Treaty 1 Nations of land and territory. At the very least, this is a clear moment for judicial co-ordination among all the Indigenous litigants because the resulting narrative benefited neither the Métis nor Treaty 1 peoples.

For their part, the MMF responded on the whole to Treaty 1 peoples by using the rules of the court to undermine the application to intervene. They argued that Treaty 1 peoples did not have an interest in the issues under appeal, that their intervention would unduly add to the time and cost of the case and that they would not make a useful contribution to the litigation.… It is a great oddity that in these interactions with people who should be natural allies by virtue of being subjects of the same processes of settler colonization, the Métis come to be the unlikely defenders of the land tenure system which dispossessed them and their kin in Treaty 1 peoples.

Canada and Manitoba also argued against Treaty 1 intervention. Each order of government used a different argumentation strategy to arrive at the same conclusion. In a troubling way, Canada's and Manitoba's agreement with the MMF did position the MMF to seem happy to work with the common oppressor of all Indigenous peoples to cut out a competing Indigenous interest for a single slice of land. The court dismissed the application stating that adding Treaty 1 peoples as interveners would unduly add to the length and cost of the case without providing a new unique perspective and their presence as interveners would likely change the nature of the litigation before the court.…

Similarly, neither are Treaty 1 peoples helping in their intervention in the MMF case. They constructed their arguments in a confrontational fashion aligning the Métis with their common oppressors while pitting themselves against the Métis for access to land that is exclusively understood as indivisible. The result is that in a single court case there is a fight on two fronts: Métis and First Nations peoples against the state and First Nations peoples against the Métis.…

Political Co-ordination and the Incentives to Exclude

In his book on the Women's Legal Education and Action Fund (LEAF), Manfredi (2004) examines [how] … LEAF forged productive legal alliances with disparate social groups like the Canadian Civil Liberties Association (CCLA), DisAbled Women's Network, Equality for Gays and Lesbians Everywhere (EGALE) and others. [*Ed. note*: See Reading 6.4.] Though on some cases these organizations may find themselves opposing LEAF, on the whole the strategic partnerships and coalitions bolstered LEAF's arguments through co-ordinated legal argumentation. The strength of this approach is that LEAF's submissions were viewed by the court as carrying more weight than that of just a single organization or social group.

These types of alliances and partnerships require the management of complex and contradictory views across social movement groups.… Strategic legal co-ordination and collaboration requires a deft hand to manage distinct interests and goals; however, when done well it seems to contribute greater strategic currency for litigants and their allies while also helping to build a broad movement. In *MMF v. Canada*, though, it appears that the case brought by the MMF was itself uncoordinated and the intervention application and the response were reactionary, inflammatory and divisive. The case and the intervention contributed ill will to an already fractured Indigenous political landscape.

One cannot, however, simply import the successes and strategies used by LEAF to bolster inter-Indigenous legal mobilization. LEAF differs in important ways from the struggle of Indigenous peoples inside and outside the legal system. As Manfredi discusses, "LEAF did not emerge in explicit opposition to the state.... Its founding document was a report commissioned by the federally funded Canadian Advisory Council on the Status of Women." Further LEAF has through its history included the Crown in right of Canada and the Crown in right of several provinces as allies. As discussed above, Indigenous peoples, by the very fact of being Indigenous in a settler state, challenge the foundation of the Crown's legitimacy claims....

While *MMF v. Canada* sought to strengthen the Métis' strategic negotiating position, it was also about relationships to, and interests in, the land. Putting aside the legal understandings of Métis title, land is a complicating factor that incentivizes zero-sum relationships between Indigenous litigants. In *Delgamuukw*, Chief Justice Lamer defined "aboriginal [*sic*] title in terms of the right to exclusive use and occupation of the land." He further rationalized his decision by saying "were it possible to prove title without demonstrating exclusive occupation, the result would be absurd, because it would be possible for more than one Aboriginal nation to have Aboriginal title over the same piece of land, and then for all of them to attempt to assert the right to exclusive use and occupation over it." This is less of an absurdity in the world of Indigenous politics where Métis people engaged in sophisticated processes of treaty making with the other Indigenous peoples sharing the same territory. Chief Justice Lamer's views here are more of an indication of his contrived effort to reconcile Indigenous peoples with the Crown and in the process make Aboriginal rights intelligible to the common law....

Lamer's findings in *Delgamuukw* set the stage for Treaty 1 peoples to not only contend with each other to gain exclusive title, but also with the Métis. Thus where Manfredi correctly noted that organizations like LEAF do not challenge the legitimacy of the state, they also are not wrapped up in complex and multilateral claims to land made by multiple Indigenous peoples. It is in these battles for land where the rewards for deploying zero-sum strategies to show exclusivity are richest....

This article has argued that Indigenous peoples are not realizing an indirect movement building effect from their legal mobilization. Instead, because of the larger structures and biases inherent in using courts, the indirect effect that accrues to Indigenous peoples is an exacerbation of the struggle to build a co-ordinated Indigenous decolonizing movement. To conclude that Indigenous peoples ought not undertake legal action to ameliorate the conditions of oppression under which they find themselves, particularly for Indigenous women, comes from a place of privilege. However, the critiques levelled by critical legal thinkers on the shortcomings of strategic Indigenous legal mobilization suggest that the goals of mobilization cannot be achieved in Canada at this time. Well-documented structural biases coupled with a steadfast, and in some cases illogical, unwillingness on the part of judges to confront those biases, significantly curtail the strategic options for Indigenous litigants in Canadian courts. Add to this the potential for exclusionary conflict between Indigenous peoples illustrated by the interaction between Métis and Treaty 1 peoples in MMF, and one is left with an institution toxic to inter-Indigenous collaboration that cannot help but find for the settler status quo. The best strategy is not to deploy courts in Indigenous struggles seeking strategic ends. The courts cannot be manipulated to produce specific outcomes to the exclusion of others. Attempting to do so not only risks collateral violence against other Métis people, but other Indigenous peoples as well....

10.6
Key Terms

Concepts
Aboriginal and treaty rights (s. 35, *Constitution Act, 1982*)

Aboriginal title

doctrine of discovery

duty to consult

First Nations

historical treaties

honour of the Crown

Indian Act (1876)

"Indians, and Land reserved for Indians" (s. 91(24), *Constitution Act, 1867*)

inter-Indigenous politics

Inuit

Métis

modern treaties

natural resources

reconciliation

residential schools system

sovereignty

stare decisis

status vs. non-status Indian

terra nullius

Institutions, Events and Documents

Calder v. British Columbia, [1973] S.C.R. 313

Charlottetown Accord (1992)

Chippewas of the Thames First Nation v. Enbridge Pipelines Inc., [2017] 1 S.C.R. 1099

Clyde River (Hamlet) v. Petroleum GeoServices Inc., [2017] 1 S.C.R. 1069

Haida Nation v. British Columbia (Minister of Forests), [2004] 3 S.C.R. 511

Indian Act (1876)

Ktunaxa Nation v. British Columbia (Forests, Lands and Natural Resource Operations), [2017] 2 S.C.R. 386

Manitoba Métis Federation (MMF)

Manitoba Métis Federation v. Canada (Attorney General) and Manitoba (Attorney General), [2013] 1 S.C.R. 623

Meech Lake Accord (1987)

Royal Proclamation (1763)

R. v. Sparrow, [1990] 1 S.C.R. 1075.

Statement of the Government of Canada on Indian Policy ("White Paper") (1969)

Treaty 1 (1871)

Truth and Reconciliation Commission of Canada (2015)

Tsilhqot'in Nation v. British Columbia, [2014] 2 S.C.R. 257

11

The Harper Conservatives and the Canadian Judiciary

After thirteen years of Liberal Party rule, Stephen Harper led the Conservative Party of Canada to power in 2006. Having merged the Progressive Conservatives and the Canadian Alliance parties three years before, this was heralded as no ordinary change in government. The Canadian Alliance's predecessor, the Reform Party, had populist roots and a strong base in Western Canada. The party's antipathy towards the Central Canadian "Laurentian consensus" that had governed Canada for much of its existence led many to hope, and others to fear, that the 2006 election would mark the beginning of significant changes to Canadian political institutions and public policy.

The Harper Conservatives spent nine and a half years in power (2006–2015), four in a majority government. After their defeat in the 2015 election, the jury is still out as to whether the Harper decade was indeed transformational; for every commentator who claims Harper fundamentally changed Canada for good or ill, there is another who says his institutional and policy changes were piecemeal, incremental and easy to reverse. The judicial process remains one such area over which the Harper legacy remains hotly debated.

As Thomas Bateman (Reading 11.6) shows, even before he became Prime Minister, there were signs that Harper's relationship with the courts would be different than his predecessors. During the 2006 election, Harper tried to reassure voters that one of the "checks on the power of a Conservative government" would be that "courts have been appointed by the Liberals." While the Harper government's subsequent defeats in the courts largely confirmed this, Bateman argues that it was nonetheless "impolitic" for Harper to say so. Canadians view their judges as independent, non-partisan and non-ideological; judges are beyond reproach, and politicians are loath to criticize them. Yet here was a political leader – on the cusp of becoming Prime Minister – suggesting that the party of appointment would influence judicial decisions. What did this portend for Canadian politics?

In hindsight, the Harper government certainly had a different conception of the role of the judiciary than its predecessors. As Emmett Macfarlane has argued,[1] Harper's skepticism pierced a bipartisan "*Charter* regime" that had existed from 1982 until 2006. Shortly after coming to office, Harper cancelled the Court Challenges Program, although he eventually restored the minority language component in 2008. This reflected a government that was less fawning in its reverence for the *Canadian Charter of Rights in Freedoms* than the other federal parties, and more partial to judges who exhibited deference to Parliament, particularly on criminal justice issues. The Harper government was, in short, the first federal government to treat with suspicion the institutional and policy changes wrought by the *Charter* Revolution.

During the Harper decade, a new relationship between the federal government and the courts emerged in three ways: first, changes to the judicial appointment process, both for lower courts and the Supreme Court of Canada; second, a more combative relationship with the Supreme Court of Canada, made manifest most clearly in the fallout after the Supreme Court's historic rejection of the appointment of Justice Marc Nadon; and third, by the sheer number of losses on major policy issues in the Supreme Court itself, even after the Court was composed of a majority of Harper-appointed judges.

Judicial Appointments to Lower Courts

One of Harper's earliest reforms was to change the composition of the Judicial Advisory Committees (JACs) that select all federally appointed judges (section 96 and 101) apart from the Supreme Court of Canada. The JACs had previously consisted of seven appointed members – three discretionary and four nominated – who ranked judicial candidates as highly recommended, recommended or not recommended (see Chapter 4). The four nominated positions – a judge, a member of a provincial law society, a member of a provincial bar association and a nominee of the provincial Attorney General – were all representatives of the legal community.

The Harper government made three changes to the JACs: it added a representative from the law enforcement community; it limited the judicial representative to a non-voting chair (except to break ties); and removed the "highly recommended" category, returning to the twofold categorization that the JACs had used from 1988 to 1991. In Reading 11.2, Rainer Knopff describes these changes, and the responses they provoked. In Knopff's words, critics railed against the Harper changes as "a startling departure from the 'merit principle' in judicial selection in favour of a dangerous ideological politicization of the judiciary." Such critics included then Chief Justice Beverley McLachlin, former Chief Justice Antonio Lamer and the Canadian Judicial Council. Knopff claims the critiques from the legal community turn on a definition of "merit" that ignores the political reality of judicial decision-making; it is a distinction that also reflects the declaratory model of judicial decision-making (see Chapter 2). The real objection, Knopff surmises, is that by removing the judicial vote and adding a law enforcement representative, the JAC majority shifted from lawyers to non-lawyers. Accordingly, the legal community's exaggerated response to the JAC changes was "the latest episode in the long-standing partisan demonization of the Harper Conservatives as anti-*Charter* and anti-court." It would not be the last.

By the time Harper had been in power for nine years, his government had passed a considerable amount of "tough-on-crime" legislation, including reforms to youth justice, an increasing number of mandatory minimum sentences and reforms to pre-trial custody. Alongside these reforms, Harper's judicial appointments to lower courts represent what Sean Fine (Reading 11.1) calls "the little-noticed half of Mr. Harper's project to toughen Canadian law." In 2007, Harper proclaimed that his government wanted "to make sure that our selection of judges is in correspondence" with its desire to "crack down on crime and make our streets and communities safer." By the end of Harper's tenure, his government had named nearly 75 per cent of the 840 full-time federally appointed judges. Fine documents how the Conservative government sought to appoint judges who would adopt an "originalist" position on the Constitution rather than the Living Tree (see Reading 12.3), accord greater deference to Parliament and accept the loss of judicial discretion entailed by Harper's crime bills. In doing so, they favoured prosecutors over criminal defence attorneys and academics. These judges, Fine argues, are "Mr. Harper's enduring legacy."

Jamie Cameron (Reading 11.3) sees a worrying trend in such appointments. She claims the latter days of the Harper government were characterized by a more overt desire to "pack" courts with judges known for their ideologically conservative views, both at the lower courts and with Harper's final Supreme Court appointment, Justice Russell Brown. Others question whether Harper's stamp on the judiciary was that influential, and whether it will actually endure. Emmett Macfarlane (Reading 11.4) contends that the reaction to Harper's lower court appointments "has been a fascinating mix of alarmism and ahistorical punditry." While Macfarlane argues that ideological diversity is just as important as other forms of diversity on the bench, he claims there is little evidence that Harper's appointments are as conservative as his detractors insist. "The real story of Harper's judicial appointments," Macfarlane writes, "has been how hard it has been for him to find clearly conservative individuals to appoint to the bench."

Whether these lower court appointments will cement Harper's legacy is an open question. However, his changes to the JACs will not endure: in its first year in power, Justin Trudeau's Liberal government reversed the Harper-era changes by removing the law enforcement representative, returning the vote to the judicial representative and reinstating the "highly recommended" category.

Appointments to the Supreme Court of Canada

Harper also introduced changes to the appointment process for the Supreme Court of Canada (see Chapter 4). Under Harper, the process was so varied that, unlike the JAC reforms, it is impossible to discern a "Harper approach" to Supreme Court appointment. After being named to a shortlist by an advisory committee including several representatives from the legal community, Justice Marshall Rothstein became, in 2006, the first Supreme Court appointee to answer questions before a parliamentary committee. However, this committee did not scrutinize Justice Thomas Cromwell's 2008 appointment (see Chapter 4). The next three Harper appointments (Justices Moldaver, Karakatsanis and Wagner) were nominated by a committee of Members of Parliament, and they answered questions before a parliamentary committee as well. Then came the appointment of Justice Marc Nadon.

In Reading 11.6, Thomas Bateman describes what came to be known as the Nadon Affair. With the impending retirement of Quebec Justice Morris Fish, Prime Minister Stephen Harper announced in 2013 that he would appoint Marc Nadon as Fish's replacement. Nadon, a Quebecker, was a semi-retired judge on the Federal Court of Appeal at the time of his appointment. He had been a member of the Federal Court for over two decades, prior to which he had been a long-standing member of the Quebec bar. However, there were questions as to whether he satisfied section 6 of the *Supreme Court Act*, which required appointments to be "among the judges of the Court of Appeal or of the Superior Court of the Province of Quebec or from among the advocates of that Province." Although Nadon was not appointed from the Court of Appeal or Quebec's Superior Court, he had been an advocate in that province several decades earlier. Complicating matters was section 5 of the *Supreme Court Act*, which stated that "Any person may be appointed a judge who is or has been a judge of a superior court of a province or a barrister or advocate of at least ten years standing at the bar of a province." As Bateman describes, "The provisions could be read to require that Quebec appointees (but not others) must be current members of the bar or current members of a s. 96 court in Québec. Nadon was neither."

The federal government sought the legal opinion of retired Supreme Court Justice Ian Binnie, who determined that Justice Nadon's appointment would be constitutional. Retired Supreme Court Justice Louise Charron and Professor Peter Hogg each reviewed Binnie's opinion for the federal government, and agreed. Nadon was formally sworn in to the Supreme Court in October 2013. Later that month, the government introduced an amendment to the *Supreme Court Act* to clarify that a person could be considered an advocate from Quebec "if, at any time, they were an advocate of at least 10 years standing at the bar of that Province." Toronto lawyer Rocco Galati (supported by the province of Quebec) challenged Nadon's appointment and the amendment, which led the Harper government to send a reference to the Supreme Court of Canada. On March 21, 2014, the Supreme Court ruled in *Reference re Supreme Court Act, ss 5 and 6*.[2] Remarkably, the same court that had sworn in Nadon voted 6–1 that his appointment violated the *Supreme Court Act*, insofar as he was neither a member of the Quebec bar nor a Quebec court at the time of his appointment. Even more remarkably, the Supreme Court declared that any changes to the statutory *Supreme Court Act* that affect the "composition" of the Supreme Court – such as the Harper government's clarifying amendment – require unanimous provincial consent under the constitutional amending formula.

Incredible as it was, neither the Supreme Court's rejection of a justice it had previously sworn in nor its constitutionalization of the *Supreme Court Act* were the most controversial part of the Nadon Affair. As Bateman recounts, less than two months after the decision, an unprecedented back-and-forth between the Prime Minister's Office (PMO) and the Supreme Court of Canada played out in the press. Conservative sources told a reporter that the Chief Justice had lobbied the government against the Nadon appointment; the Supreme Court responded that it had merely advised the government of potential issues with the appointment, but did "not express any views on the merits of the issue." The PMO then claimed the Chief Justice had initiated a call to the Minister of Justice, who in turn advised the Prime Minister that taking the call would be inappropriate; the Supreme Court responded that the Chief Justice merely sought to "flag" the issue with the Minister of Justice and the Prime Minister's Chief of Staff, that consultation with the Chief Justice was "customary" for appointments to the Supreme Court, that there was "nothing inappropriate" about this, and that the Chief Justice ultimately decided not to pursue a meeting with the Prime Minister anyhow. For court watchers, the spectacle of a sitting Prime Minister and a sitting Chief Justice engaged in a literal "he said, she said" for several days was extraordinary.

To put it lightly, Harper did not win this public relations battle with the Supreme Court of Canada. As Bateman notes, the legal community "supported the Supreme Court without exception." Leader of the Opposition Thomas Mulcair called Harper's behaviour an "unprecedented and inexplicable attack on one of our most respected democratic institutions."[3] Eleven former presidents of the Canadian Bar Association published an open letter (Reading 11.7) defending the Chief Justice's behaviour as "perfectly in line with the sort of courteous discussions which have historically occurred between the judiciary and the executive," while claiming Harper's comments "demonstrate a disrespect by the executive branch for the judicial branch of our constitutional democracy, and for the Chief Justice of Canada." These former presidents worried ominously whether the PMO's statements were a threat to judicial independence, insofar as they "may intimidate or harm the ability of the Supreme Court of Canada to render justice objectively and fairly." Even the International Commission of Jurists weighed in, claiming months later that the PMO's statements were "not well-founded and amounted to an encroachment upon the independence of the judiciary and integrity of the Chief Justice."[4]

In hindsight, concerns about threats to judicial independence seem overstated. Judicial independence in Canada is surely strong enough to withstand a few press releases from the PMO. Lorne Sossin (Reading 11.5), who is critical about the Harper government's approach to the judiciary, nevertheless argues that it demonstrates that Canadian courts remain "fiercely independent" and that the relationship between the judiciary and the executive is "more resilient than many might have thought." The swift reaction to the PMO's statements by the opposition, the media and the legal community were further proof that any hint of a critique of the Supreme Court – even as tepid as those proffered by the PMO – will be subject to intense criticism.

Yet perhaps the Prime Minister is not the only one who deserves scrutiny in the Nadon Affair. In Reading 11.7, political scientists Dennis Baker and Rainer Knopff highlight a tension between *Reference re Supreme Court Act* and the Supreme Court's official statements on the matter. On the one hand, the Supreme Court press release claims the Chief Justice called the Minister of Justice and the PMO's Chief of Staff to "flag" issues with Nadon's potential appointment, but did not "express any opinion as to the merits of the eligibility issue." On the other hand, the Chief Justice subsequently signed on to the six-judge majority that claimed the "requirement of current membership in the Quebec bar has been in place – unambiguous and unchanged – since 1875." How, Baker and Knopff ask, could the Chief Justice have no opinion on the merits of the appointment that she subsequently found "unambiguously" unconstitutional? And if the Nadon appointment so clearly violated the *Supreme Court Act*, why did the Supreme Court swear him in?

The *Reference re Supreme Court Act* was controversial, and its fallout unprecedented. However, the constitutionality of Nadon's appointment was settled; Harper appointed Clément Gascon in Nadon's stead as Justice Fish's replacement in June, 2014. Amid allegations that opposition MPs had leaked details of the Nadon appointment process to the media, Harper abandoned the MP selection panel, and used the pre-2004 criteria to appoint Gascon, with no committee scrutiny. Harper's final appointments, Suzanne Côté and Russell Brown, were appointed the same way in 2014 and 2015. In 2016, the Trudeau government reformed the Supreme Court appointment process substantially (see Chapter 4).

Limited Policy Success at the Supreme Court

Notwithstanding the failed Nadon appointment, Harper certainly had the opportunity to leave his mark on the Supreme Court of Canada. By the time of the October, 2015 election, he had named eight justices to the Court, seven of whom were still sitting. Since October, 2012, a majority of justices on the Supreme Court have been appointed by Harper; barring the death or early retirement of any of the current justices, the Court's "Harper majority" will remain until October, 2030, when Justice Karakatsanis will turn seventy-five.

Yet the post-Harper Supreme Court behaves a lot like the pre-Harper Supreme Court. Judges are undoubtedly political and bring their ideological perspectives to the cases they hear, but those perspectives are mitigated by various other factors, such as doctrine, role conceptions and a desire for institutional legitimacy (see Reading 8.3). As Harper found out to his chagrin, simply appointing justices in Canada does not guarantee they will favour government policy. Lorne Sossin (Reading 11.5) notes a number of high-profile examples where policy supported (if not created) by the Harper Conservatives was ruled unconstitutional by the Supreme Court: the 2011 reference that Vancouver's safe injection site should stay open;[5] the 2011 decision preventing the federal government from creating a national securities regulator;[6] the 2013 decision that struck down activities related to prostitution (see Reading 7.5);[7] the 2014 reference that rendered unconstitutional the Prime Minister's plan to reform the Senate (see Reading 2.6);[8] and the *Reference re Supreme Court Act*. One could add to these three different decisions (in 2008, 2010 and 2015) where the Supreme Court ruled against the government with respect to alleged terrorist Omar Khadr, an area on which the government had staked considerable political capital.[9]

The Harper government's poor record in the Supreme Court of Canada continued into its final year. As Benjamin Perrin documents, in the Supreme Court's ten most important decisions from 2015, the Harper government fared very poorly (Reading 11.8). Such losses included cases that struck down the criminal prohibition on assisted suicide (see Reading 7.5);[10] expanded collective bargaining rights for the Royal Canadian Mounted Police;[11] extended the right to medical marijuana;[12] and struck down mandatory minimum sentences.[13]

Many of these cases were part and parcel of the Harper government's tough-on-crime approach to criminal justice, yet Perrin demonstrates how the Harper government's "losing streak" continued during a year in which seven of the nine justices were Harper appointees.

Some have argued that this narrative of a "fractious relationship" between the Harper government and the Supreme Court is overstated. In Reading 11.9, Christopher Manfredi notes that when governments lose in court, they are often defending legislation passed by previous governments. Many of the above examples of Harper "losses" actually involved legislation or executive actions made by other (often Liberal) governments, including the cases concerning prostitution, assisted dying, collective bargaining and Omar Khadr. Manfredi explains how the Harper government had its own legislation invalidated by the Supreme Court at a rate that actually compares favourably to the post-*Charter* governments that preceded it. Manfredi concludes that there is "a much more complex relationship between the Court and the [Harper] government than can be captured through a simple 'scorecard' of outcomes."

Conclusion

Few would dispute that Stephen Harper desired a judiciary more deferential to legislatures and executives, one willing to engage in tougher criminal sentencing and predisposed to allow reasonable limits on *Charter* rights. Did Harper get his wish to "remake the judiciary"? Probably not. His reforms to lower court appointments, explicitly designed to encourage a greater number of "tough-on-crime" judges, were reversed by Justin Trudeau less than a year after Harper left office. Trudeau then brought in a new appointment process to the Supreme Court, the central elements of which – recommending functionally bilingual candidates regardless of region, a commitment to diversity and an advisory board with a majority of members who were lawyers or judges – would hardly have been high on Harper's wish list. Harper's institutional imprint on judicial selection has already gone.

What about the personal makeup of the judiciary – the fact that, by the time he left office, Harper had appointed seven of the nine members of the Supreme Court and nearly three-quarters of all federally appointed judges? Here again, it is too early to tell for certain, but the evidence does not suggest a revolution of deferential, tough-on-crime or even nominally "conservative" judges. While the Harper government's record at the Supreme Court of Canada may not have been that much worse than its predecessors, it certainly lost most of the major cases it fought before the Court, particularly with respect to criminal justice reform. Those losses have continued even after Harper has gone, as in *R. v. Lloyd* (2016),[14] where the Supreme Court struck down mandatory minimum sentences for drug crimes. Harper's appointees continue to strike down Harper's laws, regardless of the level of court. And the Trudeau government has also brought back the Court Challenges Program, long the scourge of critics of judicial power. The *Charter* Revolution has not been overthrown.

Harper's limited impact on the judiciary speaks to the stickiness of Canadian legal culture – its inclination towards judicial interpretative supremacy, a Living Tree approach to constitutional adjudication and a markedly different strand of criminal justice reform than Harper sought. The legal community was resolutely and uniformly anti-Harper (try finding a Canadian law professor with something positive to say about the Harper Conservatives); the characterization of the Conservatives as "anti-*Charter* and anti-court" continued throughout Harper's tenure, not always without reason. The best analogy for Harper's attempt to reshape Canada's judiciary is, as one Conservative source said in Reading 11.1, that the government was "dripping blue ink into a red pot."

Time will tell whether Harper's drop in the bucket has changed its colour. Harper's appointments no doubt brought some ideological diversity to Canadian courts, though they do not yet seem to have made a discernible impact on judicial outputs. What we can say is that the Harper years – from his appointment reforms to his willingness to challenge the judiciary in public – presented a different relationship between the federal government and the courts than Canada has ever seen. For these reasons, the Harper decade provides fascinating lessons about the institutional relationship between courts, legislatures, executives and society more broadly.

NOTES

1   Emmett Macfarlane, "'You Can't Always Get What You Want': Regime Politics, the Supreme Court of Canada, and the Harper Government," *Canadian Journal of Political Science* 51, no. 1 (2018), pp. 1–21.

2   [2014] 1 S.C.R. 433.

3   Aaron Wherry, "Stephen Harper, Beverley McLachlin and an historic mess," *Maclean's*, May 6, 2014, http://www.macleans.ca/politics/stephen-harper-beverley-mclachlin-and-historic-mess/.

4   Wilder Tayler, "Letter to Dr. Gerald Heckman," *International Commission of Jurists*, July 23, 2014, http://voices-voix.ca/sites/voices-voix.ca/files/letter_canada_230714_2_tayler_to_heckman.pdf.

5   *Canada (Attorney General) v. PHS Community Services Society*, [2011] 3 S.C.R. 134.

6   *Reference re Securities Act*, [2011] 3 S.C.R. 837.

7   *Canada (Attorney General) v. Bedford*, [2013] 3 S.C.R. 1101.

8   *Reference re Senate Reform*, [2014] 1 S.C.R. 704.

9   *Canada (Justice) v. Khadr*, [2008] 2 S.C.R. 125; *Canada (Prime Minister) v. Khadr*, [2010] 1 S.C.R. 44; *Bowden Institution v. Khadr*, [2015] 2 S.C.R. 325.

10   *Carter v. Canada (Attorney General)*, [2015] 1 S.C.R. 331.

11   *Mounted Police Association of Ontario v. Canada (Attorney General)*, [2015] 1 S.C.R. 3.

12   *R. v. Smith*, [2015] 2 S.C.R. 602.

13   *R. v. Nur*, [2015] 1 S.C.R. 773.

14   *R. v. Lloyd*, [2016] 1 S.C.R. 130.

11.1

Stephen Harper's Courts: How the Judiciary Has Been Remade

Sean Fine

The Globe and Mail, July 25, 2015, F1. Reprinted with permission.

The judge looked down at the full-bearded young man who sat relaxed and smiling before him. Omar Khadr, a former teenage terrorist, was in a Canadian courtroom for the first time.

Years earlier, through various channels, the judge had lobbied Prime Minister Stephen Harper for a promotion – and got one.

Part of his new job was assigning cases, sometimes to himself. Now, in 2013, the case before him involved an individual in whom Mr. Harper had expressed an emphatic interest. In the end, Associate Chief Justice John Rooke of the Alberta Court of Queen's Bench ruled for the government and against Mr. Khadr, deciding he had been convicted as an adult, not a juvenile.

No one, including Mr. Khadr's defence lawyer, said the judge was in any way biased or unfair.

But some familiar with the judge's lobbying said the appearance was unfortunate – that justice must also be seen to be fair.

The Rooke episode is one glimpse of a much bigger, untold story. It is the story of how Mr. Harper and the Conservatives have reclaimed the judiciary from the Liberals, who had held power for the 13 years before Harper took office and for most of the previous century.

'Dripping blue ink into a red pot,' is how one Alberta Conservative who has been involved in the appointment process described it. In the public glare of Parliament, the Conservatives have passed dozens of crime laws that reduced judges' power to decide on a sentence. Behind closed doors, the government has engaged in an effort unprecedented since 1982, when the Charter of Rights and Freedoms took effect: to appoint judges most likely to accept that loss of discretion – the little-noticed half of Mr. Harper's project to toughen Canadian law.

Mr. Harper's battles with the Supreme Court are well known. The court has struck down or softened several of his crime laws. When the Prime Minister named an outspoken conservative, Marc Nadon, to the Supreme Court in 2013, the court itself declared Justice Nadon ineligible. Mr. Harper would go on to publicly assail the integrity of Supreme Court Chief Justice Beverley McLachlin, turning an institutional dispute into a very personal battle -another Canadian first.

But while those public conflicts were playing out, the government was quietly transforming the lower courts. The Conservative government has now named about 600 of the 840 full-time federally appointed judges, or nearly three in every four judges on provincial superior courts, appeal courts, the Federal Court and Tax Court.

These are the courts that, at the appeal level, decide how the government's crime crackdown is to be implemented. At the trial level, they decide high-profile cases like Mr. Khadr's. In constitutional cases, they rule on what are called social and legislative facts – anything that establishes the real-world context in which a law plays out, such as whether prostitution laws endanger sex workers. Higher courts, including the Supreme Court, do not change these facts, unless they view them as wildly wrong. Constitutional rulings depend on these facts.

The judges, who can serve until they are 75, may be sitting long after other governments have come along and rewritten the laws. They also are a farm team or development system for the Supreme Court. They are Mr. Harper's enduring legacy.

In the course of this transformation, entire categories of potential candidates, such as criminal defence lawyers, have been neglected; prosecutors and business attorneys have been favoured. So cumbersome is the system of political scrutiny that vacancies hit record-high levels last year. And sometimes, critics say, judges and politicians, even cabinet ministers, have come into close contact in the appointment process, raising questions about neutrality and fairness.

Underlying the appointments issue is a covert culture war over who gets to define Canadian values, Parliament or the courts, and what political party puts the most indelible imprint on the nation's character.

The rules in the appointments system are few, and all previous governments have used the bench to reward party faithful.

But Mr. Harper is the first Prime Minister to be a critic of the Charter, and early on he told Parliament that he wanted to choose judges who would support his crackdown on crime.

The Globe spent months exploring the secret world of appointments to understand the extent of the changes and how the government set out to identify candidates who share its view of the judiciary's proper role. We spoke to dozens of key players – political insiders, members of judicial screening committees, academics, judges and former judges – often on a condition of anonymity, so they could talk freely.

Neither Mr. Harper nor his justice minister, Peter MacKay, would grant an interview.

Chopping at the living-tree doctrine

The appointments system has five steps, four of them political. The first – screening committees spread across the country – is intended to be neutral and independent. Its members originally consisted of lawyers nominated by law societies, bar associations, provincial governments and the federal government, and a provincial chief justice or other judge. In 2006, the Conservative government added a police representative, and took away the judge's vote ensuring that federal appointees had the voting majority on the committees.

Next, cabinet ministers responsible for patronage appointments in their regions make recommendations, chosen from the committees' lists, to the justice minister.

The minister's judicial affairs adviser scrutinizes those picks, and the minister sends his choice to the Prime Minister's Office for review. Finally, cabinet decides.

Long before he became prime minister, Mr. Harper made it clear that he objected to the judiciary this system produced, and that the deck was stacked against his view of constitutional rights. A Liberal prime minister, Pierre Trudeau, was the driving force behind the Charter. He made the first Supreme Court appointments of the Charter era, choosing liberal judges such as Brian Dickson and Bertha Wilson, who were determined that the Charter would make a difference in Canadians' lives.

Gay rights were a flashpoint. In 2003, as Canadian courts began to legalize gay marriage, Mr. Harper, then opposition leader, hired Ian Brodie as his assistant chief of staff. Mr. Brodie, at the time a political scientist at the University of Western Ontario, had just published a book in which he decried 'judicial supremacy' – the notion that Supreme Court judges had usurped the role of Parliament.

At Western, Mr. Brodie teamed up with Grant Huscroft, a young law professor who would go on to organize conferences, write articles and edit books to give life to U.S.-style 'originalism,' which holds that constitutions mean what their drafters said they meant, and don't change with the times. This is the philosophy of Antonin Scalia and Clarence Thomas, the most conservative U.S. Supreme Court justices.

That year, Mr. Harper made a daring accusation, based on originalism, in the House of Commons. The Charter's framers deliberately did not protect gays and lesbians in the equality clause, he said. Therefore, the Supreme Court, which had read such protection into the Charter back in 1995, had violated the Constitution, he argued. And now, in 2003, that decision had become the legal foundation for gay marriage.

'I would point out that an amendment to the Constitution by the courts is not a power of the courts under our Constitution,' he said.

Mr. Harper was challenging a status quo rooted in modern women's rights. In 1928, the Supreme Court ruled that women could not be appointed to the Senate because they were not 'persons' – they did not vote or run for office in 1867, when the country's founding Constitution was written. But the Judicial Committee of the Privy Council in England said on appeal that the Constitution should be seen as a 'living tree capable of growth and expansion within its natural limits.' Women were indeed persons, because constitutional interpretation changed with the times.

The living-tree idea has been at the heart of Charter legal rulings since the beginning: It has not been a matter of dispute on Canadian courts. The Supreme Court has rejected originalism in several rulings, including the landmark same-sex marriage case of 2004.

But to Mr. Harper and his circle, the living tree means rule by judges. 'We have in very significant measure ceased to be our own rulers,' Conservative MP Vic Toews told a pro-life group in Winnipeg in 2004, after quoting from a book by conservative U.S. jurist Robert Bork.

Two years later, Mr. Toews became the first justice minister in the new Conservative government. He quickly revamped the appointments process, giving the government its voting majority on the screening committees. A furor erupted. The country's chief justices complained that judicial independence was at risk.

Mr. Harper did not back down.

He got to his feet in the House of Commons and said something no prime minister in the Charter era had ever said publicly. He declared that his government wished to appoint judges who saw the world in a certain way – that is, those who would be tough on crime.

'We want to make sure that we are bringing forward laws to make sure we crack down on crime and make our streets and communities safer,' he said on Feb. 14, 2007. 'We want to make sure that our selection of judges is in correspondence with those objectives.'

But even with voting control on the screening committees, the Conservative government's choices were constrained. There were few proponents of original-ism like the Americans' Justice Scalia, who dissented bitterly from last month's landmark gay marriage ruling and as late as 2003 supported a state's right to criminalize homosexual sex.

There was nothing like the Federalist Society, a grassroots national move-ment in the U.S. that encourages young lawyers to promote conservative views and support the doctrine of original intent. There was no single defining polit-ical issue like abortion. In the U.S., judicial conservatism is much more about activism – judges trying to roll back precedents such as *Roe v. Wade*, which established women's right to abortion on demand, or to reject gun controls, or limit affirmative action policies.

In Canada, judicial conservatism tends to mean judges who accept the wishes of legislators – judges who defer to Parliament's primary role as law-maker and are reluctant to find fault with a government's choices. Judges who know their place.

Finding reliable judges

The key to the Conservative strategy is identifying prospects with the right views. The Prime Minister has eyes and ears across Canada.

These belong to the cabinet members responsible for dispensing patronage appointments (known as political ministers).

They use their local contacts, such as party fundraisers (or 'bagmen') to identify lawyers, academics and sitting judges who fit their specifications, and recommend them to the justice minister. Appointments under the Liberals, worked in much the same way: A cabinet minister opened the door.

'You always have to have a champion,' a Conservative from Alberta ex-plained. 'Nobody gets appointed without somebody walking them through, in one way or another.'

In Ontario, the political ministers are Joe Oliver in Toronto, Pierre Poilievre in Ottawa, Diane Finley in the southwest and Greg Rickford in the north. Mr. MacKay is the political minister in Nova Scotia. Defence Minister Jason Kenney and Health Minister Rona Ambrose are the political ministers in Alberta. Some political ministers are more intent on identifying conservative-minded candi-dates for the bench than others. (Strangely, three leading criminal defence law-yers have been appointed on Mr. MacKay's home turf. What he supported in his own backyard he did not foster in the rest of the country.)

Mr. Kenney has a political office in Calgary separate from his constituency office, with separate full-time staff. Both he and Ms.

Ambrose need to sign off on each candidate either one recommends for a judicial appointment, another Alberta source said. 'The person has to make it by both Jason and Rona. They both have a veto. In Calgary, there's generally a respect on Rona's part for Jason's picks and vice-versa.'

Mr. Kenney and Ms. Ambrose are not lawyers. They ask their contacts to recommend candidates.

'It's not, 'Is this person going to be tough on crime?'' the first Alberta source said. 'It's, 'Can you recommend this person, are they reliable?' There's a little bit of code in there.' Reliability means being both right-of-centre and competent – a two-level filter.

Reliability has a more nuanced meaning, too, according to an appeal court judge, not in Alberta, who follows judicial appointments closely: judges who are technically minded and stick to precedent, who won't 'play with the rules or make new rules.'

Finding reliably conservative judges is a challenge. In Alberta, roughly one-third of federal judicial appointees are not right-of-centre, the first source said, but are chosen for being competent and not left-of-centre. The ideological requirement is not a litmus test around a single issue, but around a general worldview involving a lack of sympathy for minority causes or convicted criminals – which some Conservatives see as the demarcation line between right and left.

'You either see a criminal as a victim of society or as someone who needs to pay his debt to society,' the source said. 'One's a little bit to the left, one's a little bit to the right. You don't always get that right either when you pick. People sometimes surprise you when they get up there and have no boss other than their own conscience.'

This either-or view of sentencing incenses legal observers such as Allan Wachowich, a retired chief justice of the Alberta Court of Queen's Bench. Mr. Wachowich, a long-ago Liberal 'bagman' by his own description, was a Liberal appointee who was named associate chief justice by a Progressive Conservative prime minister, Brian Mulroney. (His champion was cabinet member Don Mazankowski, but he didn't know until Mr. Mulroney told him, he said. He told the prime minister jokingly that it was all part of a 'Polish conspiracy.')

'You have to treat every case as an individual case,' Mr. Wachowich said in an interview.

'Is there any hope of redemption? Is there a prison where he isn't going to be influenced by hard-core criminals? You've got to sit there and listen and contemplate, and give it a weekend sometimes.'

About four years ago, at a time when judges had begun striking down Conservative laws on crime and drugs, political ministers such as Mr. Kenney and Ms. Ambrose came under increased pressure to choose judges who would defer to legislators.

'Deference became a buzzword when a number of laws were being struck down, mostly for Charter violations,' said former Conservative MP Brent Rathgeber, now an Independent.

As one of the few lawyers in the Alberta caucus from 2008 to 2013, he was sometimes consulted on appointments by a political minister. 'The PMO decided it would be better if we had a judiciary more deferential to Parliament's authority.'

In at least one case in Alberta, Mr. Kenney and Ms. Ambrose personally checked out a new candidate for the bench, according to a source familiar with the process.

The candidate first attended a series of get-to-know-you breakfasts and lunches with Conservative Party insiders, before a chat with the two ministers, and was ultimately named to the Court of Queen's Bench, the province's top trial court, the source said.

There are no written rules prohibiting such contacts between prospective judges and cabinet members or other politicians. A Conservative, who did not confirm that the meeting took place, said there would be nothing wrong if it did, because the appointments are for life and mistakes can't be undone.

But mention of the meeting often brings a shocked reaction from lawyers and judges, who view it as compromising independence. Peter Russell, a political science professor emeritus at the University of Toronto and a leading expert on judicial appointments, explained the sense of shock.

'Yes, the public should be concerned about partisan interviews of prospective candidates for judicial appointment,' Prof. Russell said. Such interviews mean that, in Canada, 'appointments to the highest trial courts and courts of appeal in the province remain open to blatant partisan political favouritism in selecting judges – something most provinces and most countries in the liberal democratic world have reduced or eliminated.'

Both Mr. Kenney and Ms. Ambrose refused to speak to The Globe for this story. They would not confirm or deny that they interviewed a candidate for the Court of Queen's Bench. An Alberta source said the appointment process is a matter of practice and tradition. 'It's not even really written down anywhere.'

'Interested in a promotion? Play with us'

The government's strategy is to change the judges at the same time as it toughens the Criminal Code. And sitting judges have a record that can be monitored.

Former prosecutor Kevin Phillips of Ottawa had barely taken his seat as a provincially appointed judge in the fall of 2013 when his fellow judges began rebelling openly against a new law. The victim surcharge, a financial penalty used to subsidize victim services, had just become mandatory; even the poorest criminals would have to pay. Judges in several provinces refused to force them.

In Edmonton and Vancouver, some judges allowed 50 or even 99 years to pay. In Montreal, a judge found a way to make the surcharge $1.50. An Ottawa judge ruled the law unconstitutional without even giving the government a chance to defend it.

The surcharge was typical of the government's crime laws: It removed discretion from judges, with a mandatory minimum penalty. It took from criminals and gave to victims.

Instead of joining the rebels, Justice Phillips, a police chief's son, turned against them. Thwarting the will of Parliament is a 'recipe for arbitrariness,' he said in a ruling released eight weeks after he joined the Ontario Court of Justice in Brockville, and 'arbitrariness is antithetical to the rule of law.'

His stay on that court didn't last long: On April 13, four months after Justice Phillips took his public stand, Mr. MacKay announced his promotion to the Ontario Superior Court, the top trial court in the province.

This is not to imply that Justice Phillips is less than fair-minded.

As a prosecutor, he received high praise for his fairness from criminal defence lawyers in Ottawa interviewed for this story. But his appointment sent a message to judges on lower courts – those appointed by the provinces.

As a veteran lawyer in Toronto put it, ' 'You're interested in a promotion to the Superior Court? Play with us.' '

A provincial court judge in Western Canada, speaking not about Justice Phillips but generally, says he is concerned that some judges have a 'career plan' that involves a promotion.

'I worry that some judges hear the footsteps,' he said. 'They read the headline in The Globe and Mail before it's written, and maybe, just maybe, they temper their judgment as a result. As soon as you get to that stage, the integrity of the system crumbles. But do I think that happens? Yes, I do think it happens.'

The judge, the PM and the promotion

Some judges make their case for promotion directly to politicians – despite a Canadian tradition that usually keeps judges and legislators apart to ensure that the system appears to be, and is, neutral.

On three separate occasions when he was still a Conservative MP, Mr. Rathgeber says judges came to him. 'I can tell you of one Court of Queen's Bench judge and a couple of Provincial Court judges who were seeking elevation to the Court of Appeal and Alberta Court of Queen's Bench,' he said. 'The judge would tell me why they thought they were not a good fit on the Court of Queen's Bench trial division and why their skill set might be better doing appellate [work] at the Court of Appeal. And if there's anything I can do to help that occur.'

Some in the legal community view aggressive lobbying by sitting judges as unseemly. Sometimes it backfires. Other times, though, it is rewarded – as appears to be the case with Justice Rooke.

In 2009, the judge on the Alberta Court of Queen's Bench lobbied the Prime Minister through channels for the job of chief justice, multiple sources told The Globe. He put together a dossier on his record. Jim Prentice, then the federal environment minister, spoke to Mr. Harper on Justice Rooke's behalf. Justice Rooke and Mr. Prentice had been 'little Clarkies' – party workers who had supported Progressive Conservative leader Joe Clark decades earlier. Justice Rooke also reached out personally to well-regarded figures in the legal community who tend to be consulted by the Conservative government in judicial appointments, an Alberta Conservative said.

Some of Justice Rooke's colleagues resented his lobbying, believing that Neil Wittmann of Calgary, then the associate chief justice, deserved to be chief justice. Justice Myra Bielby, the senior judge in Edmonton, would probably then become associate chief justice. According to a 100year-old tradition – never broken – if a chief justice was appointed from Calgary, the associate chief was chosen from Edmonton, and vice-versa.

A committee of his colleagues on the bench approached Justice Rooke about a rumour he had even met personally with Mr. Harper. (The Prime Minister appoints chief and associate chief justices.)

In the Canadian system, such a meeting would have been seen as irresponsible, and the committee's approach was a sign that the judges were alarmed by the prospect. Justice Rooke vehemently denied that the meeting took place, which the judges accepted.

But some made known who they felt should be chief and associate chief. 'There were a lot of 'bank shots' [from Justice Rooke's colleagues] to make sure that for an appointment like that, you have the right person, because the system has to work,' the source said. To make a bank shot is to have someone else send your message – 'you get the justice minister [of Alberta] to make a call, you get the chief of staff to make a call, you get three or four senior lawyers to make a call.'

Mr. Harper named Justice Wittmann, who joined the bench as a Liberal appointment, as chief justice. Then, despite the century old tradition, he chose Justice Rooke as associate chief. The government later promoted Justice Bielby to fill the first vacancy on the Court of Appeal.

In 2013, Justice Rooke took on the Khadr case. On the day of the hearing, Mr. Harper publicly stated his support for the most severe punishment possible.

Politicians rarely comment on cases before a court because it may look like an improper attempt to influence a judge. Still, Justice Rooke said his ruling in favour of the Canadian government – to treat Mr. Khadr as an adult – was a straightforward matter of statutory interpretation.

Six months later, the Alberta Court of Appeal overturned the ruling in a 3-0 vote. Among the three were two Conservative appointees, including Justice Bielby. This spring, the Supreme Court also ruled in Mr. Khadr's favour – adding insult by deliberating for just a half-hour.

No one has suggested that Justice Rooke was unfair, or that there was a quid pro quo for his appointment as associate chief justice. Dennis Edney, an Edmonton lawyer who represented Mr. Khadr, said he found the judge 'attentive and fair in his dealings with me and my representations. That is all I ask.'

To some Conservatives, the appointment of Neil Wittmann ahead of John Rooke showed that ability matters more than politics in Conservative appointments.

'It's a very, very good example to show where skill and talent and colleagues' confidence trumped political bias,' a party source said.

But to outside observers, when judges lobby for promotions, they undermine the appearance – and perhaps the reality – of judicial independence.

'If you're starting to get into a lobbying process, are you not then beholden to those who make the appointment?' said John Martland, a former president of the Alberta Law Society, speaking generally.

The Globe contacted Associate Chief Justice Rooke through his assistant and asked if he wanted to correct any facts or provide comments. Diana Lowe, his executive counsel, replied that judges speak only through their judgments and a response would not be appropriate.

In an ironic postscript to these events, the federal government went before the Alberta Court of Appeal in May to block Mr. Khadr's release on bail. A single judge heard the case – Justice Bielby. Mr. Khadr is now free on bail.

Tapping a 'very small pool'

Because there is rarely a straight line from what an appointing government expects to how a judge actually rules, the Conservative strategy is designed to reduce uncertainty, using broad categories as a convenient shortcut to predicting the ideological orientation of candidates for the bench.

Criminal defence lawyers are underrepresented, according to a Globe and Mail review of all appointment notices since 1984.

Academics are, as well, with some notable exceptions. So, too, is anyone who has a senior role in a group with the word 'reform' in its title. (One such group is – or was – the Law Reform Commission of Canada, later known as the Law

Commission of Canada; in the Conservative government's first year in power, it scrapped the organization.) Business lawyers are favoured. Prosecutors are favoured.

Judges appointed by Progressive Conservative prime ministers Mulroney and Kim Campbell look very much like judges appointed by Liberal prime ministers Jean Chrétien and Paul Martin, apart from the underlying political affiliations. They appointed more criminal defence lawyers than prosecutors. They did not shy away from academics, either. And Mr. Mulroney chose leading liberals such as Louise Arbour and Rosalie Abella in Ontario, and Morris Fish in Quebec; Liberal governments later named them to the Supreme Court.

The current Conservative government has appointed few judges in the past nine years who have liberal reformist credentials.

Three judges it named to the Ontario Court of Appeal since late in 2012 represented groups arguing against gay marriage at the Supreme Court in 2004. As of this winter, it has appointed 48 prosecutors, compared with 12 lawyers who did primarily criminal defence work, and 10 academics.

Conservatives say the system is no more ideological today than it was under the Liberals. 'I can't see the difference,' a Conservative said. 'When someone is a committed federal Liberal and has worked for the party for 30 years and gets to be of a certain age and a certain standing where some political heavyweights recommend them [for the bench], it's because they're ideologically framed by working for the party.'

But David Dyzenhaus, a University of Toronto law and philosophy professor, says he is deeply worried by the pattern of appointments.

'It's very clear that it's almost impossible for a judge who comes from the political centre or to the left to be appointed,' he said.

'Which means that the appointment of judges is from a very small pool of lawyers. That invariably means people of considerable ability are being passed over. The quality of the bench is going to be lower. It will invariably take its toll on the Canadian legal order.'

How to evade 'lefties'

The screening committees set minimum standards for the selection of judges. Across the country there are 17 such judicial advisory committees (JACs), as they are known, and they are the only stage of the appointment process whose rules are public.

Until 2006, the committees had three choices when presented with a candidate: highly recommend, recommend or not recommended. Mr. Toews changed that, however, stripping out the first option; now committees can only recommend, or not.

The loss of the highly recommended category 'removes a lot of the committee's ability to express to the minister its view as to who really should be appointed to these positions,' said Frank Walwyn, a Toronto business lawyer appointed by the Ontario government to the screening committee in the Greater Toronto Area.

Of the 665 applicants in 2013-14, the committee recommended 300, or nearly one in every two. Of those 300, the government anointed a chosen few – 66 judges, or roughly one in five of the recommended group. Under the last year of the old rules, 2005-6, the committees 'highly recommended' 76 applicants; if a government wished, it could find enough highly recommended judges to fill all the vacancies.

In practice, despite the changes that put federal government appointees in the voting majority, the committee members tend to seek common ground. 'What I've found is that consensus really is the order of the day,' Mr. Walwyn said. 'If you have a number of people saying this person is not balanced either in the prosecution or defence of individuals, the committee will take that very seriously.'

From the Conservative government's perspective, the committees sometimes stand in the way of the judges it wishes to appoint.

So the government has taken deliberate steps to evade the committees, at least in Alberta, a local source said. It has a kind of express lane to bypass the need for a committee recommendation: choosing from judges already serving on the Provincial Court, a lower level of court appointed by the province. (The committees comment on these judges, but make no recommendation.)

These tended to be right-of-centre judges with a known track record.

The advisory committees 'were not letting through tough-on-crime candidates because they wanted some lefties to be appointed,' the source said. 'Liberal judges had control of the screening committees. One of the ways [the government] could get around this is if you were already appointed to another court, the screening committee could not block you; they could only comment.' In this fashion, a Provincial Court judge, Brian O'Ferrall, made an unusual leap straight to Alberta's highest court, the Court of Appeal, in 2011. Several others went to the Court of Queen's Bench.

This is not against the rules. The appointments system has wide discretion.

The next steps: recommendations from the political ministers, then the judicial affairs adviser checking out the candidates. One such adviser, Carl Dholandas, was a former president of the McGill Progressive Conservative club who served as executive assistant to Nigel Wright when he was chief of staff in the PMO. The justice ministry declined to make him available for an interview. He left the post early this year, and the ministry would not even reveal the name of the new adviser. (It's Lucille Collard, who was an official at the Federal Court of Appeal.)

After the Justice Minister's recommendation goes to the PMO, an appointments adviser, Katherine Valcov-Kwiatkowski, screens the candidates yet again, before a name makes it to a cabinet vote.

This unwieldy process has slowed the system. Chief justices grew restive at the high numbers of vacancies on their courts: at record levels last year – more than 50 open seats. That number plummeted to 14 in June, with an avalanche of appointments before the official start of the federal election campaign. Quebec Court of Appeal judges were stretched so thin last fall that Chief Justice Nicole Duval Hesler asked Superior Court chief justice François Rolland if she could borrow some judges on an ad hoc basis, a source said. Chief justice Rolland said no. In his annual public address in September, chief justice Rolland complained that one of the vacancies on his court went back to August, 2013, and four others to April, 2014. Civil trials expected to take longer than 25 days must be booked four years in advance, he said. He jokingly asked if anyone could get Justice Minister MacKay on the phone, because he had tried and failed. The judge has now retired.

One seat that was filled: In 2013, an opening on the Manitoba Court of Queen's Bench went to former justice minister Vic Toews.

The judge who doesn't like Canadian law

It is easy to see why Mr. Harper would be a fan of Grant Huscroft, Ian Brodie's friend and co-editor, and why the Conservative government named the Western law professor to Ontario's highest court, effective in January. (Mr. Brodie, now at the University of Calgary, tweeted his congratulations.)

In his published work, Mr. Huscroft has rejected virtually everything at the heart of the Canadian constitutional order. He is opposed to judges reviewing rights claims under the Charter – an important part of his job. He believes it's undemocratic and judges are no better than anyone else at deciding whether a law is consistent with the rights commitments of the Charter. He has made the same point as Mr. Harper on gay rights and the Charter – that the framers deliberately did not protect gay rights. He has written that democracies do not 'grossly violate rights,' but put 'thoughtful' limits on them.

Wil Waluchow, a legal philosopher at McMaster University who strongly disagrees with Mr. Huscroft's originalism, describes him as open-minded and respectful of different viewpoints. 'He may fight against the mainstream to some extent, but I don't think it will be in a way that is disrespectful or dishonest,' Prof. Waluchow said. 'I respect Grant an enormous amount.'

Prof. Dyzenhaus, who co-edited a 2009 book of essays with Mr. Huscroft, is also familiar with his work, and has a somewhat different view. 'He's an attractive choice for Stephen Harper because he shares with Harper an antipathy for entrenched bills of rights and the way of interpreting those rights that Canadian judges have developed for 30 years,' Prof. Dyzenhaus said by phone from Cambridge University, where he is the Arthur Goodhart Visiting Professor of Legal Science.

So why does Mr. Huscroft want to be a judge? In Canada, unlike in the U.S., there is no public review of the federal appointments of new judges in which that question could be asked. Or this one: How can he stay true to his principles while respecting precedent?

Mr. Huscroft declined multiple requests for an interview. But Prof. Dyzenhaus believes Mr. Huscroft hopes to bring change from within.

'If I'm right that he thinks large chunks of the Canadian legal system are illegitimate, one reason for taking office is he wants to get involved in a kind of damage-limitation exercise. So to the extent he can, he will try to prune the living tree.'

The constitutional romance

'Constitutional romantics assume the worst of elected legislators and the best of judges,' Mr. Huscroft has written. For nearly 10 years, the Conservative government has been dripping blue ink into a red pot - attempting to expunge, bit by bit, the country's 30-year romance with the Charter, and with judges who go out of their way to be the guarantor of rights.

The moves have produced mixed results. The government is up against a culture of unanimity; when Liberal and Conservative appointees sit down together, they tend to find common ground. It also faces a tradition of judicial independence, as some Conservative-appointed judges have demonstrated in striking down tough-on-crime legislation.

'This, irrespective of who appointed you, is always the dominant culture,' one appeal court judge said.

There is no strong evidence, in a statistical sense, of more severe criminal sentencing. But there are other areas of the judicial system where the effects can be seen. Perhaps the clearest sign of change is on the Federal Court. Refugees whose claims are rejected by the immigration board can ask this court to review their case. The review is not automatic, and Conservative appointees on the Federal Court agreed to a review in just 10 per cent of cases, compared with 17.6 per cent for Liberal appointees, a study found.

David Near, a former judicial affairs adviser for the Conservatives, accepted 2.5 per cent of requests for judicial review he heard on the Federal Court. In 2013, he was appointed to the Federal Court of Appeal.

As an election approaches that will be fought in part on security from terrorism and crime, the Prime Minister and his cabinet continue their determined effort to reshape the judiciary. In June, they promoted Justice Bradley Miller, another former Western professor and proponent of originalism, to the Ontario Appeal Court. He opposes gay marriage and asks whether the Supreme Court has lost its moral centre.

Business lawyers were again prominent, criminal defence lawyers scarce.

Mr. MacKay's office has given only one answer when The Globe has asked questions over the past eight months about individual appointments and the judicial appointments process: 'All judicial appointments are based on merit and legal excellence and on recommendations made by the 17 Judicial Advisory Committees across Canada.'

11.2

The Politics of Reforming Judicial Appointments
Rainer Knopff

University of New Brunswick Law Journal 58 (2008), 44–51. Reprinted with permission.

Since the 2006 election, the minority Conservative government, led by Prime Minister Stephen Harper, has come under intense scrutiny for two reforms to the process of appointing judges. First, in making a Supreme Court appointment, the Conservatives held an innovative and highly publicized hearing that allowed an ad hoc parliamentary committee to interview the government's nominee, Justice Marshall Rothstein, before his official appointment. Second, they reformed the Judicial Advisory Committees (JACs) that screen the pool of candidates for all other federal judicial appointments into more and less qualified categories. I focus in this essay on the controversy generated by the JAC reforms. Rather than dealing with questions of institutional design – e.g. the relative merits of screening and nominating committees – I analyze the rhetorical reception of the JAC reforms. While defenders maintained that the reforms were relatively minor adjustments to the system, critics blasted them as a startling departure from the "merit principle" in judicial selection in favour of a dangerous ideological politicization of the judiciary. The minimalist defence of the reforms was wrong; they did represent significant departures from the JAC tradition. At the same time, the critique was more than a little overheated. Indeed, its exaggerations can be understood as the latest episode in the long-standing partisan demonization of the Harper Conservatives as anti-*Charter* and anti-court.

The JAC Reforms

Since the initial JACs in 1988, the committee members, all appointed by the federal Minister of Justice, have fallen into two categories: 1) a minority of discretionary ministerial appointments, and 2) a majority of nominated appointments, chosen by the minister from lists proposed by other constituencies. The size of committees went from five to seven members in 1994, with three discretionary and four nominated appointments:

- a nominee of the provincial or territorial law society; a nominee of the provincial or territorial branch of the Canadian Bar Association;

- a judge nominated by the Chief Justice or senior judge of the province or territory;

- a nominee of the provincial Attorney-General or territorial Minister of Justice.

The judicial representative, who was a full voting member, chaired the JAC. In 1988, JACs screened candidates into two categories: qualified and unqualified. In 1991, this was changed to a threefold distinction: not recommended, recommended, and highly recommended.

The Harper Conservatives made three main changes to this system:

- They added a representative of the law enforcement community to the list of nominated appointments.

- They limited the voting power of the judicial chair to breaking ties.

- They scrapped the threefold categorization, which distinguished among qualified candidates, and returned to the original twofold distinction between qualified and unqualified.

These reforms attracted considerable public comment and criticism. Indeed, it is instructive to compare the public attention generated by Harper's reforms with the 1994 Liberal government's expansion of JACs, which also included appointments for "diversity" reasons, though the particular kind of diversity was not as clearly specified as Harper's "law enforcement" appointments. Of the 277 news items turned up by a search of ProQuest databases using the term "judicial advisory committee," only 44 were written prior to the 2006 election of the Harper government, and only two of those – both relatively neutral – were about the 1994 reforms to JACs. The other 243 items all came after Harper's election and concentrated on his JAC reforms. Prominent among the critics of the Harper reforms were the Canadian Judicial Council, Chief Justice Beverley McLachlin, and former Chief Justice Antonio Lamer. The ProQuest search turned up no such high-level commentary from the legal community about the 1994 reforms.

What accounts for this startling imbalance? There are two possibilities. First, that the Harper reforms were, as the critics claimed, startling innovations that substituted blatantly political criteria for the "merit principle" in judicial selection – in short, that the reforms politicized judicial appointments in unacceptable ways. Second, that the critique was a highly partisan exaggeration, consistent with a longstanding demonization of the Conservatives as anti-*Charter* and anti-court. I maintain that, while there is some truth in the politicization charge, it is much overplayed and rests on a misleading use of the term "merit." The over-dramatized opposition between an apolitical judicial "merit" and corrupt political calculation is itself part of a broader phenomenon of rhetorical demonization.

Merit vs. Politics: An Exaggerated Distinction

Although the Conservatives sometimes defended their reforms as simple adjustments within the JAC tradition, they differed from previous reforms in important ways. Critics have highlighted three in particular:

- The reforms were not undertaken in consultation with the legal community. Such consultation had played an important role in establishing JACs in the first place and had been part of all subsequent reforms.

- The screening categories were reduced from three to two. While this could be characterized as a "return" to the original 1988 situation rather than a startling departure, it nevertheless moved away from criteria that were put in place very early in the history of JACs, and was criticized as rendering JACs "virtually useless."

- The combined effect of the new "law enforcement" representative and the reduced voting power of the judicial chair shifted the balance of power on JACs. This change was often misrepresented as tipping the balance in favour of discretionary ministerial appointments. The Canadian Judicial Council (CJC), for example, treated the "law enforcement" representative as a fourth discretionary ministerial appointment, meaning that of the "seven members who are ordinarily entitled to vote" (given the reduced voting power of the judicial chair), four are "chosen by the Minister of Justice." With "the majority of voting members now appointed by the Minister," argued the CJC, "the advisory committees may neither be, nor be seen to be, fully independent of the government." In fact, however, the "law enforcement" representative is a fifth nominated appointment, not a fourth discretionary appointment. Nominated appointments thus retain the majority, even with the reduced voting power of the judicial chair. The Harper government's reforms did not tip the balance in favour of discretionary ministerial appointments. They clearly did, however, shift the balance of power between lawyers (including judges) and non-lawyers on JACs, and this appears to have been the real objection.

For the critics, the reforms moved away from a judicial screening process with some reasonable independence from political control to one more subject to political influence and discretion. The ultimate discretion to choose was always a purely political one, of course, but in practice only "recommended" or "highly recommended" candidates were appointed. Under the Harper government's reforms, politicians would still choose from the overall pool of qualified candidates but would no longer have to contend with the embarrassment of choosing a merely "qualified" candidate over a "highly qualified" one. Moreover, in assigning candidates to the qualified and unqualified categories, non-lawyers on the JACs (including law-and-order cops) might prevail over the more expert representatives of the legal community. The result, according to the critics, would be an unhealthy politicization of appointments that would dilute the principle of "merit" in judicial selection. Had the government only followed the tradition of consulting with the legal community, this blatant error in judgment might not have happened (which, of course, is precisely why the consultation never happened).

At this point, one must distinguish between two kinds of politicization. First is run-of-the-mill patronage – the appointment of one's political friends. This hallmark of federal judicial appointments survived the introduction of the JAC screening system quite nicely, with both major national parties continuing its practice when in power. This kind of traditional patronage was not, however, the primary basis on which the reforms were criticized. In portraying the reforms as diluting the commitment to "merit" as the basis for judicial appointment, the critics were necessarily saying that the existing process, despite being patronage ridden, was more oriented to merit. The new, and egregious, attack on "merit" came, for the critics, from a second kind of politicization: ideological politicization. The appointment of political friends was one thing; the appointment of policy ideologues was quite another. The Harper government, charged the critics, was preparing to stack the courts with social conservatives who would subvert *Charter* values. It was moving its "hidden agenda" into Canadian courtrooms.

In fact, the Conservatives did very little to hide this agenda, at least as far as law-and-order issues were concerned. Emphasizing his government's desire to "crack down on crime" and to "make our streets and communities safer," Harper wanted to ensure that the "selection of judges is in correspondence with those objectives." Policy-oriented appointment was explicitly the name of the game. For the critics, it was this kind of ideological appointment that was especially objectionable, introducing an openly political bias that was highly corrosive of the merit principle in judicial appointments. But the distinction between apolitical merit and political judgment is not nearly as clean and clear as the rhetoric implies.

We can gain further insight into the concept of "judicial merit" at work here by considering the critics' claim that bringing policy considerations openly into the appointment process undermines the principles of judicial independence and impartiality on which our constitutional system rests. By judicial independence, the critics obviously have in mind more than the traditional security of salary, tenure, and administrative control that have long characterized our tradition and that remain unaffected by the Harper government's JAC reforms. These traditional protections of judicial independence enable judges to be impartial between the parties before them. But, again, when they invoke "impartiality," critics of the Harper reforms have in mind much more than impartiality between parties. They also want impartiality on the issues of legal policymaking that must sometimes be determined to resolve the case between the parties. These are two different kinds of impartiality. As a case climbs the appellate hierarchy, the significance of the parties and impartiality between them tends to fall away, with the emphasis clearly shifting to legal policymaking. Indeed, at the highest levels it is not uncommon for judges to decide issues of legal policy not raised by the factual situation of the parties or to adopt policy solutions recommended by intervenors and of little interest to the parties. It is on such matters of legal policymaking that the critics want judges to be "impartial." The capacity to be impartial in this way on policy questions is part of the "judicial merit" that they believe judicial selection should emphasize and that the Conservative reforms de-emphasize.

But what can it mean to be impartial about the highly discretionary matters of reasonable disagreement that are typically the object of judicial policymaking? If one accepts – as a great many do – that the issues resolved by judges under entrenched constitutional instruments are indeed matters of reasonable disagreement, the idea of a kind of "merit" that somehow rises above the fray to sit in objective judgment on those engaged in legitimate disagreement becomes problematic. Indeed, in a democratic context, one might even begin to see some "merit" in the attempt by those who prevail in the clash of reasonable alternatives to ensure that their victory is not overturned by a few unelected officials taking the other side.

But perhaps, there is a way of rescuing the notion of "impartiality" in the face of "reasonable disagreements." Suppose one holds – as I do – that to describe something as a matter of reasonable disagreement is not necessarily to deny the possibility of a right answer. It is, rather, simply to acknowledge that even (what one considers to be) an objectively "wrong" answer can find support among people of good will and might be reasonably chosen by the democratic process. If this is true, might one not contend that the hurly-burly of the partisan politics within the political branches is less likely to produce the right answer – even in matters of reasonable disagreement – than the more dispassionate arena of the courtroom? True, no one realistically expects judges to be blank slates, without inclinations or pre-conceived views on issues that come before them, but, like students in a seminar, one might expect them to be more open to rational persuasion than partisan politicians are. Let me concede the point for the sake of argument (though I doubt it would survive fuller examination). What do we gain? Only this: that the judgment of the judicial seminar must trump the democratic judgment on matters of reasonable disagreement because the judicial institution is more likely to choose the right – or at least better – side in a legitimate debate among people of good will. If one thinks this through, I believe, it is a fundamental rejection of democracy in favour of the rule of "philosopher kings." If that is indeed the proper criterion of judgment, the Harper Conservatives can legitimately be criticized for moving in the wrong direction with their JAC reforms. If not, the vilification of their attack on judicial merit might well be seen as just a tad overwrought.

Now, I do not claim to have settled the debate about judicial merit and politicization. The theoretical issues are too complex to be fully captured by my brief commentary. In addition, important questions can be raised about the effectiveness of ideological appointments, even if one regards them as justified in principle. One might, for example, wonder about the ideological reliability over time of judges appointed for their policy views, especially because, once appointed, judges really do enjoy considerable "independence." Nor can one discount the effect, again over time, of their integration into the existing judicial culture, which surely shapes them as much as they shape it. It must also be recognized that what is sauce for the goose is sauce for the gander, and that when the Liberals regain power, they can be expected to similarly bring their own inevitable political calculations into the open. Perhaps, as Troy Riddell has argued, it would have been better for Harper to address his law-and-order-policy preferences not through judicial appointments, but through legislative changes to, say, sentencing issues. But, of course, this neglects the ability of judges to sit in second judgment on such initiatives as mandatory minimum sentences. While I have not settled the matter, however, I hope at least to have shown that the claims of egregious villainy by the Harper Conservatives are not as starkly obvious as many of the critics suggest. The intensity of the critique, in other words, was a kind of exaggeration. The exaggerated rhetoric fits into, and is explained by, a pre-existing context of demonization of the Conservatives on judicial matters.

The Demonization Context

Demonization of the Harper Conservatives as anti-*Charter* and anti-court has become a staple in the last several federal election campaigns, as well as in the partisan maneuvering between elections. The term "demonization," which I choose advisedly, suggests an exaggerated or inflationary level of rhetoric. This exaggeration is revealed by the fact that critics of the Conservatives on *Charter* and judicial issues often vilify – that is not too strong a word – positions they themselves once held. Jean Chrétien, for example, had, during the period of *Charter*-making, insisted that the s. 33 notwithstanding clause be made available to the federal government as well as the provinces, and he later defended s. 33 against Brian Mulroney's charge that it made the *Charter* "not worth the paper it's written on." When his partisan opponents defended s. 33 during the 2000 election, however, Chrétien presented the section as appealing to "the dark side of people" and as a "nuclear bomb" that would "destroy the *Charter of Rights.*" Similarly, although Paul Martin had defended the use of s. 33 prior to the 2004 election, specifying circumstances under which he "would use it," during the election he reacted to Harper's very similar statements about s. 33 by completely rejecting the legitimacy of the clause. "My refusal to use the notwithstanding clause," he said, "is a very clear indication of the depth of the gulf between Mr. Harper and myself." In the 2006 election, Martin went so far as to propose removing the notwithstanding clause in order "to protect the *Charter* against a prime minister [i.e., Stephen Harper] who might want to use the notwithstanding clause to attack minority rights."

During the electorally charged period of the Martin minority government, 134 law professors entered the partisan fray by insisting that, were Harper to become Prime Minister, he could "honestly" enact the traditional heterosexual definition of marriage only by including a "notwithstanding clause" even though the Supreme Court in the same-sex marriage reference had explicitly refused to address the constitutionality of the heterosexual definition. Those among the 134 who were on record as opposing the very kind of "prospective" use of s. 33 they were now insisting on were no more embarrassed by their self-contradiction than Chrétien or Martin had been about theirs.

Similar about-faces were necessary to demonize the Harper Conservatives on the substantive *Charter* issues. The fact that Chrétien and Martin had voted with the huge majority of MPs who supported a 1999 parliamentary resolution in favour of keeping the heterosexual definition of marriage did not prevent them from later presenting the same position as evidence of the Conservatives social extremism (even though the latter supported the kinds of compromise civil unions in place in many other liberal democracies). Or consider Conservative MP Rob Merrifield's comment during the 2004 election that it might be useful for women contemplating an abortion to take some counselling first. The fact that Paul Martin has said the same thing earlier in the campaign did not prevent the Liberals from seeing in Merrifield's comments a "profoundly disturbing" and "very frightening hidden agenda" on social issues.

The examples could easily be multiplied, but the point is clear. In the heat of partisan politics, the Conservatives have regularly been demonized as anti-*Charter* and anti-court for taking positions the demonizers themselves have subscribed to in other contexts. The Liberals consistently insist that they are the party of the *Charter* and *Charter* values while their Conservative opponents are anti-Canadian opponents of these values. Even scholars with some conservative inclinations have described the Liberals as the *Charter* party and the Conservatives as the BNA Act party.

This highly charged and inflammatory partisan context – one that has clearly embroiled intellectuals as well as politicians – cannot be ignored in assessing the public controversy that swirled around the Conservative JAC reforms. One cannot prove counterfactuals, of course, but it is worth asking what the reaction might have been had very similar reforms been enacted by a Liberal government. It is surely plausible to think that they would have garnered more attention – and more criticism! – than the 1994 Liberal reforms, but that the level of criticism would not have been as high or intense as in the case of the Conservative reforms. Given the ongoing "demonization context" in which the Harper government launched its reforms, it is difficult to deny that the reaction was influenced not only by "what" was done but also by "who" was doing it.

Conclusion

Have we arrived at the best system of federal judicial appointments? That is not my claim. I have tried merely to identify the ways in which the reforms have been demonized out of all proportion. Whatever their weaknesses, the Harper reforms will not be the unmitigated disaster that some critics foresee. On this point, I give the last word to Marshall Crowe. Crowe, who served on a JAC, responded to a claim that going from three screening categories – not recommended, recommended, and highly recommended – back to two made the JACs worse than useless because "to be simply "recommended," a candidate had only to meet the most minimal requirements." By implication, only the "highly recommended" candidates were truly worthy. Crowe disagreed. If it were true that only "the most minimal requirements" were necessary to make it into the recommended category, "[t]hat would mean recommending virtually every applicant," when "[i]n fact, we recommended only between a third and 50 per cent of all applicants." For Crowe, in short, the bar between qualified and unqualified was reasonably high. True, "the small number of "highly recommended" individuals were almost all appointed," but the other appointees also met reasonable standards because none of them, in Crowe's memory, came from the 50 to 70 per cent of candidates screened out as unqualified. Crowe concludes that:

Criticism of the government's moderate proposals is exaggerated. I see no reason to expect the high legal quality of recommended candidates to diminish: The government will still have ample scope to make choices among those recommended. Given the unqualified constitutional authority of the executive over judicial appointments, that is how it should be.

11.3

Packing the Supreme Court

Jamie Cameron

Policy Options, October 5, 2015, http://policyoptions.irpp.org/magazines/october-2015/stephen-harper-and-the-judiciary/packing-the-supreme-court/. Reprinted with permission.

In 2006, outgoing Prime Minister Paul Martin claimed that Stephen Harper would "pack" the Supreme Court of Canada with judges who would "roll back" the Charter of Rights and Freedoms. Harper put it in more gentle terms, stating that he would choose candidates for the Supreme Court who would interpret and apply, but not rewrite, the government's laws. Five years later, *Globe and Mail* justice reporter Kirk Makin wrote about "The coming conservative court" and speculated how Harper might reshape the judiciary. Harper's appointees have formed a majority of five since October 2012, and today only two of nine Supreme Court of Canada judges were not named by this prime minister.

As yet the Charter has not been rolled back – far from it, as a number of uncomfortable setbacks for the government attests. With five of the prime minister's appointees on the panel, the Supreme Court voted 9-0 in 2013 to invalidate several *Criminal Code* provisions on prostitution-related activities. In early 2015 and with six Harper appointees sitting on the appeal, the Court unanimously invalidated criminal prohibitions relating to assisted suicide, once again by a 9-0 vote. In both instances, the judges appointed by Prime Minister Harper could have but chose not to roll the Charter back.

There is more. In 2014, another unanimous decision by eight judges, involving five Harper appointments, turned back the government's proposals for Senate reform. Four of five judges on a panel of seven also went against the government in the *Appointment Reference*, and reached the extraordinary conclusion that their colleague Justice Marc Nadon – who was already sworn in – had not been legally appointed. Meanwhile, and although with notable dissents, the Supreme Court stepped up its interpretation of the Charter in its early 2015 jurisprudence, with decisions enforcing and extending constitutional rights on labour relations, religious freedom, criminal justice and other issues.

After all that there is still more. Relations between the Court and the government were profoundly affected by the failed Nadon appointment and the outcome in the *Appointment Reference*. That is before the fallout from his ill-advised attack on Chief Justice Beverley McLachlin further hardened the Prime Minister. After the *Globe and Mail* published the short list that led to Justice

Nadon's appointment, Harper shut down what was already a modest parliamentary process and returned the matter of Supreme Court appointments to the back rooms. Those who had fretted that a process aimed at introducing a measure of transparency and accountability would politicize appointments are hard-pressed to imagine a process more political than the one we have reverted to now.

In recent months Harper has more overtly shown his determination to "pack" the courts with judges who vocally defend conservative positions and are known for their ideological convictions. This is evident in the lower courts and in the Supreme Court, with the appointment of Russell Brown to replace Justice Marshall Rothstein. More than a judge who might have conservative leanings, as Justice Rothstein did, Brown has expressed hostility toward a generous interpretation of the Charter and has written dismissive criticisms of the Court's jurisprudence. His views have been not unfairly described as voluble.

What this foretells is difficult to know. In the United States, where Supreme Court judges have life tenure, Republican presidents learned that it could take many years to put a conservative court in place. In a system where it is readily acknowledged that judges follow partisan lines, it can be irksome when some do not perform as expected. One of history's great surprises was Earl Warren, the long-time Republican governor of California, who became the most liberal chief justice of all. Some Republican appointees have enjoyed status as "swing" justices who exercise enormous power to tip the balance when the Court's liberal and conservative blocs are divided 4-4. The best examples are Sandra Day O'Connor and Anthony Kennedy.

Even after appointing seven of the Supreme Court's judges, Prime Minister Harper has realized that putting a "conservative" court in place is no easy task. Up to now, decision-making in Canada has not been ideological or partisan in nature. True enough, some judges are more "liberal" and others more "conservative," and tension can certainly build around those poles as it did during the more divisive years of the Joseph Lamer Court. That said, ideology and partisan views have mattered less than divergent conceptions of justice.

Much of the Court's current stability can be attributed to Chief Justice McLachlin – a 26-year veteran and leader of the Court since 2000 – who sets the tempo for decision-making. Neither liberal nor conservative herself, the Chief Justice models a leadership style that prioritizes collegiality among the judges and a conception of justice that is neutral in terms because it simply and deliberately seeks what is just in the circumstances.

Whether the Supreme Court will shift away from rights and roll the Charter back – and how far that could go in the days and years ahead – remains uncertain. How the Court's internal dynamics will shift and evolve is unknown, and the upcoming federal election on October 19 is another variable that could affect the institution and its work. More worrying than the prospect of divisions within the Court, a loss of consensus and collegiality, or "conservative" decisions, is the risk that decision-making based on ideology – and not the imperative of justice – might be introduced and legitimized at the Court.

11.4

Much Ado About Little

Emmett Macfarlane

Policy Options, October 5, 2015, http://policyoptions.irpp.org/magazines/october-2015/stephen-harper-and-the-judiciary/much-ado-about-little/. Reprinted with permission.

The reaction from some corners of the media and legal community to a handful of Prime Minister Stephen Harper's recent judicial appointments has been a fascinating mix of alarmism and ahistorical punditry.

Several articles in the *Globe and Mail* have emphasized the apparently conservative views held by Bradley Miller and Grant Huscroft, two recent appointees to the Ontario Court of Appeal. The revelation that Russell Brown, the Prime Minister's recently announced appointee to the Supreme Court, blogged when he was an academic and expressed sharply worded political views at the time seemed to only confirm for critics a distinctively conservative bent in Harper's judicial appointments.

The sentiment embedded in many of the criticisms directed at Harper's appointments is that the Prime Minister has inappropriately allowed political considerations to infect his selection criteria; further, there is an implication that the appointees' *conservative* political leanings are particularly problematic. Observers are rightly critical of the opaque nature of the Supreme Court appointments process, and the federal government's recent reversal of slight reforms to the process, including having appointees appear before a committee of parliamentarians to answer questions about themselves and their expected role on the Court, have only intensified the scorn. But some of these critics seem to have found the behind-the-scenes appointments process problematic only once it was Harper choosing judges; in fact, the Canadian Bar Association long opposed committee interviews for fear of "politicization" of the process.

The lack of transparency in the appointments process has always been a problem, but it has been obfuscated by a consensus that, in the modern era,

Canada has enjoyed a history of high-quality appointments, especially to the top court. It is a common error to transform this fact into the idea that appointments were somehow apolitical until Harper, a conclusion that suffers from ahistorical analysis. Pierre Trudeau, for example, famously remade the Court largely by seeking out reform-minded judges – typically small-l liberals – to fill its bench.

Worse still are some of the dubious implications being drawn about Harper's appointments. University of Toronto law professor David Dyzenhaus was quoted in one *Globe* article as saying, "It's very clear that it's almost impossible for a judge who comes from the political centre or from the left to be appointed." While it is no doubt true that Harper has avoided appointing identifiably left-wing judges – you will not find many Louise Arbours or Rosalie Abellas appointed by this prime minister – the notion that he does not appoint centrists defies reality. Indeed, the real story of Harper's judicial appointments has been how hard it has been for him to find clearly conservative individuals to appoint to the bench. That is one of the reasons why news stories about his appointments have had to rely almost exclusively on Miller and Huscroft as examples of this supposed "conservative revolution" of the judiciary. Furthermore, Harper's appointments to the Court, notwithstanding the failed appointment of Marc Nadon, who the Court itself determined was ineligible, have been consistently lauded as well-qualified.

Even more troubling is a recent op-ed by lawyers Joseph Arvay, Sean Hern and Alison Latimer arguing that there ought to be a constitutional challenge to the appointments process on the basis that politically motivated decision-making by the executive may be a threat to judicial independence. In effect, these lawyers argue that the Court itself should dictate the process by which appointments are made, notwithstanding the fact that the authority for appointments is constitutionally vested in the executive. If legally dubious, such a claim is also institutionally myopic: appellate courts, particularly the Supreme Court, are not just legal institutions but also political ones, and powerful ones at that. The Court routinely makes decisions implicating moral controversies and public policy, decisions where the justices' ideological leanings inevitably play a role. This is distinct from the false assertion that judicial ideologies are the only thing that matters; concerns that Miller's academic writings in opposition to same-sex marriage would lead him to make anti-gay rulings on the bench, for example, are likely misplaced because if anything, Miller's political and judicial philosophy makes it more likely that he would adhere to the Supreme Court's established precedents on equality rights. Ideology may not act as a one-to-one determinant of judicial behaviour, but, intermixed with legal factors and institutional norms, it can have an important impact on how courts decide.

Moreover, there is a lot of evidence that many judges may be "conservative" in one area of law and "liberal" in another area, because their broader perceptions of their role as judges provide a more coherent basis for their decision-making.

For this reason, ideological diversity is just as important for an institution like the Court as diversity along other representational grounds like gender or race (two areas, it should be noted, where there are long-standing deficiencies in representation). Critiques that treat "conservative" appointments as objectionable aberrations do more harm than good, because they reinforce a perspective that there is somehow a neutral or appropriate legal subculture to which members of the bar must belong if they are ever to be appointed to the bench.

More fundamentally, Canadians need to recognize that judicial decision-making, while necessarily distinct and independent from explicit politics, carries political weight. As a result, the judicial appointments process must be made transparent and accountable, not in a way that attempts to falsely depoliticize it but in a way that makes us aware of the nuanced ways that politics matters. And there is little evidence that this reality has changed under Harper's appointments, other than the fact that he has made a small handful of appointments of people whose political views add much-needed diversity to the bench.

11.5

Harper's Petard? The Relationship between the Courts and the Executive under the Conservative Government

Lorne Sossin

Originally published in *The Harper Decade* (May 28, 2015), http://www.theharperdecade.com/blog/2015/4/20/harpers-petard-the-relationship-between-the-courts-and-the-executive-under-the-conservative-government. Reprinted with permission.

It is hard to know at what moment Stephen Harper and his Conservative Government reached the nadir in their relationship with the Courts. Many might cite March 21, 2014, the day the Supreme Court of Canada (SCC) disqualified Justice Marc Nadon from his appointment – the first time in Canada's history that a court had turned back an executive appointment. But I would probably pick September 30, 2013, the date on which the appointment of Justice Nadon was announced. The Government knew the appointment of a Federal Court of Appeal Justice to fill one of the three "Quebec" seats on the Supreme

Court would be contentious (and had already sought an opinion from former SCC Justice Ian Binnie indicating such an appointment was not illegal). Even more so, while Justice Nadon had exhibited many commendable qualities during his service on the Federal Court of Appeal, he was nearing retirement and it was clear to most observers that his 2009 dissent in favour of the Government's position in the Khadr case was a key factor in his putative elevation. Justice Nadon's appointment on the merits, and in its process, represented a gauntlet thrown down at the feet of the Canadian judiciary.

And then, of course, it got worse. After the Supreme Court turned back the Nadon appointment (purely on eligibility grounds, without comment on the merits or the process), on May 1, 2014, "senior conservatives" leaked that Chief Justice Beverley McLachlin had lobbied against the Nadon appointment. The Chief Justice responded by stating that she had sought a call with the Prime Minister to discuss concerns about the eligibility of a Federal Court judge (concerns, which of course, did not go away). The Prime Minister, rather than climbing down from these extraordinary allegations against a sitting Chief Justice, reiterated them, pointing out that he declined the call because it would have been inappropriate to discuss the appointment with the Chief Justice. If this was not the bottom, what could possibly be next?

More to the point, how did we get here? There are two plausible explanations – one substantive and one less so. I will touch on each briefly.

The substantive reasoning relates to the many instances where Conservative ideas and policies have been stymied by Supreme Court decisions (and to a lesser extent, lower court decisions). To cite just some examples, the Supreme Court compelled an unwilling Conservative Government to fund needle exchanges in Vancouver (in 2011), and prevented an eager Conservative Government from launching a national securities regulator (in 2012). From the *Bedford* decision (2013) legalizing certain aspects of prostitution to the *Carter* decision (2015) striking down the *Criminal Code* provision making it illegal to assist someone in committing suicide, the Government appeared to ricochet from one setback to another. I should probably devote more space to the Government's significant defeat in the *Senate Reference* (2014) and the Aboriginal rights case, *Tsilhqot'in Nation* (2014), but this would simply be piling on.

Other Canadian Governments have lost significant cases at the Supreme Court or had policy proposals and positions turned back (the Liberals, for example, lost their own Senate Reference and a series of Aboriginal rights cases in the 1980s). Never before, however, has there been a partisan tinge to the narrative around Government litigation before the courts. This more American style of coverage (noting, for example, how many Harper SCC appointments voted with the majority or the dissent) represented a new and worrying turn in the relationship between the Federal Executive and the federally appointed judiciary.

The saga unfolding over the past year of the Harper decade in Canadian politics represents an extension of a broader theme. Having fought so hard in so many elections for power and ultimately for a majority mandate, it is as if for Harper's Government, other appointed bodies (whether courts, regulators or independent agencies) are viewed as less legitimate and a threat to Canada's democratic system – particularly the Supreme Court as it has interfered with or rolled back so many policy initiatives and policy preferences of the Conservative Government since 2006.

The second explanation is less political and more personal. Listening to the Conservative rhetoric, it does not appear that the Conservative Government has philosophical differences with the courts about the nature of democratic legitimacy – rather, it sounds like the Conservatives sometimes simply mistrust judges. They believe judges (though importantly not all of them) to be hostile to the Government and its value-based policy preferences.

But it is not so simple. The Government does appear to have a soft spot for the Federal Court, as suggested above. The leaked short-list for the replacement of Justice Fish on the SCC included 6 potential appointments, 3 of which emanated from the Federal Court of Appeal (including, of course, Nadon). Additionally, in the Bill C-51 debates of 2015, the Conservatives have eschewed a greater role for administrative oversight through the Security Intelligence Review Committee (SIRC) but have been content to leave key determinations in the enhanced CSIS powers in the hands of Federal Court judges. And beyond the Federal Court, the Conservatives also have used judicial appointments to advance some of their own loyalists (Vic Toews springs to mind). Like all assessments of a decade in power, the story of the Conservative Government under Prime Minister Harper and the courts is multi-faceted, and anything but one-dimensional.

As we approach 10 years of Conservative Governments under Prime Minister Harper it is fair in my view to draw some conclusions about the relationship between the Executive and Judicial branches in Canada.

The first conclusion, made ever more apparent over the past tumultuous year, is that the Courts are not beyond the reach of partisan politics and political opportunism. If the Prime Minister can go after the integrity of the Chief Justice, then no judge can truly remain beyond the fray.

The second conclusion is that, after a decade of appointments by Harper's Cabinet, the courts remain fiercely independent – tellingly, all but one of Harper's 5 appointments who took part in the Nadon decision, for example, agreed with the majority that the appointment contravened the *Supreme Court Act*.

The third conclusion is that the Conservatives have not paid an especially high price for the fights they have picked with Judges. Judges are well respected in the abstract, but not especially loved (particularly by the Conservative base) when it comes to specific issues – the public largely sides with the Government, for example, when it calls for stiffer sentences for criminals and for the discretion of the judges to be constrained in this context by mandatory minimum sentences.

While it is perhaps too early to say, my final observation is that the relationship between the Courts and the Executive is more resilient than many might have thought. Although the personal relationship may have touched rock bottom sometime over the past couple of years, the institutional relationship remains strong and largely unaffected, including Government funding for the courts and its staff, and the judicial enforcement of Government laws and policy. Unlike Statistics Canada, Elections Canada and other bodies whom the Harper Conservatives have bloodied (either for partisan reasons or simply to make a point – or both), the courts have emerged from a decade of the Harper led Conservative Government unscathed (some might say unbowed). In Canada, judges and politicians may not always like each other, but the courts and executive need each other to achieve their institutional goals – and ultimately both depend on the legitimacy conferred by Parliament and the confidence of the public.

11.6

Marc Nadon and the New Politics of Judicial Appointment

Thomas M.J. Bateman

"The Other Shoe to Drop: Marc Nadon and Judicial Appointment Politics in Post-Charter Canada," *Journal of Parliamentary and Political Law* 9 (2015), 169–187. Reproduced with permission of author and Thomson Reuters Canada Limited.

Chronicling the rise of the Harper Government to majority status in April, 2011, journalist Paul Wells asks, "What could possibly stop this man from imposing his will on the people of Canada?" The answer is clear: the courts. Wells notes in his book, *The Longer I'm Prime Minister*, that part of Harper's mission was in part to replace the ranks of Liberal-appointed boards, commission, offices, and courts with those he himself selected. To a great extent, he has done that. By the end of his government in 2015, eight justices of the SCC had been appointed by Prime Minister Harper, though one had retired. The Prime Minister went for number six in September, 2013, nominating Federal Court Justice Marc Nadon to the Court to replace the retired Morris Fish. Initially, the Liberal-established consultation and parliamentary review process unfolded as expected. Eyebrows did rise because Nadon did not make any list of likely appointees Court-watchers had drafted. But such was Canadian deference and decorum regarding things judicial that Harper's choice elicited no public criticism. It would be unseemly – un-Canadian, even – to criticize Nadon for being unqualified, incompetent, or ideologically suspect. Justice Nadon was sworn in by Chief Justice Beverley McLachlin on October 7, 2013.… In an unprecedented series of events, the Supreme Court itself on March 21, 2014 declared that Nadon could not sit on the Court. The Court reversed an appointment made by the Government of Canada to its ranks. An untutored observer might hastily conclude that the Court asserted a power to select the members of its august club.…

Stephen Harper and the Courts

Stephen Harper's Conservative Party of Canada grew out of the older western-based Reform Party of Canada and had a ballast of principles associated with free trade, smaller government, regional equity, law and order, a muscular defence policy, and a mild populism that is averse to the identity politics informing the policies of the Liberals and New Democrats.…

Some of Harper's plans for changing the country met with limited success. The government attempted to establish a national securities regulator. It attempted several measures to tip the balance against criminal offenders, including longer mandatory minimum sentences, delayed parole eligibility, stronger voices for victims in sentencing proceedings, and reductions in credits for time served before conviction by offenders. It tried to discontinue the operation of a Vancouver safe drug injection clinic, and also defended Canada's anti-prostitution provisions of the Criminal Code against Charter attack. The courts defeated the government on almost all of these measures. These defeats probably confirmed in Harper an opinion that he was impolitic enough to express publicly in early 2006, just ahead of the January federal election. Leading in the opinion polls, and now dealing with fears stoked by opponents that the Conservatives could win a majority and implement its "hidden agenda," Harper attempted to calm Canadians' nerves with this remark:

> There will be a bureaucracy appointed by the Liberals. So even with a majority, it's impossible to have absolute power for the Conservatives. The reality is that we will have for some time to

come a Liberal senate, a Liberal civil service, at least senior levels have been appointed by the Liberals, and courts have been appointed by the Liberals. So these are obviously checks on the power of a Conservative government, as I said that's why I say in the true sense there's no, certainly no absolute power for a Conservative government and no real true majority. We will have checks and limits on our ability to operate that a Liberal government would not face.

The comment implies that if Liberals appoint ideological liberals to institutions of government like the public service and the courts, Conservatives, given the chance, would themselves appoint ideological kindred spirits. When the Liberal campaign publicized the obvious implication of these remarks, Harper the following day tried to reassure voters but instead made his earlier point only clearer: "We have no alternative but to accept the checks; they're part of our system. Judges are named; judges can't be removed by governments except under extraordinary circumstances." Judges are indeed named – by governments … [and] Harper governments have installed a majority of justices in the Supreme Court: Rothstein, Cromwell, Moldaver, Karakatsanis, Wagner. Nadon would have been the sixth. Earlier appointments did not create the stir that was seen with Nadon, even though Rothstein and Moldaver were considered, by Canadian standards, more conservative jurists. Nadon's nomination seemed to tip the balance.

[*Ed. Note:* The author describes the changes to Supreme Court appointments from the Liberals in 2004 and the Conservatives from 2006–2012. See Introduction to Chapter 4.]

The Nadon Affair in Court

Nadon's nomination [to the Supreme Court of Canada] was announced September 30, 2013 [and he was formally sworn in October 7.] But the government knew long before then that there was a hitch. Nadon did practice law in Quebec many years ago but he was a sitting Federal Court justice at the time of his appointment. As is customary, as a judge he resigned his membership in the *Barreau du Quebec*. In the spring of 2013, the government asked retired Supreme Court Justice Ian Binnie to prepare an opinion on the legality of appointing a sitting Federal Court justice to a Quebec seat on the Supreme Court. Standing in the way of Nadon's straightforward appointment were the following provisions of the *Supreme Court Act*:

5.   Any person may be appointed a judge who is or has been a judge of a superior court of a province or a barrister or advocate of at least ten years standing at the bar of a province.

6.   At least three of the judges shall be appointed from among the judges of the Court of Appeal or of the Superior Court of the Province of Quebec or from among the advocates of that Province.

The provisions could be read to require that Quebec appointees (but not others) must be current members of the bar or current members of a s. 96 court in Quebec. Nadon was neither.

Binnie's opinion was that nothing in s. 6 the *Act* stood in the way of Nadon's appointment. Guided by the principle that specific provisions must always be understood in the context of the law as a whole, and that absurd implications of the literal meaning of words are to be avoided, Binnie suggested that reading s. 6 alone would mean that a person just called to the bar, and having zero years standing as a Quebec barrister could be eligible for appointment, and also that any Federal Court member was ineligible for appointment to the Court. He further suggested that substantive arguments as to the meaning of s. 6 cannot depend on changes in wording in periodic consolidations of the *Act*. The most sensible reading, he argued, is that persons who are or have been members of a provincial bar for 10 years are eligible, and that Federal Court justices are also eligible. There is no "currency requirement" for Supreme Court eligibility. Binnie did consider it inappropriate if a Federal Court justice were to rejoin the Quebec bar for a day prior to appointment, simply to qualify under s. 6. Such an expedient, he wrote, "is neither required nor compatible with the dignity of the office being filled, in my opinion."

The government had retired Supreme Court Justice Louise Charron and Professor Peter Hogg, the dean of Canadian constitutional law professors, review Binnie's opinion. Both categorically affirmed it. On the strength of these opinions, Nadon's nomination went ahead.

Toronto lawyer Rocco Galati interpreted the *Act* to mean that Nadon, a current member of the Federal Court of Appeal, could not sit on the Supreme Court. He went to court asking for an order to stay the appointment until the issue was resolved. Galati was joined in his view by the Quebec government. At the request of the Quebec bar association, the Quebec government asked the federal government to refer the matter to the Supreme Court.

On October 22 the government inserted an amendment to the *Supreme Court Act* in Bill C-4, its omnibus budget implementation bill, to clarify the meaning of ss. 5 and 6:

> 5.1   For greater certainty, for the purpose of section 5, a person may be appointed a judge if, at any time, they were a barrister or advocate of at least 10 years standing at the bar of a province.
>
> 6.1   For greater certainty, for the purpose of section 6, a judge is from among the advocates of the Province of Quebec if, at any time, they were an advocate of at least 10 years standing at the bar of that Province.

Also on October 22, the federal government announced that it would refer the legality of Nadon's appointment to the Supreme Court of Canada.

A panel of seven justices on January 14, 2014 heard the *Reference re: Supreme Court Act, ss. 5 and 6.* Justice Rothstein, elevated from the Federal Court of Canada in 2006, recused himself. The specific questions put to the Court were:

> (1)   Can a person who was, at any time, an advocate of at least 10 years standing at the Barreau du Quebec be appointed to the Supreme Court of Canada as a member of the Supreme Court from Quebec pursuant to sections 5 and 6 of the *Supreme Court Act*?
>
> (2)   Can Parliament enact legislation that requires that a person be or has previously been a barrister or advocate of at least 10 years standing at the bar of a province as a condition of appointment as a judge of the Supreme Court of Canada or enact the annexed declaratory provisions as set out in clauses 471 and 472 of the Bill entitled *Economic Action Plan 2013 Act, No. 2*?

The six-member majority in a jointly-authored opinion answered question 1 in the negative, holding that the provision respecting Quebec requires "currency" – that an appointee currently be a member of the Quebec bar or currently a member of a s. 96 court in Quebec. This is the plain meaning of the text and it goes back to the original wording of the provision in 1886; it has been consistently restrictive. More fundamentally, the special requirement for Quebec judges stems from the "historic bargain" between Canada East and the other jurisdictions that led to Confederation. Just as Quebec required a minimum number of seats on the Court to establish "the legitimacy of the Supreme Court as a federal and bijural institution" (para 55), "[r]equiring the appointment of current members of civil law institutions was intended to ensure not only that those judges were qualified to represent Quebec on the Court, but that they were perceived by Quebecers as being so qualified" (para 56). Currency ensures the representation not simply of Quebec's legal traditions but also its "social values" (para 56). The majority is not entirely clear but its sense is that only a current Quebec s. 96 judge or a current member of the Quebec bar can be assumed to have a grasp of current social values, and that such knowledge is integral to good judging. Presumably, Quebeckers are to be assured that changes in their mores will be efficiently reflected in changes to the jurisprudence of the high court....

As for question 2, the majority held that the legislation passed by Parliament in late 2013 to declare that persons who were once members of the Quebec bar are eligible for appointment to the Court touches the composition of the Court and that alterations to the composition of the Court are constitutional amendments subject to s. 41(d) of the *Constitution Act, 1982*, which requires resolutions of Parliament and each of the provincial legislatures. Here the majority repeated its reliance on the "historic bargain" between the founding communities – "still compelling" (para 93) – that prevents essential changes to the Court over Quebec's objections. The Supreme Court of Canada "is a foundational premise of the Canadian Constitution" (para 89).

Justice Moldaver dissented, stating perfunctorily that not all changes to the eligibility requirements for membership on the Court are subject to s. 41(d). He went no further on question 2. He answered question 1 in the affirmative, asking why Quebec appointees would be subject to more stringent eligibility requirements than those from other provinces. Section 6 of the *Act*, he averred, guarantees Quebec judges a minimum number of seats on the Court. In other respects, it must be read in conjunction with s. 5 which omits the currency requirement....

The currency requirement itself does nothing to promote Quebeckers' confidence in the Court, Moldaver contended. The section's object is to guarantee Quebec seats on the Court and thus to ensure that the Court has personnel versed in the civil law tradition. There is no evidence, he wrote, to suggest that the object of s. 6 is to ensure that "Quebec's ... social values" are to be represented on the Court. Further, if the majority were correct, then a person could practice law in Quebec for ten years, let his or her membership in the Quebec bar lapse, later join for one day, then be appointed to the Court. This, Moldaver wrote, is a "manifest absurdity" (para 121). Further, can one be fit for the Court if one is merely a member of the bar without practicing law (para 150)? ...

It is hard not to wonder that the government made a tactical error in amending the *Act* while referring the interpretation of ss. 5 and 6 of the *Act* to the Court. Instead of the amendment complementing the reference, it may have undermined it. While the amendment purports to clarify or "declare" the meaning the government was convinced is present in ss. 5 and 6, the amendment suggests the government thought its interpretation of the extant provision is not obvious and needs additional legislative support. In this sense the two-prong tactic was contradictory and in the event self-defeating. Instead of foreclosing a finding that Federal Court judges were ineligible to assume Quebec seats on the Supreme Court, the government gave the Supreme Court an opportunity to incorporate changes to the eligibility of appointees into the definition of "composition" of the Supreme Court for the purposes of the unanimous consent rule in Part V of the *Constitution Act, 1982*. Changes to the Constitution are now harder to achieve than they were before the amendments to the *Supreme Court Act* were attempted....

Judicial Appointment Politics in Canada

... The plot thickened on May 1, 2014 when the *National Post's* John Ivison published a column citing unnamed Conservative sources expressing frustration that the Supreme Court, and particularly the Chief Justice, has blocked the government's legislative program, lobbied the government against Nadon's appointment, and generally carried on a campaign against the government. The article contained a response from the Supreme Court denying the allegations. Specifically: "The question concerning the eligibility of a federal court judge for appointment to the Supreme Court under the Supreme Court Act was well-known in legal circles. Because of the institutional impact on the Court, the Chief Justice advised the Minister of Justice, Mr. [Peter] MacKay, of the potential issue before the government named its candidate for appointment to the Court. Her office also advised the Prime Minister's chief of staff, Mr. [Ray] Novak. The Chief Justice does not express any views on the merits of the issue." What had emerged is that after she met with Prime Minister on April 22, 2013 to present news of Justice Fish's retirement, and after she appeared before the selection committee on July 29, 2013, the Chief Justice on July 31, 2013 attempted to contact the Prime Minister to raise the eligibility issue.

The Prime Minister's Office released a statement on May 1, 2014 indicating that the Chief Justice sought to speak to the prime minister directly about Nadon's eligibility, and that this was inappropriate. Invoking a liberal definition of the *sub judice* rule, the statement read: "Neither the Prime Minister nor the Minister of Justice would ever call a sitting judge on a matter that is or may be before their court.... The Chief Justice initiated a call to the Minister of Justice. After the Minister received her call he advised the Prime Minister that given the subject she wished to raise, taking a phone call from the Chief Justice would be inadvisable and inappropriate. The Prime Minister agreed and did not take her call."

The Supreme Court immediately shot back: "On July 31, 2013, the Chief Justice's office called the Minister of Justice's office and the Prime Minister's Chief of Staff, Mr. Novak, to flag a potential issue regarding the eligibility of a judge of the federal courts to fill a Quebec seat on the Supreme Court. Later that day, the Chief Justice spoke with the Minister of Justice, Mr. MacKay, to flag the potential issue. The Chief Justice's office also made preliminary inquiries to set up a call or meeting with the Prime Minister, but ultimately the Chief Justice decided not to pursue a call or meeting." The release states that "[i]t is customary for Chief Justices to be consulted during the appointment process and there is nothing inappropriate in raising a potential issue affecting a future appointment." "The chief justice did not lobby the government against the appointment of Justice Nadon. She was consulted by the parliamentary committee regarding the government's short list of candidates and provided her views on the needs of the court." ... The legal community has supported the Supreme Court without exception. At the very least, any supporters of Harper's positon in the legal community kept their heads down....

In the wake of the Nadon debacle, the government moved quickly to fill the vacancy left by Justice Fish's retirement. The Court had been short-handed for 14 months. Citing the need to restore the Court to a full complement quickly, the government on June 3 announced that Quebec Court of Appeal Justice Clément Gascon would be the new Quebec Justice on the Court. He was indeed appointed on June 9, to the satisfaction of all concerned. Gascon's appointment was done the old way, after private consultations with legal and Quebec governmental elites, and without recourse to a selection panel of MPs. No one appeared to mind....

What has so animated the Nadon affair is that the government has challenged the ideological consensus that has defined post-Charter Canada. Commentators have long associated this ideological consensus with the central Canadian law schools of "Official Canada," the "Laurentian consensus," or the "Court Party." A majority Conservative government would naturally want to reach outside the consensus for someone comporting with its view of the country and the constitution. (How ideologically reliable nominees are upon appointment is of course another question.) It is perhaps salutary to remember that it was not the Conservatives but the Liberals who opened Pandora's Box in 2004 with Justice Minister Cotler's modest reform; a change in government was unlikely to close it....

The result of the politicization of the constitution is a constitutionalization of politics. What has largely been overlooked in the *Supreme Court Act Reference* was an enlargement of the scope of the formal amending provisions of the Constitution. The majority of the Court understood the 2013 amendments to the *Supreme Court Act* clarifying the s. 6 eligibility requirements to affect the "composition of the Supreme Court of Canada"; these require use of the unanimity rule set out in s. 41 of the *Constitution Act, 1982*. This, in conjunction with its opinion in the *Reference re Senate Reform*, expands the reach of the formal amending provisions, further constitutionalizing the politics of institutional change in Canada.

This article is no exercise in court-bashing. It is more a recognition of the Machiavellian *virtu* of Pierre Trudeau whose success in patriating the Constitution and entrenching the Charter and rigid amending formulae allowed him to rule from the grave. By constitutionalizing so many aspects of Canadian politics, Trudeau effectively insulated them from the vicissitudes of future electoral and parliamentary contest. But in the age of the Charter, it is hard to sustain the view that judges merely interpret law. They make it and shape it; they exercise political choice. Thus the personnel and the manner of their appointment are important and politically contentious. Prime Minister Harper tried to shape the Court and failed. His difficulties in rebalancing the federation stem in good part from his inability to penetrate a rigid Trudeauian constitutional edifice guarded by a judicial phalanx whose character Harper has been unable to shape. We see what Peter Russell forecast a long time ago: the entrenchment of the Charter has judicialized politics and politicized the judiciary.

11.7

Stephen Harper v. Beverly McLachlin

Harper's Disrespect for the Supreme Court Harms the Workings of Government

Canadian Bar Association Presidents

Originally published in the *Globe and Mail*, May 6, 2014. Reprinted with permission.

This statement is made by eleven former presidents of the Canadian Bar Association: L. Yves Fortier of Montreal; Thomas G. Heintzman of Toronto; Simon V. Potter of Montreal; Susan McGrath of Iroquois Falls; D. Kevin Carroll of Barrie; Bernard Amyot of Montreal; Paul Fraser of Victoria; Daphne Dumont of Charlottetown; Guy Joubert of Winnipeg; Rod Snow of Whitehorse; and William Johnson of Regina.

The recent comments by Prime Minister Stephen Harper, claiming that the Chief Justice of Canada attempted an inappropriate conversation with him, demonstrate a disrespect by the executive branch for the judicial branch of our constitutional democracy, and for the Chief Justice of Canada as the most senior member of the Canadian judiciary. This is so despite the fact that the discussion in question involved a possible new appointment to the Supreme Court of Canada, a topic well within guidelines for appropriate conversations between prime ministers and chief justices.

The judicial branch is one of the three independent components of Canada's constitutional democracy, the other two being the legislative and the executive branches. Our system can operate effectively only if each component is respectful and courteous in its relations with the others. The courtesy and respect that these relationships require are particularly important for the judicial branch because it must ultimately judge the constitutionality of the conduct of the other two branches and, yet, at the same time, must on a day-to-day administrative level have dialogue with them. Furthermore, the judicial branch, and judges generally, do not have the ability to defend themselves if those very relationships are used as grounds for attack.

The events in April to July 2013 demonstrate the usual and respectful relationship between the judicial branch and the other two branches of government. In April 2013, the Chief Justice, quite properly and according to long-standing tradition, provided her input to the appropriate parliamentary committee about proposed new appointments to the Supreme Court of Canada. In July, she provided her input to the Canadian government. These discussions occurred well before the nomination of Justice Marc Nadon. They were perfectly in line with the sort of courteous discussions which have historically occurred and which Canadians would expect to occur between the judiciary and the executive with respect to judicial appointments.

In contrast, the recent statements by the Prime Minister were made nine months after the conversations in question occurred, long after the Prime Minister could have dealt with any aspect of those discussions if there had been any good-faith reason to do so. The Prime Minister's statements were made only after the government had been a litigant in appeals before the Supreme Canada, leaving the impression that the statements were aimed at the Court as a reaction to the result of the decisions in those appeals – conduct in which no respectful private litigant should engage.

As recent press reports demonstrate, these circumstances leave us concerned that the Prime Minister's statements may intimidate or harm the ability of the Supreme Court of Canada to render justice objectively and fairly – even when the government of Canada chooses to be a litigant before it. In addition, the statement threatens to lead to abandonment of the fruitful and necessary respectful relationships between the Supreme Court of Canada and the two other branches of government and a refusal by the Court, and all courts, to have any dealings with the other two branches for fear of retribution to which the judicial branch cannot in any seemly fashion respond fully.

As former presidents of the Canadian Bar Association, we ask the Prime Minister to remedy this situation in a way which will demonstrate to our judiciary and to Canadians at large that he respects the independence of our courts and will treat with due courtesy the Chief Justice of Canada.

A Few Questions for Beverley McLachlin

Dennis Baker and Rainer Knopff

National Post, May 7, 2014, A10. Reprinted with permission.

Commentary on the tiff between the Prime Minister and the Chief Justice regarding the abortive appointment of Marc Nadon to the Supreme Court has, in the main, gone easy on Chief Justice Beverley McLachlin. Too easy.

The issue concerns calls placed by the Chief Justice to the government about the possible ineligibility of Justice Nadon for appointment to one of the three Quebec seats required under section six of the Supreme Court Act.

Section six requires the Quebec judges to be appointed "from among judges of the Court of Appeal or of the Superior Court of the Province of Quebec or from among the advocates of that province." Justice Nadon had never held one of the specified judicial positions – he was a judge of the Federal Court – so the question was whether he qualified as coming "from among" Quebec's "advocates." Was it enough that he had been trained in Quebec and practised law there for almost two decades, or did he have to be a *current* advocate in the province?

McLachlin says that she called Justice Minister Peter McKay and Stephen Harper's Chief of Staff, Ray Novak – and planned also to call or meet with the Prime Minister directly – merely to "flag" this issue of eligibility. Nadon had not yet been selected as the nominee and the case challenging his appointment had not yet been launched, so she was not communicating about an issue being litigated before her court. Knowing that the issue might come before her Court, however, McLachlin did not, at this early point, "express any opinion as to the merits of the eligibility issue"; she merely "wished to ensure that the government was aware" of it.

McLachlin's account is difficult to square with the language she (and her five colleagues in the majority) used when Justice Nadon's case was finally decided. At that point, she concluded that a "requirement of current membership in the Quebec bar has been in place – unambiguous and unchanged – since 1875."

Unambiguous! Can we believe that without also believing that McLachlin had an "opinion on the merits" at the time she made the calls, even if she did not "express" it? Can one be open-minded about a question the answer to which is "unambiguous"?

Indeed, having a strong opinion about Nadon's ineligibility might explain why McLachlin made two calls and explored direct communication with the Prime Minister. After all, only one call was needed to "ensure that the government was aware" of the issue. Several escalating calls – especially coming from the person who might help ultimately resolve the issue – suggests something more substantial than a mere "heads-up" about a still-open question, and could be perceived as a strong signal of where she stood on the eligibility controversy. Such a signal would go beyond the Chief Justice's administrative responsibility to simply alert the government of potential difficulties ahead.

Moreover, if the Chief Justice believed that Nadon was unquestionably ineligible, she probably had an obligation to do more than flag the issue or send obscure signals. As the political scientist Emmett Macfarlane has noted, if the government made the "unambiguous" mistake of proposing a non-lawyer for appointment to the Court, the sitting judges would refuse to swear in the nominee, and would presumably warn the government of this consequence. If Nadon's nomination was a similarly unambiguous error, the Chief Justice should have issued such a warning.

Instead, the Court did swear in Justice Nadon, with the Chief Justice presiding, which indicates that his ineligibility was not, in fact, "unambiguous." Certainly Justice Moldaver, in his powerful dissent, concluded that Nadon was eligible. So did former Supreme Court justices Binnie and Charron. And so did Peter Hogg, who comes close to being an honorary Supreme Court justice. There would have been no such disagreement about the truly unambiguous nomination of a non-lawyer.

So, perhaps McLachlin did have an open mind about a difficult and ambiguous issue of eligibility at the time she "flagged" it to the government. But if that was so, her subsequent portrayal of the answer to this question as "unambiguous" seems a disingenuous exaggeration – just as merely flagging a question that has an unambiguous answer seems a disingenuous evasion.

Might it be that the Prime Minister is not the only one playing political games?

11.8

Dissent From Within at the Supreme Court of Canada

Benjamin Perrin

Macdonald-Laurier Institute for Public Policy, January 2016, http://www.macdonaldlaurier.ca/files/pdf/MLI_SupremeCourt2_NewFinal.pdf. Reprinted with permission.

[In 2014], the Macdonald-Laurier Institute for Public Policy recognized the Supreme Court of Canada as its annual Policy-Maker of the Year. The Court's decisions in 2014 spanned Senate reform, prostitution, Aboriginal rights and title, tools for fighting crime and terrorism, and judicial appointments to the Court itself.... Consensus decisions were the norm that year and the federal government suffered an abysmal record of losses.

This report looks at 2015 – the final year of Prime Minister Stephen Harper's Conservative government – to see if these trends have held or not and sets the stage for some of the challenges and opportunities facing the new Liberal government under Prime Minister Justin Trudeau. The issues confronted by the top Court this year included controversial social questions like physician-assisted suicide and medical marijuana derivatives; labour relations issues including collective bargaining for the RCMP and the right to strike; and criminal law issues such as police searches of cell phones and mandatory minimum sentences for gun crimes. It also grappled with the extent to which governments should be liable to pay damages for violations of the *Canadian Charter of Rights and Freedoms* (Charter) and whether it should read-in a duty of good faith into private contracts.

Within this context and while appreciating that the work of the Court is cyclical and outcomes vary from year to year, this paper explores the recent track record of the Supreme Court of Canada and the significance of some of its landmark decisions from the last year....

[T]he one-year period selected for this review was November 1, 2014 to October 31, 2015. This period is also helpful since it roughly coincides with the formal transition of power from the Conservative to Liberal federal government on November 4, 2015. For consistency with last year's study, all judgments of the Court during this period were considered for inclusion in the analysis that follows. The top 10 cases were selected to provide a manageable, but meaningful number of cases to analyse and compare. These cases were selected based on the importance of their subject matter and broad significance to Canadians. The outcome of the decisions was not a consideration in selecting them. It is observable that the selection criteria led to a large number of public law decisions, across a wide spectrum of areas of law. However, some of these decisions have significant implications for private actors, including individuals and private corporations.

Table 1, below, provides a snapshot of these decisions and their outcomes.... The final column of "Government Win or Loss" (which refers to the federal government) requires some explanation, since the federal government is not a party to every case reaching the Court. The determination of whether a case involved a "win" or "loss" for the federal government refers to cases where the Court either agreed with, or rejected, respectively, the position taken by the federal government (which includes the Attorney General of Canada and Director of Public Prosecutions in these cases). In some instances, these federal entities were parties to the proceeding, whereas they were interveners in others (in which case their intervener's factum was consulted). The decisions are listed in chronological order....

Table 1: Top 10 Supreme Court of Canada Decisions of 2015 (Abridged)

Case	Subject	Unanimous?	Federal Government Win / Loss
Bhasin v. Hrynew	Duty of good faith in contracts	Yes (Justice Cromwell)	N/A
R. v. Fearon	Police searches of cell phones incident to arrest	No	Win
Mounted Police Association of Ontario v. Canada (Attorney General)	Collective bargaining for RCMP	No	Loss
Saskatchewan Federation of Labour v. Saskatchewan	Right to strike	No	Loss
Carter v. Canada (Attorney General)	Physician-assisted suicide	Yes (The Court)	Loss
Loyola High School v. Quebec (Attorney General)	Freedom of religion	No	N/A
Quebec (Attorney General) v. Canada (Attorney General)	Long-gun registry data from Quebec and "cooperative federalism"	No	Win
R. v. Nur	Mandatory minimum sentences	No	Loss
Henry v. British Columbia (Attorney General)	Damages for Charter violations	No	Loss
R. v. Smith	Derivatives of medical marijuana	Yes (The Court)	Loss

Main Findings

> 1. *The former federal Conservative government's losing record on major cases at the Court continued in 2015.*

In last year's report, the federal government won just one in 10 major cases in which it participated (10 percent) whereas in this year's report, it succeeded in two of eight cases in which it participated (25 percent). The federal government was either a party or intervener in each of these cases. This losing record is still substantially worse than historical trends for Charter litigation before the Court: on average, various levels of government have historically succeeded in 59 percent of Charter cases.

It is notable that the two cases that the federal government was victorious in this past year were only won narrowly – in both instances by a margin of a single judge. In *R. v. Fearon*, the Court split 4–3, while in *Quebec v. Canada*, the Court split 5–4. The win in *R. v. Fearon* was on an issue – police searches of cell phones incident to arrest – that had not featured as a policy position of the Conservative Party of Canada and it could be unpopular with libertarians in their base, so it would not have been a particularly important win from the perspective of the former federal government. On the other hand, the victory in *Quebec (Attorney General) v. Canada (Attorney General)* – on the destruction of long-gun registry data collected in Quebec – would have been considered a major political success for the former federal government given its longstanding opposition to the registry. Given it only dealt with the data from that registry from Quebec, however, its actual policy impact was negligible, particularly given that Quebec has announced it will launch its own registry.

On the other hand, the losses suffered by the former federal government included some major political and policy defeats. Losing *R. v. Nur* was particularly bad for them given that it was the first of a raft of new mandatory minimum penalties of imprisonment brought in by the former Conservative government to be challenged before the Court. The striking down of the mandatory minimums in that case, which involved a firearms violation, using an expanded application of the "reasonable hypothetical" doctrine could prove to be damaging to other recently added mandatory minimum penalties as well as favour Charter claimants more generally in other cases.

The former federal government's loss in the highly-publicized physician-assisted suicide case, *Carter v. Canada*, was taken particularly badly by supporters of its social conservative base. It created a political "hot potato" for the former government which, as discussed below, punted it before the recent federal election to an external group of experts to conduct consultations. The loss in *R. v. Smith* on derivatives of marijuana was denounced by the former federal government, which has resisted the extension of medical marijuana and opposed the legalization of marijuana – in sharp contrast with the new Liberal government that has promised to legalize marijuana.

Labour rights case losses by the former federal government stand out as having a major long-term policy impact. In *Mounted Police Association of Ontario v. Canada*, the Court recognized that RCMP members have a right to collective bargaining and in *Saskatchewan Federation of Labour v. Saskatchewan*, it recognized the right to strike. Both cases are based on freedom of association in the Charter so their impact will be longstanding.

Finally, *Henry v. British Columbia* was a major loss that extends the potential liability of all levels of government to pay damages for Charter violations. However, the decision leaves much uncertainty about how, and to what extent, such liability extends to other Charter rights beyond the right to disclosure in a criminal prosecution.

2.   *The Court has overturned its own precedents in a growing number of major Charter decisions.*

What is particularly remarkable about this year's major decisions by the Court is how many involved the Court overturning its own precedents to arrive at the outcome. These decisions add to a growing number of cases where the Court has reversed itself, often within recent decades.

In *Mounted Police Association of Ontario v. Canada*, the Court's decision was considered stunning because it overruled its 1999 decision in *Delisle v. Canada* finding that the RCMP did not have the right to collective bargaining. Likewise, in *Saskatchewan Federation of Labour v. Saskatchewan*, the Court overturned a 1987 decision (*Alberta Reference (Reference re Public Service Employee Relations Act)*) that had ruled the right to strike was not protected under freedom of association in the Charter. In this past year, the Charter has come to protect both the RCMP's right to collective bargaining and the right to strike.

The Court's decision on physician-assisted suicide in *Carter v. Canada* reversed its 1993 decision in *Rodriguez v. British Columbia*, similarly to how its recent decision on prostitution laws in *Canada v. Bedford* reversed its 1990 decision in *Reference re ss. 193 and 195.1(1)(c) of the Criminal Code (Man.)* ("Prostitution Reference").

While the Court professes to not lightly overturn its own precedents, it appears that the ability of Charter claimants to re-litigate decided constitutional cases has expanded in recent years. Some of the judges on the Court have expressed discomfort with how ready the majority of the Court has been to turn its back on recent precedents.

In *Mounted Police Association of Ontario v. Canada*, Justice Rothstein wrote a scathing dissent criticizing the majority for overturning not one, but two recent precedents to achieve the outcome in its decision. He writes: "[f]airness and certainty require that where settled law exists, courts must apply it to determine the result in a particular case. They may not identify a desired result and then search for a novel legal interpretation to bring that result about."

3. *The consensus within the Court on major decisions has not been maintained, and there are strong voices within the Court itself raising the alarm that it must not intrude into Parliament's public policy domain.*

Last year's 2014 report found that the Court's record showed a remarkably united institution with consensus decisions on significant cases being the norm and dissenting opinions rare. Of the 10 significant decisions reviewed in that previous report, only two had dissenting reasons. In other words, in eight of the 10 decisions, there was consensus on the outcome of the case (an 80 percent consensus rate) in the 2014 report. In this year's 2015 report, five of 10 decisions achieved consensus (50 percent consensus rate) with the remaining five cases involving dissenting opinions – in some cases with a deeply divided court (a 4–3 split in *R. v. Fearon*; a 5–4 split in *Quebec v. Canada*; and a 6–3 split in *R. v. Nur*). This is a major decline in consensus-based decisions by the Court compared with both last year's report (of top 10 cases) and historical trends (of all cases)....

What is even more interesting than the quantitative aspect of the rise of dissenting decisions on major cases in this year's report is that they included at times blistering criticism of majority judges for allegedly intruding on Parliament's policy-making domain. This warning of judicial restraint has been raised in reasons written by several judges appointed by former Prime Minister Stephen Harper.

In *R. v. Nur*, Justice Moldaver (with Justices Rothstein and Wagner concurring) writes in dissenting reasons that Parliament's objective in adopting mandatory penalties for firearms offences is valid and pressing and "it is not for this Court to frustrate the policy goals of our elected representatives based on questionable assumptions or loose conjecture."

In *Saskatchewan Federation of Labour v. Saskatchewan*, Justices Rothstein and Wagner dissented, writing "the majority is wrong to intrude into the policy development role of elected legislators by constitutionalizing the right to strike" (para. 105). They even went so far as to caution the Court against "usurping the responsibilities of the legislative and executive branches" (para. 114).

Finally, in *Quebec v. Canada*, it was the majority who warned that the Court must be careful not to overstep its proper role. Justices Cromwell and Karakatsanis characterize the long-gun registry data destruction as a "contentious policy choice" (para. 1) that was for Parliament to make, stating "the courts are not to question the wisdom of legislation but only to rule on its legality" (para. 3).

Conclusion

The Supreme Court of Canada continues to tackle controversial and important public policy issues. In the final year of the former federal Conservative government, it continued a losing streak observed in last year's report with just two narrow victories in the 10 major cases considered this year. However, unlike in last year's study where the Court had record levels of consensus in reaching its decisions, this recent year found a Court deeply divided with record levels of dissents on major decisions. Even more remarkable were philosophical fissures laid bare in the reasons of several judges at the Court that it must be cautious not to intrude on Parliament's legitimate role in making tough public policy decisions. It is also notable that the Court continues to overrule its own recent Charter decisions with the express disapproval of some of its members.

With the upcoming year, the new federal Liberal government is saddled with countless decisions on how to proceed with ongoing litigation involving decisions and legislation of the former federal Conservative government. It is seeking extensions of the Court's suspended declarations of invalidity to give it more time to enact legislation responding to the Court's recent decisions and preparing legislation to respond to them. In other instances, it is abandoning appeals launched by the former Conservative government that it doesn't agree with. It will be several years before law and decisions adopted by the new Liberal government will be judicially challenged and make their way eventually to the Court. Prime Minister Justin Trudeau will also have the opportunity to select the next Chief Justice during his majority mandate, which will be a significant development that could have important and lasting implications for the Court going forward.

11.9

Conservatives, the Supreme Court of Canada, and the Constitution: Judicial-Government Relations, 2006–2015

Christopher Manfredi

Osgoode Hall Law Journal 52 (2015), 951–983. Reprinted with permission.

On 20 December 2013, the Supreme Court of Canada ("SCC") unanimously declared three key sections of the *Criminal Code* that regulate prostitution unconstitutional under section 7 of the *Charter of Rights and Freedoms* ("*Charter*"). Three months later, on 21 March 2014, the Court declared that the government's nomination of a federal court judge, Justice Marc Nadon, to fill a Quebec vacancy on the Court violated the *Supreme Court Act* and that amending the *Act* to change the Court's composition could only be achieved through constitutional amendment. Just over a month after that judgment, the Court rejected the government's proposed legislation for reforming the term of Senators and the manner in which they are appointed. These three high-profile government losses in the SCC generated a growing narrative of an especially fractious relationship between the Conservative government of Prime Minister Stephen Harper and the SCC.

The narrative probably originated earlier, but it reached a crescendo in 2014 and 2015. Writing in the Globe and Mail in 2014, Lawrence Martin described the Court as having become, not by design but in effect, "the Official Opposition in Ottawa." Similarly, Vanessa Naughton described a "contentious relationship" beset by "flare-ups between the Harper government and the top court ... that have put a wrench in the Conservative government's plans." ... As Osgoode Hall Law School Dean Lorne Sossin wrote in *The Walrus*, rulings against the federal government "have become stylized as *Harper v. the Court*." The government's own reaction to some of these losses added plausibility to the narrative and suggested that any animosity might be mutual.... The purpose of this article is to analyze this narrative more rigorously by going beyond a mere tallying of government wins and losses in the Court.....

The Conservatives, the SCC, and the *Charter*

The relationship between Canadian conservatism and the *Charter* has always been ambivalent. On the one hand, conservatives were among the most vocal, if not sole, opponents of adopting the *Charter*, and conservative scholars have been strong critics of the *Charter* and its judicial application. On the other hand, conservative groups have actively participated in *Charter* litigation, including as initiators of litigation. The Reform Party – the precursor to the present-day Conservative Party – accepted the principle of a judicially enforceable *Charter* in its 1996 policy platform but advocated narrower definitions of equality rights and entrenchment of property and contract rights in the *Charter*....

The first step in understanding this aspect of the Conservative government's relationship to the SCC under the *Charter* is to step back and look at the relationship between the Court and all post-*Charter* governments. The post-*Charter* era has been one of remarkably low turnover among governments in Canada. Indeed, excluding the new Liberal government elected in October 2015, there have only been three federal governments during this period: the Progressive Conservative government (1984-1993) ("PC"), the Liberal government (1993-2006) ("LIB2"), and the Conservative Party government (2006-2015) ("CPC"). The *Charter* litigation experience of these governments before the SCC illustrates the point made above that governments often find themselves engaged in litigation over a previous government's actions.

For this article, I analyzed all SCC decisions issued up to 31 October 2015 in which the Court invalidated federal government action under the *Charter*. Table 1 shows each government's total losses and loss rate per year in office for each of three categories of cases: cases in which the government was the enactor of the invalidated measure, cases in which the government was the defender of the invalidated measure, and cases in which the government was both the enactor and defender of the invalidated measure. During this period, these three governments were on the losing side in 52 cases in which the Court declared legislation (or other government action) unconstitutional under the *Charter*. However, only 6 of those cases involved invalidation of their own legislation. For example, although the PC government found itself on the losing side in 22 *Charter* cases, 21 of those losses came in cases defending legislation enacted by previous governments, including the Liberal government of Pierre Trudeau (1968-1979, 1980-1984) ("LIB1"). Similarly, of the LIB2 government's 17 *Charter* losses, 15 involved legislation passed by previous governments. Finally, 9 of the 12 CPC government's losses in *Charter* litigation involved legislation enacted by predecessor governments.

The frequency with which the Harper government had its legislation invalidated by the Court on *Charter* grounds (0.33 per year in office) compares quite favourably to its two predecessor governments (1.00 for the PC government and 0.46 for the LIB2 government). Moreover, the rate at which the CPC government lost *Charter* cases as the defending government is almost the lowest of the three governments to date (1.33 compared to 2.56 and 1.31).... Each of these instances illustrates the general point suggested by the aggregate data in Table

1: A government's losses in *Charter* litigation may tell us very little about the relationship between that government and the Court precisely because the loss pertained to legislation enacted by a previous government.

Table 1: Invalidations by Enacting and Defending Government

Govern-ment	Period in Office	Invalidated as Enactor	Rate Per Year in Office	Invalidated as Defender	Rate Per Year in Office	Invalidated as Enactor and Defender	Rate Per Year in Office
LIB1	1968–1979, 1980–1984	12	0.80	1	0.07	0	0.00
PC	1984–1993	9	1.00	22	2.56	1	0.11
LIB2	1993–2006	6	0.46	17	1.31	2	0.15
CPC	2006–2015	3	0.33	12	1.33	3	0.33

A more detailed examination of the CPC government's experience before the Court in *Charter* cases indicates that its experience does not differ markedly from that of its predecessor governments.... This dynamic is evident in perhaps the CPC government's highest-profile early loss before the Court: *Charkaoui v. Canada (Citizenship and Immigration)....* *Charkaoui* engaged a core issue for the CPC government: national security, especially in the context of anti-terrorism measures. At issue was the constitutionality of procedures under the *Immigration and Refugee Protection Act* ("IRPA") for issuing and determining the reasonableness of security certificates and for reviewing detention under those certificates. A unanimous judgment of the Court, delivered by Chief Justice McLachlin, declared that the relevant provisions of the IRPA infringed sections 7, 9, and 10(c) of the *Charter*. The Court declared the provisions of no force or effect but suspended the declaration of invalidity for one year to give the government an opportunity to revise the legislation. While this result was clearly not welcomed by the CPC government, it cannot be characterized as a repudiation of its policy. The provisions in question had been enacted in 2001 by the Chrétien government (the LIB2 government), and the lower court proceedings began more than a year before the CPC government came to power....

The related odyssey of Omar Khadr bears similar characteristics. US forces took Khadr prisoner in Afghanistan in 2002 at the age of fifteen, transferred him to Guantanamo Bay, and charged him with murder and other terrorism-related offences. In 2003, Canadian officials questioned him at Guantanamo Bay and shared the results of those interviews with US officials. In 2008, following divided judgments by the Federal Court trial and appellate divisions, the SCC held that the Crown had an obligation under section 7 of the *Charter*, as interpreted in *R v. Stinchcombe*, to disclose the records of those interviews and the information communicated to US authorities. In 2010, the Court further found that Khadr's *Charter* rights had been violated by US interrogation techniques in 2003 and 2004 and that he was entitled to a remedy under section 24(1) of the *Charter*. However, the Court refused to order the remedy sought by Khadr – an order that Canada request his repatriation from Guantanamo Bay – and instead found that the appropriate remedy was a declaration that Khadr's rights had been violated. The Court left it to the government to determine how best to respond "in light of current information, its responsibility over foreign affairs, and the *Charter*." Finally, in 2015, the Court delivered an oral judgment from the bench affirming the Alberta Court of Appeal judgment that Khadr's sentence for his offences was a youth sentence to be served in a provincial institution.

As in *Charkaoui*, the Khadr litigation spanned both the LIB2 and CPC governments. Indeed, the constitutional violations identified by the Court in 2008 and 2010 all occurred under the LIB2 government. To be sure, the CPC government took the hardest line possible in the Khadr litigation, and its (non-) response to the Court's 2010 declaration demonstrated its disagreement with how the Court had handled the case. In that sense, the Court's summary dismissal of the CPC government's argument in 2015 might be understood as a clear rebuke of the government's position. Thus, while the CPC government was not responsible for the initial violation of Khadr's *Charter* rights, it failed to mitigate the harm flowing from those violations to the Court's satisfaction.

A similar dynamic is evident in *R v. D.B.* in 2008. At issue in *D.B.* were provisions of the *Youth Criminal Justice Act* ("YCJA") enacted by the LIB2 government in 2002 to create a category of "presumptive offences" under which Youth Court judges must impose adult sentences unless the young person demonstrates that a youth sentence would be sufficient to hold him or her accountable for the criminal act. This presumption of an adult sentence for these offences (murder, attempted murder, manslaughter, aggravated sexual assault, and "serious violent offences") reversed the standard procedure in which the Crown bears the onus of showing that the young person has lost the entitlement to a youth sentence. The provisions under review also reversed the onus with respect to publication bans in these cases by requiring youths to demonstrate why they should continue to be protected by the publication ban otherwise required by the YCJA. A five-justice majority of the Court held that these provisions infringed the right to liberty protected by section 7 of the *Charter* in a manner inconsistent with the principles of fundamental justice and that they could not be justified as a reasonable limit. It therefore rejected the Crown's appeal to set aside the youth sentence.

It should be obvious that the outcome in *D.B.* was disappointing to the CPC government, but not because it interfered with an element of its own criminal and youth justice policy. The law under review predated the CPC government by four years, the offense that precipitated D.B.'s prosecution occurred three years before the CPC's election, and the trial court judgment was rendered two years earlier. The CPC government first became involved at the provincial appellate court level but took clear ownership of the issue by pursuing the appeal to the SCC. In this sense, the CPC government was deeply invested in defending the constitutionality of the provisions even if it had not been directly responsible for enacting them. From this perspective, there is the hint of a conflict between the government and the Court, although the closeness of the judgment does not indicate a sharp conflict....

Close analysis of another of the government's 2015 losses also fails to support the narrative of high Court-government hostility. In *Mounted Police Association of Ontario v. Canada (Attorney General)*, the Court held that excluding Royal Canadian Mounted Police ("RCMP") members from the public service labour relations regime and imposing a non-unionized regime on them violated their section 2 *Charter* right to freedom of association. Although the litigation leading to MPAO began shortly after the CPC government's election, the regulations and statutes under review dated back to 1988 and 2003, respectively. Moreover, MPAO was one of two cases decided in a span of two weeks that extended *Charter* rights to organized labour in novel ways, suggesting that it was not so much directed against the federal government of the day but against a general trend in labour regulation. In addition, the Court denied a constitutional challenge against wage rollbacks imposed on RCMP members in 2009. To some degree, the CPC government was a bystander in the Court's reconsideration of its own approach to labour-management relations.

One can sense a similar, if more pronounced, dynamic at work in the Court's unanimous judgment in *Carter v. Canada (Attorney General)* in 2015. In *Carter*, the Court reconsidered its narrow 1993 decision upholding the constitutionality of the *Criminal Code*'s prohibition against assisted suicide. [*Ed. note*: See Reading 7.5] ... The relationship of *Carter* to the CPC government is analogous to the relationship of *Morgentaler* to the PC government. Both cases involved *Criminal Code* provisions regulating individuals' control over their own bodies and both sets of provisions engaged competing principles of social morality. Moreover, neither government was responsible for the policy status quo overturned by the Court, yet each government inherited the challenge of developing a new policy regime not easily reconcilable with its median ideological position....

The government's response to *Carter* was delayed but arguably moderate. On 17 July 2015, it announced the establishment of an external panel to review options for responding to the judgment. With a requirement to report by late fall 2015, the three-person panel's mandate was to consult with the public and key stakeholders, especially the interveners in *Carter*....

[*Ed. note*: Justin Trudeau's Liberals formed government after winning the October 2015 election, and in 2016 passed Bill C-14, which amends the *Criminal Code* prohibition on assisted suicide to better align with the Supreme Court decision in *Carter*. That legislation is currently being challenged in court for violating the *Charter* as well.]

If any judgments are consistent with the narrative of conflict between the Court and the CPC government, they are: *PHS* (2011), *Bedford* (2013), and *R v. Nur* (2015). At issue in *PHS* was the constitutionality of the exercise of ministerial discretion under the 1996 *Controlled Drugs and Substances Act* ("CDSA"). 69 Section 56 of the CDSA granted the federal Minister of Health the authority to grant an exemption from its application to persons or controlled substances where "in the opinion of the Minister, the exemption is necessary for a medical or scientific purpose or is otherwise in the public interest." In 2003, the LIB2 Minister of Health granted an exemption to PHS Community Services to operate Insite, a supervised safe injection site for intravenous drug users. The purpose of the exemption was to reduce the incidence of HIV/AIDS and hepatitis C among this population while assisting its members to end their dependency on drugs. In 2006 and 2007, the CPC Minister granted temporary extensions to the exemption, but in 2008, the Minister denied an application to extend the original exemption.

PHS Community Services sought to pre-empt the Minister's denial by bringing an action before British Columbia courts, arguing that denial of the exemption would infringe rights protected under section 7 of the *Charter* in a manner inconsistent with the principles of fundamental justice. In 2011, a unanimous SCC, including two justices appointed by the CPC government, declared under the Chief Justice's name that the Minister's failure to grant an exemption violated the claimants' rights to life, liberty, and security of the person and contravened the principles of fundamental justice. According to the Court, removal of the exemption infringed these rights by making it impossible for Insite clients to access the "lifesaving and health-protecting services" offered at the facility....

Not only was the Court unambiguous in rebuking the Minister's decision, it also imposed an unusually interventionist remedy. The Court determined that the special circumstance of the case merited a writ of mandamus, which is an order for a government official to take specific action. The Court thus ordered the Minister to grant an immediate exemption under section 56, and it further defined the Minister's ongoing constitutional obligations in exercising discretion under the CDSA in a way that makes it virtually impossible to deny future applications for exemptions from Insite or any other supervised injection site like it. In *PHS*, the Court chastised the CPC government for ignoring evidence "on which successive federal Ministers have relied in granting exemption orders over almost five years" and acted to protect the policy status quo from a change in government.

A similar conflict is evident in *Bedford*. At issue was whether criminal prohibitions against keeping or being in a "bawdy house," living on the avails of prostitution, and communicating for the purposes of prostitution infringe the constitutional right to security of the person under section 7 of the *Charter*. The Court unanimously held that the impugned provisions did infringe section 7 by increasing the risk that prostitutes would become victims of violence while engaging in an activity – exchanging sex for money – that is not itself prohibited. The Court further held that the infringement was inconsistent with the principles of fundamental justice because the impugned provisions were, as in *PHS*, arbitrary, overbroad, and grossly disproportionate to their objectives. [*Ed. note*: See Reading 7.5] ...

In April 2015, the Court issued a judgment that provides perhaps the closest fit with the "fractious relationship" narrative of all of the post-2006 government losses under the *Charter*. At issue in *Nur* was the constitutionality of a five-year mandatory minimum sentence for firearm-related offences that the CPC government had enacted in 2012. In a six-to-three judgment, with the Chief Justice writing for the majority, the Court held that this mandatory minimum constitutes an unjustified infringement of the right not to be subjected to cruel and unusual punishment as guaranteed by section 12 of the *Charter*. However, although the majority concluded that the five-year mandatory minimum might foreseeably be grossly disproportionate if applied to other offenders, it conceded that it was not grossly disproportionate as applied to the specific offenders involved in the appeal. Consequently, the majority invalidated the provision but upheld the sentences applied both to Nur and the other offender involved in the appeal....

In many respects, given the majority's rejection of the sentencing principles undoubtedly embraced by the CPC government (denunciation, general deterrence, and retribution), *Nur* presents itself as a clear case of the Court's repudiation of a recently-enacted core policy of the government. However, even *Nur* is more complicated than this. The Chief Justice did not reverse the sentences in the specific cases nor did she even declare mandatory minimum sentences unconstitutional per se (although she set a very high threshold for justifying them). Most obviously, unlike *PHS, Carter,* and *Bedford,* the Court was divided in *Nur.* Furthermore, the CPC government was not alone in defending the constitutionality of the mandatory minimum: Ontario defended the law as a party to the case, and British Columbia and Alberta intervened in favour of upholding its constitutionality....

The Reference Cases

Bedford, PHS, Carter, and *Nur* represent the typical situation in which governments are pulled into constitutional litigation involuntarily. The same cannot be said of most reference cases, where governments seek to advance their policy agenda by extracting a favourable advisory opinion from the Court. The three occasions on which the CPC government sought advice from the Court through the reference procedure are hybrids that combine both involuntary and purposeful elements. In each instance, actions were launched or threatened by other parties, drawing the CPC government into a legal battle over which it sought to gain greater control by initiating its own process and framing its own questions; in each instance, the tactic was unsuccessful.... It is in these cases where the strongest argument for a particularly conflictual Court-government relationship lies.

At issue in the *Securities Act Reference* of 2011 was the CPC government's proposal to implement an idea dating back to at least 2003 by establishing a single national securities regulator. Ontario – home to Canada's largest securities market – supported the project, but Quebec, Alberta, and other provinces opposed it. The question posed to the Court under the reference procedure was whether the proposed *Securities Act* fell within the federal government's legislative power to regulate trade and commerce. The federal government argued that the securities market had evolved from a provincial to a national matter, providing Parliament with legislative authority over all aspects of its regulation. The Court disagreed, finding that although "aspects of the securities market are national in scope and affect the country as a whole," the proposed legislation mostly dealt with matters that had traditionally been recognized as falling within provincial legislative authority over property and civil rights within the province. The Court therefore answered the reference question in the negative, advising the CPC government that it could not establish a national scheme to regulate the securities trade under a single regulatory body.

Although the Court expressed agnosticism with respect to "whether a single national securities scheme is preferable to multiple provincial regimes," it did express a strong preference about how federalism should function. It urged "the federal government and the provinces to exercise their respective powers over securities harmoniously, in the spirit of cooperative federalism." ... The *Securities Act Reference* is thus as much an implicit critique of the CPC government's style of intergovernmental relations as a repudiation of its preferred policy for regulating securities markets. Indeed, although there have been numerous federal-provincial-territorial meetings since 2006, the CPC government was known for its aversion to First Ministers' meetings, holding only two during its term in power and none after 2009. Unlike *PHS*, where the Court had a strong opinion about the CPC government's policy, it was largely indifferent to the substance of the proposal under review in the *Securities Act Reference* but clearly deeply concerned with how the federal government proposed to substitute a national regulatory regime for the existing local regimes. To be fair, it is arguable that this concern also extended to the provinces that intervened in the reference: The Court's message to both was cooperation rather than confrontation.

If the level of conflict was relatively mild in the *Securities Act Reference*, the same cannot be said for the *Supreme Court Act Reference* or the *Senate Reform Reference*.... The *Supreme Court Reference* and the *Senate Reform Reference* both negated initiatives of high importance to the CPC government, although the impact of the second will endure longer. [*Ed. note*: See Readings 2.6 and 11.6] ...

Conclusion

The purpose of this article has been to bring greater analytical rigour to a narrative, common among both popular and academic commentaries, that there was a particularly antagonistic relationship between the CPC government and the SCC. The narrative stems from a series of high-profile losses by the government in constitutional cases, as well as the government's and Prime Minister's reaction to those decisions. In some versions of the narrative, these losses suggest that the Court became an explicitly, and even self-consciously, oppositional force against the CPC government's "extremist" policies. In other versions of the narrative, especially in the aftermath of the Nadon appointment controversy, it was a personal conflict between Prime Minister Stephen Harper and Chief Justice Beverly McLachlin....

It is difficult to draw a direct line from losses in *Charter* cases to any particular relationship between the government and the Court. In 75 per cent of the CPC's *Charter* losses, the policy invalidated by the Court belonged to a predecessor government. Indeed, as defender or enactor, the CPC's record in *Charter* cases did not differ significantly from that of the two other post-*Charter* governments.... By contrast, the three reference cases initiated by the CPC government offer a clearer portrait of confrontation, since in all three cases the Court blocked initiatives considered important by the government....

Perhaps the most interesting development since 2006 was the adoption of a more consistently confrontational approach by the CPC government in its legislative responses compared to its predecessors. This occurred even in cases like *PHS* and *Bedford*, where the invalidated legislation or policy did not originate with the CPC government. Although other governments also refused to defer completely to the Court in certain areas, defiance appeared to emerge as the norm under the CPC government. In this sense, the CPC government may have been asserting an equal authority to interpret the Constitution's meaning, which could have brought it into much sharper conflict with the Court had it not lost the 2015 federal election.

11.10
Key Terms

Concepts
Charter revolution
composition of the Supreme Court of Canada
ideology
Judicial Advisory Committees (JACs)
judicial independence
living tree doctrine
mandatory minimum sentences
merit
notwithstanding clause
originalism
parliamentary scrutiny
politicization of the judiciary

Institutions, Events and Documents

Canada (Prime Minister) v. Khadr, [2010] 1 S.C.R. 44

Canadian Bar Association

Nadon Affair (2014)

Prime Minister's Office (PMO)

Supreme Court Act, ss. 5 and 6 (1875)

Reference re Securities Act, [2011] 3 S.C.R. 837

Reference re Senate Reform, [2014] 1 S.C.R. 704

Reference re Supreme Court Act, ss 5 and 6 [2014] 1 S.C.R. 433

12

Reconciling Judicial Review and Constitutional Democracy

The readings in this final chapter raise and address some of the fundamental questions about the practise of judicial review. Donald Smiley's contribution (Reading 12.1) emphasizes that the real question raised by an entrenched *Charter of Rights* is not whether or not Canadians shall have civil liberties, but *who* decides what is and is not a civil liberty. The principal effect of the *Charter* is to transfer the primary, although not exclusive, responsibility for such decisions to the courts, or more specifically, to Canadian judges. He notes that typically these decisions involve balancing competing rights or interests, and that every decision will have "opportunity costs." Smiley expresses skepticism over the judges' ability to make these kinds of decisions better than Canadian parliamentary legislatures. Smiley points to some of Parliament's reforms in the 1960s involving capital punishment, abortion, divorce, hate literature and official languages. Each of these legislative reforms were widely viewed as enhancing liberty, minority rights, or both. In effect, Smiley asks: What special competencies do judges have that elected legislators lack?

The late Alexander Bickel, the leading American constitutional scholar of his generation, has elaborated this question and also provided an answer. He described the requirements for a justification of judicial review on principle, rather than habit and tradition, as follows:

> The search must be for a function which might (indeed, must) involve the making of policy, yet which differs from the legislative and executive functions; which is peculiarly suited to the capabilities of the courts; which will not likely be performed elsewhere if the courts do not assume it; which can be so exercised as to be acceptable in a society that generally shares Judge [Learned] Hand's satisfaction in a "sense of common venture"; which will be effective when needed; and whose discharge by the courts will not lower

the quality of the other departments' performance by denuding them of the dignity and burden of their own responsibility.[1]

The potentially unique contribution of judicial review, according to Bickel, is the defence and articulation of a society's fundamental political and ethical principles. In the name of individual liberty, the pursuit of self-interest is given wide range in Western democracies. The executive and legislative branches are purposely made responsive to the resulting clash of interests and groups that is the stuff of democratic politics. Amidst the welter of competing self-interests, the rush and crush of practical affairs and the ensuing short-term perspective on all matters, it is prudent to have one institution, purposely distanced from the fray, to guard the principles that preserve the justice and dignity of that society. Judicial review offers this potential.

Bickel's defence of judicial review is echoed by the former Chief Justice of the Supreme Court of Canada, Beverley McLachlin (Reading 12.2). Chief Justice McLachlin explains and defends the use of unwritten constitutional principles – the "norms that are essential to a nation's history, identity, values and legal system" – by high courts around the world. Drawing from jurisprudence such as the Supreme Court's 1938 *Reference re Alberta Statutes*,[2] she claims that unwritten principles predated the *Charter* in Canada. Accordingly, the use of these principles should be viewed as a continuation, rather than a rejection, of Canada's constitutional heritage. Chief Justice McLachlin acknowledges that unwritten principles pose a challenge for judicial legitimacy. However, so long as judges do not confuse "judicial conscience" with their personal conscience, she believes this challenge can be overcome, and the judicial use of unwritten principles can be used to help ensure that the executive and legislative branches conform to established norms. However, as demonstrated by the commentary surrounding the Court's use of these principles in the *Secession Reference* (see Reading 2.5) and the *Senate Reference* (Reading 2.6), their application remains controversial, vague and subject to different interpretations. The debate over the legitimacy of judicial review under the *Charter* has changed, not disappeared.

Debates surrounding the legitimacy of judicial review can arise in the context of a specific *Charter* decision (See Justice La Forest's dissent in the *Reference re Remuneration of Judges*, Reading 5.5); or more generally, in competing approaches to constitutional interpretation, such as the Living Tree vs. originalism debate. In Reading 12.3, F.L. Morton highlights controversies over how judges choose to interpret the language of a constitutional bill of rights. Morton's history of judicial review and civil liberties in Canada, which includes cases heard under the 1960 *Bill of Rights*, demonstrates that judges have choices over how they choose to interpret rights documents. Factors such as legal culture and interest group support can certainly affect judicial interpretive strategies, yet Morton shows that the *Charter* was a game-changer. In terms of constitutional interpretation, it is fair to say the Living Tree adherents, Chief Justice McLachlin included, currently hold sway in the Canadian judiciary.

Having seen the application of decades of judicial review of the *Charter,* F.L. Morton and Rainer Knopff (Reading 12.4) argue that Canada's "*Charter* Revolution" has produced an outcome that is "deeply and fundamentally un-democratic." Interest groups with a shared desire for the growth of judicial power have helped facilitate an institutional shift whereby policies over which reasonable people disagree are definitively settled in the courtroom. Morton and Knopff worry that judicial policy-making is most corrosive to the habits and temperaments of representative democracy because it "grants the policy preferences of courtroom victors an aura of coercive force and permanence." For Morton and Knopff, enhanced judicial review under the *Charter* has harmed Canadian politics by decreasing the willingness of citizens to engage in compromise and reasonable disagreement.

The *Charter* did preserve some legislative role in rights interpretation. The section 33 "notwithstanding clause" allows Parliament or a provincial legis-lature to pass a law and declare it shall operate notwithstanding certain pro-visions (sections 2 and 7–15) of the *Charter.* As Peter Russell (Reading 12.5) describes, section 33's inclusion in the *Charter* was part of a compromise to assuage provincial premiers from all sides of the political spectrum wary of a Supreme Court that might be too activist or too pro-Ottawa. Russell reminds us that judges, like legislators, are fallible, and that the notwithstanding clause was included as a parliamentary check on such fallibility. Far from being op-posed to the *Charter,* the notwithstanding clause is an important part of the *Charter,* one that acknowledges the tradition of parliamentary rights protec-tion of which Dicey spoke.

Although the clause has been used infrequently, and never by the federal Parliament, it was thrust back into the spotlight in 2017. In *Good Spirit School Division No. 204 v. Christ the Teacher Roman Catholic Separate School Division No. 212,*[3] the Saskatchewan Court of Queen's Bench ruled that the Saskatchewan government's funding for non-Catholic children to attend Catholic schools vi-olated religious freedom and equality rights under the *Charter* (sections 2(a) and 15), and could not be saved as a reasonable limit by section 1. The judge's ruling that only Catholic students could be funded at Catholic schools raised a number of questions for a province grappling with rural depopulation and resource scarcity. The case was complicated by the fact that other parts of the Canadian Constitution allow Saskatchewan to fund separate Catholic and Protestant schools. In response, Saskatchewan Premier Brad Wall announced his government would table a bill invoking the notwithstanding clause (Reading 12.6). The government said that if the court ruling stood, roughly ten thousand non-Catholic students in Saskatchewan would be forced out of Catholic schools. Invoking the language of "school choice," the government claimed that it needed to use the clause to avoid putting other publicly funded faith-based schools at risk. Bill 89, *The School Choice Protection Act*, received Royal Assent in May, 2018.

The Saskatchewan government's response to this decision thrust the clause back into the academic and media spotlight. In Reading 12.6, Dwight Newman defends the government's use of the clause. Like Russell, Newman reminds readers that the clause was included in the *Charter* as a way to bridge an American-style, judicially enforceable bill of rights with Canada's tradition of parliamentary rights protection. Moreover, he says the "messy" Court of Queen's Bench ruling is precisely the type of case for which the notwithstanding clause was intended: rather than a case in which the state is the singular antagonist of an individual, this case involved competing social policy choices, trade-offs, budgetary decisions and no singular "aggrieved party." Far from an unconscionable infringement of rights, the Wall government was engaging in reasonable disagreement befitting of a system of judicial checks and parliamentary balances.

Not all scholars accept this assessment. Leonid Sirota (Reading 12.6) disagrees with Newman in both respects: Sirota claims the Saskatchewan Court of Queen's Bench got the decision right, and that the notwithstanding clause should never be used. Drawing comparisons to the federal power to disallow provincial legislation, which has not been used for decades, Sirota argues that the existence of a legal power does not necessarily justify its use. He also warns that normalization of the use of the notwithstanding clause could erode rights protection in Canada, and in so doing, rejects the idea that there can exist "happy Canadian middle ground between Parliamentary sovereignty and judicial enforcement of constitutional rights." Sirota's attack on section 33 demonstrates the same optimistic assessment of judges' policy capacity as found in Chief Justice McLachlin's contribution (Reading 12.2). Russell's (and Newman's) equally forceful defence of section 33 resonates with the same skepticism of judicial policy-making that animated Smiley's critique two decades earlier (see Reading 12.1). The players and the law have changed but the debate endures.

Another response to the legitimacy debate is found in the Hogg-Thornton "dialogue" theory (Reading 12.7). Peter Hogg and Allison Thornton argue that in *Charter* rulings the Supreme Court rarely has the last word. In their review of sixty-six *Charter* cases involving judicial nullification of a statute, they found that there was a "legislative sequel" to the judicial ruling in two-thirds of the cases. That is, governments responded to judicial nullifications by a variety of means – amending and re-enacting the statute, repealing the statute or invoking section 33 and reinstating the statute. Thus, rather than "activist" courts "dictating" new policies to governments, Hogg and Thornton argue that the *Charter* has created a two-way "dialogue" between courts and legislatures, in which the latter usually have the last say. Hogg and Thornton's "dialogue" theory has become a popular defence against the charge of undue judicial activism but is not without its critics. F.L. Morton's response (Reading 12.7) is that in most of these sixty-six cases, legislatures simply did what the courts told them to do – a relationship more accurately described as a "monologue." A 2013 study from Emmett Macfarlane, which defined dialogue as when legislatures respond with "independent consideration," found that such genuine dialogue occurred in fewer than 20 per cent of legislative responses to Supreme Court decisions.[4] The staying power of the judicially created status quo remains strong.

These debates are not new to democracies with a constitutional bill of rights. While the U.S. Supreme Court has exercised judicial review over that country's written *Bill of Rights* for over two hundred years, it has not always had the "final word" in constitutional disputes. The history of the United States is strewn with Supreme Court decisions that have been reversed or ignored. This has been accomplished by a variety of "court-curbing" techniques: constitutional amendment, withdrawal of jurisdiction from the Supreme Court to hear certain types of issues, statutory reversal (i.e., new legislation), court-packing and even outright disagreement with judicial majorities. Political scientist Dennis Baker argues that such disagreement is both constitutional and desirable in the Canadian context. In Reading 12.8, Baker criticizes the "judicial supremacy" orthodoxy prevalent among Canadian legal scholars, and argues that the legislative role in *Charter* conflicts should go beyond the notwithstanding clause. Drawing from the text of the *Charter* itself, Baker argues that "Parliament can and should participate in the interpretation and meaning of the Constitution." For Baker, such legislative responses convey the "real promise of dialogue": the limitation of mistakes through inter-institutional checks and balances. If all actors accept that courts have interpretive supremacy, this promise has been broken.

Of course, a constitutional change of the *Charter*'s magnitude does not just affect the branches of government: it permeates society as well. Chief Justice Glenn D. Joyal of the Manitoba Court of Queen's Bench (Reading 12.9) reflects on how the *Charter* has fundamentally changed Canadian political culture. As the broad set of "attitudes and beliefs that citizens and its specific institutional actors hold about the political system," changes in Canadian political culture have long been contested by historians and political scientists.[5] For Chief Justice

Joyal, the introduction of the *Charter* has produced another such change. Not only are political issues transformed into legal ones, as Peter Russell famously predicted in 1983,[6] but Canadians now demonstrate an "almost unconditional willingness" to accept judicial solutions to complex social problems. As Chief Justice Joyal documents, this political-cultural change, particularly the acceptance of a privileged judiciary at the expense of legislative authority, was neither anticipated nor desired by those responsible for the 1982 patriation of the Constitution. In documenting the consequences of this cultural change, Chief Justice Joyal notes an interesting irony: by employing the "living tree" metaphor to increase their scope of influence, courts may have "frozen" certain policy issues in time and immunized them from future discussion. Joyal's nuanced account stresses that any "future restoration" of the balance between courts and legislatures must occur in "what is now a new and different Canadian political culture."

In the final analysis, the debate over section 33, "dialogue" and interpretive supremacy reflects the ambiguous nature of judicial authority. That nature, and the difficult task it imposes on constitutional judges, was captured by the French philosopher Alexis de Tocqueville's analysis of American federal courts nearly 200 years ago:

> [The power of the courts] is immense, but it is power springing from opinion. They are all-powerful so long as the people consent to obey the law; they can do nothing when they scorn it. Now, of all powers, that of opinion is the hardest to use, for it is impossible to say exactly where its limits come. Often it is as dangerous to lag behind as it is to outstrip it.... Federal judges therefore must not only be good citizens and men of education and integrity, qualities necessary for all magistrates, but must also be statesmen; they must know how to understand the spirit of the age, to confront those obstacles that can be overcome, and to steer out of the current when the tide threatens to carry them away, and with them the sovereignty of the Union and obedience to its laws.[7]

The written constitution, in the end, is no stronger than the unwritten constitution. The difference is the enhanced role of judges in shaping both.

NOTES

1   *The Least Dangerous Branch: The Supreme Court at the Bar of Politics* (Indianapolis: Bobbs-Merrill, 1962), p. 24.

2   *Reference Re Alberta Statutes – The Bank Taxation Act; The Credit of Alberta Regulation Act; and the Accurate News and Information Act,* [1938] S.C.R. 100.

3   2017 SKQB 109 (CanLII).

4   Emmett Macfarlane, "Dialogue or Compliance? Measuring Legislatures' Policy Responses to Court Rulings on Rights," *International Political Science Review* 32, no.1 (2013), pp. 39–56.

5   See Janet Ajzenstat and Peter J. Smith, eds., *Canada's Origins: Liberal, Tory, or Republican?* (Montreal and Kingston: McGill-Queen's University Press, 1995).

6   Peter H. Russell, "The Political Purposes of the Canadian Charter of Rights and Freedoms," *Canadian Bar Review* 61, no. 1 (1983), p. 52.

7   Alexis de Tocqueville, *Democracy in America,* ed. J.P. Mayer (Garden City, N.Y: Anchor, 1969), pp. 150–151.

12.1

Courts, Legislatures, and the Protection of Human Rights

Donald Smiley

From M.L. Friedland, ed., *Courts and Trials: A Multidisciplinary Approach* (Toronto: University of Toronto Press, 1975) 89–101. Reprinted with permission.

This paper examines in a Canadian context the appropriateness of judicial as against legislative decision in the definition and ranking of human rights. The issue is often put within the framework of proposals for the further entrenchment of human rights in the Canadian constitution.... Most provisions related to human rights ... would necessarily be expressed in general language conferring on the courts of law the responsibility of defining and ranking rights in an ongoing process of judicial review of the constitution....

... Most discussions of legislative as against judicial decision with respect to human rights proceed according to conflicting views of what I call democratic fundamentalism.

The first view asserts that in terms of democratic theory, elected officials have better claims than courts to define and rank human rights as well as to make other important decisions about public policy. Democracy in this view is government in accord with the will of the governed, and the organs of government best able and most likely to act in accord with this will are composed of people who have successfully contested popular elections – and act in anticipation of future elections. I do not find this argument completely convincing. If we look at the operative constitution of any developed political system – the constitution in action as against the constitution of the textbooks of law or civics – we find a complex allocation of discretionary powers. Powers are wielded in various kinds of matters by judges and juries, by political executives and career bureaucrats, by elected legislatures and political parties, by the electorate, by the groups who effect constitutional amendment. And we also find different kinds of procedural rules for reaching various kinds of decisions – unanimous consent in jury verdicts, certain motions in the House of Commons and the most crucial of constitutional amendments, consensual decision-making at federal-provincial conferences and, perhaps, in cabinets, pluralities, bare majorities and extraordinary majorities as so defined, different provisions for quorums, and so on. On this basis, I would see no *a priori* reason stemming from democratic theory which would prevent a democratic community from conferring decisions involving human rights on the courts or from enacting provisions respecting such rights other than those which prevail in respect to ordinary lawmaking....

... It seems to me ... that the connection between the preferred procedures for protecting human rights and natural law is historical and psychological rather than logical in the sense that if the imperatives of natural law are binding, surely they bind legislatures as much as courts. Which of the two sets of institutions will better protect such rights is thus a matter of prudential political judgment rather than political philosophy....

... Perhaps some will agree with most of this but still maintain that, on balance, courts will be wiser and more zealous than elected bodies in defining and ranking human rights. In much of the argument for entrenchment there is the underlying premise that the community needs to be saved from the inherently liberal tendencies of public opinion because these create irresistible pressures on elected legislatures. Perhaps. It is my own impression, however, that in Canada the elected political elites are considerably more liberal than are the prevailing sentiments in their respective local, provincial, and national electorates. Again, it is my impression that when we begin to inquire carefully into those institutions of Canadian society under the direct control of the bar and the bench we will find less than a total commitment to humane values. There is a strain of absolutism in recent Canadian proposals for an entrenched *Bill of Rights*. Prime Minister Trudeau said in 1969, "To enshrine a right in a constitutional charter is to make an important judgment, to give to that right of the individual a higher order of value than the right of government to infringe it." This argument proceeds on the assumption that encroachments on human rights are always unequivocal and disinterested and liberal people will always be able to agree when such encroachments are made. Again, if we take Mr. Trudeau's statement literally, there is the assumption that under all conceivable circumstances entrenched rights are to prevail over other considerations. These absolutist premises are in practice indefensible. In the sphere of human rights there is indeed an economy, and rights have what economists call "opportunity costs," in the sense that to get something of value it is necessary to give up something else of value.

As a non-lawyer, it seems clear to me that if Canadian courts are to assume a more active role in the ranking and defining of human rights there must be profound changes in the Canadian legal culture. Canadian jurists are profoundly in the positivist tradition. But the determination of human rights in particular circumstances is in Peter Russell's terms the "delicate balancing of social priorities." I confess not to know the shape of the new jurisprudence or how judges and legal scholars are going to get us to realize it while maintaining the continuity with past traditions and lines of judicial interpretation that is surely necessary in our kind of polity. I confess also that the break proposed by Atkey and Lyon is too radical for me. But perhaps there should be a warning to enthusiasts for a socially relevant jurisprudence. This approach by its nature downgrades the technical nature of the law, and when members of bar and bench set up shop to articulate the political need and political ideals of the community they enter a world in which others make the same claims. To be blunt: as piety does not make a theologian or pugnacity a military strategist, an increasing social sensitivity among lawyers and judges is no substitute for intellectual discipline in the social sciences and political philosophy.

To return to the main argument of this paper, I quote what I said on a previous occasion:

> Apart from those times where public opinion is inflamed, the democratic legislature is uniquely equipped to make sound judgments about human rights. In my view Parliament has been at or near its best in some of the debates about human rights in the past decade, debates in respect to capital punishment, divorce, abortion, hate literature, official languages. Although the determination of the scope and nature of human rights usually involves some technical considerations, the technical content of reasoned discussion and decision is characteristically not as high as in regard to, say, defence policy or environmental pollution. Thus the major considerations in respect to human rights ordinarily

involve the clash of human values, the sense of the community
about what is acceptable and the broadest judgments of where society is going. Further, questions involving human rights tend not
to be as localized in their incidence as is true of many other public
policies and the Member of Parliament may well be more free to
act primarily as a member of a deliberative body rather than a
voice of particularized constituency interests. Elected politicians
working within an environment of public discussion and debate
are well equipped to deal wisely with questions of human rights.
It is yet to be demonstrated that the Canadian judiciary can do
better....

12.2

Unwritten Constitutional Principles: What is Going On?
Chief Justice Beverley McLachlin

Presented at the 2005 Lord Cooke Lecture in Wellington, New Zealand,
December 1, 2005. First published in *The New Zealand Journal of Public
and International Law*, 4, no. 2 (2006), 147–163. Reproduced with the
permission of the Right Honourable Beverley McLachlin, P.C., 2017.

A few years ago, a new subject emerged on the hot list of legal academe – unwritten constitutional principles. It was greeted with interest and optimism by
some, but puzzlement and scepticism by others. What were these principles?
Was the phrase "unwritten constitutional principles" not an oxymoron, given
that constitutions are generally understood to be written documents? And if
one surmounts these difficulties, how and by whom are these so-called unwritten constitutional principles to be discovered? The judges, you say? But what
gives the judges the right to set forth constitutional principles capable of invalidating laws and executive acts, when Parliament has not seen fit to set these
principles out in writing in the nation's constitution?

Yet despite these inauspicious murmurs, the subject has engaged judges,
parliamentarians and academics in countries as far flung as Israel, Australia
and the United States. It has been debated both in countries that have written
constitutions and countries that do not. In fact, many political scientists and
legal scholars observe that participation in the "rights revolution" may be less
about the precise wording of constitutional texts – or even about bills of rights
at all – but instead a reflection of a certain kind of supportive legal and political
culture. [*Ed. note*: see Readings 6.9 and 6.10] ...

What do we mean when we speak of unwritten constitutional principles? Are there some principles or norms that are so important, so fundamental, to a nation's history and identity that a consensus of reasonable citizens would demand that they be honoured by those who exercise state power? What do we mean by a constitution? Is the idea of unwritten constitutional principles really a new idea, or is it merely a new incarnation of established legal thought?

To these questions I would answer as follows. First, unwritten constitutional principles refer to unwritten norms that are essential to a nation's history, identity, values and legal system. Second, constitutions are best understood as providing the normative framework for governance. Seen in this functional sense, there is thus no reason to believe that they cannot embrace both written and unwritten norms. Third – and this is important because of the tone that this debate often exhibits – the idea of unwritten constitutional principles is not new and should not be seen as a rejection of the constitutional heritage our two countries share.

The contemporary concept of unwritten constitutional principles can be seen as a modern reincarnation of the ancient doctrines of natural law. [*Ed. note*: See Reading 1.2.] Like those conceptions of justice, the identification of these principles seems to presuppose the existence of some kind of natural order. Unlike them, however, it does not fasten on theology as the source of the unwritten principles that transcend the exercise of state power. It is derived from the history, values and culture of the nation, viewed in its constitutional context....

This "rich intellectual tradition" of natural law seeks to give the law minimum moral content. It rests on the proposition that there is a distinction between rules and the law. Rules and rule systems can be good, but they can also be evil. Something more than the very existence of rules, it is argued, is required for them to demand respect: in short, to transform rules into law. The distinction between rule by law, which is the state of affairs in certain developing countries, and rule of law, which developed democracies espouse, succinctly captures the distinction between a mere rules system and a proper legal system that is founded on certain minimum values. The debate about unwritten constitutional principles can thus be seen as a debate about the nature of the law itself and what about it demands our allegiance....

One way to confirm the link between fundamental norms and our understanding of statehood and the law is by examining the work of courts operating in systems with no written constitutional bill of rights. Even without clearly written constitutional powers of enforcement, courts have found ways to ensure fundamental justice.

In Canada, decades before the *Charter*, Rand J. of the Supreme Court alluded to enforceable – if unwritten – norms of fairness, stating that "[i]n public regulation of this sort there is no such thing as absolute and untrammelled discretion" and good faith must always be presumed. To do otherwise, he wrote, "would signalize the beginning of disintegration of the rule of law as a fundamental postulate of our constitutional structure." Nearly eighty years before Justice Rand, the courts of British Columbia struggled with a series of anti-Chinese provincial and local laws and used the division of powers in our constitution to strike them down. Members of the Supreme Court of British Columbia – a court on which I would serve a hundred years later, at the time of the introduction of the *Charter* – relied on the text of the constitution, but also on the principles of English law that underlay that text. In 1938, in the *Reference re Alberta Statutes* case, in the absence of a written guarantee, the Supreme Court held that freedom of political expression must be recognized as inherent in the nature of democracy.

At this point, you will not be surprised to hear me declare my position. As a modern natural law proponent, I believe that the world was right, in the wake of the horrors of Nazi Germany and the Holocaust, to declare that there are certain fundamental norms that no nation should transgress. I believe that it was right to prosecute German judges in the Nuremberg Trials for applying laws that sent innocent people to concentration camps and probable deaths. I believe that the drafting and adoption of the Universal Declaration of Human Rights in 1948 was a giant step forward in legal and societal thinking. And I believe that judges have the duty to insist that the legislative and executive branches of government conform to certain established and fundamental norms, even in times of trouble....

The answer to the conundrum between justice as an expression of Parliamentary will and justice as an expression of fundamental principles, sometimes unarticulated, lies in the answer to three more particular problems that arise from the concept of underlying unwritten constitutional norms. The first is the problem of how unwritten norms can be squared with the precept that law should be set out in advance of its application. The second is the problem of how to identify these fundamental unwritten principles that are capable of trumping laws and executive action. The third is the problem of judicial legitimacy.... All three are related to a central issue: the legitimacy of unwritten constitutional norms.

I turn first to the precept that the law must be known in advance of its application, and the problem that – on their face – unwritten constitutional norms violate this principle. One of the foundational concepts in law, it is said, is the importance of the "law on the books." The rule of law signifies that all actors in our society – public and private, individual and institutional – are subject to and governed by law. The rule of law excludes the exercise of arbitrary power in all its forms. It requires that laws be known or ascertainable to citizens, and ensures that laws are applied consistently to each citizen, without favouritism, thus ensuring the legitimacy of state exercise of power.…

The desire to reduce legal principles to writing is significant, but it should not be used to oversimplify the complex issue of the place of unwritten norms in our constitutions. Two points are relevant here.

First, in common law countries, it is distinctly not the case that all law must be "on the books." England's attitude to the importance of writing down the law is at best ambivalent. On the one hand, the *Magna Carta* is a foundational text designed to provide written guarantees of fundamental principles. On the other, the common law fleshed out and supplemented these principles by a catalogue of largely judge-made rules. The presumption of innocence, the rejection of the state's power to use violence against citizens implicit in the common law confessions rule, and the principle of freedom of political expression are but examples of fundamental constraints on executive power articulated by judges. While Parliament theoretically had the power to attenuate and perhaps reverse these judge-made rules, the fact that it by and large chose not to shows a relaxed attitude to the need to set laws down in writing for the citizen's guidance. Indeed, the ability of the common law to develop *ex post facto* responses to new situations is frequently cited as its genius.

Not everyone, of course, thought this lack of written laws a good thing. Jeremy Bentham decried what he saw reflected in the common law of crimes. In 1792, he wrote that it amounted to "dog law." "When your dog does any thing you want to break him of," he explained, "you wait till he does it, and then beat him for it. This is the way you make laws for your dog: and this is the way the Judges make law for you and me."

The second point that should be made about the view that all laws should be in writing, is that even when the legislature takes the trouble to write down laws, the result is almost always incomplete. Laws are necessarily stated in general terms. They are intended to apply to a wide variety of situations. Lawmakers cannot conceivably foresee all the situations to which a legal provision may apply, nor how it should do so. Judges must reduce the legislative general to the situational particular. The result is that even where laws are written down, it is often impossible to predict precisely how the law will apply in a particular situation in advance of a judicial ruling on the matter. This is as true for civil code countries where all laws are reduced to writing, as it is for common law countries. In this sense, much of the law is never "on the books." …

Even inclusive, written constitutions leave much out, requiring us to look at convention and usage. In addition, the broad, open-textured language used in constitutional documents admits of a variety of interpretations. In order to resolve the interpretational issues that may arise from this language, judges may need to resort to conventions and principles not articulated in the written constitution itself.

What then do we mean when we say law should be "on the books"? We mean, it seems to me, that applications of the law should be connected to generally accepted rules. It is not necessary that the law foretell precise results. It is sufficient that the law provide a general idea of what kind of result may ensue, and that the result, once established by judicial rulings, be justifiable in terms of what is written on the books and legal convention or usage.

Fundamental constitutional principles, whether written or unwritten, meet these requirements. Unwritten common law constitutional norms, such as the right not to be punished without a trial, to retain and instruct counsel, or to enjoy the presumption of innocence, are so fixed in convention and usage that judicial rulings based upon them will be understood and accepted as just. I conclude that while it is useful to articulate fundamental constitutional norms insofar as we can, the fact that a principle or its application does not take written form does not provide a principled reason for rejecting judicial reliance on it.

This brings us to the second problem: identifying those unwritten constitutional principles that can prevail over laws and executive action. At least three sources of unwritten constitutional principles can be identified: customary usage; inferences from written constitutional principles; and the norms set out or implied in international legal instruments to which the state has adhered.

Traditionally at common law, unwritten fundamental principles of constitutional or quasi-constitutional significance have been identified by past usage, chiefly the cases that have been decided by judges in the past.… The recourse to usage for constitutional guidance is clearly understood in post-colonial countries, such as Canada and New Zealand. Thus the preamble to Canada's 1867 constitutional text stipulates "a Constitution similar in principle to that of the United Kingdom," contemplating reference to unwritten constitutional norms derived from British history.

This brings me to the second source of unwritten constitutional principles – inference from the constitutional principles and values that have been set down in writing. While they may interpret their written constitutions, courts are never free to ignore them. Confronted with a new situation requiring a new norm, judges must look to the written constitution for the values that capture the ethos of the nation. In Canada, the 1998 *Secession Reference* provides an instructive example of how courts may draw unwritten constitutional principles from the written provisions of the constitution. [*Ed. note*: See Reading 2.5.] ... The texts of Canada's constitution are silent on whether a province can secede from the federation. No written principles set the legal framework that would govern an attempt to secede. In order to answer the question before it, the Supreme Court turned to Canada's history and conventions, as well as the values that Canadians, through their governments, had entrenched in their written constitution. It examined these in the light of a long-recognized treatment of Canada's evolving constitution as a "living tree."

The Court identified four "fundamental and organizing principles of the Constitution" which were relevant to the question: federalism; democracy; constitutionalism and the rule of law; and respect for minorities.... By examining constitutional texts in light of the principles that underlay them and gave their content meaning, the Court ensured that an important legal gap was filled. This permitted the Court to suggest concrete steps that would have to be followed in a process that would provide the certainty, stability and predictability that are cornerstones of the rule of law.

The third source that may suggest and inform unwritten constitutional principles is international law. Customary international law has been accepted as a legitimate part of the common law without controversy, largely because it is based on both usage and on an acceptance of a sense of obligation: what we call *opinio juris*. As for treaties signed by the Crown, however, the traditional "dualism" of the common law has generally required the explicit incorporation of international norms into domestic law.... Where a country adheres to international covenants, such as the UN Convention Against Torture or the International Covenant on Civil and Political Rights, it thereby signals its intentions to be bound by their principles. This may amplify indications from usage and convention and the written text of the constitution and to help to establish the boundaries of certain unwritten principles....

Having examined whether unwritten constitutional principles violate the idea that laws should be written, and having identified three sources from which these principles can be ascertained, I turn now to the final problem: the problem of judicial legitimacy.

Here we face another apparent contradiction. On the one hand, the legitimacy of the judiciary depends on the justification of its decisions by reference to a society's fundamental constitutional values. This is what we mean when we say the task of judges is to do justice. Judges who enforce unjust laws – laws that run counter to fundamental assumptions about the just society – lose their legitimacy. When judges allow themselves to be co-opted be evil regimes, they are no longer fit to be judges. This is the lesson of the Nuremberg Trials. It is also a lesson, however, that should embolden judges when faced with seemingly more mundane manifestations of injustice.

However, matters are not so simple. As judges give content to unwritten constitutional principles, they may be accused of usurping the functions of Parliament; of making the law rather than interpreting and applying it; in short, of judicial activism. We should not lightly dismiss this concern – a concern that troubles many who sincerely care about just democratic governance.... The question of judicial legitimacy returns us to the conundrum I alluded to at the outset. To be legitimate, judges must conform to fundamental moral norms of a constitutional nature. But when they do, they risk going beyond what would appear to be their judicial functions. How is the conundrum to be resolved? The answer, I would suggest, is that the conundrum is a false one; that judges must be able to do justice and at the same time stay within the proper confines of their role.

The role of judges in a democracy is to interpret and apply the law. The law involves rules of different orders. The highest is the order of fundamental constitutional principles. These are the rules that guide all other law-making and the exercise of executive power by the state. More and more in our democratic states, we try to set these out in writing. But when we do not, or when, as is inevitable, the written text is unclear or incomplete, recourse must be had to unwritten sources. The task of the judge, confronted with conflict between a constitutional principle of the highest order on the one hand, and an ordinary law or executive act on the other, is to interpret and apply the law as a whole – including relevant unwritten constitutional principles.

This presupposes that the constitutional principle is established having regard to the three sources just discussed – usage and custom; values affirmed by relevant textual constitutional sources; and principles of international law endorsed by the nation. Determining whether these sources disclose such principles is quintessential judicial work. It must be done with care and objectivity. It is not making the law, but interpreting, reconciling and applying the law, thus fulfilling the judge's role as guarantor of the Constitution.

How does the judge discharge this duty? First, it seems to me, the judge must seek to interpret a suspect law in a way that reconciles it with the constitutional norm, written or unwritten. Usually, this will resolve the problem. But in rare cases, it may not. If an ordinary law is clearly in conflict with a fundamental constitutional norm, the judge may have no option but to refuse to apply it....

Interpreting and applying constitutional principles, written and unwritten, requires that the judge hold uncompromisingly to his or her judicial conscience, informed by past legal usage, written constitutional norms and international principles to which the nation has attorned. But judicial conscience is not to be confused with personal conscience. Judicial conscience is founded on the judge's sworn commitment to uphold the rule of law. It is informed not by the judge's personal views, nor the judge's views as to what policy is best. It is informed by the law, in all its complex majesty, as manifested in the three sources I've suggested....

Lest I be accused of advocating "dog law," let me say again that the principles that guide these difficult decisions are not those of individual judges, but those implicit in the very system that gives the judges their authority. Ignoring one's judicial conscience is not about staying within one's role, but instead about abdicating one's responsibility to the law. There do indeed exist unwritten principles without which the law would become contradictory and self-defeating, and it is the duty of judges not only to discover them, but also to apply them. To forsake them, in Robert Bolt's phrase, is indeed to take the short route to chaos.

12.3

Judicial Review and Civil Liberties
F.L. Morton

Adapted from *Law, Politics and the Judicial Process*, 3rd edition (Calgary: University of Calgary Press, 2002), 479–495. Updated for the 2018 edition.

The practice of judicial review is unique to liberal democratic nations. The grounding principles of liberal democracy posit that good government is "limited government," and a written constitution enforced by judicial review is a means to that end. While all instances of judicial review are found in liberal democracies, not all liberal democracies use judicial review. Historically, Great Britain has always been a liberal democracy, but it did not have a "written constitution," and consequently English judges did not, until recently, exercise judicial review. The same was historically true for many European democracies with a written constitution, although this has changed with the European Convention on Human Rights.

The absence of a written constitution and judicial review did not mean that the government of Great Britain was "unlimited." Professor Ronald Cheffins reminds us that the starting point of the British and thus the Canadian constitution is that "an individual is free except to the extent restrained by law." The converse is also true: "a governmental official or government agency only has such power as is vested in it or him by law," as illustrated by the *Roncarelli v. Duplessis* case (Reading 1.1).

The doctrine of parliamentary sovereignty notwithstanding, A.V. Dicey makes it clear that political conventions of self-restraint and fair play, reinforced by public opinion, have operated to protect the same fundamental freedoms of Englishmen as judicial review of the U.S. *Bill of Rights* does for Americans. Dicey clearly preferred the flexibility of an "unwritten constitution" and vesting primary responsibility for the preservation of liberty in an elected, accountable, representative legislature such as Parliament. But he did not rule out the possibility of codifying the fundamental freedoms of the English people. After enumerating the fundamental components of the "rule of law" – "the right to personal freedom; the right to freedom of discussion; the right of public meeting; the use of martial law; the rights and duties of the army; the collection and expenditure of the public revenue; and the responsibility of ministers" – Dicey concludes:

> If at some future day the law of the constitution should be codified, each of the topics I have mentioned would be dealt with by the sections of the code.

In adopting the *Charter of Rights and Freedoms* in 1982, Canada did what Dicey merely speculated about some one hundred years earlier – to entrench in a written constitution the rights and freedoms that had previously been preserved through the British-style tradition of an "unwritten constitution." The preamble of the *Constitution Act, 1867*, declares that Canada shall have "a Constitution similar in Principle to that of the United Kingdom." This declaration meant not just the Westminster system of parliamentary democracy, but also the entire "unwritten constitution" that accompanied it. During its first ninety-three years Canada indeed had such a constitution, with the important exception of federalism. In 1960, the Diefenbaker government enacted the Canadian *Bill of Rights*, thus beginning the transition away from the British approach to the protection of civil liberties toward the American approach. Twenty-two years later, the Trudeau government's enactment of the *Charter of Rights* completed this transition. Parliamentary supremacy was replaced by constitutional supremacy, enforced by judicial review – or nearly replaced. The last-minute compromise leading to the section 33 "notwithstanding clause" power preserved a qualified form of parliamentary supremacy.

Since Canada adopted its *Charter of Rights* in 1982, two other Commonwealth democracies – the United Kingdom and New Zealand – have added written rights documents to their respective constitutions. While both authorize judicial interpretation and enforcement of the enumerated rights, neither nation chose to give their courts the kind of American-style "policy-veto," which is now present in Canada as well. In both countries, the court's interpretation of the rights documents are "advisory." If a court finds that a government statute or regulation is in violation of right, it is NOT deemed invalid and unenforceable. Rather, the issue returns to the respective legislative assembly for reconsideration. If the government deems it appropriate, the offending act may be revised or repealed. But if the government disagrees with the court's ruling and refuses to act, the offending statute remains on the books and is enforceable.

Civil Liberties and the Courts Prior to 1960

From Confederation until 1960, judicial protection of civil liberties was limited to two techniques. The first was the "interpretive avoidance" approach inherited from British judges. When interpreting a statute of Parliament or one of the provinces, the courts assumed that the legislature intended to respect traditional rights and liberties. If a statute was open to two interpretations, one of which infringed a right or freedom, judges would exercise their discretion to choose the other interpretation. This approach is consistent with parliamentary supremacy, in that the courts do not overrule the legislature by declaring statutes "of no force or effect." "Interpretive avoidance" simply sends a message to parliamentary lawmakers that, until they indicate otherwise, by redrafting the statute in more explicit language, the courts will interpret it as indicated. While a determined majority in Parliament could easily override such judicial attempts at protecting civil liberties, in practice this was rare. The *Roncarelli* case (Reading 1.1) and the *Boucher* case (Reading 7.3) are examples of the Canadian judiciary's use of the "interpretive avoidance" technique to protect traditional freedoms of individual Canadians.

The second method of judicial protection of civil liberties – the use of federalism limitations – was distinctly Canadian. Using this "power allocation" method, Canadian appeal court judges ruled reckless or discriminatory provincial policies *ultra vires* on section 91–92 grounds, even though the real issue was one of civil liberties. For example, in 1938, the Supreme Court struck down the euphemistically titled *Accurate News and Information Act*, which was an attempt by the Alberta Social Credit government to muzzle newspaper criticism of its economic policies. The Supreme Court ruled that this was legislation in relation to criminal law, and therefore beyond the legislative jurisdiction of any province.

A second well-known example of this technique was the 1953 case of *Saumur v. Quebec*. This was one of a series of Jehovah's Witnesses' cases from

Quebec. In this instance, Quebec City had passed a bylaw prohibiting the distribution of pamphlets in the streets without permission of the Chief of Police. Saumur and other Jehovah's Witnesses were arrested for violating this bylaw. While normally this type of legislation is within the section 92 powers of the provinces, the punitive intentions behind it were clear. In striking down the Quebec bylaw, a number of Supreme Court judges argued that it was legislation in relation to religious freedom and that this was denied to the provinces either by section 91 (criminal law) or section 93 (denominational rights) of the *Constitution Act, 1867.*

While the "power allocation" approach was successfully used to protect civil liberties on several occasions, there were drawbacks to this approach. First, whatever powers were denied to provincial governments were logically conceded to the federal government. While this technique had the disturbing implication that the federal government was free to enact the same, illiberal policy as the province, this never proved to be a practical problem. A more serious objection to this approach was that it forced the judges to use the language of federalism when dealing with the logic of civil liberties. This surreptitious method of reasoning tended to confuse the jurisprudence of both federalism and civil liberties.

There is a third strand of pre-*Bill of Rights* civil liberties jurisprudence that deserves mention, even though it has never been accepted by a Supreme Court majority. Known as the "implied *Bill of Rights*" approach, it argues that the provisions of the preamble of the *Constitution Act* – that Canada shall have "a Constitution similar in Principle to that of the United Kingdom" – imported into Canada the traditional rights and freedoms protected by Britain's "unwritten constitution." The previously cited passages from Dicey show the plausibility of this argument. In the *Alberta Press Case*, Justice Duff argued that "the right of public debate" was inherent in a parliamentary system and that the preamble provided sufficient grounds to declare the *Alberta Press Act* inoperative. Similarly, in the *Saumur* case, Justices Rand, Kellock and Locke said that the preamble implicitly protected "freedom of religion" from both levels of government. The strength of this approach lies in its correct recognition of the civil liberties dimension of the "unwritten constitution" inherited from Great Britain. This is also its weakness, since British judges never pretended to have the authority to enforce these freedoms directly against Parliament. It is widely accepted that constitutional custom and convention are not judicially enforceable, and the strength of this tradition prevented the "implied *Bill of Rights*" approach from ever gaining general acceptance on the Supreme Court or from the Canadian legal community.

Ironically, the Supreme Court resurrected this debate in its 1998 decision in the *Quebec Secession Reference* (see Reading 2.5). The Court "discovered" four unwritten "constitutional principles" – federalism, democracy, the rule of the law and constitutionalism and protection of minorities. It then used these four principles to craft its ruling that if there were a "clear majority" on a "clear question" in a Quebec referendum to secede from Canada, then there would be a "constitutional duty" for the Government of Canada to negotiate in good faith. The unanimous Court was explicit that these "constitutional principles" could be interpreted by courts to impose "substantive limitations" on government actions, i.e. judicial vetoes of government bills or actions.

Most commentators interpreted this part of the Court's ruling as an attempt to appease Quebec nationalists and to win acceptance of the ruling in Quebec, similar to the "bold statecraft, questionable jurisprudence" verdict on the 1981 *Patriation Reference* (see Reading 2.4). Others, however, pointed out that by resurrecting such broadly worded "unwritten constitutional principles" as democracy, federalism and protection of minorities and making them legally enforceable, the Court was giving itself almost unlimited discretion in future cases.

Civil Liberties and the Courts under the 1960 *Bill of Rights*

In the aftermath of the Second World War, growing awareness of the Stalinist and Nazi atrocities of the preceding decades alarmed Western democracies about the fragile nature of human rights and civil liberties in the mass societies of the twentieth century. This concern was shared by Canadian leaders, who were also troubled by their own harsh treatment of Japanese Canadians during the war years and the government's harassment of the Jehovah's Witnesses in Quebec. After a decade of committee hearings and public discussion, the Diefenbaker government adopted the Canadian *Bill of Rights* in 1960 (See Appendix B).

The 1960 *Bill of Rights* took the form of a statute of Parliament, not an amendment to the *Constitution Act*. It also applied only to the federal government. The provinces would not consent to additional restrictions on their legislative powers, and Ottawa lacked the authority to impose them unilaterally.

From the start, the *Bill of Rights* was plagued by problems of interpretation. These problems stemmed principally from its legal status as an ordinary statute and the ambiguous wording of its second section. Canadian judges, including those on the Supreme Court, could not agree on what function the *Bill of Rights* assigned to the courts. Some argued that the *Bill of Rights* conferred new authority on the courts to declare parliamentary statutes "of no force or effect," if they conflicted with enumerated rights. According to this interpretation, the

Bill of Rights armed the Canadian courts with an American-style "power denial" function. Others thought that the *Bill of Rights* was essentially a canon of statutory interpretation, a codification of the traditional "interpretive avoidance" method. They pointed to the ambiguous wording of section 2 and the statutory, as opposed to constitutional, status of the *Bill*.

The Supreme Court's landmark decision in the 1969 *Drybones* case put an end to this particular problem. A majority of the Court took the position that the *Bill of Rights* did confer authority on the judges to declare offending statutes inoperative. The Court ruled that section 94(*b*) of the *Indian Act* denied Drybones his rights to "equality before the law" because it treated him more harshly for public intoxication than other Canadians would have been treated for the same offence, simply because he was a Registered Indian under the *Indian Act*. The *Drybones* decision was hailed as a major development in Canadian constitutional evolution. It seemed to signify an important new restraint on the tradition of parliamentary supremacy and an important new role for the Canadian judiciary in policing *Bill of Rights* violations.

The high expectations created by *Drybones* were short-lived. Subsequent Supreme Court decisions indicated that the judges were still inclined to defer to Parliament's judgment on substantive issues of criminal procedure. This trend culminated in the Supreme Court's 1974 decision of the *Lavell* and *Bedard* cases. Lavell and Bedard were Indian women who had lost their Indian status pursuant to section 12(1)(*b*) of the *Indian Act*. This section provides that Indian women who marry non-Indians lose their status, but no similar disability is imposed on Indian men who marry non-Indians. Lavell and Bedard argued that this violated their right to "equality before the law," since it discriminated against them on the basis of their sex. Based on the *Drybones* precedent, which appeared to prohibit discrimination in the laws based on explicitly prohibited categories such as race and sex, their case seemed strong. The Supreme Court surprised everyone by finding otherwise. A majority of the Court ruled that the right to "equality before the law" meant "equality in the application and administration of the laws." Since there was no question that section 12(1)(*b*) was being applied to Lavell and Bedard the same as it was applied to all other Indian women, there was no violation of the *Bill of Rights*. The dissenting justices protested the apparent inconsistency of this interpretation with the *Drybones* precedent, but to no avail.

In subsequent cases, Chief Justice Laskin described the *Bill of Rights* as a "quasi-constitutional document" and exhorted his colleagues to return to the spirit of *Drybones*. Laskin's arguments were plausible but they fell on deaf ears. The fact of the matter was that a majority of the judges did not want the power of judicial review because they viewed it as inconsistent with Canada's political and legal inheritance. Justice Pigeon's opinion in *Drybones*, even though written in dissent, captured the spirit of the Court and of that generation of Canadian lawyers:

> The meaning of such expressions as "due process of law," "equality before the law," "freedom of religion," "freedom of speech," is in truth largely unlimited and undefined. According to individual views and the evolution of current ideas, the actual content of such legal concepts is apt to expand and to vary as is strikingly apparent in other countries. In the traditional British system that is our own by virtue of the *B.N.A. Act*, the responsibility for updating statutes in this changing world rests exclusively with Parliament. If the Parliament of Canada intended to depart from that principle in enacting the Bill, one would expect to find clear language expressing that intention.

Civil Liberties and the Courts under the 1982 *Charter of Rights*

By the late 1970s, Prime Minister Pierre Trudeau and his Liberal Party were increasingly interested in a constitutionally entrenched bill of rights as a potential "nation-building" device to counter the increasing intensity of conflict in federal-provincial relations. Trudeau had endorsed the idea of a constitutionally entrenched bill of rights as early as 1967. He argued that a constitutional bill of rights would enhance national unity by emphasizing what Canadians hold in common – citizenship – now to be defined by a common set of rights against both levels of government. Initially there was no market for Trudeau's idea. The attachment of Canadian political and legal elites to the tradition of parliamentary supremacy and provincial suspicions of a centralist court were too strong. (Trudeau tried to allay provincial fears by suggesting that Ottawa would be willing to abolish the federal powers of disallowance and reservation in return for provincial support of a bill of rights.) In the years following the *Lavell and Bedard* (1974) and *Morgentaler* (1975) decisions, feminists and civil libertarian groups became disillusioned with the 1960 *Bill of Rights* as an effective legal instrument to achieve the kinds of judge-led policy reforms that they observed in the United States and wanted to emulate in Canada. They were attracted to Trudeau's proposals for a new, stronger, and broader rights document. Out of these seemingly diverse interests was born the political coalition responsible for the adoption of the *Charter of Rights and Freedoms* in 1982 (Appendix C).

The *Charter* was a central part of the package of constitutional reforms adopted in 1982 and was the product of an extended process of intergovernmental and interest-group politics. The *Charter* is best understood as a compromise between the advocates and opponents of a greater role for the courts in Canadian politics and policy-making. Trudeau's initiative succeeded in strengthening the role of the courts under the *Charter* in three specific ways, relative to the 1960 *Bill of Rights*. First and foremost, the *Charter* applies to both levels of government, provincial and federal. Second, the *Charter* is constitutionally entrenched, not just a statute as the *Bill of Rights* was. Third, the *Charter* explicitly authorizes the judges to review legislation for violations of enumerated rights (s.24(1)) and to declare "any law that is inconsistent with the provisions of the Constitution ... of no force or effect" (s.52).

The opponents of too great a role for the judges extracted two concessions from the government in return for their support. The first is the "reasonable limitations" clause of section 1, which made explicit what was already understood to be implicit – that none of the enumerated rights are absolute. (Note that this objective was largely defeated when the Supreme Court operationalized section 1 in the "*Oakes* test.") The second, more important concession was the section 33 "notwithstanding clause." Section 33 allows either level of government to "veto" or override a judicial decision to which it objects, if the decision is based on the fundamental freedoms (s.2), legal rights (ss.7–14), or equality rights (s.15) sections of the *Charter*. This "legislative review of judicial review" is important because it preserves the principle of parliamentary sovereignty, albeit in a modified form. (See the debate over section 33 in Readings 12.5 and 12.6.)

With three important exceptions, the *Charter* basically amplifies the rights that were already protected by the 1960 *Bill of Rights*, and the latter only codified the rights and freedoms that already existed as common law and as constitutional conventions. The exceptions – language rights (sections 16–23), aboriginal rights (sections 25 and 35) and the exclusionary rule (section 24(2)) – did not exist before. What was new about both the *Bill of Rights* and the *Charter* was the growing transfer of the decision-making process from legislative assemblies to courts. As Russell pointed out when the *Charter* was adopted, "[A] charter of rights guarantees not rights but a particular way of making decisions about rights, in which the judicial branch of government has a much more systematic and authoritative role." The net effect of this evolution, Russell observed, is "its tendency to judicialize politics and to politicize the judiciary."[1]

Whether the addition of the *Charter* to Canada's written constitution would be an evolutionary or revolutionary development ultimately depended on the interpretation given to it by the Supreme Court. The Court's self-restrained and deferential interpretation of the 1960 *Bill of Rights* effectively prevented that document from having any significant legal or political impact. Would a similar fate meet the *Charter*? Some legal experts predicted so.

In his dissertation, Professor James Kelly analyzed the Supreme Court's first 390 decisions (1982–1999) and revealed that the answer to this question was a resounding "no."[2] Just as the Court's unreceptive attitude toward the 1960 *Bill of Rights* had the effect of discouraging litigation, the Court's activist jurisprudence under the *Charter* has stimulated litigation. The Court heard only thirty-five *Bill of Rights* cases over a twenty-two year period but it decided 395 *Charter* cases over its first seventeen years. From 1993 to 1999, *Charter* decisions accounted for twenty-six per cent of the Court's annual caseload, making the Court very much a "public law" court. Another indication of the Court's new activism was the number of statutes that it had declared invalid (in whole or in part): sixty-five by the end of 1999, compared to just one (in *Drybones*) under the 1960 *Bill of Rights*.

Other evidence of activism from this period was demonstrated by two of the Court's leading gay rights rulings – *Vriend* (1998) and *M v. H.* (1999) – which struck down statutes in Alberta and Ontario, respectively. In both cases, the Court added "sexual orientation" to the list of prohibited forms of discrimination in section 15 of the *Charter*, despite clear legislative history that proposals to add sexual orientation to section 15 were defeated when the *Charter* was being drafted. The Court in *Vriend*, rather than strike down Alberta's *Individual's Rights Protection Act*, chose as a remedy to "read in" sexual orientation. Amending legislation by judicial fiat as in *Vriend* is even more activist than striking down an offending act. Similarly in *M v. H*, the Court overruled a legislative decision that had been made by way of an all-party free vote in the Ontario Legislature not to include same-sex couples in the definition of "common law spouse" in the *Ontario Family Law Act*. *M v. H.* had a "ripple effect" of invalidating hundreds of similar provisions in the family law acts of the other nine provinces.

As Canada is in the midst of its fourth decade in "*Charter*land," the debate over the *Charter* and the courts is in full bloom. Canadians have lost the instinctive confidence in parliamentary democracy that characterized their political life from Confederation until the 1970s and that contributed to the non-development of the 1960 *Bill of Rights*. The adoption of the *Charter*, its activist interpretation by the Supreme Court, and the spirited defence of both all testify to new support for an increased judicial role in the governing process. Today there is a perception that constitutional questions are too important to be left with politicians. Contrast this attitude with the opposition to the *Supreme Court Act* in the 1870s on the grounds that constitutional questions were too important to be decided by un-elected judges (see Reading 9.1). This change reflects Canadians' growing disillusion with Parliament and democratic politics. The *Charter* is clearly here to stay. Further debate will focus not on the existence of the *Charter*, but on corollary issues such as the appointment of judges, public funding of interest-group litigation, the use of the section 33 legislative override, and proper modes of interpretation.

Constitutional Interpretation: Originalism vs. the Living Tree

Originalism and the "living tree" – two competing approaches to constitutional interpretation – have different consequences for judicial oversight of the law-making process. Both recognize that constitutional meaning must be flexible enough to keep up with social change, but they draw opposing conclusions about the permissible scope of judicial updating. The originalists stress judicial fidelity to the text and the original understanding of that text as illuminated by the framers' intent. New circumstances may require novel applications of that original meaning, but the new meaning may not contradict or overrule the original meaning. An example would be that in cases like *Vriend* and *M. v. H.*, referenced above, a judge would not add a new form of prohibited discrimination – sexual orientation – when it was clear that the original understanding of section 15 did not include it. Similarly, in Joe Borowski's epic 1980s "pro-life" *Charter* challenge to the abortion provisions of the *Criminal Code*, lower courts refused to add "the unborn child" to the section 7 right that "everyone has the right to life." Again, there were clear historical documents that the framers of the *Charter* had explicitly rejected proposals to add the right to life for the unborn to section 7, just as they had rejected proposals by "pro-choice" groups to add an explicit right for women to abort an unwanted pregnancy.[3]

Adherents to the "living tree" approach do not accept this limitation. They minimize the importance of judicial fidelity to original meaning. For Living Tree proponents, the judge's ultimate responsibility is to keep the constitution in tune with the times, not to keep the times in tune with the constitution. In the law of federalism, this approach usually supports judicial deference to legislative decisions, but in *Charter* cases it is used to encourage the judicial expansion of rights and the corollary overruling of legislative choices.

The two approaches have their respective strengths and weaknesses. The strength of the originalist approach is that it is more principled. This enhances a judicial decision's legal authority (i.e., acceptance by the losing side) because it appears that the decision is "required" by law and deductive logic, not the personal policy preferences of the judge. Judicial decisions that are firmly grounded in principle and/or original understanding allow the judge to say to critics, "Don't shoot the messenger just because you don't like the message." In constitutional cases, the implication is that it is up to the political branches of government to amend a constitutional rule if they do not like it. The liability of the originalist approach is that it may result in the enforcement of archaic, out-of-touch constitutional limitations on government action, resulting in a political backlash and loss of political authority. This problem becomes more acute the older the constitutional rule is. The negative connotations of this problem are captured by the "frozen concepts" metaphor.

The advantage of the Living Tree approach is that it avoids this liability. If a constitutional rule is clearly out of touch with society's contemporary needs or beliefs, then the judge can use discretion to "update" the rule by adding new meaning. The downside of the Living Tree approach is that it loses in legal authority (for the losing side) what it gains in political acceptance (on the winning side). Critics of decisions based on a Living Tree approach can claim that the decision is based not on law but the judges' own policy preferences. Since judges are unaccountable, this raises the problem of democratic legitimacy. In *Charter* cases, this criticism is sharpened by the fact that the *Charter*, unlike sections 91–92 of the *B.N.A. Act*, was written and adopted in 1980–81. Why do judges have to "update" constitutional meanings that are only a few decades old?

The debate between the originalists and Living Tree adherents is not simply an academic debate. In the U.S., the political battle over the appointment to fill the Supreme Court vacancy created by Justice Scalia's sudden death in January, 2016 was all about "judicial philosophy." Scalia had been the arch-defender and practitioner of the originalist philosophy, and conservatives and Republican Senators blocked Democratic President Barack Obama from making a replacement appointment before the presidential elections scheduled for November. The successful Republican presidential candidate, Donald Trump, campaigned all that year on the promise to appoint a judge with an "originalist" approach to replace Scalia. After Trump defeated the Democratic candidate Hillary Clinton, he did just that: appointing Neil Gorsuch. The Gorsuch nomination was strongly opposed by liberals and Democratic Senators who feared that Supreme Court precedents in the areas of abortion and gay rights – which depended on a "living tree" approach to constitutional interpretation – would be at risk of being overturned if Gorsuch joined the Court. The same Republican-majority in the U.S. Senate that blocked Obama's nomination a year earlier confirmed Trump's nomination of Gorsuch in April 2017.

In Canada, the debate between the originalists and Living Tree adherents is at the heart of much of the current debate over the Supreme Court's *Charter* decisions. It is what Justice Bastarache was concerned about in his 2001 interview with *The Lawyers Weekly*.[4] In response to a general question about why he was dissenting so often, Bastarache replied:

If we don't have a very principled, consistent approach to statutory interpretation we are easily going to be accused of being too subjective in our approach to legislation in order to justify a result that we want. And I don't think that that is good for the legitimacy of the court and its decisions.

When asked if "too subjective" meant the Court was being "result-oriented," Bastarache replied: "Well, yes. I think so. It's when your own values and your own personal convictions become the predominant factor in deciding the issue. The result being, of course, what you think the law should be, rather than what you think the law actually is right now as written." His interviewer then asked if it was not "almost the worst accusation you can make against a judge to say that he or she is 'result-oriented'"? Again, Bastarache did not mince his words:

> Yes. Because it means they are unprincipled, and because they favour a result they would, of course, choose to sort of create reasons according to the result already reached, instead of applying the rules and then coming to a result. So like you say, it is a very serious accusation.

In Canada, the originalists versus Living Tree debate has also spilled over into politics. It animated some of the criticisms of Prime Minister Harper's judicial appointments (see Chapter 11) and our understanding of judicial decision-making (see Chapter 8). The Living Tree was even approvingly cited by Justice Malcolm Rowe in his application to the Supreme Court of Canada (Reading 4.5). While not yet as overtly partisan as the U.S. debate, the continued politicization of the judiciary will grant the victors in this debate considerable influence over the shape and direction of Canadian politics.

NOTES

1   Peter H. Russell, "The Effect of the Charter of Rights on the Policy-Making Role of Canadian Courts," *Canadian Public Administration* 25 (1982), p. 1.

2·   James B. Kelly, "The Supreme Court of Canada's *Charter of Rights* Decisions, 1982-1999: A Statistical Analysis," *Law, Politics, and the Judicial Process in Canada,* 3rd edition (Calgary: University of Calgary Press, 2002), pp. 496–512.

3   F.L. Morton, *Morgentaler v. Borowski: Abortion, the Charter and the Courts* (Toronto: McClelland and Stewart, 1992).

4   Cristin Schmitz, "The Bastarache interview: reasoning from results at the SCC," *The Lawyers Weekly,* January 26, 2001, p. 19.

12.4

What's Wrong with the Charter Revolution and the Court Party?

F.L. Morton and Rainer Knopff

The Charter Revolution and the Court Party (Peterborough: Broadview Press, 2000), 13, 149–166. Reprinted with permission.

Just as the 1960s are remembered by Canadian historians as the decade of Quebec's "Quiet Revolution," so the 1980s and 1990s will be remembered as the period of Canada's "Charter Revolution." Since the adoption of the Charter of Rights and Freedoms in 1982, Canadian politics has been transformed. A long tradition of parliamentary supremacy has been replaced by a regime of constitutional supremacy verging on judicial supremacy. On rights issues, judges have abandoned the deference and self-restraint that characterized their pre-Charter jurisprudence and become more active players in the political process. As Chief Justice Lamer observed in 1998, "There is no doubt that [with the adoption of the Charter] the judiciary was drawn into the political arena to a degree unknown prior to 1982."

Encouraged by the judiciary's more active policymaking role, interest groups – many funded by the very governments whose laws they challenge – have increasingly turned to the courts to advance their policy objectives. As a result, policymakers are ever watchful for what a justice department lawyer describes as judicial "bombshells" which "shock ... the system." In addition to making the courtroom a new arena for the pursuit of interest group politics, in other words, Charter litigation – or its threat – also casts its shadow over the more traditional arenas of electoral, legislative, and administrative politics. Not only are judges now influencing public policy to a previously unheard-of degree, but lawyers and legal arguments are increasingly shaping political discourse and policy formation....

Our primary objection to the Charter Revolution is that it is deeply and fundamentally undemocratic, not just in the simple and obvious sense of being anti-majoritarian, but also in the more serious sense of eroding the habits and temperament of representative democracy. The growth of courtroom rights talk undermines perhaps the fundamental prerequisite of decent liberal democratic politics: the willingness to engage those with whom one disagrees in the ongoing attempt to combine diverse interests into temporarily viable governing majorities. Liberal democracy works only when majorities rather than minorities rule, and when it is obvious to all that ruling majorities are themselves coalitions of minorities in a pluralistic society. Partisan opponents, in short, must nevertheless be seen as fellow citizens who might be future allies. Representative institutions facilitate this fundamental democratic disposition; judicial power undermines it. The kind of courtroom politics promoted by the Court Party, in short, is authoritarian, not just in process but, more dangerously, in spirit.

Our concern is nicely framed by two quotations from the work of Peter Russell, one from his analysis of Canada's mega-constitutional politics, the other from his reflections on judicial policymaking. First, in *Constitutional Odyssey*, Russell infers from our constitutional history, especially from the mega-constitutional politics of recent decades, that "not all Canadians have consented to form a single people in which a majority or some special majority have, to use John Locke's phrase, 'a right to set and conclude the rest.' " This willingness to be concluded by the majority is what defines a sovereign people, at least one that wishes to govern itself democratically. Although a sovereign democratic people will certainly exhibit partisan political division, such division remains subordinate to an overarching agreement to remain a single people. As a member of a sovereign people, in other words, one must agree to treat one's partisan opponents as fellow citizens, whose rule, should they form the majority, one is willing to accept. Because not all Canadians have agreed to treat each other in this way – because, in other words, what divides us often outweighs our common citizenship – we are not, in Russell's view, a sovereign people; the subtitle of *Constitutional Odyssey* asks whether we can become one.

Second, in an oft-quoted passage from an early article on the Charter of Rights and Freedoms, Russell worries about the "negative side" of "transferring the policymaking focus from the legislative to the judicial arena." This transfer, he says, "represents a further flight from politics, a deepening disillusionment with the procedures of representative government and government by discussion as means of resolving fundamental questions of political justice." This second concern is connected to the first inasmuch as it suggests that the Charter, which the Court Party's unifiers believed would help Canadians become a sovereign people, may in fact hinder us from becoming one; indeed, it may make us even less of a sovereign people than we currently are. A people prepared to treat political opponents as legitimate surely needs to make government by discussion a leading means of settling political differences. To the extent that the Charter represents a flight from this kind of politics, it can be understood as threatening rather than promoting the unity necessary to a sovereign people....

Many of liberal democracy's early constitutionalists in Britain and the United States might have predicted the corrosive effects of the Charter. They understood what we appear to have forgotten: that even a regime dedicated to the protection of rights does not necessarily benefit from institutionalizing rights talk too prominently in public life. These pioneers put little faith in judicially enforceable bills of rights – and for good reason. They believed that representative democracy, not judicialized politics, is mainly how a sovereign people should protect rights....

Recent decades, however, have witnessed a sustained and twofold challenge to representative democracy: In Canada, as elsewhere, it is manifested by the growing popularity of both populism and constitutionally entrenched rights. To adapt Russell's formulation slightly, if populism reflects a flight from representative government and government by discussion, the Charter represents a further flight in the same direction.

Populism and the Court Party differ in obvious ways. Indeed, in contemporary Canadian politics, they inhabit opposite ends of the political spectrum, with right-wing populists launching some of the most vociferous attacks on judicial power, while the left-leaning Court Party fulminates about the tyranny of the majority entailed by populism. As important as the opposition between populists and Court Party interests, however, is their common challenge to representative democracy. When populists do not like what representatives have done, they generally do not wish to wait until a general election to "throw the rascals out"; they want to be able to recall them now. Similarly, if Court Party interests do not like legislative policies, they increasingly want courts, not elections, to reverse those policies. By the same token, populists advocate the use of initiatives and referenda to force their agenda on reluctant legislatures, just as rights advocates ask the courts to force their agenda on the legislature through such devices of positive activism as reading in. In our view, the pincer movement of populism and the Court Party against representative democracy is a problematic development....

However important and controversial the issues raised by Charter jurisprudence might be, they almost always turn out to be matters of reasonable disagreement that are unnecessarily inflated through courtroom rights talk. Courtroom rights talk, in other words, is encouraging in Canadians the same bad political instinct that Alexander Bickel criticized the US Supreme Court for fostering in American society in the 1960s: moral oversensitivity. For a democracy, being morally oversensitive is as dangerous as being morally undersensitive. It unduly lowers the threshold at which citizens feel justified in abandoning the democratic process, be it through civil disobedience, appeal to the courts, or (in the extreme case) revolt and secession. Canada would do well to heed Bickel's plea that the "morality of rights" be balanced with the "morality of consent."

We do not wish to be misunderstood. We are not suggesting that inflation of political rhetoric would disappear in the absence of a Charter of Rights and

Freedoms. To the contrary, like James Madison, we believe that the tendency to rhetorical inflation is endemic to political life. Political zealotry, Madison argued, is rooted in human nature. People will fight, he suggested, not only because their interests differ, but because they love their own opinions and wish to see them prevail, so much so that "where no substantial occasion presents itself the most frivolous and fanciful distinctions have been sufficient to ... excite [the] most violent conflicts." In other words, the temptation to inflate objectively minor disagreements into major conflicts is simply part of the human condition. The constitutional task is not to eradicate this tendency, but to find institutional ways of checking and moderating it, so that political opponents come to see each other as fellow citizens, members of a single people prepared to let the majority set and conclude the rest. Courtroom rights talk, we believe, undermines this goal by amplifying rather than moderating the inflationary tendency.

The institutional transfer of power to the courts compounds the moral inflation of rights claiming. As a logical corollary of translating reasonable disagreements into uncompromising rights talk, in other words, the responsibility for concluding these agreements moves from legislatures to courts. Because opposition to the rights claim is presented as beyond the pale, it cannot be left to the decision of representative institutions, where opposition to virtually any policy able to make it onto the agenda is a fact of life. In other words, the policy issue cannot be left to be concluded by legislative majorities because the wrong side may form the majority.

Shifting power from the legislative to the judicial arena, in short, is a way of substituting coercion for government by discussion. To be sure, we should not exaggerate the distinction between the two institutional contexts. On the one hand, much debate takes place in the courtroom. On the other, no one should romanticize the nature of parliamentary (and public) debate. We all know that there is as much posturing and inflation of claims in legislative politics as there is in the courtroom. The symbolism of having legislative partisans separated by two swords' lengths underscores the intensity and uncompromising intransigence of much of their debate. Still, important differences between legislative and judicial debate must be kept in view.

For all its sound and fury, for all its raucous and uncompromising posturing, everything about legislative debate implies the *sine qua non* of a sovereign people: the willingness to abide by the rule of majorities with which one disagrees. Thus the rules of legislative debate require its participants to use civil and decorous language even as they insult their opponents. Insults are hurled not at that "SOB" over there, but at "the honourable member" opposite. Indeed, it is not even permitted to address a member directly or by name. Debate must not be personalized and *ad hominem*, so representatives address the Speaker and use the name of other members' constituencies or offices....

Judicialized politics, especially when it concerns constitutionally entrenched rights, carries a quite different set of implications. It has a much more closed and intolerant character. True, rules of decorum also govern in the court. Nevertheless, the point of the formalized courtroom combat about constitutional rights is to determine which side holds uncompromisable trumps ... even when judicial opinions are not clear-cut, the natural inclinations of the electronic media help winners in courtroom battles present themselves as having absolute right – or "rights" – on their side; the logical corollary, of course – and it is a corollary that winners typically go out of their way to emphasize – is that the losers are not only wrong but legally illegitimate. The losers, in other words, are beyond the pale; theirs is not an eligible policy position, and, if they form the majority, it is not a majority that can be allowed to set and conclude the rest....

To transfer the resolution of reasonable disagreements from legislatures to courts inflates rhetoric to unwarranted levels and replaces negotiated, majoritarian compromise policies with the intensely held policy preferences of minorities. Rights-based judicial policymaking also grants the policy preferences of courtroom victors an aura of coercive force and permanence that they do not deserve. Issues that should be subject to the ongoing flux of government by discussion are presented as beyond legitimate debate, with the partisans claiming the right to permanent victory. As the morality of rights displaces the morality of consent, the politics of coercion replaces the politics of persuasion. The result is to embitter politics and decrease the inclination of political opponents to treat each other as fellow citizens – that is, as members of a sovereign people.

12.5

The Notwithstanding Clause: The *Charter*'s Homage to Parliamentary Democracy
Peter H. Russell

Policy Options (February 2007). http://irpp.org/wp-content/uploads/assets/po/the-charter-25/russell.pdf. Reprinted with permission.

It is surely only in Canada, besotted as we are by all things constitutional, that something called the "notwithstanding clause" could find a place in the lexicon of public debate. But it is also only in Canada that a piece of constitutional furniture known as "the Charter" (a.k.a. the Canadian Charter of Rights and Freedoms) could become a popular icon, deserving of an annual day of celebration and a virtual blowout on its 25th birthday.

These two peculiar facts about Canada are closely related. The fact that the Charter has become an object of worship – a symbol of everything right and good – has thrown the notwithstanding clause (which, believe it or not, is part of the Charter) into bad political odour. For under this strange sounding clause (even stranger when dressed up in its fancy Latin garb as the *non obstante* clause) the parliaments of Canada can insulate a piece of legislation from Charter challenge for five whole years. God forbid that those whom we have elected should have their way with our beloved Charter! No wonder Brian Mulroney, sniffing the populist breeze, once declared that so long as it contained the notwithstanding clause, the Charter of Rights "was not worth the paper it is written on."

Well, I am here to tell you that Mulroney and his fellow Charter worshippers are wrong, and to plead the case not only for retaining the notwithstanding clause but for occasionally having the guts and brains to use it. In doing so, I know that I face an uphill battle, having just witnessed another Conservative prime minister, Stephen Harper, refusing to use the notwithstanding clause even though it was needed to give effect to his legislative objective of restoring the heterosexual marriage monopoly in Canada.

My point is not to defend so-called "traditional marriage" but to defend the legitimacy of Parliament debating and deciding how marriage should be defined in Canadian law. I believe that it is wrong to deny the equal benefit of our laws to Canadians because they are gay or lesbian. Like the many Canadian judges who have examined the matter, I can see no justification in a free and democratic society for limiting the rights of gays and lesbians to enjoy the same benefits that heterosexual Canadians derive from the state's recognizing of their marriages. And I was pleased to find that a majority of our elected representatives in the House of Commons were willing to support legislation changing the traditional definition of marriage. But I would have been a lot happier if our parliamentarians had been as clear as our courts have been about the reasons for doing so, instead of simply repeating Prime Minister Martin's mantra that it was simply a matter of Charter rights. And I would have a lot more respect for Prime Minister Harper if he had the guts and – dare I say it? – the brains to be willing to use the notwithstanding clause to re-test the will of Parliament in a meaningful way.

To defend the notwithstanding clause is not to oppose the Charter. After all, it is part of the Charter. It was included in the Charter for a very good reason: a belief that there should be a parliamentary check on a fallible judiciary's decisions on the metes and bounds of our fundamental rights and freedoms. It was in the great tradition of the Canadian capacity for compromise on things fundamental. It was a compromise between the tradition of parliamentary supremacy and the prospect of judicial supremacy. And, in 1981, it was indeed a "deal-maker." Without it, Pierre Trudeau would not have had the support of nine premiers for his patriation package, and we would not have had the Charter in 1982. Premiers like Saskatchewan's Allan Blakeney, Alberta's Peter Lougheed and Manitoba's Sterling Lyon, who insisted on inclusion of the notwithstanding clause in the Charter, were no less civil libertarians than Trudeau. But they had a stronger respect than Trudeau ever evinced for the importance of parliamentary democracy to this country's freedom. As civil libertarians they welcomed the opportunity the Charter gives citizens to go to court and ask judges to test the laws and practices of government against the rights and freedoms in the Charter. They accepted that Canada's judiciary would be at the front line of decision-making in giving meaning to the abstract ideals of the Charter and applying them, with authority, to the realities of democratic governance. While most of the time the country would live with the decisions of judges on the requirements of the Charter, a clause was needed for those exceptional occasions when elected legislators, federal, provincial or territorial, after careful deliberation, conclude that the way judges have construed, or are likely to construe, a Charter right or freedom is an unreasonable constraint on democratic power or threatens a vital interest of society.

I will admit that the story of the notwithstanding clause's use and non-use through the Charter's first quarter-century has not been an encouraging story for its fans. Indeed, the most famous – or infamous – use of the legislative override seems to bolster the case of its detractors. I refer to Robert Bourassa's decision in December 1988, in the heat of the constitutional battle over the Meech Lake Accord, to invoke the notwithstanding clause to restore Quebec's French-only sign law, which had been struck down by the Supreme Court of Canada. The decision was made not through reasoned legislative debate but by Bourassa's cabinet and caucus listening to mobs in the streets howling against any federal institution that dared to touch Quebec's language law. The decision turned out to be a decisive nail in the coffin of the Meech Lake Accord, and while that may be the one good thing Trudeauites can say about the notwithstanding clause, it is not exactly an advertisement for it.

Let me add to the detractors' case by citing another quieter but nonetheless abusive use of the clause by a Quebec government. This was the blanket use of the notwithstanding clause by the PQ government to immunize all new Quebec legislation from Charter review. The Supreme Court of Canada upheld this blanket use of the legislative override in the same decision in which it struck down Quebec's sign law. But it was wrong to do so. The judges clearly had no appreciation of the notwithstanding clause's role in maintaining parliamentary democracy.

But these abusive uses of the Charter's legislative override do not justify getting rid of it or not using the clause in an appropriate manner. After all, judges too can use the Charter abusively. Not so long ago, an Ontario Superior Court judge, Paul Cosgrove, was raked over the coals by Ontario's Court of Appeal for making 150 Charter rulings in a murder trial that were "without foundation." That finding may eventually lead to Justice Cosgrove's removal from the bench. But it will not and should not lead to terminating the use of the Charter by trial judges. Judges, like legislatures, are fallible.

[*Ed. note*: The Canadian Judicial Council recommended Cosgrove's removal, but he resigned before Parliament could remove him. See introduction to Chapter 5.]

I would add that in the long term the dubious use of the legislative override by Quebec governments has not done much harm, and might even have done some good. Eventually, when nationalist tempers cooled down and a United Nations tribunal agreed that Quebec's prohibition of outdoor English signs was excessive, the province adopted the very compromise the Supreme Court had recommended – that French be the predominant although not exclusive language of outdoor advertising in Quebec. And subsequent Quebec governments, PQ and Liberal, have not returned to blanket use of the override. The Charter is alive and well and popular in Quebec. It might even be argued that the availability of the override helped to dampen down nationalist feelings that the 1982 constitutional changes had robbed Quebec of its autonomy.

There can be no doubt that the Bourassa government's use of the Charter's notwithstanding clause to protect Quebec's French-only sign law gave the clause a bad name in English Canada. But by now, nearly 20 years later, that 1988 episode is a very faded memory. We must look for deeper and more persistent factors to account for how seldom the clause has been used.

The benign reason for non-use of the notwithstanding clause is that Canadian judges have done a pretty good job in interpreting and applying the Charter. This statement, I know, will shock and offend the anti-activist critics of our judiciary. Nonetheless, on my reading of the evidence, the Supreme Court of Canada and the lower courts generally have been moderate, balanced and reasonable in their treatment of the Charter. Yes, there have been exceptions, and I will get to these in a minute, but on the whole the judiciary's interpretation of the Charter has not been counter-majoritarian and has not put pressure on elected legislators to exercise their power to insulate their laws from Charter-based judicial review. Most of the judicial-phobia has come from academic and political critics on the far right who oppose the expansion of social equality and reduction of police powers that judicial decisions in Charter cases have facilitated.

But there have been a few Charter decisions of our highest court that I find very difficult to swallow and that might well justify use of the notwithstanding clause. In my view the top candidate is the Supreme Court's decision in the judicial remuneration case. [*Ed. note:* See Reading 5.5.]

Here the Court's majority found that the Charter right of a person charged with a criminal offence to be tried by "an independent and impartial tribunal," bolstered by a reference in the original Constitution's preamble to Canada having "a Constitution similar in principle to that of the United Kingdom," requires that in setting the pay levels of Canadian judges legislatures must act on recommendations from independent commissions. If a legislature decides to pay less than a compensation commission recommends, the reasonableness of its doing so can be reviewed and overturned in the courts. In other words, according to this very far-fetched reading of our constitution, the judges have the final word in deciding how much they should be paid. The six Supreme Court justices who went along with this decision seemed not a bit disturbed by the conflict of interest inherent in their ruling. I believe that most Canadians, if they knew about this decision, would be disturbed by the judges' conflict of interest, and would support the use of the override if it is needed to protect the recent decision of Canada's parliament not to accede fully to the increases in judicial salaries recommended by the federal compensation commission.

Another deserving target of the Charter override was the Supreme Court's 1995 decision in *RJR-MacDonald Inc.* striking down (by a bare 5-4 majority) federal legislation prohibiting tobacco advertising and requiring health warnings on tobacco product packaging. The majority found the law to be an unreasonable limit on tobacco manufacturers' freedom of expression. Parliamentarians may well have found that the Supreme Court's decision was an unreasonable expansion of freedom of expression at the expense of Canadians' health. Instead, they followed the Supreme Court's hint on how an amended law might meet with its approval, and rewrote it, focusing its advertising ban on lifestyle ads.

Another close call where a Supreme Court decision in the health field might have merited invoking the notwithstanding clause was its 2005 decision in *Chaoulli* upholding a challenge to Quebec's ban on private insurance for services covered by Canada's public health plan. However, the majority judgment in this case was based on the soft and easily overridden provisions of Quebec's Charter of Human Rights. But if in subsequent cases, a majority on the Court endorses the broad substantive interpretation of fundamental justice in section 7 of the Charter advanced by Chief Justice McLachlin in *Chaoulli* as the basis for requiring a major expansion of private medicine in Canada, I hope that a majority of our elected representatives will have the guts and the brains to debate the issue and use the override if they conclude that the Supreme Court of Canada's national health policy is not good for the country.

But will they? Writing about the notwithstanding clause some years ago, Howard Leeson commented – with regret – that the notwithstanding clause appeared to be a "paper tiger" that, like the powers of reservation and disallowance, was "available in theory, but not used in practice." It is to be hoped that nothing as strong as the convention that governs non-use of reservation and disallowance will develop around section 33 of the Charter. The reason that federal governments should not use reservation or disallowance is respect for our federal system of government. The reason that our political leaders should not follow Paul Martin, who blurted out in an election debate that he would never use the notwithstanding clause, is respect for our parliamentary system of government.

I believe that maintaining a sensible attitude to use of the Charter's notwithstanding clause is more a matter of having brains than of having guts. Politicians' fear that the electorate will punish any government that uses the notwithstanding clause is not based on any solid empirical evidence about public opinion. When three colleagues and I did some in-depth interviewing of elected politicians and citizens 20 years ago, we found that support for legislatures being able to override courts on Charter issues was – interestingly – greater among elected politicians than among citizens. However, when we moved from the general to the particular and asked about applying the override in specific situations, we found shifting partisan differences in support for using the legislative override. For instance, when we asked about using it to maintain a law controlling unions, support for the legislature having the last word rose among Conservatives but fell among Liberal, NDP and PQ politicians, and vice versa when the law struck down by the courts was one that aimed at assisting the poor. Even though public regard for the Charter as icon has probably strengthened since we did our research, I very much doubt that there is a settled majority opinion against using the legislative override. The politics of any given use will depend on the policy concerns at issue.

But the real intelligence that is needed is the constitutional wisdom that led to including the notwithstanding clause in the Charter – sufficient respect for parliamentary democracy not to let the judiciary always have the last word on rights and freedoms. Let us hope that the next generation of political leaders in Canada will eschew the simplistic thinking of Mulroney and Martin and follow the wise statecraft of Blakeney, Lougheed and Lyon.

12.6

Saskatchewan Uses the Notwithstanding Clause

Government Will Use Notwithstanding Clause to Protect School Choice for Parents and Students

Government of Saskatchewan, May 1, 2017. Reprinted with permission.

Premier Brad Wall today announced the government will protect school choice in Saskatchewan by invoking the notwithstanding clause of *The Canadian Charter of Rights and Freedoms*.

The move comes in response to a recent Court of Queen's Bench ruling that, if allowed to stand, would force about 10,000 non-Catholic students out of Catholic schools. The ruling could also risk provincial funding of 26 other faith-based schools including Luther College, Regina Christian School, Saskatoon Christian School and Huda School.

"We support school choice including public, separate and faith-based schools," Wall said. "We will defend school choice for students and parents. By invoking the notwithstanding clause we are protecting the rights of parents and students to choose the schools that work best for their families, regardless of their religious faith."

Section 33 of *The Charter of Rights and Freedoms* gives provincial legislatures the authority to override certain portions of the Charter for a five year term. Invoking the notwithstanding clause requires an Act of the Legislative Assembly.

"I have asked the Ministers of Education and Justice to begin preparing legislation to invoke the notwithstanding clause to protect choice in our school system," Wall said. "We wanted to announce this now to provide clarity and provide parents with the assurance that they will be able to continue to choose the kind of school they want their children to attend."

The government's action is in response to an April 20 Court of Queen's Bench ruling on a legal challenge by the Good Spirit School Division of Christ the Teacher Catholic Schools' right to receive provincial funding for non-Catholic students. The Court ruled that the government must stop funding non-minority faith students to attend separate schools.

Wall Right in Use of 'The Clause'

Dwight Newman

National Post, May 10, 2017, A8. Reprinted with permission.

Premier Brad Wall's recent announcement that the Saskatchewan government will use the notwithstanding clause to respond to a court decision on Catholic schools has some people up in arms. Some have repeated their dislike for the notwithstanding clause, while others have claimed the clause has been incorrectly used. Both objections are based on a flawed understanding of the clause and the realities of governing. Wall actually deserves commendation for an insightful policy step.

The "notwithstanding clause" is found in Section 33 of the *Canadian Charter of Rights and Freedoms*. It allows the federal parliament or a provincial legislature to indicate in legislation that a law operates "notwithstanding" certain sections of the *Charter*.

This suspension of the *Charter*'s application expires every five years, although it can be renewed. In effect, section 33 gives legislators the last word on the application of certain rights when they profoundly disagree with the interpretations offered by judges.

The notwithstanding clause was a vital part of the constitutional negotiations that led to the *Charter* being adopted in 1982. Without it, some provinces were unwilling to come on board. Without it, there would be no *Charter* at all. Those who argue that the notwithstanding clause is somehow illegitimate actually bear the onus of explaining how the rest of the *Charter* would be legitimate without it.

The notwithstanding clause was advocated at the time by premiers of very different political stripes – notably Saskatchewan's New Democratic Party premier Allan Blakeney and Alberta's Progressive Conservative premier Peter Lougheed. These premiers had a shared vision of the supreme role of parliament in Canada's constitutional tradition, and saw the notwithstanding clause as a bridge between that vision and the vision of a constitution with a written bill of rights enforced by judges.

The notwithstanding clause was also not invented in some ad hoc way. It tracked a similar clause in the 1960 Canadian Bill of Rights. So section 33 was part of Canada's existing legal architecture, and was an important clause in bringing together different constitutional traditions.

Those who oppose its existence may be wedded to a different vision of Canada – one oriented only to individualistic – but the clause is properly part of Canadian constitutionalism.

In the *Charter*'s 35-year history, the notwithstanding clause has not been used extensively. But it has been used more than many people realize. In a 2001 journal article, constitutional scholar Tsvi Kahana identified 17 different statutes that had used it – far more than the handful of instances that are commonly cited. Most past uses have gone unnoticed because section 33 has served relatively routine purposes of enabling legislators to make a different choice than courts might have otherwise forced upon them.

That is what Wall's government has done here – in the context of a particularly nettlesome problem created by the courts. The practical effect of the recent Saskatchewan ruling was to require thousands of children to move to different schools in close to a year from now, because the court concluded that non-Catholic students could no longer be funded at Catholic schools.

The case went to court in an unusual way – over a scrap about resources between a public and Catholic school board.

The court did not receive a robust evidentiary record on the alleged rights violations or justifications for the government's infringement of those rights. The judge – a distinguished former commercial lawyer – worked valiantly with the materials he had. But the case is, quite frankly, a mess. The awkward way that the case came forward left the court with an incomplete record on how Saskatchewan funds other faith-based schools. And the judge's discussion of the equality and religious rights at play fails to mention some of the pertinent case law.

There are, then, good bases for an appeal, and an appeal should proceed. Some academics have suggested Wall ought to wait for the outcome of an appeal before turning to the notwithstanding clause. But this suggestion ignores the fact that the clause has often been used preemptively. Wall's use is simply in keeping with existing constitutional practice.

Some academics and pundits' objections also miss the realities of governing. The mere possibility that thousands of children could be hauled out of their schools creates needless anxiety for children and parents. It might affect current choices on the schools they start in. It requires the government to prepare to conduct some sort of "religion test" to determine who must be removed from Catholic schools.

To simply wait around on an appeal without promising the stability that the notwithstanding clause offers would be to shirk the responsibilities of good governance.

Wall has explained the chaos that would result from waiting for an appellate court ruling. His government is rightly acting to minimize that chaos. He is doing so through an entirely proper use of the notwithstanding clause. He should be commended for his actions.

Chekhov's Gun

Leonid Sirota

Double Aspect, May 10, 2017, https://doubleaspect.blog/2017/05/10/
chekhovs-gun/. Reprinted with permission.

Anton Chekhov liked to say that "one must never place a loaded rifle on the stage
if it isn't going to go off." And conversely, once the rifle is part of the set, then go
off it must. But must this theatrical directive apply to constitutional law? Some
evidently think so – at least when it comes to the "notwithstanding clause" of
the *Canadian Charter of Rights and Freedoms.* Dwight Newman in a National
Post op-ed [*Ed. note:* reproduced above], and Gerard Kennedy in a post for
Advocates for the Rule of Law, are the latest of those who have ventured this
opinion in the wake of Saskatchewan's decision to invoke the "notwithstanding
clause" to continue funding the education of non-Catholics at Catholic "separate" schools, despite a court finding that this is unconstitutional.

Professor Newman notes that "[t]he notwithstanding clause was a vital
part of the constitutional negotiations that led to the *Charter* being adopted
in 1982. Without it, some provinces were unwilling to come on board." In his
view, "[t]hose who argue that the notwithstanding clause is somehow illegitimate actually bear the onus of explaining how the rest of the *Charter* would
be legitimate without it." But the fact that the existence of a legal power was a
necessary part of a constitutional compromise does not justify the use of such
a power. The federal power of disallowance over provincial legislation was a
necessary part of the compromise that made Confederation possible, yet using
it now would violate a firm constitutional convention. Does Professor Newman
think that opposing the use of this power involves thinking that sections 91 and
92 of the *Constitution Act, 1867* are illegitimate too?

Professor Newman wants to bolster the propriety of using the "notwithstanding clause" by pointing out that "[i]t tracked a similar clause in the 1960
Canadian Bill of Rights … and was an important clause in bringing together
different constitutional traditions." Yet although they are worded similarly,
section 33 of the *Charter* and section 2 of the *Canadian Bill of Rights* have very
different functions. The *Charter*'s notwithstanding clause makes it possible to
deny some of its provisions the status of Supreme Law that they would otherwise
have by virtue of subsection 52(1) of the *Constitution Act, 1982.* By contrast, the
notwithstanding clause of the *Canadian Bill of Rights* serves to protect it against
implied repeal by subsequent legislation, and thus to elevate what would otherwise be an ordinary statute to what has been described as "quasi-constitutional" status. Though they can both be described as reconciling the protection

of individual rights with Parliamentary sovereignty, the two notwithstanding clauses are thus motivated by opposite concerns. That of the *Canadian Bill of Rights* is rights-protecting; the *Charter*'s is legislation-protecting.

Professor Newman makes some substantive criticisms of the court decision Saskatchewan wishes to override. For my part, I am still of the view that the decision on the issue of religious freedom was quite obviously correct. Professor Newman also claims that those who criticize Saskatchewan's use of the notwithstanding clause "miss the realities of governing" – notably the need to prevent the uncertainty about the eventual application of the court decision, indeed the "chaos" that would result from its application. Of course, uncertainty is not eliminated, but merely postponed by invoking the notwithstanding clause, which has to be renewed every five years. More importantly though, the government has a way to avoid creating "chaos" while complying with the constitution. It only needs to fund all non-public schools equally, without discrimination in favour of the Catholic ones.

More importantly still, the "realities of governing" objection, and the concern about uncertainty, could be applied to any number of *Charter* decisions. Uncertainty has followed the Supreme Court's decisions declaring unconstitutional the blanket ban on assisted suicide and extreme trial delays, for instance, to name only two. If uncertainty, or public concern, is enough to set aside a judicial decision about rights, then we should drop the pretense of having a judicially enforced *Charter of Rights*, and go back to the good pre-1982 days of Parliamentary sovereignty. Mr. Kennedy is perhaps more forthright about this, arguing that anyone "who seeks to have a court expand" – or simply declare – "the meaning of *Charter* rights must be prepared to have the scope of those rights subsequently narrowed by the legislature."

This is really the heart of the debate. Do we want a judicially enforced constitution, or should we go back to Parliamentary sovereignty? I'm not saying, by the way, that turning the clock back to 1982 would be some sort of catastrophe. Canada was a free country in 1982 – albeit a free country where the *Lord's Day Act* was good, unassailable law. New Zealand, which does not have rights protections enforceable against Parliament, is a free country, freer than Canada in some ways, though not in others. I think that abandoning judicially enforced rights would be a step backwards, which is why I am so critical of those who want to do it, but it would not be a step into the abyss.

But even though it would not be a crazy thing to do, giving up on judicial enforcement of constitutionally guaranteed rights would involve a substantial change to our constitutional arrangements. Professor Newman claims that those opposed to the use of the "notwithstanding clause" "may be wedded to a different vision of Canada – one oriented only to individualistic rights." But in truth, however exactly we count them, uses of the "notwithstanding clause" have been a marginal phenomenon for 29 years, ever since Québec gave in to nationalist protests to prevent the use of English in advertising. Professor Newman's individualistic dystopia is actually our reality. It is he and his fellows, not Andrew Coyne or I, who are "wedded to a different vision of Canada" from that in which we live.

Ostensibly, Professor Newman and Mr. Kennedy might not see themselves as advocating a complete *de facto* reversal of the 1982 constitutional settlement as it has been implemented by political actors as well as courts over 35 years. They might think that they are only defending occasional uses of the notwithstanding clause in response to particularly problematic judicial decisions. But as I've explained before, I do not think there is a *tertium quid*, some sort of happy Canadian middle ground between Parliamentary sovereignty and judicial enforcement of constitutional rights. If the norm against using the notwithstanding clause disappears, then it will be used proactively, profusely, and promiscuously. Like the Saskatchewan government now, others will use it whenever they think their policy ends justify the means, without paying attention to the rights the constitution is supposed to protect.

As Chekhov knew, placing a loaded rifle on the stage creates an unstable situation. A good dramatist will resolve the instability with a bang – and probably some casualties. But constitutional actors are not comedians. Even if they are put in a position where a loaded gun is within their reach, their responsibility is not to fire it, but to keep it safe if they cannot unload it, and to instruct those who follow them to do likewise. As for constitutional critics, they should not be cheering for the most theatrical resolution. They might enjoy a drama, but the shots, when fired, are likely to be aimed at the audience.

12.7

Dialogue or Monologue? Hogg and Thornton versus Morton

The Charter Dialogue between Courts and Legislatures
Peter W. Hogg and Allison A. Thornton

Policy Options, April 1999. Reprinted with permission.

Judicial review is the term used to describe the action of courts in striking down laws. Lawyers and political scientists, especially those employed at universities, love to debate the question of whether judicial review is legitimate. In Canada, the question arises because our *Charter of Rights* vests judges, who are neither elected to their offices nor accountable for their actions, with the power to strike down laws that have been made by the duly elected representatives of the people. Is this a legitimate function in a democratic society? Is the *Charter of Rights* itself legitimate, inasmuch as it provides the authority for a much expanded role for judicial review?

The conventional answer to these questions is that judicial review is legitimate in a democratic society because of our commitment to the rule of law. All of the institutions in our society must abide by the rule of law, and judicial review simply requires obedience by the legislative bodies to the law of the Constitution. When, for example, the Supreme Court of Canada strikes down a prohibition on the advertising of cigarettes (as it did in the *RJR-MacDonald* case, 1995), it is simply forcing the Parliament of Canada to abide by the *Charter*'s guarantee of freedom of expression. Similarly, when the Court adds sexual orientation to the list of prohibited grounds of discrimination in Alberta's human rights legislation (as it did in the *Vriend* case, 1998), it is simply forcing the Legislature of Alberta to observe the *Charter*'s guarantee of equality.

The difficulty with this conventional answer is that the *Charter of Rights* is for the most part couched in such broad, vague language that in practice judges have a great deal of discretion in applying its provisions to laws that come before them. The process of applying the *Charter* inevitably involves interpreting its provisions into the likeness favoured by the judges. This problem has been captured in a famous American aphorism: "We are under a Constitution, but the Constitution is what the judges say it is!"

In this article, we argue that, in considering the legitimacy of judicial review, it is helpful to think of such review as part of a "dialogue" between judges and legislatures. At first blush, this concept of dialogue may not seem particularly apt. Given that the Supreme Court of Canada's decisions must be obeyed by the legislatures, one may ask whether a dialogue between judicial and legislative institutions is really possible. Can a legislature "speak" when its laws are subject to the constitutional views of the highest Court? The answer, we suggest, is "Yes, it can," certainly in the vast majority of cases where a judicial decision is open to reversal, modification or avoidance by the competent legislative body. Thus a judgment can spark a public debate in which *Charter* values are more prominent than they would have been otherwise. The legislative body is then in a position to decide on a course of action – the re-enactment of the old law, the enactment of a different law, or the abandonment of the project – that is informed by both the judgment and the public debate that followed it.

Dialogue will not work, of course, if the effect of a judicial decision is to prevent the legislative body whose law has been struck down from pursuing its legislative objective. But this is seldom the case. The first reason why a legislative body is rarely disabled by a judicial decision is the existence in the *Charter of Rights* of the override power of s. 33, under which a legislature can simply insert a "notwithstanding" clause into a statute and thereby liberate the statute from most of the provisions of the *Charter*, including the guarantees of freedom of expression (s. 2(b)) and equality (s. 15). Section 33 was added to the *Charter of Rights* late in the drafting process at the behest of provincial premiers who feared the impact of judicial review on their legislative agendas, and it is the most powerful tool legislatures can use to overcome a *Charter* decision they do not accept.

When the Supreme Court of Canada struck down a Quebec law forbidding the use of English in commercial signs on the ground that the law violated the guarantee of freedom of expression (*Ford*, 1988), Quebec answered by enacting a law that continued to ban the use of English on all outdoor signs. The new law violated the *Charter*'s guarantee of freedom of expression as much as the previous one had, but the province protected it from challenge by inserting a s. 33 notwithstanding clause into it. The Quebec National Assembly recognized that it was restricting the freedom of expression of its anglophone citizens, but concluded that the enhancement of the French language in the province was important enough to justify overriding the *Charter* value.

More recently, when the Supreme Court of Canada held that Alberta's human rights legislation violated the guarantee of equality by not providing protection for discrimination on the ground of sexual orientation (*Vriend*, 1998), there was much debate in the province about re-enacting the law in its old form under the protection of a s. 33 notwithstanding clause. In the end, the Alberta government decided to live with the decision of the Court. But because using the notwithstanding clause to override the decision had been an option, it is clear that this outcome was not forced on the government, but rather was its own choice based on, among other things, what the Court had said about the equality guarantee in the *Charter of Rights*.

Both these cases are examples of the dialogue that s. 33 permits. Admittedly, because of the political climate of resistance to the use of the clause, "notwithstanding" is a tough word for a legislature to use. But making tough political decisions is part of a legislature's job. In the dialogue between courts and legislatures, "notwithstanding" is therefore at least a possible legislative response to most judicial decisions.

The second element of the *Charter of Rights* that facilitates dialogue is Section 1, which provides that the guaranteed rights are subject to "such reasonable limits prescribed by law as can be demonstrably justified in a free and democratic society." In other words, Parliament or a legislature is free to enact a law that infringes on one of the guaranteed rights, provided the law is a "reasonable limit" on the right.

Since 1982, the Supreme Court has established rules for determining whether a law is such a reasonable limit. The rules can be boiled down to: (1) The law must pursue an objective that is sufficiently important to justify limiting a *Charter* right, and (2) it must limit the right no more than is necessary to accomplish the objective. In practice, the Court usually holds that the first requirement is satisfied – that is, the objective of the law is sufficiently important to justify limiting a *Charter* right – and in most cases the area of controversy concerns the second requirement, whether the law limits the right by a means that is the least restrictive of the right.

When a law is struck down because it impairs a *Charter* right more than is necessary to accomplish the legislative objective, then it is obviously open to the legislature to fashion a new law that accomplishes the same objective with provisions that are more respectful of the *Charter* right. Moreover, since the reviewing court that struck down the original law will have explained why the law did not satisfy the s. 1 justification tests, the court's explanation will often suggest to the legislative body exactly how a new law can be drafted that will pursue the desired ends by *Charter*-justified means.

In the Quebec language case, for example, the Supreme Court acknowledged that protection of the French language was a legislative objective that was sufficiently important to justify limiting freedom of expression. However, the Court also held that a complete ban on the use of other languages in commercial signs was too drastic a means of accomplishing the objective, and it suggested that the province could make the use of French mandatory without banning other languages, and could even require that the French wording be predominant on the sign. Such a law, the Court implied, would be justified under s. 1.

As we have explained, the province was not initially inclined to follow this suggestion and simply re-enacted the outright ban under the protection of the notwithstanding clause. However, five years later, when language passions had died down a bit, the province did enact a law of the sort the Supreme Court had suggested, requiring that French be used on commercial signs and be predominant, but permitting the use of other languages.

Many other examples could be given of laws which have been modified and re-enacted following a *Charter* decision. The point is that s. 1 allows dialogue to take place between the courts and the legislatures. Section 1 dialogue facilitates compromise between legislative goals and the courts' judgment on what the *Charter* requires.

Several of the rights guaranteed by the *Charter* are expressed in qualified terms. For example, s. 8 guarantees the right to be secure from "unreasonable" search or seizure. Section 9 guarantees the right not to be "arbitrarily" imprisoned. Section 12 guarantees against "cruel and unusual" punishment. When these rights are violated, the offending law can always be corrected by substituting a law that is not unreasonable, arbitrary, or cruel and unusual.

For example, the enforcement provisions of the *Competition Act* have been struck down on the grounds that they authorized unreasonable searches and seizures contrary to s.8 of the *Charter* (*Hunter*, 1984). So have the comparable provisions of the *Income Tax Act* (*Kruger*, 1984). But in both cases the Supreme Court also laid down guidelines as to how s. 8 could be complied with. What was required was the safeguard of a warrant issued by a judge before government officials could search for evidence. Parliament immediately followed this advice and amended both acts so that they now authorize searches and seizures only on the basis of a warrant issued by a judge. The legislative objective is still achieved, but in a way that is more respectful of the privacy of the individual.

Once again, many other examples could be given, but the essential point is that the very language of the qualified rights encourages a continuing dialogue between the courts and the legislatures.

The proof of the pudding is in the eating, and our research has indicated that most of the decisions of the Supreme Court of Canada in which laws have been struck down for breach of a *Charter* right have in fact been followed by the enactment of a new law. In a study published in 1997 in the *Osgoode Hall Law Journal*, we found that there had been 66 cases in which a law had been struck down by the Supreme Court of Canada for breach of the *Charter of Rights and Freedoms*. Only 13 of these had prompted no legislative response at all, and these 13 included both recent cases, in which there may have been little time to react, and cases in which corrective action was under discussion. In seven of the 66 cases, the legislature simply repealed the law that had been found to violate the *Charter*. In the other 46 cases, a new law was enacted to accomplish the same general objective as the law struck down.

A critique of the *Charter of Rights* based on its supposed usurpation of democratic legitimacy simply cannot be sustained. To be sure, the Supreme Court of Canada is a non-elected, unaccountable group of middle-aged lawyers. To be sure, from time to time the Court strikes down statutes enacted by elected, accountable, representative legislative bodies. But the decisions of the Court almost always leave room for a legislative response, and they usually receive a legislative response. In the end, if the democratic will is there, a legislative way will be found to achieve the objective, albeit with some new safeguards to protect individual rights. Judicial review is not "a veto over the politics of the nation" but rather the beginning of a dialogue on how best to reconcile the individualistic values of the *Charter* with the accomplishment of social and economic policies enacted for the benefit of the community as a whole.

Dialogue or Monologue? A Reply to Hogg and Thornton

F.L. Morton

Policy Options, April 1999. Reprinted with permission.

Peter Hogg argues that the alleged illegitimacy of the courts' new power under the *Charter* is much ado about nothing. According to his theory, the *Charter* encourages a "dialogue" between courts and legislatures. Courts scrutinize legislative means not ends. If courts do try to block an important legislative objective, governments have the option of the final say via the use of the section 33 override power. The result is a democratic process enriched by a new rights dialogue between independent judges and accountable legislators. I will briefly address three of the principal problems that I see in Hogg's "dialogue" defence of the Supreme Court's activist exercise of *Charter* review.

1. Dialogue is a two-way street

Hogg uses a self-serving definition of "dialogue." Obeying orders is not exactly what most of us consider a dialogue. If I go to a restaurant, order a sandwich, and the waiter brings me the sandwich I ordered, I would not count this as a "dialogue." Yet this is how the concept is used in the Hogg-Bushell 1987 study. Hogg counts as dialogue any legislative response to the judicial nullification of a statute. If a government repeals the offending legislation or amends it according to specifications laid out by the Court, this is counts as "dialogue." No wonder Professor Hogg found a two-thirds incidence of dialogue!

This lax operationalization of the concept of dialogue also obscures important differences between types of legislative response. When Parliament added a new search warrant requirement to the *Anti-Combines Act* after *Hunter v. Southam*, it simply did what the Court told it to do. After *Daviault*, by contrast, Parliament created a new offence that explicitly rejected the Court's ruling that self-induced intoxication can be used as a *mens rea defence* against assault charges. Similarly, Quebec's 1988 use of section 33 to avoid compliance with the Court's ruling in the "French-only" public signs case is clearly not on par with the same government's decision in 1993 to comply with the Court's ruling. Yet in the Hogg-Bushell study, these very different responses are all counted equally as "dialogue."

Hogg anticipated this response and declared that even if one excludes cases in which governments simply followed judicial directions," there would still be a significant majority of cases in which the competent legislative body has responded to a *Charter* decision by changing the outcome in a substantive way." It would have been reassuring to have an actual number to attach to "significant majority." It is also hard to reconcile this assertion with Hogg's earlier claim that, "In most cases, relatively minor amendments were all that was required in order to respect the *Charter*." Were most of the 46 legislative responses "minor" or "substantive"? Were governments delivering the sandwich the judges had ordered or were they changing the menu?

2. The means/ends distinction does not bear scrutiny

Another essential element of the dialogue theory is the means/ends distinction. By this account, *Charter* review only impinges on the "how" not the "what" of government policy. Under the "reasonable limitations" provisions of section 1 of the *Charter*, as operationalized by the now famous *Oakes* test, judges review government policy to ensure that legislators have chosen the "least restrictive means" of achieving their policy objectives. When judges believe a policy fails the "least restrictive means" test, it remains open to the responsible government to redraft the legislation to achieve its original goal with more carefully tailored means.

As Rainer Knopff and I have argued elsewhere, the means/ends distinction sounds fine in theory but breaks down in practice. First, politics is as much about means as ends. Everyone wants equal employment opportunities for women and racial minorities, but not everyone favours preferential treatment or quotas as the way to achieve this goal. No respectable person is willing to defend child pornography, but many will argue that restrictions on it must be balanced with our respect for freedom of expression and privacy.

Second, apparent disagreement about means sometimes turns out to be disagreement about ends. Everything depends on the purpose(s) a judge attributes to the statute. The broader the purpose(s), the easier it is to find that the legislation passes the "least restrictive means" test. In fact, any half-clever judge can use procedural objections as a pretense to strike down legislation that he opposes for more substantive reasons. As examples, I would point to the very cases used by Hogg: those involving voluntary religious instruction in Ontario schools and the federal prisoner-voting cases. In both instances, courts initially struck down policies for failing the "least restrictive means" test. In both instances, the responsible governments redrafted the legislation to restrict its impact on religious freedom and voting rights, respectively. And in both instances, the courts again ruled that the new legislation was still "too restrictive" of the rights at stake. In cases such as these, the means/ends distinction becomes a charade for substantive disagreement about public policy.

Perhaps the best example of this instrumental use of procedural objections comes from the Chief Justice of Canada. In the 1988 *Morgentaler* case, Justice Lamer joined Justice Dickson in an opinion striking down the abortion provisions of the Criminal Code because the procedures required to attain a legal abortion were too restrictive and ambiguous. However, speaking on the tenth anniversary of the *Morgentaler* decision, Lamer told law students at the University of Toronto in 1998 that he voted to strike down the abortion law for a very different reason: because a majority of Canadians were against making it a criminal offence. Does this mean that his 1988 procedural objections were simply after-the-fact rationalizations to justify striking down a law that he opposed for other reasons?

3. The staying power of the policy status quo

Hogg assumes that if a government is unhappy with a judicial nullification of one of its policies, then it has the means to reverse it – either by enacting revised legislation or, more emphatically, by re-instating the old law through the use of the section 33 notwithstanding clause. "If the democratic will is there, there will be a legislative way," he declares (p. 4). If a government fails to use the tools at its disposal, that's the government's fault, not the court's.

This account fails to recognize the staying power of a new, judicially created policy status quo (PSQ), especially when the issue cuts across the normal lines of partisan cleavage and divides a government caucus. I develop this argument by adapting Thomas Flanagan's recent analysis of the Mulroney government's response to the Court's 1988 *Morgentaler* ruling.

Contrary to Chief Justice Lamer's beliefs, in 1988 the majority of Canadians were not opposed to the abortion policy that he voted to strike down. Under that policy, abortion was deemed wrong in theory but available in practice. (Dr. Morgentaler and his lawyers could not produce a single witness who had actually been prevented from getting an abortion.) This compromise accurately reflected Canadians' conflicting opinions on the abortion issue. In 1988, 24 percent said that abortion should be legal under any circumstances; 14 percent illegal under any circumstances; and 60 percent legal under certain circumstances.

A recently published study of abortion politics in Canada and the U.S. found that from the late Sixties through the early 1990s "the contours of public opinion towards abortion have been generally unchanged. What exists is a situation where two intense minorities have polarized views of abortion policy that do not represent the feelings of a majority of Americans or Canadians. In both countries, the majority stands to the right of the strongest pro-choice position but left of the absolutist pro-life position."

This pattern of support was replicated in House of Commons voting on the Mulroney government's efforts to enact a new abortion policy after the 1988 *Morgentaler* ruling. The new policy was designed to meet the procedural problems identified in the written judgment of Justices Dickson and Lamer. (The government mistakenly believed that these were the "real" reasons for Justice Lamer's vote.) It left abortion in the Criminal Code, but would have significantly widened access. In its final form, Bill C-43 would have abolished the requirement of committee approval; broadened the definition of health to include "mental and psychological" health; and lifted the "hospitals only" restriction.

The government's "compromise" approach was opposed by both pro-choice and pro-life factions within Parliament, albeit for opposite reasons. Two pro-choice amendments – which basically affirmed the new judicially created policy status quo of "no abortion law" – were easily defeated in the House by votes of 191–29 and 198–20. A strong pro-life amendment, which would have created a more restrictive policy than the one struck down by the Court, received much more support but was narrowly defeated by a vote of 118–105. A paradoxical coalition of pro-choice and pro-life MPs then combined to defeat the government's own compromise proposal by a vote of 147–76.

The following session, the government re-introduced a new compromise abortion policy – Bill C-43. To avoid a repeat of the earlier disaster, Mulroney invoked party discipline for his forty cabinet ministers and warned pro-life MPs that this would be his last attempt. The House then approved the bill by a vote of 140–131. However, it was subsequently defeated by a tie vote (43–43) in the Senate. As in the House of Commons the year before, the pro-choice and pro-life minorities combined to vote against the policy compromise, but in the Senate there were no Cabinet ministers to save it. The new judicially created PSQ of "no law" thus continued by default, not because it commanded majority support in either Parliament or the public.

The defeat of Bill C-43 illustrates a common dynamic between public opinion and Supreme Court decisions on contemporary rights issues. Contrary to the rhetoric of majority rule and minority rights, on most contemporary rights issues there is an unstable and unorganized majority or plurality opinion, bracketed by two opposing activist minorities. In terms of political process, the effect of a Supreme Court *Charter* ruling declaring a policy unconstitutional is to transfer the considerable advantages of the PSQ from one group of minority activists to the other. The ruling shifts the burden of mobilizing a new majority coalition (within voters, within a government caucus and within a legislature) from the winning minority to the losing minority.

This transfer is a significant new advantage for the winning minority. Just as it was impossible for pro-choice activists to persuade either the Trudeau or Mulroney governments to amend Parliament's compromise abortion law of 1969 prior to the Court's *Morgentaler* decision; so after the ruling, it has been equally impossible for pro-life activists to interest the Chrétien government in amending the new judicially created PSQ of no abortion law. The reasons are the same: the issue is not a priority for the government, the opposition parties or the public.

Indeed, the priority for most governments on such "moral issues" is to avoid them as much as possible. Such issues cross-cut normal partisan cleavages and thus fracture party solidarity, from the cabinet to the caucus to the rank and file membership. Nor do they win any new supporters among the (disinterested) majority. To act risks losing support from the activist policy minority you abandon, without securing the support of the activists you help. (After all, you only did what was "just.") On such issues, political self-interest favours government inaction over action.

A similar pattern occurred in Alberta after the Supreme Court's *Vriend* ruling in April, 1998. The Klein Government – and the Conservative Party of Alberta – were deeply divided on whether to add sexual orientation to the *Alberta Human Rights Act*. Two previous task forces had recommended against it, but with minority reports. Gay rights groups had lobbied aggressively for the reform. Social conservatives – a force to be reckoned with in Alberta politics – were just as strongly opposed. For the majority of Albertans, it was an issue of secondary importance.

When the Supreme Court "read in" sexual orientation to the *Alberta Human Rights Act*, there was a strong public outcry – especially among the rural wing of the Alberta Tories – to invoke section 33. After a week of public debate, the Cabinet was as divided as before. In the end, Premier Klein declared that his personal preference was not to invoke section 33 and a majority of the caucus fell into line.

Describing the Alberta government's decision to "live with" the *Vriend* ruling, Hogg writes: "But because 'notwithstanding' was an option, it is clear that this outcome was not forced on the Government, but was the Government's own choice." Hogg is only half right in this assertion. He ignores that the Court's decision decisively changed the government's options. The government's preferred choice was not to act at all – to simply leave the old PSQ in place. The Court destroyed this and – with the clever use of the "reading in" technique – created a new PSQ.

Prior to the ruling, the government could safely ignore the issue – upsetting only a small coalition of activists, few of whom were Tory supporters in any case. After the ruling, the government had to choose between accepting the judicially created PSQ or invoking the notwithstanding clause – a decision that it knew would be strongly criticized in the national media and that risked creating a backlash among otherwise passive government supporters. The judicial ruling significantly raised the political costs of saying "no" to the winning minority. For the same reason that the Klein government had refused to alter the old PSQ, it now accepted the new judicially created PSQ. In both instances, the safest thing to do was to do nothing.

Hogg writes that judicial nullification of a statute "rarely raises an absolute barrier to the wishes of democratic institutions." He is right in his observation, but wrong in his conclusion. It does not have to be an absolute barrier. Depending on the circumstances, a small barrier may suffice to permanently alter public policy.

To conclude, Hogg's theory must be qualified to account for different circumstances. A government's ability to respond to judicial nullification of a policy depends on a variety of factors. When the policy is central to the government's program, the government should have little difficulty mustering the political will to respond effectively. Examples of this pattern of dialogue would include the Quebec government's use of notwithstanding in response to Ford and the Devine government's overruling of the Saskatchewan Court of Appeal's rejection of its back-to-work legislation.

By contrast, when the issue cuts across partisan allegiances and divides the government caucus; when public opinion is fragmented between a relatively indifferent middle bracketed by two opposing groups of policy activists – the judicial creation of a new PSQ may suffice to tip the balance in favour of one minority interest over that of their adversaries. Both *Morgentaler* and *Vriend* illustrate this pattern of response. Some of course will applaud these practical results. Others, such as my colleague Rainer Knopff, would see them as further examples of how courts are "more apt to intensify than moderate the tendency to Tupperism in political life."

To conclude, what Professor Hogg describes as a dialogue is usually a monologue, with judges doing most of the talking and legislatures most of the listening. Hogg suggests that the failure of a government to respond effectively to judicial activism is a matter of personal courage, or the lack thereof, on the part of government leaders. The fault, if there is any, rests with individuals.

By contrast, I am suggesting that legislative paralysis is institutional in character: that legislative non-response in the face of judicial activism is the "normal" response in certain circumstances. When the issue in play is

cross-cutting and divides a government caucus, the political incentive structure invites government leaders to abdicate responsibility to the courts – perhaps even more so in a parliamentary as opposed to a presidential system. If
I am correct, the Canadian tradition of "responsible government" is in for a
rough ride in our brave new world of *Charter* democracy.

12.8

Checking the Court: Justifying Parliament's Role in Constitutional Interpretation
Dennis Baker

Supreme Court Law Review 73, no. 2 (2016), 1–16. Reproduced with
permission by LexisNexis Canada Inc.

For some, particularly within the Canadian legal and chattering classes, the
Supreme Court of Canada (SCC) has been viewed as the "oracular" source of
Canadian constitutional law. It is treated as "supreme" not only in the sense that
it is the top of the judicial hierarchy – with lower courts applying its judgments
to new cases as they arise – but also "supreme" as the authoritative and exclusive interpreter of what the Constitution demands and requires. Non judicial
actors, like executives and the legislatures, must operate within constitutional
boundaries that only the Court can identify. Or so it is commonly assumed.

This "judicial supremacy" orthodoxy misstates the relationship between
Canada's institutions and delegitimizes non-judicial sources of constitutional
law. An increasingly popular view is that constitutional law may come from
only two sources: the formal constitutional documents and the judicial interpretations of them. Whereas once Parliament was clearly an accepted source
of constitutional law, it is now more commonly perceived as the subject being
bound or limited by constitutional law, and rarely thought of as an active participant in its creation. Parliament continues to be recognized as part of the
broad constitutional machinery and every statute is presumed constitutional
until proven otherwise, but many reject the proposition I wish to advance: that
Parliament can and should participate in the interpretation and meaning of the
Constitution. Moreover, it can do so through ordinary legislation....

In 2007, [Supreme Court] Justices LeBel and Rothstein would bluntly tell
us that "in our system, the Supreme Court has the final word on the interpretation of the Constitution." The Court now speaks as if its interpretive authority
is certain. But where does this power come from? It is not textual: section 52 of

the *Constitution Act, 1982*, affirms the Constitution as the "supreme law" but says nothing about its interpretation and fails to mention the judicial branch at all; section 24 of the same *Act* does refer to "courts of competent authority" but makes it clear the broad remedial power ("any such remedy the court considers appropriate and just in the circumstances") is to be exercised in discrete cases for particular litigants. While these textual provisions ensure the judiciary plays a leading role in the implementation and enforcement of the Constitution, they are a weak foundation for an authoritative power of interpretation that excludes all other governing institutions. The failure of the text to assign an interpretive power was unlikely to be an oversight.... The 1982 Framers could have cut short any Canadian variant of this debate with a provision that would simply say "The Constitution of Canada shall be interpreted by the Supreme Court of Canada." Instead, the constitutional silence on the interpretive power allows space for an inter-institutional approach that ensures that even the institution most likely to wield interpretive power regularly remains not quite supreme. While courts are always going to be the institution of first resort for interpretive controversies, a parliamentary check is constitutionally appropriate.

Such a parliamentary check on judicial interpretive authority is useful for at least three reasons: (1) judges make mistakes, (2) judges takes sides in reasonable disagreements and (3) judges make ambiguous rulings. Each of these justifications can be illustrated by a case sequence that demonstrates how a parliamentary intervention – in the form of an ordinary statute – made for better constitutional law.

1. Judges Make Mistakes: *Daviault*

Because they are human, judges will make mistakes. The Supreme Court of Canada has made some clear, incontrovertible errors: the 30,000 criminal charges dropped in the wake of the Court's wonky social science in *Askov* and the *Marshall* decision on aboriginal treaty rights, which required a "clarification" two months after it was delivered, are obvious examples. We should not be surprised by the reality of judicial error. The simple fact is that institutions make mistakes whenever humans are involved in decision-making. Parliament, of course, makes errors too – perhaps even more frequently. As economist Neil Komesar argues, the question of judicial versus legislative decision-making is really the choice between "imperfect alternatives." One strategy for addressing the inevitable errors is to allow for iterative institutional responses.

An example of iterative correction is the judicial-legislative sequence arising out of the Supreme Court's very unpopular and troubling decision in *R. v. Daviault*. In 1994, the Court ordered a new trial for Henri Daviault, who had been convicted of sexually assaulting a 65-year-old and partially paralyzed woman. Abandoning earlier common law precedent, the Court found that Daviault had unconstitutionally been denied the defence of intoxication – that he was too drunk to form the mental element of the offence – at trial. The bottom line was that the Court made extreme intoxication a constitutionally guaranteed defence to sexual assault. Needless to say, the public face of the decision – the notion that drunken men should be allowed to rape with impunity – proved controversial.

Jean Chrétien's Liberal Government responded to the decision nine months later with s.33.1 of the *Criminal Code of Canada*.... Far from completely rejecting *Daviault*, the provision distinguishes between two kinds of situations: 1) if the offence is an assault or interference with bodily integrity, no intoxication defence is available; 2) where bodily integrity is not at issue, the defence remains viable. *Daviault* remains "good law" even after the enactment of s.33.1, but it is confined to certain types of offences – so, for example, extreme intoxication remains a defence to offences related to property damage. Parliament overturned the specific result in *Daviault* – on sexual assault – but did so in a thoughtful and respectful way that recognized the general importance of the offender's mental state but accommodated the societal judgment that an extreme drunkenness defence was inappropriate for violent and sexual offences....

It is often suggested that if the Government holds a different understanding of the Constitution than the one offered by the Court, the legitimate expression of that differing opinion is through the section 33 notwithstanding clause and, if it has any questions about a creative response to a judicial decision, it should refer its new legislation to the Court. In the case of the *Daviault* response, Justice Minister Rock considered but rejected calls to refer the legislation to the Supreme Court, and, despite the suggestion that the notwithstanding clause could be invoked, Rock decided to proceed with ordinary legislation on the basis that it was the most appropriate response. He preferred a factual record in any lower court challenges to an abstract reference, and he implied that the legislation did not require a pre-emptive use of s.33.... Invoking section 33 would leave the legislature vulnerable to the charge that it does not value section 7 – or the due process it protects – when it is simply offering a competing vision of how the right might be better implemented. While the use of ordinary legislation to achieve constitutional ends has been referred to as "notwithstanding-by-stealth," there is nothing secretive or hidden about a publicly promulgated statute contesting a judicially-invented extension of the constitutional text....

Despite the initial expectations of legal observers that the legislation would provide the next big opportunity for the Court to engage in "dialogue," a straight-up challenge to the provision has never reached the Supreme Court, largely because cases invoking the defence are, for strategic reasons, rarely appealed. Several lower courts in Ontario have found s.33.1 to be unconstitutional while several others (particularly in Quebec) have found it to be constitutional. But there are no cases where an appellate court has found s.33.1 to be unconstitutional and acquitted the accused on the basis of the intoxication defence. So the defence has proven to be *practically* unavailable. Moreover, in the 2011 case of *Bouchard-Lebrun* the Supreme Court, sidestepping the constitutional issue for technical reasons, approved the use of s.33.1 to convict an accused. It is difficult to believe that the Court would permit a law they considered unconstitutional to cause a serious conviction. It is far more likely … that the Court has tacitly changed its mind about the drunkenness defence in bodily integrity cases....

2. Judges Take Sides in Reasonable Disagreements: *Mills*

While *Daviault* might be considered a case where the Court simply got it wrong, the controversies raised by judicial decisions are more often related to the Court's taking a position on a matter where reasonable disagreement is possible. In these cases, Parliament can play an important – and sometimes decisive – role in challenging the Court's attempted resolution of a controversy where both sides present positions compliant with the Constitution. Since they are insulated from public pressures by design, courts may be ill-suited for choosing between legally-defensible policy alternatives, especially if the policy area involves the articulation of broad societal choices. By comparison, Parliament, as the representative institution, has a greater claim to being able to speak for the nation and resolve – at least temporarily – reasonable disagreements. To some extent, this is recognized by even shallow versions of the dialogue approach, with Parliament selecting from options within the constitutional boundaries identified by the Court. Where it becomes more contentious is when there are reasonable disagreements among the judges themselves as to what is constitutionally permissible. In such cases, Parliament may assist the Court in resolving its own internal disagreements.

A second sequence of cases, the *O'Connor-Mills* sequence, is illustrative of the potential role for Parliament in settling constitutional disputes. In *O'Connor* and *Mills*, the admissibility of therapeutic records of sexual assault held by third parties was at stake. Essentially, the question in both cases was whether the accused in a sexual assault case can get access to the records that are held not by the Crown but by rape counselors the victim has visited....

In the 1995 case of *O'Connor*, the Court made its first attempt at striking that balance. They divided 5-4 on the issue. Everyone on the bench agreed that two major values were at stake: (1) the accused's constitutional right to "full answer and defence" – basically the right to make the best defense possible to the charge, and (2) the complainant's privacy rights. Neither side accepted the extremes – no defendant is entitled to a fishing expedition into the records, nor should there be an absolute prohibition against admitting such records. Both sides of the 5-4 split agreed that balancing is necessary and each side came up with a process for arriving at the balance. For the majority, the balance must be tipped to the accused, largely to be consistent with the general asymmetrical norms of criminal justice, which presume innocence and require a greater evidentiary burden to be put upon the prosecution than the accused. For the 4-judge minority, the balance must reflect the societal interest of encouraging victims to seek out therapeutic services and thus the balance must skew towards privacy. What is clear from any reading of *O'Connor*, however, is the absence of any incontrovertible *legal* reason to favor one side or the other. The 5-4 split is entirely dependent on how one orders the interests to be protected. This is an *inherently* political choice.

The *O'Connor* majority decision favouring the accused over the victim with respect to the use of sexual counselling records at trial was as publicly unpopular as the *Daviault* decision in favour of the accused, and, once again, the Chrétien Government passed new legislation to challenge the judicial decision. Its new legislation, Bill C-46, *An Act to Amend the Criminal Code on the Production of Record in Sexual Offence Proceeding*, essentially adopted – sometimes word for word – the position of the 4-judge judicial minority, allowing trial judges to consider the societal impact of admitting the records. This is perhaps the best Canadian example of the two institutions working together to develop constitutional law, with the Court effectively setting out a menu of plausible legal alternatives – none of them obviously correct – and Parliament choosing between them. While this sequence of institutional interactions seems appropriate to some, it causes proponents of judicial interpretive supremacy to react in dismay: "how can Parliament be allowed to reverse a 5-4 judgment?!" The answer is that the majoritarian processes of the Court are important internally – so that each judge is equal to every other judge – but of *no* significance externally. If we are prepared to accept the proposition that any opinion supported by four judges of the Court is at least a *reasonable* answer to a legal question, then it is hard to suggest that Parliament's pursuit of that reasonable legal alternative is impermissible.

And, indeed, this is what the Court itself accepted. In the subsequent case of *Mills*, the Court upheld the constitutionality of Bill C-46 even though it clearly departed from the majority opinion that ought to have been legally determinative from the standpoint of judicial supremacy. Most tellingly, two of the judges in the 5-judge majority of *O'Connor* (Justices Iacobucci and Major) are also in the *Mills* majority, thus endorsing the policy they had already voted against when it was originally put forward by the *O'Connor* dissenters. These Justices do not explain their switch, but the most likely explanation is that, in the context of striking a difficult balance between competing interests, Parliament's judgment should be given some weight. Just as in *Daviault*, Parliament was able to substantially change the interpretation of the Constitution through ordinary legislation.

3. Judges Make Ambiguous Decisions: *Bedford*

Parliament can play an even more productive role in forcing the Court to clarify its own decisions and justify its own premises. The Harper Government's response to the 2013 *Bedford* prostitution decision, Bill C-36, *The Protection of Communities and Exploited Persons Act*, is a good example of an effective response to what is an ambiguous decision. The Court ruled that certain criminal laws regulating prostitution are unconstitutional under section 7 of the *Charter* because they made a legal activity – prostitution – unsafe. For example, prohibiting a bawdy-house prevents sex workers from collectively creating a safe working environment and prohibiting living off the avails of prostitution prevents the hiring of bodyguards. What is unclear or ambiguous in the Court's formulation is whether the Constitution requires prostitution to remain a legal activity and to what extent the Court's result is contingent on the continued legality of prostitution. On the one hand, the Court noted that the case was "not about whether prostitution should be legal or not," which suggests that it might be open to the government to make it explicitly illegal....

On the other hand, there is much in the decision that suggests that prostitution cannot be constitutionally criminalized. The judgment begins starkly by noting that "[i]t is not a crime in Canada to sell sex for money" and then peppers this notion throughout the decision, repeating that it is legal to engage in prostitution at least seven more times. Moreover, in a key passage, Chief Justice McLachlin, writing for a unanimous Court, equates the freedom to prostitute one's self to any other obviously legal freedom: "[a]n analogy could be drawn to a law preventing a cyclist from wearing a helmet. That the cyclist chooses to ride her bike does not diminish the causal role of the law in making that activity riskier." In other words, a law prohibiting helmets makes cycling unconstitutionally dangerous in the same way that prohibiting bawdy houses and "living off the avails" endangers prostitutes. But this analogy works only if the constitutional criminalization of prostitution is as inconceivable as the prohibition of cycling. If prostitution *can* be constitutionally criminalized – as cycling obviously could not be – then we are back to the oddity of complaining about unsafe conditions for an illegal activity. In short, McLachlin's helmet analogy strongly suggests that prostitution cannot be directly prohibited....

In Bill C-36, the government has taken a clear stand on this interpretive ambiguity by making the act of prostitution itself illegal. In this way, the response to *Bedford* would make what was *implicit* in the earlier legal framework *explicit*: all acts of prostitution are to be discouraged and would now be illegal but, in the public interest, sex workers will not be prosecuted (the customers – or "Johns" – are not similarly immune from prosecution).... It is clear from the drafting of the *Act* that [prostitution] is surely criminal, even if one party – presumed to be a vulnerable person – is shielded from criminal consequences.

With these new provisions, the entire context of the *Bedford* decision is radically shifted. In terms of its compliance with *Bedford*, it was difficult for even opponents of the legislation to call it an outright repudiation of the Court's decision.... In any future challenge, the Court will be prevented from making the "legal act" argument that was part of its *Bedford* decision. The new legislation makes clear Parliament's view that the commodification of sex is undesirable and all ancillary measures should be understood as part of a general strategy to deter participation in the activity. Regardless of whether one approves of the direction taken by the legislation, it is a "dialogic" response to the Court's decision.... Any [future] decision by the Court will need to be more clear about what section 7 demands and, if the Constitution requires legalized prostitution, then the Court will have to say precisely that....

An Unequal but Persistent Dialogue

In each of the circumstances discussed above – when the judiciary makes mistakes, when they weigh in on one side of a reasonable disagreement, and when they make ambiguous rulings – a parliamentary check is justified. This does not mean that, when it comes to the interpretation of the constitution, Parliament and the Courts must be treated as equals. Given their expertise and more frequent encounters with interpretive controversies, it is quite understandable that the Court would take a *leading* role in interpretive matters. Such leadership, however, need not preclude the participation of other institutions, and, indeed, an exclusive power over interpretation would leave Canadians with little practical recourse when confronted with questionable rulings from the Supreme Court. The real promise of dialogue is its potential to limit institutional mistakes and confine their damage through iterations of inter-institutional responses. As an added benefit of such an approach, any concerns about parliamentary participation in constitutional law can be assuaged with the knowledge that there can be subsequent judicial review of that participation. As long as no institution can claim final interpretive supremacy, our politics and our laws can constantly interact, in concert or in conflict, to produce constitutional law that best serves the nation and its citizens.

12.9

The Charter and Canada's New Political Culture: Are We All Ambassadors Now?

Chief Justice Glenn D. Joyal, Manitoba Court of Queen's Bench

Originally delivered at the Canadian Constitution Foundation's Law and Freedom Conference, January 6, 2017. Reprinted with permission.

Tonight, ladies and gentlemen, I feel very much like the shy and timid church organist who, on a rare Friday night, gets to sneak out to a local smoky bar and play electric piano with a group of exciting but somewhat subversive jazz musicians.

I say that in part because my talk this evening will not address many of the more mundane administrative or operational subjects about which a Chief Justice typically speaks out. Instead, my topic this evening is a topic of a more foundational nature, touching important aspects of public law.

I have entitled my talk: "The Charter and Canada's New Political Culture: Are We All Ambassadors Now?"

As the title might suggest, tonight, I want to talk to you about Canada's current political culture, the Charter and the somewhat uneasy and uneven institutional relationship that exists as between the judiciary and the legislative branch.

It is my position that the new Canadian political culture has been in part, both caused by and now, very much reflects, what has been over the last 35 years, an increasing judicial dominance in that judicial/legislative institutional relationship.

The subtextual and sometimes explicit question that I want to raise this evening, is whether the state of that relationship should be so reflexively applauded and, in different ways, promoted.

Regrettably, my position this evening will be advanced with all of the superficiality and conclusory reasoning that the limits of time require and that judges generally abhor. Nonetheless, I should feel more than satisfied if my remarks provide any of you some source or reference for future reflection.

So let's start with some context.

Many many years ago, in my misspent youth, I completed a Master's Thesis entitled "Traditional Canadian Political Culture Adrift in the Era of the Charter." "Adrift" as in floating somewhat aimlessly and with uncertainty. That thesis was written in the comparatively early days of the Canadian Charter of Rights and Freedoms. Fast forward to the present day.

In 2017 and in the current era of the Charter, Canadian political culture is no longer adrift. Canadian political culture, in my humble view ladies and gentlemen, has now fundamentally changed.

For those who are concerned about maintaining an institutional balance as between a strong and robust judiciary and an equally purposeful and respected legislative branch, this fundamental change in the Canadian political culture is not without consequence.

This evening, I hope to explain why.

Political culture is an extraordinarily useful and relevant concept, especially for keen students, like yourselves, who are interested in the evolution of the Canadian Constitution and constitutional history generally.

What is political culture? Broadly defined, a political culture reflects the attitudes and beliefs that citizens and its specific institutional actors hold about the political system. Political culture can also be seen as the conglomeration of ideas and attitudes which set the parameters in which debate over policy justifications take place. A political culture is in part revealed and transmitted through a polity's public discourse. In this context, language can both encode and shape attitudes, outlooks and assumptions about politics and institutions.

Strong hints about a political culture can also be revealed through legislation. National or local laws will frequently reflect a polity's values and beliefs and will in the process, depending upon the manner in which the legislative "solution" is formulated and defined, highlight, emphasize and reinforce a society's prioritization of values, attitudes and beliefs.

Political culture shapes the perception of politically relevant problems and further affects what people perceive are the appropriate areas of governmental and institutional action.

Tonight, I will suggest that Canada's new political culture is largely dominated by attitudes and beliefs now held by a broad cross-section of the Canadian citizenry and its institutional actors, which attitudes and beliefs suggest an almost unconditional willingness to accept or endorse the idea of judicial adjudications in respect of what are often complex and even insoluble social and political problems. What were once political issues are now frequently transformed into legal issues.

This transformation of political issues into legal issues, often on the basis of new rights, has led to a new institutional dynamic as between the judiciary and the legislative branch.

Given the principle of constitutional supremacy, it is now an institutional relationship in which the legislative branch frequently occupies a diminished and even inferior role. It is in the discussions surrounding this new institutional relationship and dynamic, that incendiary questions are sometimes raised about the judicialization of politics and the politicization of the judiciary.

While this new reality may be both a cause and now, a reflection of Canada's new political culture, it is for many who study Canadian history, an unanticipated development that was not envisioned nor necessarily desired by the 1982 compromise that led to the adoption of the Charter.

Indeed, as I will explain, the 1982 compromise was, in part, a response to those who raised institutional concerns about an enhanced policy-making role for the judiciary under the Charter. Many, like the Canadian constitutional scholar Peter Russell, feared that an enhanced judicial policy-making role would precipitate "a flight from politics." A "flight from politics" that Russell said would cause "a deepening disillusionment with the procedures of representative government, and government by discussion as a means of resolving fundamental questions of political justice."

You'll hear more about the "flight from politics" later.

I set out a few minutes ago the quixotic title of this evening's talk, "The Charter in Canada's New Political Culture: Are We All Ambassadors Now?" The somewhat incongruous reference to the ambassadorial role comes from a speech recently given at the University of British Columbia by Canada's Attorney General and Minister of Justice, The Honourable Jody Wilson-Raybould. In a very genuine and earnest reference, Minister Wilson-Raybould explained to the students, that she saw herself as being "the ambassador for the Charter."

It should be noted that the definition of the ambassadorial task includes the acts of "promoting," "championing" and "protecting." With her reference to the ambassadorial role, the Minister was perhaps spontaneously demonstrating through her rhetorical enthusiasm, the very institutional and attitudinal changes that so reflect the new political culture.

The Minister is hardly alone in her celebration of the Charter. To the contrary, most institutional actors in the Canadian polity seem similarly unconditional in their willingness to play a role championing and promoting the Charter.

Whether one speaks of the legal profession, the legal academy, the opposition parties of the day, the citizenry, the media and, of course, the judiciary, the spirit of "Charter values" has been enthusiastically adopted and endorsed. In other words, "Charter values" – whatever that means – is now not only an interpretative term of art emanating from Supreme Court of Canada jurisprudence, it also now serves as a somewhat self-congratulatory reference point for defining the Canadian identity.

An enthusiasm for the Charter or, as Professor Alan Cairns called it a "Charter patriotism," is on one level, certainly understandable. The Charter is in many ways a unique and potentially nuanced constitutional instrument that in 1982, grew out of what Edmund Burke might have identified as the particular harmony and hidden wisdom of a nation's social and political history. There is much to admire in a document which provides important protections in relation to areas of criminal justice, minority rights, group rights, equality, and the lines demarcating the public and private sphere, more generally. Indeed, there is much to admire about how the judiciary has generally applied and enforced those rights.

Put simply, as a foundational part of Canada's constitutional architecture, the Charter deserves our respect and demands our compliance.

Yet, to the extent that we, as Canadian citizens and we as institutional actors, rarely raise questions about the resulting new and imbalanced relationship between the judiciary and the legislative branch, and to the extent that we rarely raise connected questions about the broader implications for the Canadian polity, we risk a consequential intellectual complacency.

In a political culture without such foundational questions being raised, it is not unreasonable to ask whether we are not all ambassadors now, through complacency or by default.

Tonight, in the face of so many domestic Canadian ambassadors, I ask the question whether in Canada's new political culture, there remains any intellectual space in which genuine concerns can be raised and debated about a potential institutional imbalance that has, and will continue to have, implications for the Canadian polity.

For the rest of my talk, I want to deal with the question I have raised by breaking it down and addressing two points:

First, I wish to address in slightly more detail, how Canadian political culture has changed and, in that context, why, the somewhat uneven judicial/legislative institutional relationship has to a significant degree, contributed to that change.

Second, I want to address the implications and consequences of this uneven institutional relationship as it relates to the broader Canadian polity.

So let's start with what I allege is the change in Canadian political culture, a change that I also say is both caused by and reflects the current uneven institutional relationship that exists between the judicial and legislative branch.

***

If one is going to describe a change, one must be able to point to what existed before the change.

So let me take a moment to describe what I suggest was the traditional Canadian political culture in the years prior to the era that has followed the 1982 entrenchment of the Charter. I do so with some humility as I must acknowledge that the nature of Canada's political culture has always been the subject of much debate.

The degree to which liberal, collectivist and communitarian values have been seen to dominate or share Canada's political culture has depended upon the manner in which Canadian intellectual and ideological history has been interpreted.

That debate, however, in no way questions or casts doubt on the comparatively strong role of the legislative branch in Canadian history.

Indeed, throughout its history, Canadian citizens have respected and deferred to the role of their federal and provincial governments to act in purposeful ways, irrespective of whether those governments were situated in or on the centre, left or right of the political spectrum.

That sort of "purposeful" governance was expected to include and achieve on the one hand, the realization of big and bold federal and provincial objectives. On the other hand, it was also expected to assist in the accommodation and brokering of the diverse and conflicting interests underlying the various societal ills and problems that regularly presented in a physically vast and politically complex federation.

This Canadian version of purposeful governance was inextricably linked to a concern for the larger community, a concern that cohered not to the perceived American commitment to "life, liberty and the pursuit of happiness," but rather to what became the Canadian constitutional cliché of "peace, order and good government."

Despite this obvious concern for the concept of a broader national or provincial community, and the purposeful role of the accompanying governments who nurtured it, it is my contention and the contention of many Canadian historians, that prior to the era of the Charter, traditional Canadian political culture can be explained as having been shaped largely by attitudes which were consistent with and sympathetic to the core of the liberal ideal – attitudes which convey respect for the individual and for liberty.

Importantly, however, and it is important, there was at the same time in this Canadian political culture, another very significant, idiosyncratic and enduring quality. That idiosyncratic and enduring quality related to the general degree to which Canadian political culture remained ideologically open. This ideological openness permitted a distinctly Canadian liberal and non-liberal value mix.

Let me try to be more concrete.

Some Canadian social historians believe, for example, that the loyalist settlement was a formative event that was part of a counter-revolution to the American revolution. This counter-revolution created in Canada, what some have called the "tory touch." This "tory touch" implies that despite a dominant attachment to the ideal of individual liberty, Canada did, during its evolution, adopt from European conservatism, a sensibility that tolerated a degree of state intervention in certain spheres of societal life. That "tory touch," along with subsequent phases of immigration that brought significant social democratic influences from the European left, created in Canada an ideological diversity similar to European societies, but one with a decidedly more liberal cast.

This instinctively esteemed liberal element, tempered as it was with note-worthy strains of European Toryism and the rudiments of a social democratic emphasis on the collective, enabled Canadians to value their freedoms as jeal-ously as the Americans, and at the same time, to point to important distinctions.

These distinctions were based on and fostered by, amongst other things, the nature of Canadian legislation and the prevailing public discourse. Canadian legislation and its prevailing public discourse frequently reflected the collec-tivist and communitarian aspects of Canada's incoming European ideologies. That legislation and public discourse, revealed as well, an attitudinal tone which in part, shaped what Canadians thought about their political system and its institutions.

So it's in the context of this traditional political culture – where the leg-islative branch was both highly respected and comparatively strong and bold – that Canada's less dominant but always present tory, social democratic and collectivist-communitarian strains were so well served.

At the risk of seeming to romanticize a golden age that never completely existed, I am going to nonetheless suggest that these less dominant ideological strains were well served by the coexisting processes of conciliation, compro-mise and consensus. These processes were an integral part of the usually mod-erate ideological party positioning which takes place in a liberal democracy where an elected Parliament remains purposeful, accountable and supreme.

***

So if what I have just discussed constitutes more or less what had been, prior to 1982, Canada's traditional political culture, how, in the years following 1982, did the fundamental change occur? More specifically, why do I say that the change is both caused by and is now reflected in the new relationship between the judiciary and the legislative branch?

Any attempt to understand the nature and cause of the post-1982 changes in Canadian political culture begins with a recognition of what was the 1982 Constitutional compromise and the accompanying common understandings that made the adoption of the Charter possible. It is only by acknowledging some of those common understandings that one sees how the judicial branch de-emphasized those understandings. By failing to more fully shape its role in light of those common understandings, the judiciary has created an unantici-pated new relationship as between itself and the legislative branch.

Time does not permit an adequate review of the background and context of the 1982 repatriation initiative which led to the adoption of the Charter. It is enough to remember that the repatriation of the Constitution and the ultimate entrenchment of the Charter had been for some time prior to 1982, a goal of the Federal Government. The goal of entrenching a Charter of Rights was seen as a key ingredient in the Federal Government's nation building strategy from 1967 to 1982. This strategy coincided with what were admittedly, certain emerging international trends in relation to the recognition of universal human rights, new norms of statehood, and more expansive notions of citizenship.

Despite these trends, it should never be forgotten that in the context of the Federal Government's initiatives from 1968 to 1981, most provincial gov-ernments, to a greater or lesser degree, opposed the adoption of the sort of Charter that the Federal Government wanted as the centrepiece of any patria-tion package. Some of the provincial opposition was based on hesitation which arose from an intense loyalty to what was perceived as Canada's British parlia-mentary tradition. The Charter was seen by these opponents as an instrument which was irreconcilable with the concept of legislative supremacy. These op-ponents were also mindful of some of what occurred during the development of American constitutional law and the extent to which an entrenched Bill of Rights had created an extremely potent judiciary. These premiers and provin-cial officials were very concerned by what they were witnessing in the United States in terms of the manner of judicial interpretation and innovation which they believed served to circumvent the power of elected representatives.

In addition to the institutional or parliamentary purists and those who feared the sort of innovation associated with the American Supreme Court, there were still other premiers who simply felt that duly elected legislatures were better positioned than appointed judges when it came to the matter of protecting individual and community rights.

So with that opposition in mind, the agreement ultimately reached by Pierre Elliott Trudeau and nine provinces in November of 1981, must be seen as the negotiated accord that it was. As with any such agreement, it contains the results of a "give and take," a "give and take" that was required to win over opposition. When one examines the nature of the negotiations and the tradeoffs leading up to the agreement, it should be clear that the patriation package constitutes a tough political compromise. That compromise brokered certain common understandings which, amongst other things, were able to assuage the concerns and interests of those on both the right and the left who worried about both the loss of legislative supremacy and what they realized was going to be, inevitably, a new judicial/legislative relationship.

The tough political compromise that was attained nonetheless succeeded in mirroring much of the liberal and non-liberal value mix that had historically made up traditional Canadian political culture. The very inclusion of s. 1 and s. 33 represented an effort to find an acceptable balance between individual rights and majoritarian democracy.

By its nature, the compromise of 1982 envisioned, through its included balancing mechanisms and terminology, what the framers thought would now be, by necessity, a more nuanced but still balanced relationship as between the judiciary and the legislative branch. The essence of the 1982 compromise and some of the accompanying common understanding can be summarized as follows:

Common Understanding No. 1
(1) Concessions were made to both the communitarian and liberal elements as they found expression in both the individual rights guarantees, and those provisions guaranteeing group rights.

Common Understanding No. 2
(2) The compromise was based on a premise of positivism grounded on a consensus as to the necessarily limited number of specifically enumerated individual and group rights identified. That is to say, there was an understanding that the legal protections, while requiring some eventual interpretation and particularization, would be those that were enacted by the framers. There was no suggestion of hidden rights or principles that awaited discovery by human reason. The drafters wanted the courts to be mindful of what rights were specifically prescribed and which were excluded.

Common Understanding No. 3
(3) The specifically chosen phrase for s. 7, "fundamental justice," was intended to be interpreted so as to limit the judiciary's review only to the procedural adequacy of legislation. The drafters and the framers of the Charter were not prepared to relinquish to the courts the right to question the substantive adequacy

of their legislation. In fact, no section caused the drafters more concern than what was to become s. 7. One of the drafters of the Charter was, at the time, Federal Assistant Deputy Minister of public law, Mr. Barry Strayer, Q.C., who later went on to become a much respected judge of the Federal Court of Appeal.

Mr. Strayer, as he then was, testified before a joint Parliamentary committee about what was understood and intended by the drafters in respect of the phrase "fundamental justice." Fearing the worst excesses of the American experience with the phrase "due process of law," the drafters specifically chose the phrase "fundamental justice" which was specifically meant to not go beyond procedural fairness. Put simply and perhaps bluntly, the drafters wanted to avoid any language that would mandate substantive review and that would have the effect of permitting s. 7 to be interpreted to mean just about anything that could attract five votes on the Supreme Court of Canada.

Common Understanding No. 4

(4) The inclusion of s. 1 expressly recognized that individual rights will sometimes yield to the broader collective good.

Common Understanding No. 5

(5) The inclusion of s. 33 – the notwithstanding clause – was meant to signal to the courts a caution, a caution in respect of any misconception that the judiciary might have were they, the judiciary, inclined to give the absolutely most expansive scope to the enumerated Charter rights. It is reasonable to assume that it was expected that the interpretation of those substantive Charter rights would be restrained by and discerned with reference to the liberal, non-liberal value mix characteristic of Canada's political culture.

In this regard, as Chief Justice Dickson would later and properly note in *R. v. Big M Drug Mart Ltd.*, [1985] 1 S.C.R. 295 at 344, while a substantive Charter right deserved a generous interpretation, it was nonetheless important to not "overshoot" the actual purpose of the right. It would be necessary for the judiciary to recall that the Charter was "not enacted in a vacuum."

Those are some of the common understandings of the 1982 compromise.

Irrespective of whether one agrees or disagrees with the intellectual merits of the ideas or the motivations that underlie those common understandings, as facts, they can be substantiated a priori or by the historical record. They do constitute the background and context for the 1982 compromise, a compromise that made the adoption of the Charter possible. Accordingly, those common understandings should now inform, at the very least, any study of Canada's constitutional history and the subsequent evolution of the judicial/legislative relationship.

I'll acknowledge again that the framers of the Charter would have been realistic enough to realize that the Charter did contain many open-ended provisions. Those open-ended provisions, with undefined terminology, would eventually have to be particularized by the courts. Nonetheless, it was thought that the public debate of the day and the specifically limited number of purposely-included rights would provide sufficient guide posts for the judiciary, a judiciary that I would contend was expected in certain areas in the years ahead to be more restrained than turned out to be the case.

***

So if that was the nature of the 1982 compromise, a compromise that seemed to reflect in many respects the traditional liberal and non-liberal value mix along with the desired institutional balance between the judicial and legislative branches, what happened in the following 35 years?

Well, a few things actually. While time does not permit a catalogue review of the specific, relevant and related cases, certain judicial approaches and analytical choices must be mentioned.

Let's start with the judiciary's approach to the concept of justiciability, which expanded the breadth of issues and subjects that could now be dealt with by the courts. There was also the judiciary's new approach under the Charter to "standing," which significantly relaxed previously existing rules, thereby permitting the participation of non-governmental intervenors in Charter litigation.

Then, there was of course the foundational interpretive approaches. In this regard, I note the elimination of the presumption of constitutionality, the metaphor of the living tree, and as Justice David Stratas identified last year in his keynote address, the court's repeated use of the purposive approach to interpret and expand in different cases substantive Charter rights that had already been the subject of a purposive analysis. Justice Stratas' point is obvious but important and it is consistent with what I identified was Chief Justice Dickson's approach in Big M. Drug Mart. Assuming a completely thorough and robust purposeful analysis has already been conducted in respect of a given Charter right, it is reasonable to conclude that the analysis need not frequently be repeated for that same right on the questionable basis that its meaning may have changed (or requires updating) within a decade or two of its last analysis. To repeat such an analysis is to suggest that the Charter was enacted in a vacuum and/or that a great deal remains "up for grabs." Such a repeated use of the purposive approach for the same right risks as well the inconsistency that comes with the seeming discovery of new and significant enhanced meanings.

Perhaps most fatefully, as it relates to interpretive approaches and choices, I note the Supreme Court of Canada's decision in Reference re: British Columbia Motor Vehicle Act. It was in that case that the court reasoned and determined that in relation to s. 7 of the Charter, the principles of fundamental justice need be interpreted substantively as well as procedurally. In making that determination, Justice Lamer specifically ignored the intention of those who so carefully crafted the language of s. 7 to not go beyond procedural protection. Justice Lamer did so by determining that the evidence of those "present at the creation" – those involved in the drafting – should be given minimal weight, since statements by "civil servants" were not sufficiently indicative of the intentions of the legislative bodies that adopted the Charter. It can be said that since Justice Lamer's fateful decision in the Motor Vehicle Branch reference, s. 7 has become, particularly in recent years, the single most fertile source for the discovery of new rights and the de facto constitutionalization of political and social issues.

The resulting judicial incursion into subject areas and issues of profound political, moral and social complexity has the potential effect of removing these issues from the civic and political realms where ongoing and evolving debate and discussion may have taken place.

As it relates to s. 1, it is worth noting that its impact on judicial power has been mitigated because as with every section of the Charter, the operational meaning of s. 1 was subject to judicial definition. The judiciary's formulation of the proportionality test under s. 1 somewhat incongruously places the judiciary in the discretionary position of, amongst other things, measuring rationality, assessing legislative means, and considering and balancing the relative costs and benefits of national or provincial legislative regulation. Despite the structured nature of the discretion, the proportionality test still places the judiciary into a process of ad hoc interest balancing and cost benefit analysis.

For many, it's not obvious that courts are always institutionally equipped to conduct this traditionally legislative function. To the extent that the identified judicial approaches and accompanying reasoning may have been restrained by such things as the consistency and predictability that comes with precedent, or by such developments like the "dialogue theory," those potential restraints had in their application sometimes uneven and ineffective influence.

Precedent under the Charter for example, has become less reliable as a source of consistent and stabilizing constitutional doctrine. This was never better illustrated than in the recent Supreme Court of Canada judgments in Bedford and Carter. In those cases, the Supreme Court has all but invited trial judges to overturn Supreme Court of Canada's decisions if and where an evidentiary record suggests that enough circumstances have changed. [*Ed. note*: See Reading 7.5.]

In the case of the dialogue theory, rather than offering the legislative branch a truly equal voice by way of its legislative responses, the theory proved to be more useful as a means by which the scope of Canadian judicial review could be legitimated. In the end, the so-called dialogue theory left little doubt about who alone could end the institutional conversation.

It should be acknowledged that during this period where the judiciary was opting to deploy the approaches and reasoning it did, the Canadian citizenry was becoming increasingly cynical and distrustful of their elected governments. In this context, governments quickly proved reluctant to use the notwithstanding clause, which had become the constitutional equivalent of the nuclear option.

***

So that's some of what happened since 1982.

The interpretive approaches adopted and the analytical choices made by the judiciary throughout the 1980s and 1990s and indeed, those that continue to this day, have led without question to a level of judicial potency that was not anticipated back in 1982.

As suggested, this new judicial potency evolved and now continues to exist, concurrent with the comparatively less respected and the less celebrated standing of the legislative branch. Canadians, more quickly than some expected, have accustomized themselves to the dispositions of societal problems by Charter litigation and judicial adjudication.

I suggested earlier that such a development was not without consequence for the Canadian polity. What are some of those consequences? I see five.

Consequence No. 1

(1) The traditional role that the legislative branch played in the crafting of legislation which reflected some combination of the main ideological strains of Canadian political history is increasingly more difficult. The now new and ever-expanding judicially-inspired criteria for constitutionality is more and more difficult for the legislative branch to anticipate and meet. The sometimes technical and legalistic nature of such criteria does not always mesh or reconcile with the compromises or solutions that need regularly be made in the legislative forum where efforts are typically made to accommodate differing ideological positions. These compromises and solutions had historically helped shape a particular and distinctive Canadian identity.

Consequence No. 2
(2) In a political culture where its citizens and institutional actors have become undeniably comfortable with Charter litigation and judicial adjudication of political and social issues, there is now less room for long-term legislative results and solutions premised upon the tools of negotiation, persuasion, bargaining and compromise. That development is significant in a country like Canada where such legislative results could be seen historically as having been faithful to certain particular national and cultural realities. Those decidedly nonlegalistic compromises had worked to preserve shades of grey that defined a diverse Canadian society, a complex federation and a unique political culture.

Consequence No. 3
(3) With the expansion of judicial policy-making and the ability by individuals and groups to now make more stark sorts of claims on the state, there has indeed been a flight from politics. It is a flight from what is now a less potent and less influential legislative branch that seldom has the final word. This flight from politics toward the zero-sum game of Charter litigation is shaped by a public discourse dominated by the concept of "rights." This flight from politics and the accompanying rights-inspired public discourse often leaves the broader citizenry on the sidelines in a potentially disempowered state not always able to understand, discuss or debate the highly technical and legalistic formulations and tests which now often form the basis of a final determination concerning a significant societal issue.

Consequence No. 4
(4) For both the broader citizenry and members of the legislative branch, there is, in the new Canadian political culture, a tendency to ground one's interests and rationalize one's behaviour on the basis of what is constitutional. In such a political culture, constitutionality may be conflated with wisdom. In the case of lawmakers, as former law dean and professor Douglas A. Schmeiser has noted, they, the law makers, may themselves become distracted from pursuing what should be their proper goal. According to Schmeiser, a legislator should be concerned primarily with the rightness of his or her legislation, not with its constitutionality.

In connection to the sometimes reflexively invoked concept of constitutionality, governments may now be alternately more timid or opportunistic. The timidity and opportunism can manifest in the manner in which governments may take, delay or avoid policy positions in the name of ensuring "constitutionality."

Consequence No. 5

(5) With the "constitutionalizing" of more and more political and social issues into fundamental rights, the Canadian judiciary has all but removed those issues, in a fairly permanent way, from the realm of future civic engagement and future political debate. Given the often invoked rationale underlying the use of the living tree metaphor, it is ironic indeed that in constitutionalizing these political and social issues, the courts have "frozen" those issues in time, and thereby immunized those issues from future and evolving civic engagement, discussion and debate.

In my view, ladies and gentlemen, those five consequences to the Canadian polity are not insignificant. They all flow from what I suggest is a now uneasy and somewhat more imbalanced institutional relationship under the Charter.

So I repeat the question with which I started my remarks: In the context of Canada's celebration of the Charter, should the state of the resulting judicial/ legislative relationship be so reflexively applauded and promoted? For those who find the intellectual space in Canada to ask that question, it may lead you to inquire as to how an institutional balance might be restored?

To that question I can say only the following. Any future restoration of a peculiarly Canadian institutional balance in the judicial/legislative relationship, if it is to take place, will have to occur in what is now a new and different Canadian political culture.

Yet even if Canadians are now and will remain comfortable with the addressing of political and social problems through Charter adjudication, I remain hopeful that my institution – the judiciary – will increasingly perform its task with the type of principled restraint, consistency and predictability that can and should come from identifiable constitutional and legal doctrine.

Part of my hopeful scenario would include continuing efforts at renewal of parliamentary and political institutions.

The resulting enhanced public confidence would leave considerable room for a resuscitated and bold legislative branch to once again assertively shape attitudes and policies. This more assertive posture could include a Parliament that would itself begin to play an increasing coordinate role in articulating and promoting its own interpretation of the meaning, for example, of the Charter right to life, liberty and security of the person. I would hope, and have every reason to believe, that this would signal the beginning of a true dialogue with the courts, where the resulting policies would, I suspect, reflect a traditionally pragmatic and uniquely Canadian mix of liberal and non-liberal values.

Those values had always infused into any conception of individual liberty, an accompanying emphasis on the concept of a broader collective good.

When I was at Oxford many years ago, they used to say that the definition of a good debate is one where no one opportunistically mentions Adolf Hitler. In that same spirit, I suppose one could say that a definition of a good Canadian speech is one where no one opportunistically invokes Canada's differences with the United States in a subtle claim to Canadian superiority.

Alas, at the risk of being accused of doing just that, let me conclude by making one final point. Canadian attitudes and policies are currently in this, the era of the Charter, increasingly shaped by judicial formulations and tests, many of which find inspiration in a more absolutist notion of liberty. That less nuanced notion of liberty is more consistent with the ideological strains and doctrines that find their origins in the political culture of the United States. This more American liberal/rationalist approach to rights protection gives expression to what used to be a very un-Canadian distrust of government. It is an approach to rights protection that arguably removes more and more areas from legitimate spheres of government action and influence. With this removal of issues from the appropriate spheres of government action and influence, there is a potentially impoverishing effect on traditional Canadian notions of the public and national good. This is especially so at a time when our laws are now increasingly shaped by a more narrow, legalistic and rights-inspired concept of constitutionality.

The theme of much of Canadian history has been the assertion and survival of a distinct Canadian identity in North America. It may be one of the bitter ironies of Pierre Elliott Trudeau's Nation Building strategy of the 1980s, that despite the celebration and promotion of the Charter, it has led to an institutional imbalance that dilutes a source of Canadian distinctiveness.

While no one would seriously suggest that Canadians value, desire or ought to receive protection of their fundamental freedoms in a manner more abridged or diminished than that of their American neighbours, it is nonetheless important to remember Chief Justice Dickson's observation in Big M Drug Mart that the Charter was not to be interpreted in a vacuum. In that spirit, we are also well to recall Canada's traditional liberal and non-liberal value mix which had reflected the longstanding Canadian esteem for liberty and the accompanying concern for the complex realities that underlie the broader Canadian notion of "community." As I've tried to contend, this communitarian strain was in no small way cultivated and nurtured by the purposeful role of Canadian governments, their legislation and the resulting and prevailing public discourse.

Without a restoration of a more equal judicial/legislative relationship, it remains uncertain as to whether there will be the type of nuanced and balanced institutional dynamic envisioned by the framers in the 1982 compromise. Yet, without such a balance, it is far from certain that the Canadian legislative branch will be in a position to do that which it has always done: maintain and nurture those distinguishing ideological traits that shape policies and solutions that have been so uniquely Canadian.

Can the judicial/legislative institutional relationship be restored to a state of nuanced balance as envisioned by the framers of 1982? If it can, a necessary starting point for the realization of that objective will be the sort of inquiry that some might say I have presumptuously imposed upon you tonight.

I thank you for your attention and your kind invitation.

12.10
Key Terms

Concepts

Charter revolution

constitutional "architecture"

constitutional supremacy

Court Party

democratic legitimacy

dialogue theory

frozen concepts

judicial activism

judicial independence

judicial supremacy

living tree doctrine

notwithstanding clause (section 33)

originalism

parliamentary supremacy

patriation of the Constitution (1982)

political culture

populism

unwritten constitutional principles

Institutions, Events and Documents

Canadian Charter of Rights and Freedoms (1982)

Good Spirit School Division No. 204 v. Christ the Teacher Roman Catholic Separate School Division No. 212, 2017 SKQB 109 (CanLII)

Reference re Alberta Statutes, [1938] S.C.R. 100

Ref re Remuneration of Judges of the Prov. Court of P.E.I.; Ref re Independence and Impartiality of Judges of the Prov. Court of P.E.I., [1997] 3 S.C.R. 3

Reference re Secession of Quebec, [1998] 2 S.C.R. 217

Appendix

Constitution Act, 1867, ss. 91–95, 133.
VI. – Distribution of Legislative Powers.

Legislative Authority of Parliament of Canada.

91. It shall be lawful for the Queen, by and with the Advice and Consent of the Senate and House of Commons, to make laws for the Peace, Order, and good Government of Canada, in relation to all Matters not coming within the Classes of Subjects by this Act assigned exclusively to the Legislatures of the Provinces; and for greater Certainty, but not so as to restrict the Generality of the foregoing Terms of this Section, it is hereby declared that (notwithstanding anything in this Act) the exclusive Legislative Authority of the Parliament of Canada extends to all Matters coming within the Classes of Subjects next hereinafter enumerated; that is to say, –

1. Repealed.
1A. The Public Debt and Property.
2. The Regulation of Trade and Commerce.
2A. Unemployment insurance.
3. The raising of Money by any Mode or System of Taxation.
4. The borrowing of Money on the Public Credit.
5. Postal Service.
6. The Census and Statistics.
7. Militia, Military and Naval Service, and Defence.
8. The fixing of and providing for the Salaries and Allowances of Civil and other Officers of the Government of Canada.

9.   Beacons, Buoys, Lighthouses, and Sable Island.

10. Navigation and Shipping.

11. Quarantine and the Establishment and Maintenance of Marine Hospitals.

12. Sea Coast and Inland Fisheries.

13. Ferries between a Province and any British or Foreign Country or between Two Provinces.

14. Currency and Coinage.

15. Banking, Incorporation of Banks, and the Issue of Paper Money.

16. Savings Banks.

17. Weights and Measures.

18. Bills of Exchange and Promissory Notes.

19. Interest.

20. Legal Tender.

21. Bankruptcy and Insolvency.

22. Patents of Invention and Discovery.

23. Copyrights.

24. Indians, and Lands reserved for the Indians.

25. Naturalization and Aliens.

26. Marriage and Divorce.

27. The Criminal Law, except the Constitution of Courts of Criminal Jurisdiction, but including the Procedure in Criminal Matters.

28. The Establishment, Maintenance, and Management of Penitentiaries.

29. Such Classes of Subjects as are expressly excepted in the Enumeration of the Classes of Subjects by this Act assigned exclusively to the Legislatures of the Provinces.

And any Matter coming within any of the Classes of Subjects enumerated in this section shall not be deemed to come within the Class of Matters of a local or private Nature comprised in the Enumeration of the Classes of Subjects by this Act assigned exclusively to the Legislatures of the Provinces.

Exclusive Powers of Provincial Legislatures.

92. In each Province the Legislature may exclusively make Laws in relation to Matters coming within the Classes of Subject next hereinafter enumerated; that is to say, –

1. Repealed.

2. Direct Taxation within the Province in order to the raising of a Revenue for Provincial Purposes.

3. The borrowing of Money on the sole Credit of the Province.

4. The Establishment and Tenure of Provincial Offices and the Appointment and Payment of Provincial Officers.

5. The Management and Sale of the Public Lands belonging to the Province and of the Timber and Wood thereon.

6. The Establishment, Maintenance, and Management of Public and Reformatory Prisons in and for the Province.

7. The Establishment, Maintenance, and Management of Hospitals, Asylums, Charities, and Eleemosynary Institutions in and for the Province, other than Marine Hospitals.

8. Municipal Institutions in the Province.

9. Shop, Saloon, Tavern, Auctioneer, and other Licences in order to the raising of a Revenue for Provincial, Local, or Municipal Purposes.

10. Local Works and Undertakings other than such as are of the following Classes: –

    (a) Lines of Steam or other Ships, Railways, Canals, and other Works and Undertakings connecting the Province with any other or others of the Provinces, or extending beyond the Limits of the Province;

    (b) Lines of Steam Ships between the Province and any British or Foreign Country;

    (c) Such Works as, although wholly situate within the Province, are before or after the Execution declared by the Parliament of Canada to be for the general Advantage of Canada or for the Advantage of Two or more of the Provinces.

11. The Incorporation of Companies with Provincial Objects.

12. The Solemnization of Marriage in the Province.

13. Property and Civil Rights in the Province.

14. The Administration of Justice in the Province, including the Constitution, Maintenance, and Organization of Provincial Courts, both of Civil and of Criminal Jurisdiction, and including Procedure in Civil Matters in those Courts.

15. The Imposition of Punishment by Fine, Penalty, or Imprisonment for enforcing any Law of the Province made in relation to any Matter coming within any of the Classes of Subjects enumerated in this Section.

16. Generally all Matters of a merely local or private Nature in the Province.

Non-Renewable Natural Resources, Forestry Resources and Electrical Energy.

92A. (1) In each province, the legislature may exclusively make laws in relation to

    (a) exploration for non-renewable natural resources in the province;

    (b) development, conservation and management of non-renewable resources natural resources and forestry resources in the province, including laws in relation to the rate of primary production therefrom; and

    (c) development, conservation and management of sites and facilities in the province for the generation and production of electrical energy.

(2) In each province, the legislature may make laws in relation to the export from the province to another part of Canada of the primary production from non-renewable natural resources and forestry resources in the province and the production from facilities in the province for the generation of electrical energy, but such laws may not authorize or provide for discrimination in prices or in supplies exported to another part of Canada.

(3) Nothing in subsection (2) derogates from the authority of Parliament to enact laws in relation to the matters referred to in that subsection and, where such a law of Parliament and

a law of a province conflict, the law of Parliament prevails to the extent of the conflict.

(4)   In each province, the legislature may make laws in relation to the raising of money by any mode or system of taxation in respect of

    (a)   non-renewable natural resources and forestry resources in the province and the primary production therefrom, and

    (b)   sites and facilities in the province for the generation of electrical energy and the production therefrom, whether or not such production is exported in whole or in part from the province, but such laws may not authorize or provide for taxation that differentiates between production exported to another part of Canada and production not exported from the province.

(5)   The expression "primary production" has the meaning assigned by the Sixth Schedule.

(6)   Nothing in subsections (1) to (5) derogates from any power or rights that a legislature or government of a province had immediately before the coming into force of this section.

Education.

93.   In and for each Province the Legislature may exclusively make Laws in relation to Education, subject and according to the following Provisions: –

(1)   Nothing in any such Law shall prejudicially affect any Right or Privilege with respect to Denominational Schools which any Class of Persons have by Law in the Province at the Union:

(2)   All the Powers, Privileges and Duties at the Union by Law conferred and imposed in Upper Canada on the Separate Schools and School Trustees of the Queen's Roman Catholic Subjects shall be and the same are hereby extended to the Dissentient Schools of the Queen's Protestant and Roman Catholic Subjects in Quebec:

(3)   Where in any Province a System of Separate or Dissentient Schools exists by Law at the Union or is thereafter established by the Legislature of the Province, an Appeal shall lie to the Governor General in Council from any Act or Decision of any Provincial Authority affecting any Right or Privilege of the Protestant or Roman Catholic Minority of the Queen's Subjects in relation to Education:

(4)   In case any such Provincial Law as from Time to Time seems to the Governor General in Council requisite for the Execution of the Provisions of this Section is not made, or in case any Decision of the Governor General in Council on any Appeal under this Section is not duly executed by the proper Provincial Authority in that Behalf, then and in every such Case, and as far as the Circumstances of each Case require, the Parliament of Canada may make remedial Laws for the due Execution of the Provisions of this Section and of any Decision of the Governor General in Council under this Section.

93A. Paragraphs (1) to (4) of section 93 do not apply to Quebec.

Uniformity of Laws in Ontario, Nova Scotia and New Brunswick.

94.   Notwithstanding anything in this Act, the Parliament of Canada may make Provision for the Uniformity of all or any of the Laws relative to Property and Civil Rights in Ontario, Nova Scotia, and New Brunswick, and of the Procedure of all or any of the Courts in Those Three Provinces, and from and after the passing of any Act in that Behalf the Power of the Parliament of Canada to make Laws in relation to any Matter comprised in any such Act shall, notwithstanding anything in this Act, be unrestricted; but any Act of the Parliament of Canada making Provision for such Uniformity shall not have effect in any Province unless and until it is adopted and enacted as Law by the Legislature thereof.

Old Age Pensions.

94A. The Parliament of Canada may make laws in relation to old age pensions and supplementary benefits, including survivors' and disability benefits irrespective of age, but no such law shall affect the operation of any law present or future of a provincial legislature in relation to any such matter.

Agriculture and Immigration.

95.   In each Province the Legislature may make Laws in relation to Agriculture in the Province, and to Immigration into the Province; and it is hereby declared that the Parliament of Canada may from Time to Time make Laws in relation to Agriculture in all or any of the Provinces, and to Immigration into all or any of the Provinces; and any Law of the Legislature of a Province relative to Agriculture or to Immigration shall have effect in and for the Province as long and as far only as it is not repugnant to any Act of the Parliament of Canada.

IX. – Miscellaneous Provisions.

General.

133.   Either the English or the French Language may be used by any Person in the Debates of the Houses of the Parliament of Canada and of the Houses of the Legislature of Quebec; and both those Languages shall be used in the respective Records and Journals of those Houses; and either of those Languages may be used by any Person or in any Pleading or Process in or issuing from any Court of Canada established under this Act, and in or from all or any of the Courts of Quebec.

The Acts of the Parliament of Canada and of the Legislature of Quebec shall be printed and published in both those Languages.

Appendix

Canadian Bill of Rights, 1960

Preamble

The Parliament of Canada, affirming that the Canadian Nation is founded upon principles that acknowledge the supremacy of God, the dignity and worth of the human person and the position of the family in a society of free men and free institutions;

Affirming also that men and institutions remain free only when freedom is founded upon respect for moral and spiritual values and the rule of law;

And being desirous of enshrining these principles and the human rights and fundamental freedoms derived from them, in a Bill of Rights which shall reflect the respect of Parliament for its constitutional authority and which shall ensure the protection of these rights and freedoms in Canada:

Therefore Her Majesty, by and with the advice and consent of the Senate and House of Commons of Canada, enacts as follows:

PART I

Bill of Rights

1. It is hereby recognized and declared that in Canada there have existed and shall continue to exist without discrimination by reason of race, national origin, colour, religion or sex, the following human rights and fundamental freedoms, namely,

    (a) the right of the individual to life, liberty, security of the person and enjoyment of property, and the right not to be deprived thereof except by due process of law;

    (b) the right of the individual to equality before the law and the protection of the law;

(c)   freedom of religion;

(d)   freedom of speech;

(e)   freedom of assembly and of association; and

(f)   freedom of the press.

2.   Every law of Canada shall, unless it is expressly declared by an Act of Parliament of Canada that it shall operate notwithstanding the *Canadian Bill of Rights*, be so construed and applied as not to abrogate, abridge or infringe or to authorize the abrogation, abridgment or infringement of any of the rights or freedoms herein recognized and declared, and in particular, no law of Canada shall be construed or applied so as to

(a)   authorize or effect the arbitrary detention, imprisonment or exile of a person;

(b)   impose or authorize the imposition of cruel and unusual treatment or punishment;

(c)   deprive a person who has been arrested or detained

   (i)   of the right to be informed promptly of the reason for his arrest or detention,

   (ii) of the right to retain and instruct counsel without delay, or

   (iii) of the remedy by way of *habeas corpus* for the determination of the validity of his detention and for his release if the detention is not lawful;

(d)   authorize a court, tribunal, commission, board or other authority to compel a person to give evidence if he is denied counsel, protection against self-crimination or other constitutional safeguards;

(e)   deprive a person of the right to a fair hearing in accordance to the principles of fundamental justice for the determination of his rights and obligations;

(f)   deprive a person charged with a criminal offence of the right to be presumed innocent until proved guilty according to the law in a fair and public hearing by an independent and impartial tribunal, or of the right to reasonable bail without just cause; and

(g)   deprive a person of the right to the assistance to an interpreter in any proceedings in which he is involved or in which he is a party or a witness, before a court, commission, board or other tribunal, if he does not understand or speak the language in which such proceedings are conducted.

3. (1) Subject to subsection (2), the Minister of Justice shall, in accordance with such regulations as may be prescribed by the Governor General in Council, examine every regulation transmitted to the Clerk of the Privy Council for registration pursuant to the *Statutory Instruments Act* and every Bill introduced in or presented to the House of Commons by a Minister of the Crown in order to ascertain whether any of the provisions thereof are inconsistent with the purposes and provisions of this Part and he shall report any such inconsistency to the House of Commons at the first convenient opportunity.

(2) A regulation need not be examined in accordance with subsection (1) if prior to being made it was examined as a proposed regulation in accordance with section 3 of the *Statutory Instruments Act* to ensure that it was not inconsistent with the purposes and provisions of this Part.

4. The provisions of this Part shall be known as the *Canadian Bill of Rights*.

PART II

5. (1) Nothing in Part I shall be construed as to abrogate or abridge any human right or fundamental freedom not enumerated therein that may have exist in Canada at the commencement of this Act.

(2) The expression "law of Canada" in Part I means an Act of the Parliament of Canada enacted before or after the coming into force of this Act, any order, rule or regulation thereunder, and any law in force in Canada or in any part of Canada at the commencement of this Act that is subject to be repealed, abolished or altered by the Parliament of Canada.

(3) The provisions of Part I shall be construed as extending only to matters coming within the legislative authority of the Parliament of Canada.

Appendix

Constitution Act, 1982, ss. 1–35, 38–49, 52.

PART I

Canadian Charter of Rights and Freedoms

Whereas Canada is founded upon the principles that recognize the supremacy of God and the rule of law:

Guarantee of Rights and Freedoms

1.   The Canadian Charter of Rights and Freedoms guarantees the rights and freedoms set out in it subject only to such reasonable limits prescribed by law as can be demonstrably justified in a free and democratic society.

Fundamental Freedoms

2.   Everyone has the following fundamental freedoms:
   (*a*)   freedom of conscience and religion;
   (*b*)   freedom of thought, belief, opinion and expression, including freedom of the press and other means of communication;
   (*c*)   freedom of peaceful assembly; and
   (*d*)   freedom of association.

Democratic Rights

3.   Every citizen of Canada has the right to vote in an election of members of the House of Commons or of a legislative assembly and to be qualified for membership therein.

4.   (1)   No House of Commons and no legislative assembly shall continue for longer than five years from the date fixed for the return of the writs at a general election of its members.

        (2)   In time of real or apprehended war, invasion or insurrection, a House of Commons may be continued by Parliament and a legislative assembly may be continued by the legislature beyond five years if such continuation is not opposed by the votes of more than one-third of the members of the House of Commons or the legislative assembly, as the case may be.

5.   There shall be a sitting of Parliament and of each legislature at least once every twelve months.

Mobility Rights

6.   (1)   Every citizen of Canada has the right to enter, remain in and leave Canada.

        (2)   Every citizen of Canada and every person who has the status of a permanent resident of Canada has the right

            (*a*)   to move to and take up residence in any province; and

            (*b*)   to pursue the gaining of livelihood in any province.

        (3)   The rights specified in subsection (2) are subject to

            (*a*)   any laws or practices of general application in force in a province other than those that discriminate among persons primarily on the basis of province of present or previous residence; and

            (*b*)   any laws providing for reasonable residency requirements as a qualification for the receipt of publicly provided social services.

        (4)   Subsections (2) and (3) do not preclude any law, program or activity that has as its object the amelioration in a province of conditions of individuals in that province who are socially or economically disadvantaged if the rate of employment in that province is below the rate of employment in Canada.

Legal Rights

7.   Everyone has the right to life, liberty and security of the person and the right not to be deprived thereof except in accordance with the principles of fundamental justice.

8.   Everyone has the right to be secure against unreasonable search or seizure.

9.   Everyone has the right not to be arbitrarily detained or imprisoned.

10.   Everyone has the right on arrest or detention

     (*a*)   to be informed promptly of the reason therefor;

     (*b*)   to retain and instruct counsel without delay and to be informed of that right; and

     (*c*)   to have the validity of the detention determined by way of *habeas corpus* and to be released if the detention is not lawful.

11.   Any person charged with an offence has the right

     (*a*)   to be informed without unreasonable delay of the specific offence;

     (*b*)   to be tried within a reasonable time;

     (*c*)   not to be compelled to be a witness in proceedings against that person in respect of the offence;

     (*d*)   to be presumed innocent until proven guilty according to law in a fair and public hearing by an independent and impartial tribunal;

     (*e*)   not to be denied reasonable bail without cause;

     (*f*)   except in the case of an offence under military law tried before a military tribunal, to the benefit of trial by jury where the maximum punishment for the offence is imprisonment for five years or a more severe punishment;

     (*g*)   not to be found guilty on account of any act or omission unless, at the time of the act or omission, it constituted an offence under Canadian or international law or was criminal according to the general principles of law recognized by the community of nations;

     (*h*)   if finally acquitted of the offence, not to be tried for it again and, if finally found guilty and punished for the offence, not to be tried or punished for it again; and (*i*)   if found guilty of the offence and if the punishment for the offence has been varied between the time of commission and the time of sentencing, to the benefit of the lesser punishment.

12.   Everyone has the right not to be subjected to any cruel or unusual treatment or punishment.

13.   A witness who testifies in any proceedings has the right not to have any incriminating evidence so given used to incriminate that witness in any other proceedings, except in a prosecution for perjury or for the giving of contradictory evidence.

14.   A party or witness in any proceedings who does not understand or speak the language in which the proceedings are conducted or who is deaf has the right to the assistance of an interpreter.

Equality Rights

15.   (1)   Every individual is equal before and under the law and has the right to the equal protection and equal benefit of the law without discrimination and, in particular, without discrimination based on race, national or ethnic origin, colour, religion, sex, age or mental or physical disability.

    (2)   Subsection (1) does not preclude any law, program or activity that has as its object the amelioration of conditions of disadvantaged individuals or groups including those that are disadvantaged because of race, national or ethnic origin, colour, religion, sex, age or mental or physical disability.

Official Languages of Canada

16.   (1)   English and French are the official languages of Canada and have equality of status and equal rights and privileges as to their use in all institutions of the Parliament and government of Canada.

    (2)   English and French are the official languages of New Brunswick and have equality of status and equal rights and privileges as to their use in all institutions of the legislature and government of New Brunswick.

(3)   Nothing in this Charter limits the authority of Parliament or a legislature to advance the equality of status or use of English and French.

16.1 (1)   The English linguistic community and the French linguistic community in New Brunswick have equality of status and equal rights and privileges, including the right to distinct educational institutions and such distinct cultural institutions as are necessary for the preservation and promotion of those communities.

(2)   The role of the legislature and government of New Brunswick to preserve and promote the status, rights and privileges referred to in subsection (1) is affirmed.

17. (1)   Everyone has the right to use English or French in any debates and other proceedings of Parliament.

(2)   Everyone has the right to use English or French in any debates and other proceedings of the legislature of New Brunswick.

18. (1)   The statutes, records and journals of Parliament shall be printed and published in English and French and both language versions are equally authoritative.

(2)   The statutes, records and journals of the legislature of New Brunswick shall be printed and published in English and French and both language versions are equally authoritative.

19. (1)   Either English or French may be used by any person in, or in any pleading in or process issuing from, any court established by Parliament.

(2)   Either English or French may be used by any person in, or in any pleading in or process issuing from, any court of New Brunswick.

20. (1)   Any member of the public in Canada has the right to communicate with, and to receive available services from, any head or central office of an institution of the Parliament or government of Canada in English or French, and has the same right with respect to any other office of any such institution where

(a)   there is a significant demand for communications with and services from that office in such language; or

(b) due to the nature of the office, it is reasonable that communications with and services from that office be available in both English and French.

(2) Any member of the public in New Brunswick has the right to communicate with, and to receive available services from, any office of an institution of the legislature or government of New Brunswick in English or French.

21. Nothing in sections 16 to 20 abrogates or derogates from any right, privilege or obligation with respect to the English and French languages, or either of them, that exists or is continued by virtue of any other provision of the Constitution of Canada.

22. Nothing in sections 16 to 20 abrogates or derogates from any legal or customary right or privilege acquired or enjoyed either before or after the coming into force of this Charter with respect to any language that is not English or French.

Minority Language Educational Rights

23. (1) Citizens of Canada

(a) whose first language learned and still understood is that of the English or French linguistic minority population of the province in which they reside, or

(b) who have received their primary school instruction in Canada in English or French and reside in a province where the language in which they received that instruction is the language of the English or French linguistic minority population of the province, have the right to have their children receive primary and secondary school instruction in that language in that province.

(2) Citizens of Canada of whom any child has received or is receiving primary or secondary school instruction in English or French in Canada, have the right to have all their children receive primary and secondary school instruction in the same language.

(3) The right of citizens of Canada under subsections (1) and (2) to have their children receive primary and secondary

school instruction in the language of the English or French linguistic minority population of a province

(*a*) applies wherever in the province the number of children of citizens who have such a right is sufficient to warrant the provision to them out of public funds of minority language instruction; and

(*b*) includes, where the number of those children so warrants, the right to have them receive that instruction in minority language educational facilities provided out of public funds.

Enforcement

24. (1) Anyone whose rights or freedoms, as guaranteed by this Charter, have been infringed or denied may apply to a court of competent jurisdiction to obtain such remedy as the court considers appropriate and just in the circumstances.

(2) Where, in proceedings under subsection (1), a court concludes that evidence was obtained in a manner that infringed or denied any rights or freedoms guaranteed by this Charter, the evidence shall be excluded if it is established that, having regard to all the circumstances, the admission of it in the proceedings would bring the administration of justice into disrepute.

General

25. The guarantee in this Charter of certain rights and freedoms shall not be construed so as to abrogate or derogate from any aboriginal, treaty or other rights or freedoms that pertain to the aboriginal peoples of Canada including

(*a*) any rights or freedoms that have been recognized by the Royal Proclamation of October 7, 1763; and

(*b*) any rights or freedoms that now exist by way of land claims agreements or may be so acquired.

26. The guarantee in this Charter of certain rights and freedoms shall not be construed as denying the existence of any other rights or freedoms that exist in Canada.

27. This Charter shall be interpreted in a manner consistent with the preservation and enhancement of the multicultural heritage of Canadians.

28. Notwithstanding anything in this Charter, the rights and freedoms referred to in it are guaranteed equally to male and female persons.

29. Nothing in this Charter abrogates or derogates from any rights or privileges guaranteed by or under the Constitution of Canada in respect of denominational, separate or dissentient schools.

30. A reference in this Charter to a province or to the legislative assembly or legislature of a province shall be deemed to include a reference to the Yukon Territory and the Northwest Territories, or to the appropriate legislative authority thereof, as the case may be.

31. Nothing in this Charter extends the legislative powers of any body or authority.

Application of Charter

32. (1) This Charter applies

   (a) to the Parliament and government of Canada in respect of all matters within the authority of Parliament including all matters relating to the Yukon Territory and Northwest Territories; and

   (b) to the legislature and government of each province in respect of all matters within the authority of the legislature of each province.

   (2) Notwithstanding subsection (1), section 15 shall not have effect until three years after this section comes into force.

33. (1) Parliament or the legislature of a province may expressly d eclare in an Act of Parliament or of the legislature, as the case may be, that the Act or a provision thereof shall operate notwithstanding a provision included in section 2 or sections 7 to 15 of this Charter.

   (2) An Act or a provision of an Act in respect of which a declaration made under this section is in effect shall have such operation as it would have but for the provision of this Charter referred to in the declaration.

   (3) A declaration made under subsection (1) shall cease to have effect five years after it comes into force or on such earlier date as may be specified in the declaration.

(4)   Parliament or the legislature of a province may re-enact a declaration made under subsection (1).

(5)   Subsection (3) applies in respect of a re-enactment made under subsection (4).

Citation

34.   This Part may be cited as the *Canadian Charter of Rights and Freedoms*.

PART II

Rights of the Aboriginal Peoples of Canada

35.   (1)   The existing aboriginal and treaty rights of the aboriginal peoples of Canada are hereby recognized and affirmed.

(2)   In this Act, "aboriginal peoples of Canada" includes the Indian, Inuit and Métis peoples of Canada.

(3)   For greater certainty, in subsection (1) "treaty rights" includes rights that now exist by way of land claims agreements or may be so acquired.

(4)   Notwithstanding any other provision of this Act, the aboriginal and treaty rights referred to in subsection (1) are guaranteed equally to male and female persons.

35.1   The government of Canada and the provincial governments are committed to the principle that, before any amendment is made to Class 24 of section 91 of the "Constitution Act, 1867", to section 25 of this Act or to this Part,

(*a*)   a constitutional conference that includes in its agenda an item relating to the proposed amendment, composed of the Prime Minister of Canada and the first ministers of the provinces, will be convened by the Prime Minister of Canada; and

(*b*)   the Prime Minister of Canada will invite representatives of the aboriginal peoples of Canada to participate in the discussions on that item.

...

PART V

Procedure for Amending the Constitution of Canada

38. (1) An amendment to the Constitution of Canada may be made by proclamation issued by the Governor General under the Great Seal of Canada where so authorized by

(*a*) resolutions of the Senate and House of Commons; and

(*b*) resolutions of the legislative assemblies of at least two-thirds of the provinces that have, in the aggregate, according to the then latest general census, at least fifty per cent of the population of all the provinces.

(2) An amendment made under subsection (1) that derogates from the legislative powers, the proprietary rights or any other rights or privileges of the legislature or government of a province shall require a resolution supported by a majority of the members of each of the Senate, the House of Commons and the legislative assemblies required under subsection (1).

(3) An amendment referred to in subsection (2) shall not have effect in a province the legislative assembly of which has expressed its dissent thereto by resolution supported by a majority of its members prior to the issue of the proclamation to which the amendment relates unless that legislative assembly, subsequently, by resolution supported by a majority of its members, revokes its dissent and authorizes the amendment.

(4) A resolution of dissent made for the purposes of subsection (3) may be revoked at any time before or after the issue of the proclamation to which it relates.

39. (1) A proclamation shall not be issued under subsection 38(1) before the expiration of one year from the adoption of the resolution initiating the amendment procedure thereunder, unless the legislative assembly of each province has previously adopted a resolution of assent or dissent.

(2) A proclamation shall not be issued under subsection 38(1) after the expiration of three years from the adoption of the resolution initiating the amendment procedure thereunder.

40. Where an amendment is made under subsection 38(1) that transfers provincial legislative powers relating to education or other cultural matters from provincial legislatures to Parliament, Canada shall provide reasonable compensation to any province to which the amendment does not apply.

41. An amendment to the Constitution of Canada in relation to the following matters may be made by proclamation issued by the Governor General under the Great Seal of Canada only where authorized by resolutions of the Senate and House of Commons and of the legislative assembly of each province:

    (*a*) the office of the Queen, the Governor General and the Lieutenant Governor of a province;

    (*b*) the right of a province to a number of members in the House of Commons not less than the number of Senators by which the province is entitled to be represented at the time this Part comes into force;

    (*c*) subject to section 43, the use of the English or the French language;

    (*d*) the composition of the Supreme Court of Canada; and

    (*e*) an amendment to this Part.

42. (1) An amendment to the Constitution of Canada in relation to the following matters may be made only in accordance with subsection 38(1):

    (*a*) the principle of proportionate representation of the provinces in the House of Commons prescribed by the Constitution of Canada;

    (*b*) the powers of the Senate and the method of selecting Senators;

    (*c*) the number of members by which a province is entitled to be represented in the Senate and the residence qualifications of Senators;

    (*d*) subject to paragraph 41(d), the Supreme Court of Canada;

    (*e*) the extension of existing provinces into the territories; and

    (*f*) notwithstanding any other law or practice, the establishment of new provinces;

(2)   Subsections 38(2) to (4) do not apply in respect of amendments in relation to matters referred to in subsection (1).

43.   An amendment to the Constitution of Canada in relation to any provision that applies to one or more, but not all, provinces, including

    (*a*) any alteration to boundaries between provinces, and

    (*b*) any amendment to any provision that relates to the use of the English or the French language within a province,may be made by proclamation issued by the Governor General under the Great Seal of Canada only where so authorized by resolutions of the Senate and House of Commons and of the legislative assembly of each province to which the amendment applies.

44.   Subject to sections 41 and 42, Parliament may exclusively make laws amending the Constitution of Canada in relation to the executive government of Canada or the Senate and House of Commons.

45.   Subject to section 41, the legislature of each province may exclusively make laws amending the constitution of the province.

46.   (1)   The procedures for amendment under sections 38, 41, 42 and 43 may be initiated either by the Senate or the House of Commons or by the legislative assembly of a province.

    (2)   A resolution of assent made for the purposes of this Part may be revoked at any time before the issue of a proclamation authorized by it.

47.   (1)   An amendment to the Constitution of Canada made by proclamation under section 38, 41, 42 or 43 may be made without a resolution of the Senate authorizing the issue of the proclamation if, within one hundred and eighty days after the adoption by the House of Commons of a resolution authorizing its issue, the Senate has not adopted such a resolution and if, at any time after the expiration of that period, the House of Commons again adopts the resolution.

    (2)   Any period when Parliament is prorogued or dissolved shall not be counted in computing the one hundred and eighty day period referred to in subsection (1).

48. The Queen's Privy Council for Canada shall advise the Governor General to issue a proclamation under this Part forthwith on the adoption of the resolutions required for an amendment made by proclamation under this Part.

49. A constitutional conference composed of the Prime Minister of Canada and the first ministers of the provinces shall be convened by the Prime Minister of Canada within fifteen years after this Part comes into force to review the provisions of this Part.

...

PART VII

General (Supremacy Clause)

52. (1) The Constitution of Canada is the supreme law of Canada, and any law that is inconsistent with the provisions of the Constitution is, to the extent of the inconsistency, of no force or effect.

    (2) The Constitution of Canada includes

    (a) the Canada Act, 1982, including this Act;

    (b) the Acts and orders referred to in the Schedule; and

    (c) any amendment to any Act or order referred to in paragraph (a) or (b).

    (3) Amendments to the Constitution of Canada shall be made only in accordance with the authority contained in the Constitution of Canada.

Appendix

Chief Justices of the Supreme Court of Canada

	Name of Chief Justice	Term on court as Chief Justice
1)	Hon. Sir William Buell Richards	September 30, 1875–January 10, 1879
2)	Hon. Sir William Johnston Ritchie	January 11, 1879–September 25, 1892
3)	Rt. Hon. Sir Samuel Henry Strong	December 13, 1892–November 18, 1902
4)	Rt. Hon. Sir Henri-Elzéar Taschereau	November 21, 1902–May 2, 1906
5)	Rt. Hon. Sir Charles Fitzpatrick	June 4, 1906–October 21, 1918
6)	Rt. Hon. Sir Louis Henry Davies	October 23, 1918–May 1, 1924
7)	Rt. Hon. Francis Alexander Anglin	September 16, 1924–February 28, 1933
8)	Rt. Hon. Sir Lyman Poore Duff	March 17, 1933–January 7, 1944
9)	Rt. Hon. Thibaudeau Rinfret	January 8, 1944–June 22, 1954
10)	Hon. Patrick Kerwin	July 1, 1954–Feb. 2, 1963
11)	Rt. Hon. Robert Taschereau	April 22, 1963–Sept. 1, 1967
12)	Rt. Hon. John Robert Cartwright	September 1, 1967–March 23, 1970
13)	Rt. Hon. Joseph Honoré Gérald Fauteux	March 23, 1970–December 23, 1973
14)	Rt. Hon. Bora Laskin	December 27, 1973–March 26, 1984
15)	Rt. Hon. Robert George Brian Dickson	April 18, 1984–June 30, 1990
16)	Rt. Hon. Antonio Lamer	July 1, 1990–January 6, 2000
17)	Rt. Hon. Beverley McLachlin	January 7, 2000–December 15, 2017
18)	Rt. Hon. Richard Wagner	December 18, 2017–

Province from	Appointed by
Ontario	Alexander Mackenzie (Liberal)
New Brunswick	Sir John A. Macdonald (Conservative)
Ontario	Sir John Thompson (Conservative)
Quebec	Sir Wilfrid Laurier (Liberal)
Quebec	Sir Wilfrid Laurier (Liberal)
Prince Edward Island	Sir Robert Borden (Conservative/Unionist
Ontario	Mackenzie King (Liberal)
British Columbia	Richard B. Bennett (Conservative)
Quebec	Mackenzie King (Liberal)
Ontario	Louis St. Laurent (Liberal)
Quebec	Lester Pearson (Liberal)
Ontario	Lester Pearson (Liberal)
Quebec	Pierre Trudeau (Liberal)
Ontario	Pierre Trudeau (Liberal)
Manitoba	Pierre Trudeau (Liberal)
Quebec	Brian Mulroney (Progressive Conservative)
British Columbia	Jean Chrétien (Liberal)
Quebec	Justin Trudeau (Liberal)

Appendix

Puisne Justices of the Supreme Court of Canada

	Name of Supreme Court Justice	Term served on the court
1)	Hon. William Johnstone Ritchie*	September 30, 1875–January 11, 1879*
2)	Hon. Samuel Henry Strong*	September 30, 1875–December 13, 1892*
3)	Hon. Jean-Thomas Taschereau	September 30, 1875–October 6, 1878
4)	Hon. Télesphore Fournier	September 30, 1875–September 12, 1895
5)	Hon. William Alexander Henry	September 30, 1875–May 3, 1888
6)	Hon. Sir Henri-Elzéar Taschereau*	October 7, 1878–November 21, 1902*
7)	Hon. John Wellington Gwynne	January 14, 1879–January 7, 1902
8)	Hon. Christopher Salmon Patterson	October 27, 1888–July 24, 1893
9)	Hon. Robert Sedgewick	February 18, 1893–August 4, 1906
10)	Hon. George Edwin King	September 21, 1893–May 8, 190
11)	Hon. Désiré Girouard	September 28, 1895–March 22, 1911
12)	Hon. Sir Louis Henry Davies*	September 25, 1901–October 23, 1918*
13)	Hon. David Mills	February 8, 1902–May 8, 1903
14)	Hon. John Douglas Armour	November 21, 1902–July 11, 1903
15)	Hon. Wallace Nesbitt	May 16, 1903–October 4, 1905
16)	Hon. Albert Clements Killam	August 8, 1903–February 6, 1905
17)	Hon. John Idington	February 10, 1905–March 31, 1927
18)	Hon. James Maclennan	October 5, 1905–February 13, 1909
19)	Hon. Lyman Poore Duff*	September 27, 1906–March 17, 1933*
20)	Hon. Francis Alexander Anglin*	February 23, 1909–September 16, 1924*
21)	Hon. Louis-Philippe Brodeur	August 11, 1911–October 10, 1923
22)	Hon. Pierre-Basile Mignault	October 25, 1918–September 30, 1929
23)	Hon. Arthur Cyrille Albert Malouin	January 30, 1924–October 1, 1924
24)	Hon. Edmund Leslie Newcombe	September 16, 1924–December 9, 1931

Province from	Appointed by
New Brunswick	Alexander Mackenzie (Liberal)
Ontario	Alexander Mackenzie (Liberal)
Quebec	Alexander Mackenzie (Liberal)
Quebec	Alexander Mackenzie (Liberal)
Nova Scotia	Alexander Mackenzie (Liberal)
Quebec	Alexander Mackenzie (Liberal)
Ontario	Sir John A. Macdonald (Conservative)
Ontario	Sir John A. Macdonald (Conservative)
Nova Scotia	Sir John Thompson (Conservative)
New Brunswick	Sir John Thompson (Conservative)
Quebec	Sir Mackenzie Bowell (Conservative)
September 25, 1901–October 23, 1918*	Sir Wilfrid Laurier (Liberal)
Ontario	Sir Wilfrid Laurier (Liberal)
Ontario	Sir Wilfrid Laurier (Liberal)
Ontario	Sir Wilfrid Laurier (Liberal)
Manitoba	Sir Wilfrid Laurier (Liberal)
Ontario	Sir Wilfrid Laurier (Liberal)
Ontario	Sir Wilfrid Laurier (Liberal)
British Columbia	Sir Wilfrid Laurier (Liberal)
Ontario	Sir Wilfrid Laurier (Liberal)
Quebec	Sir Wilfrid Laurier (Liberal)
Quebec	Sir Robert Borden (Conservative/Unionist)
Quebec	Mackenzie King (Liberal)
Nova Scotia	Mackenzie King (Liberal)

Puisne Justices of the Supreme Court of Canada (continued)

Name of Supreme Court Justice	Term served on the court
25) Hon. Thibaudeau Rinfret*	October 1, 1924–January 8, 1944*
26) Hon. John Henderson Lamont	April 2, 1927–March 10, 1936
27) Hon. Robert Smith	May 18, 1927–December 7, 1933
28) Hon. Lawrence Arthur Dumoulin Cannon	January 14, 1930–December 25, 1939
29) Hon. Oswald Smith Crocket	September 21, 1932–April 13, 1943
30) Hon. Frank Joseph Hughes	March 17, 1933–February 13, 1935
31) Hon. Henry Hague Davis	January 31, 1935–June 30, 1944
32) Hon. Patrick Kerwin*	July 20, 1935–July 1, 1954*
33) Hon. Albert Blelloch Hudson	March 24, 1936–January 6, 1947
34) Hon. Robert Taschereau*	February 9, 1940–April 22, 1963*
35) Hon. Ivan Cleveland Rand	April 22, 1943–April 27, 1959
36) Hon. Roy Lindsay Kellock	October 3, 1944–January 15, 1958
37) Hon. James Wilfred Estey	October 6, 1944–January 22, 1956
38) Hon. Charles Holland Locke	June 3, 1947–September 16, 1962
39) Hon. John Robert Cartwright*	December 22, 1949–September 1, 1967*
40) Hon. Joseph Honoré Gérald Fauteux*	December 22, 1949–March 23, 1970*
41) Hon. Douglas Charles Abbott	July 1, 1954–December 23, 1973
42) Hon. Henry Gratton Nolan	March 1, 1956–July 8, 1957
43) Hon. Ronald Martland	January 15, 1958–February 10, 1982
44) Hon. Wilfred Judson	February 5, 1958–July 20, 1977
45) Hon. Roland Almon Ritchie	May 5, 1959–October 31, 1984
46) Hon. Emmett Matthew Hall	November 23, 1962–March 1, 1973
47) Hon. Wishart Flett Spence	May 30, 1963–December 29, 1978
48) Hon. Louis-Philippe Pigeon	September 21, 1967–February 8, 1980
49) Hon. Bora Laskin*	March 19, 1970–December 27, 1973*
50) Hon. Robert George Brian Dickson*	March 26, 1973–April 18, 1984*
51) Hon. Jean Beetz	January 1, 1974–November 10, 1988
52) Hon. Louis-Philippe de Grandpré	January 1, 1974–October 1, 1977
53) Hon. Willard Zebedee Estey	September 29, 1977–April 22, 1988
54) Hon. Yves Pratte	October 1, 1977–June 30, 1979
55) Hon. William Rogers McIntyre	January 1, 1979–February 15, 1989

Province from	Appointed by
Quebec	Mackenzie King (Liberal)
Saskatchewan	Mackenzie King (Liberal)
Ontario	Mackenzie King (Liberal)
Quebec	Mackenzie King (Liberal)
New Brunswick	Richard B. Bennett (Conservative)
Ontario	Richard B. Bennett (Conservative)
Ontario	Richard B. Bennett (Conservative)
Ontario	Richard B. Bennett (Conservative)
Manitoba	Mackenzie King (Liberal)
Quebec	Mackenzie King (Liberal)
New Brunswick	Mackenzie King (Liberal)
Ontario	Mackenzie King (Liberal)
Saskatchewan	Mackenzie King (Liberal)
British Columbia	Mackenzie King (Liberal)
Ontario	Louis St. Laurent (Liberal)
Quebec	Louis St. Laurent (Liberal)
Quebec	Louis St. Laurent (Liberal)
Alberta	Louis St. Laurent (Liberal)
Alberta	John Diefenbaker (Progressive Conservative)
Ontario	John Diefenbaker (Progressive Conservative)
Nova Scotia	John Diefenbaker (Progressive Conservative)
Saskatchewan	John Diefenbaker (Progressive Conservative)
Ontario	Lester Pearson (Liberal)
Quebec	Lester Pearson (Liberal)
Ontario	Pierre Trudeau (Liberal)
Manitoba	Pierre Trudeau (Liberal)
Quebec	Pierre Trudeau (Liberal)
Quebec	Pierre Trudeau (Liberal)
Ontario	Pierre Trudeau (Liberal)
Quebec	Pierre Trudeau (Liberal)
British Columbia	Pierre Trudeau (Liberal)

Puisne Justices of the Supreme Court of Canada (continued)

	Name of Supreme Court Justice	Term served on the court
56)	Hon. Julien Chouinard	September 24, 1979–February 6, 1987
57)	Hon. Antonio Lamer*	March 28, 1980–July 1, 1990*
58)	Hon. Bertha Wilson	March 4, 1982–January 4, 1991
59)	Hon. Gerald Eric Le Dain	May 29, 1984–November 30, 1988
60)	Hon. Gérard V. La Forest	January 16, 1985–September 30, 1997
61)	Hon. Claire L'Heureux-Dubé	April 15, 1987–July 1, 2002
62)	Hon. John Sopinka	May 24, 1988–November 24, 1997
63)	Hon. Charles Doherty Gonthier	February 1, 1989–August 1, 2003
64)	Hon. Peter deCarteret Cory	February 1, 1989–June 1, 1999
65)	Hon. Beverley McLachlin*	March 30, 1989–January 7, 2000*
66)	Hon. William Stevenson	September 17, 1990–June 5, 1992
67)	Hon. Frank Iacobucci	January 7, 1991–June 30, 2004
68)	Hon. John C. Major	November 13, 1992–December 25, 2005
69)	Hon. Michel Bastarache	September 30, 1997–June 30, 2008
70)	Hon. William Ian Corneil Binnie	January 8, 1998–October 21, 2011
71)	Hon. Louise Arbour	September 15, 1999–June 30, 2004
72)	Hon. Louis LeBel	January 7, 2000–November 30, 2014
73)	Hon. Marie Deschamps	August 7, 2002–August 7, 2012
74)	Hon. Marris J. Fish	August 5, 2003–August 31, 2013
75)	Hon. Rosalie Abella	October 4, 2004–
76)	Hon. Louise Charron	October 4, 2004–August 30, 2011
77)	Hon. Marshall Rothstein	March 1, 2006–August 31, 2015
78)	Hon. Thomas Cromwell	December 22, 2008–September 1, 2016
79)	Hon. Michael J. Moldaver	October 21, 2011–
80)	Hon. Andromache Karakatsanis	October 21, 2011–
81)	Hon. Richard Wagner*	October 21, 2011–December 18, 2017*
82)	Hon. Clément Gascon	June 9, 2014–
83)	Hon. Suzanne Côté	December 1, 2014–
84)	Hon. Russell Brown	August 31, 2015–
85)	Hon. Malcolm Rowe	October 28, 2016–
86)	Hon. Sheilah Martin	December 18, 2017–

*Asterisk denotes date of appointment as Chief Justice; Term as Chief Justice in Appendix D.

Province from	Appointed by
Quebec	Joe Clark (Progressive Conservative)
Quebec	Pierre Trudeau (Liberal)
Ontario	Pierre Trudeau (Liberal)
Ontario	Pierre Trudeau (Liberal)
New Brunswick	Brian Mulroney (Progressive Conservative)
Quebec	Brian Mulroney (Progressive Conservative)
Ontario	Brian Mulroney (Progressive Conservative)
Quebec	Brian Mulroney (Progressive Conservative)
Ontario	Brian Mulroney (Progressive Conservative)
British Columbia	Brian Mulroney (Progressive Conservative)
Alberta	Brian Mulroney (Progressive Conservative)
Ontario	Brian Mulroney (Progressive Conservative)
Alberta	Brian Mulroney (Progressive Conservative)
New Brunswick	Jean Chrétien (Liberal)
Ontario	Jean Chrétien (Liberal)
Ontario	Jean Chrétien (Liberal)
Quebec	Jean Chrétien (Liberal)
Quebec	Jean Chrétien (Liberal)
Quebec	Jean Chrétien (Liberal)
Ontario	Paul Martin (Liberal)
Ontario	Paul Martin (Liberal)
Manitoba	Stephen Harper (Conservative)
Nova Scotia	Stephen Harper (Conservative)
Ontario	Stephen Harper (Conservative)
Ontario	Stephen Harper (Conservative)
Quebec	Stephen Harper (Conservative)
Quebec	Stephen Harper (Conservative)
Quebec	Stephen Harper (Conservative)
Alberta	Stephen Harper (Conservative)
Newfoundland and Labrador	Justin Trudeau (Liberal)
Alberta	Justin Trudeau (Liberal)

Appendix

Online Resources

Supreme Court of Canada	www.scc-csc.gc.ca
Supreme Court of Canada Decisions	https://scc-csc.lexum.com
Canadian Legal Information Institute (CanLII)	www.canlii.org/en
Canadian Judicial Council	www.cjc-ccm.gc.ca
National Judicial Institute	www.nji-inm.ca
Office of the Commissioner for Federal Judicial Affairs	www.fja.gc.ca
Policy Options	http://policyoptions.irpp.org
Double Aspect: A Canadian Constitution Blog by Leonid Sirota	https://doubleaspect.blog
TheCourt.ca: Commentary on the Supreme Court of Canada	www.thecourt.ca
Centre for Constitutional Studies: University of Alberta	http://ualawccsprod.srv.ualberta.ca
The Docket: A Podcast by Michael Spratt	www.michaelspratt.com/poadcast-legal-matters/
Oyez: A United States Supreme Court Resource	www.oyez.org

Rights Advocacy Organizations

Women's Legal Education and Action Fund (LEAF)	www.leaf.ca
Canadian Civil Liberties Association	www.ccla.org
British Columbia Civil Liberties Association	www.bccla.org
National Citizens Coalition	www.nationalcitizens.ca
Egale Canada	www.egale.ca
Canadian Constitution Foundation	www.theccf.ca
Criminal Lawyers' Association	www.criminallawyers.ca

Index

bilingualism, 88, 124, 128, 23n, 244, 511
bill of rights (see Canadian Bill of Rights; United States Bill of Rights)
Bill 101 (Charter of the French Language), 70-71, 252, 308
Binnie, Ian, 447, 477, 507-508, 541, 545-546, 555, 680
Blakeney, Allan, 421, 607, 610, 612
Bork, Robert, 184n, 516
Borovoy, Alan, 248-249, 262-269
Borowski v. Canada (Attorney General) (1989), 245, 254n, 279, 598, 600n
Boucher v. the King (1951), 12, 332, 351-355, 591
Brandeis, Louis, 278
British North America (BNA) Act, 1867 (also see Constitution Act, 1867), 5, 6, 47n, 66, 101-102, 106, 174, 260, 405-406, 416-417, 421, 423, 430, 433, 441-442, 454, 460n, 534
Brodie, Ian, 251-252, 254n, 304, 308, 515, 525
Brown, Russell, 127, 129, 133-135, 506, 510, 537-538, 680
Bushnell, S.I., 97, 100n, 371, 376n
Bzdera, André, 412, 415n

Cairns, Alan, 262n, 414n, 415n, 637
Calder v. British Columbia (1973), 454, 471, 477
Camp, Robin, 179-181, 226-241
Canada (AG) v. Ontario (AG) (1937) (see *Labour Conventions Case*)
Canada (Attorney General) v. Bedford (2013), 338-339, 363-368, 541, 559, 567-571, 632-633, 644-645
Canada (Attorney General) v. Downtown Eastside Sex Workers United Against Violence Society (2012), 245
Canada (Prime Minister) v. Khadr (2010), 510
Canadian Advisory Council on the Status of Women, 249, 313, 501
Canadian Association of Law Teachers (CALT), 121-122

Canadian Bar Association (CBA), 120-121, 138, 140, 143, 157, 178, 194, 197, 199-205, 250, 290, 509, 528, 538, 552-553
Canadian Bill of Rights (1960), 5, 42-43, 106, 109-110, 263, 267, 313, 319, 574, 590, 592-597, 612, 614-615, 658-660
Canadian Civil Liberties Association (CCLA), 133, 248-249, 262-269, 282, 290, 313, 322, 500, 683
Canadian Council of Churches v. Minister of Employment and Immigration (1992), 245, 254n, 290
Canadian Jewish Congress, 267, 290
Canadian Judicial Council (CJC), 34-35, 61, 175, 177, 184n, 188, 193-199, 202-205, 209-210, 221-241, 505, 529-530, 608, 682
Canadian Labour Congress, 290, 428-429
Capital Cities Communication v. C.R.T.C. (1978), 414n
Cardozo, Benjamin, 41, 56, 107, 343-344
Carter v. Canada (Attorney General) (2015), 338-339, 363, 367-368, 541, 557-559, 566-567, 569, 644
cattle trespass case (see *Fleming v. Atkinson*)
Central Canada Potash v. Government of Saskatchewan (1979), 414n, 440-441
Charlottetown Accord (1992), 73, 80, 260, 453-456, 466
Charron, Louise, 120, 125, 129, 447, 508, 546, 555, 680
Charter Canadians, 250, 287, 289-290, 292-304
Charter revolution, 24, 33, 374, 380, 399, 505, 512, 575, 601-605
Charter values, 8, 27, 29-30, 33-36, 531, 534, 617, 636
checks and balances, 25, 577, 627-633
Chippewas of the Thames First Nation v. Enbridge Pipelines Inc. (2017), 458
CIGOL v. Government of Saskatchewan (1978), 414n, 440-443
civil law, 92, 94-98, 130, 184n, 330, 548
civil society, 8, 23-36, 322
Clark, Joe, 141, 521

clerks (*see* law clerks)

codification, 333-334

collegiality, 105-106, 371-375, 377-379, 384, 391, 394, 402, 537-538

Colonial Laws Validity Act, 406

Commissioner for Federal Judicial Affairs, 117, 122-124, 127, 143, 156, 165, 175, 682

Committee on the Judiciary, 120-122, 143

common law, 3, 23, 29-31, 41, 55, 57, 95, 103, 106, 118-120, 166-168, 171, 173, 184n, 191, 243, 264, 279, 288, 291, 294-295, 300, 319, 330-338, 342-351, 361, 363, 370, 384, 386, 407, 474-475, 501, 585-587, 596-597, 629

conference (*see* judicial conference)

Conservative Party of Canada, 80, 125, 239, 504, 519, 544, 558, 563-571, 625

Constitution Act, 1867 (also see British North American (BNA) Act, 1867), 5, 40, 93, 95-96, 110, 117, 176, 211-212, 217-219, 256, 314, 405, 412, 445, 447, 460n, 462, 590, 592, 614, 651-658

Constitution Act, 1982, 44-47, 73, 82, 88, 90, 99, 169, 177, 212, 218, 245, 248, 256, 260, 421-422, 453, 455, 459, 460n, 463-464, 476, 478, 502, 548-551, 614, 628, 61-672

constitutional architecture, 84, 86, 612, 637

constitutional convention, 4, 44, 64-70, 82, 84, 411, 596, 614

constitutional law, 4, 22, 39-42, 47, 65, 68, 73, 119, 171, 186, 188-189, 223, 243-244, 253, 256, 313-324, 338, 356, 363, 384, 407, 416, 422, 424, 426, 484, 546, 614, 627-628, 631, 633, 640

constitutional supremacy, 75-76, 590, 601, 635

cooperative federalism, 168, 557, 570

Cosgrove, Paul, 179, 181, 608

Côté, Suzanne, 127, 129, 680

Court Challenges Program (CCP), 251, 253, 306-310, 314, 321, 412, 505, 512

court packing, 133, 536-538, 577

Court Party, 23, 254, 287, 313, 398-399, 550, 601-605

Court of Queen's Bench, 94-95, 111-115, 139, 179, 498, 513, 518-521, 524-525, 575-577, 611-616, 634

Criminal Code of Canada, 31, 94, 106, 113, 167, 171, 227-228, 234, 275, 278-280, 283, 286, 300, 334-335, 338, 354, 364-366, 445, 519, 536, 541, 544, 562, 566-567, 598, 623-624, 629, 631

criminal law, 60-61, 92-97, 103, 134, 167, 184n, 266, 275, 279, 291, 334, 335, 412, 440, 444-451, 555, 591-592, 632, 652

Cromwell, Thomas, 98, 126-129, 131, 170, 448, 507, 545, 557, 561, 680

Crown sovereignty, 454, 456-459, 460n, 469-475, 488-494, 499

declaration of incompatibility, 6-7

Declaration of Independence, 2, 18, 74, 174

declaratory model, 39-43, 107, 506

democratic legitimacy (*also see* institutional legitimacy), 89, 402, 542, 599, 620

dialogue theory, 7, 22-23, 336, 375, 397, 399, 402-403, 576-578, 616-633, 644-647

Dicey, A.V., 2, 4, 18-22, 217, 331, 340n, 575, 590, 592

Dickson, Brian, 40, 43-44, 56, 66, 97, 99, 183, 373, 385-387, 394, 429, 515, 623-624, 642, 643, 648, 674, 678

direct sponsorship, 272

disallowance (*also see* reservation), 252-253, 405-406, 414n, 417-420, 595, 610, 614

distinct society clause, 463

docket, 96, 97, 238, 253, 292, 310, 312-313, 315, 321, 323-325, 370, 391, 394, 435

doctrine of discovery, 454, 456, 469, 474-475

Doré v. Barreau du Québec (2012), 34-35

Douglas, Lori, 179-180, 221-226

dual court system, 92, 102

Duplessis, Maurice, 1, 10-15, 191, 244, 590

human rights, 2-29, 32-33, 36, 63, 199, 231, 271-272, 284, 298, 309, 313, 321, 386, 579-581, 584, 589, 593, 597, 617-618, 640, 658

Human Rights Act 1998 (United Kingdom), 3, 6

identity politics, 124, 128, 134, 182, 252, 544,

ideological judicial appointments, 46, 120, 133-135, 169, 179, 375, 391-393, 504-506, 510, 512, 518, 522-523, 527, 531, 533, 537, 539-540, 544-545

impartiality, 13, 53, 58-61, 119, 178, 192, 194-195, 203, 212, 216, 219-220, 226, 231-232, 236, 241, 411, 419, 531, 532

implied bill of rights, 592

independence (*see* judicial independence)

Indian Act, 299, 454, 460n, 463, 594

Indians (see First Nations; non-status Indians; status Indians)

indictable offence, 94-95, 113-114

influencing the influencers, 249, 269-272, 336

inherent national importance, 409, 412-413, 425-426, 430, 432-433, 436, 445-447, 451

institutional capacity, 299, 338

institutional delay, 361-362

institutional legitimacy (*also see* democratic legitimacy), 338, 468, 510

interest groups, 23, 33, 74, 133, 179, 182, 243-255, 262-323, 336-337, 348-349, 354, 397-401, 427, 435, 459, 462, 467, 575, 596, 598, 601, 683

interpretive avoidance, 591, 594

intervenor, 33, 69, 74, 247-250, 262-269, 273-279, 282-285, 290-291, 294, 300, 303, 320, 338, 372, 402, 409, 421, 459, 486, 496-501, 531, 556, 558, 567, 569-570, 643

Inuit, 193, 453, 459, 460n, 463, 467, 669

iron law of politics, 119, 337

Jefferson, Thomas, 2-3, 18, 311

Jehovah's Witnesses, 1, 9n, 10, 244, 352, 592-593

judicial accountability (*see* accountability)

judicial activism, 4, 134, 251, 287, 294-5, 303-304, 306, 400-401, 517, 577, 588, 597, 603, 626

Judicial Advisory Committees (JACs), 122-124, 135n, 142, 158-159, 165, 505, 507, 523, 527-530, 535

judicial appointments, 41, 45-46, 59, 62, 84, 92, 98-99, 102, 117-172, 180, 183, 200-201, 214, 231, 239, 250, 286, 389-390, 410-412, 441, 484, 504-555, 570, 598-600

  public hearings for, 125-129, 136n, 286, 390, 527

Judicial Committee of the Privy Council (JCPC), 42, 93, 96, 133, 256, 259, 333, 338, 377, 394, 406, 409, 416-426, 445, 516

judicial compensation commissions, 176, 183, 184n, 213-220

judicial conference, 115, 202, 370-372, 378-379, 388

judicial democrats, 251, 254, 288, 297-302, 305

judicial discretion, 331-335, 390, 506

judicial education, 61, 181-182, 233-241, 336, 578

judicial independence, 43, 95, 99, 105, 108, 117, 173-242, 261, 346, 372, 378-379, 399, 417-419, 504, 509, 515-516, 519, 522, 526, 531, 533, 539-543, 552-553, 609, 621

judicial nationalism, 42, 93, 409

judicial policy-making, 253, 311, 332, 403, 575-576, 602, 605, 636, 646

judicial realism, 42-43, 132, 332

judicial restraint, 42, 134, 191, 560, 601, 647

judicial supremacy, 399, 417, 422, 515, 577, 601, 607, 627, 631

judicialization of politics, 304-305, 384, 468, 636

justiciability, 97, 105, 266

Karakatsanis, Andromache, 126, 129, 131, 507, 510, 545, 561, 680
Khadr, Omar, 510-511, 513-514, 521-522, 541, 564-565
Key, V.O., 119, 135n, 340n
Knopff, Rainer, 22-23, 33, 123, 313-314, 399-400, 505-506, 509, 527, 553, 575, 601, 622, 626
Ktunaxa Nation v. British Columbia (2017), 458, 461n

Labatt Breweries of Canada Ltd. v. Canada (1980), 437-440, 443
Labour Conventions Case (1937), 408, 423-424
labour law and labour unions, 29, 58, 85, 216, 250, 258-259, 270, 287, 288, 290-292, 295, 351, 362, 425, 427-429, 435, 536, 555, 559, 561, 566
Lamer, Antonio, 66, 97, 99, 123, 176, 385-386, 394, 501, 505, 429, 537, 601, 623-624, 644, 674, 680
language rights, 70-71, 251-252, 292, 306, 308-309, 314, 321, 398, 414n, 596, 666-668
Laskin, Bora, 43-44, 56, 66, 96-98, 100, 131, 133, 178, 189, 194, 196, 199, 244-245, 248, 333, 371-373, 379, 385, 409-411, 414n, 424, 429-435, 594, 674, 678
Lavell and Bedard (1974), 494-495
Law v. Canada (1999), 31, 362, 374
law clerks, 374, 378, 401-402
law of nature (*see* natural law)
LEAF (*see* Women's Legal Education and Action Fund)
leave to appeal (*see* appeal by leave)
Lederman, William R., 95, 174, 184, 186, 407, 417, 430, 433-435
legal model of decision-making, 375, 389-396
legal positivism, 39-40, 48, 50, 390, 581, 641
legal realism, 40-43, 53
legal rights, 9n, 167, 282, 422, 596, 663-664

legal view (*see* legal model of decision-making)
legislative facts (*see* social facts)
legislative history, 444, 448, 450, 597
Lévesque, René, 65, 71-72, 193, 197
LGBTQ rights, 36, 179, 182, 209-210, 245, 286-287, 289, 306, 336, 456, 459, 500, 515-516, 525, 597, 599, 606, 625
L'Heureux-Dubé, Claire, 179, 182, 185n, 205-210, 278, 390, 680
liberal constitutionalism, 8, 23-36, 310
Liberal Party of Canada, 45, 80, 92, 121, 124, 128, 138, 161-162, 259, 424, 446, 504, 595
living tree doctrine, 41, 85, 90, 168, 303, 364, 408, 423, 506, 512, 515-516, 526, 574-575, 578, 587, 598-600, 643, 647
lis, 243-244, 246-247
Locke, John, 2–3, 9n, 15, 39, 602

MacKeigan v. Hickman (1989), 183, 189n
Magna Carta, 2, 9n, 585
Mahoney, Kathleen, 181
mandatory minimum sentences, 403, 506, 510, 520, 533, 543-544, 557-558, 568-569
Mandel, Michael, 44-45, 64, 411
Manitoba Métis Federation v. Canada and Manitoba (2013), 459, 461n, 495-502
Marbury v. Madison (1803), 4
Marshall, Thurgood, 120, 391
Martin, Paul, 120, 125, 133, 161, 523, 533-534, 536, 606, 610
Martin, Sheilah, 98, 127-129, 135, 680
McClung Affair, 178-179, 181, 205-210
McCormick, Peter, 97, 118, 335, 373-374, 380
McNaught, Kenneth, 248
McPhedran, Marilou, 271, 274
Meech Lake Accord, 73, 80, 90, 99, 135n, 260, 411-412, 453, 463, 465, 468, 607
mega-constitutional politics, 88, 247, 258-260, 602
merit, 123-124, 126, 134, 137n, 138, 157, 164, 505-506, 527-532

Métis, 193, 453, 455, 459, 460n, 461n, 463, 466, 495-502, 669

minority language groups (MLGs), 250-252, 309, 505

minority language rights (*see* language rights)

Minister of Justice (Canada) v. Borowski (1981), 244-245

Miranda v. Arizona (1966), 265-266

modern treaties, 480, 482, 484-485, 488

Moldaver, Michael, 86, 126, 129, 131, 170, 461n, 507, 545, 548, 555, 560, 680

Monahan, Patrick, 337, 413, 436

mootness, 243-247, 253

Mulroney, Brian, 83, 99, 121-122, 139, 142-143, 145, 149, 150, 251, 306, 308, 414n, 444, 463, 465, 518, 523, 533, 606, 610, 623-625

multiculturalism, 251, 314, 668

multinational, 46, 75-77

Nadon, Marc, 84, 126-130, 403, 505, 507-510, 514, 536-537, 539-555, 562, 570

Nadon Reference (*see Reference re Supreme Court Act, ss. 5 and 6*)

National Action Committee on the Status of Women (NAC), 118, 133, 313

National Association for the Advancement of Colored People (NAACP), 273, 278, 312

National Citizens' Coalition (NCC), 314, 683

National Committee on the Judiciary, 143

national concern branch (*see* inherent national importance)

natural justice, 109, 191, 313, 319-320

natural law, 2, 15-16, 580, 583

natural resources, 256, 260, 262n, 288, 300, 414n, 440-443, 473, 477-478, 484-485, 654

natural rights theory of government, 2–3

neutral umpire (*see* umpire)

nominating committee, 118, 125-127, 133-134, 135n, 140, 159, 164, 527

non-status Indians, 460n

notwithstanding clause, 6, 7, 71, 193, 263, 340n, 363, 414n, 422, 455, 464, 533-534, 575-578, 590, 596, 598, 605-616, 618-619, 621, 623, 625, 626, 629, 642, 645

Nova Scotia Board of Censors v. McNeil (1976), 244

Oakes test, 35, 278, 367, 596, 622

obiter dicta, 179, 499

O'Connor Report, 42, 409

Ontario Judicial Appointments Advisory Committee (JAAC), 118, 131-133, 159

Operation Dismantle v. The Queen (1985), 246

oral argument, 128, 147, 149, 264, 266-268, 290, 370, 372, 380

originalism, 41, 120, 506, 515-517, 525, 527, 574, 598-600

panel size, 101, 180, 371-373, 378, 394, 401, 536

parliamentary scrutiny, 126-127, 134, 507

parliamentary sovereignty, 6, 19, 306, 576, 590, 596, 615-616

parliamentary supremacy, 4–6, 39, 43, 338, 391, 417-422, 590-591, 594-545, 601, 607

Parti Québécois, 45, 87, 252, 308, 435

Patriation Reference (1981), 9n, 44-47, 64-73, 81, 87-88, 130, 169, 247, 255, 260, 411, 457, 593

patronage (*see* judicial appointments), 87, 118-124, 130, 138-143, 149, 165, 515, 517, 530-531

peace, order and good government (POGG), 408, 410, 412-413, 424-426, 429-436, 445-451, 638, 651

per legem terrae, 2, 9n

per saltum appeal, 93, 406

Persons Case (1930), 408, 423

plurinational, 77

policy-making model of judging, 43, 54, 119, 183, 339

rights advocacy organizations (*see* interest groups)
Roe v. Wade (1973), 41, 517
role conceptions, 394-396, 510
Roman Law, 330
Roncarelli v. Duplessis (1959), 1–2, 9n, 10-15, 109, 191, 590
Rosenberg, Gerald, 281, 459, 497
Rothstein, Marshall, 125-126, 129, 131, 362-363, 448, 507, 527, 537, 545, 547, 560-561, 627, 680
Rowe, Malcolm, 40, 42, 98, 127-130, 165-172, 461n, 600, 680
royal commissions, 185n, 192-193, 199, 271, 302, 350, 351, 412, 444-451, 465, 465
Royal Proclamation (1763), 454-455, 667
rule of law, 1–9, 14, 18-21, 45, 83, 89, 107, 168-171, 184, 186, 191, 227, 231, 331, 346, 434, 520, 583-585, 587-590, 617, 658, 661
Russell, Peter H., 27, 81, 118, 142-150, 260, 398, 409, 411, 415n, 422, 424, 519, 551, 575-576, 578, 581, 596, 602-603, 605, 636

Saskatchewan Judges Affair, 121, 138-141
Saumur v. Quebec (1953), 244, 591-592
screening committee, 117-118, 122-124, 135n, 136n, 142, 144-145, 150, 515-517, 523-524
Secession Reference (*see Reference re Secession of Quebec*)
section 33 of the *Charter* (*see* notwithstanding clause)
section 92 courts, 92-95, 111-115, 117, 174, 176, 408
section 96 courts, 92-95, 111-115, 121, 122, 124, 126-127, 131, 135n, 139, 174, 176-177, 505-506
security of tenure, 173-175, 188-189, 200, 391, 531, 537
seditious libel, 12, 332, 351, 353-355
separation of powers, 3, 25, 287, 195, 246, 310-311

seriatim opinion-writing, 372
sexual assault, 28, 178, 181-182, 205-206, 226-241, 250, 270, 278, 282-286, 300, 336, 565, 629-630
sexual orientation, 32, 33, 85, 123, 250, 277, 284-286, 309, 336, 597-598, 617-618, 625
Shapiro, Martin, 336-337, 412
Smiley, Donald, 573, 576, 579
social facts, 337-339, 356-368, 435, 514
sovereignty (*see* Crown sovereignty; parliamentary sovereignty; Quebec sovereignty)
standing, 243-247, 294, 303, 427, 435, 643
stare decisis (*also see* precedent), 56, 107, 167, 330-335, 338, 341-344, 361-368, 407, 459, 498
state action, 8, 24-26, 29-30, 33
statute, 6, 23, 39, 57-58, 106-107, 114, 119, 167-169, 171, 174, 189, 191-192, 295, 235-326, 330-370, 407, 576-577, 591, 593-596
Statute of Westminster (1931), 408
status Indians, 248, 454, 460n, 461n, 594
strategic model of decision-making, 375, 393-396, 480
Strayer, Barry, 416-417, 420, 642
strong-form judicial review, 22-23
summary conviction offence, 94–95, 113
supervisory function, 71, 89, 97, 104-105, 191, 219
support structure for legal mobilization (SSLM), 253, 311-315, 321, 323, 325
Supreme Court Act (1875), 84, 96, 98-99, 124, 127, 130, 246, 253, 255, 256, 370-371, 406, 413, 420, 507-510, 542, 545, 547, 549, 551, 553, 562, 597
systematic litigation, 249, 251, 336

Tax Court of Canada, 96, 117, 144, 151, 514
terra nullius, 454, 456, 460n, 469-476,
test case, 11, 249, 273-274, 309, 314
The Queen. v. Beauregard (1986), 175, 183, 212